HARCOURT HORIZONS

HARCOURT HORIZONS

The Pledge of Allegiance

I pledge allegiance to the Flag

of the United States of America,

and to the Republic

for which it stands,

one Nation under God, indivisible,

with liberty and justice for all.

HARCOURT HORIZONS

United States History:

From Civil War to Present

Orlando   Austin   Chicago   New York   Toronto   London   San Diego

Visit *The Learning Site!*
www.harcourtschool.com

HARCOURT HORIZONS

UNITED STATES HISTORY: FROM CIVIL WAR TO PRESENT

General Editor

Dr. Michael J. Berson
Associate Professor
Social Science Education
University of South Florida
Tampa, Florida

Contributing Authors

Dr. Robert P. Green, Jr.
Professor
School of Education
Clemson University
Clemson, South Carolina

Dr. Thomas M. McGowan
Chairperson and Professor
Center for Curriculum and Instruction
University of Nebraska
Lincoln, Nebraska

Dr. Linda Kerrigan Salvucci
Associate Professor
Department of History
Trinity University
San Antonio, Texas

Series Consultants

Dr. Robert Bednarz
Professor
Department of Geography
Texas A&M University
College Station, Texas

Dr. Barbara Caffee
Coordinator, K–12 Social Studies
Carrollton–Farmers Branch Independent
    School District
Carrollton, Texas

Dr. Asa Grant Hilliard III
Fuller E. Callaway Professor
    of Urban Education
Georgia State University
Atlanta, Georgia

Dr. Thomas M. McGowan
Chairperson and Professor
Center for Curriculum and Instruction
University of Nebraska
Lincoln, Nebraska

Dr. John J. Patrick
Professor of Education
Indiana University
Bloomington, Indiana

Dr. Cinthia Salinas
Assistant Professor
Department of Curriculum and Instruction
University of Texas at Austin
Austin, Texas

Dr. Philip VanFossen
Associate Professor,
    Social Studies Education,
    and Associate Director,
    Purdue Center for Economic Education
Purdue University
West Lafayette, Indiana

Dr. Hallie Kay Yopp
Professor
Department of Elementary, Bilingual, and
    Reading Education
California State University, Fullerton
Fullerton, California

Content Reviewers

United States Geography

Dr. Phillip Bacon
Professor Emeritus
Geography and Anthropology
University of Houston
Houston, Texas

Native Americans and European Exploration

Dr. Susan Deans-Smith
Associate Professor
Department of History
University of Texas at Austin
Austin, Texas

Dr. John Jeffries Martin
Professor
Department of History
Trinity University
San Antonio, Texas

Richard Nichols
President
Richard Nichols and Associates
Fairview, New Mexico

Early Settlement and the American Revolution

Dr. John W. Johnson
Professor and Head
Department of History
University of Northern Iowa
Cedar Falls, Iowa

Dr. John P. Kaminski
Director, Center for the Study of
    the American Constitution
Department of History
University of Wisconsin
Madison, Wisconsin

Dr. Elizabeth Mancke
Associate Professor of History
Department of History
University of Akron
Akron, Ohio

The Constitution and United States Government

Dr. James M. Banner, Jr.
Historian
Washington, D.C.

Carol Egbo
Social Studies Consultant
Waterford Schools
Waterford, Michigan

Dr. John P. Kaminski
Director, Center for the Study of
  the American Constitution
Department of History
University of Wisconsin
Madison, Wisconsin

Dr. John J. Patrick
Professor of Education
Indiana University
Bloomington, Indiana

The National Period and Westward Expansion

Dr. Ross Frank
Professor
Department of Ethnic Studies
University of California at San Diego
La Jolla, California

Civil War and Reconstruction

Dr. Judith Giesburg
Assistant Professor
Department of History
Northern Arizona University
Flagstaff, Arizona

The United States in the Twentieth Century

Dr. Carol McKibben
Visiting Professor
Monterey Institute of International Studies
Monterey, California

Dr. Albert Raboteau
Henry W. Putnam Professor
Department of Religion
Princeton University
Princeton, New Jersey

Classroom Reviewers

Anne Hall
Teacher
Indian Prairie School District #204
Aurora, Illinois

Jennie Haynes
Teacher
A. Brian Elementary
Augusta, Georgia

Dr. Tom Jaeger
Assistant Superintendent:
  Curriculum/Instruction
Warren County R-III School District
Warrenton, Missouri

Ann Johnstone
Teacher
Stone-Robinson Elementary School
Charlottesville, Virginia

Betty Morgan
Teacher
Hayes Elementary School
Kennesaw, Georgia

Deborah Neal
Teacher
Windsor Hill Elementary
North Charleston, South Carolina

Sondra Pair
Teacher
Johnson Elementary School
Pinson, Alabama

Debra Smallwood
Teacher
Dupont Elementary School
Hopewell, Virginia

Melody Wysong
Teacher
Big Valley Elementary School
Rupert, Idaho

Maps
researched and prepared by

Readers
written and designed by

Take a Field Trip
video tour segments provided by

Printed in the United States of America

ISBN 0-15-321350-7

2 3 4 5 6 7 8 9 10 048 10 09 08 07 06 05 04 03

Contents

· UNIT ·

2

Civil War Times

Reference

Features You Can Use

Time Lines

Reading Your Textbook

Getting Started

Your textbook is divided into seven units.

Each unit has a Unit Preview that gives facts about important events. The Preview also shows where and when those events took place.

Each unit is divided into chapters, and each chapter is divided into lessons.

Each unit begins with a song, poem, story, or other special reading selection.

The Parts of a Lesson

This statement gives you the lesson's main idea. It tells you what to look for as you read.

This statement tells you why it is important to read the lesson.

These are the new vocabulary terms you will learn in the lesson.

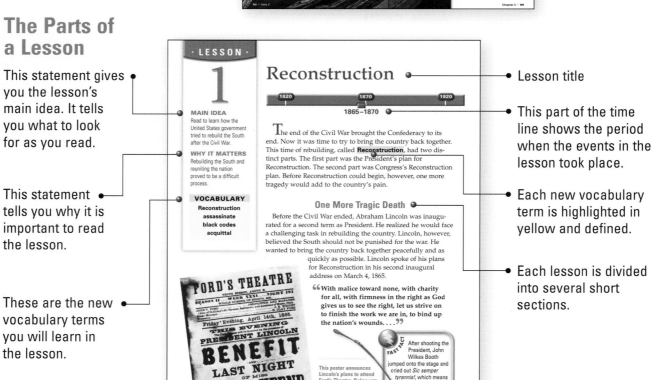

Lesson title

This part of the time line shows the period when the events in the lesson took place.

Each new vocabulary term is highlighted in yellow and defined.

Each lesson is divided into several short sections.

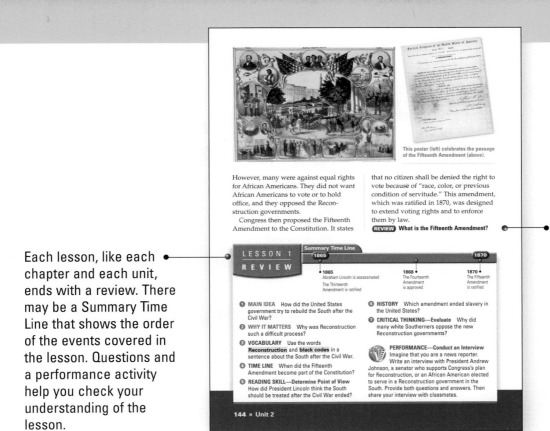

Each lesson, like each chapter and each unit, ends with a review. There may be a Summary Time Line that shows the order of the events covered in the lesson. Questions and a performance activity help you check your understanding of the lesson.

Each short section ends with a **REVIEW** question that will help you check whether you understand what you have read. Be sure to answer this question before you continue reading the lesson.

Skills

Your textbook has lessons that will help you build your reading, citizenship, chart and graph, and map and globe skills.

This statement tells you why it is important to learn the skill.

You will be able to practice and apply the skills you learn.

Special Features

The feature called
Examine Primary
Sources shows
you ways to learn
about different kinds
of objects and
documents.

The Visit feature lets
you "visit" many
interesting places.

Atlas

The Atlas provides maps
and a list of geography
terms with illustrations.

For Your Reference

At the back of your textbook, you will find
the reference tools listed below.

- Almanac
- American Documents
- Biographical Dictionary
- Gazetteer
- Glossary
- Index

You can use these tools to look up words
and to find information about people,
places, and other topics.

Atlas

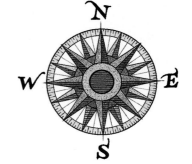

·SKILLS·

MAP AND GLOBE

Read a Map

VOCABULARY		
map title	grid system	compass rose
map key	locator	cardinal directions
inset map	map scale	intermediate directions

▶ WHY IT MATTERS

Maps provide many kinds of information about the world around you. Knowing how to read maps is an important social studies skill.

▶ WHAT YOU NEED TO KNOW

A map is a drawing that shows all of or part of the Earth on a flat surface. Mapmakers add certain features to most of the maps they draw.

Mapmakers sometimes need to show places marked on the map in greater detail or places that are beyond the area shown on the map. Find Alaska and Hawaii on the map of the United States on pages A10–A11. This map shows the location of those two states in relation to the rest of the country.

- A **map title** tells the subject of the map. It may also identify the kind of map.
  - Political maps show cities, states, and countries.
  - Physical maps show kinds of land and bodies of water.
  - Historical maps show parts of the world as they were in the past.

- A **map key**, or legend, explains the symbols used on a map. Symbols may be colors, patterns, lines, or other special marks.

- An **inset map** is a small map within a larger map.

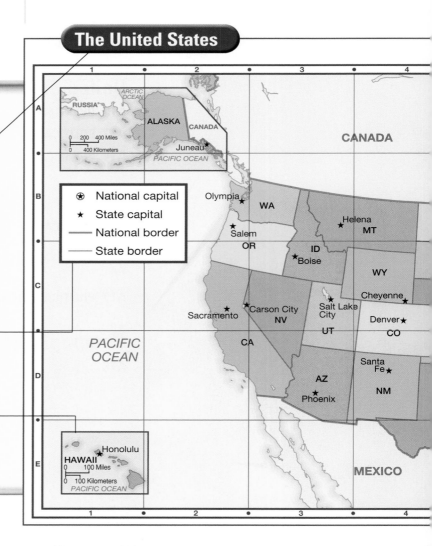

The United States

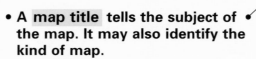

RUSSIA
ARCTIC OCEAN
ALASKA
CANADA
0 200 400 Miles
0 400 Kilometers
Juneau★
PACIFIC OCEAN

CANADA

⊛ National capital
★ State capital
— National border
— State border

Olympia★
WA
Helena★
MT
Salem★
OR
Boise★
ID
WY
Cheyenne★
Sacramento★
Carson City★
NV
Salt Lake City★
UT
Denver★
CO
PACIFIC OCEAN
CA
AZ
Phoenix★
Santa Fe★
NM

HAWAII
Honolulu
0 100 Miles
0 100 Kilometers
PACIFIC OCEAN

MEXICO

A2

Now find Alaska and Hawaii on the map below. To show this much detail for these states and the rest of the country on one map, the map would have to be much larger. Instead, Alaska and Hawaii are each shown in a separate **inset map**, or a small map within a larger map.

To help people find places on a map, mapmakers sometimes add lines that cross each other to form a pattern of squares called a **grid system**. Look at the map of the United States below. Around the grid are letters and numbers. The columns, which run up and down, have numbers. The rows, which run left and right, have letters. Each square on the map can be identified by its letter and number. For example, the top row of squares in the map includes square A1, square A2, and square A3.

▶ PRACTICE THE SKILL

Use the map of the United States to answer the following questions.

❶ What cities can be found in square B7?

❷ In which direction would you travel to go from Phoenix, Arizona, to Richmond, Virginia?

❸ About how many miles is it from Austin, Texas, to Baton Rouge, Louisiana?

❹ Which two oceans border Alaska?

▶ APPLY WHAT YOU LEARNED

Choose one of the maps in the Atlas. With a partner, identify the parts of the map and discuss what the map tells you. Ask each other questions that can be answered by reading the map.

- A **locator** is a small map or picture of a globe that shows where the place on the main map is located.

- A **map scale** compares a distance on the map to a distance in the real world. It helps you find the real distance between places on a map.

- A **compass rose**, or direction marker, shows directions.
  - The **cardinal directions**, or main directions, are north, south, east, and west.
  - The **intermediate directions**, or directions between the cardinal directions, are northeast, northwest, southeast, and southwest.

The World
POLITICAL

ARCTIC OCEAN

180° 160°W 140°W 120°W 100°W 80°W 60°W

80°N

Greenland
(DENMARK)

ALASKA
(U.S.)

60°N

CANADA

**NORTH
AMERICA**

40°N

UNITED STATES

Azores
(PORTUGAL)

Midway
Islands
(U.S.)

Area of inset

Bermuda
(U.K.)

ATLANTIC
OCEAN

20°N

Tropic of Cancer

MEXICO

CAPE VERDE

HAWAII
(U.S.)

PACIFIC
OCEAN

VENEZUELA GUYANA
SURINAME

COLOMBIA

FRENCH GUIANA
(FRANCE)

Equator

ECUADOR

0°

Tokelau
(N.Z.)

KIRIBATI

Galápagos
Islands
(ECUADOR)

BRAZIL

**SOUTH
AMERICA**

SAMOA

American
Samoa
(U.S.)

Cook
Islands
(N.Z.)

French
Polynesia
(FRANCE)

PERU

BOLIVIA

TONGA

20°S

Tropic of Capricorn

PARAGUAY

Pitcairn
(U.K.)

Easter Island
(CHILE)

CHILE

Niue
(N.Z.)

URUGUAY

ARGENTINA

Falkland
Islands
(U.K.)

40°S

PACIFIC

South
Georgia
(U.K.)

OCEAN

60°S

Antarctic Circle

180° 160°W 140°W 120°W 100°W 80°W 60°W

Central America and the Caribbean

100°W

30°N

N
W E
S

ATLANTIC
OCEAN

Gulf of Mexico

BAHAMAS

Tropic of Cancer

20°N

Turks and
Caicos (U.K.)

CUBA

Cayman
Islands
(U.K.)

HAITI

DOMINICAN
REPUBLIC

Puerto
Rico
(U.S.)

Anguilla (U.K.)
St. Martin (FRANCE AND NETH.)

ANTIGUA AND BARBUDA
Montserrat (U.K.)
Guadeloupe (FRANCE)

BELIZE

JAMAICA

Virgin Islands
(U.S. AND U.K.)

ST. KITTS
AND NEVIS

DOMINICA
Martinique (FRANCE)

GUATEMALA

HONDURAS

Caribbean Sea

ST. LUCIA
BARBADOS

EL SALVADOR

NICARAGUA

Aruba
(NETH.)

Netherlands
Antilles
(NETH.)

GRENADA

ST. VINCENT AND
THE GRENADINES

PACIFIC OCEAN

10°N

Panama
Canal

TRINIDAD AND
TOBAGO

10°N

0   200   400 Miles
0   200   400 Kilometers
Azimuthal Equal-Area Projection

COSTA
RICA

PANAMA

90°W

80°W

70°W

60°W

National
border

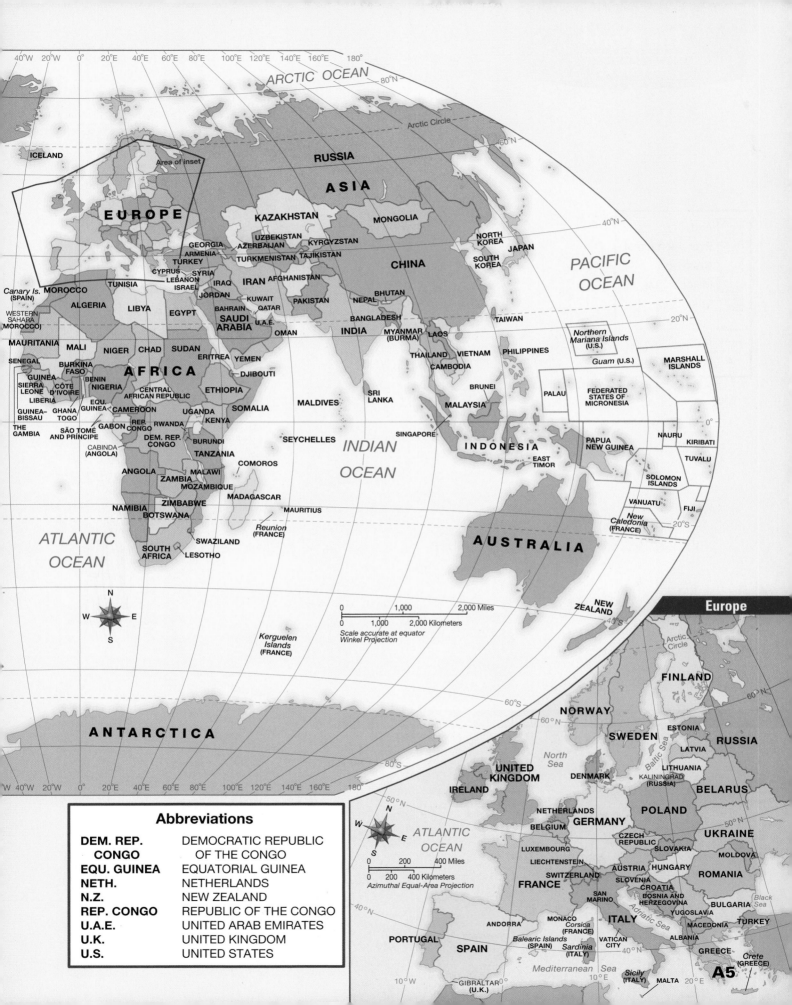

Abbreviations

DEM. REP. CONGO	DEMOCRATIC REPUBLIC OF THE CONGO
EQU. GUINEA	EQUATORIAL GUINEA
NETH.	NETHERLANDS
N.Z.	NEW ZEALAND
REP. CONGO	REPUBLIC OF THE CONGO
U.A.E.	UNITED ARAB EMIRATES
U.K.	UNITED KINGDOM
U.S.	UNITED STATES

Europe

A5

The World
PHYSICAL

Legend:
- Arid
- Evergreen forest
- Grassland
- Mixed forest
- Mountains
- Tundra
- National border
- ▲ Mountain peak

ARCTIC OCEAN

Beaufort Sea
Denali (Mt. McKinley) 20,320 ft. (6,194 m) ▲
Yukon R.
Queen Elizabeth Islands
Great Bear Lake
Baffin Island
Mackenzie R.
Bering Sea
Mt. Logan 19,550 ft. (5,959 m) ▲
Great Slave Lake
Hudson Bay
Aleutian Islands
Gulf of Alaska
NORTH AMERICA
Vancouver Island
Columbia R.
ROCKY MOUNTAINS
Missouri R.
Great Lakes
Newfoundland
Mt. Whitney 14,495 ft. (4,418 m) ▲
Colorado R.
GREAT PLAINS
Mississippi R.
Ohio R.
APPALACHIAN MTS.
Bermuda
ATLANTIC OCEAN
Rio Grande
Gulf of California
Tropic of Cancer
Gulf of Mexico
Bahamas
Hawaiian Islands
Pico de Orizaba 18,855 ft. (5,747 m) ▲
Yucatán Peninsula
Cuba
Hispaniola
West Indies
Caribbean Sea

PACIFIC OCEAN

Equator
Galápagos Islands
Orinoco River
Guiana Highlands
AMAZON BASIN
Amazon R.
SOUTH AMERICA
Polynesia
Brazilian Highlands
ANDES MOUNTAINS
Atacama Desert
Gran Chaco
Paraná River
Tropic of Capricorn
Mt. Aconcagua 22,834 ft. (6,960 m) ▲
Pampa
PACIFIC OCEAN
Patagonia
Falkland Islands
Strait of Magellan
Cape Horn
Tierra del Fuego
Antarctic Circle
Antarctic Peninsula
Ross Sea

Northern Polar Region

Sea of Okhotsk
ASIA
EUROPE
Kamchatka Peninsula
Novaya Zemlya
Severnaya Zemlya
Barents Sea
New Siberian Is.
Baltic Sea
ARCTIC OCEAN
North Pole
Norwegian Sea
North Sea
Wrangel Island
Svalbard
British Isles
Bering Sea
Bering Strait
North Magnetic Pole
Queen Elizabeth Islands
Greenland Sea
Iceland
ATLANTIC OCEAN
BROOKS RANGE
Beaufort Sea
Greenland
Baffin Bay
PACIFIC OCEAN
NORTH AMERICA

0   400   800 Miles
0   400   800 Kilometers
Azimuthal Equidistant Projection

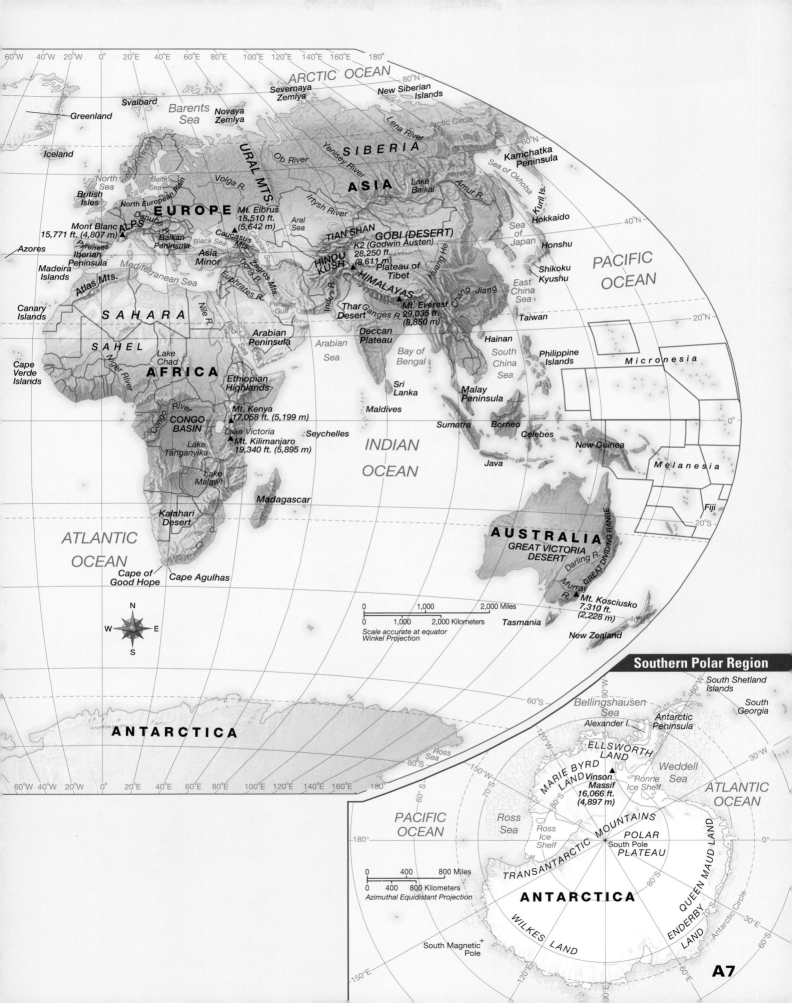

Western Hemisphere
POLITICAL

ARCTIC OCEAN

Beaufort Sea

Viscount Melville Sound

Baffin Bay

Greenland
(DENMARK)

Bering Strait

ALASKA
(U.S.)

Yukon River

Fairbanks

Foxe Basin

Arctic Circle

Great Bear Lake

Mackenzie River

Anchorage

Whitehorse

Yellowknife

Davis Strait

60°N

Gulf of Alaska

Juneau

Liard River

Peace River

Great Slave Lake

CANADA

Hudson Strait

Labrador Sea

Hudson Bay

Edmonton

Athabasca R.

Saskatchewan R.

Lake Athabasca

Lake Winnipeg

James Bay

St. John's

Calgary

Saskatoon

Regina

Winnipeg

Thunder Bay

Gulf of St. Lawrence

Vancouver

Seattle

UNITED STATES

Ottawa

Quebec

St. John

Halifax

Puget Sound

St. Lawrence River

Great Lakes

Portland

Columbia R.

Snake R.

Boise

Missouri R.

Chicago

Detroit

Toronto

Montreal

Albany

Boston

Salt Lake City

Great Salt Lake

Cleveland

New York City

Reno

Denver

St. Louis

Indianapolis

Philadelphia

Washington, D.C.

San Francisco

Las Vegas

Colorado R.

Memphis

Richmond

Norfolk

Los Angeles

Phoenix

Atlanta

Raleigh

Charleston

ATLANTIC OCEAN

San Diego

Tucson

El Paso

Dallas

Mississippi R.

Savannah

30°N

Hermosillo

Rio Grande

San Antonio

Houston

New Orleans

Tampa

Jacksonville

Orlando

Gulf of California

Chihuahua

MEXICO

Monterrey

Gulf of Mexico

Miami

BAHAMAS

Nassau

Tropic of Cancer

Durango

Havana

CUBA

HAITI

Port-au-Prince

Honolulu

León

Tampico

Santo Domingo

HAWAII
(U.S.)

Guadalajara

Mexico City

Veracruz

JAMAICA

Puerto Rico **(U.S.)**

PACIFIC OCEAN

Acapulco

Puebla

BELIZE

Belmopan

Kingston

DOMINICAN REPUBLIC

GUATEMALA

Guatemala City

HONDURAS

Caribbean Sea

San Salvador

Tegucigalpa

EL SALVADOR

Managua

Maracaibo

NICARAGUA

San José

Caracas

GUYANA

COSTA RICA

Panama City

VENEZUELA

SURINAME

PANAMA

Medellín

Georgetown

Paramaribo

Cayenne

Cali

Bogotá

FRENCH GUIANA (FRANCE)

0°

Quito

COLOMBIA

Rio Negro

Amazon R.

Belém

Equator

Galápagos Islands
(ECUADOR)

Guayaquil

Manaus

Fortaleza

ECUADOR

Iquitos

Recife

Trujillo

PERU

Tapajós River

Xingu R.

Tocantins R.

BRAZIL

Lima

Cuzco

Brasília

Salvador

French Polynesia
(FRANCE)

Lake Titicaca

La Paz

São Francisco R.

Papeete

Arequipa

BOLIVIA

Goiânia

Belo Horizonte

Sucre

Campo Grande

Rio de Janeiro

Tropic of Capricorn

Antofagasta

PARAGUAY

São Paulo

Paraguay R.

Salta

Asunción

Curitiba

San Miguel de Tucumán

Paraná R.

Pôrto Alegre

CHILE

Córdoba

URUGUAY

30°S

Valparaíso

Rosario

Santiago

Buenos Aires

Montevideo

Concepción

La Plata

Rio de la Plata

Mar del Plata

Valdivia

Bahía Blanca

0   1,000   2,000 Miles

0   1,000   2,000 Kilometers

Miller Cylindrical Projection

ARGENTINA

National border

National capital

City

Punta Arenas

Falkland Islands
(U.K.)

South Georgia
(U.K.)

N
W   E
S

A8

150°W   120°W   90°W   60°W   30°W

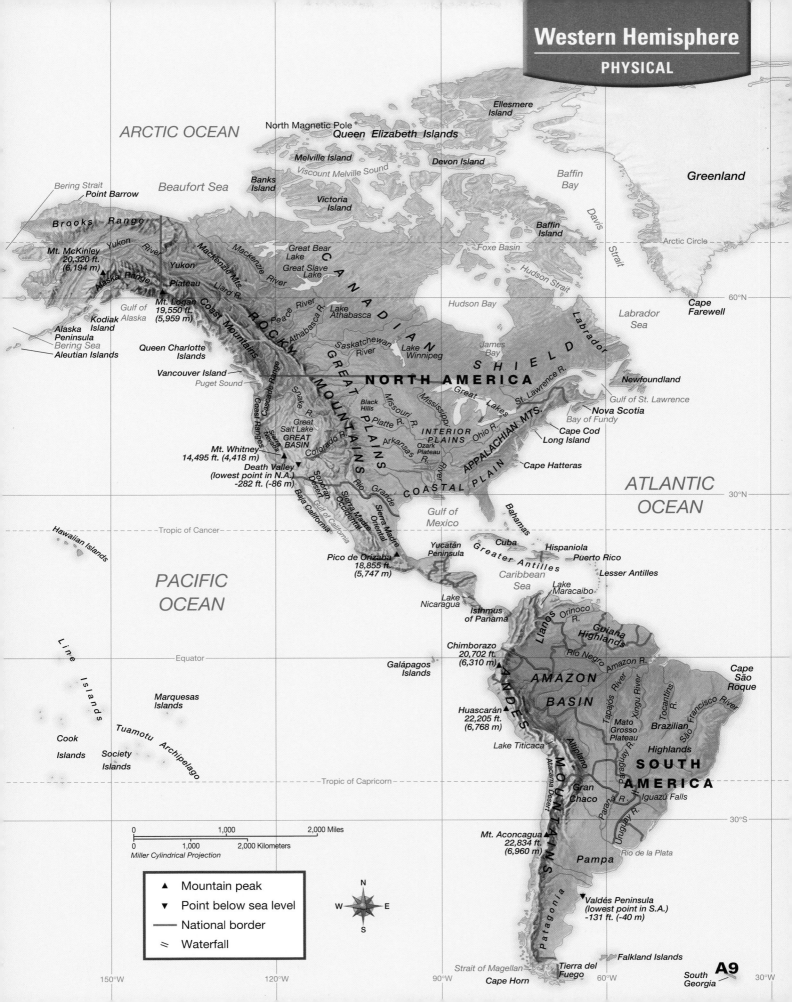

Western Hemisphere
PHYSICAL

ARCTIC OCEAN

North Magnetic Pole +

Ellesmere Island

Queen Elizabeth Islands

Melville Island

Viscount Melville Sound

Devon Island

Baffin Bay

Greenland

Bering Strait
Point Barrow

Beaufort Sea

Banks Island

Victoria Island

Baffin Island

Davis Strait

Arctic Circle

Brooks Range

Mt. McKinley 20,320 ft. (6,194 m)

Yukon River

Alaska Range

Yukon Plateau

Mackenzie Mts.

Mackenzie River

Great Bear Lake

Great Slave Lake

Foxe Basin

Hudson Strait

60°N

Mt. Logan 19,550 ft. (5,959 m)

Liard R.

Peace River

Athabasca R.

Lake Athabasca

Hudson Bay

Hudson Bay

Cape Farewell

Gulf of Alaska

Coast Mountains

CANADIAN

ROCKY

Saskatchewan River

Lake Winnipeg

James Bay

Labrador Sea

Alaska Peninsula

Kodiak Island

Bering Sea

Aleutian Islands

Queen Charlotte Islands

Vancouver Island

Puget Sound

Cascade Range

Coast Ranges

Snake R.

GREAT

MOUNTAINS

NORTH AMERICA

Great Lakes

SHIELD

Labrador

Newfoundland

Gulf of St. Lawrence

St. Lawrence R.

Nova Scotia

Bay of Fundy

PACIFIC OCEAN

Sierra Nevada

Great Salt Lake

GREAT BASIN

Black Hills

PLAINS

Missouri R.

Platte R.

Mississippi R.

INTERIOR PLAINS

Ohio R.

Ozark Plateau

Arkansas R.

APPALACHIAN MTS.

Cape Cod

Long Island

Cape Hatteras

ATLANTIC OCEAN

Mt. Whitney 14,495 ft. (4,418 m)

Death Valley (lowest point in N.A.) -282 ft. (-86 m)

Colorado R.

Sonoran Desert

Sierra Madre Occidental

Rio Grande

Sierra Madre Oriental

COASTAL PLAIN

30°N

Gulf of California

Baja California

Gulf of Mexico

Bahamas

Hawaiian Islands

Tropic of Cancer

Pico de Orizaba 18,855 ft. (5,747 m)

Yucatán Peninsula

Cuba

Greater Antilles

Hispaniola

Puerto Rico

Lesser Antilles

Caribbean Sea

PACIFIC OCEAN

Lake Nicaragua

Isthmus of Panama

Lake Maracaibo

Llanos

Orinoco R.

Guiana Highlands

Line Islands

Equator

Galápagos Islands

Chimborazo 20,702 ft. (6,310 m)

ANDES

Rio Negro

Amazon R.

AMAZON BASIN

Cape São Roque

Marquesas Islands

Huascarán 22,205 ft. (6,768 m)

Tapajós R.

Xingu River

Tocantins R.

Mato Grosso Plateau

Brazilian

São Francisco River

Cook Islands

Tuamotu Archipelago

Society Islands

Lake Titicaca

Altiplano

Atacama Desert

Paraguay R.

Highlands

SOUTH AMERICA

Tropic of Capricorn

Gran Chaco

Paraná R.

Iguazú Falls

Uruguay R.

30°S

0   1,000   2,000 Miles

0   1,000   2,000 Kilometers

Miller Cylindrical Projection

Mt. Aconcagua 22,834 ft. (6,960 m)

Pampa

Rio de la Plata

Valdés Peninsula (lowest point in S.A.) -131 ft. (-40 m)

▲ Mountain peak

▼ Point below sea level

—— National border

≈ Waterfall

N
W   E
S

Patagonia

Falkland Islands

Strait of Magellan

Tierra del Fuego

Cape Horn

South Georgia

150°W   120°W   90°W   60°N   30°W

A9

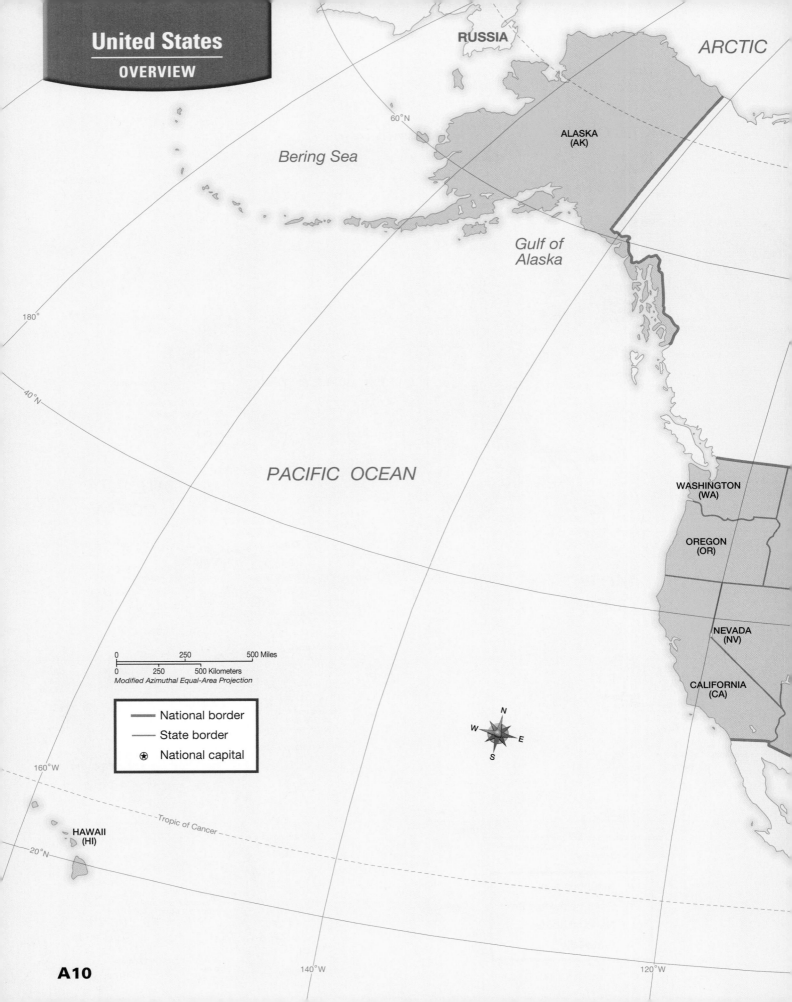

United States
OVERVIEW

RUSSIA

ARCTIC

60°N

Bering Sea

ALASKA
(AK)

Gulf of
Alaska

180°

40°N

PACIFIC OCEAN

WASHINGTON
(WA)

OREGON
(OR)

0   250   500 Miles
0   250   500 Kilometers
Modified Azimuthal Equal-Area Projection

NEVADA
(NV)

CALIFORNIA
(CA)

N
W — E
S

——— National border
——— State border
⊛ National capital

160°W

Tropic of Cancer

HAWAII
(HI)

20°N

140°W

120°W

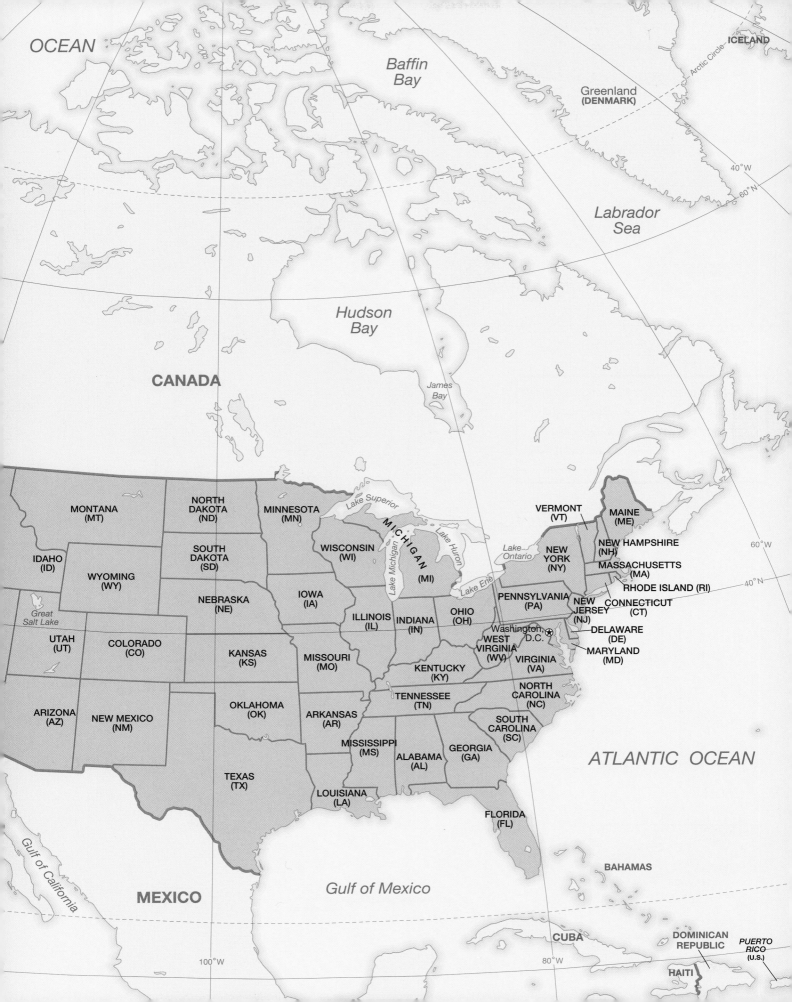

United States
POLITICAL

CANADA

RUSSIA

ARCTIC OCEAN

ALASKA

CANADA

Arctic Circle

Yukon River

Fairbanks

Bering Sea

Anchorage

Yukon River

Gulf of Alaska

Juneau ★

PACIFIC OCEAN

70°N
170°E
60°N
180°
50°N
60°N
120°W
130°W
0 250 500 Miles
0 250 500 Kilometers

Seattle
Tacoma
Olympia ★
WASHINGTON
Spokane

Great Falls

Portland
Columbia River
Salem ★
Helena ★
MONTANA

Eugene
OREGON
Billings
Yellowstone R.

IDAHO

Boise
WYOMING

Snake River
Pocatello
Casper

Great Salt Lake
Ogden
Cheyenne ★

NEVADA
Lake Tahoe
Reno
Salt Lake City
Provo

Sacramento
Carson City ★
UTAH

San Francisco
Oakland
COLORADO
Denver ★

San Jose
Colorado Springs

Fresno
Colorado River
Pueblo

CALIFORNIA
Las Vegas
COLORADO

Bakersfield

PACIFIC OCEAN

Flagstaff
Santa Fe ★
Albuquerque

Los Angeles
San Bernardino
ARIZONA
Phoenix ★
NEW MEXICO

San Diego
Roswell

Tucson

El Paso

Rio Grande

MEXICO

Legend

▢ Northeast	✪ National capital
▢ South	★ State capital
▢ Middle West	• Major city
▢ West	━ National border
	─ State border

PACIFIC OCEAN

Honolulu ★
HAWAII
Hilo

160°W 155°W
20°N
0 100 200 Miles
0 100 200 Kilometers

30°N
130°W
20°N
120°W
110°W

N
W E
S

0 250 500 Miles
0 250 500 Kilometers
Albers Equal-Area Projection

A12

CANADA

Lake of the Woods

NORTH DAKOTA
Grand Forks •
★ Bismarck   Fargo •
• Duluth

Lake Superior

Sault Sainte Marie •

MICHIGAN

Lake Huron

MAINE
• Augusta ★

Lake Champlain

MINNESOTA

St. Paul ★
Minneapolis •

WISCONSIN

Green Bay •

Lake Michigan

VERMONT
Burlington • ★ Montpelier
NEW HAMPSHIRE
★ Concord
• Portland

SOUTH DAKOTA

Rapid City •

★ Pierre

Sioux Falls •

Madison ★

• Milwaukee

Grand Rapids •

Lansing ★

• Flint

Detroit •

Lake St. Clair

Lake Erie

Lake Ontario

Buffalo •

NEW YORK
Rochester •
Syracuse ★ Albany

Manchester •

Worcester •
★ Boston
MASSACHUSETTS
• Providence
RHODE ISLAND

Hartford ★
CONNECTICUT

IOWA

Sioux City •

Cedar Rapids •
Davenport •
★ Des Moines

Rockford •
Chicago •
Gary •
South Bend •

Toledo •

Cleveland •
Akron •

PENNSYLVANIA
Harrisburg ★
Pittsburgh •

Newark •
NEW JERSEY
★ Trenton
• New York City
Philadelphia •
Wilmington •
DELAWARE
• Dover

NEBRASKA

Omaha •

Lincoln ★

Platte River

ILLINOIS
• Peoria
Decatur •
★ Springfield

INDIANA
Indianapolis ★

OHIO
Columbus ★
Dayton •
Cincinnati •

Wheeling •

WEST VIRGINIA
Charleston ★

Washington, D.C. ★
Baltimore •
Annapolis ★
MARYLAND

Missouri River

KANSAS
Topeka ★
Wichita •

Kansas City •

St. Louis •

Jefferson City ★

MISSOURI
Springfield •

Louisville •
Evansville •

Frankfort ★
Lexington •

Ohio River

KENTUCKY

VIRGINIA
Richmond ★
Roanoke •

• Newport News
• Norfolk

Arkansas River

OKLAHOMA
Oklahoma City ★   Tulsa •

ARKANSAS

Arkansas River

Fort Smith •
Little Rock ★

Memphis •

Knoxville •
★ Nashville
Chattanooga •

TENNESSEE

Winston-Salem •
Charlotte •

Greensboro •
★ Raleigh

NORTH CAROLINA

Amarillo •

Lubbock •

Red River

Lake Texoma

Shreveport •

MISSISSIPPI

Meridian •

Jackson ★

Huntsville •

Birmingham •

ALABAMA

Montgomery ★

Atlanta ★

GEORGIA
Macon •
Columbus •

SOUTH CAROLINA
Columbia ★

• Charleston

Savannah •

Odessa •

Abilene •

Fort Worth •
Dallas •

LOUISIANA

Mississippi River

Biloxi •

Mobile •

Baton Rouge ★
New Orleans •

★ Tallahassee

Jacksonville •

FLORIDA
Orlando •

Tampa •
St. Petersburg •

Lake Okeechobee

West Palm Beach •

ATLANTIC OCEAN

TEXAS

Austin ★
Houston •

San Antonio •

Laredo •   Corpus Christi •

Rio Grande

Gulf of Mexico

Miami •

BAHAMAS

80°W

CUBA

100°W   90°W   80°W   70°W

50°N

40°N

70°W

30°N

100°W   90°W

A13

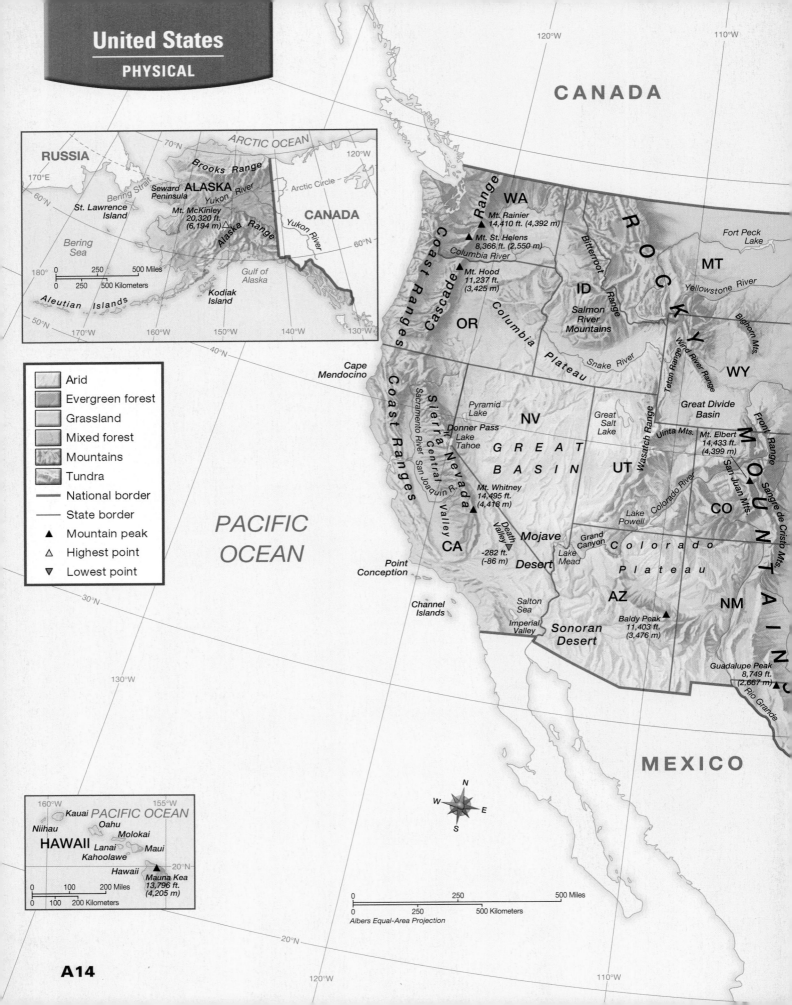

United States
PHYSICAL

CANADA

RUSSIA

ARCTIC OCEAN

70°N

Brooks Range

Seward
Peninsula   ALASKA
Yukon
River

Mt. McKinley
20,320 ft.
(6,194 m) △

St. Lawrence
Island

Bering
Sea

Bering Strait

Alaska Range

Arctic Circle

120°W

CANADA

Yukon River

60°N

Gulf of
Alaska

Kodiak
Island

Aleutian Islands

50°N

180°   170°E

60°N

170°W   160°W   150°W   140°W   130°W

0   250   500 Miles
0   250   500 Kilometers

Legend

- Arid
- Evergreen forest
- Grassland
- Mixed forest
- Mountains
- Tundra
- ——— National border
- ——— State border
- ▲ Mountain peak
- △ Highest point
- ▽ Lowest point

**PACIFIC
OCEAN**

Cape
Mendocino

40°N

Coast Ranges

Coast Ranges

Sierra Nevada

Central Valley

Sacramento River

San Joaquin R.

Donner Pass
Lake
Tahoe

Pyramid
Lake

Mt. Whitney
14,495 ft.
(4,418 m) ▲

CA

Death
Valley
-282 ft.
(-86 m)

Mojave
Desert

Point
Conception

Channel
Islands

Salton
Sea

Imperial
Valley

Sonoran
Desert

WA

Mt. Rainier
14,410 ft. (4,392 m) ▲

Mt. St. Helens
8,366 ft. (2,550 m) ▲

Columbia River

Mt. Hood
11,237 ft.
(3,425 m) ▲

Cascade Range

Range

OR

Columbia Plateau

Bitterroot Range

Salmon
River
Mountains

Snake River

ID

NV

G R E A T
B A S I N

Great
Salt
Lake

Wasatch Range

Uinta Mts.

UT

Lake
Powell

Colorado River

Grand
Canyon

Lake
Mead

C o l o r a d o
P l a t e a u

AZ

Baldy Peak
11,403 ft.
(3,476 m) ▲

CANADA

Fort Peck
Lake

MT

Yellowstone River

Bighorn Mts.

R O C K Y

Teton Range

Wind River Range

WY

Great Divide
Basin

Mt. Elbert
14,433 ft.
(4,399 m) ▲

San Juan Mts.

CO

M O U N T A I N S

Front Range

Sangre de Cristo Mts.

NM

Guadalupe Peak
8,749 ft.
(2,667 m) ▲

Rio Grande

MEXICO

N
W   E
S

110°W

120°W

130°W

30°N

20°N

HAWAII

160°W   PACIFIC OCEAN   155°W

Kauai

Niihau

Oahu

Molokai

Lanai   Maui

Kahoolawe

Hawaii

Mauna Kea
13,796 ft.
(4,205 m) ▲

20°N

0   100   200 Miles
0   100   200 Kilometers

0   250   500 Miles
0   250   500 Kilometers

Albers Equal-Area Projection

A14

110°W

100°W   90°W   80°W   70°W

50°N

CANADA

Lake of
the Woods

Upper
Red Lake

Lower
Red Lake

Lake Sakakawea

ND

Isle
Royale

Lake Superior

Keweenaw
Peninsula

Mesabi
Range

Leech
Lake

Mille
Lacs
Lake

MN

Upper Peninsula

St. Lawrence River

ME

Moosehead
Lake

Mt. Katahdin
5,269 ft.
(1,606 m)

Mt. Washington
6,288 ft.
(1,917 m)

Lake
Champlain

VT

Green Mts.

White Mts.

NH

Cape Ann

NY

Adirondack
Mountains

MA

Cape
Cod

CT

RI

**G
R
E
A
T**

Lake
Oahe

SD

Black
Hills

WI

Wisconsin River

Lake
Winnebago

Mississippi River

Lake Michigan

Lower Peninsula

MI

Lake
St. Clair

Lake Huron

Lake Ontario

Niagara
Falls

Finger
Lakes

Hudson R.

Lake Erie

Long
Island

NJ

40°N

North Platte R.

Sand Hills

NE

Platte River

South Platte R.

IA

**INTERIOR
PLAINS**

Illinois River

Wabash River

OH

PA

Allegheny Mts.

MD

Potomac R.

DE

Delaware
Bay

70°W

IL

IN

CENTRAL PLAINS

Ohio River

WV

**A
P
P
A
L
A
C
H
I
A
N**

**P
I
E
D
M
O
N
T**

VA

Cape
Charles

Chesapeake
Bay

KS

Smoky Hills

Red Hills

MO

Missouri River

Lake of
the Ozarks

Harry S. Truman
Reservoir

Ozark Plateau

KY

Lake
Barkley

Cumberland
Gap

Mt. Mitchell
6,684 ft.
(2,037 m)

**M
O
U
N
T
A
I
N
S**

James R.

Roanoke R.

Albemarle
Sound

NC

Cape
Hatteras

**P
L
A
I
N
S**

Arkansas

OK

Canadian River

River

Ouachita
Mountains

Lake
Texoma

Red River

AR

Mississippi River

TN

Cumberland R.

Tennessee R.

Stone
Mountain

Clark
Hill Lake

SC

Cape Fear River

Cape
Fear

**P
L
A
I
N
S**

Llano
Estacado

TX

Edwards
Plateau

Pecos River

Rio Grande

Colorado River

Brazos River

Sabine River

Red River

Sam
Rayburn
Reservoir

Toledo
Bend
Reservoir

LA

MS

AL

Tombigbee R.

Alabama R.

Chattahoochee R.

Savannah River

Oconee R.

Ocmulgee R.

GA

Altamaha R.

Okefenokee
Swamp

**C
O
A
S
T
A
L**

St. Johns River

Cape
Canaveral

Galveston
Bay

Lake
Maurepas

Lake
Pontchartrain

COASTAL PLAIN

Mobile
Bay

Mississippi
Delta

**ATLANTIC
OCEAN**

30°N

BAHAMAS

FL

Tampa
Bay

Lake
Okeechobee

Everglades

Cape
Sable

Florida Keys

Straits of Florida

Gulf of Mexico

CUBA

100°W   90°W   80°W

A15

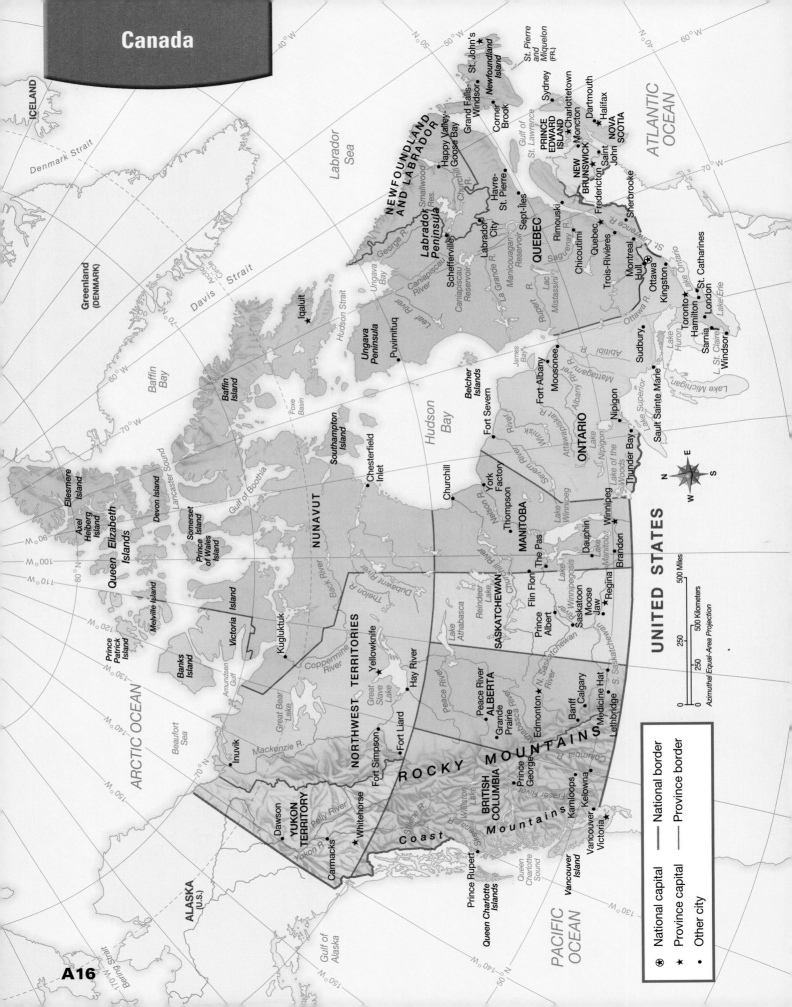

Canada

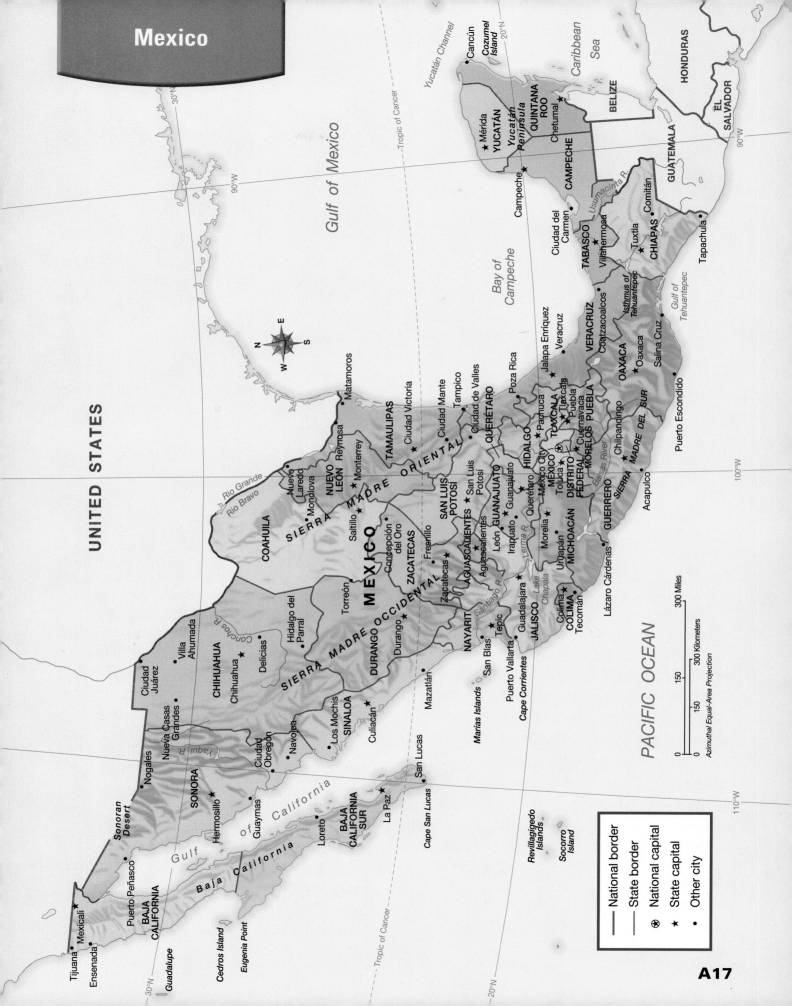

Geography Terms

1. **basin** bowl-shaped area of land surrounded by higher land

2. **bay** an inlet of the sea or some other body of water, usually smaller than a gulf

3. **bluff** high, steep face of rock or earth

4. **canyon** deep, narrow valley with steep sides

5. **cape** point of land that extends into water

6. **cataract** large waterfall

7. **channel** deepest part of a body of water

8. **cliff** high, steep face of rock or earth

9. **coast** land along a sea or ocean

10. **coastal plain** area of flat land along a sea or ocean

11. **delta** triangle-shaped area of land at the mouth of a river

12. **desert** dry land with few plants

13. **dune** hill of sand piled up by the wind

14. **fall line** area along which rivers form waterfalls or rapids as the rivers drop to lower land

15. **floodplain** flat land that is near the edges of a river and is formed by silt deposited by floods

16. **foothills** hilly area at the base of a mountain

17. **glacier** large ice mass that moves slowly down a mountain or across land

18. **gulf** part of a sea or ocean extending into the land, usually larger than a bay

19. **hill** land that rises above the land around it

20. **inlet** any area of water extending into the land from a larger body of water

21. **island** land that has water on all sides

22. **isthmus** narrow strip of land connecting two larger areas of land

23. **lagoon** body of shallow water

24. **lake** body of water with land on all sides

25. **marsh** lowland with moist soil and tall grasses

№	Term	Definition
26	**mesa**	flat-topped mountain with steep sides
27	**mountain**	highest kind of land
28	**mountain pass**	gap between mountains
29	**mountain range**	row of mountains
30	**mouth of river**	place where a river empties into another body of water
31	**oasis**	area of water and fertile land in a desert
32	**ocean**	body of salt water larger than a sea
33	**peak**	top of a mountain
34	**peninsula**	land that is almost completely surrounded by water
35	**plain**	area of flat or gently rolling low land
36	**plateau**	area of high, mostly flat land
37	**reef**	ridge of sand, rock, or coral that lies at or near the surface of a sea or ocean
38	**river**	large stream of water that flows across the land
39	**riverbank**	land along a river
40	**savanna**	area of grassland and scattered trees
41	**sea**	body of salt water smaller than an ocean
42	**sea level**	the level of the surface of an ocean or a sea
43	**slope**	side of a hill or mountain
44	**source of river**	place where a river begins
45	**strait**	narrow channel of water connecting two larger bodies of water
46	**swamp**	area of low, wet land with trees
47	**timberline**	line on a mountain above which it is too cold for trees to grow
48	**tributary**	stream or river that flows into a larger stream or river
49	**valley**	low land between hills or mountains
50	**volcano**	opening in the earth, often raised, through which lava, rock, ashes, and gases are forced out
51	**waterfall**	steep drop from a high place to a lower place in a stream or river

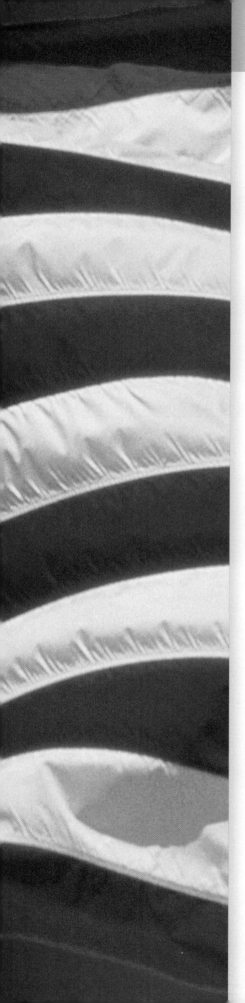

Introduction

"It is history that teaches us hope."

— Robert E. Lee, letter to Charles Marshall, 1866

Learning About Our Country

This year in social studies, you will be studying United States history. You will learn about past events and the places where those events occurred. You will also read about the people who helped shape our country. You will see how the people of the United States have worked together to govern themselves and to meet their needs. You will learn why social studies matters.

Civics and Government

Culture and Society

What Is Social Studies?

History

Economics

Geography

Why History Matters

VOCABULARY

history   oral history   historical empathy   analyze

chronology   point of view   frame of reference

History , or what happened in the past, helps you see links between the past and the present. History also helps you understand how events that happen today can affect the future. As you learn to recognize these links, you will think more like a historian, a person who studies the past.

Measuring Time

By studying the chronology (kruh•NAH•luh•jee) of events, historians can see connections in history. **Chronology** is the order in which events happen. This helps historians learn how the past is connected to the present.

Finding Evidence

Historians study the past by looking for clues in the objects and documents that people have left behind. They read journal entries, newspaper articles, and other writings by people who experienced past events. They also listen to or read records of oral histories. An **oral history** is a story of an event or an experience told aloud by a person who did not have a written language or who did not write down what happened. Historians also look at photographs, films, and artwork. By examining such clues, historians can piece together what took place in the past and explain why events happened as they did.

Historians can learn about the Great Depression in the United States by studying the crash of the stock market in 1929 (bottom), stock certificates (below), and photographs of how the crash affected people's lives (above).

Identifying Points of View

Historians examine people's points of view. A person's **point of view** is how he or she sees things. It can depend on whether that person is old or young, a man or a woman, rich or poor. A point of view is also shaped by a person's background, experiences, culture, and race. People with different points of view may see the same event differently.

Historians learn about the times and places in which people lived. They study how scientific discoveries and innovations affected people's lives. In that way, historians can understand earlier people's actions and feelings. This understanding is called **historical empathy** (EM•puh•thee).

Understanding Frames of Reference

Historians also work hard to understand people's **frames of reference**. A frame of reference includes where people were when an event took place and what part they took in it. Historians must be careful not to judge the actions of people in the past based on the way people of today would act.

Drawing Conclusions

Many events in history are connected to other events. To **analyze** an event, historians look closely at how the parts of it connect with one another and how the event is connected to other events. Analyzing an event allows historians to summarize it or draw conclusions about how and why it happened.

REVIEW Why is it important to study history?

During the Great Depression people like President Herbert Hoover (above) and this couple (top) had different experiences. This may have led them to have different points of view.

Compare Primary and Secondary Sources

VOCABULARY
primary source
secondary source

▶ WHY IT MATTERS

To find out what really happened in the past, you need proof. You can find proof by studying and comparing two kinds of sources—primary sources and secondary sources.

▶ WHAT YOU NEED TO KNOW

Primary sources are the records made by people who saw or took part in an event. These people may have written down their thoughts in a journal, or they may have told their story in a letter or a poem. They may have made a speech, produced a film, taken a photograph, or painted a picture. Primary sources may also be objects or official documents that give information about the time in which they were made or written. A primary source gives people of today a direct link to a past event.

This letter **Ⓐ**, photograph **Ⓑ**, and name tag **Ⓒ** are all primary sources from the time of World War II.

A **secondary source** is not a direct link to an event. It is a record of the event written by someone who was not there at the time. A magazine article, newspaper story, or book written by someone who only heard about or read about the event is a secondary source. So is an object made at a later time.

Some sources can be either primary or secondary, depending on how the event is reported. A newspaper might print the exact words of a person who saw the event take place. It might also print an article about the event, written by a reporter who was not there. Oral histories, textbooks, and online resources can also be either primary or secondary sources.

▶ **PRACTICE THE SKILL**

Look at the photographs of objects and printed materials that give information about World War II. Then answer these questions.

1 How are Items A and F alike and different?

2 What kind of information might be found in item A but not in item D?

3 Why might secondary sources D and F also be considered primary sources?

▶ **APPLY WHAT YOU LEARNED**

Look through a newspaper for examples of primary and secondary sources. Explain to a classmate what makes each source you selected a primary source or a secondary source.

D

E

F

This newspaper **D**, recent photograph of people dressed as World War II soldiers **E**, and World War II Web site **F** are secondary sources.

Why Geography Matters

VOCABULARY

geography	physical feature	region
modify	human feature	
adapt	location	

Each event in this textbook has a setting, and part of the setting is the place where the event happened. Learning about places is an important part of **geography**—the study of Earth's surface and the way people use it. People who study geography are called geographers.

The Five Themes of Geography

Geographers often speak of five main themes when they study a place. You will find that most of the maps in this book focus on one of these themes. Keeping these themes in mind as you read will help you think like a geographer.

Human-Environment Interactions
Humans and their surroundings interact, or affect each other. People's activities may **modify**, or change, the environment. The environment may affect people, causing them to **adapt**, or adjust, to their surroundings.

Location
Everything on Earth has its own **location**—the place where it can be found.

GEOGRAPHY THEME

Movement
Each day, people in different parts of the country and around the world exchange products and ideas.

Place
Every location has features that make it different from all other locations. **Physical features** are formed by nature. **Human features** are created by people.

Regions
Areas of Earth that share features that make them different from other areas are called **regions**. A region can be described by its physical features or human features.

Essential Elements of Geography

Geographers also use six other topics when they study a place. These six topics are called the six essential elements of geography. Thinking about them will also help you understand the world around you.

• GEOGRAPHY •

The World in Spatial Terms
Geographers use maps and other kinds of information to study relationships among people and places. They want to know why things are located where they are.

Places and Regions
People are linked to the places and regions in which they live. Places and regions have both physical and human features.

Physical Systems
Physical processes, such as wind and rain, shape Earth's surface. Living things interact with physical features to create and change environments.

Human Systems
People's activities include where they settle, how they earn a living, and the laws they make. All these help shape Earth's surface.

Environment and Society
People's activities often affect the environment, and the environment affects people's activities.

The Uses of Geography
Knowing how to use maps, globes, and other geographic tools helps people in their everyday lives.

REVIEW What is geography?

Why Economics Matters

Have you ever earned money for doing chores? Did you use the money to buy something you needed or wanted? When you do these things, you are taking part in the economy. An **economy** is the way people of a state, a region, or a country use resources to meet their needs. The study of how people meet their needs is called **economics**.

In this textbook you will read about how people in the past made, bought, sold, and traded goods to meet their needs. You will also learn how the economy of the United States has become one in which businesses are free to sell many kinds of goods and services.

REVIEW How are resources important?

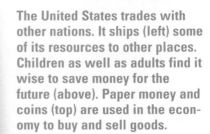

The United States trades with other nations. It ships (left) some of its resources to other places. Children as well as adults find it wise to save money for the future (above). Paper money and coins (top) are used in the economy to buy and sell goods.

Why Civics and Government Matter

VOCABULARY

civics

civic participation

government

"Your country needs you!" This World War I slogan is an example of another key area of social studies—civics. **Civics** is the study of citizenship. In this textbook you will read about the rights and responsibilities of citizens of the United States. You will also learn about the importance of **civic participation**. Civic participation is being concerned with and involved in issues related to your community, state, or country or to the entire world.

In the United States, citizens have an important part in making government work. A **government** is a system of leaders and laws that helps people live together in their community, state, or country. It protects citizens and settles disagreements among them. In this textbook you will read about how the United States government works today.

REVIEW How is civics different from government?

The voting sticker (top) is a symbol of civic participation. The White House (below) is a symbol of the United States government.

Why Culture and Society Matter

In this textbook you will learn about people of the past who helped shape the present. You will learn about their customs and beliefs, their families and communities, and the ways they made a living. All these things make up a **culture**, or way of life.

Each human group, or **society**, has a culture This textbook will help you discover the many cultures of the United States, both now and in the past. You will also learn about our country's **heritage**, or culture that has come from the past and continues today.

REVIEW What will you learn when you study a group's culture?

These people (above) are celebrating their Ukrainian heritage. Visiting museums, like the Metropolitan Museum of Art in New York, allows people to see works of art from people of many different cultures.

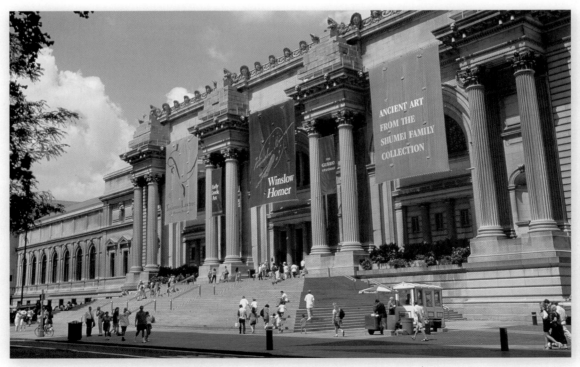

Making a New Nation

Paul Revere's
lantern

Statue of Paul Revere in front of the
Old North Church, Boston, Massachusetts

PAUL REVE

Making a New Nation

❝ The fate of a nation was riding that night. ❞

—Henry Wadsworth Longfellow, "The Landlord's Tale: Paul Revere's Ride," in *Tales of a Wayside Inn,* 1863

Preview the Content

Read the lesson titles. Then fill in the first two columns of the chart with information about early United States history. After you have read the unit, fill in the last column.

K (What I Know)	W (What I Want to Know)	L (What I Have Learned)

Preview the Vocabulary

Related Words Words that are related have meanings that are connected in some way. Make a chart of words that are related to the vocabulary words **migration, navigation, technology,** and **colony.**

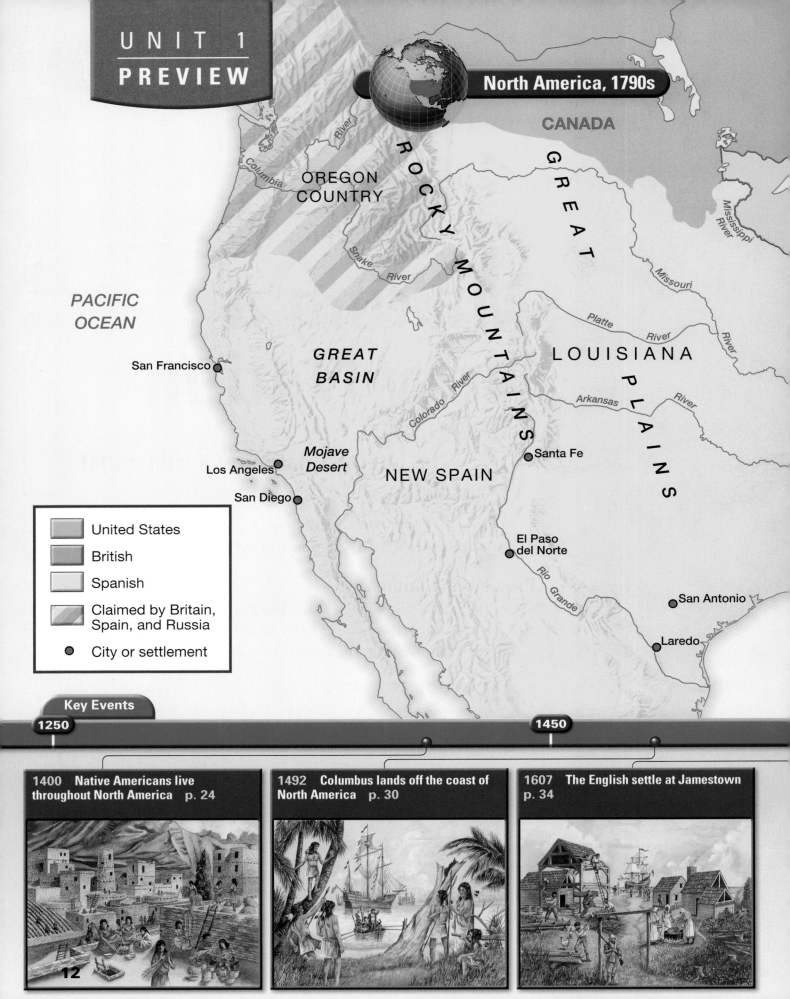

North America, 1790s

CANADA

ROCKY MOUNTAINS

GREAT PLAINS

OREGON COUNTRY

PACIFIC OCEAN

Columbia River

Snake River

GREAT BASIN

Mojave Desert

San Francisco

Los Angeles

San Diego

NEW SPAIN

Colorado River

Santa Fe

El Paso del Norte

Rio Grande

San Antonio

Laredo

LOUISIANA

Platte River

Arkansas River

Missouri River

Mississippi River

Legend

- United States
- British
- Spanish
- Claimed by Britain, Spain, and Russia
- City or settlement

Key Events

1250

1450

1400 Native Americans live throughout North America p. 24

1492 Columbus lands off the coast of North America p. 30

1607 The English settle at Jamestown p. 34

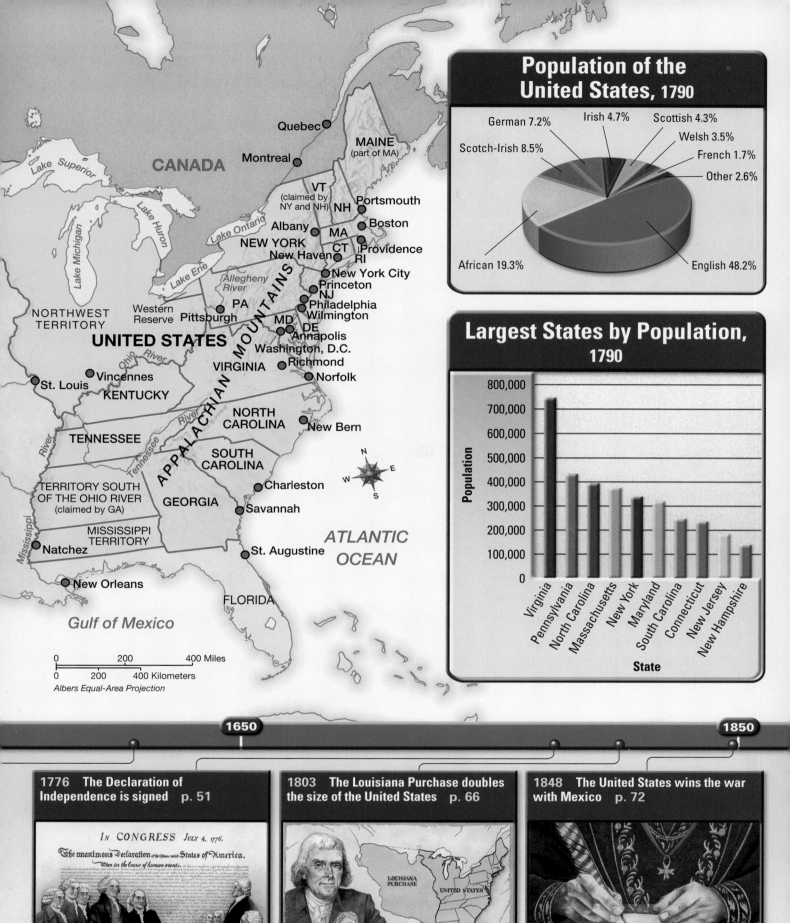

Population of the United States, 1790

- German 7.2%
- Scotch-Irish 8.5%
- Irish 4.7%
- Scottish 4.3%
- Welsh 3.5%
- French 1.7%
- Other 2.6%
- African 19.3%
- English 48.2%

Largest States by Population, 1790

Population (y-axis): 0, 100,000, 200,000, 300,000, 400,000, 500,000, 600,000, 700,000, 800,000

States (x-axis): Virginia, Pennsylvania, North Carolina, Massachusetts, New York, Maryland, South Carolina, Connecticut, New Jersey, New Hampshire

Map labels

CANADA
Quebec
Montreal
MAINE (part of MA)
Lake Superior
Lake Huron
Lake Michigan
Lake Ontario
Lake Erie
VT (claimed by NY and NH)
NH
Portsmouth
Albany
MA
Boston
NEW YORK
CT
Providence
New Haven
RI
New York City
Allegheny River
Princeton
NJ
Philadelphia
PA
Wilmington
Western Reserve
Pittsburgh
MD
Annapolis
DE
Washington, D.C.
NORTHWEST TERRITORY
UNITED STATES
Richmond
VIRGINIA
Norfolk
Ohio River
St. Louis
Vincennes
KENTUCKY
NORTH CAROLINA
New Bern
APPALACHIAN MOUNTAINS
TENNESSEE
Tennessee River
SOUTH CAROLINA
TERRITORY SOUTH OF THE OHIO RIVER (claimed by GA)
GEORGIA
Charleston
Savannah
MISSISSIPPI TERRITORY
Mississippi
Natchez
New Orleans
St. Augustine
FLORIDA
ATLANTIC OCEAN
Gulf of Mexico

N W E S

0   200   400 Miles
0   200   400 Kilometers
Albers Equal-Area Projection

1650   1850

1776 **The Declaration of Independence is signed** p. 51

IN CONGRESS. JULY 4, 1776.
The unanimous Declaration of the thirteen united States of America.

1803 **The Louisiana Purchase doubles the size of the United States** p. 66

LOUISIANA PURCHASE
UNITED STATES

1848 **The United States wins the war with Mexico** p. 72

13

Betsy Ross
Patriot of Philadelphia
by Judith St. George

The year 1776 was an exciting time in North America. The 13 British colonies broke away from British rule to form their own country. During their struggle for independence, they became united under one flag— the Stars and Stripes. Before this struggle took place, there had been many changes in North America. Read now about the flag that came to represent the United States of America.

Betsy Ross and workers sew the United States flag.

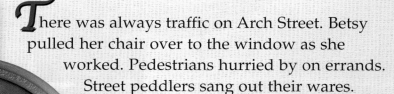
George Washington

There was always traffic on Arch Street. Betsy pulled her chair over to the window as she worked. Pedestrians hurried by on errands. Street peddlers sang out their wares. Wagons, carts, coaches, and carriages bumped and clattered over the cobblestones. Betsy looked up and saw three distinguished-looking gentlemen approaching the house.

Betsy recognized all of them. Uncle George Ross, of course, was a familiar figure. And everyone in Philadelphia knew the wealthy businessman Robert Morris by sight. As for their companion, he was taller than the others. Broad-shouldered and handsomely dressed, with freshly powdered hair, the third man was the person all Philadelphia was talking about, General George Washington.

Betsy hurried to the door and opened it. The three men removed their three-cornered hats, greeted her, and entered. Signs of Betsy's trade were everywhere. The upholstered chair was still displayed in the front window. A sofa pillow was half-stuffed with horsehair. Muslin curtains were draped over a chair. Pattern books, ledger books, and sketches were stacked on Betsy's desk. Trying her best not to appear flustered, Betsy invited the men into her back parlor. The shop was too public a place to talk.

Betsy's parlor, with its flowered wallpaper and freshly sanded floor, was simple and neat. It was a pleasant room with a tall chest, a few chairs, a gateleg table, and a looking glass. A corner cupboard was filled with Betsy's prize possessions, books, pewter pieces, and glassware. The fireplace was framed in cheerful blue tiles and covered by a handsome firescreen that Betsy had embroidered.

The three men didn't waste any time. General Washington pulled a chair up to the table and sat down. Taking out a piece of paper, he unfolded it. Could Mistress Ross copy the flag in the picture?

Betsy studied the rough drawing. Like the Grand Union flag, this flag had red and white stripes. But instead of the British Union Jack in the canton, there were thirteen six-pointed stars. Betsy considered General Washington's request. She had never made a flag before but she saw no reason why she couldn't.

"I'll try," she replied.

Betsy had a good sense of design, and right away she saw how the flag could be improved. She hesitated before giving her opinion to these important gentlemen, but only for a moment. Although she knew that most regimental flags were square, she suggested that this flag be made in the shape of a rectangle. And five-pointed stars would be more practical. To demonstrate, she took a square piece of paper and folded it four different ways. With the scissors from her chatelaine, she made one cut. When she opened the paper, she held up a perfect five-pointed star.

The committee of three agreed with her changes. As General Washington altered his drawing to follow her suggestions, George Ross asked when she could finish the flag. General Washington was leaving Philadelphia soon, and they were in a hurry.

Betsy replied that she would start working immediately and finish as soon as she could. George Ross gave Betsy money for her expenses. Robert Morris told her the name of a ship's merchant who could show her sample flags and outfit her with supplies.

Betsy had a lot to do in very little time. Closing up her shop, she hurried to the shipping merchant's store. The merchant lent her an old flag. Betsy examined it closely. It was made from wool bunting

Thousands of people each year come to see the Betsy Ross flag (bottom) at her house on Arch Street (below).

canton   the top corner of a flag
chatelaine   a hook or chain worn to carry things on

fabric and had extra rows of stitching with sturdy linen thread. The edges were bound with heavy sailcloth. She could see right away that the flag had been made strong enough to withstand severe winds and weather.

Betsy took great care in measuring and cutting the stripes. But when she began to hand-stitch them together, she discovered that she needed a different set of needles for the heavy wool bunting and tough sailcloth. Sewing a flag certainly wasn't anything like turning up a lady's silk hem or tacking ruffles on a shirt.

As soon as Betsy was finished, she got in touch with George Ross, who came by to pick up the flag. When he returned the next day, he reported that General Washington had been pleased with her work and had given his approval. George Ross paid Betsy and told her to make as many flags as she could and as quickly as possible. Money would be advanced to her from time to time.

The flag had seven red stripes and six white ones. The canton had thirteen white five-pointed stars arranged in a circle on a blue background, or field. Forever after, the new American flag would be known as the Betsy Ross flag.

There are no records to indicate that Betsy Ross sewed the first Stars and Stripes flag. However, both her daughter and her niece recalled Ross telling them of the day when Washington, Morris, and Ross visited her shop on Arch Street with a request for a flag.

Analyze the Literature

❶ What changes did Betsy want to make to the flag's design?

❷ Why do you think General Washington wanted a flag before he left Philadelphia?

❸ Why do many people call the first United States flag the Betsy Ross flag?

READ A BOOK

START THE UNIT PROJECT

A History Play With the class, write a play about one of the historical events in this unit. As you read the unit, take notes about the key people and events. Your notes will help you decide what to include in your play.

USE TECHNOLOGY

Visit The Learning Site at **www.harcourtschool.com/ socialstudies** for additional activities, primary sources, and other resources to use in this unit.

LIBERTY BELL PAVILION

On July 8, 1776, the Liberty Bell was rung to celebrate the first public reading of the Declaration of Independence. The bell was rung each year after that until it cracked in 1835. Today the Liberty Bell is a symbol of freedom to people in the United States.

LOCATE IT

PENNSYLVANIA

Philadelphia

Early People to Independence

" Proclaim liberty throughout the land unto all the inhabitants thereof. "

—Bible, Leviticus 25:10 (inscribed on the Liberty Bell, 1752)

CHAPTER READING SKILL

Main Idea and Supporting Details

The most important thought of a chapter, lesson, or paragraph is the **main idea**. The main idea may be stated in a sentence, or it may only be suggested. Facts or examples that provide information to support a main idea are known as **supporting details**.

As you read this chapter, list the main ideas of each lesson. Then write down details that support each main idea.

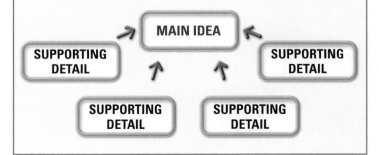

MAIN IDEA
Read to find out how the environment affected the ways of life of the first peoples in the Americas.

WHY IT MATTERS
Today the environment continues to affect how and where people live.

VOCABULARY
theory
migration
technology
agriculture
civilization
diversity
confederation

The Earliest Americans

12,000 years ago	6,000 years ago	Present

12,000 years ago–600 years ago

Thousands of years ago, people lived in the Americas—North America and South America. Scientists have many **theories**, or possible explanations, about how, when, and from where those early people came. However, few of those theories have been proved.

There is one thing that scientists do know about early people. They know that they formed groups as they slowly moved through the Americas over thousands of years. These groups settled in different places and lived different ways of life.

Arrival Theories

In its long history, the Earth has had long periods of freezing cold. During those times, known as Ice Ages, the Earth's climate became so cold that huge glaciers formed. So much water was trapped in glaciers that the water level of the oceans dropped. In some places it dropped so low that land under the sea was uncovered.

A "bridge" of dry land was exposed that connected the continents of Asia and North America. Scientists have given this land bridge the name

FAST FACT Today glaciers still cover one-tenth of the Earth's land area. These glaciers also store almost three-fourths of the world's fresh water.

Beringia (buh•RIN•jee•uh) because it appeared where the Bering Strait is today. There, Asia and North America are only about 50 miles (80 km) apart.

Some scientists believe that between 12,000 and 40,000 years ago, groups of hunters from Asia began to follow animals across Beringia to North America. These wandering people became part of a great **migration**, or movement of people, as they followed the ever-moving animal herds. Over thousands of years, the hunters' children and their children's children spread out all over the Americas. They became the first Americans, or Native Americans.

Other scientists support an "early arrival" theory. They think Beringia appeared during an earlier Ice Age and that people have lived in the Americas much longer than once believed. Some scientists think that early people may not have crossed a land bridge at all. Instead, they believe early people may have used boats to reach the Americas from Asia.

Some people believe that the first Americans did not come from Asia or anywhere else. Many present-day Native Americans, or American Indians, believe that their ancestors have always lived in the Americas.

REVIEW Where was the land bridge located?

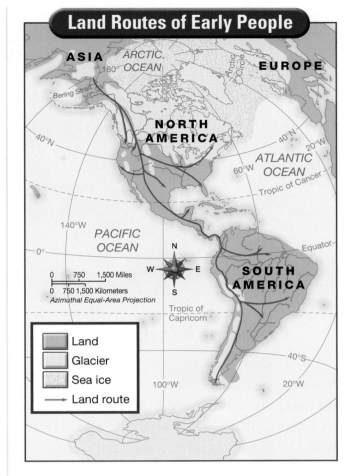

Land Routes of Early People

Movement Over the centuries, early people made their way to the tip of South America—a distance of close to 10,000 miles (16,000 km).

❖ Which continent had more glaciers— North America or South America?

Ears of corn appear on this carving of a god (right) believed to help bring good harvests. Early corn, or maize (far right), was an important part of many ancient Indians' diets.

Changing Ways of Life

Most of the first Americans, or ancient Indians, as archaeologists call them, were nomads who lived and hunted together in small groups. To survive, they gathered fruits and nuts and hunted mammoths and other large animals that wandered the land. They ate the meat and used the animals' fur, skins, and bones to make clothing, shelters, and tools.

At first, people may have faced these large animals armed only with sharp sticks. Then, about 12,000 years ago, they learned how to shape stones into spear points. This was an important change in technology for the ancient Indians. **Technology** is the use of scientific knowledge or tools to make or do something.

Over time, the Earth's climate became warmer and drier. Many of the plants that the large animals ate could no longer grow, so the large animals began to

Pitchers like this were used to hold food or water.

die out. By about 10,000 years ago, most of them had become extinct.

The ancient Indians now had to look for other food sources. They hunted smaller animals, they fished, and they ate many more plants. They later found ways to store food in containers they made from wood, clay, and other materials.

Between 7,000 and 4,700 years ago, some ancient Indians changed their way of life even more. They began to plant seeds and grow their own food. This change marked the beginning of **agriculture**, or farming, in the Americas.

Agriculture made it possible for people to settle in one place. About 5,000 years ago, some ancient Indians began to gather in villages for part of the year. Some people formed what are today called tribes. Over time, each of these tribes came to have a culture that set it apart from other tribes.

REVIEW When did agriculture begin in the Americas?

Early Civilizations

Some ancient Indian groups developed civilizations. A **civilization** is a culture that usually has cities and well-developed forms of government, religion, and learning.

The Olmec (OHL•mek) civilization developed in what is now southeastern Mexico. It lasted from about 1500 B.C. to A.D. 300. During that time the Olmecs developed calendars, a number system, and a form of writing.

Other groups nearby, such as the Maya, learned from the Olmecs. These groups learned so much from the Olmecs that the Olmec culture became known as the "mother civilization" of the Americas.

At about the same time that early civilizations were growing in Mexico and Central America, the Adenas (uh•DEE•nuhz), the Hopewells, and the Mississippians were growing in what is now the eastern half of the United States. Because the people in all these civilizations made large mounds of earth as burial sites and as places of worship, they became known as Mound Builders.

Another important ancient civilization grew up in the dry lands of what is now the southwestern United States.

• GEOGRAPHY •

Chaco Culture National Historical Park

Understanding Places and Regions

Chaco Culture National Historical Park is located in northwestern New Mexico. The park was established to preserve the many ancient Indian sites found there, such as Anasazi (ah•nuh•SAH•zee) pueblos. The largest of these pueblos is Pueblo Bonito (boh•NEE•toh), shown below. It is located in the park's large canyon. Pueblo Bonito is five stories high and made up of 800 rooms. The walls were made of blocks carved out of the surrounding canyon. Pueblo Bonito was once home to more than 1,200 Anasazis.

371
Blanco Trading Post
Nageezi
550
Pueblo Bonito Ruins
N
W E
S
CHACO CULTURE NATIONAL HISTORICAL PARK
371
197
509
0   10   20 Miles
0   10   20 Kilometers
Crownpoint

The civilization of the Anasazi (ah•nuh•SAH•zee), or the "Ancient People," lasted from about 100 B.C. to A.D. 1300. Anasazi houses were built on top of one another and beside each other like our present-day apartment buildings. These houses are known today as pueblos (PWEH•blohs), which is the Spanish word for "villages."

REVIEW What civilizations became known as the Mound Builders?

Native Americans in North America

Over time, early cultures in the Americas gave way to new ones. By about 600 years ago, North America had already become a land of great **diversity**—a land of great differences among the people. There were hundreds of Native American tribes, and each one had its own culture. Groups that lived near one another often shared similar ways of life.

In the Southwest region, many groups of Native Americans continued to live in pueblos. Over time, all the groups who lived in pueblos, such as the Hopis (HOH•peez) and the Zunis (ZOO•neez), became known as the Pueblo peoples. The Pueblo peoples were farmers. To grow crops on their dry lands, they collected water from springs and rain to irrigate their crops.

The Indians of the Northwest Coast lived in a region with thick forests and many rivers. Instead of farming, Northwest Coast tribes such as the Chinooks (shih•NUKS) and Kwakiutls (kwah•kee•OO•tuhlz) used other natural resources to live. For food they hunted animals and gathered plants from the forests. The Indians used wood from the trees to build houses and dugouts—boats made from large, hollowed-out logs. They used their dugouts to fish both in the rivers of the Northwest Coast and in the Pacific Ocean. A few groups hunted whales.

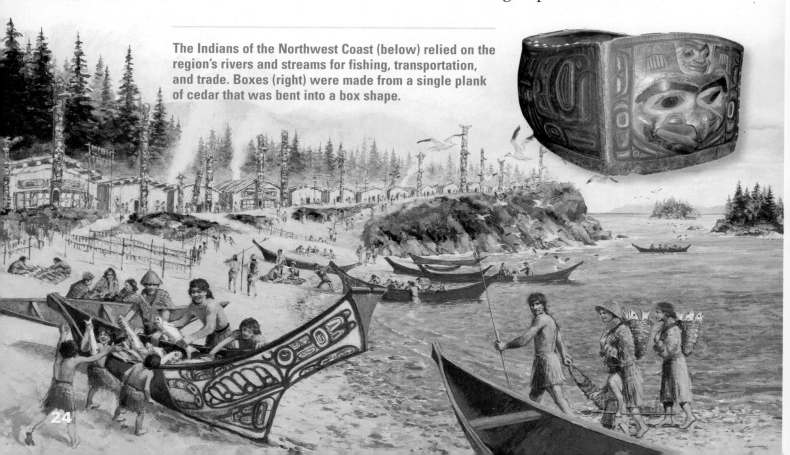

The Indians of the Northwest Coast (below) relied on the region's rivers and streams for fishing, transportation, and trade. Boxes (right) were made from a single plank of cedar that was bent into a box shape.

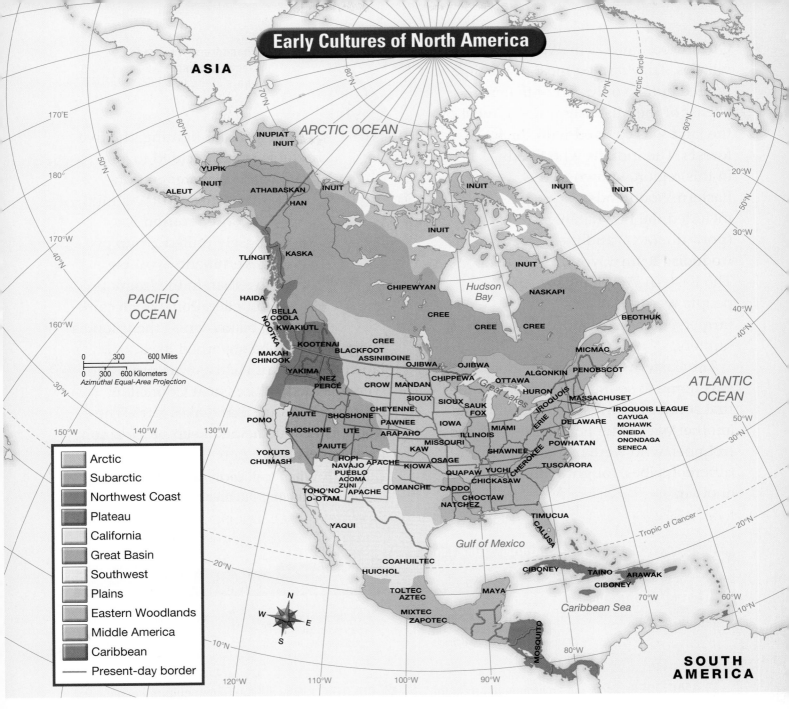

Early Cultures of North America

ASIA

ARCTIC OCEAN

INUPIAT
INUIT

YUPIK
INUIT
ALEUT
ATHABASKAN   INUIT
HAN

INUIT   INUIT   INUIT

INUIT

TLINGIT   KASKA

PACIFIC
OCEAN

HAIDA

CHIPEWYAN

Hudson
Bay

NASKAPI

INUIT

CREE

BELLA
COOLA
KWAKIUTL
NOOTKA

CREE   CREE   CREE

BEOTHUK

KOOTENAI   CREE
BLACKFOOT
MAKAH   ASSINIBOINE
CHINOOK
YAKIMA   OJIBWA   OJIBWA
NEZ
PERCÉ   CHIPPEWA   OTTAWA
CROW   MANDAN   HURON

MICMAC

ALGONKIN   PENOBSCOT

IROQUOIS   MASSACHUSET

POMO
PAIUTE
SHOSHONE

SIOUX
CHEYENNE   SIOUX
SAUK
SHOSHONE   UTE   PAWNEE   FOX
ARAPAHO   IOWA
PAIUTE   KAW   MISSOURI   ILLINOIS
YOKUTS   HOPI
CHUMASH   NAVAJO   APACHE   KIOWA   OSAGE
PUEBLO
ACOMA
ZUNI
TOHO'NO-   APACHE   COMANCHE   CADDO
O-OTAM

ERIE
DELAWARE

MIAMI

SHAWNEE

QUAPAW   YUCHI
CHICKASAW

POWHATAN

IROQUOIS LEAGUE
CAYUGA
MOHAWK
ONEIDA
ONONDAGA
SENECA

TUSCARORA

ATLANTIC
OCEAN

YAQUI

COAHUILTEC
HUICHOL

TOLTEC
AZTEC
MIXTEC
ZAPOTEC

CHEROKEE

CHOCTAW
NATCHEZ

TIMUCUA
CALUSA

Gulf of Mexico

CIBONEY   TAINO   ARAWAK
CIBONEY

MAYA

Caribbean Sea

MOSQUITO

SOUTH
AMERICA

0   300   600 Miles
0   300   600 Kilometers
Azimuthal Equal-Area Projection

Legend:
- Arctic
- Subarctic
- Northwest Coast
- Plateau
- California
- Great Basin
- Southwest
- Plains
- Eastern Woodlands
- Middle America
- Caribbean
- Present-day border

N
W   E
S

Tropic of Cancer

GEOGRAPHY THEME

Regions Many of the names for United States cities, states, rivers, and regions come from Native American languages.

❓ What connections do you see between the names of the Native American cultures on the map and the names of places today?

The environment also affected the way of life of the many Plains Indians groups, who lived on the Interior Plains between the Mississippi River and the Rocky Mountains. There, miles of flat land were covered by grasses. These grasses fed buffalo, which the Plains Indians hunted for food. They used buffalo skins to make clothing and shelters. Some tribes, such as the Blackfeet and the Comanches (kuh•MAN•cheez), lived a nomadic life, following the buffalo as they crossed the land.

Other tribes, such as the Mandans, settled in villages. They farmed most of the time and hunted buffalo only part of the time.

East of the Mississippi River, most of the land was covered with thick forests. The Indians who lived in this region, known as the Eastern Woodlands, included the Powhatans (pow•uh•TANZ) and the Iroquois (IR•uh•kwoy). The Eastern Woodlands people were mostly farmers, gatherers, and hunters.

The Eastern Woodlands region was home to so many different peoples that sometimes tribes fought with one another over land. For many years the Iroquois, who were made up of five different tribes, fought with one another.

After years of fighting, the five Iroquois tribes decided to join together in a confederation (kuhn•feh•duh•RAY•shuhn). A **confederation** is a loosely united group of governments working together. In the Iroquois confederation, which came to be known as the Iroquois League, each tribe governed itself. However, matters such as war and trade were decided by the Great Council. A council is a group that makes laws. The Iroquois League helped keep peace among its members.

REVIEW When had North America already become a land of great diversity?

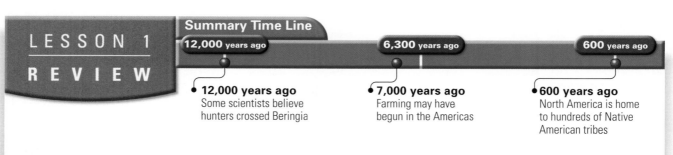

LESSON 1 REVIEW

Summary Time Line

12,000 years ago	6,300 years ago	600 years ago
12,000 years ago Some scientists believe hunters crossed Beringia	**7,000 years ago** Farming may have begun in the Americas	**600 years ago** North America is home to hundreds of Native American tribes

1 **MAIN IDEA** How did environment affect the way ancient Americans lived?

2 **WHY IT MATTERS** How might the forests in the Northwest affect how people live there today?

3 **VOCABULARY** Write two sentences about early people, using the terms **technology** and **agriculture**.

4 **TIME LINE** When might farming have begun in the Americas?

5 **READING SKILL—Main Idea and Supporting Details** What details in the Native Americans in North America section support the main idea of the lesson?

6 **CULTURE** Why did the Olmec culture become known as the "mother civilization" of the Americas?

7 **CRITICAL THINKING—Analyze** How did the Indians survive in the environment of the Northwest Coast?

PERFORMANCE—Create a Brochure Imagine you are visiting one of the Native American groups discussed in this lesson. Create a travel brochure that includes a description of the region's environment and of the people who live there. Then share your brochure with a classmate.

·SKILLS· READING

Identify Causes and Effects

VOCABULARY

cause   effect

▶ WHY IT MATTERS

To find links between events in history, you need to identify cause-and-effect relationships. A **cause** is an event or an action that makes something else happen. An **effect** is what happens as a result of that event or action. Knowing about causes and effects can help you make more thoughtful decisions.

▶ WHAT YOU NEED TO KNOW

The cause of events in history can have more than one effect. An effect can also have more than one cause. You can use these steps to help you identify the causes and the effects of an event.

Step 1 Look for the effects.

Step 2 Look for the causes of those effects.

Step 3 Think about how the causes relate to the effects.

▶ PRACTICE THE SKILL

Iroquois leaders worried that fighting would destroy their people. They helped the tribes end their fighting by forming the Iroquois League.

Follow the arrows on the chart and follow the steps above to help you understand what led to the formation of the Iroquois League.

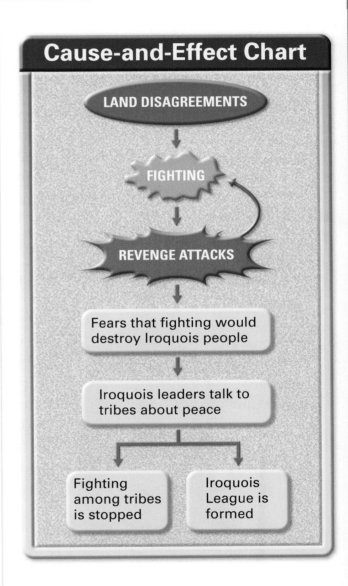

Cause-and-Effect Chart

LAND DISAGREEMENTS

↓

FIGHTING

↓

REVENGE ATTACKS

↓

Fears that fighting would destroy Iroquois people

↓

Iroquois leaders talk to tribes about peace

↓

Fighting among tribes is stopped   Iroquois League is formed

▶ APPLY WHAT YOU LEARNED

Examine pages 20–26 and identify at least two other cause-and-effect relationships. Share your findings with a classmate.

MAIN IDEA
Read to find out why Europeans explored and settled the Americas in the late 1400s and the 1500s.

WHY IT MATTERS
The people who settled different areas of the Americas helped shape the cultures found there today.

VOCABULARY
navigation
expedition
conquistador
empire
colony
missionary
mission
slavery
legislature

Exploration and Settlement

1250–1700

For a long time most Europeans knew nothing about the Americas. The first Europeans known to have explored them were people known as the Vikings. In about A.D. 1000 they sailed to North America from what is now the country of Norway, in northern Europe. The Vikings did not stay long, and few Europeans heard about their trip. About 500 years passed before other Europeans sailed to the Americas.

Early Voyages of Exploration

In 1271 an Italian trader named Marco Polo traveled to Asia. He returned from his trip with exciting stories of the great riches he saw there, especially in China. Those riches included gold, jewels, silk, spices, and perfumes. Trade soon began between Europeans and Asians. European traders did not have to travel all over Asia, as Marco Polo had. Instead, they traveled to cities in what the Europeans called the

This model of a Viking helmet (above) from the A.D. 700s shows how some helmets were designed to protect both a person's head and neck. Viking longships, such as the one below, could travel on rough, open seas.

The Caravel

Sailors at Prince Henry's school learned how to sail a new kind of ship, the caravel. This ship used square or triangular sails to travel long distances quickly. The new kind of sails also made the caravel able to sail against the wind. The caravel was better able to survive stormy seas. Since the caravel was easier to sail and could carry larger cargoes than earlier kinds of ships, it was the preferred ship for ocean exploration in the late 1400s and early 1500s.

Middle East—the region made up of North Africa and Southwest Asia. There, the Europeans traded their goods for other goods that traders had brought from Asia.

Trade over land came to an end in 1453 when the Ottoman Turks took control of the Middle East. They captured the trading city of Constantinople and closed the trade routes to Asia.

Portugal's king, John I, had already decided to look for a water route to Asia. He asked his son, Prince Henry, to start a school in which sailors could be trained in navigation (na•vuh•GAY•shuhn). **Navigation** is the study or act of planning and controlling the course of a ship. At Prince Henry's school, sailors, shipbuilders, and mapmakers worked to make better maps, faster ships, and improved sailing tools.

Prince Henry, who became known as Henry the Navigator, thought the most direct water route to Asia from Europe was to sail south around Africa and then east across the Indian Ocean. In 1488 a Portuguese sailor, Bartolomeu Dias (DEE•ahsh), became the first European to sail to Africa's southern tip, the Cape of Good Hope. Ten years later another Portuguese sailor, Vasco da Gama (dah GA•muh), sailed around the cape and to India.

Italian explorer Christopher Columbus had a different idea—instead of sailing around Africa, Columbus wanted to sail west. He believed that Asia was on the other side of the Atlantic Ocean.

REVIEW Why did King John I want to find a water route to Asia?

Henry the Navigator

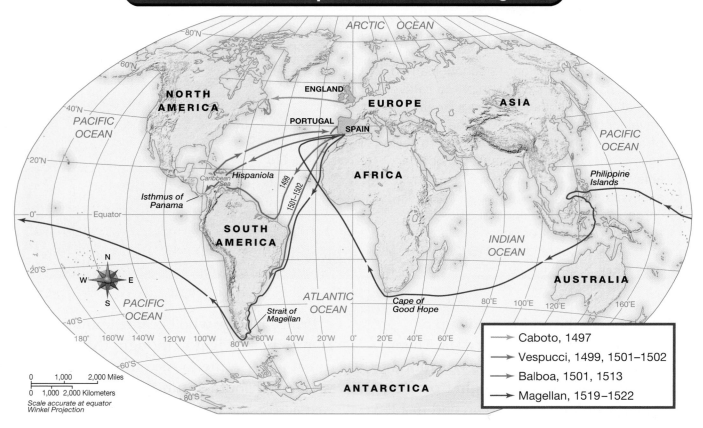

Movement Caboto, Vespucci, Balboa, and Magellan were among the first Europeans to sail across the Atlantic.

❖ Where did Vespucci sail in 1499?

Exploring the Americas

In 1492 Christopher Columbus convinced Spain's King Ferdinand and Queen Isabella to support his **expedition**, or journey, across the Atlantic. Columbus set sail with three ships in August. On October 12 he landed on an island in the present-day Bahamas, off the east coast of North America, and claimed the land for Spain. He called the people who lived there *Indians* because he thought he had sailed to the East Indies, a group of islands in Asia.

With the news of Columbus's success, other European monarchs, or kings and queens, paid to send explorers across the Atlantic. These explorers claimed the lands they visited for the country for which they sailed.

In 1497 the king of England hired an Italian explorer named Giovanni Caboto (joh•VAH•nee kah•BOH•toh) to lead an expedition. Caboto, called John Cabot by the English, may have reached the coast of present-day Newfoundland, in Canada. He, too, thought he had reached Asia.

In 1499, and again in 1501, Spain sent the Italian explorer Amerigo Vespucci (uh•MAIR•ih•goh veh•SPOO•chee) to explore lands south of where Columbus had first landed. Because Vespucci did not see anything that matched the stories that Marco Polo had told about Asia, he said that Columbus had not reached Asia at all. Instead, Vespucci believed Columbus had reached a continent unknown to Europeans. In 1507 a German mapmaker drew a map of the continent and called it *America*, for Amerigo Vespucci.

A Spanish helmet

The first to prove Vespucci's theory about an unknown continent was Vasco Núñez de Balboa (NOON•yays day bahl•BOH•ah). In 1513 Balboa crossed the Isthmus of Panama, the narrow strip of land that connects the continents we know today as North America and South America. He became the first European to see the Pacific Ocean from the Americas.

In 1519 Spain sent Ferdinand Magellan (muh•JEH•luhn) to find a route to Asia around or through the Americas. Magellan did not live to complete his voyage. The 18 sailors who finished the journey became the first people to sail around the world. They proved what Columbus had believed—that Europeans could reach Asia by sailing west.

REVIEW **What did Magellan's voyage prove?**

The Spanish Conquerors

In the 1500s Spain sent explorers to conquer and claim large areas of North America and South America. These explorers and the soldiers with them became known as **conquistadors** (kahn•KEES•tuh•dawrz), which comes from the Spanish word for "conquerors." Some conquistadors wanted to serve their country and win fame. Some dreamed of finding gold and other riches, while others hoped to teach Native Americans about Christianity.

The first conquistador to explore land in what is today the mainland United States was Juan Ponce de León (POHN•say day lay•OHN). In 1513 he landed in what is now Florida and claimed the land for Spain. Later, in 1565, the first permanent European settlement in the present-day United States—St. Augustine, Florida—was built north of where Ponce de León first landed.

Other conquistadors also explored parts of the present-day United States. In 1539 Hernando de Soto (day SOH•toh) landed in Florida.

This painting, titled *Ponce de Leon in Florida*, was painted by Thomas Moran in 1877.

He soon traveled into present-day Georgia, South Carolina, North Carolina, Tennessee, Alabama, Arkansas, and Louisiana. A year later, explorer Francisco Vásquez de Coronado (VAHS•kez day kawr•oh•NAH•doh) began an expedition farther west. He traveled through what are now the states of Arizona, New Mexico, Texas, Oklahoma, and Kansas.

Spain was interested in other parts of the Americas, too. In 1519 Hernando Cortés (kawr•TEZ) landed on the east coast of present-day Mexico and marched to Tenochtitlán (tay•nohch•teet•LAHN), the capital city of the Aztecs. Many years earlier, the Aztecs had conquered other Native American groups in the region and had set up a powerful empire there. An **empire** is a conquered land of many people and places governed by one ruler.

At first the Aztecs' ruler, Motecuhzoma (maw•tay•kwah•SOH•mah), welcomed Cortés and his army. But about two years after they came, the Spanish destroyed the Aztecs' capital and built Mexico City on that site.

To protect its own growing empire in the Americas, Spain built presidios (pray•SEE•dee•ohz), or forts, there. It also formed colonies. A **colony** is a settlement ruled by another country. Spain's first colony in the Americas, New Spain, included all lands north of Panama, the islands of the Caribbean, and parts of South America. Mexico City was its capital.

To help settle New Spain, Spain sent **missionaries**, or people sent out by a church to spread its religion. Most were Catholic priests who believed it was their job to teach Native Americans about

This Spanish mission in New Mexico was founded in 1622. Spain also established missions in what are now the states of Georgia, Florida, Texas, Arizona, and California.

LOCATE IT

Albuquerque

NEW MEXICO

Salinas Pueblo Missions National Monument

This map of what is today the eastern coast of Canada was designed by Samuel de Champlain (right) in 1607.

Christianity. These missionaries built many **missions**, or small religious settlements, in many parts of New Spain.

Many of the colonists who first came to New Spain started huge farms, or plantations. They also started gold and silver mines. But the colonists needed more and more workers for these businesses. So the Spanish chose to force some of the Indian peoples into slavery. **Slavery** is the practice of holding people against their will and making them carry out orders. Many Indians had already died fighting the Spanish. Now millions died from hunger, disease, and too much work. So many Indians died that the colonists decided to find other workers. In time they began to use people who had been taken from their homes in Africa as slaves. So many Africans were taken as slaves that part of Africa's west coast became known as the Slave Coast.

REVIEW Which Spanish conquistadors explored the present-day United States?

The French and the Dutch

The Spanish had claimed most of the land in the Americas. However, both the French and the Dutch hoped to find the Northwest Passage—a water route to Asia that they thought lay north of the Spanish lands. In 1534 the French king sent Jacques Cartier (ZHAHK kar•TYAY) to search for this waterway. He did not find it, but he claimed for France much of what is today eastern Canada. Then, in 1603, Samuel de Champlain (sham•PLAYN) began his explorations of what is now eastern Canada and the state of New York. In 1608 he founded Quebec (kwih•BEK), one of France's earliest permanent settlements in North America.

Other explorers claimed lands farther south for France. In 1673 missionary Jacques Marquette (mar•KET), fur trader Louis Joliet (zhohl•YAY), and five other adventurers explored the upper part of the Mississippi River. They traveled about 2,500 miles (4,023 km) on their journey.

Later, in 1682, René-Robert Cavelier (ka•vuhl•YAY), known as Sieur de La Salle, or "Sir" La Salle (luh•SAL), claimed the whole Mississippi River valley for France and named it Louisiana for the French king, Louis XIV. Many of the French explorers traded with the Indians, exchanging European goods for animal furs.

During the early 1600s, the Dutch were also busy exploring North America. A Dutch company hired Henry Hudson, an English sea captain, to search for the Northwest Passage. Hudson sailed up the coast of North America and into what is now New York Bay. Then he sailed up a river, later named the Hudson River, to present-day Albany. Hudson claimed all this land for the Dutch.

In 1621 the Dutch government set up a company to build settlements along the Hudson River and to trade with the

Henry Hudson

Indians. These settlements became the colony of New Netherland. It included parts of present-day New York and New Jersey. The capital, New Amsterdam, was built at the mouth of the Hudson River. New Amsterdam later became New York City.

REVIEW Why did a Dutch company send Henry Hudson to North America?

Early English Settlements

Jamestown was England's first permanent settlement in North America. It was founded in 1607, in present-day Virginia. Jamestown almost failed because the people who settled there wanted to search for gold to get rich quick. Because they gave little thought to preparing for the coming winter, many died of hunger and cold.

Captain John Smith helped the Jamestown Colony survive. Smith made an important new rule. He said that colonists who did not work could not eat.

By 1619 Virginia had more than 1,000 colonists. That year, they set up an assembly, or legislature, for the colony. A **legislature** is the lawmaking branch of a government. Virginia's legislature was called the House of Burgesses.

Present-day Plymouth, Massachusetts, was the site of England's second permanent North American colony. It was settled mostly by a group of Separatists, or people who had separated from the Church of England because of their beliefs. These Separatists, who became known as Pilgrims, traveled to North America in search of religious freedom.

Located in the village of Sleepy Hollow, New York, this Dutch church dates back to 1685.

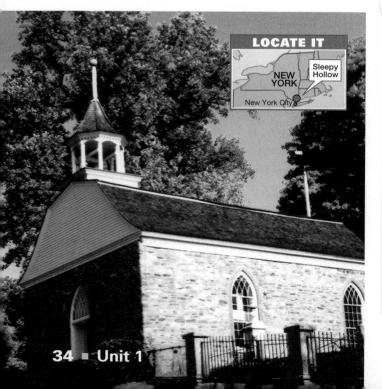

LOCATE IT

NEW YORK

Sleepy Hollow

New York City

This painting, titled *The First Thanksgiving*, was painted by Jennie A. Brownscombe. Foods served at the first Thanksgiving feast included pumpkins, turkeys, fish, clams, oysters, and lobsters.

The Pilgrims were sailing toward Virginia, but a storm blew their ship, the *Mayflower*, off course. When the Pilgrims decided to settle at Plymouth, they wrote an agreement to make laws for the good of the colony and promised they would obey those laws. The agreement became known as the Mayflower Compact.

The Pilgrims arrived at Plymouth on December 21, 1620. They faced a very hard first winter. Half of the settlers died. The whole colony might have failed without the help of an Indian named Tisquantum (tuh•SKWAHNT•uhm), or Squanto, as the English called him. He taught the settlers where to fish and how to plant crops. He also helped keep peace between the local Indian tribes and the Pilgrims. The groups got along for many years. As more English colonists came, however, terrible wars broke out between the colonists and the Indians.

REVIEW Why did the Pilgrims want to start a colony in the Americas?

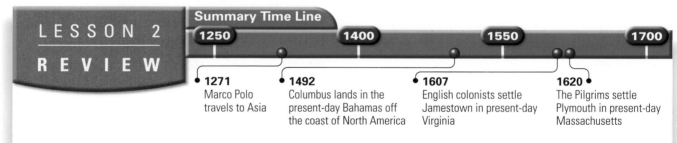

LESSON 2 REVIEW

Summary Time Line

| 1250 | 1400 | 1550 | 1700 |

1271 Marco Polo travels to Asia

1492 Columbus lands in the present-day Bahamas off the coast of North America

1607 English colonists settle Jamestown in present-day Virginia

1620 The Pilgrims settle Plymouth in present-day Massachusetts

1. **MAIN IDEA** Why did Europeans explore and settle in the Americas?

2. **WHY IT MATTERS** Why do you think there are parts of Canada today where many people speak French?

3. **VOCABULARY** Write a sentence that compares and contrasts the terms **empire** and **colony**.

4. **TIME LINE** Which North American settlement was founded first—Jamestown or Plymouth?

5. **READING SKILL—Main Idea and Supporting Details** How did Spain protect its growing empire in the Americas?

6. **HISTORY** Why was Portugal's Prince Henry known as Henry the Navigator?

7. **CRITICAL THINKING—Synthesize** Why do you think the Pilgrims thought it was important to write an agreement to make laws and promise to obey them?

PERFORMANCE—Report the News Suppose that you are a writer in the early days of European exploration. You have been assigned to travel with Christopher Columbus on his voyage in 1492. Write an article that describes one part of the voyage, such as the ships' departure, the days at sea, or the moment when land is first sighted.

·SKILLS· MAP AND GLOBE

Use Latitude and Longitude

▶ WHY IT MATTERS

The numbers in a global address stand for lines of latitude and lines of longitude. You can use these lines to help you describe the **absolute location**, or exact location, of any place on the Earth.

▶ WHAT YOU NEED TO KNOW

Mapmakers use a system of imaginary lines to form a grid on maps and globes. The lines that run east and west are the **lines of latitude**. Lines of latitude are also called **parallels** (PAIR•uh•lelz). This is because they are parallel, or always the same distance from one another. Parallel lines never meet.

Lines of latitude are measured in degrees north and south from the equator, which is labeled 0°, or *zero degrees*. The parallels north of the equator are marked *N* for *north latitude*. This means that they are in the Northern Hemisphere. The parallels south of the equator are marked *S* for *south latitude*. This means they are in the Southern Hemisphere. The greater the number of degrees marking a parallel, the farther north or south of the equator it is.

The lines that run north and south on a map are the **lines of longitude**, or **meridians**. Each meridian runs from the North Pole to the South Pole. Unlike parallels, which never meet, meridians

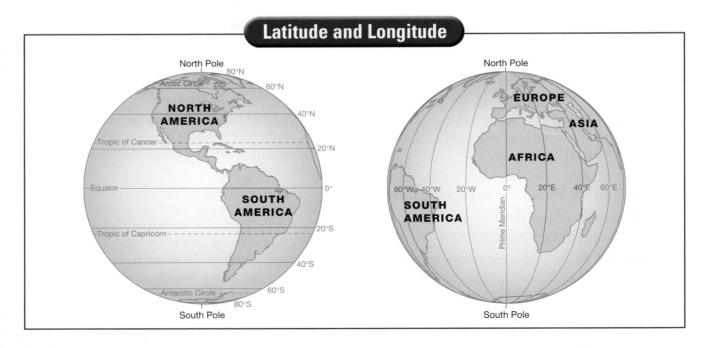

Latitude and Longitude

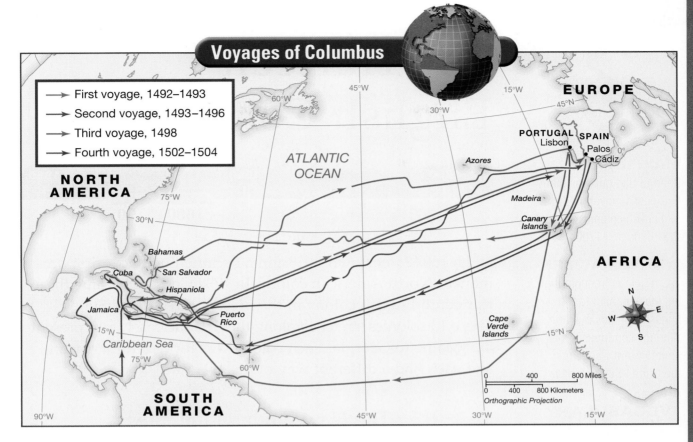

Voyages of Columbus

→ First voyage, 1492–1493
→ Second voyage, 1493–1496
→ Third voyage, 1498
→ Fourth voyage, 1502–1504

NORTH AMERICA

ATLANTIC OCEAN

EUROPE

PORTUGAL SPAIN
Lisbon
Palos
Cádiz

Azores

Madeira

Canary Islands

AFRICA

Bahamas
Cuba
San Salvador
Hispaniola
Jamaica
Puerto Rico
Caribbean Sea

Cape Verde Islands

SOUTH AMERICA

0   400   800 Miles
0   400   800 Kilometers
Orthographic Projection

meet at the poles. Meridians are farthest apart at the equator.

Meridians are numbered in much the same way as parallels are numbered. The meridian marked 0° is called the **prime meridian**. It runs north and south. Lines of longitude to the west of the prime meridian are marked *W* for *west longitude*. They are in the Western Hemisphere. The meridians to the east of the prime meridian are marked *E* for *east longitude*. They are in the Eastern Hemisphere.

▶ PRACTICE THE SKILL

The map above shows Christopher Columbus's voyages to the Americas. Like most maps, it does not show every parallel and meridian. Use the lines of latitude and lines of longitude that are labeled on the map to find an absolute location. At the left-hand side of the map,

find 30°N. At the top or bottom find 15°W. Use one finger of each hand to trace these lines to the point where they cross each other. The Canary Islands are not far from this point.

Use the map to answer these questions.

1 Which trip took Columbus closest to the line of longitude marked 90°W?

2 Columbus's first voyage closely followed which line of latitude?

3 Which location is farther north, 45°N, 60°W or 30°N, 90°W?

▶ APPLY WHAT YOU LEARNED

Use latitude and longitude to tell where you live or where someone else lives in the United States. Write a description that tells how you found the location.

Practice your map and globe skills with the **GeoSkills CD-ROM**.

MAP AND GLOBE SKILLS

3

MAIN IDEA
Read to find out why many Europeans moved to the 13 English colonies during the 1600s and 1700s.

WHY IT MATTERS
The religious freedom that led many people to the English colonies in North America continues to be an important freedom in the United States today.

VOCABULARY

charter
constitution
proprietary colony
trial by jury
immigrant
import
cash crop
royal colony
indentured servant

The Thirteen English Colonies

1250　　　　　　1550　　　　　　1850

1600–1750

In 1607 Jamestown in Virginia became England's first permanent North American colony. In 1732 Georgia became the thirteenth English colony in the present-day United States. These 13 colonies stretched along the Atlantic coast from present-day Maine to Georgia. Each colony was formed for a reason, and each had a different way of life.

The New England Colonies

Not long after the Pilgrims settled at Plymouth, another religious group sailed to the region that English explorers called New England. It includes the present-day states of Maine, Vermont, New Hampshire, Massachusetts, Connecticut, and Rhode Island. Like the Pilgrims, these settlers did not like some of the teachings of the Church of England. However, they did

The painting below shows School Street in Salem, Massachusetts, in 1765.

Analyze Primary Sources

Hornbooks, like the one shown here, were used during colonial times to teach children to read. A hornbook was a flat board with a handle. Pasted on the board was a sheet of paper with reading exercises.

1 The alphabet is shown in lowercase and capital letters.

2 Vowels begin the next section, followed by combinations of vowels and consonants.

3 The Lord's Prayer completes the page.

❷ Why do you think learning to read was important to many colonists?

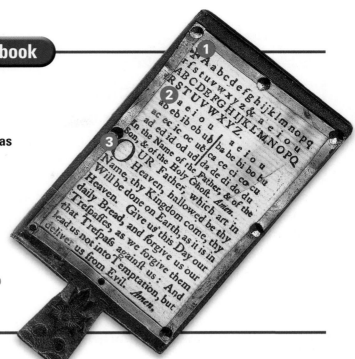

not want to separate from the church. Instead, they wanted to make it simpler, or more "pure." For this reason they became known as Puritans. The Puritans wanted a place where they could freely practice their religion.

In 1628 a group of Puritans and some other English people formed the New England Company. This company received a charter from the king of England that allowed it to start a colony in New England. A **charter** is an official paper in which certain rights are given by a government to a person or business. That same year a group of Puritans sailed to New England and started a settlement named Salem in an area they called Massachusetts Bay.

In 1629 the New England Company became the Massachusetts Bay Company. In 1630 the Puritans' new leader, John Winthrop, brought a large group to settle in Massachusetts Bay. This group of more than 1,000 colonists started several settlements, including Boston, which became the Puritans' main

town. Together the settlements became known as the Massachusetts Bay Colony.

Puritan life centered on religion. At the center of each town was a meetinghouse, where people worshiped and held town meetings. The government was controlled by a few powerful male church members.

The Puritans came to North America so they could worship the way they chose. Yet those who did not share the Puritans' religious beliefs were not welcome in the Massachusetts Bay Colony. Some colonists who disagreed with the Puritan leaders left on their own. Others were expelled, or forced to leave.

Roger Williams, a popular minister from Salem, was one of the people the Puritans expelled. Williams believed that the church and the government should be separate from each other. He also believed that people should not be punished if their religious beliefs were different from those of the Puritan leaders.

In 1635 Roger Williams and his family went to Narragansett (nair•uh•GAN•suht) Bay, in what is present-day Rhode Island.

Anne Hutchinson 1591–1643

Character Trait: Courage

When Anne Hutchinson arrived in the Massachusetts Bay Colony, she began to hold meetings in her home. At those meetings, she talked about ways in which she disagreed with some of the religious teachings of the colony's ministers. She knew these meetings would get her into trouble. Yet she continued to hold them until she was made to leave the colony.

Today, in Boston, there stands a statue of Anne Hutchinson. Words on the base of the statue honor her as "a courageous exponent [champion] of civil liberty and religious toleration."

MULTIMEDIA BIOGRAPHIES
Visit The Learning Site at **www.harcourtschool.com/biographies** to learn about other famous people.

There the Narragansett Indians provided them with food and protection. The following year many of Williams's followers joined him at Narragansett Bay. Williams founded the settlement he called Providence. England's King Charles I later gave Williams a charter for the colony of Rhode Island.

Anne Hutchinson was also forced to leave the Massachusetts Bay Colony. She questioned the authority of the Puritan leaders and spoke out against some of their teachings. In response, the Puritan leaders expelled her. Like Williams, Hutchinson and her followers moved to Narragansett Bay, where they founded a settlement near Providence. Their settlement later became part of the Rhode Island Colony.

Reverend Thomas Hooker decided on his own to leave Massachusetts Bay Colony. He believed that a colony's

Narragansett Bay in Rhode Island is named after the Narragansett Indians. Today most members of the Narragansett tribe still make their home in Rhode Island.

LOCATE IT

Providence
RHODE ISLAND
Narragansett Bay

government should be guided by what its people wanted, not by what its leaders wanted. So in 1636 Hooker and a group of followers left Massachusetts and moved southwest into the Connecticut River valley. There they started several settlements, including present-day Hartford, which became the Connecticut Colony in 1638.

In 1639 the rest of the people in the Connecticut Colony accepted Hooker's beliefs and signed a document called the Fundamental Orders. It was a **constitution**, or plan of government, for Connecticut. It was the first written constitution in North America.

REVIEW Why did the Puritans found the Massachusetts Bay Colony?

The Middle Atlantic Colonies

English colonies also were started in what are now the states of New York, New Jersey, Pennsylvania, and Delaware. These colonies became known as the Middle Atlantic Colonies. They attracted people from many countries and many religious backgrounds.

Even as English colonies grew all around them, the Dutch continued to control New Netherland. In 1664, however, England's King Charles II decided that New Netherland should be made part of the English colonies. He promised New Netherland to his brother, James, the duke of York, and sent warships to take the colony by force.

The colonists, who were unhappy with their leader, gave up without fighting. Both the colony of New Netherland and its capital of New Amsterdam were named New York, for the duke of York.

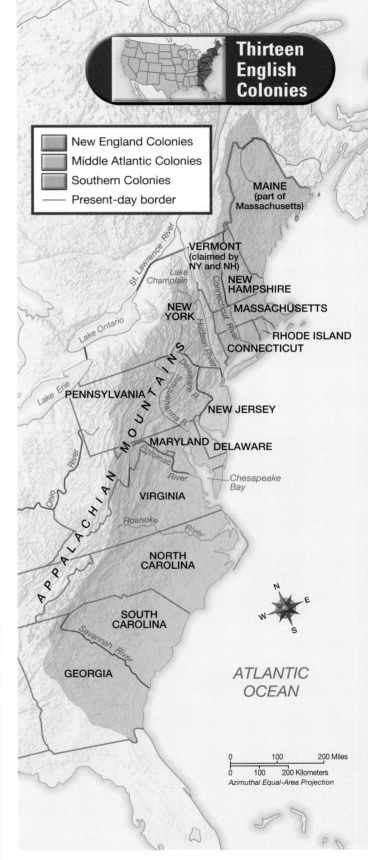

Thirteen English Colonies

- New England Colonies
- Middle Atlantic Colonies
- Southern Colonies
- Present-day border

MAINE (part of Massachusetts)

St. Lawrence River

VERMONT (claimed by NY and NH)

Lake Champlain

NEW HAMPSHIRE

Lake Ontario

NEW YORK

Connecticut River

MASSACHUSETTS

Hudson River

RHODE ISLAND

CONNECTICUT

Lake Erie

PENNSYLVANIA

Delaware R.

Susquehanna R.

NEW JERSEY

APPALACHIAN MOUNTAINS

MARYLAND

DELAWARE

Potomac River

Chesapeake Bay

Ohio River

VIRGINIA

Roanoke River

NORTH CAROLINA

N E W S

SOUTH CAROLINA

Savannah River

GEORGIA

ATLANTIC OCEAN

0   100   200 Miles
0   100   200 Kilometers
Azimuthal Equal-Area Projection

GEOGRAPHY THEME

Regions The 13 English colonies were located along the Atlantic Coast.

❷ Why do you think Georgia was the last English colony to be founded?

The duke helped start the New Jersey Colony when he gave the lands between the Hudson River and the Delaware River to two friends.

William Penn received a charter for a new colony from the king of England in 1681. This charter said Penn could set up a **proprietary colony** to the west of New Jersey. This meant that the king said one person owned the colony and could rule it. Penn's colony was named Pennsylvania, which means "Penn's woods."

William Penn belonged to the Society of Friends, a religious group also known as the Quakers. He believed in freedom

This statue of William Penn stands in front of Pennsylvania Hospital, the oldest hospital in the United States.

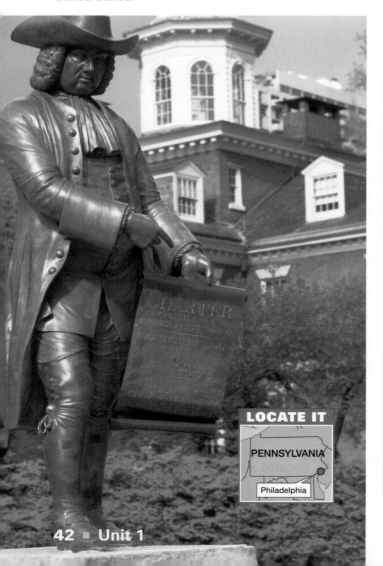

LOCATE IT

PENNSYLVANIA

Philadelphia

of religion and promised settlers that in Pennsylvania they could worship as they pleased. He also said they would have many other freedoms, such as freedom of speech and the right to a trial by jury. **Trial by jury** guaranteed a person accused of breaking a law the right to be judged by a jury of fellow colonists.

The first English settlers arrived in Pennsylvania in 1682. That same year Penn also became the owner of what is now Delaware, which he governed as part of Pennsylvania.

Cheap land and the promise of religious freedom attracted many settlers to the area. Among these settlers were Catholics from Ireland, Lutherans from Germany, and Jews from several countries. Most of these **immigrants**, or people from one country who come to live in another country, sailed into the port of Philadelphia. Penn had founded Philadelphia—a word that is Greek for "brotherly love"—on the Delaware River. Philadelphia soon became a busy port and Pennsylvania's main settlement.

Most of the immigrants who settled in Pennsylvania and the other Middle Atlantic Colonies farmed for a living. They grew fruits, vegetables, and many kinds of grains. The Middle Atlantic Colonies grew so many crops for making bread that they were called the "bread-basket" colonies.

After the harvest farmers would bring their extra crops to market towns. There they would trade their crops for **imports**, or goods brought in from other countries. These imports were tea, sugar, spices, cloth, and shoes.

REVIEW What attracted many settlers to Pennsylvania?

In early colonial Virginia, women often worked in the tobacco fields alongside men.

The Southern Colonies

The settlement of Jamestown in 1607 marked the beginning of Virginia, the earliest of the Southern Colonies. Jamestown had been founded by the Virginia Company, a company formed by English merchants who hoped to make money by starting trading posts in Virginia. The colony did not make money until settlers began to grow tobacco as a **cash crop**—a crop that they could grow to sell.

The Virginia Company made a lot of money selling Virginia tobacco to countries all over Europe. However, the company was poorly managed, and in 1624 it went out of business. The king then made Virginia a **royal colony**, a colony ruled directly by a monarch.

In 1632 Charles I, England's king at that time, gave a charter to start a colony north of Virginia with Cecilius Calvert, Lord Baltimore, as owner. He named the new colony Maryland for the queen.

Lord Baltimore gave some early colonists large pieces of land, on which they started tobacco plantations. Most of the colonists who moved to the Maryland Colony were indentured servants. An **indentured servant** was a person who agreed to work for another person for a certain length of time in exchange for passage to North America.

Lord Baltimore, who was Catholic, wanted to build a colony in North America that not only made money but also was a refuge for Catholics. At that time, Catholics in England were often treated unfairly because they did not belong to the Church of England.

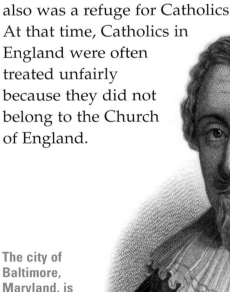

The city of Baltimore, Maryland, is named for Lord Baltimore.

In 1663 King Charles II granted a charter for another Southern Colony. That colony, known as Carolina, was south of Virginia. Colonists there prepared naval stores, and they grew cash crops, such as tobacco and grapes. Carolina did not begin to make money until people started growing rice. Later, on drier land, they also grew indigo, a plant from which blue dye was made.

In 1712 the northern two-thirds of the Carolina Colony was divided into two colonies—North Carolina and South Carolina. North Carolina was a colony of small farms. In South Carolina colonists started large plantations on the coastal plain. Charles Town became the colony's largest city and most important port.

Plantations in South Carolina and the other Southern Colonies needed many workers to plant and harvest cash crops. The plantation owners chose to depend on African slaves to do the work. The work was hard, and the life of a slave was difficult.

As the need for workers grew, so did the slave trade. Africa became part of the regular trade routes followed by ships doing business with the colonies and England, or Britain, as it became known. The paths these ships followed became known as the triangular trade routes. That is because the routes linking Britain, the British colonies in North America, and the west coast of Africa formed great imaginary triangles in the Atlantic Ocean. Traders carried manufactured goods from Britain, raw materials from the colonies, and enslaved people from Africa.

Georgia became the last North American colony to be founded by the British. It was created from the southern third of what had been Carolina. In 1732 James Oglethorpe (OH•guhl•thawrp) led a group to settle the colony, which he named Georgia to honor King George II. Oglethorpe founded Georgia to help debtors, or people who owed money. In Britain, debtors were often put in prison. Oglethorpe offered extra land to

A CLOSER LOOK
Charles Town

Charles Town, later called Charleston, was first built as a fort to protect the South Carolina Colony from the Spanish in Florida. Over time, Charles Town became one of the busiest ports in the 13 colonies.

❶ English ships sailed into Charles Town, bringing goods from Britain and leaving with tobacco, rice, and other products.

❷ Rowboats were often used to load and unload a ship's cargo.

❸ Cannons were set up in Charles Town's harbor to protect it against pirate raids.

❓ Why do you think rowboats were used to load and unload cargo?

settlers who agreed to bring debtors with them. His plan did not work because few people accepted his offer, but many other settlers came.

The colony's charter did not allow traders to take slaves to Georgia, so most farms there were small. In 1752 the law was changed. Many large plantations were started, and many slaves were brought in to work on them.

REVIEW What cash crop made the Virginia Colony rich?

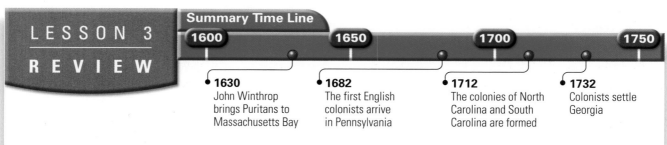

LESSON 3
REVIEW

Summary Time Line

| 1600 | 1650 | 1700 | 1750 |

1630 John Winthrop brings Puritans to Massachusetts Bay

1682 The first English colonists arrive in Pennsylvania

1712 The colonies of North Carolina and South Carolina are formed

1732 Colonists settle Georgia

❶ **MAIN IDEA** Why did people in Europe move to the English colonies in North America during the 1600s and the 1700s?

❷ **WHY IT MATTERS** How is religious freedom still important in the United States today?

❸ **VOCABULARY** Write two or three sentences that compare the terms **royal colony** and **proprietary colony**.

❹ **TIME LINE** Which colony was founded first, Massachusetts or Georgia?

❺ **READING SKILL—Main Idea and Supporting Details** What are some details about the Middle Atlantic Colonies that support the main idea of the lesson?

❻ **ECONOMICS** Why were the Middle Atlantic Colonies known as the "breadbasket" colonies?

❼ **CRITICAL THINKING—Evaluate** What role did religion play in the founding of the English colonies in North America?

PERFORMANCE—Write a Diary Entry Imagine that you are a settler living in the Georgia Colony. Write a diary entry describing a day in your life as a colonist. Read your entry aloud to your classmates.

MAIN IDEA
Read to find out how unhappiness with the way Britain governed the colonies led to the American Revolution.

WHY IT MATTERS
The American Revolution decided whether the 13 colonies would remain tied to Britain or become a separate nation.

VOCABULARY

revolution
representation
boycott
declaration
competition
independence
treaty

The American Revolution

1250   1550   1850

1750–1790

Each of the 13 British colonies had its own legislature to make its laws. However, each legislature's authority was limited. No colonial law could violate British law. All colonial laws also had to be approved by the colony's governor and then by the king and his council. The governor also tried to make the colonists obey laws passed by Parliament, the British lawmaking body in London.

Over time, many people in the 13 colonies grew unhappy with the way the British monarch and Parliament governed them. They decided to break away from Britain and become independent states—the United States of America.

This painting shows the Battle of Quebec in the French and Indian War.

This painting shows a meeting of the members of the British Parliament in the late 1700s. Parliament is the main lawmaking body in Britain.

Disagreements in the Colonies

The events that led to the American Revolution began about 20 years before the colonies cut their ties with Britain. A **revolution** is a sudden, complete change, such as the overthrow of an established government. The first of these events began in 1754, when war broke out between Britain and France over control of the Ohio Valley. This conflict was called the French and Indian War because both sides were helped by Indian allies. Britain won the war in 1763.

After the war the French gave the British new lands in North America, including lands in present-day Canada and Florida and the lands between the Appalachian Mountains and the Mississippi River. Many settlers from the 13 colonies wanted to move to the lands west of the Appalachians. The British government decided that stopping them was the only way to prevent fighting between the settlers and Native Americans.

To do this, King George III issued the Proclamation of 1763. It ordered that the colonists could not buy or settle on land west of the Appalachians.

The colonists ignored the king's proclamation, but it angered them. They became angrier still when they learned that Britain had decided that the colonists should be taxed to help pay for the cost of the French and Indian War and to keep British soldiers in North America to protect the colonies.

The first of these tax laws was passed in 1764. It came to be known as the Sugar Act because it added a tax on sugar and molasses coming into the colonies. The next year Parliament passed the Stamp Act. It made colonists buy a tax stamp for all kinds of paper goods—everything from newspapers to playing cards. The stamp had to be on the paper goods to show the tax had been paid.

REVIEW What was the purpose of the Proclamation of 1763?

Protesting the Taxes

Colonists resented the new taxes because they had no **representation** in Parliament. No one was speaking for them there. One colonist, James Otis, asked why colonists should pay taxes to a government in which they were not represented. Colonists soon began repeating Otis's words,

66 No taxation without representation. 99

Some colonists responded to these new taxes by starting **boycotts**. That is, they refused to buy British goods—especially the paper goods that needed stamps. Other colonists protested in more violent ways. They attacked the homes of tax collectors.

In October 1765, representatives from 9 of the 13 colonies met in New York City to discuss what to do about the Stamp Act.

That meeting became known as the Stamp Act Congress. The Congress approved a **declaration**, or official statement, called the Declaration of Rights and Grievances (GREE•vuhns•ez), which it sent to the British government. The declaration listed the colonists' rights as British citizens and their grievances, or complaints, against the British government. It stated that the British government had no right to tax the colonists without giving them representation.

The colonists' boycotts hurt some British businesses. So, in 1766, Parliament voted to repeal, or do away with, the Stamp Act. But Parliament soon passed new laws that taxed other goods, such as paint, lead, and glass. To enforce these new tax laws and show its authority, Britain sent more tax collectors and more soldiers to the colonies.

LOCATE IT

Boston

MASSACHUSETTS

The picture (below) shows what happened at the Boston Massacre. The photograph (left) shows the area of Boston where the Boston Massacre took place.

Having British soldiers in their cities further angered many colonists, and fighting sometimes broke out between them and the soldiers. On March 5, 1770, a fight started in Boston, Massachusetts. On one of the city's streets, tensions grew as a group of colonists insulted British soldiers and threw rocks at them. Suddenly, when the crowd moved forward, the soldiers opened fire, and five colonists were shot and killed. Americans called this event the Boston Massacre.

The three years following the Boston Massacre were quiet in the 13 colonies. That changed when the British Parliament passed a new law that again made the colonists angry. This law, called the Tea Act, allowed a British company, called the East India Company, to sell its tea to colonists at a lower price than the price charged by colonial companies. That meant that the colonial merchants who sold tea now lost money in their competition with British companies. In business, **competition** is the contest among companies to get the most customers or sell the most goods.

In Boston, on the night of December 16, 1773, some colonists showed just how angry they were about the Tea Act. That night, members of a group known as the Sons of Liberty, disguised as Mohawk Indians, boarded ships docked in Boston Harbor. In what became known as the Boston Tea Party, the Sons of Liberty dumped all the ships' tea into the harbor.

The British government decided to punish the entire colony of Massachusetts for the Boston Tea Party. A new law stopped ships from loading or unloading cargo in Boston Harbor until the colonists paid for all the tea lost by the East India

In the Boston Tea Party, members of the Sons of Liberty dumped chests of tea into Boston Harbor to protest the Tea Act.

Company. Another law ordered the colonists to quarter, or to feed and house, British soldiers. These new laws became known as the Intolerable Acts because the colonists found them impossible to bear.

The colonists knew that something had to be done about the Intolerable Acts. In 1774, representatives from 12 of the 13 colonies met in Philadelphia. The colonists called the meeting the Continental Congress. Members of the Continental Congress agreed to write a statement of rights, which they recorded in a petition that they sent to Parliament. At the same time, they agreed to stop most trade with Britain until Parliament repealed the Intolerable Acts.

REVIEW What were the Intolerable Acts?

John Hancock, president of the
Second Continental Congress

Samuel Adams, a member of the
Second Continental Congress

Independence Is Declared

On April 19, 1775, British General Thomas Gage sent 700 troops toward two towns in Massachusetts. In Lexington, Gage hoped to capture Patriot leaders John Hancock and Samuel Adams. A Patriot was a colonist who was against British rule. Other colonists, known as Loyalists, supported the British monarch and laws. In Concord, Gage hoped to seize Patriot weapons.

In both towns the British troops found armed Patriots waiting for them. The Patriots had been warned by Paul Revere and William Dawes, who rode through the night to tell them that British soldiers were coming.

In May 1775 the Second Continental Congress met. This Second Continental Congress sent a letter to the king, asking for peace. At the same time, it formed an army—the Continental Army. Congress appointed George Washington to lead the army. Before Washington could take command, fighting broke out again in Massachusetts. The first major battle of the Revolutionary War, the Battle of Bunker Hill, took place near Boston on June 17, 1775. The colonists killed or wounded more than 1,000 British soldiers before the British drove the colonists off.

Even as guns were being fired in Massachusetts, many of the colonists still hoped for peace. However, in January 1776 Thomas Paine published a paper that changed many minds. He titled it *Common Sense,* and in it he called for the colonists to cut their ties with Britain.

In June 1776 the Second Continental Congress formed a committee to write a declaration explaining why the American colonies no longer wished to be ruled by Britain.

This statue of Paul Revere is located near Old North Church in Boston.

William Dawes, a Patriot

Mercy Otis Warren, a Patriot, poet, and playwright

The colonies wanted **independence**—the freedom to govern on their own.

Committee member Thomas Jefferson, from Virginia, did most of the writing of the document called the Declaration of Independence. In the Preamble, or the first part, he stated why the Declaration was needed. In the second part he described the colonists' main ideas about government. He explained that "all men are created equal" and that they have "certain unalienable rights." Those rights include "Life, Liberty and the pursuit of Happiness." He then listed the colonists' grievances. The last part of the Declaration said that the colonies were "free and independent states." Congress approved the Declaration on July 4, 1776.

REVIEW What was the significance of the Battle of Bunker Hill?

Benjamin Franklin (left), John Adams (center), and Thomas Jefferson (right) stated in the Declaration that a government gets its power from the consent of the people.

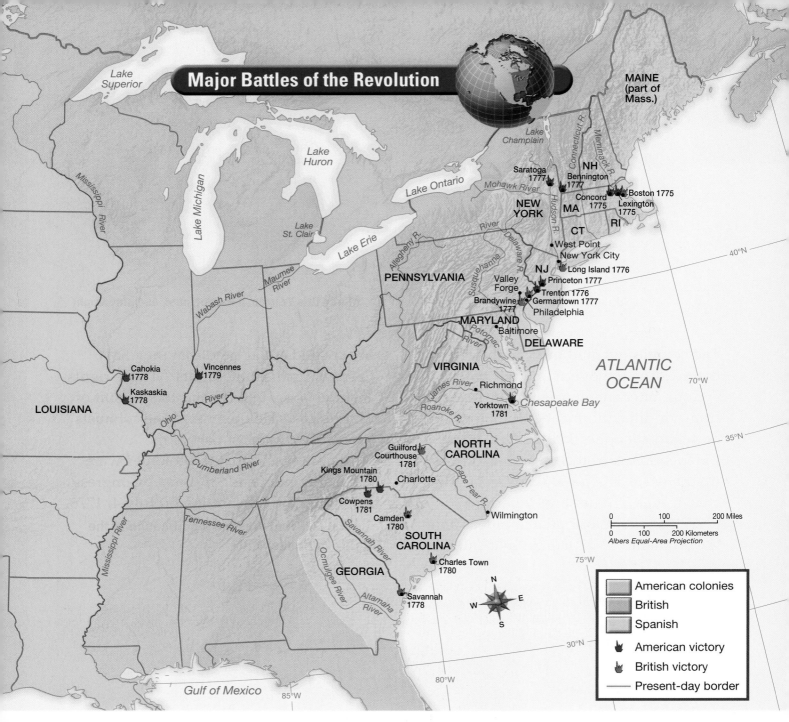

Major Battles of the Revolution

MAINE (part of Mass.)

Lake Superior

Lake Huron

Lake Michigan

Lake St. Clair

Lake Erie

Lake Ontario

Lake Champlain

Connecticut R.

Merrimack R.

NH

Saratoga 1777

Bennington 1777

Mohawk River

Concord 1775

Boston 1775

Lexington 1775

NEW YORK

MA

RI

CT

Hudson R.

West Point

New York City

Long Island 1776

Allegheny R.

PENNSYLVANIA

Delaware R.

Susquehanna R.

NJ

Princeton 1777

Valley Forge

Trenton 1776

Brandywine 1777

Germantown 1777

Philadelphia

MARYLAND

Baltimore

DELAWARE

Maumee River

Wabash River

Cahokia 1778

Vincennes 1779

Kaskaskia 1778

LOUISIANA

Ohio River

VIRGINIA

Potomac River

James River

Richmond

Yorktown 1781

Chesapeake Bay

ATLANTIC OCEAN

Roanoke R.

Cumberland River

Guilford Courthouse 1781

NORTH CAROLINA

Cape Fear R.

Kings Mountain 1780

Charlotte

Tennessee River

Cowpens 1781

Camden 1780

Wilmington

SOUTH CAROLINA

Savannah River

Ocmulgee River

Charles Town 1780

GEORGIA

Altamaha River

Savannah 1778

Mississippi River

Gulf of Mexico

40°N

70°W

35°N

75°W

30°N

80°W

85°W

0   100   200 Miles
0   100   200 Kilometers
Albers Equal-Area Projection

N W E S

	American colonies
	British
	Spanish
	American victory
	British victory
—	Present-day border

GEOGRAPHY THEME

Regions   **This map shows the major battles of the Revolutionary War.**

❓ **In which region did most of the early battles take place? In which region did the later battles take place?**

The Fight for Freedom

In early 1776 George Washington and the Continental Army forced the British out of Boston. The British then went to New York, and Washington and his army followed them. Washington's army lost several battles in New York, such as the Battle of Long Island. By the fall of 1776, the Continental Army had retreated into Pennsylvania. It later won major battles at Trenton and Princeton, in New Jersey.

More good news came the following year. On October 17, 1777, the Americans won a victory at Saratoga, New York. After this battle the French began to help the Americans in the war. They sent guns, ships, and soldiers to help the Patriots.

The Continental Army was encouraged by its victory at Saratoga and by the help from the French. But it still faced hardships. In December 1777 Washington set up headquarters at Valley Forge, Pennsylvania, near Philadelphia. That winter almost destroyed his Continental Army. Many soldiers became ill, and many died. However, the winter gave Washington time to get his army trained.

In October 1781 the Americans and the French attacked the British by land at Yorktown, Virginia, on Chesapeake Bay. The French fleet blocked British ships from bringing in soldiers and supplies. The British were trapped. On October 19, 1781, they surrendered.

John Trumbull's painting shows the British surrender at Yorktown.

Yorktown was the last major battle of the war. The war officially ended on September 3, 1783, when both sides signed a **treaty**, or an agreement between countries. This treaty was called the Treaty of Paris, because it was signed in the city of Paris, France. With this treaty, Britain officially recognized a new and separate country—the United States of America.

REVIEW What treaty ended the war?

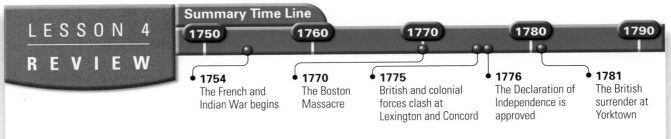

LESSON 4
REVIEW

Summary Time Line

| 1750 | 1760 | 1770 | 1780 | 1790 |

1754
The French and Indian War begins

1770
The Boston Massacre

1775
British and colonial forces clash at Lexington and Concord

1776
The Declaration of Independence is approved

1781
The British surrender at Yorktown

① **MAIN IDEA** Why did the British colonists become unhappy with British rule?

② **WHY IT MATTERS** How would life be different if the 13 colonies had remained part of Britain?

③ **VOCABULARY** Use the word **boycott** to describe the colonists' reaction to British taxes.

④ **TIME LINE** When did the British surrender at Yorktown?

⑤ **READING SKILL—Main Idea and Supporting Details** How did the colonists break away from Britain?

⑥ **GEOGRAPHY** Where was the last major battle of the Revolutionary War fought?

⑦ **CRITICAL THINKING—Hypothesize** What might have happened if the French had won the French and Indian War?

PERFORMANCE—Play a Part With a partner, act out an argument between a colonial merchant and a British governor over taxes on the colonies. Repeat the argument for the class.

1 Review and Test Preparation

• 12,000 years ago
Some scientists believe hunters from
Asia migrated to the Western Hemisphere

USE YOUR READING SKILLS

Complete this graphic organizer to show that you
have identified the main ideas and supporting details
in this chapter. A copy of this graphic organizer
appears on page 14 of the Activity Book.

Environment and Early People of the Americas

SUPPORTING DETAILS

SUPPORTING DETAILS

MAIN IDEA

Environmental
conditions affected the
ways of life of
America's early people.

SUPPORTING DETAILS

SUPPORTING DETAILS

THINK & WRITE

Write a Theory   Imagine you are a scientist studying the migration patterns of early
people in the Americas. Write your own theory about how early people first came to the
Americas. Then, give reasons to support your theory.

Write a Report   Research a colonial
American charter such as the Massachusetts
Bay Company Charter. Write a one-page
report about the charter. Include in the report
who wrote the charter, the general contents
of the charter, and the purpose of the charter.

1492
Christopher Columbus
arrives in the Americas

1565
St. Augustine
is settled

1607
English settlers
arrive at Jamestown

1620
English Pilgrims
settle in Plymouth

1754
The French
and Indian
War begins

1776
The Declaration
of Independence
is approved

1783
The Revolutionary
War ends

USE THE TIME LINE

Use the chapter summary time line to answer these questions.

1 When was St. Augustine settled?

2 What happened in 1754?

USE VOCABULARY

Use each term in a sentence that explains its meaning.

3 **agriculture** (p. 22)

4 **missionaries** (p. 32)

5 **constitution** (p. 41)

6 **cash crop** (p. 43)

7 **boycotts** (p. 48)

RECALL FACTS

Answer these questions.

8 Which Native American tribes formed a confederation?

9 Who were the first known Europeans to have explored the Americas?

10 Where was England's first permanent North American colony?

11 What were the 13 original British colonies in what is now the United States?

Write the letter of the best choice.

12 **TEST PREP**   Which of the following is an ancient North American civilization?
 A Roman
 B Olmec
 C Egyptian
 D Viking

13 **TEST PREP**   Why did many Europeans begin searching for a water route to Asia in 1453?
 F King John I closed trade routes through Portugal.
 G Trade routes were overcrowded.
 H The Ottoman Turks closed the trade routes to Asia.
 J Traveling by water cost less than traveling by land.

THINK CRITICALLY

14 How might European exploration have been affected if Marco Polo had not traveled to Asia in 1271?

15 Do you think that boycotting was a good way for the colonists to protest the new taxes? Why or why not?

APPLY SKILLS

Identify Causes and Effects
Use the chart on page 27 to answer these questions.

16 What caused the Iroquois to fight?

17 What was one effect of the fighting?

Use Latitude and Longitude
Use the map on page 37 to answer these questions.

18 Between which lines of longitude is Hispaniola located?

19 Which location is farther south, 15°N, 75°W or 30°N, 60°W?

20 Which location is closer to Europe, 45°N, 15°W or 30°N, 75°W?

THE GATEWAY ARCH

The Gateway Arch, in St. Louis, Missouri, was completed in 1965 and stands 630 feet (192 m) tall. This monument was built to honor the pioneers who settled the west.

LOCATE IT

St. Louis

MISSOURI

The Nation Grows

❝ The Gateway to the West ❞

—name given in 1843 to the city of St. Louis

CHAPTER READING SKILL

Draw Conclusions

A conclusion is a decision or idea reached by using evidence from what you read and information you already know about a subject. To **draw a conclusion**, you combine new facts with the facts you already know.

As you read this chapter, use new facts and facts you already know to draw conclusions about the United States.

A New Government for a New Nation

MAIN IDEA
Read to find out how the American people worked together to change the government of the United States.

WHY IT MATTERS
Without change, the government of the United States could not continue to meet the needs of the American people.

VOCABULARY
republic
compromise
federal system
legislative branch
executive branch
judicial branch
ratify
amendment
electoral college

1785–1791

Even before the Revolutionary War had ended, the 13 former colonies—now independent states—were busy writing their own state constitutions, or plans of government. At the same time, the Continental Congress knew that the country also needed a national framework that would allow the 13 states to act together as one nation. The Continental Congress wrote the Articles of Confederation to serve as the nation's first plan of government.

The Confederation Period

The writers of the Articles of Confederation planned for a weak central government. Because of their experiences under British rule, many colonists feared a government with a lot of power. The central government created by the Articles of Confederation, however, was too weak. George Washington even described it as "a half-starved, limping government."

John Dickinson headed the committee that wrote the first draft of the Articles of Confederation.

ARTICLES

OF

CONFEDERATION AND PERPETUAL

BETWEEN THE COLONIES OF

NEW-HAMPSHIRE,
MASSACHUSETTS-BAY,
RHODE-ISLAND,
CONNECTICUT,
NEW-YORK,
NEW-JERSEY,
PENNSYLVANIA,

THE COUNTIES OF NEW-C
KENT AND SUSSEX OF
MARYLAND,
VIRGINIA,
NORTH-CAROLI
SOUTH-CAROLI
GEORGIA.

ART. I. THE Name of this Confe
"THE UNITED
OF AMERICA."

ART. II. The said Colonies unite themselves to as never to be divided by any Act whatever, and hereby severally enter into a firm League of Friendship with each other, for their common Defence, the Security of their Liberties, and their mutual and general Welfare, binding the said Colonies to assist one another against all Force offered to or attacks made upon them

FAST FACT When the Articles of Confederation were ratified on March 1, 1781, the President of the Continental Congress officially became President of the United States in Congress Assembled. As a result, Samuel Huntington was the first President of the United States in Congress Assembled.

The Articles did not give Congress the power to raise an army or make laws about trade or taxes. It had to ask the states for the power to do these things. It also had to ask the states for the money it needed to run the central government.

An event known as Shays's Rebellion showed many American leaders that the country needed a stronger central government. After the American Revolution many people had money troubles. All over the country many farmers did not have enough money to pay their debts or their state taxes. If they did not pay their debts or their taxes, the state could take away their farms or put them in prison.

Shays's Rebellion was named for Daniel Shays, a farmer in Massachusetts who thought he would soon lose his farm. Shays, a former Continental Army captain, led an uprising of other farmers like himself. In January 1787 they attacked an arsenal, or building used for storing weapons. There was no national army at that time, so the Massachusetts militia, the state's volunteer army, stopped Shays's Rebellion.

Shays's Rebellion showed just how little power Congress had to stop unrest in the nation. The rebellion and concerns about commerce, or trade, between the states led Congress to call a meeting to talk about changing the Articles of Confederation.

REVIEW Why did the Articles of Confederation limit the powers of Congress?

Planning the Constitution

In May 1787 all states except Rhode Island sent delegates to a meeting in Philadelphia. The delegates discussed whether changing the Articles of Confederation might help solve some of the nation's problems. Instead of changing the Articles, they decided the country needed a new plan of government. For the next four months, delegates met almost every day to work on writing a new constitution for the United States.

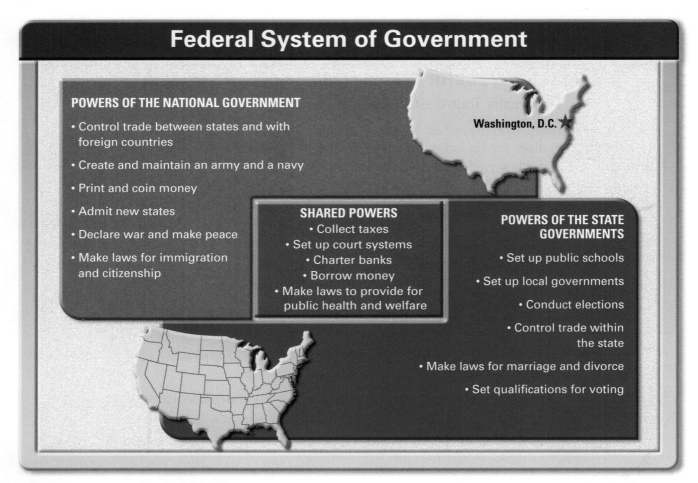

Federal System of Government

POWERS OF THE NATIONAL GOVERNMENT

- Control trade between states and with foreign countries
- Create and maintain an army and a navy
- Print and coin money
- Admit new states
- Declare war and make peace
- Make laws for immigration and citizenship

Washington, D.C. ★

SHARED POWERS
- Collect taxes
- Set up court systems
- Charter banks
- Borrow money
- Make laws to provide for public health and welfare

POWERS OF THE STATE GOVERNMENTS

- Set up public schools
- Set up local governments
- Conduct elections
- Control trade within the state
- Make laws for marriage and divorce
- Set qualifications for voting

Analyze Charts In a federal system some powers are shared.
◈ Which level of government sets qualifications for voting?

Like the Articles of Confederation, the Constitution of the United States would create a republic. A **republic** is a form of government in which people elect representatives to govern the country. In other ways the Constitution was very different from the Articles.

The delegates working on the Constitution realized that one document would never please everyone. Instead, they knew they needed to **compromise**, or give up some of what they wanted in order to reach an agreement.

Their willingness to compromise helped the delegates create a federal system of government. In a **federal system**, the authority to govern is shared by the national, or federal, government and the state governments. The states rule over their own affairs, while the national government acts on matters that concern the whole country. Also, the federal and the state governments share certain powers, such as the power to make laws and the power to tax.

The delegates decided the new federal government would have three branches. The **legislative branch** would make the laws. The **executive branch** would carry out the laws. And the **judicial branch** would settle differences about the meaning of the laws.

None of the delegates wanted any one branch of the government to have too much power. So, they gave each branch of the government ways to check, or limit, the power of the other two branches. This system of checks and balances helps all three branches work together as equal partners.

Although the delegates were able to agree that the government would have three branches, they continued to debate many other issues. One of the most important of these issues dealt with how each state would be represented in Congress. Large states wanted to adopt the Virginia Plan, created by Edmund Randolph and other Virginia delegates. According to the Virginia Plan, the number of representatives each state had would depend on the number of free people living in that state. Small states, on the other hand, wanted to adopt the New Jersey Plan, created by William Paterson and other New Jersey delegates. According to the New Jersey Plan, every state would have equal representation in Congress.

After long, heated debates, delegates were able to reach a compromise. This compromise, which came to be known as the Great Compromise, allowed for two houses in the Congress. In one house, called the House of Representatives, membership would be based on the population of each state. In the other house, known as the Senate, each state would be represented equally.

On September 17, 1787, all of the debates and all of the compromises finally came to an end. On that day, the Constitution of the United States was signed. The Constitution then went to the 13 states for their approval.

REVIEW What was the Great Compromise?

Approving the Constitution

For the Constitution to become law, 9 of the 13 states had to **ratify**, or approve, it. To decide whether to ratify the Constitution, each state held a convention. At each convention, elected delegates would vote for or against the Constitution.

Immediately, people began to take sides. Those who supported the Constitution were called Federalists. They wanted a strong federal government. Those who did not support the Constitution were called Anti-Federalists. Both Federalists and Anti-Federalists gave speeches and wrote newspaper articles and pamphlets to try to persuade others to support their point of view.

Gouverneur (guh•ver•NIR) Morris spent long hours polishing each sentence of the Constitution.

In New York three well-known Federalists—Alexander Hamilton, James Madison, and John Jay—wrote essays that supported the Constitution. Later, the essays were published as a book called *The Federalist*.

In each state the delegates debated whether to ratify the Constitution. One point on which most of the delegates agreed was that the Constitution needed to preserve people's basic rights. Most of the delegates came from states whose state constitutions had such lists of rights to protect their citizens. The Federalists promised that after the Constitution was ratified, a bill, or list, of rights would be added.

By the middle of 1790, all 13 states had ratified the Constitution. By the end of 1791, ten **amendments**, or changes, to the Constitution were adopted. These ten amendments became known as the Bill of Rights. They describe freedoms the government cannot take away and actions the government is not allowed to take.

REVIEW **What did almost all state delegates want added to the Constitution?**

CITIZENSHIP

DEMOCRATIC VALUES
Individual Rights

On September 25, 1789, Congress gave the state legislatures 12 proposed amendments. Two were not adopted. The other 10 amendments became the Bill of Rights. Thomas Jefferson fought hard to get the Bill of Rights added to the Constitution. He felt strongly that the Bill of Rights protected the individual rights and freedoms of United States citizens. These rights, including freedom of religion, freedom of speech, and freedom of the press, are still considered to be the most basic and important rights in a democratic society.

Analyze the Value

1 What is the Bill of Rights?

2 **Make It Relevant** Write a paragraph about why it is important to have a Bill of Rights.

Thomas Jefferson

The New Government Begins

Once the Constitution had officially become the law of the land, it was time to create the government that it outlined. Voters—all property-owning white male citizens—elected the first members of the House of Representatives. In addition, each state legislature chose two United States senators to represent its state.

To choose the nation's first President, state legislatures first voted for people who were called electors. Then the electors, who together are known as the **electoral college**, voted for President. They chose George Washington. Runner-up John Adams became the first Vice President.

On April 30, 1789, George Washington stood on a balcony at Federal Hall in New York City, where the new Congress was to meet for the first time. There he took the oath of office, as it is written in the Constitution. When he finished, the man who had led the oath turned to the crowd and shouted, "Long live George Washington, President of the United States!" The new nation now had its President.

Soon, however, disagreements started. This could be seen clearly between two men whom Washington had chosen to be part of his Cabinet, or group of the President's advisers. They were Thomas Jefferson, secretary of state, and Alexander Hamilton, secretary of the treasury. Jefferson wanted the national government to limit itself to the powers

Alexander Hamilton favored a strong national government.

already outlined in the Constitution. He thought the nation's economy should continue to rely mostly on agriculture. Hamilton wanted a strong national government and thought that the government should encourage manufacturing.

Members of Congress began to take sides. The two sides became the nation's political parties. Hamilton and his followers formed the Federalist party. Jefferson's followers started the Democratic-Republican party.

This painting shows George Washington taking the oath of office in New York City.

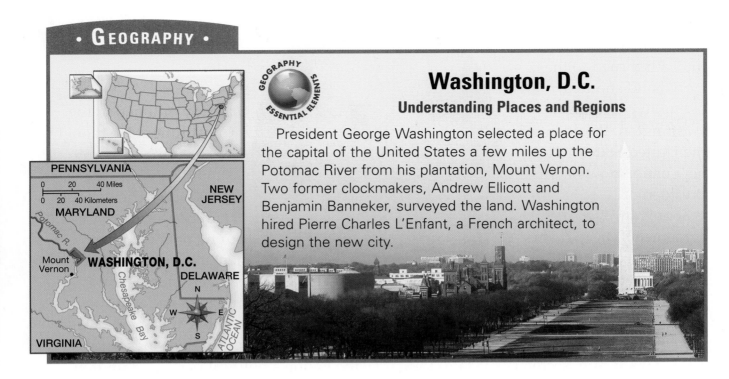

Washington, D.C.
Understanding Places and Regions

President George Washington selected a place for the capital of the United States a few miles up the Potomac River from his plantation, Mount Vernon. Two former clockmakers, Andrew Ellicott and Benjamin Banneker, surveyed the land. Washington hired Pierre Charles L'Enfant, a French architect, to design the new city.

It was sometimes called the Republican party, but it was not like the party with that name today.

Often the leaders in Congress had to compromise so that laws could get passed. In one compromise, they agreed that a national capital would be built that would not be part of any one state.

REVIEW What two political parties formed?

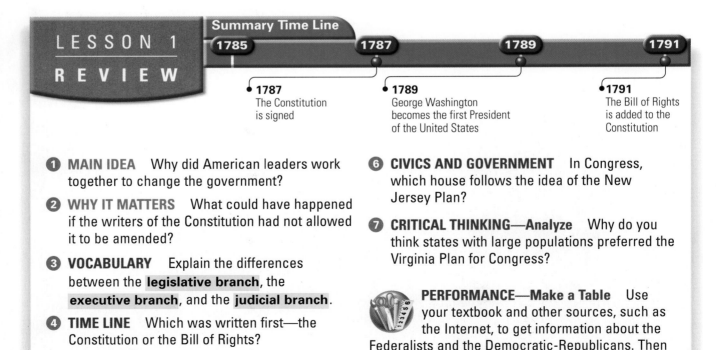

LESSON 1 REVIEW

Summary Time Line

1785 — 1787 — 1789 — 1791

1787 The Constitution is signed

1789 George Washington becomes the first President of the United States

1791 The Bill of Rights is added to the Constitution

1. **MAIN IDEA** Why did American leaders work together to change the government?

2. **WHY IT MATTERS** What could have happened if the writers of the Constitution had not allowed it to be amended?

3. **VOCABULARY** Explain the differences between the **legislative branch**, the **executive branch**, and the **judicial branch**.

4. **TIME LINE** Which was written first—the Constitution or the Bill of Rights?

5. **READING SKILL—Draw Conclusions** Why did people begin to take sides before the Constitution was ratified?

6. **CIVICS AND GOVERNMENT** In Congress, which house follows the idea of the New Jersey Plan?

7. **CRITICAL THINKING—Analyze** Why do you think states with large populations preferred the Virginia Plan for Congress?

PERFORMANCE—Make a Table Use your textbook and other sources, such as the Internet, to get information about the Federalists and the Democratic-Republicans. Then make a table that shows the differences between these two parties. Display your table in the classroom.

From Ocean to Ocean

1250   1550   1850

1750–1850

MAIN IDEA
Read to find out how the United States expanded its lands to stretch from the Atlantic Ocean to the Pacific Ocean.

WHY IT MATTERS
If people had not explored and settled the western lands, the United States as we know it today might have been much smaller.

VOCABULARY

pioneer
territory
nationalism
doctrine
democracy
manifest destiny
dictator

After the Revolutionary War ended, the United States grew. Before the war the western border of the colonies was the Appalachian Mountains. After the war the Treaty of Paris set the new nation's western border at the Mississippi River.

Across the Appalachians

Some Americans, such as Daniel Boone, had settled lands west of the Appalachians before those lands became part of the United States. Boone was a **pioneer**, or person who first settles a place. In 1769 Boone went to what is now Kentucky by following an Indian trail known as the Warrior's Path through a gap in the Appalachians. People became interested in Kentucky as Boone's stories about its natural riches spread.

Six years later, the route Boone followed was made wider for wagons. It came to be known as the Wilderness Road. Over the next few years, thousands of pioneers followed the Wilderness Road. Some settled in Kentucky. Others moved south into what is now Tennessee.

Daniel Boone (leading the horse) led settlers through the Cumberland Gap and into Kentucky.

LOCATE IT

Lexington
KENTUCKY
Cumberland Gap

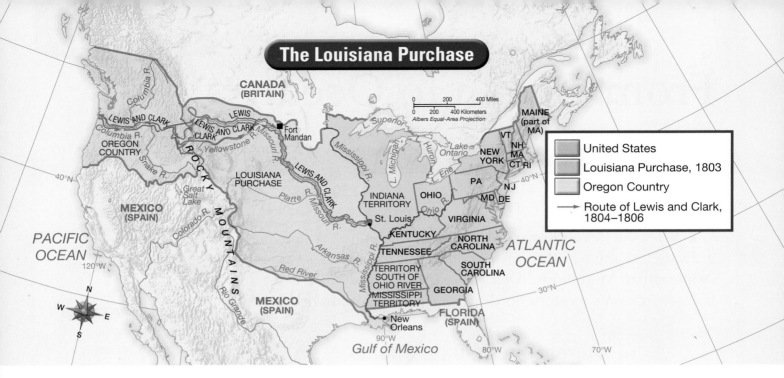

The Louisiana Purchase

Regions The United States purchased Louisiana from France in 1803.
❖ What formed the eastern border of Louisiana?

While more and more people settled in Kentucky and Tennessee, others traveled to lands north of the Ohio River, an area that was then known as the Northwest Territory. A **territory** is land that belongs to a national government but is not a state and is not represented in Congress. The Northwest Territory was made up of the present-day states of Ohio, Michigan, Indiana, Illinois, Wisconsin, and a part of Minnesota.

REVIEW What present-day states made up the Northwest Territory?

The Louisiana Purchase

The large area that the French were now calling Louisiana was bordered by the Mississippi River in the east, the Rocky Mountains in the west, New Orleans in the south, and Canada in the north. This land was also home to many Native American groups.

When Thomas Jefferson became the President in 1801, Spain controlled Louisiana, including the port city of New Orleans. Because the United States had no ports on the Gulf of Mexico, farmers in Kentucky, Tennessee, and parts of the Northwest Territory had to ship their goods down the Mississippi River to New Orleans. At first the Spanish allowed farmers to use this port free of charge. When that changed, it became costly for the farmers to sell their goods. Jefferson wanted to make sure that they could get their products to market.

Not long after he became President, Jefferson heard that Spain had secretly given Louisiana back to France. The President sent representatives to meet with France's leader, Napoleon Bonaparte (nuh•POH•lee•uhn BOH•nuh•part). They asked Bonaparte to sell to the United States land along the east bank of the Mississippi River, including New Orleans.

The representatives could offer as much as $10 million for the land.

Originally, Bonaparte hoped to use Louisiana to once again make France a power in North America. But France was preparing for a war with Britain, and troubles in the French colonies in the West Indies made him change his mind. So he offered to sell all of Louisiana for about $15 million. Louisiana, which was more than 800,000 square miles (2,071,840 sq km) of land, would double the size of the United States.

The Louisiana Purchase, as the territory came to be called, became part of the United States on April 30, 1803. This addition made the United States one of the largest nations in the world.

The government wanted Americans to learn more about the lands of the Louisiana Purchase. So President Jefferson asked Meriwether Lewis and

William Clark carried this compass on his journey through Louisiana.

William Clark to lead an expedition to find out all they could about the territory. In May 1804 Lewis and Clark led about 30 frontier soldiers from their camp near St. Louis, in what is now Missouri, northwest up the Missouri River.

By October the group, which Lewis and Clark called the Corps of Discovery, had reached present-day North Dakota. They built a camp near a Mandan Indian village and spent the winter there. In the spring, they set out again. They hired a French fur trader to go with them and translate the languages of the Indians they met along the way.

Meriwether Lewis (right) and William Clark (far right) spent a winter in Fort Clatsop, in what is now Oregon. This copy of the fort was built in 1955.

The fur trader's wife, a Shoshone (shoh•SHOH•nee) Indian named Sacagawea (sa•kuh•juh•WEE•uh), went with them, too. She agreed to guide the expedition when it reached Shoshone land near the Rocky Mountains.

In November 1805, after traveling more than 3,000 miles (4,828 km), the Corps of Discovery finally reached the Pacific Ocean. In March 1806 the group started back to St. Louis, which they reached in September. The stories they told made others want to travel west, too.

REVIEW **Who were Lewis and Clark?**

The War of 1812

While Lewis and Clark were exploring the Louisiana Purchase, American settlers were pushing the frontier farther west. Many Indians grew angry that settlers were taking their land. They attacked settlers and tried to keep them off their lands. Many Americans in the West blamed the British in Canada for the Indian attacks. The British had been selling the Indians guns and encouraging them to fight American settlers.

Other Americans were angry with the British, too. The British did not want Americans trading with France and other Europeans, so they stopped American merchant ships at sea. They took sailors off the ships and forced them to work on British ships. Taking workers this way is called impressment.

In 1812 Congress declared war against Britain. Many Indians helped the British fight against the Americans. The War of 1812 ended with the signing of a peace treaty in December 1814.

The war ended with no clear winner, but the Indians in the western lands suffered the greatest losses. Many Indians had died in the fighting. After the war new settlers met with little Indian resistance as settlers moved farther and farther west of the Appalachians.

News that the war was over did not reach New Orleans until after the Battle of New Orleans was fought.

This painting, *Birth of the Monroe Doctrine*, by Clyde DeLand, shows Monroe and some members of his Cabinet.

Soon a wave of **nationalism**, or pride in the country, swept through the nation. The United States had proved it was equal to Britain. More than ever before, people took great pride in the fact that they were Americans. For this reason, the years from 1817 to 1825 are often called the Era of Good Feelings.

With this rise in nationalism, the government began to take a stronger stand with other nations. James Monroe, the nation's fifth President, helped set a new United States–Canada border. He also convinced Spain to give up its claims to West Florida, which had been annexed, or added on, to the United States earlier. These actions helped stop the growth of the European colonies in North America.

In 1823 Monroe took another step toward limiting Europe's activity in the Americas. He announced a new **doctrine**, or government plan of action. The doctrine warned Europe and the rest of the world that the United States was willing to go to war to keep nations from starting more American colonies. This plan came to be known as the Monroe Doctrine.

REVIEW Why was the period between 1817 and 1825 known as the Era of Good Feelings?

The Age of Jackson

By 1826 the United States had grown from the original 13 states to 24 states. Its land area had more than doubled in size. Ideas about democracy also were growing with the nation. In a **democracy** the people rule, and they are free to make choices about their lives and government.

In 1828 Andrew Jackson of Tennessee was elected the seventh President of the United States. The first six Presidents had all come from either Massachusetts or Virginia. Now for the first time a person from a western state had been elected. It was also the first election in which all white American men could vote. Before this time, only white males who owned land could vote.

While serving in the military, Jackson had gotten the nickname Old Hickory.

"He's tough," said his soldiers, "tough as hickory"—hickory being a very hard wood. During the War of 1812, Jackson became a national hero after his troops defeated the British at the Battle of New Orleans.

As President, Andrew Jackson continued to be tough. His toughness led to the harsh and unfair Indian Removal Act of 1830. This act said that all Indians east of the Mississippi had to move to the Indian Territory. This area spread across most of what is now the state of Oklahoma.

Many tribes refused to leave their lands. They chose to fight the soldiers sent to remove them. Many Native Americans were either killed or forced to leave their homes.

Instead of fighting on the battlefield, the Cherokee Nation chose to fight in the United States courts. They had many towns in the Southeast, including New Echota (ih•KOH•tuh), Georgia, the capital of the Cherokee Nation.

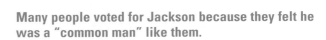

Many people voted for Jackson because they felt he was a "common man" like them.

By 1832 the Cherokees' case had gone to the United States Supreme Court. The Court's ruling said that Georgia had no say over Cherokee lands. The ruling was ignored, and federal troops were ordered to remove the Cherokees.

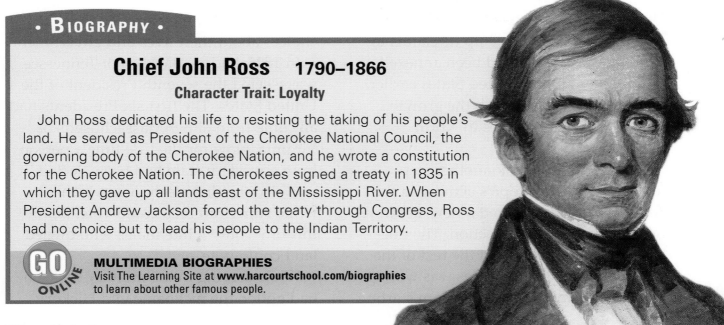

· **BIOGRAPHY** ·

Chief John Ross   1790–1866
Character Trait: Loyalty

John Ross dedicated his life to resisting the taking of his people's land. He served as President of the Cherokee National Council, the governing body of the Cherokee Nation, and he wrote a constitution for the Cherokee Nation. The Cherokees signed a treaty in 1835 in which they gave up all lands east of the Mississippi River. When President Andrew Jackson forced the treaty through Congress, Ross had no choice but to lead his people to the Indian Territory.

GO ONLINE

MULTIMEDIA BIOGRAPHIES
Visit The Learning Site at www.harcourtschool.com/biographies to learn about other famous people.

The Growth of the United States

CANADA

TREATY WITH BRITAIN 1842

TREATY WITH BRITAIN 1818

OREGON TERRITORY 1846

LOUISIANA PURCHASE 1803

Present-day border

MEXICAN CESSION 1848

PACIFIC OCEAN

UNITED STATES 1783

ATLANTIC OCEAN

0   200   400 Miles
0 200 400 Kilometers
Albers Equal-Area Projection

GADSDEN PURCHASE 1853

TEXAS ANNEXATION 1845

1810

1812   1813

FLORIDA 1819

MEXICO

Gulf of Mexico

GEOGRAPHY THEME

Regions By 1848 the United States gained all the land needed to reach the Pacific Ocean.

◆ When did the United States first gain land on the Pacific coast?

In late 1838 federal troops forced the last large group of Cherokees to leave North Carolina and Georgia. They traveled more than 800 miles (about 1,300 km) to the Indian Territory. By March 1839, more than 4,000 Cherokees had died. The Cherokees called their long journey the Trail Where They Cried. It later became known as the Trail of Tears.

REVIEW How did the Cherokees' fight against being forced from their land differ from that of other Indian tribes?

Moving Westward

Settlers continued to push into the lands between the Appalachians and the Mississippi and beyond the nation's borders. Americans who believed in **manifest destiny** felt the nation should stretch from the Atlantic to the Pacific.

One of the areas that American settlers began moving into was Texas, which was then owned by Mexico. In 1821 Stephen F. Austin led a large group of

American settlers to Texas. By 1830, however, Mexico became worried that it was losing control of Texas. So the Mexican government said that no more Americans could settle in Texas. Mexican leaders also said settlers had to pay taxes on goods brought in from the United States.

Fighting broke out between Texans and Mexican troops, which were led by General Antonio López de Santa Anna, Mexico's dictator. A **dictator** is a leader who has total authority to rule. In 1836 Santa Anna and a huge army marched to San Antonio. There they attacked the Alamo, an old Spanish mission that was being defended by about 189 Texans and Americans who came to support them. After more than a week of fighting, the Alamo fell. All 189 Texans and most of their supporters died there. Other Texans fought on. Soon Texas gained its independence from Mexico. It remained an independent country until it became part of the United States in 1845.

Pioneers also pushed west into the Oregon Country. This region included the present-day states of Washington, Oregon, and Idaho, as well as parts of Montana and Wyoming. To reach the Oregon Country, many settlers followed the Oregon Trail, which stretched 2,000 miles (3,219 km) west from Missouri.

People faced many obstacles as they traveled west.

While more and more people moved west, an argument about Texas's southern border led to a war between the United States and Mexico. In 1848 the United States won the war, and Texas's border was set at the Rio Grande. Also, all of present-day California, Nevada, Utah, and parts of present-day Arizona, New Mexico, Colorado, and Wyoming, became part of the United States.

About the same time that California became part of the United States, gold was found there. During 1849 more than 80,000 people went to California from all over, hoping to strike it rich. The movement was called the gold rush, and the gold seekers were called forty-niners. In the next year California became a state.

REVIEW What attracted many people to California?

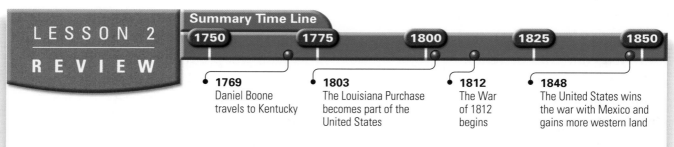

LESSON 2 REVIEW

Summary Time Line

1750 — 1775 — 1800 — 1825 — 1850

1769 Daniel Boone travels to Kentucky

1803 The Louisiana Purchase becomes part of the United States

1812 The War of 1812 begins

1848 The United States wins the war with Mexico and gains more western land

1 **MAIN IDEA** What did Americans believe was the manifest destiny of the United States?

2 **WHY IT MATTERS** How might the United States be different today if Jefferson had not bought Louisiana?

3 **VOCABULARY** Use **manifest destiny** in a sentence about westward expansion.

4 **TIME LINE** Did Louisiana become a part of the United States before or after the War of 1812?

5 **READING SKILL—Draw Conclusions** How did more Americans get involved with the government after the election of 1828?

6 **HISTORY** What was different about the presidential election of 1828?

7 **CRITICAL THINKING—Analyze** How is a government run by a dictator different from the government of a republic?

PERFORMANCE—Write a Report Go to the library and do research on life on the Oregon Trail. Use what you learn to write a report called "A Day on the Oregon Trail." In your report, include details such as what the pioneers ate, where they slept, and what dangers they faced.

Determine Point of View

VOCABULARY

bias

➤ WHY IT MATTERS

You can get information from many sources—television, newspapers, and the Internet. Before you use this information, however, you need to decide if it is reliable.

➤ WHAT YOU NEED TO KNOW

As you study history, pictures provide important information. Some may show an accurate description from many points of view. Others may show one person's point of view. Some points of view are based on fact, but some may show bias. To show **bias** is to show favor either for or against someone or something.

To find the point of view in a picture, follow these steps:

Step 1 **Find out who made the picture. Did that person see what happened or learn about it from accounts of others?**

Step 2 **Think about the audience. The audience it was made for may have affected what was drawn or the way it was drawn.**

Step 3 **Check for bias. Watch for clues that show a one-sided view.**

Step 4 **Compare pictures of the same event. Comparing sources can help you identify bias.**

➤ PRACTICE THE SKILL

Use the picture below and the picture on page 72 to answer these questions.

1 In what ways are the pictures alike? How are they different?

2 Which picture shows a more positive view of moving west?

➤ APPLY WHAT YOU LEARNED

With a partner, look at the pictures in a magazine article. Follow the steps listed here to study the pictures. Describe whether the pictures show bias. Explain.

READING SKILLS

The Corps of Discovery

Not long after President Thomas Jefferson chose Meriwether Lewis to lead the Corps of Discovery, Lewis and William Clark began preparing for their journey. Part of the preparation was gathering supplies that the expedition was going to need, including clothing, tools, weapons, maps, and books. The following pictures show some of the supplies taken west by the Corps of Discovery.

FROM THE LIBRARY OF CONGRESS
ONLINE EXHIBIT "THOMAS JEFFERSON: THE WEST"

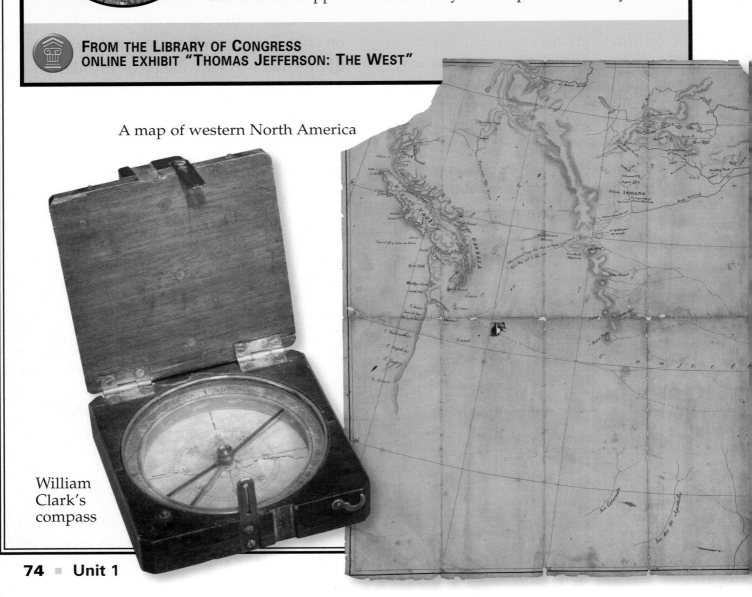

A map of western North America

William Clark's compass

Supply summary with costs

Medals that Lewis and Clark would give to Indian chiefs they met

ACTIVITY

Compare and Contrast   Make a list of supplies that you might need today on a cross-country expedition of 30 people. Gather information about costs for your supplies, and estimate the total cost of your expedition.

RESEARCH

Visit The Learning Site at **www.harcourtschool.com/ primarysources** to research other primary sources.

3

MAIN IDEA

Read to find out how new inventions changed life in the United States in the early to mid-1800s.

WHY IT MATTERS

The Industrial Revolution helped the United States become one of the richest, most powerful nations in the world.

VOCABULARY

Industrial Revolution
textile
interchangeable parts
mass production

The Industrial Revolution

1250   1550   1850

1770–1850

While the United States was growing in size during the early 1800s, it was also going through economic changes. The United States remained mostly an agricultural nation. Industry, however, became more important as new inventions changed the way goods were made. People began using machines instead of hand tools. This **Industrial Revolution** affected the way Americans lived, worked, and traveled.

Industries Grow and Change

In the late 1700s Britain was the only country in the world that had machines for spinning thread and weaving **textiles**, or cloth. These machines were so valuable to Britain's economy that the British government said that none of the machines or

Visitors to the Slater Mill Historic Site can see how water was used to power the mill.

LOCATE IT

Pawtucket

RHODE ISLAND

the plans for building them could leave the country. Even the textile workers who used the machines could not leave Britain.

A man named Samuel Slater lived in Britain and worked in a factory there. He memorized how all the machines in the factory were built and how they worked. In 1789 he sneaked out of Britain and took some of Britain's manufacturing secrets to the United States. By doing this, he helped bring the Industrial Revolution to the nation. A year later Slater built a textile mill in Pawtucket, Rhode Island. The mill's machines were built as Slater remembered them. Slater's mill marked the beginning of large-scale manufacturing in the United States.

Before the Industrial Revolution most products were made by hand by skilled workers. That meant that no two products were exactly alike. Even the muskets, or guns, used by the United States Army were handmade. Every piece of every musket was made individually. Parts of one musket would not fit into another musket. If one part of a soldier's musket broke, the soldier needed a whole new gun.

In 1798 Eli Whitney, who had invented the cotton gin, began to make machines that could make identical copies of each part of a musket. Because all the machine-made parts were identical, they were **interchangeable parts**. That is, any one of these identical pieces could be used to make or repair any musket.

Samuel Slater

• SCIENCE AND TECHNOLOGY •

Water Power

The early water-powered mills used during the Industrial Revolution used water from nearby rivers or streams to turn wooden water wheels. These wheels then powered the millstones. The amount of water needed in those days was much less than the amount needed to run many of the machines today. For example, each spindle, or machine that twisted cotton fibers into thread, used only 10 watts of power. This is about the same amount of power needed to light a bulb on a present-day Christmas tree. Today there are many different ways to harness the energy in moving water. The most common way is hydroelectric power, or electricity created by moving water that has been trapped by a dam.

The idea of interchangeable parts spread to other industries, too. Because of this idea, factories could produce large amounts of goods at one time. This system of producing large amounts of goods at one time became known as **mass production**. Factories could use unskilled workers to do the work because it was easy to train them to run the machines.

The nation's growing industries needed more workers. Some of these workers were people who left the nation's farms to work in the cities, where many factories were located. Other workers came from other countries.

REVIEW How did Samuel Slater help bring the Industrial Revolution to the United States?

New Roads and Waterways

As Americans moved west, the need for roads grew. Eastern factories needed better ways to get their goods to western markets. Western farmers needed reliable roads to get their produce to eastern markets. Congress could see that improved ways of transportation were needed. In 1803 Congress voted to build a paved road to Ohio, which had just become a state. This route became known as the National Road.

In 1811 work began on the National Road. The first part of it ran from Maryland to western Virginia. By 1841 the National Road had passed through Ohio and ended in Vandalia, Illinois.

Canal building also became widespread at this time. Boats or barges traveling on canals could carry larger loads at less cost than wagons could traveling on roads. Canals were built all over the United States. The Erie Canal in New York became one of the most important canals built during this time. It was the longest canal in the world.

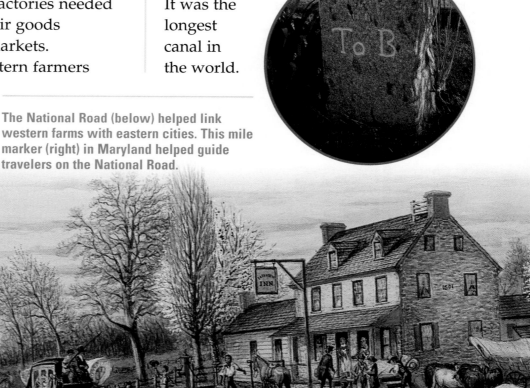

The National Road (below) helped link western farms with eastern cities. This mile marker (right) in Maryland helped guide travelers on the National Road.

Much of its 363 miles (584 km) was dug by immigrants. Most of the work was done by about 3,000 Irish immigrants. Each was paid 80 cents a day, which was three times what they could have earned working in their homeland. However, the hours were long and they worked hard.

The finished canal connected the city of Buffalo, on Lake Erie, with the city of Troy, on the Hudson River. Goods that reached Troy by the Erie Canal then could be shipped down the Hudson River to the port at New York City. In fact, the opening of the Erie Canal helped make New York City the nation's leading trading port.

REVIEW Why did Congress vote to build the National Road?

New Transportation

Canal building lasted only a short time in the United States. Soon people developed faster ways to move people and goods. The invention of the steam engine changed the way many Americans moved from place to place. That is because the steam engine was used both by steamboats for water travel and by railroads for land travel.

In 1807 Robert Fulton sailed his new steamboat, named the *Clermont,* on the Hudson River. The people watching from the riverbanks were amazed.

Movement In 1850 roads, canals, and railroads connected cities.

❖ What forms of transportation connected northern and southern cities?

Transportation in the East, 1850

—— Major road

········ Major canal

········ Major railroad

Because it was powered by a steam engine, the *Clermont* could easily travel up the Hudson against the flow of the river. By the 1820s steamboats had become the main way that people and goods traveled on rivers. By 1860 there were more than 1,000 paddle wheel steamboats traveling the nation's large rivers and lakes.

While travel by steamboat was growing, a faster way to travel by land was being developed. In 1830 a manufacturer named Peter Cooper built the *Tom Thumb*, the first locomotive, or railroad engine, made in the United States. With the help of the locomotive, railroads became a cheap and easy way for both people and goods to travel by land.

By 1850 about 9,000 miles (14,500 km) of track had been laid in the United States, and most of the large cities in the East were connected by railroads.

REVIEW How did the steamboat improve river travel?

Because steamboats were powered by steam engines, they could travel against the flow of a river. Until this time, boats had not been able to travel easily upstream.

1 paddle wheel
2 steam engine
3 lifeboats
4 steam escape valves
5 smokestacks
6 pilot house
7 pilot
8 officers' cabins
9 hurricane deck
10 boiler deck
11 boiler
12 main deck

❖ Why do you think the pilot house was located on top of the boat?

LESSON 3 REVIEW

Summary Time Line

| 1770 | 1790 | 1810 | 1830 | 1850 |

1789
Samuel Slater brings manufacturing secrets to the United States

1807
Robert Fulton sails his steamboat, the *Clermont*, on the Hudson River

1811
Work begins on the National Road

1850
About 9,000 miles of railroad track have been laid in the United States

1 **MAIN IDEA** How did new inventions change the ways people lived, worked, and traveled in the 1800s?

2 **WHY IT MATTERS** How might the development of businesses have been different if new forms of transportation had not been created?

3 **VOCABULARY** Use the vocabulary terms **interchangeable parts** and **mass production** in a sentence about how manufacturing changed during the Industrial Revolution.

4 **TIME LINE** When did work begin on the National Road?

5 **READING SKILL—Draw Conclusions** How do you think the use of railroads affected communication in the United States?

6 **HISTORY** How did Samuel Slater contribute to the Industrial Revolution in the United States?

7 **GEOGRAPHY** What was the National Road?

8 **CRITICAL THINKING—Synthesize** What kinds of transportation connect parts of the United States today?

9 **CRITICAL THINKING—Analyze** How did better transportation lead to the building of more factories?

PERFORMANCE—Draw a Poster
Review what you learned in this lesson about roads, canals, steamboats, and railroads. Choose one of these topics. Then draw an advertising poster that would make people want to use the form of travel you are illustrating.

·SKILLS·
Use a Double-Bar Graph

CHART AND GRAPH

▶ WHY IT MATTERS

Double-bar graphs can help you see how something has changed over time. They also can help you compare how two things have changed as the years passed.

Imagine that you have a business. A double-bar graph can show you how sales of two products have changed over time. The graph also can allow you to compare the money made from one product with that made from another.

▶ WHAT YOU NEED TO KNOW

The double-bar graph on page 83 shows how the rural and urban populations of the United States changed between 1790 and 1850. The title of the graph shows

this. So does the way the graph is set up. Look at the labels across the bottom. You see years listed by decades, or ten-year periods, starting with 1790 and ending with 1850. Now look on the left-hand side of the graph. The numbers of people are shown by the bars.

Color helps you read the information on the double-bar graph, because it tells which bars represent which populations. On this graph the gold bars show urban populations. The blue-green bars show rural populations.

You can use this graph to find the urban or rural population for any of the given years. Place your finger on the top of a chosen bar, and then move your finger left to the population number to find out how many people that bar represents. Sometimes the top of a bar is between the numbered lines. In those cases, estimate the correct number.

New York City, New York

Urban

PRACTICE THE SKILL

Use the double-bar graph on this page to answer these questions.

1 For which years are populations shown on the graph?

2 During this time, how did the number of Americans living on farms compare with the number living in cities?

3 Was there a time between 1790 and 1850 in the United States when more people lived in cities than in the country? If so, when?

APPLY WHAT YOU LEARNED

Make a double-bar graph that will show your test scores in social studies and in another subject for the next five weeks. Label the bottom of your graph by week for five weeks. Label the left-hand side of your graph by tens, starting with 0 and ending with 100. Then, each week for the next five weeks, keep track of your test scores in those two subjects by making for each subject a bar that shows that week's score. Use one color for social studies bars and another color for the other subject's bars. At the end of the five weeks, write a sentence comparing your social studies scores with your scores in the other subject, based on what your double-bar graph tells you.

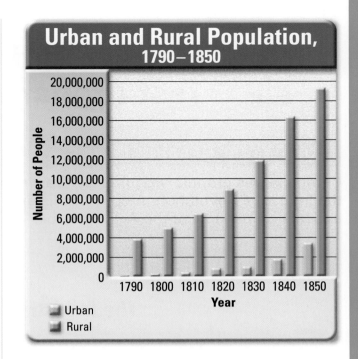

Urban and Rural Population, 1790–1850

Number of People / *Year*

☐ Urban
☐ Rural

Rural

Forbestown, California

2 Review and Test Preparation

Summary Time Line
1750

● **1787**
Shays's Rebellion

● **1789**
George Washington becomes President

USE YOUR READING SKILLS

Complete this graphic organizer by drawing conclusions about the Industrial Revolution. A copy of this graphic organizer appears on page 24 of the Activity Book.

The Industrial Revolution

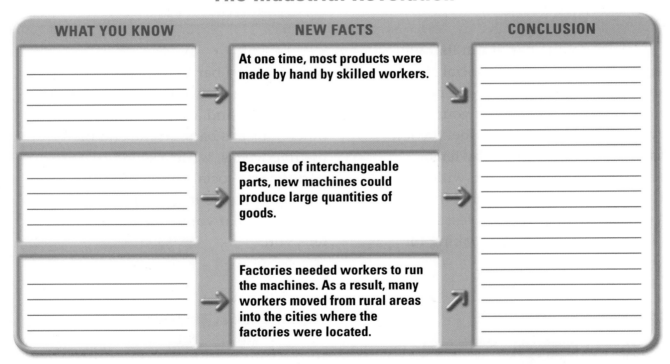

WHAT YOU KNOW → **NEW FACTS** → **CONCLUSION**

At one time, most products were made by hand by skilled workers.

Because of interchangeable parts, new machines could produce large quantities of goods.

Factories needed workers to run the machines. As a result, many workers moved from rural areas into the cities where the factories were located.

THINK & WRITE

Write a Patriotic Essay   Imagine you are a soldier, a pioneer, or a politician in the United States in the year 1817. The Era of Good Feelings has just begun. Write a short essay about why you are proud to be an American citizen.

Write a Proposal   Research an item invented during the Industrial Revolution. Then write a proposal, or plan, about why the invention would benefit people in the United States. Include in your proposal a description of the invention and what it does.

1790
The Constitution is ratified by all thirteen states

1803
The Louisiana Purchase is made

1807
Robert Fulton develops the steamboat

1811
Work begins on the National Road

1836
The Battle of the Alamo

1848
The United States wins the war with Mexico

USE THE TIME LINE

Use the chapter time line to answer these questions.

1 What happened in 1803?

2 When was the Battle of the Alamo fought?

USE VOCABULARY

Use each pair of terms in a sentence that explains the meanings of the terms.

3 **republic, federal system** (p. 60)

4 **ratify, amendment** (pp. 61, 62)

5 **pioneer, territory** (pp. 65, 66)

6 **democracy, dictator** (pp. 69, 71)

7 **Industrial Revolution, mass production** (pp. 76, 78)

RECALL FACTS

Answer these questions.

8 What was the nation's first plan of government?

9 What is the electoral college?

10 What was the Wilderness Road? Where was it located?

11 What was the Monroe Doctrine?

Write the letter of the best choice.

12 **TEST PREP**   Which of the following does not describe a republic?
  A a form of government
  B governed by the people
  C the government followed in the United States
  D led by a dictator

13 **TEST PREP**   Which of the following areas was included in the Louisiana Purchase?
  F West Florida
  G Appalachian Mountains
  H New Orleans
  J Northwest Territory

THINK CRITICALLY

14 What might have happened to the United States if the Constitution had not replaced the Articles of Confederation?

15 Why do you think some products are still made by hand by skilled workers in the United States?

APPLY SKILLS

Determine Points of View
Use the picture on page 73 to answer these questions.

16 What is shown in the picture?

17 What do you think is the artist's point of view?

Use a Double-Bar Graph
Use the graph on page 83 to answer these questions.

18 How many people lived in rural areas in 1790?

19 How many people lived in urban areas in 1810?

20 In which year did more people live in urban areas, 1800 or 1850?

21 Did the United States' total population increase or decrease between 1790 and 1850? How do you know?

Provincetown

GET READY

Provincetown, Massachusetts, is a quaint town filled with little shops and seaside homes. It is located at the place where the Pilgrims first landed hundreds of years ago. Here the Pilgrims wrote and signed the Mayflower Compact, the first agreement by American colonists to govern themselves.

Visitors to this charming community can explore the town's historical past. The Provincetown Museum and the Pilgrim Monument honor the place of the first landing of the Pilgrims in 1620.

WHAT TO SEE

A model of the *Mayflower* sails into Provincetown.

LOCATE IT

MASSACHUSETTS

Provincetown

This painting shows the signing of the Mayflower Compact.

The view from the top of the Pilgrim Monument shows Cape Cod curving into the Atlantic Ocean.

If you visit Provincetown, you can climb to the top of the Pilgrim Monument for a spectacular view.

THE FIRST LANDING PLACE
OF THE
PILGRIMS, NOV. 11, 1620. O.S.
THE MAP IN MOURT'S RELATION
SHOWS THAT NEAR THIS SPOT
THE PILGRIMS
FIRST TOUCHED FOOT ON AMERICAN SOIL

ERECTED BY THE RESEARCH CLUB OF PROVINCETOWN
1917

This plaque marks the spot where the Pilgrims landed.

TAKE A FIELD TRIP

A VIRTUAL TOUR
Visit The Learning Site at **www.harcourtschool.com/tours** to find virtual tours of other historic places in the United States.

A VIDEO TOUR
Check your media center or classroom library for a videotape tour of Provincetown, Massachusetts.

1 Review and Test Preparation

VISUAL SUMMARY

Write a Story Look at the Visual Summary below and choose one of the events to write a story about. Use your imagination and what you have learned in your reading to decide what is taking place in the picture. In your story, tell what the characters in the picture are doing and how they might be feeling.

USE VOCABULARY

Identify the term that correctly matches each definition.

technology (p. 22)

navigation (p. 29)

compromise (p. 60)

textile (p. 76)

1 to give up something to reach an agreement

2 cloth

3 the use of scientific knowledge or tools to make or do something

4 the study or act of planning and controlling the course of a ship

RECALL FACTS

Answer these questions.

5 Where was the Anasazi civilization located?

6 In what year did Columbus make his first journey west across the Atlantic Ocean?

7 Why did the Spanish conquistadors explore the Americas?

8 What is a federal system of government?

9 What was the name of the group led by Lewis and Clark to explore the Louisiana Purchase?

Write the letter of the best choice.

10 **TEST PREP** Who was the first European to see the Pacific Ocean from the Americas?
 A Henry the Navigator
 B Vasco Núñez de Balboa
 C Ferdinand Magellan
 D Amerigo Vespucci

11 **TEST PREP** The first President of the United States was—
 F Alexander Hamilton.
 G Benjamin Franklin.
 H Thomas Jefferson.
 J George Washington.

Visual Summary

| 1250 | | 1450 | |

1400 Native Americans live throughout North America   p. 24

1492 Columbus lands off the coast of North America   p. 30

1607 The English settle at Jamestown   p. 34

12 What do you think is the world's most important advance in technology? Why?

13 How do you think the American Revolution affected the rest of the world?

14 Why did President James Monroe develop the Monroe Doctrine?

15 How do you think the Industrial Revolution changed family life in the United States?

APPLY SKILLS

Use Latitude and Longitude

Use the map of the Thirteen English Colonies on this page to answer the following questions.

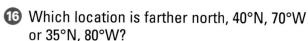

16 Which location is farther north, 40°N, 70°W or 35°N, 80°W?

17 What line of latitude is closest to the border between North Carolina and South Carolina?

18 What city is located closest to the location, 40°N, 75°W?

19 What cities on the map are located to the south of 35°N latitude?

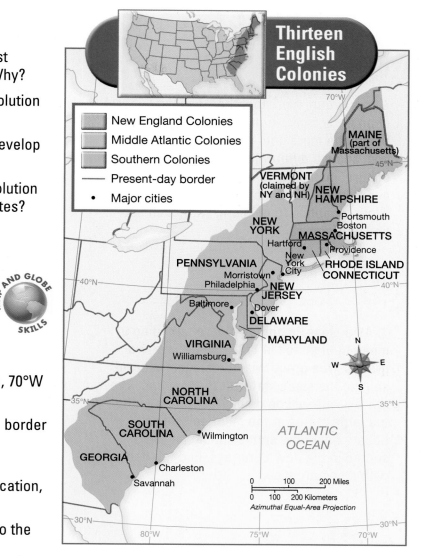

Thirteen English Colonies

- New England Colonies
- Middle Atlantic Colonies
- Southern Colonies
- — Present-day border
- • Major cities

MAINE (part of Massachusetts)

VERMONT (claimed by NY and NH)

NEW HAMPSHIRE

NEW YORK

MASSACHUSETTS

Portsmouth
Boston

Hartford
Providence

New York City

RHODE ISLAND
CONNECTICUT

PENNSYLVANIA

Morristown
Philadelphia

NEW JERSEY

Baltimore

Dover

DELAWARE

MARYLAND

VIRGINIA
Williamsburg

NORTH CAROLINA

SOUTH CAROLINA

Wilmington

ATLANTIC OCEAN

GEORGIA

Charleston

Savannah

0 100 200 Miles
0 100 200 Kilometers
Azimuthal Equal-Area Projection

1650

1850

1776 The Declaration of Independence is signed p. 51

1803 The Louisiana Purchase doubles the size of the United States p. 66

1848 The United States wins the war with Mexico p. 72

89

Unit Activities

Make a Mural

In a group, work together to make a mural of an early civilization in North America. Divide the mural into sections. In each section, show a different part of the civilization's culture, including its cities, its people, its agriculture, its religion, and its government. Write a caption to go along with each section of the mural.

Act as Delegates

As a class, imagine you are attending a meeting of states in 1787. Divide into two groups. One group will be delegates representing the small states at the meeting. The other group will be delegates representing the large states at the meeting. Hold a debate over how states should be represented in the new Congress. End the debate with a compromise.

VISIT YOUR LIBRARY

■ **Dear Mr. President: Letters from a Philadelphia Bookworm** by Jennifer Armstrong. Winslow Press.

■ **The Stone Age News: The Greatest Newspaper of All Time** by Fiona MacDonald. Candlewick Press.

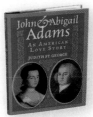

■ **John & Abigail Adams: An American Love Story** by Judith St. George. Holiday House.

COMPLETE THE UNIT PROJECT

A History Play Work as a class to complete the unit project—a history play. Review the notes you took during your reading. Then, decide on the event you want to write your play about. Begin writing your play by making a list of characters. Next, divide your play into two or three different scenes. Each scene should tell about a different part of the event. Invite students from other classes to see your play.

Civil War Times

President Abraham
Lincoln's hat

The Lincoln Memorial, Washington, D.C.

·UNIT·

2

Civil War Times

" A house divided against itself cannot stand. "

—Abraham Lincoln,
Republican State Convention,
Springfield, Illinois, June 16, 1858

Preview the Content

Scan the unit and read the chapter and lesson titles. Use what you have read to make a unit outline. Once you have finished, write down any questions you may have about the Civil War.

Preview the Vocabulary

Compound Words   A compound word is a combination of two or more words that form a new word. Use the meanings of the smaller words below to figure out the meanings of the compound words. Then use the Glossary to check the meanings.

SMALLER WORD		SMALLER WORD		COMPOUND WORD	POSSIBLE MEANING
under	+	ground	=	**underground**	_____
rail	+	road	=	**railroad**	_____
share	+	cropping	=	**sharecropping**	_____
carpet	+	bagger	=	**carpetbagger**	_____

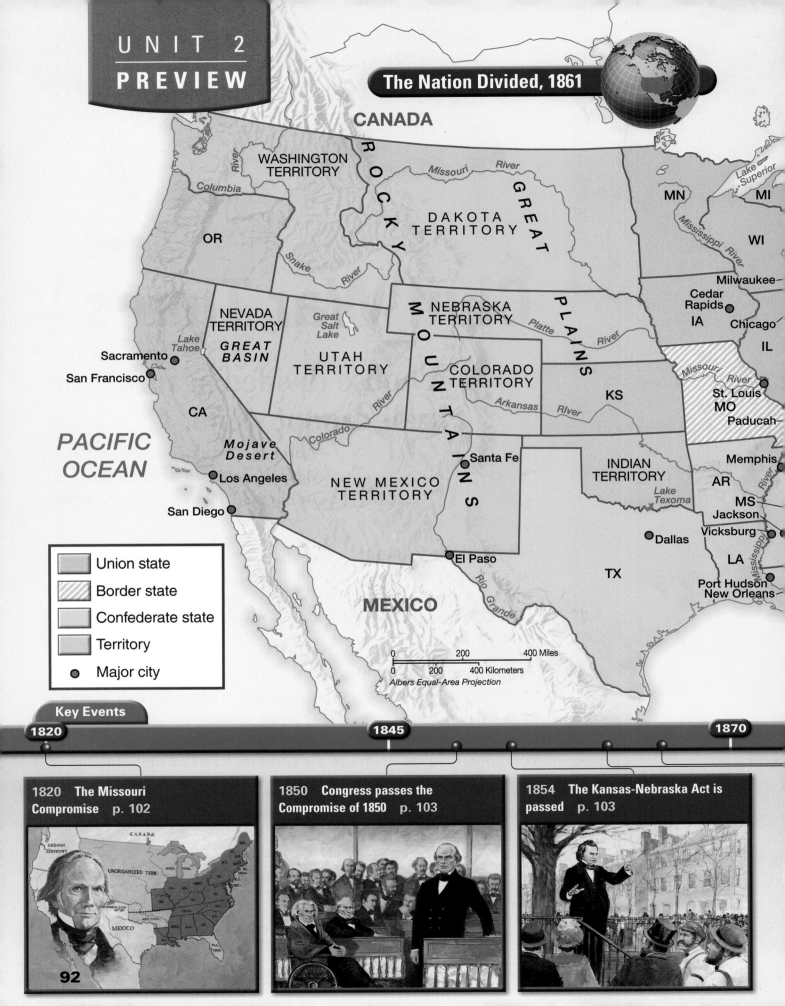

The Nation Divided, 1861

CANADA

WASHINGTON TERRITORY

Columbia River

OR

Snake River

ROCKY

Missouri River

DAKOTA TERRITORY

GREAT

MN

MI

WI

Lake Superior

Mississippi River

Milwaukee

Cedar Rapids

IA

Chicago

IL

NEVADA TERRITORY

GREAT BASIN

Great Salt Lake

Lake Tahoe

Sacramento

San Francisco

CA

UTAH TERRITORY

NEBRASKA TERRITORY

Platte River

COLORADO TERRITORY

Colorado River

Arkansas River

M O U N T A I N S

PLAINS

KS

St. Louis

MO

Paducah

Missouri River

PACIFIC OCEAN

Mojave Desert

Los Angeles

San Diego

NEW MEXICO TERRITORY

Santa Fe

INDIAN TERRITORY

Lake Texoma

Memphis

AR

MS

Jackson

Mississippi River

El Paso

Dallas

Vicksburg

LA

TX

Rio Grande

Port Hudson

New Orleans

MEXICO

Legend:
- Union state
- Border state
- Confederate state
- Territory
- ● Major city

0   200   400 Miles
0   200   400 Kilometers
Albers Equal-Area Projection

Key Events

1820 ——————————— **1845** ——————————— **1870**

1820 The Missouri Compromise p. 102

1850 Congress passes the Compromise of 1850 p. 103

1854 The Kansas-Nebraska Act is passed p. 103

CANADA
OREGON COUNTRY
UNORGANIZED TERR.
MEXICO

92

CANADA

ME

Lake Champlain

Portland

VT NH

Boston

Troy
Albany

MA

Providence

NY

CT

RI

Buffalo

New York City

NJ

Philadelphia

PA

Baltimore

MD

DE

Annapolis

Washington, D.C.

WV (1863)

Richmond

VA

Norfolk

IN

Cincinnati

Ohio River

Louisville
Perryville

KY

Raleigh

Tennessee River

Nashville

NC

TN

Wilmington

SC

Atlanta

AL

GA

Charleston

Savannah

Montgomery

Mobile

Jacksonville

Pensacola

St. Augustine

FL

Lake Okeechobee

Gulf of Mexico

ATLANTIC OCEAN

MI

Lake Huron

Lake Michigan

Lake St. Clair

Detroit

Cleveland

Pittsburgh

OH

Lake Ontario

Lake Erie

APPALACHIAN MOUNTAINS

N E S W

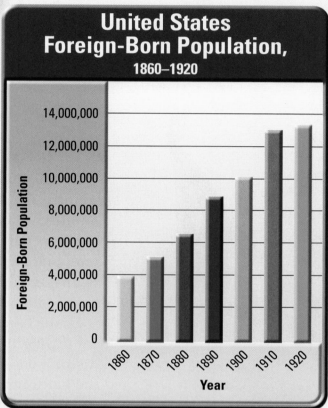

United States Foreign-Born Population,
1860–1920

Foreign-Born Population

14,000,000

12,000,000

10,000,000

8,000,000

6,000,000

4,000,000

2,000,000

0

1860 1870 1880 1890 1900 1910 1920

Year

1895

1920

1861 The Civil War begins p. 118

1865 General Lee surrenders at Appomattox Court House p. 133

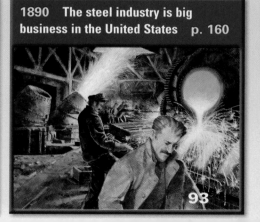

1890 The steel industry is big business in the United States p. 160

93

START with a JOURNAL

All for the Union

THE CIVIL WAR DIARY AND LETTERS OF ELISHA HUNT RHODES

edited by Robert H. Rhodes

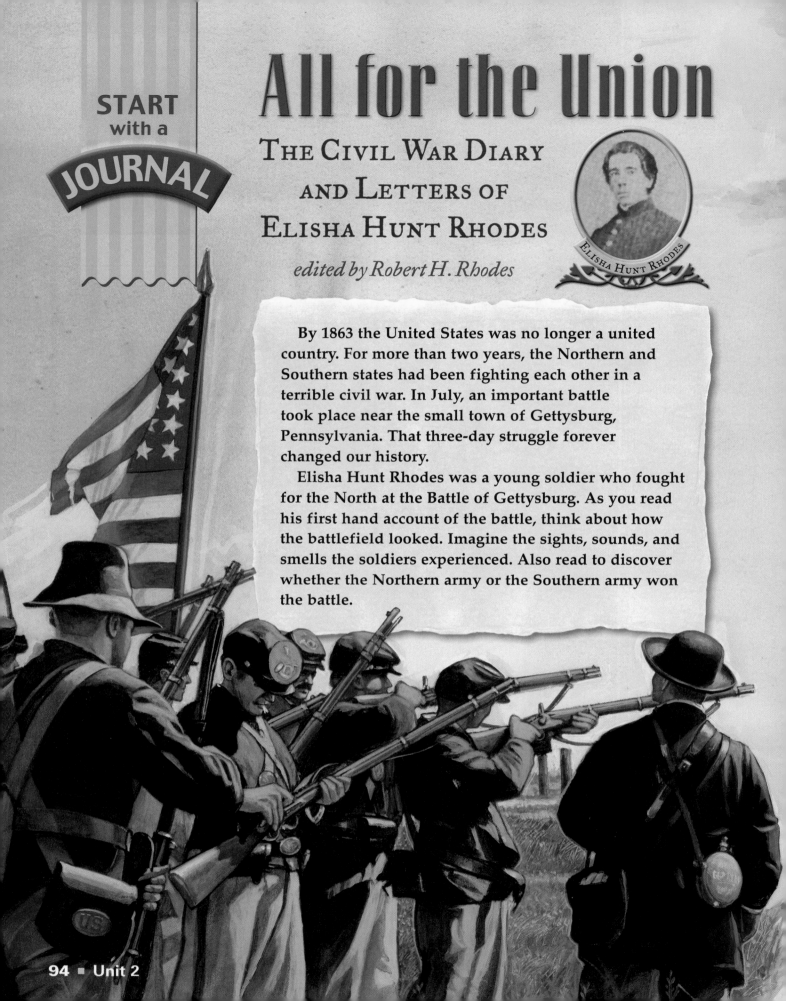

ELISHA HUNT RHODES

By 1863 the United States was no longer a united country. For more than two years, the Northern and Southern states had been fighting each other in a terrible civil war. In July, an important battle took place near the small town of Gettysburg, Pennsylvania. That three-day struggle forever changed our history.

Elisha Hunt Rhodes was a young soldier who fought for the North at the Battle of Gettysburg. As you read his first hand account of the battle, think about how the battlefield looked. Imagine the sights, sounds, and smells the soldiers experienced. Also read to discover whether the Northern army or the Southern army won the battle.

July 3rd 1863—This morning the troops were under arms before light and ready for the great battle that we knew must be fought. The firing began, and our Brigade was hurried to the right of the line to reinforce it. While not in the front line yet we were constantly exposed to the fire of the Rebel Artillery, while bullets fell around us. We moved from point to point, wherever danger to be imminent until noon when we were ordered to report to the line held by Gen. Birney. Our Brigade marched down the road until we reached the house used by General Meade as Headquarters. The road ran between ledges of rocks while the fields were strewn with boulders. To our left was a hill on which we had many batteries posted. Just as we reached Gen. Meade's Headquarters, a shell burst over our heads, and it was immediately followed by showers of iron. More than two hundred guns were belching forth their thunder, and most of the shells that came over the hill struck in the road on which our Brigade was moving. Solid shot would strike the large rocks and split them as if exploded by gunpowder. The flying iron and pieces of stone struck men down in every direction. It is said that this fire continued for about two hours, but I have no idea of the time. We could not see the enemy, and we could only cover ourselves the best we could behind rocks and trees. About 30 men of our Brigade were killed or wounded by this fire. Soon the Rebel yell was heard, and we have found since that the Rebel General Pickett made a charge with his Division and was repulsed after reaching some of our batteries. Our lines of Infantry in front of us rose up and poured in a terrible fire. As we were only a few yards in rear of our lines we saw all the fight. The firing gradually died away, and but for an occasional shot all was still. But what a scene it was. Oh the dead and the dying on this bloody field. The 2nd R.I. lost only one man killed and five wounded. One of the latter belonged to my Co. "B". Again night came upon us and again we slept amid the dead and dying.

Brigade a large body of troops
Rebel the Southern army or a Southern soldier
imminent ready to take place

batteries groupings of big guns
repulsed driven back
R.I. Rhode Island

July 4, 1863— Was ever the Nation's Birthday celebrated in such a way before. This morning the 2nd R.I. was sent out to the front and found that during the night General Lee and his Rebel Army had fallen back. It was impossible to march across the field without stepping upon dead or wounded men, while horses and broken Artillery lay on every side. We advanced to a sunken road (Emmitsburg Road) where we deployed as skirmishers and lay down behind a bank of earth. Berdan's Sharpshooters joined us, and we passed the day in firing upon any Rebels that showed themselves. At 12 M. a National Salute with shotted guns was fired from several of our Batteries, and the shells passed over our heads toward the Rebel lines. At night we were relieved and went to the rear for a little rest and sleep.

skirmishers scouts

July 5th 1863— Glorious news! We have won the victory, thank God, and the Rebel Army is fleeing to Virginia. We have news that Vicksburg has fallen. We have thousands of prisoners, and they seem to be <u>stupified</u> with the news. This morning our Corps (the 6th) started in pursuit of Lee's Army. We have had rain and the roads are bad, so we move slow. Every house we see is a hospital, and the road is covered with the arms and equipments thrown away by the Rebels.

stupified stunned

Analyze the Literature

1. What brigade did Elisha Hunt Rhodes belong to?

2. Where did the Southern army flee after losing the Battle of Gettysburg?

3. How can reading a first hand account of a historical event help you better understand it?

READ A BOOK

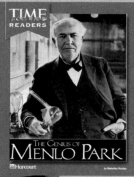

START THE UNIT PROJECT

The Hall of Fame With your classmates, create a Hall of Fame about the key people in the unit. As you read take notes on the contributions key people made. Your notes will help you create your Hall of Fame.

USE TECHNOLOGY

Visit The Learning Site at **www.harcourtschool.com/ socialstudies** for additional activities, primary sources, and other resources to use in this unit.

ANTIETAM NATIONAL BATTLEFIELD

The Battle of Antietam claimed more American lives in a single day than any other one day battle in United States history. Nearly 4,700 Union and Confederate soldiers were lost on September 17, 1862. Visitors to Antietam National Battlefield can tour over 90 monuments built to honor those fallen soldiers.

LOCATE IT

MARYLAND

Antietam National Battlefield

3

The Nation Divided

" Yes, we'll rally 'round the flag, boys, we'll rally once again, Shouting the battle cry of freedom. "

—George Frederick Root,
The Battle Cry of Freedom, 1863

CHAPTER READING SKILL

Categorize

To **categorize** is to classify information by category. You can place people, places, and events into categories to make it easier to find facts.

As you read this chapter, categorize information about regional conflicts and the Civil War.

UNION ARMY

CONFEDERATE ARMY

MAIN IDEA
Read to learn how regional differences caused conflict between Northern and Southern states.

WHY IT MATTERS
If regional differences are strong enough, they can tear a nation apart.

VOCABULARY
sectionalism
tariff
states' rights
free state
slave state

People in the South used money from the cash crops they sold to buy goods from Europe.

Regional Disagreements

1820–1860

As the United States expanded its borders in the first half of the 1800s, strong differences developed among the various regions. Because of those differences, it was difficult for Americans to agree on many issues. In Congress, representatives from the North, South, and West often made decisions based on helping their own section, or region, rather than the country as a whole. This regional loyalty is called **sectionalism** (SEK•shuhn•uh•lih•zuhm), and the disagreements it caused threatened to tear the country apart.

Debate over State Authority

Sectionalism in the United States became a serious problem in 1828, when Congress set a high **tariff**, or tax, on some imports. The tariff made goods from Europe cost more than goods made in the United States. This protected factory owners and workers in the United States from foreign competition and made it easier for factories to sell their products.

The tariff helped the North because most of the nation's factories were located there. However, it did little to help the South, which remained mostly an agricultural region. People in the South sold many of their cash crops to businesses in Europe. In return, they bought many European manufactured goods. Southerners generally opposed the tariff because they did not like having to pay higher prices for those goods.

In 1829 Andrew Jackson became President, and John C. Calhoun of South Carolina became Vice President. Calhoun argued against the tariff. He believed in **states' rights**, or the idea that the states, not the federal government, should have the final authority over their own affairs. Calhoun believed that states had the right to refuse to accept a law passed by Congress.

Although President Jackson was known to support states' rights, he still believed that the federal government had the constitutional right to collect the tariff, even if South Carolina thought it was too high. President Jackson made his feelings clear when he spoke at a dinner honoring the memory of former President Thomas Jefferson. Jackson, looking straight at Calhoun, firmly said, "Our Federal Union—It must and shall be preserved!" Calhoun, who was just as determined, answered, "The Union, next to our liberty most dear. May we all remember that it can be preserved only by respecting the rights of the states."

The debate over states' rights continued after Congress passed another tariff in 1832. Sectionalism grew stronger, and it further divided the people of the United States.

REVIEW Why did most people in the South oppose tariffs? _They did not like to pay higher prices for goods._

Division over Slavery

Another issue that had long divided the nation was slavery. Northern and Southern states had argued about it since the writing of the Constitution. The same argument flared up again with the rapid settlement of the western frontier. As settlers moved west into territories such as Arkansas, Illinois, Iowa, and Missouri, they took with them their own ways of life. For settlers from the North, this meant a way of life without slavery. For settlers from the South, this meant taking along their enslaved workers.

Arguments soon broke out over the spread of slavery to the West. Most

For political advice Jackson sometimes relied on a group of unofficial advisers, whom many referred to as Jackson's "Kitchen Cabinet."

Northerners thought that slavery should go no farther than where it already was—in the South. Most Southern slave owners believed that they had the right to take their slaves wherever they wanted. As the new western territories grew, settlers there asked to join the Union as new states. In each case, the same question arose. Would the new state be a free state or a slave state? A **free state** did not allow slavery. A **slave state** did.

For a time there were as many free states as slave states. This kept a balance between the North and the South in the Senate. Then, in 1819, settlers in the Missouri Territory, a part of the Louisiana Purchase, asked to join the Union as a slave state. If this happened, slave states would outnumber free states for the first time since the founding of the country.

The Missouri Compromise, 1820

CANADA

OREGON COUNTRY

UNORGANIZED TERRITORY

MICHIGAN TERRITORY

MEXICO

MAINE
VT
NH
NEW YORK
MA
CT
RI
40°N
PENNSYLVANIA
NJ
INDIANA OHIO
MD
DE
ILLINOIS
VIRGINIA
MISSOURI
KENTUCKY
NORTH CAROLINA
TENNESSEE
ARKANSAS TERRITORY
SOUTH CAROLINA
ATLANTIC OCEAN
ALABAMA
GEORGIA
MISSISSIPPI
80°W
30°N
LOUISIANA
FLORIDA TERRITORY
Gulf of Mexico
90°W

Legend:
- Free state
- Free territory
- Admitted as a free state
- Slave state
- Slave territory
- Admitted as a slave state
- Missouri Compromise line

0   200   400 Miles
0 200 400 Kilometers
Albers Equal-Area Projection

Regions
The Missouri Compromise line divided lands that could join the Union as free states from lands that could join as slave states.

❓ Which two states were admitted to the Union as part of the compromise?

The Missouri question was debated in Congress for months. Henry Clay, a member of Congress from Kentucky, found himself in the middle of these heated arguments about slavery. Clay himself owned slaves, but he did not want to see the issue of slavery divide the country. He worked day and night to help solve the problem. Finally, in 1820, Clay persuaded Congress to agree to a plan known as the Missouri Compromise.

Under this plan Missouri would be allowed to join the Union as a slave state. Maine, which had also asked to become a state, would join as a free state. This would keep the balance between free states and slave states. Then a line would be drawn on a map of the rest of the lands gained in the Louisiana Purchase. Slavery would be allowed in places south of the line. It would not be allowed in places north of the line.

REVIEW How did the Missouri Compromise keep the balance between free states and slave states? Miss. joined the Union as a slave state   Maine - free state

Henry Clay became known as the Great Compromiser because of his work to settle differences between the North and the South.

A New Compromise

The Missouri Compromise kept the peace for nearly 30 years. During this time six new states joined the Union. The number of free states and slave states remained equal. Then, in 1848, the United States gained new lands after winning the war with Mexico. Settlers in California, a part of these new lands, asked to join the Union as a free state. Once again arguments about the spread of slavery broke out. The Missouri Compromise did not apply to lands outside of the Louisiana Purchase.

Henry Clay again worked toward a compromise—the Compromise of 1850. Under this compromise, California joined the Union as a free state. The rest of the lands gained from Mexico were divided into two territories—New Mexico and Utah. The people in those territories would decide for themselves whether to allow slavery.

Henry Clay, who became known as the Great Compromiser, died in 1852. He never gave up hope that the country would find a peaceful way to settle its differences. On his grave marker in Lexington, Kentucky, are the words *I know no North—no South—no East—no West.* Two years after Clay's death, however, bad feelings between free states and slave states turned to violence.

REVIEW Who became known as the Great Compromiser? Henry Clay

Bleeding Kansas

In 1854 Congress passed the Kansas–Nebraska Act, which changed the rules of the Missouri Compromise. Under the Missouri Compromise, slavery would not have been allowed in the territories of Kansas and Nebraska. Under the Kansas–Nebraska Act, however, people in those territories were given the opportunity to decide for themselves whether to allow slavery. They would decide by voting.

The Kansas Territory quickly became the center of attention in the nation. People for and against slavery rushed into the territory. They hoped to help decide the outcome by casting their votes.

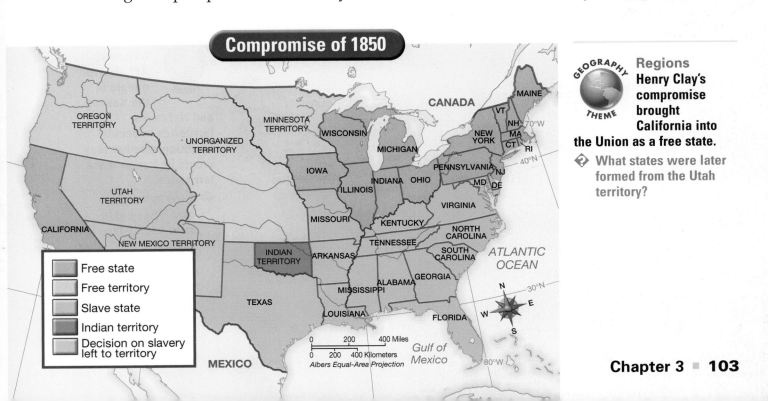

Compromise of 1850

Free state
Free territory
Slave state
Indian territory
Decision on slavery left to territory

GEOGRAPHY THEME

Regions Henry Clay's compromise brought California into the Union as a free state.

❓ What states were later formed from the Utah territory?

Analyze Primary Sources

This poster was used to announce a meeting of those who supported the Kansas–Nebraska Act.

1. The headline states what type of meeting was being held.
2. The date shows when the meeting was held.
3. The phrase indicates that many people were to attend the meeting.

❓ Why do you think quotations are included on the poster?

"UNION IS STRENGTH."

FREE STATE CONVENTION!

①

All who are favorable to union of effort, and a permanent organization of all those who desire to make Kansas a Free State, and who wish to secure, upon the broadest platform, the co-operation of all who agree upon this point, are requested to meet in their respective districts, and appoint Delegates who shall meet in general Convention at

BIG SPRING, THIRD DISTRICT.

② On Wednesday, September 5th,

For the purpose of adopting a Platform upon which all may act harmoniously. The nomination of a Delegate to Congress, will also come up before the General Convention.

Every District will be entitled to five Delegates for each Representative apportioned to the Governor previously to the last election.

Let us see that all our Free State men, without distinction or party issues, are absolutely necessary to success. The proslavery party are fully and effectually organized. No jars nor minor issues divide them. And to contend against them successfully, we also must be united. Without prudence and harmony of action we are certain to fail.

Let every man then do his duty and we are certain of victory.

All Free State men, without distinction, are earnestly requested to take every proper steps to insure a full and correct representation for every District in the Territory.

The Delegates to represent the First and Second Districts in the Convention, will be chosen on the occasion of the

Mass Meeting

③ To be held at Lawrence on August 14th. The residents of these Districts are requested to attend this meeting.

"United we stand; divided we fall."

By order of the meeting held at Lawrence, July 17, 1855.

It was not long before fighting broke out between the two sides. More than 200 people were killed in the bitter conflict that is known as "Bleeding Kansas."

Kansas eventually joined the Union as a free state, but the bloodshed there was a sign of things to come. Many people on both sides of the slavery issue no longer saw compromise as a possible solution. Some in the South began to speak of leaving the Union.

REVIEW What did the Kansas–Nebraska Act do? *it would give K and N the oppurtunity to decide from themselves wether to allow slavery by voting*

The Dred Scott Decision

In 1857 the United States Supreme Court decided the case of an enslaved African American named Dred Scott. Scott had asked the Court for his freedom. The Court said no.

Scott was the slave of an army doctor. His owner moved often and always took Scott with him. For a time they lived in Illinois, a free state. Then they lived in

Regions The Kansas–Nebraska Act allowed people in the Kansas and Nebraska territories to decide by voting whether they would be free or slave territories.

❓ How many territories could now decide for themselves whether to allow slavery?

4

WASHINGTON TERRITORY

OREGON TERRITORY

CALIFORNIA

UTAH TERRITORY

NEW MEXICO TERRITORY

MINNESOTA TERRITORY

NEBRASKA TERRITORY

KANSAS TERRITORY

INDIAN TERRITORY

TEXAS

CANADA

WISCONSIN

IOWA

MISSOURI

ARKANSAS

LOUISIANA

MICHIGAN

ILLINOIS INDIANA OHIO

KENTUCKY

TENNESSEE

MISSISSIPPI ALABAMA

MAINE

VT NH

NEW YORK MA CT RI

PENNSYLVANIA NJ

MD DE

VIRGINIA

NORTH CAROLINA

SOUTH CAROLINA

GEORGIA

FLORIDA

ATLANTIC OCEAN

Gulf of Mexico

40°N

30°N

90°W 80°W

Legend:
- Free state
- Free territory
- Slave state
- Indian territory
- Decision on slavery left to territory

0   200   400 Miles
0   200   400 Kilometers
Albers Equal-Area Projection

Wisconsin, a free territory under the Missouri Compromise.

After his owner died, Scott took his case to court. He argued that he should be free because he had once lived on free land. The case moved up through the federal court system until it reached the Supreme Court. There, Chief Justice Roger B. Taney (TAH•nee) said that because Scott was a slave, he had "none of the rights and privileges" of an American citizen. Having lived in a free territory did not change that.

Taney also declared that Congress had no right to forbid slavery in the Wisconsin Territory. He felt that the United States Constitution protected the right of people to own slaves. Slaves, he wrote, were property. He believed that the Missouri Compromise was keeping people from owning property. This, Taney wrote, was unconstitutional.

Many people had hoped the Dred Scott decision would finally settle the disagree-

In 1857 the Supreme Court decided that Dred Scott should not be given his freedom.

ments among sections of the country over slavery once and for all. Instead, it made the problem worse.

REVIEW Why did the Supreme Court deny freedom to Dred Scott?

b/c he was a slave, he has none of the rights and privileges of an american citizen.

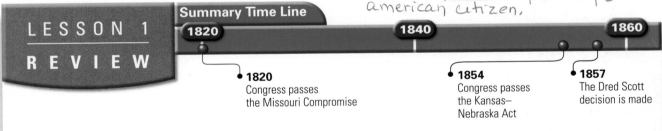

LESSON 1 REVIEW

Summary Time Line

1820 — 1840 — 1860

- **1820** Congress passes the Missouri Compromise
- **1854** Congress passes the Kansas–Nebraska Act
- **1857** The Dred Scott decision is made

1 MAIN IDEA   What were some of the regional differences causing conflict between the North and the South?

2 WHY IT MATTERS   How did regional differences threaten to tear the nation apart?

3 VOCABULARY   What was the difference between a **slave state** and a **free state**?

4 TIME LINE   When was the Kansas–Nebraska Act passed?

5 READING SKILL—Categorize   What states were affected by the Missouri Compromise?

6 GEOGRAPHY   In what region of the country were tariffs helpful?

7 CRITICAL THINKING—Analyze   How was the Missouri Compromise changed by the Kansas–Nebraska Act and the Dred Scott decision?

PERFORMANCE—Write a Plan   Imagine that you are Henry Clay and it is 1850. You need to write a plan that will help the country find a peaceful way to settle its differences. Describe in your plan how the country can settle its regional disagreements without tearing itself apart. Share your plan with the rest of the class.

Identify Frame of Reference

VOCABULARY

frame of reference

▶ WHY IT MATTERS

When you read something that people have written about an event or listen to them tell about it, you need to consider their **frame of reference**—where they were when the event happened or what role they played in it. A person's frame of reference can influence how he or she sees an event or feels about it. It can also influence how a person describes an event. Considering a person's frame of reference as you read or listen can help you better understand what happened.

▶ WHAT YOU NEED TO KNOW

In the 1800s, people's opinions about slavery and other issues were often influenced by where they lived. People who lived in the South, North, and West all had different frames of reference.

SENATOR JAMES HENRY HAMMOND, South Carolina, 1858

❝The greatest strength of the South arises from the harmony of her political and social institutions. This harmony gives her a frame of society, the best in the world, and an extent of political freedom, combined with entire security, such as no other people ever enjoyed upon the face of the earth. . . . In all social systems there must be a class to do the menial [unskilled] duties.❞

The statements on these pages were made in 1858 by Senator James Henry Hammond of South Carolina and Senator William Seward of New York. Senator Hammond owned a cotton plantation and had served as governor of South Carolina in 1842. Senator Seward was born, raised, and educated in New York State. He served as governor of New York from 1839 to 1843 and established a strong antislavery stand.

As you read the statements, consider how each senator's frame of reference might have affected what he said.

▶ PRACTICE THE SKILL

Answer these questions.

❶ What was Senator Hammond's position on slavery? How might his frame of reference have affected it?

❷ How was Senator Seward's position on slavery different from the one held by Senator Hammond? In what way was Seward's frame of reference different?

❸ How might a Southerner's opinion of Senator Seward's description of the "slave system" be different from that of a person from the North? of a person from the West?

▶ APPLY WHAT YOU LEARNED

Think about a present-day example of how frames of reference cause differences in opinions and beliefs. Write a paragraph that describes this present-day example and explains why the people involved may think the way they do. Share your paragraph with a classmate.

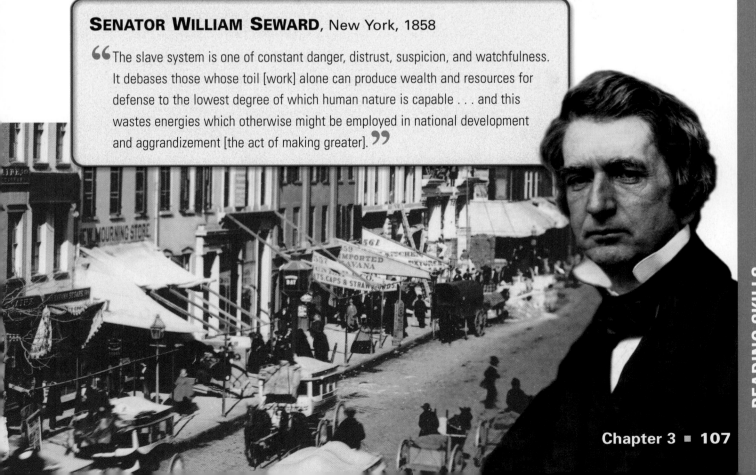

SENATOR WILLIAM SEWARD, New York, 1858

"The slave system is one of constant danger, distrust, suspicion, and watchfulness. It debases those whose toil [work] alone can produce wealth and resources for defense to the lowest degree of which human nature is capable . . . and this wastes energies which otherwise might be employed in national development and aggrandizement [the act of making greater]."

MAIN IDEA
Read to learn what some
people did to try to end
slavery.

WHY IT MATTERS
As conflict over slavery
grew, divisions between
the North and the South
became deeper.

VOCABULARY
emancipation
resist
code
fugitive
underground
abolitionist
equality

Slavery and Freedom

1820	1870	1920

1820–1860

By 1860 there were nearly 4 million slaves in the United States, an increase from 900,000 in 1800. This growth of slavery was due chiefly to the growing importance of cotton as a cash crop in the South. The worldwide demand for cotton had made many Southern planters rich. It had also created a demand for more enslaved workers.

The Slave Economy

Slavery had been a part of American life since colonial days. Some people thought that slavery was wrong. Other people could not make money using enslaved workers. The cost of feeding, clothing, and housing slaves was too great.

In the South, however, slavery continued because owners had come to depend on the work of enslaved people. Slaves were made to work as miners, carpenters, factory workers, and house servants. Some, however, were taken to large plantations. There they raised many acres of cotton and other cash crops, such as rice, tobacco, and sugarcane. Cash crops

Many slaves had to wear identification badges (above). This scene (right) shows a plantation on the Mississippi River.

While wealthy planters owned more than half the slaves in the South, most white Southerners owned no slaves at all. By 1860 one of every four white Southern families owned slaves.

REVIEW Why was slavery important to the South? *It depended on the work of slaves*

Slavery and the Law

Until the 1820s most people in the South thought slavery was wrong but necessary. In 1832, members of the Virginia legislature even debated **emancipation** (ih•man•suh•PAY•shuhn), or the freeing of slaves, in their state.

The debate started because many Virginians had been frightened by a slave rebellion the year before. The rebellion took place in Southampton County, Virginia. A slave named Nat Turner led an attack that killed more than 50 people, among them his owner. In turn, slave owners trying to end the rebellion killed more than 100 slaves.

Most slaves never took part in such rebellions, but they did whatever they could to **resist**, or act against, slavery. They broke tools, pretended to be sick, or acted as if they did not understand what they had been told. Such actions were dangerous, however, and slaves had to be careful to avoid punishment.

The Virginia legislature voted not to end slavery. To prevent future uprisings, Virginia joined with other slave states who had passed laws that put more controls on slaves. These laws were called slave codes. Under these **codes**, or sets of laws, slaves were not allowed to leave their owners' land, to meet in groups, or to buy or sell goods. Most slaves were not allowed to learn to read or write, and speaking against slavery became a crime.

The federal government also passed laws about slavery. One of these laws was called the Fugitive Slave Act. A **fugitive** is a person who is running away from something. Under this law, anyone caught helping a slave escape could be punished. People who found runaway slaves had to return them to the South.

REVIEW What were slave codes? *Slaves were not allowed to leave their owners land, to meet in groups, or to buy or sell goods.*

Analyze Graphs Many people did not own slaves.
❖ What percent of Southerners owned no slaves?

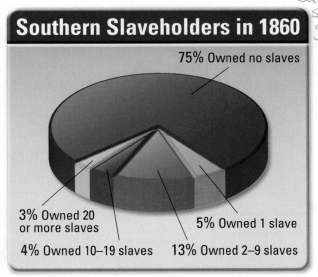

Southern Slaveholders in 1860

75% Owned no slaves

3% Owned 20 or more slaves

5% Owned 1 slave

4% Owned 10–19 slaves

13% Owned 2–9 slaves

The Underground Railroad

By 1860 there were more than 500,000 free African Americans living in the United States. Some had been born to parents who were free. Some had bought their freedom or had been freed by their owners. Others had escaped slavery by running away.

Over the years thousands of slaves tried to gain their freedom by running away. Some ran away alone. Others tried to escape with their families or friends.

Once away from their owners' land, runaway slaves had to find safe places to hide. Many slaves helped each other along the way. Native American groups helped slaves by giving them shelter. Some slaves hid in forests, swamps, or mountains, sometimes for years.

Many runaway slaves continued moving for months until they reached Canada or Mexico or free states in the North. Some found helpers who led the way—the brave men and women of the Underground Railroad. The word **underground** is often used to describe something done in secret.

The Underground Railroad was a system of secret escape routes leading to free

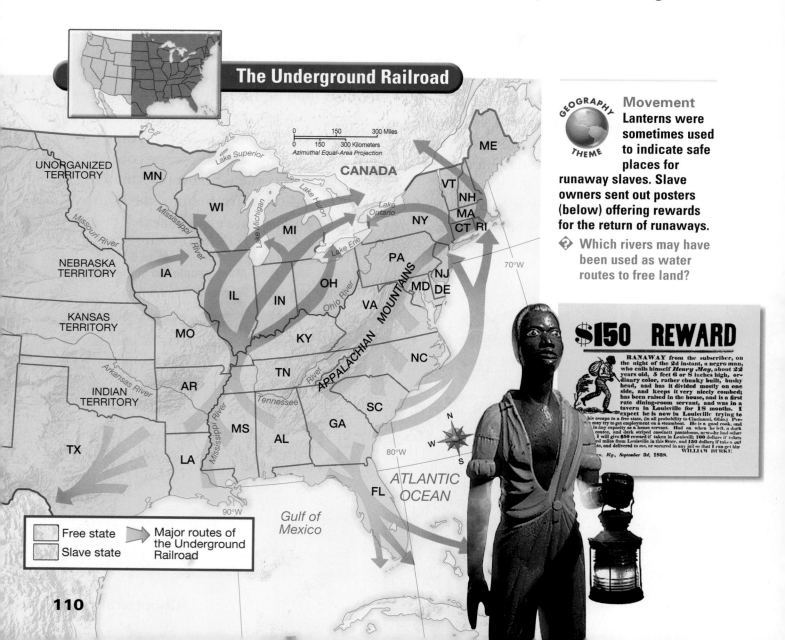

The Underground Railroad

0   150   300 Miles
0   150   300 Kilometers
Azimuthal Equal-Area Projection

Free state
Slave state
Major routes of the Underground Railroad

GEOGRAPHY THEME

Movement
Lanterns were sometimes used to indicate safe places for runaway slaves. Slave owners sent out posters (below) offering rewards for the return of runaways.

❖ Which rivers may have been used as water routes to free land?

$150 REWARD

RANAWAY from the subscriber, on the night of the 2d instant, a negro man, who calls himself *Henry May*, about 22 years old, 5 feet 6 or 8 inches high, ordinary color, rather chunky built, bushy head, and has it divided mostly on one side, and keeps it very nicely combed; has been raised in the house, and is a first rate dining-room servant, and was in a tavern in Louisville for 18 months. I expect he is now in Louisville trying to ... his escape to a free state, (in all probability to Cincinnati, Ohio.) Per... may try to get employment on a steamboat. He is a good cook, and in any capacity as a house servant. Had on when he left, a dark ... coatee, and dark striped cassinett pantaloons, new—he had other ... I will give $50 reward if taken in Louisville; 100 dollars if taken ... ed miles from Louisville in this State, and 150 dollars if taken out ... te, and delivered to me, or secured in any jail so that I can get him
WILLIAM BURKE.
..., Ky., September 3d, 1838.

lands. Most routes led from the South to free states in the North or to Canada. Some led to Mexico and to islands in the Caribbean Sea.

Working mostly at night, conductors, or helpers along the Underground Railroad, led runaway slaves from one hiding place to the next along the routes. These hiding places—barns, attics, storage rooms—were called stations. There the runaways could rest and eat, preparing for the journey to the next station.

Most conductors were free African Americans and white Northerners who opposed slavery. Harriet Tubman, an African American who had escaped from slavery herself, was one of the best-known conductors of the Underground Railroad. During the 1850s Tubman returned to the South 20 times and guided about 300 people to freedom. She proudly claimed, "I never lost a single passenger."

REVIEW **What was the Underground Railroad?** A system of secret escape routes leading to free lands.

Harriet Tubman helped enslaved African Americans escape to free lands.

Women Work for Change

Many of the people who worked to free slaves were themselves not entirely free. White women, many of whom spoke out against slavery, were generally not accepted as men's equals. They could not vote, hold public office, or sit on juries.

In 1840, a group of American women went as delegates to a world antislavery convention in London, England. They were denied the right to participate and could only watch the proceedings from the balcony.

One of the women who took part in the convention in London also played an important role at another convention eight years later. Elizabeth Cady Stanton, a defender of the rights of both women and slaves, participated at the first women's rights convention, held in Seneca Falls, New York. Stanton wrote a statement listing women's grievances.

This mural by Hames Michael Newell shows runaway slaves on the Underground Railroad.

In her statement, she demanded that women "have immediate admission to all the rights and privileges which belong to them as citizens of the United States."

In 1852 Harriet Beecher Stowe worked for change by publishing a novel that turned many people against slavery. The book, *Uncle Tom's Cabin*, told the heartbreaking story of slaves being mistreated by a cruel overseer. The book quickly became a best-seller and was made into a play.

Many of the same people who fought for equal rights for women also fought to end slavery. They often united antislavery and women's rights to form a double crusade for freedom.

REVIEW What book turned many people against slavery?

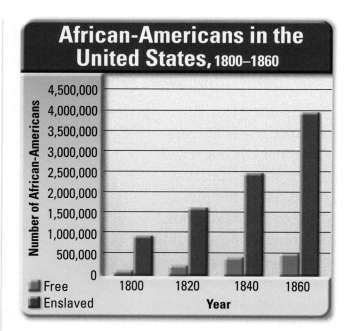

African-Americans in the United States, 1800–1860

Analyze Graphs This graph shows the numbers of free and enslaved African Americans in the United States.

◆ What trend does this graph show?

Abolitionists

People who opposed slavery worked to abolish, or end, it. Those who wanted to abolish slavery were called **abolitionists** (a•buh•LIH•shuhn•ists). Among the first to speak out, as early as the 1680s, were members of the Society of Friends, commonly known as the Quakers. In 1775, Quakers formed the first organized group to work against slavery.

In 1827 two free African Americans, Samuel Cornish and John Russwurm, started a newspaper that called for **equality**, or equal rights, for all Americans. The newspaper, *Freedom's Journal*, was the first to be owned and written by African Americans. In it Cornish and Russwurm wrote, "Too long have others spoken for us."

A few years later another abolitionist, William Lloyd Garrison, a white Northerner, founded a newspaper called *The Liberator*. Garrison called for a complete end to slavery, saying, "On this subject I do not wish to think, or speak, or write with moderation. I am earnest . . . I will not excuse. I will not retreat a single inch—AND I WILL BE HEARD."

While some abolitionists were writing, others were giving speeches. One of the

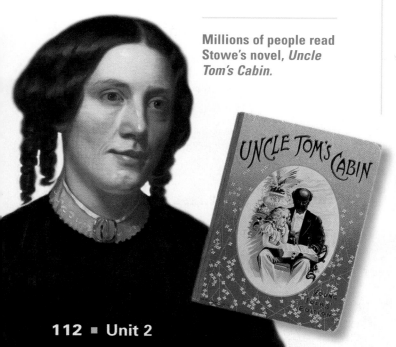

Millions of people read Stowe's novel, *Uncle Tom's Cabin*.

best-known abolitionist speakers was Frederick Douglass, a runaway slave. In 1841 Douglass attended a convention of the Massachusetts Antislavery Society. He delivered a speech so moving that everyone cheered. He often told his audiences, "I appear this evening as a thief and a robber. I stole this head, these limbs, this body from my master [slave owner], and ran off with them."

Like Douglass, another former slave named Isabella Van Wagener (WAI•guh•nur) traveled the country speaking out against slavery. Van Wagener believed that God had called her to "travel up and down the land" to preach. She changed her name to reflect her path. She chose *Sojourner*, which means "traveler," for her first name and *Truth* as her last name.

Frederick Douglass was a runaway slave and an abolitionist.

Sojourner Truth believed that slavery could be ended peacefully. Other abolitionists did not. On the night of October 16, 1859, an abolitionist named John Brown and a group of followers seized a government storehouse at Harpers Ferry, in what is now West Virginia. The storehouse was filled with guns. Brown planned to give the guns to slaves so they could fight for their freedom. Brown was caught, put on trial, and hanged.

Over time, more people had come to believe that only the use of force could end slavery. By 1860 it appeared that they were right. The nation was soon to be divided by civil war.

REVIEW Who were abolitionists?
abolish slavery

LESSON 2
REVIEW

Summary Time Line

1830 — 1850 — 1860

● **1831** Nat Turner leads African slave rebellion

● **1850** The Fugitive Slave Act is passed

● **1852** *Uncle Tom's Cabin* is published

❶ **MAIN IDEA** What did some people do to try to end slavery?

❷ **WHY IT MATTERS** How did tensions between the North and South grow as the conflict over slavery grew?

❸ **VOCABULARY** Use the words **fugitive** and **resist** in a sentence about slavery.

❹ **TIME LINE** In what year was *Uncle Tom's Cabin* published?

❺ **READING SKILL—Categorize** Why did abolitionists work for change?

❻ **GEOGRAPHY** Where did the Underground Railroad system lead?

❼ **CRITICAL THINKING—Analyze** Why did *Uncle Tom's Cabin* have such a strong influence on the people who read it?

PERFORMANCE—Write a Report Use library sources to learn more about the Underground Railroad or how abolitionists worked for change. Then write a report about what you have learned and share it with the rest of your classmates.

3

MAIN IDEA
Read to learn how the election of 1860 affected the United States.

WHY IT MATTERS
The outcomes of elections often have long-lasting consequences.

VOCABULARY

secede
Confederacy

The Union Breaks Apart

1820   1870   1920

1855–1865

In the 1850s, new national leaders, such as Abraham Lincoln, began to speak out on the slavery issue. Abraham Lincoln was not an abolitionist, but he was against the spread of slavery. He did not think that the federal government had the right to abolish slavery in the United States. Instead, he hoped that if slavery were not allowed to spread, it would one day die out.

Young Abe Lincoln

Abraham Lincoln was named for his grandfather, who had been a friend of Daniel Boone. Lincoln's grandfather had followed Boone to Kentucky, on the western frontier. He had a son named Thomas, who eventually married Nancy Hanks. They lived in a small log cabin with a dirt floor. Abraham Lincoln was born in that cabin in 1809.

The Lincolns left their home in Kentucky in 1816 and moved to the Indiana Territory. One reason they left Kentucky was that many people there owned slaves. Because slaves did most of the work, there were few paying jobs available. The Lincolns

People today can visit a replica of Abraham Lincoln's boyhood home at the Lincoln Boyhood National Memorial near Little Pigeon Creek, Indiana.

LOCATE IT

INDIANA
• Indianapolis

Lincoln Boyhood
National Memorial

Stephen Douglas and Abraham Lincoln held seven debates in 1858. This painting shows Lincoln (standing) and Douglas (to Lincoln's right) debating in Charleston, Illinois.

lived in Indiana for 14 years. By then, Indiana seemed crowded to them, so they moved to the Illinois Territory.

As a young man, Abraham Lincoln held several jobs. All the while, he studied law. In the 1830s he became a lawyer and opened a law office in Illinois.

In 1834 Abraham Lincoln entered public service. He served first in the Illinois legislature. Later, in 1846, he was elected to the United States Congress, where he served one term in the House of Representatives. After returning to Illinois, Lincoln became concerned about the spread of slavery to the West. He joined a new political party formed to fight the spread of slavery. This party was called the Republican party.

In 1858 Lincoln decided to run again for government office. On June 17, Lincoln was nominated, or chosen, by the Republican party to be its candidate for the United States Senate. In his acceptance speech, Lincoln used words from the Bible to explain his beliefs about the spread of slavery and the future of the United States. He said, "A house divided against itself cannot stand. I believe this government cannot endure permanently half slave and half free." Lincoln hoped that his strong stand would not cost him the election.

REVIEW What newly formed political party did Abraham Lincoln join? *Republican Party*

Lincoln and Douglas

Abraham Lincoln ran against Senator Stephen A. Douglas, the person who had written the Kansas–Nebraska Act. Lincoln and Douglas were very different from each other. Abraham Lincoln was very tall and thin, while Stephen Douglas was heavy and a full foot shorter than Lincoln.

Because Douglas was already serving in the Senate, he was well known across the country. Few people in places other than Illinois had ever heard of Lincoln.

Despite their differences, Lincoln and Douglas were alike in one important way. Both were talented public speakers. In the summer of 1858, the two candidates traveled around the state of Illinois and debated questions that were important to voters. Huge crowds turned out to listen to them, and newspapers printed what each man had to say.

Stephen Douglas argued that each new state should decide the slavery question for itself. That was what the nation's founders had allowed, he said, and that was what the new Kansas–Nebraska Act allowed.

THE UNION, CONSTITUTION AND THE FLAG MUST AND SHALL BE UPHELD.

Posters in the North were made to show people's support for the Union.

Abraham Lincoln responded that "the framers of the Constitution intended and expected" slavery to end. The problem, Lincoln pointed out, was more than a question of what each state wanted. It was a question of right and wrong. Slavery should not spread to the West, Lincoln said, because slavery was wrong.

Although Stephen Douglas won reelection to the Senate for another term, people all over the country now knew who Lincoln was. Two years later, in 1860, the two men faced each other in another election. This one would decide the next President of the United States.

REVIEW How were the positions of Lincoln and Douglas on the spread of slavery different?

Lincoln - slavery wrong
Douglas - each state should decide slavery for itself

The Election of 1860

In the 1860 election for the presidency Abraham Lincoln represented the Republican party, which firmly opposed the spread of slavery. The Democratic party was divided in its views. Some members of the party supported Stephen Douglas, who continued to argue that western settlers should decide for themselves whether to allow slavery. Other

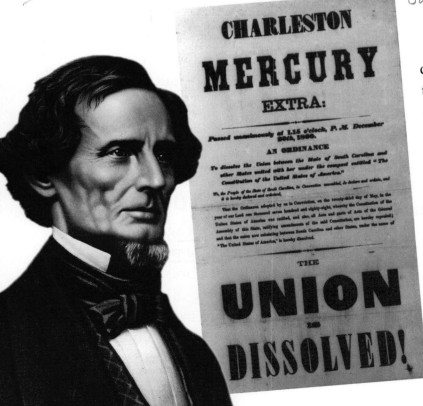

CHARLESTON MERCURY
EXTRA:

Passed unanimously at 1.15 o'clock, P. M. December 20th, 1860.

AN ORDINANCE

To dissolve the Union between the State of South Carolina and other States united with her under the compact entitled "The Constitution of the United States of America."

THE UNION IS DISSOLVED!

The first notice of South Carolina's secession was printed in the *Charleston Mercury.* Jefferson Davis (left) was elected president of the Confederacy.

members, mostly Southerners, backed John Breckinridge of Kentucky. Breckinridge thought that the federal government should allow slavery everywhere in the West.

The division within the Democratic party made Lincoln's election almost certain. Although Lincoln promised not to abolish slavery in the South, he said he hoped it would end there one day. Many Southerners feared that Lincoln was attacking their whole way of life. Some leaders in the South said that their states would **secede** from, or leave, the Union if Lincoln became President. Like most Southerners, they believed that states could freely leave the Union since the states had created the Union in the first place.

On Election Day in November 1860, Lincoln did not win a single state in the South. However, he won enough states in the North and the West to win the presidency. Southern leaders did not wait long before carrying out their threat to secede. On December 20, South Carolina seceded from the Union.

Five other states—Alabama, Florida, Georgia, Louisiana, and Mississippi—soon followed. Together these six states formed their own government at Montgomery, Alabama, early in February 1861. They called themselves the Confederate States of America, or the **Confederacy**. Jefferson Davis, a United States senator from Mississippi, was elected president. Alexander Stephens of Georgia became vice president. That month Texas seceded and later joined the Confederacy.

> **REVIEW** What did seven Southern states do after Lincoln was elected President? *Seceded from the union.*
> *1. S.C.* *4. Georgia* *7. TEXAS.*
> *2. Alabama* *5. Louisiana*
> *3. Florida* *6. Mississippi*

POINTS OF VIEW
Union or Secession

JOHN C. CALHOUN, a senator from South Carolina

66 What is the cause of this discontent? It will be found in the belief in the people of the Southern States. . . that they can not remain, as things are now. . . . If you who represent the stronger portion [the North], can not agree to settle [these differences] on the broad principle of justice and duty, say so; and let the states we both represent agree to separate and part in peace. 99

SAM HOUSTON, the governor of Texas

66 I tell you that, while I believe with you in the doctrine of State's Rights, the North is determined to preserve this Union. They are not a fiery, impulsive people as you are, for they live in colder climates. But when they begin to move in a certain direction. . . they move with the steady momentum and perseverance of a mighty avalanche. 99

Analyze the Viewpoints

1. What views about secession did each Southerner hold?
2. What other viewpoints might Southerners have held on the matter of secession?
3. **Make it Relevant** Look at the Letters to the Editor section of your newspaper. Find two letters that express different viewpoints about the same issue, and summarize the viewpoints of each letter.

Fort Sumter was one of many forts built by the United States after the War of 1812.

1. stair tower
2. soldiers' barracks
3. officers' quarters
4. wall facing Charleston
5. fort lantern
6. mess hall
7. cannons
8. wharf

❖ **Why do you think cannons were placed on nearly every side of the fort?**

Crisis at Fort Sumter

On March 4, 1861, Abraham Lincoln took the oath of office as President of the United States. In his inauguration speech, he declared, "I have no purpose directly or indirectly to interfere with the institution of slavery in the states where it exists." Yet he firmly stated, "No state, upon its own mere action, can lawfully get out of the Union." Like many Northerners, Lincoln believed the United States could not be divided.

For one month after Lincoln's inauguration, the tension built. Americans everywhere wondered what Lincoln would do about the seceding states. Some people thought he should let them go. Others said that he should accept the Southern position on the slavery question and hope that the Southern states would return. Still others felt that Lincoln should use the army to end the revolt. The country's fate was soon determined at Fort Sumter, which is located on an island off the coast of South Carolina.

When the Southern states seceded, they had taken over post offices, forts, and other federal government property within their borders. Fort Sumter was one of the few forts in the South that remained under Union control. By April 1861, however, supplies at the fort were running out. The fort's commander, Major Robert Anderson, feared that if more supplies were not sent soon, he would have to surrender the fort to the Confederacy.

Lincoln had promised to hold onto all property that belonged to the United States. He sent supply ships to the fort and waited to see how the Confederate leaders would react. On April 12, 1861, Confederate leaders demanded that Union forces surrender. When Major Anderson refused, Confederate troops fired their cannons on the fort. They bombarded the fort for the next 34 hours, until the Union troops surrendered.

Learning of the fall of Fort Sumter, President Lincoln called for 75,000 Americans to join an army to stop the Southern rebellion and preserve the United States. Four more states—Arkansas, North Carolina, Tennessee, and Virginia—seceded and joined the

Confederacy. This brought the number of Confederate states to 11. Tensions between the Union and the Confederate States—the North and the South—had reached their breaking point. The Civil War had begun.

REVIEW Who was in command of Fort Sumter when it was fired upon?

Robert Anderson

LESSON 3 REVIEW

Summary Time Line

1855 — 1860 — 1865

- **1860** Abraham Lincoln is elected President
- **1861** The Civil War begins

1. **MAIN IDEA** What issue defined the presidential election of 1860?

2. **WHY IT MATTERS** What long-lasting consequences did the election of 1860 have on the United States?

3. **VOCABULARY** Use the words **Confederacy** and **secede** in a sentence.

4. **TIME LINE** When did the Civil War begin?

5. **READING SKILL—Categorize** What states made up the Confederacy?

6. **HISTORY** What event led South Carolina's leaders to secede from the Union?

7. **GEOGRAPHY** How many states in the South did Lincoln win in the election of 1860?

8. **CRITICAL THINKING—Analyze** Why do you think Fort Sumter was important to both Abraham Lincoln and Jefferson Davis?

PERFORMANCE—Write a Newspaper Headline Write two newspaper headlines, one from a Northern newspaper and one from a Southern newspaper, as they would have appeared the day after the election of 1860. Think about what each paper might have printed as a headline.

· SKILLS ·
MAP AND GLOBE

Compare Maps with Different Scales

▶ **WHY IT MATTERS**

Have you ever helped your family plan a trip? You may have wanted to know how far you had to travel.

A map scale helps you find out how far one place is from another. The map scale compares a distance on a map to a distance in the real world. Map scales are different depending on how much area is shown. This means that different maps are drawn to different scales. Knowing about map scales can help you choose the best map for gathering the information you need.

▶ **WHAT YOU NEED TO KNOW**

Look at the map below and the map on page 121. They both show Fort Sumter and the surrounding area, but with different scales. On Map A, Fort Sumter looks larger. For that reason the scale is said to be larger. When the map scale is larger, more details can be shown. On Map B, Fort Sumter appears smaller, and the scale is said to be smaller.

Although they have different scales, Maps A and B can both be used to measure the distance between the same two places.

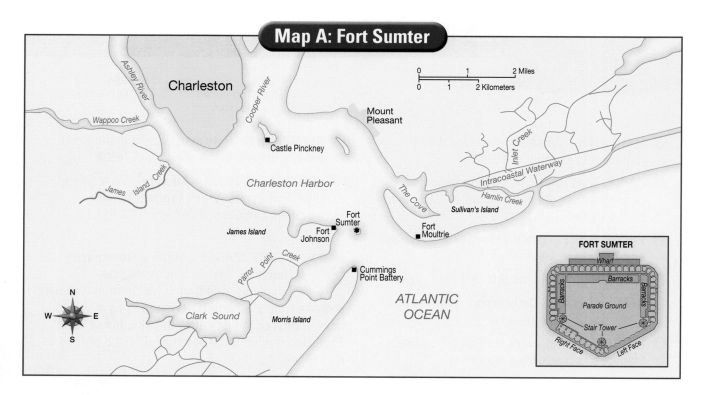

Map A: Fort Sumter

PRACTICE THE SKILL

On April 12, 1861, Confederate troops opened fire on Fort Sumter from Fort Moultrie, Fort Johnson, Castle Pinckney, and various batteries around Charleston Harbor. This act signaled the beginning of the Civil War.

Use the maps below to find the real distance in miles between Fort Sumter and Castle Pinckney.

1 On Map A, use a ruler to measure the exact length of the scale, or use a pencil to mark off the length on a sheet of paper. How long is the line that stands for one mile?

2 Still using Map A, find Fort Sumter and Castle Pinckney. Using the ruler or the sheet of paper you marked, measure the distance between these two places. What is the real distance in miles between Fort Sumter and Castle Pinckney?

3 Now go through the same steps for Map B. How long is the scale length that stands for one mile? Use that scale length to measure the distance between Fort Sumter and Castle Pinckney on the map. What is the real distance in miles? Are the real distances you found on the two maps the same? You should see that even when map scales are different the real distances shown on the maps are the same.

APPLY WHAT YOU LEARNED

Find two maps with different scales—perhaps a map of your state and a map of a large city within your state. Compare the real distances between two places that are on both maps.

Practice your map and globe skills with the **GeoSkills CD-ROM**.

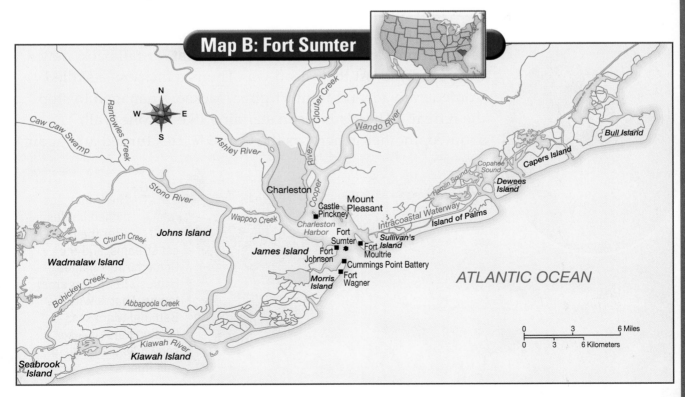

Map B: Fort Sumter

MAIN IDEA
Read to learn about the key events that happened in the early years of the Civil War.

WHY IT MATTERS
As the war continued, the North hoped to end slavery in the Confederate states as well as save the Union.

VOCABULARY
retreat
border state
strategy
casualty

Civil War

| 1820 | | 1870 | | 1920 |

1861–1863

Afer Confederate troops fired on Fort Sumter, hopes for peace between the North and the South ended. Both the Union and the Confederacy prepared for war. Men and boys eagerly joined regiments made up of their neighbors and friends.

The Fighting Begins

The first of the major battles between the Union and the Confederacy was fought in July 1861. The battle took place at Bull Run, a stream near the town of Manassas Junction, Virginia. On the day of the battle, crowds of enthusiastic sight-seers came in carriages from nearby Washington, D.C. They brought picnic lunches as if to watch a sporting event. A Union soldier said, "We thought it wasn't a bad idea to have the great men from Washington come out to see us thrash the Rebs [Confederate troops]."

At Bull Run two untrained armies clashed in a confusing bat-tle. At first it appeared that the Union army would win. Then, as the Confederate army started to **retreat**, or fall back, new troops arrived. At their head was Thomas Jackson, a skilled Confederate general from Virginia. Jackson managed to stop the retreat. "There's Jackson standing like a stone wall," shouted another general as the Confederates turned and again

General Thomas Jackson

FAST FACT The Union named battles after the near-est streams, and the Confederates named battles after the nearest towns. That is why the Battle of Manassas (shown here) is also known as the Battle of Bull Run.

Northern soldiers
wore blue uniforms.

Advantages in the Civil War

NORTHERN ADVANTAGES
Advanced industry
Advanced railroad system
Strong navy

SOUTHERN ADVANTAGES
Large number of military leaders
Troops experienced in outdoor living
Familiar with the environment of the South

Analyze Graphs This graph compares the advantages of the North and South.

❓ What advantages did the North have?

Southern soldiers
wore gray uniforms.

attacked the Union army. From that day on, General Jackson was known as Stonewall Jackson.

The Confederates won the Battle of Manassas, also called the Battle of Bull Run. The defeat shocked the Union. The South had proved more powerful than most Northerners had expected. Americans came to realize that this war would last far longer than they had first believed.

Most Northerners supported the Union, while most white Southerners supported the Confederacy. For some Americans, however, the choice between the Union and the Confederacy was not an easy one. The war had deeply divided people in all regions. People in the **border states**—Delaware, Kentucky, Maryland, and Missouri—were especially torn between the two sides. These states, which were located between the North and the South, permitted slavery but had not seceded.

REVIEW Where did the first major battle of the Civil War take place? *Bull Run Manassas, Virginia*

Battle Plans

The Union **strategy**, or long-range plan, for winning the war was first to weaken the South and then to invade it. To weaken the South, Lincoln and his advisers came up with a strategy that some people called the Anaconda (a•nuh•KAHN•duh) Plan. An anaconda is a large snake that squeezes its prey to death. The Union would squeeze the South by not letting it ship its cotton or bring in goods. If the South could not sell its cash crops, it would not have the money to buy supplies for its army.

The purpose of the plan was to block all imports from reaching the South. The plan called for winning control of the Mississippi River and for establishing a naval blockade of Confederate ports. Not everyone in the North liked the idea of a blockade, however. Many people thought it would take too long to set up. They wanted the Union army to invade the South. "On to Richmond!" they shouted.

The Union and the Confederacy

CANADA

WASHINGTON TERRITORY

OREGON

DAKOTA TERRITORY

MINNESOTA

MAINE

Lake Superior

MICHIGAN

WISCONSIN

Lake Huron

VT

NH

Lake Ontario

NEW YORK

MA

70°W

CT

RI

NEVADA TERRITORY

IOWA

PENNSYLVANIA

NJ

40°N

40°N

UTAH TERRITORY

NEBRASKA TERRITORY

OHIO

MD

DE

ILLINOIS

INDIANA

WEST VIRGINIA (1863)

CALIFORNIA

COLORADO TERRITORY

KANSAS

MISSOURI

KENTUCKY

VIRGINIA

NORTH CAROLINA

PACIFIC OCEAN

TENNESSEE

SOUTH CAROLINA

ATLANTIC OCEAN

30°N

120°W

NEW MEXICO TERRITORY

INDIAN TERRITORY

ARKANSAS

GEORGIA

ALABAMA

30°N

MISSISSIPPI

N

TEXAS

E

W

LOUISIANA

FLORIDA

S

MEXICO

Gulf of Mexico

90°W

80°W

0   200   400 Miles

0   200   400 Kilometers

Albers Equal-Area Projection

Union state
Border state
Confederate state
Territory

Regions   The Civil War had divided the nation. In western Virginia, feelings for the Union were so strong that the people voted to break away from Virginia. West Virginia joined the Union in 1863.

❖ Which states were border states?

Richmond, Virginia, had become the capital of the Confederacy by this time.

At first the most important strategy of the Confederate states was simply to protect their lands. This strategy was based on the belief that Britain and France would help the South. Both countries depended on Southern cotton to keep their textile mills going. The South also hoped that the North would tire of the war. Many Southerners, however, were impatient. Cries of "On to Washington!" were soon answered with plans to invade the North.

REVIEW What was the Anaconda Plan?

The union will squeeze the S, by no letting them export the cotton or

The Battle at Antietam

As the Civil War dragged on into 1862, the Anaconda Plan seemed to be working. The blockade brought trade in the South to a halt, and supplies there ran

This cannon was used in the Battle of Antietam.

very low. This made life increasingly difficult for Southern troops, who became poorly equipped, fed, and clothed. Even so, many Northerners became discouraged by the long lists of war casualties. A **casualty** is a person who has been killed or wounded in a war.

Then, in September 1862, the Union and the Confederates fought a major battle at Antietam (an•TEE•tuhm) Creek, near Sharpsburg, Maryland. By that time Robert E. Lee was Confederate commander of the Army of Northern Virginia. General Lee had led his army from Virginia into Maryland, intending to reach Harrisburg, Pennsylvania. There, Lee planned to cut off railroad communication between the states in the East and those in the West. Lee also hoped to find in Pennsylvania supplies that his troops badly needed.

At Antietam Creek, Lee's army was stopped by Union troops. The battle that followed resulted in the highest number of casualties in one day of the whole war. Union casualties numbered more than 2,000 killed and 9,500 wounded. Confederate casualties totaled 2,700 killed and over 9,000 wounded. "Never before or after in all the war were so many men shot on one day," historian Bruce Catton wrote. Having lost one-fourth of his army, Lee retreated to Virginia.

Although the battle at Antietam was really a draw, or tie, it had an important result. Five days later, on September 22, 1862, President Lincoln announced his decision to issue an order freeing the slaves in areas that were still fighting against the Union.

REVIEW Why was General Lee leading his army to Pennsylvania? _planning to cut off railroad communication b/t the E. & W. To find supplies_

The Emancipation Proclamation

To President Lincoln, the purpose of the war had been to keep the country together—to save the Union. It had not been to abolish slavery. In 1862 President Lincoln wrote a letter explaining his view to Horace Greeley, publisher of the *New York Tribune*. "My [main] object in this struggle is to save the Union, and is not either to save or destroy slavery."

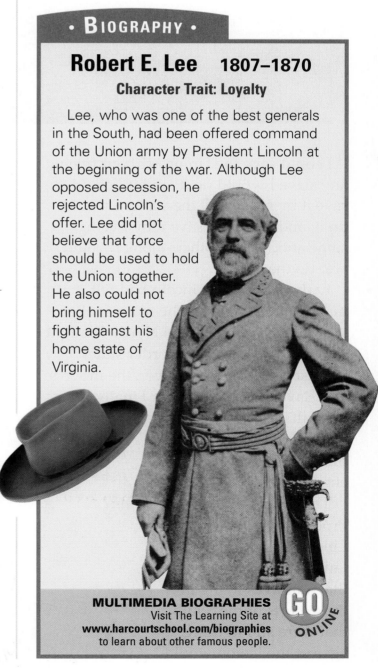

• BIOGRAPHY •

Robert E. Lee   1807–1870
Character Trait: Loyalty

Lee, who was one of the best generals in the South, had been offered command of the Union army by President Lincoln at the beginning of the war. Although Lee opposed secession, he rejected Lincoln's offer. Lee did not believe that force should be used to hold the Union together. He also could not bring himself to fight against his home state of Virginia.

MULTIMEDIA BIOGRAPHIES
Visit The Learning Site at
www.harcourtschool.com/biographies
to learn about other famous people.
GO ONLINE

This painting shows Abraham Lincoln meeting with his cabinet to discuss the Emancipation Proclamation.

If I could save the Union without freeing any slave I would do it; and if I could save it by freeing all the slaves I would do it; and if I could save it by freeing some and leaving others alone I would also do that."

Early in the war Lincoln had felt that making emancipation the main goal of the war might divide the North. It might also turn people in the border states against the Union. However, the move to end slavery grew stronger. Finally, after the Battle of Antietam Creek, Lincoln decided the time had come for an emancipation order.

The Emancipation Proclamation, which Lincoln issued on January 1, 1863, said that all slaves living in those parts of the South that were still fighting against the Union would

be "then, thenceforward, and forever free." The proclamation did not give all enslaved people instant freedom. The order was meant only for the states that had left the Union, not for the border states or for areas that had already been won back by the Union.

The Emancipation Proclamation hurt the South's hopes of getting help from Britain and France. Now that the war had become a fight against slavery, most British and French citizens, who opposed slavery, gave their support to the Union. Confederate President Jefferson Davis called Lincoln's proclamation "the most execrable [terrible] measure recorded in the history of a guilty man."

To celebrate the proclamation, it was reprinted on this poster.

As the Union troops advanced farther and farther into the Confederacy, they carried out the Emancipation Proclamation. Thousands of enslaved people fled to freedom behind the Northern battle lines, where they worked as laborers or joined the Union army or navy. By allowing freed slaves to serve in the military, the Emancipation Proclamation helped ease the Union army's shortage of soldiers.

REVIEW **What was the Emancipation Proclamation?** *All slaves living in those parts of the South that were still fighting against the union would be free.*

Contributions from All

In both the North and the South, only men were allowed to join the army. Women, however, found many ways to help. They took over factory, business, and farm jobs that men left behind. They sent food to the troops, made bandages, and collected supplies. Many women, such as Clara Barton and Sally Tompkins, worked as nurses. A few served as spies, and some even dressed as men, joined the army, and fought in battles.

About 180,000 African Americans eventually served in the Union army during the Civil War as well. They served in separate regiments, mostly under the command of white officers. At first they were not paid as much as white soldiers. They were also given poor equipment, and they often ran out of supplies. Despite these hardships, African American soldiers proved themselves on the battlefield. They led raids behind Confederate lines, served as spies and scouts, and fought in almost every major battle of the war.

The Union navy was open to African American men when the Civil War began. During the war the Union navy enlisted about 20,000 African American sailors. Among those who served was Robert Smalls. In 1862 Smalls and some other slaves took over a Confederate steamer in Charleston Harbor and surrendered it to Union forces.

• **BIOGRAPHY** •

Clara Barton   1821–1912

Character Trait: Compassion

"While our soldiers stand and fight, I can stand and feed and nurse them." Clara Barton followed the fighting from battle to battle, caring for sick and wounded Union soldiers. Barton had always tried to help people in need. She taught school for a time and then worked as a government clerk. When the Civil War broke out, she wanted to help. Her work is still carried on by the American Red Cross. Barton founded the American branch of this world organization in 1881.

MULTIMEDIA BIOGRAPHIES
Visit The Learning Site at www.harcourtschool.com/biographies
to learn about other famous people.

African American troops (left) played a key role in support of the Union. Thousands of Hispanic Americans also took part in the war, with some fighting for the Union and others fighting for the Confederacy. Unlike African American soldiers, most Hispanic Americans served in regular army units.

European immigrants who came to this country for a better life marched off to preserve the Union, as well. There were Irishmen in the Fighting 69th, the Irish Zouaves, Irish Volunteers, and St. Patrick Brigade. Italians fought with the Garibaldi Guards and Italian Legion. Germans fought with the Steuben Volunteers, German Rifles, Turner Rifles, and DeKalb Regiment. In fact, the immigrant population in the Northern states helped the Union army replenish itself and eventually wear out a depleted Confederate army.

REVIEW How did African American soldiers help the Union during the war?

They led raids, served as spies and fought in almost every major battle of the war.

LESSON 4 REVIEW

Summary Time Line

1860 — 1865

1861 The Battle of Bull Run is fought

1862 The Battle of Antietam is fought

1863 President Lincoln issues the Emancipation Proclamation

1. **MAIN IDEA** Why did the first major battle of the Civil War shock the Union? *The Confederates won!*

2. **WHY IT MATTERS** Why did Lincoln avoid making emancipation the main goal of the war? *He just wanted to preserve the Union*

3. **VOCABULARY** Use the word **retreat** in a sentence.

4. **TIME LINE** What Civil War battle occurred first, Antietam or Bull Run?

5. **READING SKILL—Categorize** Name the border states. *Delaware, Kentucky, Missouri, Maryland*

6. **HISTORY** What were the results of the Battle of Antietam? *President Lincoln issue an order to free slaves.*

7. **HISTORY** How did women in both the North and South help the troops? *Spies, farm jobs, Nurses. They took over factory, business*

8. **CRITICAL THINKING—Evaluate** How did the Emancipation Proclamation affect the Confederates' strategy?

PERFORMANCE—Write a Letter Imagine that you are living in the South during the Civil War. Write a letter to a friend describing how the Union's blockade is changing your life. Then share your letter with a classmate.

The Road to Union Victory

1820   1870   1920
1863–1865

The Emancipation Proclamation gave new hope to enslaved people and new spirit to the North. In fact, in the months following the Emancipation Proclamation, the Union seemed to be winning the war. Across the South, younger and younger men joined the army to take the places of Confederate soldiers who had been killed or wounded. The war, however, was far from over.

Vicksburg and Chancellorsville

By May 1863 the Union army finally had a general as effective as Confederate General Robert E. Lee. His name was Ulysses S. Grant. One of Grant's first important battles began in May at Vicksburg, Mississippi, the Confederate headquarters on the Mississippi River.

Grant laid siege to the city. The Union guns pounded Vicksburg, and the Union army cut off all supplies to the city. The trapped Confederates, both soldiers and townspeople, soon ran out of food. Conditions were so bad that they had to tear down houses for firewood and dig caves in hillsides for shelter. Yet the people of Vicksburg were determined to endure whatever Grant had in store for them. One Vicksburg woman wrote, "We'll just burrow into these hills and let them batter away as hard as they please."

Ulysses S. Grant (right) used this box to carry his saddle and other field equipment.

129

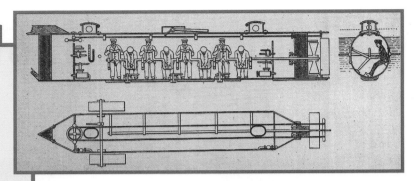

The *H. L. Hunley*

In 1864 the *H. L. Hunley* became the first submarine to sink an enemy ship during wartime. Measuring just over 39 feet (12 m) long and just under 4 feet (1 m) wide, the *Hunley* was powered by crew members who cranked a propeller by hand. The submarine was built to ram a torpedo into a target and then back away, causing a trip line to set off the explosion. The design of the *Hunley* proved to be successful when it sank the Union warship *Housatonic*.

The diagram (above) shows the inside of the Hunley (below).

However, by July 4, 1863, the people of Vicksburg could hold out no longer. They finally surrendered.

Vicksburg proved to be a key victory. Its location gave the Union control of the Mississippi River. This, in turn, cut the Confederacy into two parts. The western states of the Confederacy were no longer able to communicate easily with the states to the east or to supply many reinforcements to them.

At about the same time that Grant started to lay siege to Vicksburg, General Lee and his army defeated a Union army at Chancellorsville, Virginia. In winning, however, Lee lost one of the South's best generals. In the confusion of battle, Stonewall Jackson was accidentally shot by one of his own troops and later died.

Despite Jackson's death, the victory at Chancellorsville gave the Confederacy confidence to try again to invade the North. The Confederates' goal was to win a victory on Northern soil.

If they could do so, the Confederates hoped people in the North would demand an end to the war. In June 1863, General Lee's troops headed north. They reached the small town of Gettysburg, Pennsylvania, on July 1.

REVIEW **Why was the victory at Vicksburg so important for the Union army?**

union control of the Mississippi River

The Battle of Gettysburg

General Robert E. Lee believed that victory at Gettysburg might turn the war in favor of the Confederacy. However, after two days of fighting, victory did not seem possible. In a final attempt on July 3, 1863, Lee ordered General George Pickett's entire division—15,000 soldiers—to make a direct attack. They were to charge across open country toward a stone fence at the Union army's center.

Marching shoulder to shoulder, Pickett's troops formed a line half a mile (0.8 km) wide. Steadily, the wall of soldiers in what came to be called Pickett's Charge moved forward. As the Confederates moved closer, they were met by the fire of Union guns, which controlled the higher ground of the battlefield. "Men were falling all around us, and cannon and muskets were raining death upon us," remembered a Confederate officer. "Still on and up the slope toward the stone fence our men steadily swept."

Pickett's soldiers reached the fence but were stopped there in fierce fighting. The charge had failed, and Pickett's men retreated, leaving behind half their number dead or wounded.

The Battle of Gettysburg was one of the deadliest battles of the Civil War. In fighting between July 1 and 3, 1863, more than 3,000 Union soldiers and nearly 4,000 Confederates were killed. More than 20,000 on each side were wounded or reported missing.

The fate of the Fourteenth Tennessee Regiment tells the story. When the battle began, there were 365 men in the unit. When the battle ended, there were only 3.

The Union victory at Gettysburg marked a turning point in the war. After

This pin was worn on the hats of Civil War soldiers to indicate that they were foot soldiers.

the battle, General Lee's army retreated to Virginia. It would never again be able to launch a major attack against the Union.

REVIEW What was Pickett's Charge?

The Gettysburg Address

On November 19, 1863, President Lincoln went to Gettysburg to dedicate a cemetery for the Union soldiers who had died in the battle. A crowd of nearly 6,000 people gathered for the ceremony.

Lincoln gave a short speech, or **address**, that day. In fact, he spoke for less than three minutes. Lincoln's Gettysburg Address was so short that many people in the crowd were disappointed. Soon, however, people realized that this short speech was one of the most inspiring speeches ever given by a United States President.

In his address, Lincoln spoke to the heart of the war-weary North.

This scene, painted by James Walker, shows the battle at Gettysburg.

THE GETTYSBURG ADDRESS

Four score and seven years ago our fathers brought forth on this continent a new nation, conceived in Liberty, and dedicated to the proposition that all men are created equal.

Now we are engaged in a great civil war, testing whether that nation or any nation so conceived and so dedicated, can long endure. We are met on a great battlefield of that war. We have come to dedicate a portion of that field, as a final resting place for those who here gave their lives that that nation might live. It is altogether fitting and proper that we should do this.

But, in a larger sense, we can not dedicate—we can not consecrate—we can not hallow—this ground. The brave men, living and dead, who struggled here, have consecrated it, far above our poor power to add or detract. The world will little note nor long remember what we say here, but it can never forget what they did here. It is for us the living, rather, to be dedicated here to the unfinished work which they who fought here have thus far so nobly advanced. It is rather for us to be here dedicated to the great task remaining before us—that from these honored dead we take increased devotion to that cause for which they gave the last full measure of devotion—that we here highly resolve that these dead shall not have died in vain—that this nation, under God, shall have a new birth of freedom—and that government of the people, by the people, for the people, shall not perish from the earth.

He spoke of the ideals of liberty and equality on which the nation had been founded. He honored the many soldiers who had died defending those ideals. He also called on the people of the Union to try even harder to win the struggle those soldiers had died for—to save the "government of the people, by the people, for the people" so that the Union would be preserved.

REVIEW Why did Lincoln give the Gettysburg Address?

The Road to Appomattox

In March 1864 Lincoln gave command of all the Union armies to General Ulysses S. Grant. Grant soon devised a plan to invade the South and destroy its will to fight. The plan called for an army under Grant's command to march to Richmond, the Confederate capital. At the same time a second army under General William Tecumseh Sherman was to march from Chattanooga, Tennessee, to Atlanta, Georgia.

As Sherman captured Atlanta, much of the city burned to the ground. The destruction of Atlanta, a manufacturing center and junction of several railroads, was a great loss for the Confederacy.

From Atlanta, Sherman's army of 62,000 men headed toward Savannah in a march that has become known as the March to the Sea. The army cut a path of destruction 60 miles (97 km) wide and 300 miles (483 km) long. Union soldiers burned homes and stores, destroyed crops, wrecked bridges, and tore up railroad tracks. When Sherman reached Savannah on December 22, 1864, he sent a message to President Lincoln. He wrote, "I beg to present you as a Christmas gift the city of Savannah."

From Georgia, Sherman turned north and marched through South Carolina, destroying even more than he had in Georgia. At the same time, General Grant moved south into Virginia. In his pursuit of General Lee's army, Grant cut off Lee's supply lines and kept pushing the Confederates in retreat. In early April 1865, Richmond was evacuated and set on fire by retreating Confederates. More than 900 buildings were destroyed and hundreds more were badly damaged. Union troops took control of the city.

General Lee's army moved west, with General Grant in constant pursuit. Lee's men were starving, and they were now outnumbered by 10 to 1. Lee could retreat no farther, nor could he continue to fight. Lee said, "There is nothing left for me to do but to go and see General Grant, and I would rather die a thousand deaths."

On the afternoon of April 9, 1865, Lee surrendered to Grant at Appomattox (a•puh•MA•tuhks) Court House, Virginia.

This painting shows General Lee (seated at left) surrendering to General Grant (seated at right) at the home of Wilmer McLean.

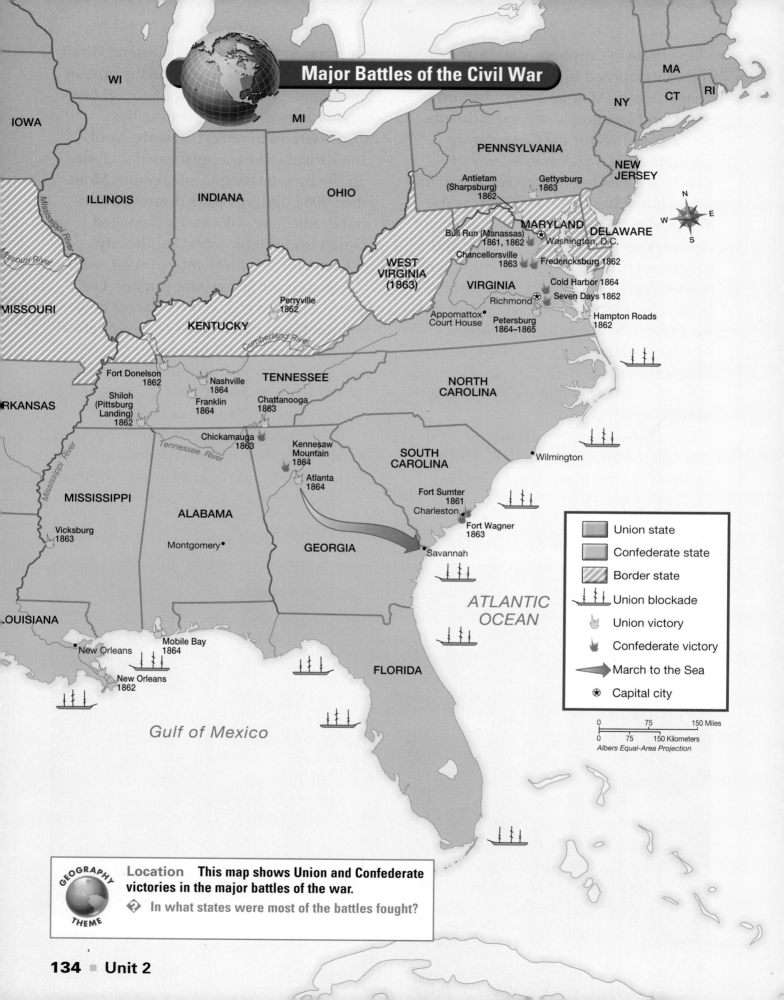

Major Battles of the Civil War

WI

MA

NY

CT

RI

IOWA

MI

PENNSYLVANIA

NEW JERSEY

ILLINOIS

INDIANA

OHIO

Antietam (Sharpsburg) 1862

Gettysburg 1863

MARYLAND

DELAWARE

N
W E
S

MISSOURI

WEST VIRGINIA (1863)

Bull Run (Manassas) 1861, 1862

Washington, D.C.

Perryville 1862

Chancellorsville 1863

Fredericksburg 1862

KENTUCKY

VIRGINIA

Richmond

Cold Harbor 1864

Seven Days 1862

Appomattox Court House

Petersburg 1864–1865

Hampton Roads 1862

Fort Donelson 1862

Nashville 1864

TENNESSEE

NORTH CAROLINA

RKANSAS

Shiloh (Pittsburg Landing) 1862

Franklin 1864

Chattanooga 1863

Chickamauga 1863

Kennesaw Mountain 1864

SOUTH CAROLINA

Wilmington

MISSISSIPPI

ALABAMA

Atlanta 1864

Fort Sumter 1861

Charleston

Vicksburg 1863

Montgomery

GEORGIA

Fort Wagner 1863

Savannah

ATLANTIC OCEAN

LOUISIANA

New Orleans

Mobile Bay 1864

New Orleans 1862

FLORIDA

Gulf of Mexico

	Union state
	Confederate state
	Border state
	Union blockade
	Union victory
	Confederate victory
	March to the Sea
	Capital city

0   75   150 Miles
0   75   150 Kilometers
Albers Equal-Area Projection

GEOGRAPHY THEME

Location This map shows Union and Confederate victories in the major battles of the war.

❓ In what states were most of the battles fought?

Memorial Day

On May 5, 1866, people in Waterloo, New York, honored those who died in the Civil War. The people closed businesses for the day and decorated soldiers' graves with flowers. This was the beginning of the holiday known as Memorial Day, or Decoration Day. On this day Americans remember those who gave their lives for their country in all wars. Today most states observe Memorial Day on the last Monday in May.

People often celebrate this holiday by holding parades.

In a meeting at the home of Wilmer McLean, the two generals agreed to the terms of the Confederate army's surrender. After signing the surrender, Lee mounted his horse Traveller and rode back to his men.

In the next few weeks, as word of General Lee's surrender reached them, other Confederate generals surrendered, too. After four years of bloodshed the Civil War was over. The Union had been preserved, but at a horrible cost.

More than 600,000 soldiers had died during the war. Many died as a result of battle. Others, however, had died from disease. Thousands of soldiers also returned home wounded, scarred both physically and emotionally from the terrible devastation the war had brought.

REVIEW Why did Lee surrender to Grant?

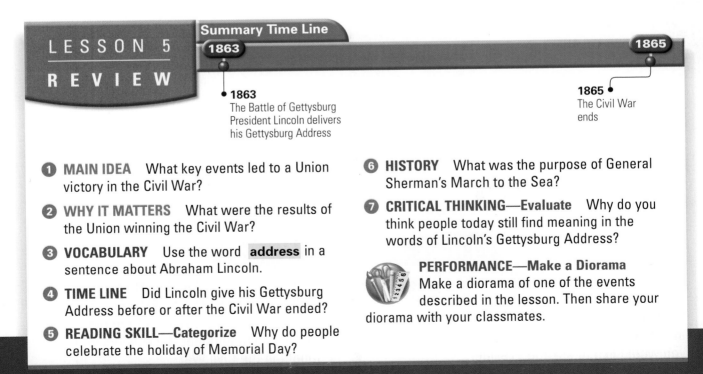

LESSON 5 REVIEW

Summary Time Line

1863 — 1865

1863
The Battle of Gettysburg
President Lincoln delivers his Gettysburg Address

1865
The Civil War ends

① **MAIN IDEA** What key events led to a Union victory in the Civil War?

② **WHY IT MATTERS** What were the results of the Union winning the Civil War?

③ **VOCABULARY** Use the word address in a sentence about Abraham Lincoln.

④ **TIME LINE** Did Lincoln give his Gettysburg Address before or after the Civil War ended?

⑤ **READING SKILL—Categorize** Why do people celebrate the holiday of Memorial Day?

⑥ **HISTORY** What was the purpose of General Sherman's March to the Sea?

⑦ **CRITICAL THINKING—Evaluate** Why do you think people today still find meaning in the words of Lincoln's Gettysburg Address?

PERFORMANCE—Make a Diorama
Make a diorama of one of the events described in the lesson. Then share your diorama with your classmates.

3 Review and Test Preparation

1820
Congress
passes the
Missouri
Compromise

USE YOUR READING SKILLS

Complete this graphic organizer by categorizing important leaders and battles of the Civil War. A copy of this graphic organizer appears on page 34 of the Activity Book.

Important Leaders and Battles of the Civil War

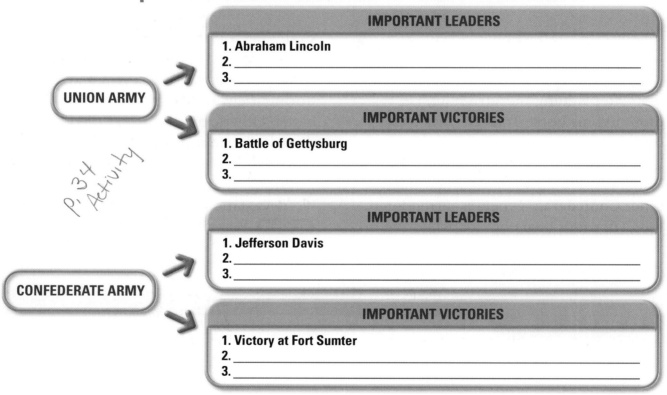

UNION ARMY

IMPORTANT LEADERS
1. Abraham Lincoln
2. _____
3. _____

IMPORTANT VICTORIES
1. Battle of Gettysburg
2. _____
3. _____

P. 34 Activity

CONFEDERATE ARMY

IMPORTANT LEADERS
1. Jefferson Davis
2. _____
3. _____

IMPORTANT VICTORIES
1. Victory at Fort Sumter
2. _____
3. _____

THINK & WRITE

Write a List of Questions   Imagine you are a newspaper reporter in 1863. You have the opportunity to interview President Lincoln at the White House. Write a list of questions you would like to ask the President.

Write a Song   The Civil War inspired the writing of many patriotic American songs, such as "The Battle Hymn of the Republic." Write a song to honor the soldiers who fought in the Civil War.

1850
Congress passes the Compromise of 1850

1854
Congress passes the Kansas-Nebraska Act

1860
Abraham Lincoln is elected President

1861
The Civil War begins

1863
The Emancipation Proclamation is issued

1865
Lee surrenders at Appomattox Court House

USE THE TIME LINE

Use the chapter summary time line to answer these questions.

1 In what year did the Civil War end? *1865*

2 How many years after the Missouri Compromise did the Civil War begin? *11*

USE VOCABULARY

Use these terms to write a story about life in the United States during the Civil War.

states' rights (p. 100)

abolitionist (p. 112)

equality (p. 112)

secede (p. 117)

Confederacy (p. 117)

RECALL FACTS

Answer these questions.

3 What effect did the Kansas-Nebraska Act have on life in the Kansas Territory? *K will decise by voting.*

4 How did Harriet Tubman contribute to the abolitionist cause? *She help slaves to escape to free land.*

5 What were some of the causes of the Civil War? *i*

Write the letter of the best choice.

6 TEST PREP One effect of the worldwide demand for Southern cotton was that —
A it made Southern planters want to end slavery.
B many new public schools were built in the South.
C it created a need for more enslaved workers.
D many new factories were built in the South.

7 TEST PREP During the Civil War, many European immigrants helped preserve the Union by—
F serving as members of Congress.
G working as Union spies.
H donating money to the war effort.
J serving in the Union army.

THINK CRITICALLY

8 How did changes brought about by the Industrial Revolution lead to conflicts between different regions in the United States?

9 Why do you think the North and South were not able to reach a compromise over slavery in 1861?

10 What do you think would have happened if Abraham Lincoln had waited until after the Civil War to issue the Emancipation Proclamation?

APPLY SKILLS

Identify Frame of Reference

11 The debate over states' rights was one of the issues that led to the Civil War. Explain how a Southern politician's view of states' rights might have been different from a Northern politician's.

Compare Maps with Different Scales
Study the two maps of Fort Sumter on pages 120 and 121. Then answer the following question.

12 Which map would you use if you wanted to see a more detailed view of Fort Sumter and the surrounding area? Explain.

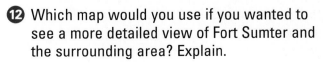

DRAYTON HALL

During the Civil War, many of the South's plantation homes were destroyed or badly damaged. Drayton Hall managed to survive the conflict and today serves as a living history museum. Visitors can learn about its various buildings, farming methods, and the daily lives of those who once lived there.

LOCATE IT

SOUTH CAROLINA

Charleston

Drayton Hall

The Nation Reunited

" **The war is over—the rebels are our countrymen again.** "
— Ulysses S. Grant, April 9, 1865, silencing his cheering troops after Robert E. Lee surrendered

CHAPTER READING SKILL

Determine Point of View

When you determine someone's **point of view** on a subject, you identify that person's way of looking at it.

As you read this chapter, determine different people's points of view about Reconstruction, industrial growth, and immigration.

WHO SAID IT → WHAT THEY SAID

↓

POINT OF VIEW ← WHY THEY SAID IT

MAIN IDEA
Read to learn how the United States government tried to rebuild the South after the Civil War.

WHY IT MATTERS
Rebuilding the South and reuniting the nation proved to be a difficult process.

VOCABULARY
Reconstruction
assassinate
black codes
acquittal

Reconstruction

1820 — 1870 — 1920

1865–1870

The end of the Civil War brought the Confederacy to its end. Now it was time to try to bring the country back together. This time of rebuilding, called **Reconstruction**, had two distinct parts. The first part was the President's plan for Reconstruction. The second part was Congress's Reconstruction plan. Before Reconstruction could begin, however, one more tragedy would add to the country's pain.

One More Tragic Death

Before the Civil War ended, Abraham Lincoln was inaugurated for a second term as President. He realized he would face a challenging task in rebuilding the country. Lincoln, however, believed the South should not be punished for the war. He wanted to bring the country back together peacefully and as quickly as possible. Lincoln spoke of his plans for Reconstruction in his second inaugural address on March 4, 1865.

66 **With malice toward none, with charity for all, with firmness in the right as God gives us to see the right, let us strive on to finish the work we are in, to bind up the nation's wounds. . . .** 99

FORD'S THEATRE
TENTH STREET, ABOVE E.
SEASON 11 .... WEEK XXXI .... NIGHT 191
WHOLE NUMBER OF NIGHTS, 495.
JOHN T. FORD .... PROPRIETOR AND MANAGER
(Also of Holliday's St. Theatre, Baltimore, and Academy of Music, Phila
Stage Manager .... J. B. WRIGHT
Treasurer .... H. CLAY FORD
Friday • Evening, April 14th, 1865.
THIS EVENING
The Performance will be honored by the presence of
PRESIDENT LINCOLN
BENEFIT
—AND—
LAST NIGHT
OF MISS
LAURA KEENE
THE DISTINGUISHED MANAGERESS, AUTHORESS, and ACTRESS
Supported by
MR. JOHN DYOTT
AND
MR. HARRY HAWK
TOM TAYLOR'S CELEBRATED ECCENTRIC COMEDY
As originally produced in America by Miss Keene, and performed by her upwards of
OUSAND NIGH

This poster announces Lincoln's plans to attend Ford's Theatre. Below are the glasses he wore that night.

FAST FACT After shooting the President, John Wilkes Booth jumped onto the stage and cried out *Sic semper tyrannis!*, which means "Thus ever for tyrants" in Latin.

140

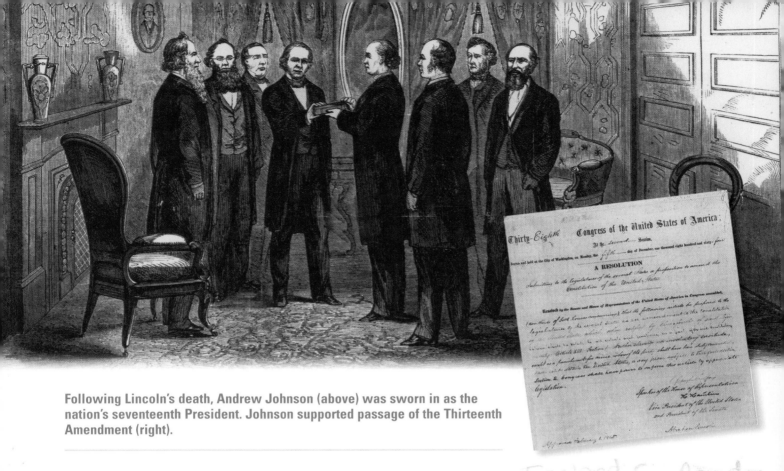

Following Lincoln's death, Andrew Johnson (above) was sworn in as the nation's seventeenth President. Johnson supported passage of the Thirteenth Amendment (right).

The President's plans were tragically cut short. On April 14, 1865, just five days after Lee's surrender, Lincoln went with Mary Todd Lincoln, his wife, to watch a play at Ford's Theatre in Washington, D.C. There he was **assassinated**—murdered in a sudden or secret attack—by John Wilkes Booth. Booth, an actor at Ford's Theatre, supported the Confederate cause.

Lincoln's death shocked the nation. Northerners had lost the leader who had saved the Union. Southerners had lost the leader who had promised an easy peace between the North and the South. Mary Chesnut, a Southerner, feared the worst. When she learned of Lincoln's death, Chesnut wrote in her diary, "Lincoln—old Abe Lincoln—killed. . . . I know this foul murder will bring down worse miseries on us."

REVIEW Why might many Southerners be upset by Lincoln's death?

The President's Plan

After Lincoln's death, the Vice President, Andrew Johnson, became President. Johnson returned the rights of citizenship to most Confederates who pledged loyalty to the United States. Their states then held elections, and state governments went back to work.

Johnson also said that the former Confederate states had to abolish slavery before they could rejoin the Union. To that end, the Thirteenth Amendment to the Constitution was ratified in December 1865. It ended slavery in the United States and its territories.

Such easy terms for rejoining the Union made many Northerners angry. They felt the Confederates were not being punished for their part in the war. White Southerners were again being elected to office and running state governments.

However, few people talked about the rights of the former slaves.

It was not long before the newly elected state legislatures in the South passed laws to limit the rights of former slaves. These laws, called **black codes**, differed from state to state. In most states, however, former slaves were not allowed to vote. In some they were not allowed to travel freely. They could not own certain kinds of property or work in certain businesses. They could be forced to work without pay if they could not find other jobs.

REVIEW **Why was the Thirteenth Amendment to the Constitution ratified?** *Because Conf. states had to abolish slavery b/f they could rejoin the union.*

Congress's Plan

Many members of Congress were upset about what was happening in the South. As a result, Congress replaced the President's Reconstruction plan with one of its own.

As part of its plan, Congress did away with the new state governments and put the Southern states under military rule. Union soldiers kept order, and army officers were appointed to be governors. Before any Southern state could reestablish its state government, it had to write a new state constitution giving all men, both black and white, the right to vote.

Under its plan for Reconstruction, Congress sent Union troops to the Southern states. The troops in the photograph below are standing in front of a house in Atlanta, Georgia.

Johnson was the first President to be impeached. His trial in the Senate (above) drew large crowds of people.

• BIOGRAPHY •

Edmund G. Ross 1826–1907
Character Trait: Courage

Edmund G. Ross moved to Kansas in 1856 to lead the "free state" movement. He started two Kansas newspapers, the *Topeka Tribune* and the *Kansas State Record*, both of which supported this cause. During the Civil War, Ross became a major in the Union army. In 1866 he was appointed to the Senate, where despite pressure from other senators, he voted to acquit President Johnson.

MULTIMEDIA BIOGRAPHIES
Visit The Learning Site at
www.harcourtschool.com/biographies
to learn about other famous people.

GO ONLINE

To return to the Union, a state also had to approve the Fourteenth Amendment. The Fourteenth Amendment states that all persons born in the United States, except Native Americans, and those who later become citizens are citizens of the United States and of the state in which they live. The amendment also protects the rights of all citizens.

President Johnson was very angry about this plan and about other laws Congress had passed to limit his authority as President. After Johnson fired a popular member of his cabinet in 1868, the House of Representatives voted to impeach him. The Senate put Johnson on trial. By just one vote, the Senate failed to get the two-thirds majority needed to remove Johnson from office. The final and deciding vote for **acquittal**, or a verdict of not guilty, was cast by Senator Edmund G. Ross of Kansas. Although Andrew Johnson stayed in office, he was no longer respected as a strong leader.

REVIEW What rights are provided by the Fourteenth Amendment?

Reconstruction Governments

As the Southern states began to write new state constitutions and approve the Fourteenth Amendment, new elections were held. For the first time African Americans, such as Blanche K. Bruce and Hiram R. Revels of Mississippi, were elected to the United States Congress.

Many African Americans also served in the new Reconstruction governments in the Southern states. Jonathan C. Gibbs became secretary of state in Florida and helped set up Florida's public school system. Before this time, most schools in the South were privately run. Francis L. Cardozo, another African American, was secretary of state and, later, state treasurer in South Carolina.

Most Confederates accepted their defeat and the abolition of slavery.

This poster (left) celebrates the passage of the Fifteenth Amendment (above).

However, many were against equal rights for African Americans. They did not want African Americans to vote or to hold office, and they opposed the Reconstruction governments.

Congress then proposed the Fifteenth Amendment to the Constitution. It states that no citizen shall be denied the right to vote because of "race, color, or previous condition of servitude." This amendment, which was ratified in 1870, was designed to extend voting rights and to enforce them by law.

REVIEW What is the Fifteenth Amendment?

right to vote

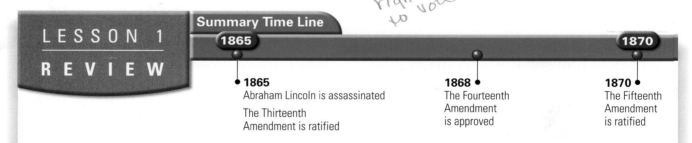

LESSON 1 REVIEW

Summary Time Line

1865		1870

1865
Abraham Lincoln is assassinated

The Thirteenth Amendment is ratified

1868
The Fourteenth Amendment is approved

1870
The Fifteenth Amendment is ratified

1. **MAIN IDEA** How did the United States government try to rebuild the South after the Civil War?

2. **WHY IT MATTERS** Why was Reconstruction such a difficult process?

3. **VOCABULARY** Use the words **Reconstruction** and **black codes** in a sentence about the South after the Civil War.

4. **TIME LINE** When did the Fifteenth Amendment become part of the Constitution?

5. **READING SKILL—Determine Point of View** How did President Lincoln think the South should be treated after the Civil War? *quickly and easy*

6. **HISTORY** Which amendment ended slavery in the United States? *13*

7. **CRITICAL THINKING—Evaluate** Why did many white Southerners oppose the new Reconstruction governments? *They were against equal rights*

PERFORMANCE—Conduct an Interview
Imagine that you are a news reporter. Write an interview with President Andrew Johnson, a senator who supports Congress's plan for Reconstruction, or an African American elected to serve in a Reconstruction government in the South. Provide both questions and answers. Then share your interview with classmates.

The South After the War

1820 ——————— 1870 ——————— 1920

1865–1877

MAIN IDEA
Read to learn about
the many challenges the
South faced after the war.

WHY IT MATTERS
The refusal of many white
Southerners to accept the
reconstruction of Southern
society caused conflict.

VOCABULARY
freedmen
sharecropping
carpetbagger
scalawag
secret ballot
segregation

When the Civil War ended, much of the South was in ruins. The money issued by the Confederacy was worthless, and most Confederate banks were closed. Entire cities had been burned, and many railroads, bridges, plantations, and farms had been destroyed. As one Southerner remembered, "All the talk was of burning homes, houses knocked to pieces, . . . famine, murder, desolation."

The years following the war were hard ones for all people in the South. For the more than 4 million former slaves living there, however, those years also brought new hope.

The Freedmen's Bureau

In March 1865, even before the war ended, the United States Congress set up the Bureau of Refugees, Freedmen, and Abandoned Lands—the Freedmen's Bureau, as it was called. It aided all needy people in the South, although **freedmen**—men, women, and children who had been slaves—were its main concern.

Many former slaves, like those shown outside this Freedmen's Bureau school (below), were eager to learn to read and write. Many of the teachers in those schools were Northern women.

145

Many former slaves were wandering through the country looking for the means to start a new life. The Freedmen's Bureau gave food and supplies to these people. It also helped some white farmers rebuild their farms. The most important work of the Freedmen's Bureau, however, was education. Newly freed slaves were eager to learn to read and write. To help meet this need, the Freedmen's Bureau built more than 4,000 schools and hired thousands of teachers.

The Freedmen's Bureau also wanted to help former slaves earn a living by providing them with land to farm, but this plan did not work. The land was to have come from the plantations taken or abandoned during the war, but the federal government decided to give those plantations back to their original owners. In the end, most former slaves were not given any land. Without money to buy land of their own, they had to find work where they could.

REVIEW Why was the Freedmen's Bureau set up?

This photograph (left) shows people going to an early Juneteenth celebration. Many people, such as those participating in this parade in Austin, Texas (below), celebrate Juneteenth.

• HERITAGE •

Juneteenth

Abraham Lincoln had issued the Emancipation Proclamation on January 1, 1863. But because Union troops did not control Texas at the time, the order had little effect there. On June 19, 1865, Union soldiers landed in Galveston, Texas. On that day Union General Gordon Granger read an order declaring that all slaves in Texas were free. Today people in Texas and across the country celebrate June 19, or Juneteenth, as a day of freedom. It is a holiday marked by picnics, parades, and family gatherings.

Sharecropping

In their search for jobs, many former slaves went back to work on plantations. Planters welcomed them. Fields needed to be plowed, and crops needed to be planted. Now, however, planters had to pay the former slaves for their work.

Because there was not much money available in the years following the war, many landowners paid workers in shares of crops rather than in cash. Under this system, known as **sharecropping**, a landowner gave a worker a cabin, mules, tools, and seed. The worker, called a sharecropper, then farmed the land. At harvesttime the landowner took a share of the crops plus enough extra to cover the cost of the worker's housing and supplies. What was left was the worker's share.

Sharecropping gave landowners the help they needed to work the fields. It also gave former slaves work for pay. Yet few people got ahead through sharecropping. When crops failed, both landowners and workers suffered. Even in good times, most workers' shares were very little, if anything at all.

REVIEW How were workers paid in a sharecropping system?

Using tools like this plow, many former slaves worked as share-croppers in the years following the Civil War.

Carpetbaggers and Scalawags

To rebuild bridges, buildings, and railroads, the South's Reconstruction governments had to increase taxes. In Louisiana, for example, taxes almost doubled. Mississippi's taxes were 14 times higher than they had been. White Southerners blamed the higher taxes on African American state legislators and on other state government leaders they called carpetbaggers and scalawags.

Carpetbaggers were people from the North who moved to the South to take part in Reconstruction governments. They were called carpetbaggers because many of them carried their belongings in suitcases made of carpet material. Some of them truly wanted to help. Others were looking for an opportunity for personal gain.

James Longstreet believed that building factories would help the South rebuild its economy.

A **scalawag** (SKA•lih•wag) is a rascal, someone who supports a cause for his or her own gain. Many scalawags were white Southerners who had opposed the Confederacy. Some were thinking only of themselves. Others felt they were doing what was best for the South.

Among the most famous of the scalawags was James Longstreet, a former Confederate general. Longstreet believed that the South needed to cooperate with the North in order to prosper. He and other leading business people wanted to build factories to lessen the South's dependence on agriculture.

REVIEW How did the Reconstruction governments raise money to rebuild bridges, buildings, and railroads?

increase taxes

Reconstruction Ends

Many white Southerners did not want their way of life to change. Burdened by heavy taxes and a changing society, they began to organize to regain their authority. One way to do so was to control the way people voted.

In the 1860s there was no secret ballot, as there is today. A **secret ballot** is a voting method that does not allow anyone to know how a person has voted. Before the secret ballot was used, the names of voters and how they voted were published in newspapers.

Secret societies were formed to keep African Americans from voting or to make sure they voted only in certain ways. Those who joined the secret societies included white Southerners who resented the fact that African Americans were now considered their equals. Members of one secret society, the Ku Klux Klan, used violence to keep African Americans from voting or to make sure they voted as they were told.

Over time, white Southerners once again took control of their state governments and society. Despite the Fifteenth Amendment, new state laws were passed that made it very difficult, if not impossible, for African Americans to vote. African Americans also were required to go to separate schools and churches and to sit in separate railroad cars. Laws such as these led to **segregation**, or the

Many carpetbaggers who came to the South during Reconstruction carried their belongings in bags made of carpet material.

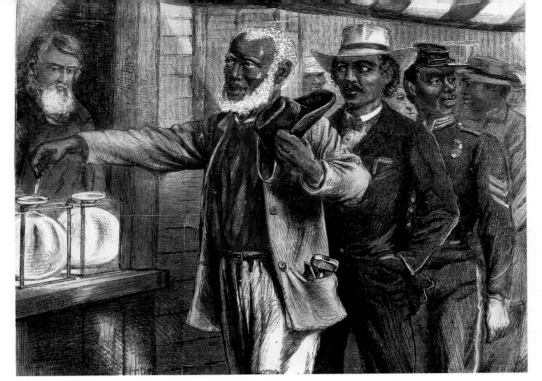

The Fifteenth Amendment guaranteed African Americans the right to vote, as seen in this illustration. With the end of Reconstruction, however, that right was again denied to most African Americans living in the South.

practice of keeping people in separate groups based on their race or culture.

Reconstruction was over by 1877. In that year the last of the Union troops left the South. The rights and freedoms that African Americans had won were again being taken away in the South. By 1900 African Americans in many of the Southern states were not allowed to vote, and few held public office.

REVIEW How did white Southerners take back control of their state governments and society? *Secret society, pass laws that made it impossible for A. A to vote*

LESSON 2 REVIEW

Summary Time Line

1865 — 1869 — 1873 — 1877

1865
The Freedmen's Bureau is founded

1877
Reconstruction ends

1. **MAIN IDEA** What challenges did the South face after the Civil War? *No money, no housing, no jobs*

2. **WHY IT MATTERS** How did the refusal of many white Southerners to accept Reconstruction cause conflict?

3. **VOCABULARY** Use the words **carpetbagger** and **scalawag** in a sentence about the South after the Civil War.

4. **TIME LINE** When did Reconstruction end? *1877*

5. **READING SKILL—Determine Point of View** How did members of the Ku Klux Klan feel about African Americans being allowed to vote? *they didn't*

6. **ECONOMICS** Why was it difficult for sharecroppers to get ahead?

7. **CRITICAL THINKING—Analyze** In what ways did the Freedmen's Bureau help African Americans? In what ways did it fail? *It help them read/write /No land was given.*

PERFORMANCE—Write a List Write a list of things you would have done to help rebuild the South after the Civil War. Be sure to include ways in which you would have helped the newly freed slaves, as well as the economies of the Southern states. Share your list with the rest of the class.

Settling the Last Frontier

MAIN IDEA
Read to learn why many people decided to move to the West after the Civil War.

WHY IT MATTERS
The West offered Americans a new place to explore and settle.

VOCABULARY
boom
refinery
prospector
bust
long drive
homesteader
open range
reservation

1820   1870   1920

1850–1890

The years following the Civil War saw the full-scale settlement of the West. Many Americans moved to settle this last frontier, which included the Great Plains, the Rocky Mountains, and the Great Basin.

Miners

After the California gold rush of 1849, new discoveries of gold and silver brought more miners to the West and supplied new sources of mineral wealth for the nation. Thousands of miners hurried to Colorado after gold was found near Pikes Peak in 1858. The next year, news of huge deposits of silver in the area known as the Comstock Lode drew thousands to what is now Nevada. Between 1862 and 1868, other finds in present-day Arizona, Idaho, Montana, and Alaska added to the West's **boom**, or time of fast economic or population growth.

When gold or silver was discovered in a place, miners moved into the area hoping to strike it rich. They claimed

Many stores in towns that were abandoned in the late 1800s are once again open for business. Stores, such as the one mentioned in this poster (left), were closed.

land and set up camps, which often grew into towns. Some towns sprang up almost overnight as people quickly started businesses and farms and built refineries. A **refinery** is a factory where metals, fuels, and other materials are cleaned and made into usable products.

Fights often broke out among the **prospectors**, or those searching for gold, silver, and other mineral resources. The towns had no sheriffs, and law and order did not exist. "Street fights were frequent," one writer reported, "and . . . everyone was on his guard against a random shot." As mining towns grew, families began to arrive. Many mining towns set up governments and started schools, hospitals, and churches.

In most places all of the gold or silver was mined in just a few years. When that happened, the miners left to look for new claims and the mining town was often abandoned. Just as quickly as a boom built a town, a **bust**, or time of fast economic decline, left a town lifeless. Some of these abandoned towns, called ghost towns, can still be seen in the West today.

REVIEW What brought miners to the West?

Ranchers

The West's vast grasslands attracted many ranchers to the region. Large-scale cattle ranching had begun in Texas in the early 1800s. Ranchers there raised cattle mostly for leather and for tallow, or fat, which was used for making candles and soap. After the Civil War, however, as cities in the East grew, the demand for beef increased. Cattle sold there for ten times as much as they did in Texas. Ranchers could make more money if they could get their cattle to those markets.

At first Texas ranchers drove, or herded, their cattle to port cities, such as Galveston, Texas, and Shreveport, Louisiana, for shipment to New Orleans and to cities in the East. This method was both slow and costly. In the late 1860s, a cheaper, faster method became available when the first railroads were built out West. Between 1867 and 1890, ranchers drove about 10 million head of cattle north to the railroads on **long drives**.

The long drives followed cattle trails such as the Sedalia Trail, which went from Texas to Sedalia, Missouri.

Cattle Trails

Movement **This map shows the four major cattle trails used by ranchers in the 1880s.**

❖ Which trail led to both Abilene and Ellsworth?

Saddles and hats like these were used by ranchers on long drives.

Other trails—the Chisholm, the Western, and the Goodnight-Loving—led to other "cow towns" along the railroads. Abilene, Kansas; Ogallala, Nebraska; and Cheyenne, Wyoming, were towns that grew at the end of cattle trails. At each town the cattle were loaded onto railroad cars and sent to Chicago. There the animals were prepared for market. The meat was then sent in refrigerated freight cars to markets in the East.

REVIEW How were railroads important to Texas ranchers?

Barbed wire was used to build fences on the Great Plains.

Homesteaders

In 1862 Congress passed the Homestead Act. This law opened the Great Plains to settlers by giving 160 acres of land to any head of a family who was over 21 years of age and who would live on the land for five years. Thousands of Americans, as well as about 100,000 immigrants from Europe, rushed to claim those plots of land called homesteads. The people who settled them were known as **homesteaders**.

Living on the Great Plains was very difficult. There were few streams for water or trees for wood. Many settlers used sod to build their houses, but sod houses were difficult to keep clean. Dirt often fell from the sod ceiling onto the furniture. Drought and dust storms were common in the summer, and homesteaders worried about prairie fires. In winter, snow and bitterly cold temperatures froze the region. Insects, too, were a problem. In 1874, grasshoppers came by the millions, turning the sky black and eating anything that was green.

Many homesteaders saw the Great Plains as a "treeless wasteland." They believed that the tough sod and dry soil were unsuited for farming, and they left. Those who stayed used new technologies to solve some of the challenges the land presented. They used an improved steel plow, invented by James Oliver of Indiana, to cut through the thick sod. They used new models of windmills to pump water from the ground. They planted Russian wheat, which needed less water, and used reapers to harvest it.

Relations with ranchers posed another problem for farmers. It was difficult to grow crops in the same area where cattle ranchers kept their herds. To keep the cattle out of their fields, farmers began using wire with steel points, known as barbed wire, to build fences. Some ranchers also built fences to keep their cattle from wandering off the ranches.

Fences often kept farmers from reaching the water they needed for their crops and kept ranchers from reaching the water they needed for their cattle. Fences also blocked some cattle from reaching the millions of acres of government land that ranchers used as **open range**, or free grazing land.

GEOGRAPHY THEME

Movement This map shows the areas of the United States that were settled by 1870 and 1890. Among the settlers was this Nebraska family (right), who used sod to build their home.

❖ What happened to the frontier as settlers moved west?

Settlers Move West, 1870–1890

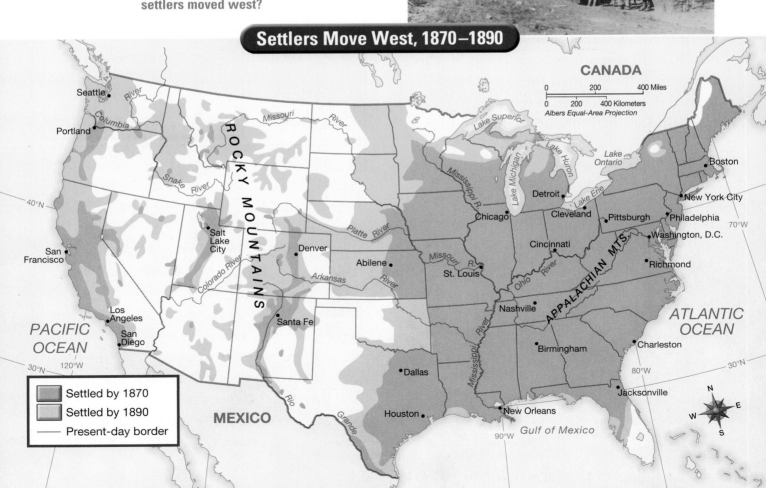

Settled by 1870
Settled by 1890
Present-day border

Farmers and ranchers began cutting one another's fences. Some people even started shooting one another. These fights, called range wars, went on through the 1880s until ranchers were told they had to move their cattle off government land.

In spite of these problems, about 5 million homesteaders had migrated to the Great Plains by 1890. So many people had moved there and to lands farther west, in the Rocky Mountains and the Great Basin, that in 1890 the Census Bureau declared the last frontier "closed."

REVIEW What hardships did homesteaders moving west face? No enough H2O, No trees praires fire extreme temperatures

Conflict in the West

Many of the Native American groups on the Great Plains had long depended on the buffalo for their basic needs. As settlers began using the land for farming and ranching, the buffalo began to die out. In addition, hunters working for the railroads killed large numbers of buffalo to feed the workers who were laying track. In the 1860s about 15 million buffalo lived on the Great Plains. Within 20 years, fewer than 1,000 were left.

With fewer buffalo and the loss of their hunting lands, many groups of Plains Indians signed treaties with the United States. Those treaties set up reservations for the Indians. A **reservation** is an area of land set aside by the government for use only by Native Americans.

· GEOGRAPHY ·

Little Bighorn Battlefield
Understanding Places and Regions

Among the soldiers killed at the Little Bighorn Battlefield in June 1876 were five members of the Custer family—George, his two brothers Thomas and Boston, their nephew, and their brother-in-law. The Little Bighorn Battlefield was made a national military cemetery in 1879, and in 1946 it was designated a national monument.

In 1868 the Sioux Nation signed a treaty that created the Great Sioux Reservation in the Black Hills region of present-day South Dakota and Wyoming. Some Indians, however, continued to roam the lands west of the reservation in search of buffalo. After gold was discovered in the Black Hills, the United States sent soldiers to move all the Indians to reservations.

In June 1876 Lieutenant Colonel George Custer led an attack against the Sioux and their Cheyenne allies at the Little Bighorn River. Two of the chiefs leading the Sioux were Sitting Bull and Crazy Horse. As many as 2,000 Indian warriors quickly surrounded Custer and his men. In the battle that followed, about 225 soldiers were killed. Crazy Horse and

Chief Joseph

Sitting Bull were later defeated, and the Indians were forced onto reservations.

In 1877 the United States government also ordered the Nez Perce (NES PERS) Indians in eastern Oregon to move to a reservation in Idaho. The Nez Perce leader, Chief Joseph, led a group of 800 men, women, and children in an attempt to escape to Canada. They were stopped and surrendered without a fight. Chief Joseph told his people, "I am tired of fighting."

By 1880 almost all Native Americans in the United States had been moved onto reservations. In 1924 Congress granted citizenship to all Native Americans. In 1934 it gave Indians living on reservation lands the right to govern themselves.

REVIEW **Why did Custer attack the Sioux?**

To move all the indians into reservation.

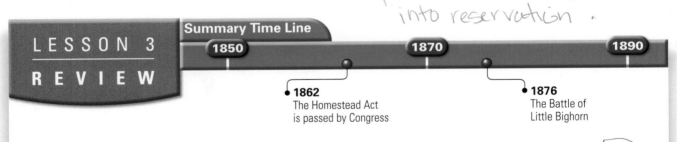

LESSON 3 REVIEW

Summary Time Line

1850 — 1870 — 1890

1862
The Homestead Act is passed by Congress

1876
The Battle of Little Bighorn

❶ **MAIN IDEA** Why did settlers migrate to the West after the Civil War?

❷ **WHY IT MATTERS** How did settlement of the West affect the growth of the United States?

❸ **VOCABULARY** How did **prospectors** cause **booms** in some areas?

❹ **TIME LINE** When was the Homestead Act passed?

❺ **READING SKILL—Determine Point of View** How did ranchers and farmers think differently about cattle ranching?

❻ **ECONOMICS** What were the main ways that settlers in the west earned their living?

❼ **CRITICAL THINKING—Analyze** How do you think the destruction of the buffalo affected Native Americans? *It was their main living*

PERFORMANCE—Write a List of Questions Imagine that it is 1870 and that you are going to move out west to become a homesteader. Write a list of questions that you would want to ask a homesteader or cattle rancher that will make your journey easier and help you live in an unfamiliar land.

Use a Climograph

VOCABULARY
climograph

▶ WHY IT MATTERS

In the late 1800s many Americans who moved from eastern cities to the Great Plains were surprised by much of what they found there. However, probably nothing surprised them more than the extremes of temperature and precipitation.

If you and your family were moving to another place, you would want to know more about its climate before you moved there. One way to learn about the climate of a place is to study a climograph, or climate graph. A **climograph** shows on one graph the average monthly temperature and the average monthly precipitation for a place. Comparing climographs can help you understand differences in climates.

▶ WHAT YOU NEED TO KNOW

The climographs on page 157 show the average monthly temperature and precipitation for Omaha, Nebraska, and Philadelphia, Pennsylvania. The temperatures are shown as a line graph. The amounts of precipitation are shown as a bar graph. The months are listed along the bottom of each climograph, from January to December.

Along the left-hand side of each climograph is a Fahrenheit scale for temperature. A point is shown on the climograph for the average temperature for each month. These points are connected with a red line. By studying the line, you can see which months are usually warm and which are usually cold.

Along the right-hand side of each climograph is a scale for precipitation. The average monthly amounts of precipitation are shown in inches. By studying the heights of the blue bars, you can see which months are usually dry and which are usually wet.

Pioneers who settled on the Great Plains sometimes experienced ice storms. These storms covered fences, plants, and the ground with a layer of ice.

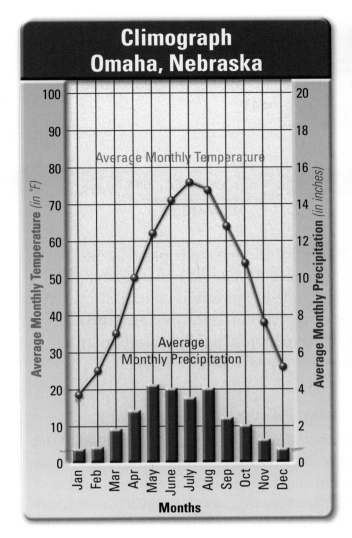

Climograph
Omaha, Nebraska

Average Monthly Temperature

Average Monthly Precipitation

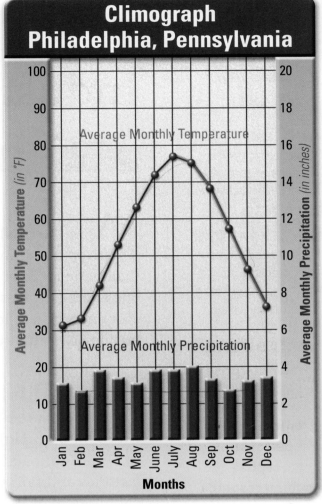

Climograph
Philadelphia, Pennsylvania

Average Monthly Temperature

Average Monthly Precipitation

▶ PRACTICE THE SKILL

Use the climographs above to answer the following questions. *July-P*

1 Which is the warmest month in each of these cities? Which is the coolest?

2 What is the wettest month in each city?

3 What is the driest month in each city?

4 Which city receives more precipitation during the year?

5 What is the average temperature for each place in January?

6 How much precipitation falls during January in each place?

▶ APPLY WHAT YOU LEARNED

Use an almanac, an encyclopedia, or the Internet to create a climograph for your city or for a city close to where you live. Compare your climograph with the ones shown on this page. Which place shows the greatest changes in temperature and precipitation? Share your findings with a family member or friend. Then discuss why people might need to know this kind of information.

The Rise of New Industries

1820   1870   1920

1860–1900

After the Civil War great changes took place in the American economy. Inventors developed new technologies that made it easier for people to travel and communicate with one another. It was an important time for **free enterprise**—an economic system in which people are able to start and run businesses with little control by the government.

The Transcontinental Railroad

From 1860 to 1900, the railroad network in the United States was built up rapidly in order to move people from place to place. Railroads were also needed to move raw materials to factories and finished products to market. By 1900 the country had more than 193,000 miles (311,000 km) of track. That included the **transcontinental railroad**, which crossed the entire continent of North America. The transcontinental railroad was actually made up of a number of different lines,

including the Union Pacific Railroad and the Central Pacific Railroad. Together they linked the Atlantic and Pacific coasts and opened the nation's vast interior to people who wanted to settle there. They also made trade between different parts of the country easier, which caused the economy to grow.

One reason for the growth of railroads was the development of new inventions that improved rail transportation. George Westinghouse's air brake made trains safer by stopping not only the locomotive but also each car. Granville T. Woods improved the air brake and also developed a telegraph system that allowed trains and stations to communicate.

The transcontinental railroad crossed both the Rocky Mountains and the Sierra Nevada. Workers had to build bridges across valleys, cut ledges on mountainsides, and blast tunnels through mountains. At Promontory, Utah, on May 10, 1869, workers laid the last of the transcontinental railroad. A ceremonial golden spike was driven into place.

REVIEW How did the transcontinental railroad help the economy grow?

The Steel Industry

Railroads needed strong, long-lasting tracks. At first, iron rails were used. With bigger and heavier locomotives, however, iron rails were no longer strong enough. Steel rails would be harder and last longer than iron, but steel was much more expensive to make.

In 1872 Andrew Carnegie, an entrepreneur (ahn•truh•pruh•NER) from Pittsburgh, Pennsylvania, visited Britain. An **entrepreneur** is a person who sets up and runs a business. In Britain, Carnegie saw a new process for making steel. Invented by Henry Bessemer, this process melted iron ore and other metals and materials together in a new kind of coal-fired furnace, called a blast furnace.

A CLOSER LOOK
Transcontinental Railroad

To complete the transcontinental railroad, workers often worked long hours in dangerous conditions. Most of the workers were Chinese and Irish immigrants.

1 Workers used tools, such as pickaxes and shovels, to clear tunnels.

2 A small locomotive powered machines that hauled dirt and rock to the surface.

3 Explosives were used to blast through rock.

4 Workers stayed behind a protective wall during tunnel blasting.

5 Workers on the transcontinental railroad laid more than 1,776 miles (2,858 km) of track.

❖ What kinds of work did immigrant workers have to do to build the transcontinental railroad?

It was called a blast furnace because blasts of air were forced through the molten metal to burn out the impurities. This process made the steel stronger.

Back in Pennsylvania, Carnegie found investors to help him build a steel mill. Western Pennsylvania and nearby areas of Ohio and West Virginia had all the resources needed to make steel. By the early 1870s, Carnegie's steel business was so successful that he built more steel mills and bought coal and iron mines to supply them. Then he bought ships to carry these natural resources to his mills. With his mines and ships, he could make a greater supply of steel at a lower cost than other mills could.

By the 1890s Andrew Carnegie had become one of the wealthiest people in the world. Carnegie, who had come to the United States as an immigrant from Scotland in 1848, gave much of his wealth to build libraries and schools.

Other industries quickly discovered new uses for steel. In the 1880s William Jenney used steel frames to build taller buildings. People called these tall buildings skyscrapers because they seemed to scrape the sky.

John Roebling, a German immigrant, used steel cables and beams to build suspended bridges. One of his bridges, the Brooklyn Bridge, still links Manhattan with Brooklyn, in New York City.

As the demand for steel increased, more steel mills were built. In the late 1800s, large deposits of iron ore were discovered in the Mesabi Range, west of Lake Superior. To be nearer to those resources, the steel industry spread to cities along the Great Lakes, such as Cleveland, Ohio, and Chicago, Illinois.

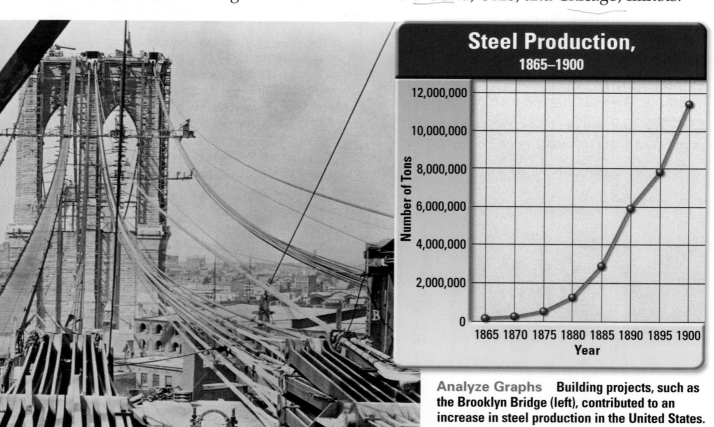

Steel Production, 1865–1900

Analyze Graphs Building projects, such as the Brooklyn Bridge (left), contributed to an increase in steel production in the United States.

◆ Between which years did steel production increase the most?

Ships and railroads carried raw materials to steel mills and carried steel to factories and cities across the nation.

REVIEW Why did the steel industry spread to cities along the Great Lakes?

Iron ore was discovered

The Oil Industry

For years people had been aware of the **petroleum**, or oil, that gathered on ponds in western Pennsylvania and other places. Then, in the 1840s, a Canadian scientist named Abraham Gesner discovered that petroleum burned well. When kerosene, a fuel made from petroleum, became widely used for lighting lamps, the demand for petroleum increased. This caused its price to rise.

In 1859 Edwin Drake drilled an oil well in Titusville, Pennsylvania. When the well began producing large amounts of oil, an oil boom took place. Oil towns soon sprang up all over western Pennsylvania and eastern Ohio.

John D. Rockefeller was 23 years old in 1863 when he invested money to build an oil refinery near Cleveland. The money needed to set up or improve a business is called **capital**. Rockefeller steadily invested more capital, buying up some of the other 30 refineries in the Cleveland area. In 1867 he combined his refineries into one business, which he called the Standard Oil Company.

To cut costs and be more efficient, Rockefeller bought other businesses. His company built its own barrels, pipelines, warehouses, and tank cars. As a result, it could produce and distribute oil products at the lowest prices.

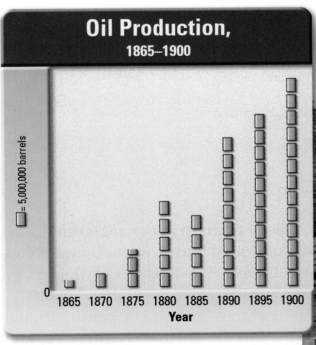

Oil Production, 1865–1900

= 5,000,000 barrels

Year: 1865 1870 1875 1880 1885 1890 1895 1900

Analyze Graphs Drake's oil well (right) produced large amounts of oil. Such discoveries led to increases in oil production in the United States.

❖ About how many barrels of oil were produced in 1900?

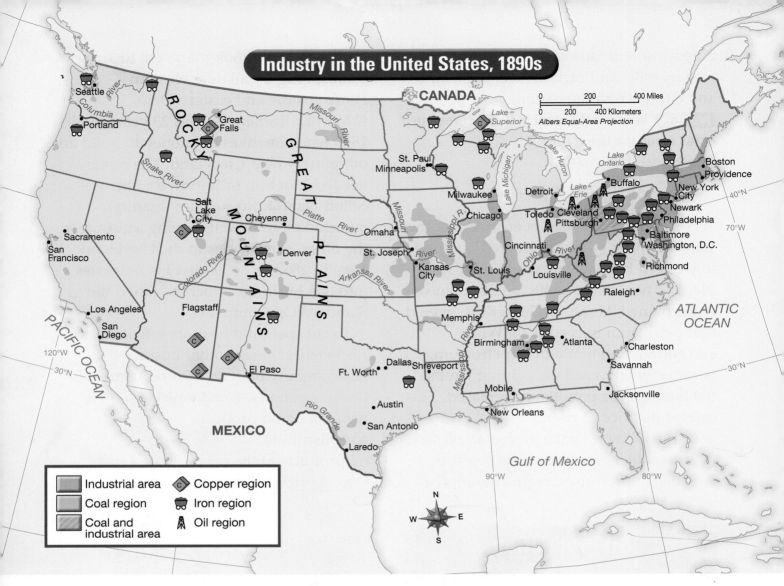

Industry in the United States, 1890s

CANADA

Seattle
Portland
ROCKY
Great Falls
Columbia River
Snake River
GREAT
Salt Lake City
Cheyenne
Sacramento
San Francisco
MOUNTAINS
Denver
Flagstaff
Los Angeles
San Diego
El Paso
PLAINS
Missouri River
Platte River
Colorado River
Arkansas River
St. Paul Minneapolis
Milwaukee
Chicago
Omaha
St. Joseph
Kansas City
Memphis
Ft. Worth
Dallas Shreveport
Austin
San Antonio
Laredo
Rio Grande
MEXICO

Lake Superior
Lake Michigan
Lake Huron
Detroit
Lake Erie
Toledo Cleveland
Chicago
Pittsburgh
Cincinnati
St. Louis
Louisville
Ohio River
Mississippi River
Missouri
Birmingham
Atlanta
Mobile
New Orleans

Lake Ontario
Buffalo
Boston
Providence
New York City
Newark
Philadelphia
Baltimore
Washington, D.C.
Richmond
Raleigh
Charleston
Savannah
Jacksonville

ATLANTIC OCEAN

PACIFIC OCEAN

Gulf of Mexico

120°W   30°N   90°W   80°W   30°N
40°N   70°W

0   200   400 Miles
0   200   400 Kilometers
Albers Equal-Area Projection

N
W   E
S

Legend:
- Industrial area
- Coal region
- Coal and industrial area
- Copper region
- Iron region
- Oil region

Regions   This map shows industrial areas and resource regions in the United States about 1890.

❓ In which part of the United States were most industrial areas found?

Other companies could no longer compete and were driven out of the oil business.

By 1882 the Standard Oil Company controlled almost all of the oil refining and distribution in the United States and much of the world's oil trade as well. After the gasoline engine was invented and automobiles came into use, Rockefeller's oil refineries turned to producing gasoline and engine oil.

REVIEW What did John D. Rockefeller do to make his company more profitable?

Thomas Alva Edison

One of the most important inventors and industrial leaders in the United States was Thomas Alva Edison. Growing up, Edison had learned about the telegraph. Samuel Morse's telegraph, patented in the 1840s, was the nineteenth century's equivalent of the World Wide Web.

While studying the telegraph, Edison learned some of the practical uses of electricity. This knowledge led to his first serious invention in 1869, an electrical vote recorder for the Massachusetts State Legislature. Two years later, in 1871, Edison started a laboratory in Newark, New Jersey. At the time, Newark was known for its many fine machinists. Those machinists were just the kind of **human resources**—the workers and the ideas and skills they bring to their jobs—that Edison needed.

In 1874 Edison's laboratory developed a telegraph system that could send more than one message over a single wire. With the money he earned from selling that telegraph system, Edison opened a laboratory in Menlo Park, New Jersey, in 1876. That

laboratory averaged one patented invention every five days. The best known was the first practical electric lightbulb. Among the others was an improved telephone, an invention that Alexander Graham Bell had patented in 1876.

In 1882 Edison set up the first central power station in New York City. It made electricity available to large parts of the city. Less than 10 years later, hundreds of communities all over the United States had Edison power stations. With Edison's help, electricity soon became an important source of power for American homes, offices, and industries.

REVIEW What was Edison's best known patented invention at Menlo Park?
Electric light bulb

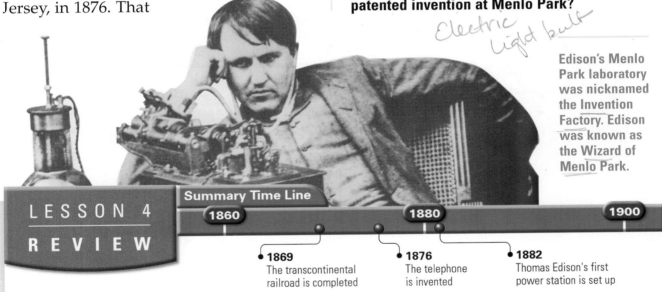

Edison's Menlo Park laboratory was nicknamed the Invention Factory. Edison was known as the Wizard of Menlo Park.

LESSON 4 REVIEW

Summary Time Line

1860	1880	1900

- **1869** The transcontinental railroad is completed
- **1876** The telephone is invented
- **1882** Thomas Edison's first power station is set up

1. **MAIN IDEA** How did the United States economy change in the years after the Civil War? *Industrial*

2. **WHY IT MATTERS** How did changes in the United States economy encourage growth? *Free Enter*

3. **VOCABULARY** Use the word **entrepreneur** in a sentence about **free enterprise**.

4. **TIME LINE** When was the transcontinental railroad completed? *1869*

5. **READING SKILL—Determine Point of View** How do you think John D. Rockefeller felt about the benefits of the free enterprise system?

6. **ECONOMICS** How did the discovery of oil help the United States economy grow?

7. **CRITICAL THINKING—Analyze** How did Andrew Carnegie contribute to the growth of cities?

PERFORMANCE—Write "Who Am I" Questions Write a list of "Who Am I" questions about some of the people you read about in this lesson. Ask your classmates the "Who Am I" questions and see if they can identify who you are.

Edison's Inventions

In his lifetime, Thomas Edison obtained more than 1,000 patents, the most the United States Patent Office has ever issued to one person. Edison invented items that were just for pleasure, as well as devices to solve problems people faced in their everyday lives. These are some of the inventions Edison and his workers produced.

 FROM THE HENRY FORD MUSEUM AND GREENFIELD VILLAGE AND THE SMITHSONIAN INSTITUTION NATIONAL MUSEUM OF AMERICAN HISTORY

The electric lightbulb (left) was invented in 1879. The electric pen (right) was invented in 1874.

The Kinetoscope, invented in 1892, was a machine that showed motion pictures.

Analyze the Primary Source

❶ Which of these inventions looks familiar to you?

❷ Identify the purpose of each invention. Which inventions do you think made people's lives easier?

❸ Explain how one or more of Edison's inventions might work.

The phonograph (left), patented in 1878, is still thought of as Edison's most original invention. The electronic stock ticker (below) was used to print out stock information.

ACTIVITY

Think Critically Make a list of tasks or jobs that you do often. Beside each item on your list, name the tools or appliances that you use to help make the task easier. Do you think you would be able to do the same tasks if the tools or appliances had not been invented?

RESEARCH

GO ONLINE Visit The Learning Site at **www.harcourtschool.com/sources** to research other primary sources.

A Changing People

1880–1920

MAIN IDEA
Read to learn about some of the problems that immigrants to the United States faced in the past.

WHY IT MATTERS
Many immigrants worked hard to overcome their problems and to make a better life for themselves in the United States.

VOCABULARY
old immigration
new immigration
advertisement
tenement
prejudice
regulation

Like its economy, the population of the United States grew and changed after the Civil War. Between 1860 and 1910, about 23 million immigrants arrived on our shores. Those from Europe settled mostly in the cities of the East and Middle West. Those from Asia, Mexico, and parts of Central America and South America settled mostly in the West. Immigrants from all over the world played an important part in the growth of industry and agriculture in the United States.

Immigrants Old and New

European immigrants were by far the largest group to come to the United States. Before 1890 most immigrants from Europe came from northern and western Europe. They were part of the **old immigration**. That is, they came from the same parts of the world as earlier immigrants. The largest groups were from Britain, Germany, and Ireland. Others came from countries such

Between 1890 and 1920, nearly 16 million immigrants from Europe arrived in the United States. The passport below belonged to the Flinck family, from Sweden.

Irving Berlin (left) was one of the millions of immigrants who came to the United States. As a result of immigration, many cities, like New York City (above), grew very quickly.

as Denmark, Norway, and Sweden. These were the immigrants who helped build the Erie Canal and transcontinental railroad and who took part in settling the West.

Beginning about 1890, a period of **new immigration** began. People still came from the countries of northern and western Europe, but now most came from countries in southern and eastern Europe and from other parts of the world. Those from Europe came from countries such as Austria, Hungary, Italy, Greece, Poland, and Russia.

Most of the new immigrants from Europe were poor, and they had few opportunities in their homelands. They came to the United States hoping to find a better life. Many of them learned about jobs in the United States through advertisements. An **advertisement** is a public announcement that tells people about a product or an opportunity. Railroad, coal, and steel companies in the United States placed advertisements in other countries to attract new workers.

Most of the new immigrants settled in cities. They tended to live among people from their own country, with whom they shared a common language and familiar customs. Many lived with relatives, crowded together in poorly built apartment buildings called **tenements**. Wages were so low that everyone in the family—even young children—had to work to earn enough money for food.

In spite of the difficult conditions, many new immigrants succeeded. One of these people was Irving Berlin. He and his family moved to New York City from Russia in 1893. While Berlin was a boy, his father died. To help support his family, Berlin performed as a street singer and singing waiter. He began to write song lyrics and published his first song in 1907. During his life, Berlin wrote more than 800 songs, including "God Bless America," perhaps his most famous song.

REVIEW How did many immigrants learn about jobs in the United States?

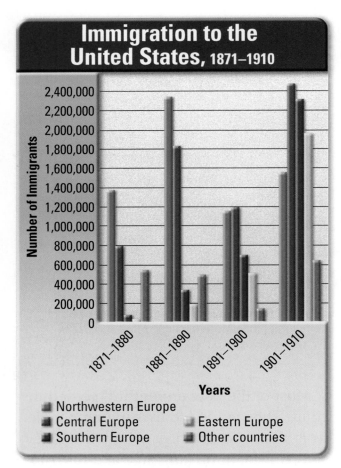

Immigration to the United States, 1871–1910

Number of Immigrants

2,400,000
2,200,000
2,000,000
1,800,000
1,600,000
1,400,000
1,200,000
1,000,000
800,000
600,000
400,000
200,000
0

1871–1880 1881–1890 1891–1900 1901–1910

Years

- Northwestern Europe
- Central Europe
- Southern Europe
- Eastern Europe
- Other countries

Analyze Graphs This graph compares the number of immigrants for different periods of time.

❖ When did the number of immigrants from central Europe first become larger than the number from northwestern Europe?

Immigrants from Asia

Immigrants from China first came to the United States in large numbers after the California gold rush. By 1852 about 25,000 Chinese were working in the goldfields.

As less and less gold was found, some Chinese immigrants returned home. But most stayed and looked for other kinds of work. They often worked for low wages because above all they wanted to stay in the United States. In the 1860s Chinese workers played an important part in building the transcontinental railroad. Some Chinese immigrants set up businesses in California or other parts of the West.

Immigrants from Japan and other countries in Asia also began to enter the United States and find opportunities in the West. Most found jobs in agriculture, mainly in California. Some bought their own land.

Over time, thousands of immigrants came to the United States from Asia. However, the number of Asian immigrants remained small when compared to the number of immigrants who came from Europe.

REVIEW Why did large numbers of Chinese people first come to the United States?

Reaction to Immigrants

Many people born in the United States reacted harshly to the immigrants. Some Americans felt that because many of the immigrants had little education, they were not qualified to take part in a democracy. Others worried that the newcomers would take jobs away from American workers. As a result, many immigrants faced prejudice. **Prejudice** is an unfair feeling of hate or dislike for

These three children and their families came to the United States from Asia. Most immigrants were searching for new opportunities and a better life.

members of a certain group because of their background, race, or religion.

Immigrants were sometimes taunted and called unkind names. They were denied jobs by many businesses, and certain businesses even posted signs that said things such as "Irish need not apply." Jewish immigrants were denied access to the better universities and often found it difficult to get jobs. Some immigrants also suffered physical attacks, and many were ridiculed for their religious beliefs. These anti-immigrant feelings led to the formation of groups that pressured Congress to pass laws that would limit the number of immigrants who could enter the country.

In the West there had been opposition to Asian immigrants for a long time. Their language, appearance, and customs were unfamiliar to most native-born Americans. As feelings against the Chinese grew, numerous **regulations**, or controls, were set up. Some states in the West passed laws that made life harder for the Chinese. Chinese people could not

get state jobs, and their lawsuits would not be heard by state courts.

In 1882 the United States Congress passed the Chinese Exclusion Act. This act excluded, or kept out, all new Chinese workers. It prevented any Chinese workers from coming to the United States for ten years. By the early 1900s many Americans were calling for a stop to all immigration from Asia. Instead of passing such laws, however, the United States government persuaded Asian countries such as Japan to allow only a small number of its people to come to the United States.

REVIEW Why did many Americans react harshly to immigrants?

African Americans on the Move

Even as immigrants were moving to the United States from other countries, people within the United States were moving from place to place. This was true of many different groups of Americans, including African Americans. Many African Americans were looking for new places to live and work.

Many African Americans migrated from the South to the West. There they started farms or found job opportunities they did not have in the South. Some African Americans who had fought in the Civil War stayed in the Army and became part of units formed to fight against Native Americans in the West. The Indians gave the African American troops the name buffalo soldiers because they saw the same fighting spirit in the soldiers that they saw in the buffalo.

Most African Americans who did not move after the end of the Civil War found jobs in the South, often as sharecroppers. Few African Americans moved to the cities because they could not find work there. That changed between 1915 and 1930, however, when many African Americans moved north. This movement of people came to be known as the Great Migration.

One of the main reasons for the Great Migration was that many African Americans working on farms in the South were going through hard times. Floods had damaged many farms, and year after year an insect called the boll weevil had

This painting by artist Jacob Lawrence depicts the Great Migration. In it African Americans are shown leaving the South for cities in the North.

destroyed the cotton crop. At the same time, jobs began to open up in the North.

Many African Americans found factory jobs in large cities such as Boston, Chicago, Cleveland, Detroit, New York, Pittsburgh, Cincinnati, and St. Louis. Newspapers owned by African Americans in those cities actively encouraged this migration. "Get out of the South," advised the *Chicago Defender*. "Come north." As many as 500,000 people did.

Before the early 1900s nearly 90 percent of African Americans lived in the South. Because of the Great Migration, more than half of all African Americans now live in the North and in the Middle West. Most have parents, grandparents, or great-grandparents who were part of the huge movement north.

Jacob Lawrence's parents moved to the North in the early 1900s as part of the Great Migration.

Jacob Lawrence's parents moved north in the early 1900s. Lawrence went to art school in New York City and became a painter. He wrote in his book *The Great Migration*, "Life in the North brought many challenges, but the migrants' lives had changed for the better. The children were able to go to school, and their parents gained the freedom to vote. And the migrants kept coming. Theirs is a story of African-American strength and courage. I share it now as my parents told it to me, because their struggles and triumph ring true today. People all over the world are still on the move, trying to build better lives for themselves and for their families."

REVIEW What was the Great Migration?

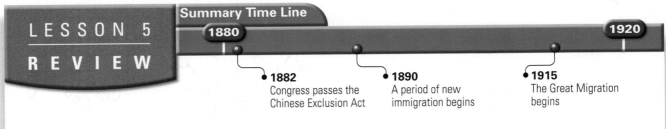

LESSON 5 REVIEW

Summary Time Line

1880 — 1920

1882
Congress passes the Chinese Exclusion Act

1890
A period of new immigration begins

1915
The Great Migration begins

① **MAIN IDEA** What were some of the problems immigrants to the United States faced?

② **WHY IT MATTERS** How did some immigrants overcome the problems associated with coming to the United States?

③ **VOCABULARY** How did **prejudice** lead to the **regulation** of some immigrants?

④ **TIME LINE** In what year did Congress pass the Chinese Exclusion Act? 1882

⑤ **READING SKILL—Determine Point of View** How did many people born in the United States feel about immigrants?

⑥ **GEOGRAPHY** Where did most people come from during the old immigration? N. W. Europe

⑦ **CRITICAL THINKING—Evaluate** How do you think African Americans felt about the Great Migration?

PERFORMANCE—Write an Advertisement
Imagine that you are the owner of a railroad company in 1890. Write an advertisement to attract immigrant workers to your company. Share your advertisement with your classmates.

Review and Test Preparation

Summary Time Line

1860

1862
The Homestead Act is passed

1869
The Transcontinental Railroad is completed

1870
The Fifteenth Amendment becomes law

1877
Reconstructio ends

USE YOUR READING SKILLS

Complete this graphic organizer by describing different points of view about Reconstruction. A copy of this graphic organizer appears on page 44 of the Activity Book.

Abraham Lincoln and Reconstruction

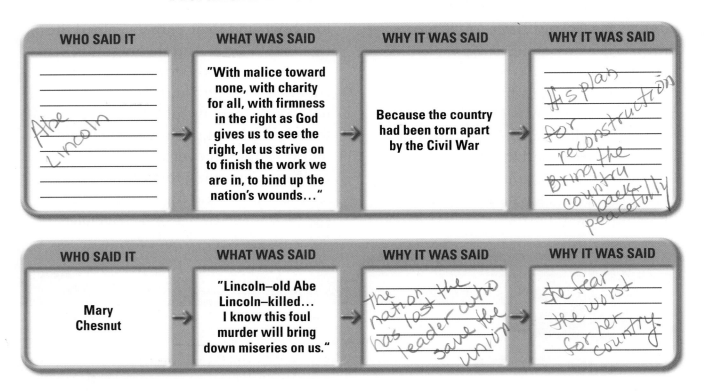

WHO SAID IT	WHAT WAS SAID	WHY IT WAS SAID	WHY IT WAS SAID
Abe Lincoln (handwritten)	"With malice toward none, with charity for all, with firmness in the right as God gives us to see the right, let us strive on to finish the work we are in, to bind up the nation's wounds…"	Because the country had been torn apart by the Civil War	*His plan for reconstruction bring the country back peacefully* (handwritten)

WHO SAID IT	WHAT WAS SAID	WHY IT WAS SAID	WHY IT WAS SAID
Mary Chesnut	"Lincoln—old Abe Lincoln—killed… I know this foul murder will bring down miseries on us."	*The nation has lost the leader who save the union* (handwritten)	*she fear the worst for her country* (handwritten)

THINK & WRITE

Write a Folktale Many American folktales grew out of the nation's western experience. Imagine you are hiking in the west when you come upon a ghost town. Write a folktale about your discovery and the miners and business owners who once lived there.

Write a Letter Immigrants to the United States have always been presented with both opportunities and challenges. Imagine you are a nineteenth century immigrant trying to adjust to your new home. Write a letter to a friend describing your situation and hopes for the future.

1915
The Great
Migration
begins

USE THE TIME LINE

Use the chapter summary time line to answer these questions.

1 When was the Transcontinental Railroad completed? *1869*

2 Did Reconstruction end before or after the Fifteenth Amendment was passed? *after*

USE VOCABULARY

For each pair of terms, write a sentence that explains how the terms are related.

3 **freedmen** (p. 145), **segregation** (p. 148)

4 **long drive** (p. 151), **open range** (p. 153)

5 **entrepreneur** (p. 159), **capital** (p. 161)

6 **new immigration** (p. 167), **tenement** (p. 167)

RECALL FACTS

Answer these questions.

3 to enforce them by law. To extend voting rights

7 Why was the Fifteenth Amendment passed?

8 What challenges did Native Americans face in the years after the Civil War?

9 What was the main reason for the Great Migration? *New place to live and work a fresh start*

Write the letter of the best choice.

10 **TEST PREP** The Fourteenth Amendment was passed to—
  A end slavery in the United States.
  B establish the Freedmen's Bureau.
  C give citizenship to all people born in the United States—including former slaves.
  D give every United States citizen the right to vote regardless of his or her race.

11 **TEST PREP** The most important work of the Freedmen's Bureau was—
  F to ensure voting rights for all African American males.
  G to promote African American political candidates.
  H to decide whether President Johnson should be removed from office.
  J to educate newly freed slaves.

12 **TEST PREP** The main reason oil production greatly increased in the late ninteenth century was because—
  A ranchers often traded their herds for oil.
  B people used kerosene to light their lamps.
  C homesteaders used petroleum to kill insects.
  D oil was used to fuel trains.

THINK CRITICALLY

They were against equal rights for slaves

13 Why do you think Southern state legislatures passed black codes after the Civil War?

To limit the rights of former slaves

14 How do you think the Great Migration affected the economy of the United States?

15 Why do you think many homesteaders chose to move west despite all the difficulties? *To own land*

APPLY SKILLS

Use a Climograph
Study the climographs on page 157. Then answer the following questions.

16 What is the average temperature for each city in August?

17 How much precipitation falls during August in each city?

THE GETTYSBURG

NATIONAL MILITARY PARK

GET READY

The largest battle of the Civil War was fought near the town of Gettysburg, Pennsylvania. Today, nearly 6,000 acres of that battlefield have been preserved. On a visit to the Gettysburg National Military Park, a guide can lead you on an informative tour that highlights significant events of the Battle of Gettysburg. At the battlefield you can see more than 1,400 monuments and markers dedicated to the soldiers who fought and lost their lives during the three-day battle.

LOCATE IT

PENNSYLVANIA

Gettysburg National Military Park

WHAT TO SEE

The Pennsylvania Memorial (left) is the largest monument at the Gettysburg National Military Park. It honors the Pennsylvania soldiers who fought at Gettysburg. The Gettysburg National Cemetery (below) was dedicated by President Abraham Lincoln in 1863.

Actors dressed as Union and Confederate soldiers reenact Civil War battles at the Gettysburg National Military Park.

TAKE A FIELD TRIP

A VIRTUAL TOUR
Visit The Learning Site at **www.harcourtschool.com/tours** to find virtual tours of historical sites in the United States.

A VIDEO TOUR
Check your media center or classroom library for a videotape tour of the Gettysburg National Military Park.

2 Review and Test Preparation

VISUAL SUMMARY

Write a Letter Study the pictures and captions below to help you review Unit 2. Then choose one of the events shown. Write an informative letter to a friend describing the event and how you think it will change the country.

USE VOCABULARY

Use a term from this list to complete each of the following sentences.

| tariffs (p. 100) |
| acquittal (p. 143) |
| homesteaders (p. 152) |

1. Senator Edmund G. Ross cast the deciding vote for the _acquittal_ of Andrew Johnson.

2. Before the Civil War, the North and South disagreed on the issue of _slavery_.

3. Nearly 100,000 European immigrants became _homesteaders_ on the Great Plains.

RECALL FACTS

Answer these questions.

4. How did enslaved people resist slavery?

5. What is the free enterprise system?

Write the letter of the best choice.

6. **TEST PREP** The conflict that started the Civil War took place at—
   A Williamsburg, Virginia.
   B Fort Sumter, South Carolina.
   C Gettysburg, Pennsylvania.
   D Antietam Creek, Maryland.

7. **TEST PREP** One major effect of the Civil War was that—
   F the United States never again admitted a new state to the Union.
   G Northerners were not allowed to settle in the South.
   H Southerners were not allowed to vote.
   J the Southern economy suffered many hardships.

Visual Summary

1820   1845   1870

1820 **The Missouri Compromise** p. 102

1850 **Congress passes the Compromise of 1850** p. 103

1854 **The Kansas–Nebraska Act is passed** p. 103

176

South Carolina Coast, 1861

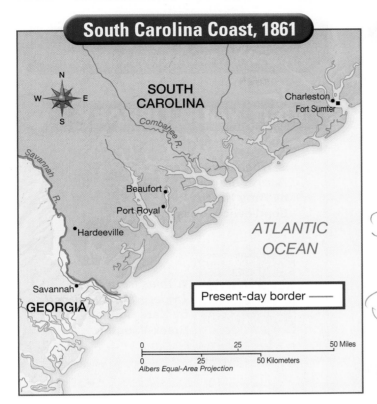

SOUTH CAROLINA

Charleston
Fort Sumter

Combahee R.

Savannah R.

Beaufort

Port Royal

Hardeeville

ATLANTIC OCEAN

Savannah

GEORGIA

Present-day border ——

0   25   50 Miles
0   25   50 Kilometers
Albers Equal-Area Projection

8 TEST PREP During Reconstruction the Southern states were under military rule because—

A the Fourteenth Amendment to the Constitution allowed Congress to do so.

B Abraham Lincoln's assassination angered many Northerners.

C legislators began to pass laws limiting the rights of former slaves.

D it was a way to return the rights of American citizenship to most Confederates.

THINK CRITICALLY

9 Lincoln once was called "the miserable tool of traitors and rebels." Today he is thought of as a great leader. Why might someone at the time have been so critical of him?

10 What do you think would have happened if the South had won the Battle of Gettysburg? *They made trade easier*

11 How did the growth of railroads in the United States play an important role in the growth of the country? Explain your answer. *The west will send beef to feed the east, a lot quicker and cheaper than before.*

12 Why did many immigrants come to the United States? *To make a better life for themselves.*

APPLY SKILLS

Compare Maps with Different Scales

Use the map on this page and the maps on pages 120–121 to answer the following questions.

13 Compare the map on this page to Map B on page 121. Which map would you use to find the distance between Fort Sumter and the city of Charleston, South Carolina?

14 Compare the map on this page to Map A on page 120. Which map would you use to find the South Carolina–Georgia border?

1895

1920

1861 The Civil War begins p. 118

1865 General Lee surrenders at Appomattox Court House p. 133

1890 The steel industry is a big business in the United States p. 160

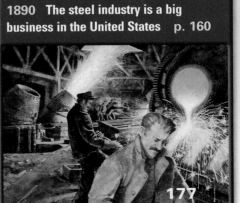

Unit Activities

 GO ONLINE Visit The Learning Site at www.harcourtschool.com/socialstudies/activities for additional activities.

Draw a Map

Work together to draw a map of the United States at the time of the Civil War. Use different colors for the states of the Union, the states of the Confederacy and the border states. Write the date on which each Southern state seceded. Draw diagonal lines on the border states. Label the capitals of the North and the South and the major battle sites. Use your map to tell your classmates about the Civil War.

Make a Chart

Work together in a group to make a chart titled *How New Laws Affected the Lives of Americans After the Civil War*. The first section of your chart should show how new national and state laws affected African Americans. The second section should show how new laws affected Southerners. The third section should show how new laws affected Northerners. Present your completed chart to your classmates.

VISIT YOUR LIBRARY

■ *When Jessie Came Across the Sea* by Amy Hest. Candlewick Press.

■ *Tales from the Underground Railroad* by Kate Connell. Steck-Vaughn.

■ *Across the Lines* by Carolyn Reeder. Simon & Schuster.

COMPLETE THE UNIT PROJECT

Hall of Fame Work with a group of your classmates to finish the unit project—a hall of fame honoring individuals who showed strength and bravery before, during, or after the Civil War. Your group should choose five people from this unit to include in your hall of fame. Then design a poster that includes short biographies as well as drawings or pictures of the people you have chosen. Display your group's finished poster together with those of your classmates.

Becoming a World Power

United States
Navy anchor pin

3

Becoming a World Power

66 **Whether they will or no, Americans must now begin to look outward.** 99

—Alfred T. Mahan, *The United States Looking Outward,* 1890

Preview the Content

Scan the pictures and other illustrations in each chapter and lesson. Use them to create a list of topics you will learn about in this unit.

Preview the Vocabulary

Word Meanings   Write what you think each word below means and why. Use the Glossary to check your answers.

WORD	POSSIBLE MEANING	WHY
panhandle		
political boss		
no-man's-land		

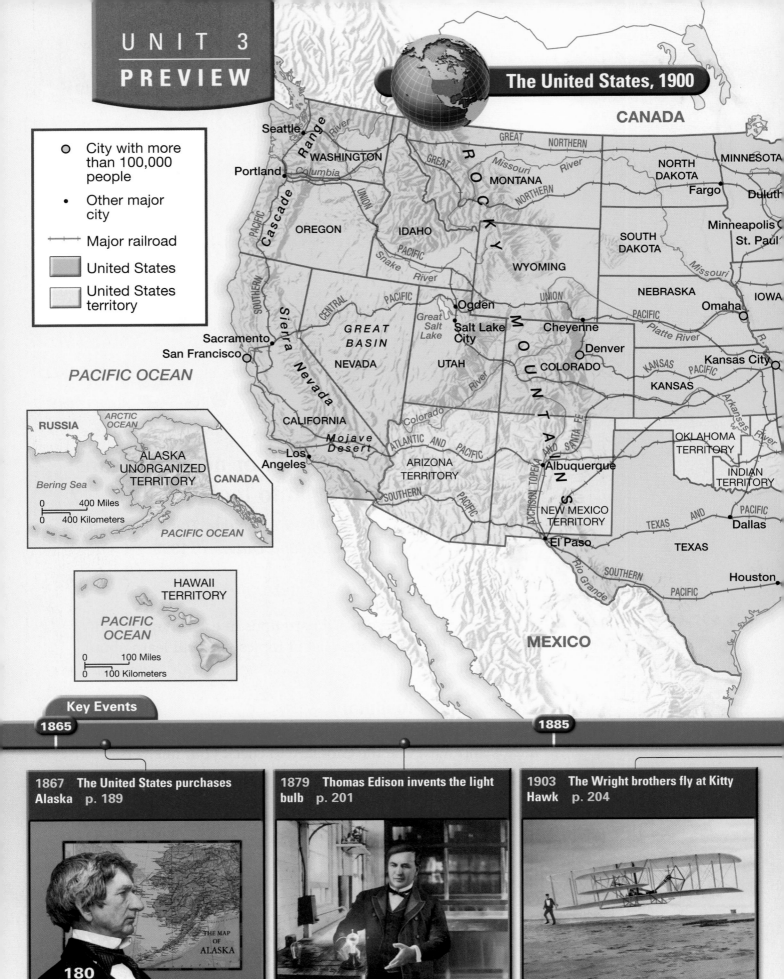

The United States, 1900

CANADA

Legend:
- ○ City with more than 100,000 people
- • Other major city
- ┼┼┼ Major railroad
- United States
- United States territory

Seattle
WASHINGTON
Portland
Columbia
OREGON
Cascade Range
PACIFIC
SOUTHERN
Sacramento
Sierra Nevada
San Francisco
CALIFORNIA
Los Angeles
Mojave Desert

PACIFIC OCEAN

GREAT NORTHERN
Missouri River
MONTANA
NORTHERN
IDAHO
UNION PACIFIC
Snake River
WYOMING
ROCKY
Ogden
Great Salt Lake
Salt Lake City
NEVADA
UTAH
GREAT BASIN
CENTRAL PACIFIC
Colorado River
ATLANTIC AND PACIFIC
ARIZONA TERRITORY
SOUTHERN PACIFIC
MOUNTAINS
Cheyenne
Denver
COLORADO
UNION
ATCHISON TOPEKA AND SANTA FE
NEW MEXICO TERRITORY
Albuquerque
El Paso
Rio Grande
SOUTHERN PACIFIC
MEXICO

NORTH DAKOTA
Fargo
SOUTH DAKOTA
Missouri
NEBRASKA
Omaha
PACIFIC
Platte River
KANSAS
Kansas City
PACIFIC
KANSAS
Arkansas River
OKLAHOMA TERRITORY
INDIAN TERRITORY
TEXAS AND PACIFIC
Dallas
TEXAS
Houston
PACIFIC

MINNESOTA
Duluth
Minneapolis
St. Paul
IOWA

Inset (Alaska):
RUSSIA
ARCTIC OCEAN
ALASKA UNORGANIZED TERRITORY
CANADA
Bering Sea
0 400 Miles
0 400 Kilometers
PACIFIC OCEAN

Inset (Hawaii):
HAWAII TERRITORY
PACIFIC OCEAN
0 100 Miles
0 100 Kilometers

Key Events

1865

1885

1867 The United States purchases Alaska p. 189

180

1879 Thomas Edison invents the light bulb p. 201

1903 The Wright brothers fly at Kitty Hawk p. 204

THE MAP OF ALASKA

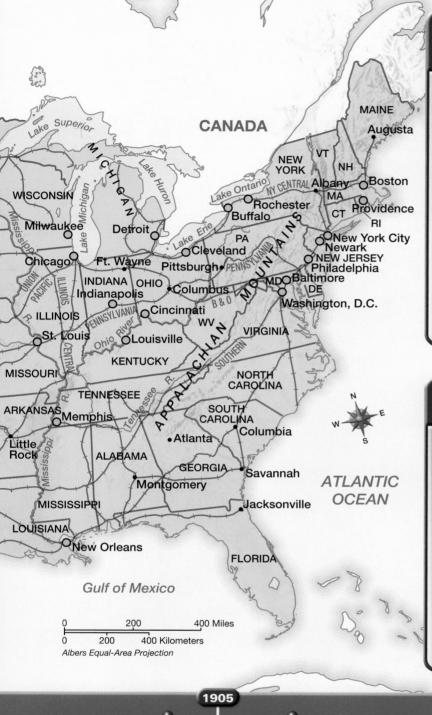

CANADA

Lake Superior

MICHIGAN

Lake Huron

Lake Michigan

WISCONSIN

Milwaukee

Detroit

Chicago

Ft. Wayne

INDIANA

Indianapolis

ILLINOIS

St. Louis

MISSOURI

ARKANSAS

Memphis

Little Rock

MISSISSIPPI

LOUISIANA

New Orleans

Mississippi

UNION PACIFIC R.R.

ILLINOIS CENTRAL

Ohio River

OHIO

Cleveland

Pittsburgh

Columbus

Cincinnati

Louisville

KENTUCKY

TENNESSEE

ALABAMA

Montgomery

GEORGIA

Atlanta

PENNSYLVANIA

B & O

WV

VIRGINIA

Tennessee R.

SOUTHERN

NORTH CAROLINA

SOUTH CAROLINA

Columbia

Savannah

Jacksonville

FLORIDA

Gulf of Mexico

APPALACHIAN MOUNTAINS

PA

PENNSYLVANIA MOUNTAINS

MD

Baltimore

DE

Washington, D.C.

Lake Ontario

Lake Erie

Rochester

Buffalo

NEW YORK

NY CENTRAL

Albany

New York City

Newark

NEW JERSEY

Philadelphia

VT

NH

MA

Boston

CT

Providence

RI

MAINE

Augusta

ATLANTIC OCEAN

N

S

E

W

0   200   400 Miles

0   200   400 Kilometers

Albers Equal-Area Projection

United States Population Growth, 1850–1920

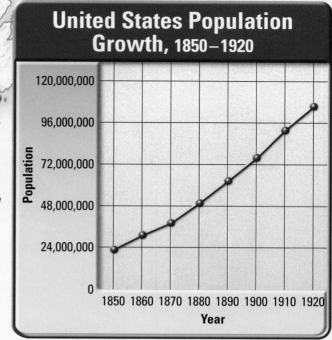

Population

120,000,000

96,000,000

72,000,000

48,000,000

24,000,000

0

1850 1860 1870 1880 1890 1900 1910 1920

Year

United States Patents, 1850–1920

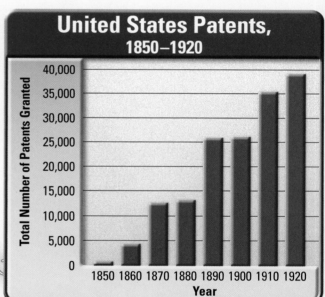

Total Number of Patents Granted

40,000

35,000

30,000

25,000

20,000

15,000

10,000

5,000

0

1850 1860 1870 1880 1890 1900 1910 1920

Year

1905

1925

1908   Henry Ford introduces the Model T
p. 202

1914   World War I begins
p. 228

1920   The Nineteenth Amendment gives American women the right to vote
p. 248

181

Jason's GOLD

by Will Hobbs • illustration by Rich Nelson

When the United States purchased Alaska in 1867, nobody, especially Jason Hawthorn, thought that one day thousands of people would journey to that northern land. In 1896 Hawthorn had left Seattle, Washington, and headed east. His plan was to return home in a year. After ten months, however, he rushed back west with plans to head to Alaska. Read now why Jason Hawthorn, and many others from across the country, raced to Alaska.

When the story broke on the streets of New York, it took off like a wildfire on a windy day.

"Gold!" Jason shouted at the top of his lungs. "Read all about it! Gold discovered in Alaska!"

The sturdy fifteen-year-old newsboy waving the paper in front of Grand Central Depot had arrived in New York only five days before, after nearly a year spent working his way across the continent.

"Gold ship arrives in Seattle!" Jason yelled. "EXTRA! EXTRA! Read all about it! Prospectors from Alaska. Two tons of gold!"

The headline, GOLD IN ALASKA, spanned the width of the entire page, the letters were so enormous.

People were running toward him like iron filings to a magnet. He was selling the *New York Herald* hand over fist. His sack was emptying so fast, it was going to be only a matter of minutes before he was sold out.

"Prospectors from Alaska arrive in Seattle! Two tons of gold!"

Jason wanted to shout, Seattle is where I'm from! but instead he repeated the cry "Gold ship arrives in Seattle," all the while burning with curiosity. Beyond the fact that the ship had arrived this very day—this momentous seventeenth of July, 1897—he knew nothing except what was in the headlines. He hadn't even had a chance to read the story yet.

It was unbelievable, all this pushing and shoving. A woman was giving a man a purse-beating over his head for knocking her aside. "Skip the change!" a man in a dark suit cried amid the crush, pressing a silver dollar into Jason's hand for the five-cent newspaper. "Just give me the paper!"

When there was only one left, Jason took off running with it like a dog with a prize bone. In the nearest alley, he threw himself down and began to devour the story.

At six o'clock this morning a steamship sailed into Seattle harbor from Alaska with two tons of gold aboard. Five thousand people streamed from the streets of Seattle onto Schwabacher's Dock to meet the gold ship, the Portland.

Five thousand people at Schwabacher's Dock! He knew Schwabacher's like the back of his hand. Mrs. Beal's rooming house was only six blocks away! Were his brothers, Abraham and Ethan, among the five thousand? Maybe, but probably not. At that hour they would have been on their way to work at the sawmill. Would they have risked being fired for arriving late? He didn't think so. His older brothers were such cautious sorts. Hurriedly, Jason read on:

"Show us your gold!" shouted the crowd as the steamer nosed into the dock.

The prospectors thronging [crowding] the bow obliged by holding up their riches in canvas and buckskin sacks, in jars, in a five-gallon milk can, all manner of satchels and suitcases. One of the sixty-eight, Frank Phiscator, yelled, "We've got millions!"

Jason closed his eyes. He could picture this just as surely as if he were there. He'd only been gone for ten months. Suddenly he could even smell the salt water and hear the screaming of the gulls above the crowd.

Imagine, he told himself, *millions in gold*. His eyes raced back to the newsprint:

Another of the grizzled prospectors bellowed, "The Klondike is the richest goldfield in the world!"

"Hurrah for the Klondike!" the crowd cheered.

"Ho for the Klondike!"

Klondike. Jason paused to savor the word. "Klondike," he said aloud. The name had a magical ring to it, a spellbinding power. The word itself was heavy and solid and dazzling, like a bar of shiny gold.

Analyze the Literature

1 Why did thousands of people gather at Schwabacher's Dock?

2 Why was Jason especially excited by the newspaper article?

3 Write a newspaper article about the discovery of gold in the Klondike. Then share your article with a classmate.

READ A BOOK

START THE UNIT PROJECT

Make a Scrapbook With your classmates, make a scrapbook. As you read this unit, make a list of key people, places, and events. This list will help you select people, places, and events to feature in the scrapbook.

USE TECHNOLOGY

Visit The Learning Site at **www.harcourtschool.com/ socialstudies** for additional activities, primary sources, and other resources to use in this unit.

MOUNT McKINLEY, DENALI NATIONAL PARK

Mount McKinley is part of the Alaska Range. It is located in the Denali National Park in Alaska. At a height of 20,320 ft (6,194 m), it is the tallest mountain in North America. Visitors to the mountain enjoy hiking, skiing, and snowshoeing. Others visit to see grizzly bears, wolves, Dall sheep, and moose.

LOCATE IT

ALASKA

Denali National Park

America Grows and Changes

❝ We step upon the threshold of 1900 . . . facing a still brighter dawn for human civilization. ❞

—*The New York Times*, editorial, December 31, 1899

CHAPTER READING SKILL

Summarize

To **summarize**, restate the most important ideas or key points in your own words.

As you read this chapter, think about the key points of each lesson. Then write them down in your own words.

| KEY POINTS | | SUMMARY |

MAIN IDEA
Read to find out how the United States added new lands in the late 1800s and early 1900s.

WHY IT MATTERS
The new lands gained by the United States continue to add to the richness and diversity of the nation today.

VOCABULARY
panhandle

New Lands for the United States

| 1865 | 1885 | 1905 | 1925 |

1865–1915

As the 1800s came to an end, the frontier seemed to have come to an end in the United States. Americans now lived on both coasts and were quickly filling up the lands in between.

The end of the frontier worried some Americans. They knew that the challenges of settling the frontier had helped the nation be strong. Some Americans began to look for frontiers outside the borders of the United States. These Americans hoped that new frontiers would bring new business opportunities that would help the nation's economy grow. Others saw new frontiers as opportunities for finding wealth and adventure.

Alaska

Alaska once belonged to Russia. In the early 1700s, the Russians were the first Europeans to send explorers to the area. For years Russian traders went to Alaska to hunt sea otters for their furs. Over time, the sea otters died out in that region.

FAST FACT
Alaska is one-fifth the size of the continental United States and 488 times larger than the state of Rhode Island.

Thousands of people rushed to Skagway, Alaska, when gold was discovered in the Klondike region of Canada.

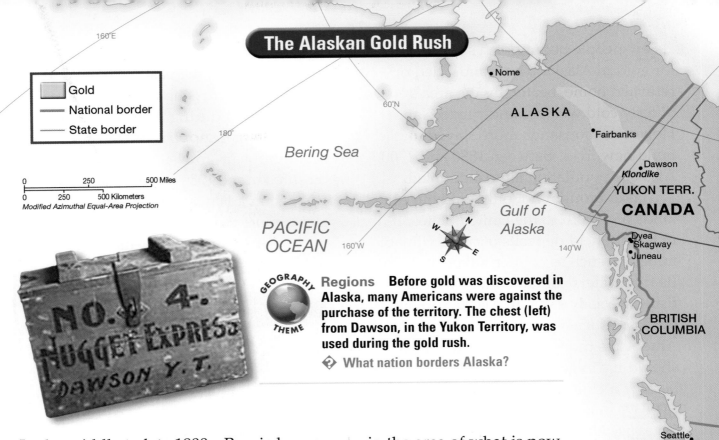

Gold
National border
State border

0   250   500 Miles
0   250   500 Kilometers
Modified Azimuthal Equal-Area Projection

Nome

60°N   ALASKA

Bering Sea   •Fairbanks

180   •Dawson
                                          Klondike
                                      YUKON TERR.

PACIFIC   160°W   Gulf of   CANADA
OCEAN   Alaska
                                          Dyea
                             140°W   •Skagway
                                          •Juneau

                                          BRITISH
                                          COLUMBIA

GEOGRAPHY THEME

Regions Before gold was discovered in Alaska, many Americans were against the purchase of the territory. The chest (left) from Dawson, in the Yukon Territory, was used during the gold rush.

What nation borders Alaska?

NO. 4. NUGGET EXPRESS DAWSON Y.T.

Seattle,
WASHINGTON

OREGON

Sacramento,
San Francisco•

CALIFORNIA

Los Angeles,

San Diego •

In the middle to late 1800s, Russia began to lose interest in the area because of economic problems. In addition, Russia knew that it would be hard to defend its far-off Alaskan lands from the nearby United States or other nations. For all these reasons, in 1867 Russia offered to sell Alaska to the United States for about $7 million—about two cents an acre!

Americans had different opinions about buying Alaska. Some who were against the purchase thought Alaska was a barren place of no value. Others liked the idea of buying Alaska, including Secretary of State William Seward. Seward believed in expanding the nation's borders. His support helped persuade Congress to agree to buy Alaska. This decision was nicknamed Seward's Folly by those who were against the purchase. A folly is a foolish idea.

Many who spoke against the Alaska purchase changed their minds when gold was found there in 1880. Gold was found in the area of what is now the city of Juneau (JOO•noh), on Alaska's **panhandle**, or portion of land that sticks out like the handle of a pan. Then gold was discovered in the present-day city of Nome, on the western coast, and near the present-day city of Fairbanks. All three cities were built because of the gold found in those areas. These discoveries started a gold rush like the one in California in 1849. Thousands of people went to Alaska hoping to make their fortunes.

The finding of gold in Canada's Klondike region, in the Yukon Territory, also added to Alaska's population growth. Its population grew because thousands of gold seekers came through Alaskan ports like Skagway and Dyea (DY•ay) on their way to the Yukon.

Few people became rich searching for gold in Alaska. Thousands died or returned home, beaten by the area's bitterly cold weather and rugged land. However, thousands more stayed to build new lives. Between 1880 and 1900, Alaska's population almost doubled.

Alaska brought not only gold but other kinds of wealth to the United States. Its rich earth held deposits of other valuable minerals, such as copper, silver, and zinc. Its rich waters contained many kinds of fish, especially salmon. Alaska turned out to be such a good buy that many Americans thought the United States should try to get more new lands. Alaska became a United States territory in 1912.

REVIEW **From what country did the United States buy Alaska?** Russia

The Hawaiian Islands

The Hawaiian Islands are in the Pacific Ocean, about 2,500 miles (4,023 km) southwest of California. Polynesian people from other places in the Pacific migrated to Hawaii in about the 700s. The islands were ruled by Polynesian kings and queens for centuries.

Tourists visit Honolulu to see its many attractions, including Waikiki (wy•kih•KEE) Beach and Diamond Head, a hill made of volcanic ash.

Some have called Hawaii the gateway to the Pacific. In the past, whaling and trading ships crossing the Pacific Ocean often stopped during their months-long voyages to get supplies in Hawaii. The first Europeans to visit the islands arrived on ships in the 1780s. Soon, many sailors stopped at a Hawaiian port. In 1846 alone, more than 400 ships stopped at the busy port on the Hawaiian island of Maui.

· GEOGRAPHY ·

Honolulu, Hawaii
Understanding Places and Regions

Honolulu (hah•nuhl•OO•loo) is a harbor city along the southern shore of Oahu (oh•AH•hoo), the most visited island of the Hawaiian Islands. The city lies about 2,500 miles (4,023 km) southwest of Los Angeles, California, and 3,860 miles (6,210 km) southeast of Tokyo, Japan. European merchant and whaling ships made Honolulu a meeting place for trade between North America and Asia in the early 1800s. Today, Honolulu is Hawaii's capital city and the center of business and culture.

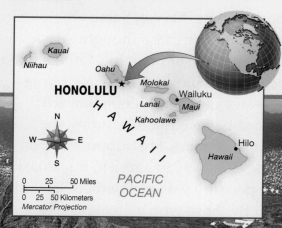

Hawaii was not only a stopping point. For many, Hawaii was the end of the journey. This was true of Christian missionaries, who traveled from New England to the islands in 1820 and tried to convert the Hawaiians to Christianity. The missionaries were among the first Americans to settle in Hawaii. Other Americans followed, and many started cattle ranches, sugar plantations, and other businesses. In just a few decades, this group controlled large parts of Hawaii's land and trade. The Americans took over much of the political power on the islands.

Like many European countries, Hawaii was ruled by a monarch. However, the power of Hawaii's monarchs had been weakened by the Americans.

Queen Liliuokalani (far left), wrote the well-known song "Aloha Oe," or "Farewell to Thee." The royal crest (left) is still shown on some buildings in Hawaii.

In 1891 Hawaii's ruling king, Kalakaua (kah•lah•KAH•ooh•ah), died, and his sister became the queen. Queen Liliuokalani (lih•lee•uh•woh•kuh•LAH•nee) tried to bring back the monarchy's authority. In 1893, however, a group led by Americans overthrew Queen Liliuokalani's government. Hawaii became a United States–controlled republic. Five years later, in 1898, the United States Congress decided to annex Hawaii to the United States. In 1900 Hawaii became a United States territory.

REVIEW Why was Hawaii sometimes called the gateway to the Pacific?

ships crossing the Pacific O. will stop there to get supplies.

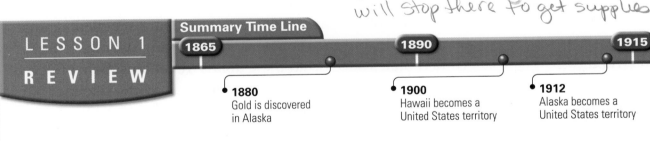

LESSON 1 REVIEW

Summary Time Line

| 1865 | 1890 | 1915 |

1880
Gold is discovered in Alaska

1900
Hawaii becomes a United States territory

1912
Alaska becomes a United States territory

① **MAIN IDEA** How did the United States acquire Alaska and Hawaii?

② **WHY IT MATTERS** In what ways do you think Alaska and Hawaii add to the richness and diversity of our nation today?

③ **VOCABULARY** Use the term **panhandle** in a sentence about Alaska.

④ **TIME LINE** Which became part of the United States first—Alaska or Hawaii?

⑤ **READING SKILL—Summarize** What kinds of wealth did Alaska bring to the United States?

⑥ **CULTURE** What group of people first settled the Hawaiian Islands?

⑦ **CRITICAL THINKING—Analyze** One of Alaska's nicknames is the Last Frontier. Why do you think this is so?

PERFORMANCE—Have a Debate With a partner, read more about Alaska and Hawaii. When you have finished your reading, debate with your partner which territory was the more valuable addition to the United States—Alaska or Hawaii.

2

MAIN IDEA
Read to find out how a war with Spain and other events helped the United States become a world power in the early 1900s.

WHY IT MATTERS
Events in the early 1900s helped shape the role the United States would play in world events throughout the twentieth century.

VOCABULARY

imperialism
yellow journalism
siege
armistice
anarchist
isthmus

A New Role for the United States

1865   1885   1905   1925

1895–1905

After the United States took control of Alaska and Hawaii, some people accused the nation's leaders of **imperialism**, or empire building. By the late 1800s, the United States had many new lands, including more islands in the Pacific Ocean. This brought the United States into conflict with European nations that had also spread beyond their borders—especially Spain.

War with Spain

By the end of the 1800s, Spain had lost most of its overseas lands. Its once-large empire was now made up of only a few places in Africa and several islands in the Atlantic and Pacific Oceans. Spain had only two colonies left in the Western Hemisphere—Cuba and Puerto Rico.

Many Cubans wanted their island to be independent from Spain. In 1868 and again in 1895, the Cubans rebelled against Spanish rule, but the rebellions failed. Many people in the United States supported the Cubans' rebellions. Some felt that Cuba's struggle for independence was a little like the American Revolution. Others supported Cuba because they wanted to keep the plantations and mills they owned on the island.

Many other Americans supported Cuba because of stories they read in American newspapers. These stories told of the cruel way the Spanish treated the Cubans. Some of these stories were true, and some were not. Many were exaggerated to sell newspapers. This kind of reporting, in which newspapers do not tell the truth and

José Martí (mar•TEE) was a leader in the Cuban revolution. Martí traveled to Florida to win the support of the Cubans who were living there.

When the *Maine* exploded, 260 American sailors were killed. The photograph (top) shows the wreckage of the ship. Some newspapers (left) did not print all the facts.

exaggerate the facts, came to be known as **yellow journalism**. Two New York newspapers were especially known for their yellow journalism. They were Joseph Pulitzer's *New York World* and William Randolph Hearst's *New York Journal*.

At first, the United States tried to help end Spain's rule in Cuba through peaceful means. It even offered to buy Cuba, but Spain refused to sell it.

On February 15, 1898, the American battleship *Maine* sailed into Havana's harbor. The ship had come to protect American-owned businesses and the lives of United States citizens in Cuba.

On its first night in the harbor, the *Maine* exploded, killing 260 seamen. No one knows for sure what happened. However, American newspapers—and many others—blamed Spain. "Remember the *Maine*!" was the cry heard across the United States, as Americans demanded that war be declared on Spain. On April 25, Congress declared war.

The very first battle of the Spanish-American War was fought in the Pacific in the Philippines, a Spanish territory. On May 1, 1898, under the leadership of Commodore George Dewey, American ships fired on the Spanish fleet in Manila Bay.

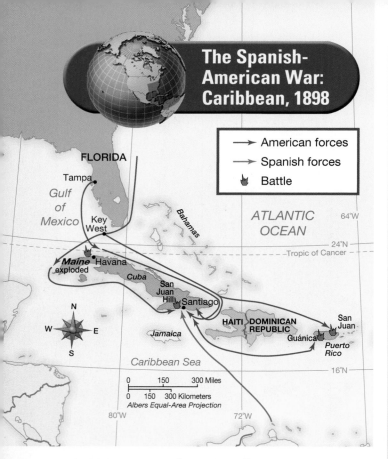

The Spanish-American War: Caribbean, 1898

American forces
Spanish forces
Battle

FLORIDA
Tampa
Gulf of Mexico
Key West
Bahamas
ATLANTIC OCEAN
64°W
24°N
Tropic of Cancer
Maine exploded
Havana
Cuba
San Juan Hill
Santiago
HAITI
DOMINICAN REPUBLIC
San Juan
Jamaica
Guánica
Puerto Rico
Caribbean Sea
16°N

0   150   300 Miles
0   150   300 Kilometers
Albers Equal-Area Projection
80°W   72°W

GEOGRAPHY THEME

Movement Part of the Spanish-American War was fought in and near Cuba.

◆ From which cities in Florida did American forces leave?

The battle lasted for seven hours. When the smoke cleared, Spain's fleet had been defeated, and all its ships had been captured, damaged, or destroyed.

Meanwhile, in the Atlantic Ocean, other United States Navy ships fought Spain's Atlantic fleet. The United States Army placed the Cuban city of Santiago under siege. A **siege** is a long-lasting attack. On July 17, 1898,

Commodore George Dewey commanded the United States fleet in the Pacific.

the 24,000 Spanish troops at Santiago surrendered, and the Spanish leaders there signed an armistice. An **armistice** is an agreement to stop fighting a war.

The Spanish-American War was over in less than four months. More than 5,000 American soldiers died, mostly from diseases such as malaria and yellow fever. The war, however, helped the United States become a world power.

Under the peace treaty that was signed, Spain agreed to give the United States control of Cuba, Puerto Rico, Guam, and the Philippine Islands. Cuba became an independent country in 1902. The Philippine Islands gained independence in 1946. Puerto Rico and Guam remain territories of the United States today.

REVIEW Where did the first battle of the Spanish-American War take place?

Phillipines

Theodore Roosevelt

The Spanish-American War made heroes of two well-known Americans. Commodore Dewey became a hero for his leadership in the Pacific. The other hero, a volunteer in the United States Army, became famous for his leadership in the siege of Santiago. His name was Theodore Roosevelt.

At the beginning of the war, Roosevelt was the assistant secretary of the navy. It was Roosevelt who ordered Commodore Dewey to be ready to attack the Spanish at Manila, the Philippine capital city. However, Roosevelt wanted to help fight the war, too. So he gave up his job with the navy and

This painting shows Roosevelt and the Rough Riders charging San Juan Hill. However, the charge was really made on foot.

helped form a volunteer fighting company. The Rough Riders, as this group became known, was made up mostly of western cowhands and college athletes who had responded to Roosevelt's advertisement for "young, good shots, and good riders." The Rough Riders helped the United States win several important battles in Cuba.

Soon after Theodore Roosevelt came back from Cuba, he was elected governor of New York. Two years later he was elected Vice President of the United States, serving under President William McKinley. On September 6, 1901, President McKinley was shot by an anarchist. An **anarchist** (A•ner•kist)

This canteen was carried by a Rough Rider in Cuba.

is a person who is against any kind of government. Eight days later, President McKinley died, and Theodore Roosevelt became the President.

Roosevelt was a man of action, who felt that the United States should be a nation of action. He believed strongly that the people of the United States should take part in international events because they affected the nation.

In 1907 President Roosevelt decided to remind other countries that he was the leader of a powerful military force. He sent a fleet of warships, painted white, on a world cruise. Roosevelt said that the Great White Fleet showed the world that "the Pacific was as much our home as the Atlantic."

REVIEW Who were the Rough Riders?

Volunteer fighting co made up of western cowhands + college athletes.

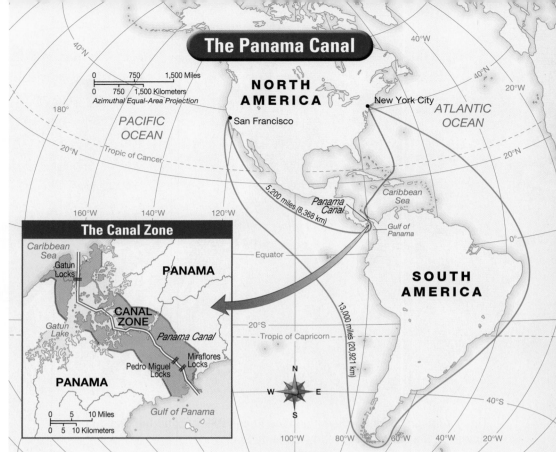

The Panama Canal

Location The Panama Canal opened in 1914. The first ship sailed through it in August of that year. Today the Panama Canal, which is now under Panama's control, continues to help move people and goods from the Atlantic to the Pacific.

❖ How long is the route from New York City to San Francisco by way of the Panama Canal?

The Panama Canal

President Roosevelt wanted to build a canal in Panama, in Central America. At that time, the only way to make the trip from the Atlantic Ocean to the Pacific Ocean was to sail around South America. This trip would be much shorter if a canal were cut across the isthmus (IS•muhs) that joined North America and South America. An **isthmus** is a narrow strip of land that connects two larger landmasses.

The United States had many reasons to build a canal. Its interests in the lands in the Pacific and in trading with nations across that ocean had grown. Also, the war with Spain had taught Americans how hard it would be for United States ships in the Atlantic and the Pacific to help each other quickly.

In 1903 Congress voted to build a canal across the Isthmus of Panama. However, Colombia would not give the United States permission to build it. At the time, Panama was part of Colombia.

The people of Panama tried but failed to become independent from Colombia. In 1903 they tried again. This time, the United States sent warships to protect Panama. This revolution succeeded, and the people of Panama formed a new nation. The United States and Panama made a deal that gave the United States the needed land.

Work on the canal started in 1904. It took ten long years of hard work to build the canal across Panama—a distance of just over 40 miles (64 km) from shore to shore. One reason for this was disease. A French company had tried earlier to build a canal through the isthmus.

It lost 20,000 workers to yellow fever and malaria before the company gave up.

In 1904 Colonel William C. Gorgas became chief sanitation officer for the Panama Canal Zone. He knew that both yellow fever and malaria were carried by certain kinds of mosquitoes. All along the planned canal path, he had workers clear areas where mosquitoes laid eggs. As a result, the number of deaths by these diseases dropped.

When the Panama Canal was finished, it had cost the United States about $380 million and about 5,600 lives. The United States had joined the two oceans.

REVIEW Why was the United States interested in building the Panama Canal?

Workers used large machines and heavy equipment to clear the land in Central America and to construct the locks of the Panama Canal.

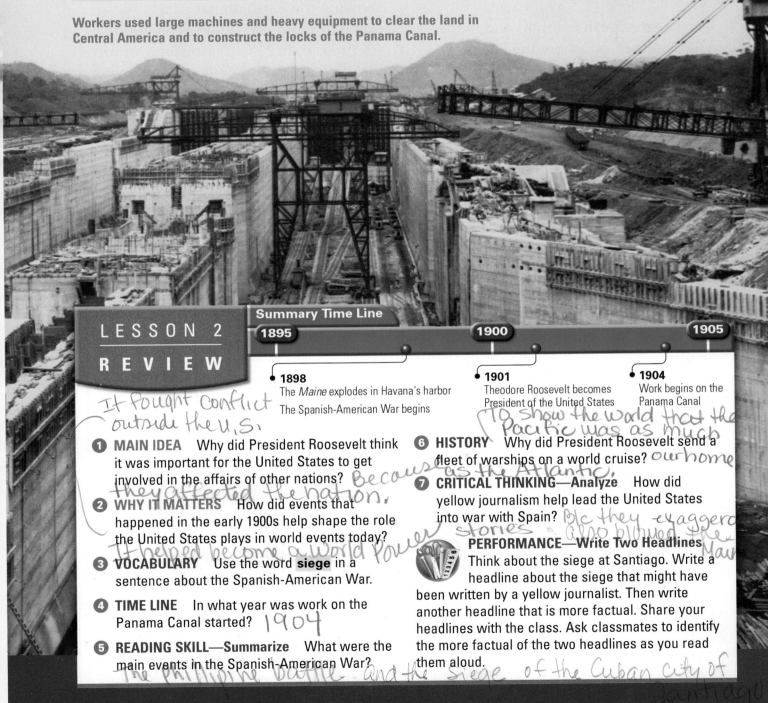

LESSON 2 REVIEW

Summary Time Line

1895 — 1900 — 1905

1898
The *Maine* explodes in Havana's harbor
The Spanish-American War begins

1901
Theodore Roosevelt becomes President of the United States

1904
Work begins on the Panama Canal

It fought conflict outside the U.S.

1 **MAIN IDEA** Why did President Roosevelt think it was important for the United States to get involved in the affairs of other nations? *Because they affected the nation.*

2 **WHY IT MATTERS** How did events that happened in the early 1900s help shape the role the United States plays in world events today? *It helped become a world power*

3 **VOCABULARY** Use the word **siege** in a sentence about the Spanish-American War.

4 **TIME LINE** In what year was work on the Panama Canal started? *1904*

5 **READING SKILL—Summarize** What were the main events in the Spanish-American War? *The Phillipine battle and the siege of the Cuban city of Santiago*

6 **HISTORY** Why did President Roosevelt send a fleet of warships on a world cruise? *To show the world that the Pacific was as much our home as the Atlantic.*

7 **CRITICAL THINKING—Analyze** How did yellow journalism help lead the United States into war with Spain? *B/c they exaggerated stories. Also blamed the Maine*

PERFORMANCE—Write Two Headlines Think about the siege at Santiago. Write a headline about the siege that might have been written by a yellow journalist. Then write another headline that is more factual. Share your headlines with the class. Ask classmates to identify the more factual of the two headlines as you read them aloud.

·SKILLS·

MAP AND GLOBE

Compare Map Projections

▶ WHY IT MATTERS

Because the Earth is round and maps are flat, no map can show the Earth's shape exactly. Only on a globe can the Earth be shown as it really is. As a result, cartographers have different ways of showing the Earth on flat paper. These different views are called **projections**. All projections have **distortions**, or areas that are not accurate. Identifying how a map is distorted can help you understand how different maps can be used.

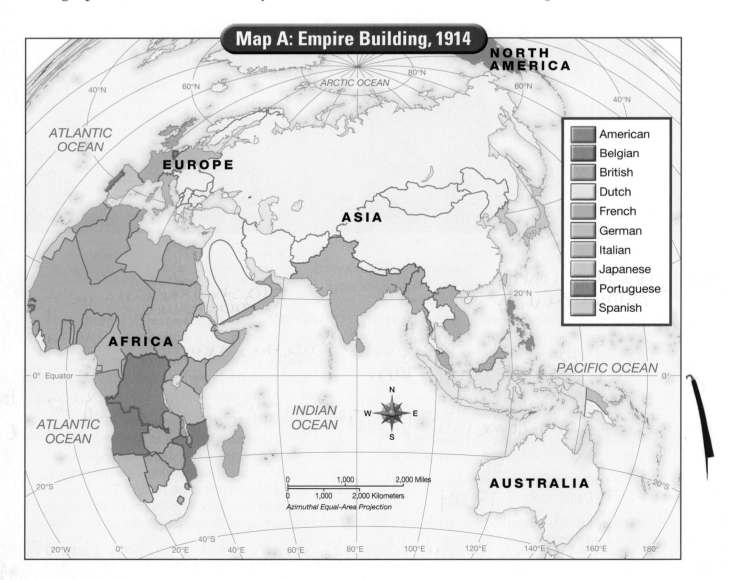

Map A: Empire Building, 1914

NORTH AMERICA

ARCTIC OCEAN

ATLANTIC OCEAN

EUROPE

ASIA

	American
	Belgian
	British
	Dutch
	French
	German
	Italian
	Japanese
	Portuguese
	Spanish

AFRICA

PACIFIC OCEAN

ATLANTIC OCEAN

INDIAN OCEAN

AUSTRALIA

0   1,000   2,000 Miles
0   1,000   2,000 Kilometers
Azimuthal Equal-Area Projection

WHAT YOU NEED TO KNOW

Map A and Map B both show the same information. They show the world's empires in 1914. But each map uses a different projection. Map A is an equal-area projection map. Equal-area projections show the sizes of regions in correct relation to one another. However, they distort the shapes of the areas shown on them.

Map B is a cylindrical projection map, a kind of conformal projection map. On this kind of map, the lines of longitude are equal distances apart. This "equal distance" causes the distortion. Conformal projections show directions correctly, but they distort sizes, especially near the poles.

PRACTICE THE SKILL

Use Maps A and B to answer these questions.

1 On which parts of Maps A and B do the shapes of the land areas appear to be the same?

2 On which map is the size of Asia more accurate?

APPLY WHAT YOU LEARNED

Write a sentence explaining when you would use an equal-area projection map. Then write a sentence explaining when you would use a conformal projection map.

 Practice your map and globe skills with the **GeoSkills CD-ROM.**

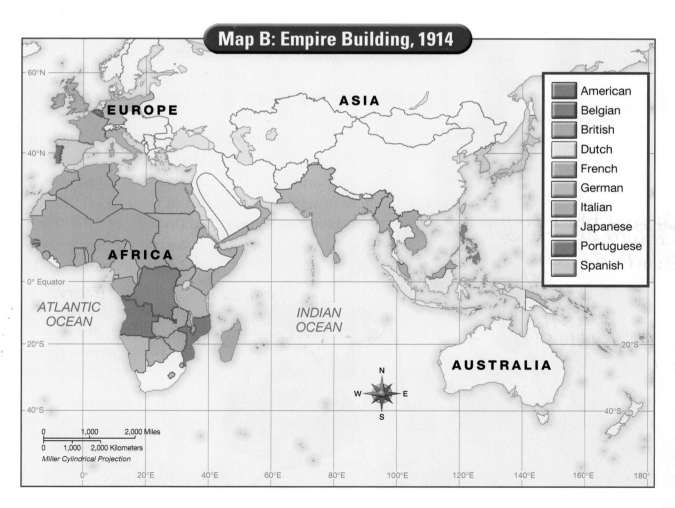

Map B: Empire Building, 1914

American
Belgian
British
Dutch
French
German
Italian
Japanese
Portuguese
Spanish

EUROPE

ASIA

AFRICA

ATLANTIC OCEAN

INDIAN OCEAN

AUSTRALIA

60°N
40°N
0° Equator
20°S
40°S

0° 20°E 40°E 60°E 80°E 100°E 120°E 140°E 160°E 180°

0   1,000   2,000 Miles
0   1,000   2,000 Kilometers
Miller Cylindrical Projection

N
W   E
S

MAP AND GLOBE SKILLS

New Directions

1875–1920

MAIN IDEA
New inventions changed
life in the United States in
the late 1800s and early
1900s.

WHY IT MATTERS
Inventions continue
to change the way
Americans live today.

VOCABULARY
assembly line
aviation

The early 1900s were not only years when the United States was becoming a world power. They were also years of great change for the people of the United States. New inventions changed industry and the daily lives of the American people. Inventions that improved industry helped make life easier for many Americans. Many kinds of work that were once done by hand could now be done faster and with less difficulty by machines. Faster ways of travel and new ways of communication saved people valuable time. New inventions helped many people have more time to enjoy their lives.

Signs of Change

In 1860 only about one out of every six Americans lived in cities. By 1900 that number had changed to about one in three. Many people moved to the cities partly because of new machines.

Some of these machines improved farming. For example, before the Civil War, farmers spent many hours planting, caring for, and harvesting an acre of wheat. By the end of the 1800s, different kinds of machines could do each of those farming tasks more quickly.

Many farmers found that fewer farmers were needed since the machines were

Like today, telephone wires were connected at poles (far left). The telephone (left) has changed the way people communicate.

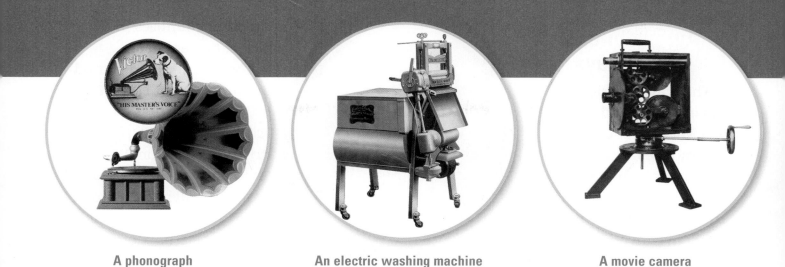

A phonograph   An electric washing machine   A movie camera

so efficient, so the farmers headed toward the cities to find new kinds of work.

Other machines were changing the way almost everyone in the United States lived. In 1876 the invention of the telephone by Alexander Graham Bell had started a revolution in communications. By 1900 more than 1 million telephones were being used in the United States.

In 1877 Thomas Edison carried the revolution even further with his invention of the phonograph, a machine that could record and play back sound. In 1879 he introduced the world to the lightbulb, which changed how people lit their homes. His power stations produced electricity for many homes, offices, and factories and allowed people to use other inventions powered by electricity.

In September 1899 the Italian inventor Guglielmo Marconi (gool•YEL•moh mahr•KOH•nee) tried out a new invention to send reports of a sailing race while he watched it at sea. His reports of the race were the first use of radio in the United States. Twenty years later the first radio stations began broadcasting news and entertainment in Detroit and Pittsburgh. Around the same time that the radio was

invented, several inventors were working on motion-picture cameras that could make movies. By the 1920s silent movies made in Hollywood, California, became popular all over the world.

New inventions also helped people shorten the amount of time it took to do housework. In the mid-1800s treadle (TREH•duhl), or foot-powered, sewing machines reduced the time needed to make clothes. Washing machines that people worked by turning a crank made doing laundry easier and saved time. By the early 1900s some homes had sewing machines and washing machines that were powered by electricity.

Even shopping changed in the late 1800s and early 1900s. Department stores became common in big cities. In 1890 the first shopping mall, a single building with many different stores, opened in Cleveland, Ohio.

Shopping also changed for people who lived in America's rural areas. They now could buy many of the same items as people in the cities through new mail-order catalogs.

REVIEW What inventions helped shorten the time it took to do housework?

Automobiles and Highways

The way Americans traveled changed because of a Michigan builder of automobiles, or cars. His name was Henry Ford. Ford did not build the first automobile, but he made many improvements on how automobiles were made. The first automobiles were built in the late 1800s. In 1894 Indiana inventor Elwood Haynes test-drove one of the first gasoline-powered automobiles.

The first automobiles were very expensive because each was made by hand. It took workers more than 12 hours to make just one automobile. Handmade automobiles also cost a lot to repair.

Early carmakers in the United States used the ideas of mass production and interchangeable parts in their car factories. As a result, the prices of automobiles were lower in the United States than they were in other countries in which cars were made.

Then Henry Ford started building cars in Detroit, Michigan. At first, his cars cost a lot, too. He decided to build an automobile that many people could afford. "I will build a motor car for the great multitude (large numbers of people)," he promised. Ford kept his promise by using technology to build a car he called the Model T.

Ford and his engineers tried many different ideas to save time in building the Model T. One of the ideas that saved the most time was to use an **assembly line**, in which moving belts carried car parts from worker to worker. Each worker was given one task. The workers did the same tasks over and over as the belt moved parts past them. Because of the assembly lines, Ford could build a car in less than 2 hours, instead of the 12 or more hours it once took.

Henry Ford

These workers (below), on a Ford factory assembly line, are installing an engine on a Model T (right).

As more and more people bought Model Ts (above), signs (right) were posted to remind drivers to maintain safe speeds.

TRAVEL AT A SAFE SPEED

WATCH YOUR SPEEDOMETER

FATALITIES FOR YESTERDAY

TOTAL FOR YEAR

TOTAL FOR WEEK

Stewart

MAKE ST. LOUIS SAFE

Each time a new idea saved money, Ford would pass the savings on to the buyer. In time this lowered the cost of the Model T. By 1927 the Model T sold for just $290. This was less than one-third of its original cost of $950 in 1908. In the years between 1908 and 1927, Ford sold more than 15 million Model Ts!

In 1914 Ford announced more changes. But these were not changes in his cars. Instead, they were changes in his company's working conditions. Ford said that he would now pay most of his workers $5 a day. This was more than twice the wages earned by workers in other car factories. He also said his workers would have to work only eight hours a day, instead of the usual nine hours. These changes helped improve the workers' lives.

Ford made these changes because he knew that many people would want to work for him under these conditions. He also knew that paying a good wage would help his employees buy cars.

Because more people were buying cars, many new roads were built. In 1900 the nation had only about 128,000 miles (206,000 km) of hard-surfaced roads. By 1916 that number had jumped to almost 300,000 miles (483,000 km). Just eight years later, there were more than 500,000 miles (805,000 km) of hard-surfaced roads in the nation.

Aviation

Orville and Wilbur Wright experimented for four years with kites and engines before they made their first successful flight near Kitty Hawk, North Carolina, in 1903. The key to their success was learning how to master the basic principles of flight. Flight may seem difficult to understand, but it is actually based on some simple laws of nature. An airplane's wings are designed to create lift, which holds the airplane up in the air. In order for an airplane to climb, lift must be greater than gravity, the force that holds objects on the Earth. The force of forward movement is called thrust, which is created by an engine-driven propeller or a jet engine. An airplane has horizontal and vertical surfaces called stabilizers that enable it to move up and down and right and left. The pilot, who steers the plane, controls these stabilizers.

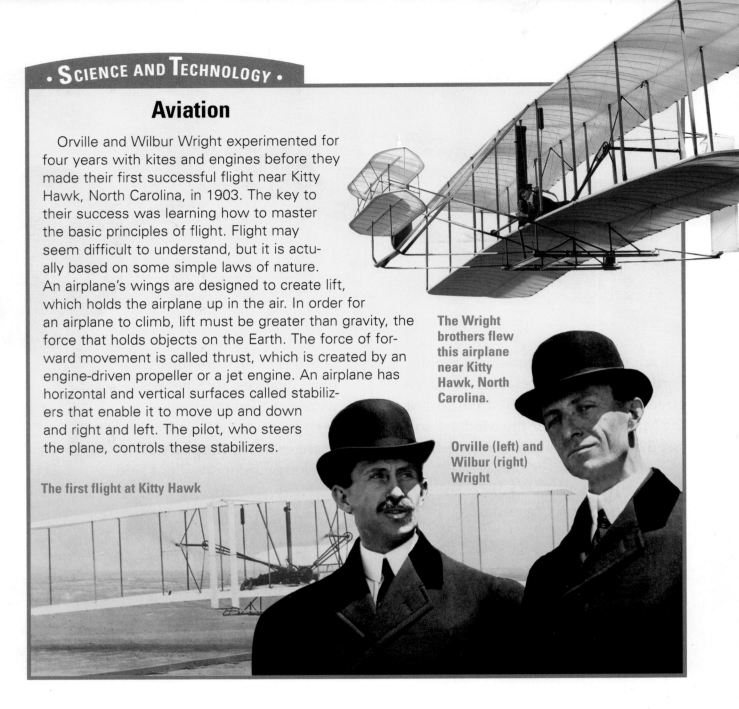

The Wright brothers flew this airplane near Kitty Hawk, North Carolina.

Orville (left) and Wilbur (right) Wright

The first flight at Kitty Hawk

Henry Ford's automobiles changed everything from where people lived and worked to where people went on vacation. Automobiles also helped connect the nation's rural areas with the urban areas. The automobile, which was once only a luxury item, had become an important part of everyday life in the United States for more Americans.

REVIEW Why did the price of the Model T drop over the years?

Early Aviation

At about the same time that Henry Ford was working to improve travel by land, two brothers from Dayton, Ohio, were thinking about travel by air, or **aviation**. Orville and Wilbur Wright, who ran a bicycle shop in Dayton, also worked on a machine in which people could fly.

They studied what others had written about flight. They did experiments to see

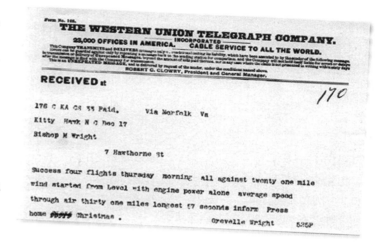

how an airplane heavier than air could carry an engine as well as a person.

First, the brothers practiced in Ohio by building and testing three different gliders, which are airplanes that glide on the air and do not have engines to propel them. Later, they built their first engine-driven plane.

On December 17, 1903, the Wright brothers made history on a beach called Kill Devil Hill, near Kitty Hawk, North Carolina. They had tested gliders there before, and they knew that the area's steady winds would lift their airplane.

Orville Wright was the pilot of the first successful flight. The first flight using the two-winged plane they named *Flyer* lasted only 12 seconds. Orville traveled a distance of 120 feet (37 m). A later flight that same day, with Wilbur Wright at the controls, lasted almost a whole minute.

A few years after Americans realized what the Wright brothers had done, many people began building airplanes. By the 1920s the first scheduled airlines were flying people from place to place. Aviation had become an important industry in the United States.

REVIEW When and where did the first airplane flight take place? 1903

Kill Devil Hill near Kitty Hawk N.C.

LESSON 3 REVIEW

Summary Time Line

1875 — 1890 — 1905 — 1920

1876 Alexander Graham Bell invents the telephone

1877 Thomas Edison invents the phonograph

1879 Thomas Edison invents the lightbulb

1903 The Wright brothers fly at Kitty Hawk

1. **MAIN IDEA** How did new inventions change life in the United States in the late 1800s and early 1900s?

2. **WHY IT MATTERS** How might your life be different if the computer had not been invented?

3. **VOCABULARY** Use the term **aviation** in a sentence about how American life changed in the early 1900s.

4. **TIME LINE** Which was invented first—the telephone or the lightbulb?

5. **READING SKILL—Summarize** How did the automobile and the airplane change the way people traveled?

6. **HISTORY** In what ways did Henry Ford change working conditions for his employees?

7. **CRITICAL THINKING—Analyze** In what ways do you think the idea of the assembly line affected other industries?

PERFORMANCE—Make a Time Line Make a time line that shows the same years as the time line above. Reread the lesson, and choose three inventions or three events to show on your time line. Draw a picture for each invention or event, and attach the pictures in the appropriate places on your time line. Share your finished time line with the class.

The Growth of Cities

| 1865 | 1885 | 1905 | 1925 |

1870–1900

By the beginning of the twentieth century, cities in the United States were growing fast. Some people thought they were growing too fast. No one had expected such growth, and no one had planned for it. Millions of Americans were moving to cities from farms, and millions of immigrants were coming to American cities from other countries. As cities grew, so did their problems.

City Problems

One problem was the overcrowded tenements where many immigrants and other city dwellers lived. Tenements were apartment houses. Because tenements were so crowded, when one person became ill, disease spread quickly. In one Chicago tenement, three out of every five children born in 1900 died before they were three years old. A newspaper reporter named Jacob Riis (REES) described the same kind of poor living conditions in New York City tenements.

These photographs show the crowded conditions that existed in tenement buildings.

This painting (left) shows the Great Chicago Fire of 1871. The fire destroyed whole city blocks (above).

Riis saw that when someone died in a tenement, a ribbon tied into a bow was hung on the tenement door—black for an adult and white for a child. Riis wrote,

66 Listen! that short hacking cough, that tiny, helpless wail—what do they mean? They mean that the soiled bow of white you saw on the door downstairs will have another story to tell—Oh! a sadly familiar story—before the day is at an end. The child is dying with measles. With half a chance it might have lived; but it had none. 99

Insects and rats in the garbage spread the germs of disease. With so many people in the cities, garbage piled up. At this time there was no regular garbage collection. Even in the largest cities, garbage was eaten by pigs in the streets.

The danger of fire became greater as new buildings went up. Most buildings were made partly of wood. Terrible fires burned down whole city blocks. The Great Chicago Fire of 1871 was one of the worst. The fire burned for 24 hours, killing at least 300 people and leaving more than 90,000 people homeless. Few cities at that time had full-time fire departments.

Crime was another problem in cities. Because of the crowded conditions, it was often hard for the police to find lawbreakers. Sometimes a gang would take over an entire neighborhood in a city, and even the police would be afraid to go into that neighborhood.

REVIEW What problems did many people living in cities face?

Help for the Cities' Poor

Some people who lived in cities tried to solve the problems they saw around them. Jane Addams was one of these people. Addams came from a wealthy family and had gone to college, something few women did in the late 1800s. She worried about the growing problems of the tenements in Chicago.

While traveling in Britain, Jane Addams had visited a place called Toynbee Hall.

In addition to taking classes, people at Hull House gathered to sing songs.

It was a **settlement house**, a community center where people could learn new skills. Addams took the idea back to Chicago. She said,

> **It is hard to tell just when the very simple plan . . . began to form itself in my mind. . . . But I gradually became convinced that it would be a good thing to rent a house in a part of the city where many . . . needs are found.**

In 1889 Jane Addams started Hull House in Chicago with a friend, Ellen Gates Starr. The workers in the settlement house ran a kindergarten for children whose mothers worked. The Hull House workers also taught classes in sewing, cooking, and the English language. Later they made other efforts to help people living in cities. They worked to improve conditions in tenements and health and safety conditions in factories. They also tried to get laws passed to put limits on child labor.

Hull House became a model for other settlement houses. In 1890 an African American teacher, Janie Porter Barrett, founded one in Hampton, Virginia. Three years later, Lillian Wald started the Henry Street Settlement in New York City. By 1900 almost 100 settlement houses had opened in American cities.

REVIEW Why were settlement houses important to people in the cities?

They worked to improve conditions

The Changing City

Even with their many problems, cities came to stand for much that was good in industrial America. Besides factories, stores, and tenements, cities had parks, theaters, schools, zoos, railroad stations, and tall office buildings.

Before this time, buildings could not be built taller than four or five stories because their walls were made only of bricks. The bricks on the bottom had to hold up the weight of all the bricks above them. In the 1880s an engineer named William Jenney found a way to build taller buildings. Jenney used steel frames to hold up a building the way a skeleton holds up a body. In 1885 Jenney finished building the ten-story Home Insurance Company Building in Chicago. It was the world's first tall steel-frame building, or **skyscraper**.

As buildings were made taller and taller—20 floors, then 50 floors, then 100 floors—fast, safe elevators were needed. The first electric elevator was put into a skyscraper in New York City in 1889.

As cities grew upward, they also grew outward. When the first cities were built in the United States, people walked to work. As people began moving away from the center of the city, transportation was needed to help them get to their jobs.

In 1865 most cities had streetcars that were pulled by horses. Horses could go only about 6 miles (10 km) an hour on flat ground. Each horse cost about $200—about the price of a car in today's money. In San Francisco the horses had to pull the cars up very steep hills. This was hard for the horses and slow for the passengers. An inventor named Andrew S. Hallidie worked on the problem. In 1871 he invented the cable car.

This cable car in San Francisco, California, helped transport people to the center of the city.

• BIOGRAPHY •

Scott Joplin 1868–1917
Character Trait: Individualism

By the early 1900s, many people were listening to new kinds of music that helped them forget about the problems of city life. Scott Joplin was an African American composer whose music became very popular during this time. Joplin was born in Texarkana, Arkansas, and moved to St. Louis, Missouri, while he was still a teenager. Joplin's first important songs, including the popular "Maple Leaf Rag," used the ragged rhythm and complicated melodies of a kind of music called ragtime. Before long, Joplin became known as the King of Ragtime.

MULTIMEDIA BIOGRAPHIES
Visit The Learning Site at
www.harcourtschool.com/biographies
to learn about other famous people.

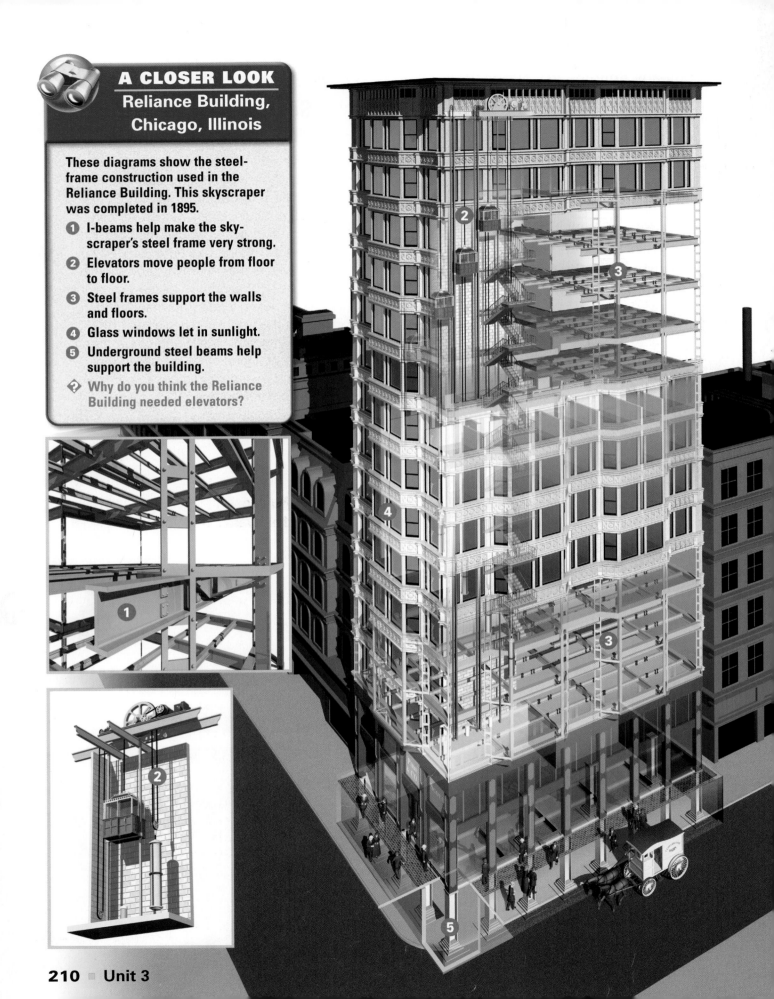

A CLOSER LOOK
Reliance Building, Chicago, Illinois

These diagrams show the steel-frame construction used in the Reliance Building. This skyscraper was completed in 1895.

1. I-beams help make the skyscraper's steel frame very strong.
2. Elevators move people from floor to floor.
3. Steel frames support the walls and floors.
4. Glass windows let in sunlight.
5. Underground steel beams help support the building.

❖ Why do you think the Reliance Building needed elevators?

Today the Reliance Building is home to the Hotel Burnham Chicago.

Cable cars ran on tracks and were fastened to a steam-powered cable, or strong wire, that ran in a slot in the street. The cable pulled the cars at about 9 miles (15 km) an hour up and down steep hills. Fifteen cities put in cable cars. Chicago alone had 710 of them!

Then, in the late 1880s, Frank Sprague built an electric streetcar that was first used in Richmond, Virginia. His streetcar was powered by electricity instead of steam. On a pole called a trolley, on top of the car, a small wheel rode along an overhead electric wire. The new streetcar was called a trolley car. By 1890 more than 50 cities had trolley systems.

As more trolley tracks were laid, many people moved farther and farther from the center of the city. They could ride the trolley cars to their jobs in the city and live away from the inner city's problems.

REVIEW **What inventions helped cities grow upward and outward during the late 1800s?**

skycraper
electric streetcar

LESSON 4 REVIEW

Summary Time Line

1870	1880	1890	1900

1871
The Great Chicago Fire kills hundreds

1885
The first skyscraper is completed

1889
Jane Addams starts Hull House in Chicago

1890
More than 50 cities have trolley transportation systems

① **MAIN IDEA** What problems did people face as cities grew larger, and how did some people work to solve them?

② **WHY IT MATTERS** What problems do people face in cities today?

③ **VOCABULARY** Use the terms **settlement house** and **skyscraper** to write two sentences about city life in the early 1900s.

④ **TIME LINE** When was the first skyscraper completed?

⑤ **READING SKILL—Summarize** In what ways did people try to help poor people in the cities?

⑥ **GEOGRAPHY** How did trolley cars affect where some city workers chose to live?

⑦ **CRITICAL THINKING—Evaluate** How did the inventions you read about in this lesson affect the way people lived in cities?

PERFORMANCE—TV Report Activity With several classmates, prepare an outline for a television program on life in the cities in the late 1800s. Write down topics for your program. Then list ideas for interviews, pictures, maps, charts, and graphs. Present your outline to the class.

· SKILLS ·
Solve a Problem

WHY IT MATTERS

All people face problems at one time or another. Think about a problem you have faced recently. How did you know you had a problem? Were you able to solve it? Did you wish you could have found a better way to solve the problem? Knowing how to solve problems is a skill that you will use your whole life.

WHAT YOU NEED TO KNOW

Here are some steps you can use to help solve a problem.

Step 1 Identify the problem.

Step 2 Gather information.

Step 3 Think of and list possible solutions.

Step 4 Consider the advantages and disadvantages of possible solutions.

Step 5 Choose the best solution.

Step 6 Try your solution.

Step 7 Think about how well your solution helps solve the problem.

PRACTICE THE SKILL

You have read about the many problems that made city life difficult in the late 1800s and early 1900s. Think again about these problems and how Jane Addams tried to solve them.

1 What problems did Jane Addams see in Chicago?

2 What solution did Addams learn about at Toynbee Hall?

3 What did Addams decide was a good way to solve the problems in Chicago?

4 How did Addams carry out her solution?

5 How did Addams's solution help solve the problems of city life?

APPLY WHAT YOU LEARNED

Look around your school or neighborhood. What problems do you see? Use the steps listed on this page to think of ways to solve one of the problems. Share your ideas with your classmates.

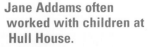

Jane Addams often worked with children at Hull House.

CITIZENSHIP SKILLS

Progressives and Reform

| 1865 | 1885 | 1905 | 1925 |

1900–1920

MAIN IDEA
Around the turn of the century, many people worked to improve life in the United States.

WHY IT MATTERS
During this time, many Americans began to believe that they, along with the government, were responsible for the quality of life of all Americans.

VOCABULARY
progressive
political boss
commission
merit system
monopoly
conservation
civil rights
prohibition

Many Americans profited from the growth in American business and inventions in the late 1800s and early 1900s. However, many others did not. Some Americans set out to improve life for those who did not share in the nation's wealth. These reformers, who wanted to bring progress, or cause changes to help others, called themselves **progressives**.

Progressives did not all share the same beliefs. However, they all wanted to make life for Americans better in some way. Some progressives worked for economic changes, while others tried to change their state governments. President Theodore Roosevelt worked to reform the national government.

City and State Reforms

Many city governments needed to be reformed. In many cities, political bosses controlled the government. A **political boss** is an elected official—often a mayor—who has many dishonest employees and who is able to control the government with the help of those employees. Often these political bosses were elected or reelected in illegal ways—with votes counted more than once or votes paid for with money or favors. Some political bosses were able to remain in power by doing favors for immigrant groups. They helped immigrants get jobs and find good housing in exchange for their votes in elections. Some immigrants benefited from this, but it was still a dishonest way of winning votes.

The cartoon (right) shows that money was used to influence political decisions in New York City. Political boss William Tweed (far right) ran New York City.

Robert M. La Follette made so many reforms in Wisconsin that President Roosevelt called the state a "laboratory of democracy."

One of the best-known political bosses was William Tweed. "Boss" Tweed, as he was called, ran New York City for years and robbed it of millions of dollars. He protected himself by controlling the city police department.

One way to put a stop to boss rule was to make a new kind of city government in which one person could not have too much power. Around 1900 some cities began to try a commission form of government. A **commission** is a special committee. In this kind of government, each member of the commission is in charge of one part of city government, such as the police department, the fire department, or water services. Before long, more than 400 cities across the United States had set up commission governments.

Progressives also worked to improve state governments. Robert M. La Follette (luh FAH•luht), who became governor of Wisconsin in 1900, worked for reforms at the state level. For example, until La Follette became governor, candidates for elected state offices were chosen by political party delegates. La Follette changed the system so that the people themselves could vote to decide who the candidates would be.

• BIOGRAPHY •

Ida Tarbell   1857–1944

Character Trait: Fairness

Ida Tarbell was one of the leading reporters during the progressive movement. She was born in western Pennsylvania and was among the first women to graduate from Allegheny College, in 1880. In 1902 she began her investigation of John D. Rockefeller's Standard Oil Company. Two years later, what she learned led to the publication of her book, *History of the Standard Oil Company*. Her uncovering of Rockefeller's unfair business practices made her the most famous woman journalist of her time. In 1906 she founded the *American Magazine*, for which she continued to write about important social and political issues. She later worked to expose the terrible working conditions many women faced at the time.

MULTIMEDIA BIOGRAPHIES
Visit The Learning Site at www.harcourtschool.com/biographies
to learn about other famous people.

Another problem in many state governments was that elected officials often gave jobs to people who did favors for them. La Follette made sure that in Wisconsin's government, people were chosen based on a merit system. This **merit system** tested a person to make sure that he or she was qualified for the job. The person with the highest test score got the job.

La Follette also wanted to help workers. He asked the state legislature to pass a law that said that a workday could be no more than ten hours long. A second law was passed listing jobs that children could not be hired to do. A third law said that the state would pay workers who were hurt while working on their jobs. To raise the money to do this, factory owners had to make payments to the state.

REVIEW What governor helped make reforms in Wisconsin? *La Follette*

The Square Deal

President Theodore Roosevelt also believed in the progressive movement. In his first months as President, Roosevelt started a government program called the Square Deal to make sure that all Americans were given the same opportunities to succeed.

One of the first targets of Roosevelt's progressive policies was big business. Some businesses had become so big that they were the only businesses supplying a certain kind of good or service.

A company that has very little or no competition is called a **monopoly**.

Some monopolies acted in the best interests of their customers. However, other monopolies charged very high prices or made poor goods because they knew the goods could not be bought from another company. Some monopolies used their power to force smaller companies out of business.

The first monopoly Roosevelt turned his attention to was the Northern Securities Company, in 1902. This was a very large railroad company that was made up of several smaller railroad companies. Together they controlled the western rail lines. In time, Roosevelt succeeded in breaking up the Northern Securities Company. Another company he helped break up was John D. Rockefeller's Standard Oil Company.

This cartoon shows Roosevelt working to break up monopolies, or trusts, that did not act in the best interests of their customers.

United States National Parks

North Cascades (1968)

Olympic (1938)

WA

Mount Rainier (1899)

Glacier (1910)

CANADA

MT

Voyageurs (1975)

ND

Theodore Roosevelt (1978)

Isle Royale (1931) Lake Superior

Albers Equal-Area Projection

ME

Acadia (1919)

OR

Crater Lake (1902)

ID

Yellowstone (1872)

MN

SD

Badlands (1978)

MN

WI

MI

Lake Huron

Lake Ontario

VT NH

NY

MA CT

RI

Redwood (1968)

Grand Teton (1929)

Wind Cave (1903)

Lake Michigan

Lake Erie

PA

NJ

Lassen Volcanic (1916)

CA

NV

Capitol Reef (1971)

WY

Rocky Mountain (1915)

NE

IA

Cuyahoga Valley (2000)

IL

IN

OH

MD DE

Yosemite (1890)

Great Basin (1986)

Arches (1971)

CO

Black Canyon of the Gunnison (1999)

WV

VA

Shenandoah (1935)

Kings Canyon (1890)

UT

Zion (1919)

Canyonlands (1964)

KS

Great Sand Dunes (2000)

MO

Mammoth Cave (1941)

KY

Sequoia (1890)

Death Valley (1994)

Bryce Canyon (1924)

Grand Canyon (1919)

Mesa Verde (1906)

TN

Great Smoky Mountains (1934)

NC

ATLANTIC OCEAN

Channel Islands (1980)

Joshua Tree (1994)

AZ

Petrified Forest (1962)

NM

Carlsbad Caverns (1930)

OK

AR

Hot Springs (1921)

SC

PACIFIC OCEAN

Saguaro (1994)

Guadalupe Mts. (1972)

TX

MS

AL

GA

RUSSIA

ARCTIC OCEAN

Kobuk Valley (1980)

Gates of the Arctic (1980)

AK

Denali (1917)

Wrangell-St. Elias (1980)

MEXICO

Big Bend (1944)

Gulf of Mexico

FL

Lake Clark (1980)

Bering Sea

Katmai (1980)

Kenai Fjords (1980)

Glacier Bay (1980)

CANADA

PACIFIC OCEAN

Haleakala (1916) HI

Hawaii Volcanoes (1916)

PACIFIC OCEAN

American Samoa (1988)

AMERICAN SAMOA

National park

Everglades (1947)

Biscayne (1980)

Dry Tortugas (1992)

ATLANTIC OCEAN

Puerto Rico

Virgin Islands

Virgin Islands (1956)

Caribbean Sea

GEOGRAPHY THEME

Regions Most of the United States' national parks are located in the western region of the country.

❓ When and where was the nation's first national park opened?

During his time as President, Roosevelt went after many more monopolies. He had no wish to destroy American businesses. He just wanted them to be fair to the American people.

Roosevelt also worked toward making foods and medicines safe for people. In 1906 Congress passed the Pure Food and Drug Act. The law said that all foods and medicines had to meet government safety standards. Congress also passed the Meat Inspection Act. This law said that inspectors would go to all factories that packaged meat to make sure the meat was handled safely.

President Roosevelt also felt strongly about **conservation**, or the protection of the environment by keeping natural resources from being wasted or destroyed. Roosevelt's conservation efforts were aided by his belief that as President, he could take action if there was no law against it. In 1903, for example, he asked, "Is there any law that will prevent me from declaring Pelican Island (in Florida) a Federal Bird Reservation?" When told there was not, Roosevelt said, "Very well, then I so do declare it." With those words, Roosevelt created

Before the Pure Food and Drug Act, companies often indicated that their foods were safe or pure, even if they were not.

the nation's first wildlife refuge, or nature preserve. He also set aside millions of acres of land around the country as national parks.

REVIEW What was the first monopoly that President Roosevelt broke up?

Northern Security Co.

Other Federal Reforms

The Constitution's Sixteenth Amendment reformed the way government collected some of its money. Until this time, many taxes were based on how much property people owned. However, some people hid their property ownership to avoid paying taxes. Progressives wanted to tax people on their income, or how much money they make. The Sixteenth Amendment, ratified in 1913, put in place a national income tax.

The Seventeenth Amendment to the Constitution, also ratified in 1913, had the support of the progressives. This amendment allowed the people, rather than the state legislatures, to elect their

The writer John Muir helped persuade Congress to establish Yosemite National Park. Muir (right) met there with Roosevelt (left) in 1903.

United States senators. The amendment's supporters believed that it would give more power to the people.

REVIEW What constitutional amendment requires Americans to pay a national income tax? *16th*

DEMOCRATIC VALUES
Popular Sovereignty

CITIZENSHIP

The Seventeenth Amendment to the Constitution of the United States provides for the direct popular election of United States senators by the people of each state. This allows the people, rather than the state legislatures, to elect their senators. Before the ratification of the amendment in 1913, upper and lower houses in state legislatures would often wind up in a deadlock, or tie vote, that would prevent them from appointing senators in a timely manner. The Seventeenth Amendment solved this problem by giving this electoral power to the voters.

Analyze the Value

❶ How does the Seventeenth Amendment support the idea of popular sovereignty?

❷ **Make It Relevant** Research another amendment to the United States Constitution, and write a paragraph about the way this amendment supports a democratic value.

Early Civil Rights

The progressive movement led to better lives for many Americans. However, there were groups that did not always benefit directly from many of the progressive efforts. They were still working for their **civil rights**—the rights guaranteed to all citizens by the Constitution.

African Americans made up one of the largest groups of people who were working for their civil rights. In the early 1900s they were still facing segregation in many parts of their lives. Segregation laws existed throughout the South and in much of the North. The laws applied to all places where people gathered. Under these laws, African Americans had to go to separate schools, churches, theaters, and restaurants. African Americans who broke these laws were sent to jail.

Segregation laws became known as Jim Crow Laws. Jim Crow was an imaginary African American character who acted silly and never stood up for himself. Many white Americans who were prejudiced wanted all African Americans to be like Jim Crow.

One leader who worked for civil rights was an African American named W. E. B. Du Bois (doo•BOYS). In 1909 Du Bois and other progressive leaders—both black and white—organized a group known as the National Association for the Advancement of Colored People, or NAACP. Members of the NAACP, which is still active today, worked to change state laws that did not give full civil rights to African Americans and any other minority groups who lived in the United States.

A year later, another group formed to help African Americans. This group was called the National Urban League. Its purpose was to help African Americans living in the cities find jobs and housing.

REVIEW What two groups worked for civil rights for African Americans?

Booker T. Washington (left) and W. E. B. Du Bois (below right) worked to end prejudice in the United States.

Improving Society

Because many people were looking for work in the cities, factory owners were able to hire those who were willing to work for little pay. Soon many factory workers could no longer support their families. Many parents had to send their children to work. By the late 1800s more than 1 million children worked in mines and factories instead of going to school.

People were upset that children were working long hours—often in dangerous conditions. In the early 1900s some progressive leaders tried but failed to get the federal government to pass laws against hiring children. However, by 1914 almost every state had passed laws that limited child labor and stated that children must attend school. Some employers ignored the state laws.

Other progressives believed that alcoholic beverages were the cause of many of the problems in the United States.

Children sometimes worked up to 14 hours per day in factories such as this cotton mill.

These progressives were part of what was known as the temperance movement. Their plan, known as **prohibition**, was to stop, or prohibit, people from drinking alcoholic beverages. They worked to pass an amendment to prohibit the making and selling of alcoholic beverages in the United States.

REVIEW **What did some progressives do to help put an end to child labor?**

LESSON 5 REVIEW

Summary Time Line

| 1900 | 1910 | 1920 |

1903
President Roosevelt creates the first national wildlife refuge

1909
The NAACP is created

1913
The Sixteenth and Seventeenth Amendments are ratified

merit system

1 **MAIN IDEA** How did the progressives work to improve life in the United States?

work shorter day labour

2 **WHY IT MATTERS** How do Americans today work to improve people's lives? *merit system*

3 **VOCABULARY** Write a sentence explaining how **commission** governments took power away from **political bosses**.

16 & 17

4 **TIME LINE** What two progressive amendments were both ratified in 1913?

5 **READING SKILL—Summarize** What was President Roosevelt's Square Deal?

All Americans were given the same opportunities to succeed

6 **HISTORY** What were the goals of the National Urban League? *to help African American living in cities find jobs & housing*

7 **CRITICAL THINKING—Evaluate** Governor La Follette wanted to make Wisconsin "a happier and better state to live in." Do you think he succeeded? Why or why not? *yes*

 PERFORMANCE—Make a Plan Imagine you are a progressive reformer living in the United States in the early 1900s. Choose one of the problems identified in this lesson. Then make a plan to help solve the problem. Your plan should include several steps.

Jacob Riis's Photographs

Jacob Riis is considered America's first photojournalist. The Danish-born photographer traveled throughout New York City during the 1880s and 1890s, taking thousands of photographs. Riis documented the lives of men, women, and children of all nationalities at home, at work, and at leisure. His photographs appeared in newspapers and in his books, such as *How the Other Half Lives*.

FROM THE MUSEUM OF THE CITY OF NEW YORK

This camera is similar to one of the cameras Jacob Riis used.

Baxter Street Alley in Mulberry Road
"At 59 Baxter Street . . . is an alley leading in from the sidewalk with tenements on either side crowding so close as to almost shut out the light of day. On one side they are brick and on the other wood, but there is little difference in their ricketiness and squalor."
— from the *New York Sun*, February 12, 1888

Necktie Workshop

"The bulk of the sweater's work is done in the tenements, which the law that regulates factory labor does not reach. . . . Ten hours is the legal work-day in the factories, and nine o'clock the closing hour at the latest. Forty-five minutes at least must be allowed for dinner, and children under sixteen must not be employed unless they can read and write English; none at all under fourteen. . . . But the tenement has defeated its benevolent purpose. In it the child works unchallenged from the day he is old enough to pull a thread."
— from *How the Other Half Lives*, 1890

A "Slide" in Hamilton Street

"A dozen years ago [1890], I gave a stockbroker a good blowing up for hammering his cellar door full of envious nails to prevent the children using it as a slide. It was all the playground they had."
— from *The Battle with the Slum*, 1902

ACTIVITY

Compare and Contrast Describe the people, the activities, and the scenes of life in most cities today. If Jacob Riis were taking pictures today, how would they differ from his older pictures? How might they be similar?

RESEARCH

Visit The Learning Site at **www.harcourtschool.com/ primarysources** to research other primary sources.

Analyze the Primary Source

1. **What are the people doing in each photograph?**

2. **What does Jacob Riis say about each photograph?**

3. **What do the photographs tell you about life among the poor in New York City in the 1890s?**

USE YOUR READING SKILLS

Complete this graphic organizer by summarizing the following facts about Progressives and civil rights. A copy of this graphic organizer appears on page 54 of the Activity Book.

Progressives and Civil Rights

FACTS → SUMMARY

1. Many people became wealthy from the growth of business and technology in the United States.
2. Reformers, called Progressives, wanted to improve life for those who did not share in America's wealth.
3. Progressives worked for economic and political changes at the city, state, and national level.

_____
_____
_____
_____
_____
_____

_____
_____
_____
_____
_____
_____
_____

At one time, laws existed that denied full civil rights to African Americans and other minorities. A group of leaders started the NAACP, which worked to change the laws and secure full civil rights for African Americans and all minorities.

THINK & WRITE

Write a Newspaper Article Imagine you are a journalist assigned to cover the arrival of the battleship *Maine* in Havana, Cuba, in 1898. Write a newspaper article about the explosion on the *Maine*. Try to use as many facts as possible.

Write a Story Choose one of the inventions mentioned in Lesson 3 to write a story about. Your story could be about how the invention was discovered, how people reacted to the invention, or why the invention is important today.

1889
Jane Addams
opens Hull House

1898
The Spanish-American
War

1901
Theodore Roosevelt
becomes President

1903
The Wright
brothers make
their first flight

1909
The NAACP
is founded

1913
The Sixteenth and
Seventeenth Amendments
are ratified

1914
The Panama
Canal opens

USE THE TIME LINE

Use the chapter summary time line to answer these questions.

1 In what year did the Wright brothers make their first flight? *1903*

2 When did the Panama Canal open? *1914*

USE VOCABULARY

Identify the term that correctly matches each definition.

imperialism (p. 192)

settlement house (p. 208)

monopoly (p. 215)

conservation (p. 216)

3 a community center where people can learn new skills

4 the protection of the environment

5 empire building

6 a company that has little or no competition

RECALL FACTS

Answer these questions.

7 Who were among the first Americans to settle in Hawaii? *The missionaries*

8 Who were the Rough Riders?

9 What were Jim Crow laws? *segregation laws*

Write the letter of the best choice.

10 **TEST PREP** Which of the following was not invented by Thomas Edison?
A radio
B power stations
C phonograph
D lightbulb

11 **TEST PREP** In the 1800s, streetcars in the United States were not powered by—
F horses.
G steam.
H electricity.
J gasoline.

THINK CRITICALLY

we were recognized by the super power

12 How did the Spanish-American War help make the United States a world power?

13 How did Theodore Roosevelt help change life in the United States? *square deal* *p. 215-216*

APPLY SKILLS

Compare Map Projections
Review the information on pages 198 and 199 to answer these questions.

14 Why do flat maps have distortions? *you are trying to round to flat*

15 What is an equal-area projection map? *show the sizes in correct*

16 What is a conformal projection map? *relation to one the lines of longitude are equal distance to another*

Solve a Problem
Reread pages 204 and 205 about early aviation. Then use the steps listed on page 212 to help answer these questions.

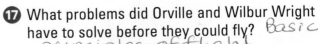

17 What problems did Orville and Wilbur Wright have to solve before they could fly? *Basic principles of flight*

18 What did the Wright brothers discover in their testing of gliders on Kill Devil Hill? *flying*

19 How did the Wright brothers help improve transportation? *revolutionized the way people travel.*

Chapter 5 ■ **223**

TOMB OF THE UNKNOWN SOLDIER

The Tomb of the Unknown Soldier was built in 1921 to honor an unidentified American soldier from World War I. Unknown soldiers from World War II and the Korean War are also buried there. The Tomb, located in Arlington National Cemetery, is guarded 24 hours a day by specially chosen United States Army soldiers.

LOCATE IT

Arlington

VIRGINIA

The Great War

" The world must be made safe for democracy. "

—Woodrow Wilson, in a speech to the United States Congress asking for a declaration of war, April 2, 1917

CHAPTER READING SKILL

Sequence

The order in which events occur is their **sequence**. The sequence tells what happened first, next, and last.

As you read this chapter, try to put the major events related to the Great War in the correct sequence.

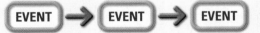

EVENT → EVENT → EVENT

MAIN IDEA
President Wilson and
other American leaders
reluctantly guided the
United States into World
War I.

WHY IT MATTERS
The United States
continues to be involved in
international matters
because what happens in
the rest of the world often
affects the United States.

VOCABULARY
militarism
alliance
ally
dollar diplomacy
neutral
military draft

The War Begins

| 1865 | 1885 | 1905 | 1925 |

1913–1917

The United States went through many changes in the early 1900s, but events in Europe were about to change the lives of the nation's people even more. In 1914, conflicts among European nations led to war. At first, most people saw the war as a European problem. In time, however, the nation was drawn into the war. This war was at first known as the Great War. It would later be called World War I.

Causes of the War

A belief in imperialism and a need for more raw materials led some European nations to build great empires. Other European countries wanted to build empires also. This led to problems between the countries that had colonies and the countries that did not.

Militarism also contributed to the problems among the countries of Europe. **Militarism** is the belief that using military force is a good way to solve problems. Militarism had led some

Archduke
Ferdinand
and Duchess
Sophie

FAST FACT When the Great War broke out in 1914, Germany had been preparing for a major European war for years.

European countries to begin building up their armies and navies. Other countries, afraid of the military strength of their neighbors, also built up their military forces.

European countries began to form secret **alliances**, or formal agreements, with one another. **Allies**, or partners in an alliance, promised to help defend any other member in case of attack. Europeans hoped that these alliances would prevent war, but the opposite happened.

Nationalism led to tensions in Europe. For some Europeans, nationalism was pride in the country in which they lived. For others, though—especially members of ethnic groups whose countries had been swallowed by empires—it meant something different. To them, nationalism meant pride in a new country they hoped to create for the people of their own ethnic group.

Many European countries seemed ready for war. This description of Germany by a United States diplomat might have also fit some of Germany's neighbor nations: "The whole of Germany is charged with electricity," reported the diplomat, who was stationed in the German capital, Berlin. "Everybody's nerves are tense. It only requires a spark to set the whole thing off." That "spark" would come from an assassin's gun.

Gavrilo Princip assassinated the Archduke and the Duchess.

Serbia was a small European country that bordered the large empire of Austria-Hungary. Many Serbs had strong feelings of nationalism. Some Serbs lived in the southern part of Austria-Hungary. They wanted the land on which they lived to be part of Serbia, too.

Archduke Francis Ferdinand was heir to Austria-Hungary's throne. On June 28, 1914, he was visiting parts of his empire.

• GEOGRAPHY •

GEOGRAPHY ESSENTIAL ELEMENTS

Serbia
Understanding Places and Regions

In 1914 Serbia was one of a group of countries in the region known as the Balkans. The Balkans were located in southeastern Europe on the Balkan Peninsula. Austria-Hungary, Romania, Bulgaria, Greece, Albania, and Montenegro surrounded Serbia. The location of Serbia put the country in the middle of national conflicts that helped start World War I. In 1992 Serbia and Montenegro together formed an independent state that is slightly smaller than the state of Kentucky. The capital of Serbia is Belgrade, and the capital of Montenegro is Podgorica (PAHD•guh•reet•suh).

He and Duchess Sophie, his wife, hoped to show friendship toward the Serbs who lived in the southern city of Sarajevo (sar•uh•YAY•voh). During their drive, an assassin fired two shots at their carriage. Both Ferdinand and Sophie were killed. The assassin was one of seven Serbs who had come that day to try to assassinate the Archduke.

Analyze Charts The Allied Powers fought the Central Powers during the Great War.

What countries were members of the Allied Powers?

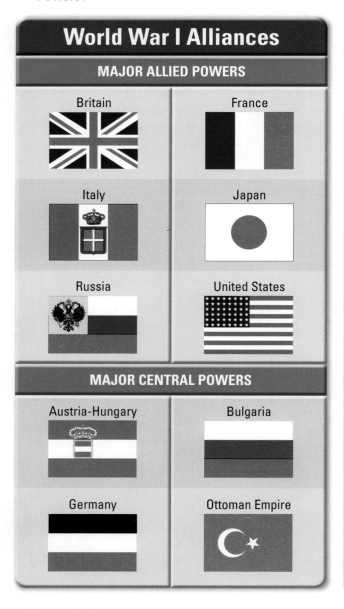

World War I Alliances

MAJOR ALLIED POWERS

Britain

France

Italy

Japan

Russia

United States

MAJOR CENTRAL POWERS

Austria-Hungary

Bulgaria

Germany

Ottoman Empire

Exactly one month after the murders, on July 28, 1914, Austria-Hungary declared war on Serbia. Because of alliances that had formed across Europe, other nations soon were drawn into the war. Siding with Serbia were Britain, France, Russia, and Belgium. Their alliance was known as the Allied Powers, or Allies. Italy joined the Allies the following year. Against the Allied Powers was an alliance called the Central Powers. It was made up of the countries of Germany, Austria-Hungary, Bulgaria, and the Ottoman Empire.

REVIEW What countries were members of the Central Powers?

The United States Enters the War

The relationship between the United States and other countries of the world had changed over time. Imperialism was part of President Theodore Roosevelt's foreign policy. When William Howard Taft became President after Roosevelt, he started a different kind of foreign policy. Under Taft's policy, the United States government gave money to other nations in return for some control over the actions of those nations. Taft's policy was known as **dollar diplomacy**.

In 1913 Woodrow Wilson became President. Wilson did not agree with dollar diplomacy. He thought the nation should never become involved with another country for its own gain.

President Wilson wanted the United States to stay out of Europe's troubles. His ideas did not change when, in 1914, those troubles turned into war. In 1916 Wilson ran for a second term, using the slogan "He kept us out of war."

Many people in the United States had come from the countries involved in the conflict. However, President Wilson asked people not to take sides. Still, the United States was not able to stay **neutral**, or take no sides, for long.

As the war dragged on, Germany again and again acted in ways that angered the United States. On May 7, 1915, a German submarine sank the British passenger ship *Lusitania*. More than 1,000 people, including 128 United States citizens, were killed when the *Lusitania* sank. The United States might have joined the Allies in the war right then, but Germany agreed not to attack any more passenger ships.

Germany honored its agreement for more than a year. Early in 1917, however, it decided to begin firing upon any ships—even passenger ships—that tried to sail to Britain. German leaders knew this decision would make the United States angry. Nevertheless, they hoped to starve Britain by cutting off the ships that delivered food supplies. The Germans also thought Britain would give up long

President Wilson wanted the United States to stay out of the war.

before the United States could be ready for war.

Then Britain told the United States that a telegram written in a secret code had been found. Germany's foreign secretary, Arthur Zimmermann, had sent the telegram to a German representative in Mexico.

Before the *Lusitania* was attacked, a warning (right) was printed in newspapers.

NOTICE!

TRAVELLERS intending to embark on the Atlantic voyage are reminded that a state of war exists between Germany and her allies and Great Britain and her allies; that the zone of war includes the waters adjacent to the British Isles; that, in accordance with formal notice given by the Imperial German Government, vessels flying the flag of Great Britain, or of any of her allies, are liable to destruction in those waters and that travellers sailing in the war zone on ships of Great Britain or her allies do so at their own risk.

IMPERIAL GERMAN EMBASSY
WASHINGTON, D. C., APRIL 22, 1915.

The agents decoded the secret message. Part of it said,

> **We intend to begin . . . unrestricted submarine warfare. We shall endeavour [try] to keep the United States of America neutral. In the event of this not succeeding, we make Mexico a proposal of alliance on the following basis: make war together, make peace together, generous financial support, and an understanding . . . that Mexico is to reconquer . . . Texas, New Mexico, and Arizona.**

Germany had asked Mexico to go to war against the United States if the United States entered the war. Then, when the Central Powers won, Mexico would receive money and part of the United States. The Mexican government did not accept Germany's offer.

President Wilson still hoped to avoid war. Then, in the nine days between March 12 and March 21, German submarines sank five United States merchant ships. Now Wilson felt there was no choice—the United States must join the war.

On the evening of April 2, 1917, President Wilson asked Congress to declare war on Germany. Wilson said, "The world must be made safe for democracy." With the support of Congress, the United States declared war on Germany on April 6, 1917.

The United States had been at peace for a number of years. It was not prepared for war. The army was made up of fewer than 200,000 soldiers. To increase the number of soldiers in the army, Congress passed the Selective Service Act. This act put into place a military draft. A **military draft** is a way of making the people of a nation join its armed forces. The act required every male between the ages of 21 and 30 to sign up for the draft. The following year the age range would change to between 18 and 45. Those who

The Zimmermann Telegram

Analyze Primary Sources

Arthur Zimmermann sent a telegram, written in a secret code, to Germany's representative in Mexico.

1. The coded telegram as received by the German representative. The numbers represent different words.

2. British agents had to identify what word each group of numbers stood for.

3. The final decoded telegram.

◆ What states are listed on the document the British agents used to decode the message?

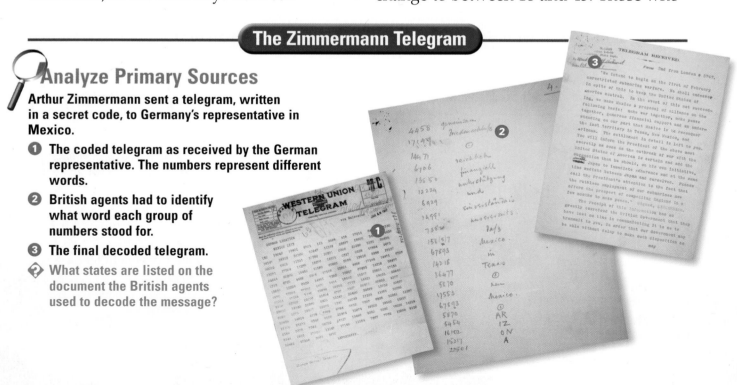

United States soldiers (above) leave to fight the war in Europe. Soldiers who were drafted were chosen by lottery (right).

would have to serve were chosen by lottery, or drawing.

The first sign-up day for the draft was June 5, 1917. On that day more than 9 million men registered at centers all over the United States. At each center, numbers were given to the men. Then a drawing took place in which many numbers were drawn. The men who held those numbers were the ones who would begin serving in the military.

As the draft was being held, the army rushed to build training camps and get the equipment the new soldiers would need. Before the year ended, the first United States soldiers arrived in France.

REVIEW What was the purpose of the Selective Service Act?

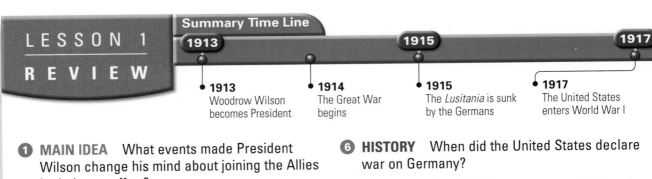

LESSON 1 REVIEW

Summary Time Line

1913 — 1915 — 1917

1913 Woodrow Wilson becomes President

1914 The Great War begins

1915 The *Lusitania* is sunk by the Germans

1917 The United States enters World War I

1. **MAIN IDEA** What events made President Wilson change his mind about joining the Allies in their war effort?

2. **WHY IT MATTERS** In what ways does the United States get involved in world affairs today?

3. **VOCABULARY** Write one or two sentences using the vocabulary terms **militarism** and **alliance**.

4. **TIME LINE** Was the *Lusitania* sunk before or after the start of the Great War?

5. **READING SKILL—Sequence** What events led to the beginning of the Great War?

6. **HISTORY** When did the United States declare war on Germany?

7. **CRITICAL THINKING—Hypothesize** When do you think the Great War became known as World War I?

PERFORMANCE—Role-Play the President Imagine that you are President Wilson. It is the afternoon of April 2, 1917, and you are preparing to ask Congress to declare war on Germany. Write your speech, based on what you learned in the lesson. Practice your speech by reading it aloud several times. Then read your speech to a classmate.

Predict a Likely Outcome

VOCABULARY

prediction
propaganda

➡ WHY IT MATTERS

A **prediction** is a decision about what might happen next, based on the way things are. A prediction is not just a guess about the future. Instead, a prediction is based on what you already know and on any new information that you gather. Using old and new information allows you to predict a likely outcome.

➡ WHAT YOU NEED TO KNOW

Think about what you already know about World War I. For the first several years, the United States stayed out of the war. Many Americans believed the United States should not take sides in Europe's conflicts. Then, in 1915, the *Lusitania* was sunk by a German submarine. United States citizens were angry, but most still did not want to get involved in the war. Two years later, in early 1917, German submarines sank several United States merchant ships. Many United States citizens were killed. On April 6, 1917, Congress declared war on Germany.

Now think about this new information. After the United States declared war, President Wilson set up the Committee on Public Information. George Creel headed the committee. His job was to convince United States citizens that the nation had been right to join the war. He did this by using propaganda. **Propaganda** is information designed to help or hurt a cause. Creel hired artists and writers to create propaganda in favor of the war. He had millions of leaflets and posters printed. These materials praised United States soldiers for defending democracy. The materials also said that the German government carried out terrible crimes in its effort to win the war.

➡ PRACTICE THE SKILL

Based on the information you read in the lesson and this new information, what do you predict happened to the way most people in the United States felt about the war?

Step 1 **Think about what you already know. Many people wanted the United States to stay out of the war. However, they were angry when German submarines sank the *Lusitania* and attacked United States ships. Soon after the attacks Congress declared war on Germany.**

During the war, posters encouraged people to support the war effort in different ways.

Step 2 Review any new information you may have learned. The government set up a committee to develop propaganda that praised the United States' role in the war and accused Germany of terrible crimes.

Step 3 Make a prediction, based on what you know.

Step 4 As you gather more information, ask yourself if your prediction still seems likely to be correct.

Now see if your prediction was correct. Many Americans became very patriotic after the United States entered the war. Millions of people volunteered to fight in the nation's armed forces. Millions more helped the war effort at home.

▶ **APPLY WHAT YOU LEARNED**

As you read the next lesson, follow the steps listed here to predict what would happen to the world after World War I ended.

MAIN IDEA
The United States helped the Allied Powers win World War I.

WHY IT MATTERS
If the Central Powers had won World War I, our government and way of life might be very different today.

VOCABULARY
no-man's-land
communism

FAST FACT To help the war effort, American school children collected peach pits for the Allies. The pits were burned and made into charcoal. This peach-pit charcoal was used for the filters in gas masks.

The War Years

1865   1885   1905   1925

1916–1918

After the United States Congress started a military draft, many new soldiers were added to the nation's military forces. These soldiers and the people who worked for the war effort at home helped the Allied Powers win World War I. These soldiers also faced a war unlike any other in their nation's history.

New Ways of Warfare

In earlier times soldiers fought face to face—sometimes hand to hand. New weapons, though, changed the way war was fought, both on land and at sea. New weapons also carried the Great War to the air.

One of the powerful new weapons used in this war was a machine gun developed by the Germans that could fire 600 bullets per minute at a target 3,000 feet (910 m) away. Tanks and flamethrowers were also introduced. The most feared of the new weapons was poison gas, which killed soldiers by making them unable to breathe.

1

Germany used submarines, known as U-boats, to fight at sea.

New weapons made World War I one of history's bloodiest wars. One especially terrible battle was the battle of the River Somme, in France. More than 22,000 soldiers died on the battle's first day. During the five months that the battle lasted, more than 500,000 soldiers from both sides died.

World War I was a war fought in trenches. A trench is a ditch dug into the ground. France, where much of the fighting took place, was crisscrossed with trenches. Soldiers from the Central Powers would stay in one group of trenches, and Allied soldiers would stay in another. A no-man's-land stretched between them. This **no-man's-land** was an area not controlled by either side. It was filled with barbed wire and land mines, or bombs buried in the ground. Any soldier who tried to cross no-man's-land or even just stick his head outside of the trench could be killed by enemy fire.

A CLOSER LOOK
World War I Trenches

Thousands of soldiers fought in trenches during World War I.

1 Soldiers lived in the trenches for weeks.
2 Between enemy trenches was a no-man's-land filled with barbed wire and land mines.
3 Tanks protected soldiers from gunfire.
4 Masks protected soldiers against poison gas.
5 Airplanes were used in war for the first time. Pilots dropped bombs by hand.

◈ What kinds of hardships do you think the soldiers faced living in the trenches?

Submarines were changing the way war was fought at sea. The Germans did not invent the submarine, but they knew what powerful weapons submarines could become. Many nations had submarines in their navies during the war, but the German *unterseeboot,* or U-boat, seemed to rule the Atlantic. By the end of the war, U-boats had destroyed 10 million tons of Allied ships and supplies.

To prevent Germany's U-boats from sinking so many ships, the Allies sent merchant ships to sea in groups. Along with them, they sent powerful warships to protect them. This was called a convoy, and it helped make the Atlantic a safer ocean for the Allies. Convoys also helped get the nation's soldiers safely to Europe. The United States Navy also planted mines under the ocean's surface. Any U-boat bumping into one of these mines would be damaged or destroyed when the mine exploded.

World War I was the first war in which airplanes were used. At first, planes were used to scout out enemy locations. Then a machine gun was invented that could be mounted on an airplane. It was mounted so that it would fire through the plane's propellers without hitting them. Planes then became weapons of war.

REVIEW **What were some of the new weapons introduced in World War I?**

U-boat   machine guns
airplanes
poison gas

Changes at Home

World War I helped the economy of the United States. As the war dragged on, European nations needed more and more goods from the United States. The United States also increased its trade with Latin American countries. These countries had lost their European trading partners because of the war. During the war years the amount of wheat and flour exported from the United States more than tripled. The value of meat from the United States sent overseas rose from $68 million in 1913 to $668 million in 1918. The war also helped other industries develop in the United States. For example, the weapons industry grew as it helped supply the

Many United States ships were built to help deliver supplies and soldiers to Europe.

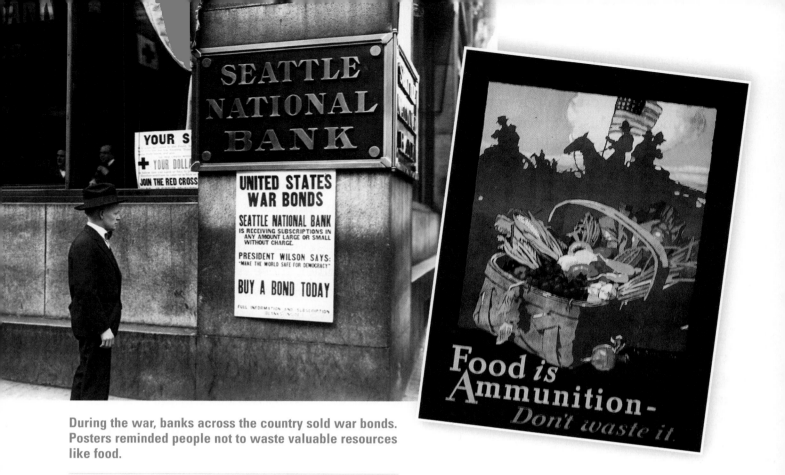

During the war, banks across the country sold war bonds. Posters reminded people not to waste valuable resources like food.

Allies with guns and ammunition. The growing weapons industry needed lots of iron and steel, so the nation's iron and steel industry also grew.

To help meet the needs created by the war, other United States companies that had made goods for everyone now turned out goods for the military instead. Women's clothing factories started making signal flags. Automobile factories manufactured plane engines. Still other companies, such as the big railroad lines, were used by the government until the war ended.

In the United States, many industries were producing more goods than ever before because of the war. Yet the Allies kept needing more. The needs of the United States Army also continued to grow as its number of soldiers reached into the millions.

The United States government called on the American people for help, and the people quickly answered the call. To help meet the great need for food overseas, President Wilson asked people to eat less. In response, people had "wheatless" days and "meatless" days every week. They also planted vegetable gardens, called victory gardens, to grow their own food.

Energy saving, too, was a great concern. Americans saved coal by having "heatless Mondays." They saved gasoline and oil by having "gasless Sundays." In other words, there were no more Sunday drives in their new Model Ts.

People at home also supported the United States war effort with their money. During the war years men, women, and children loaned the government more than $20 billion by buying Liberty Bonds and Victory Bonds.

A war bond was a paper showing that the buyer had loaned a certain amount of money to the government. In return, the government promised to pay back the cost of each bond, with interest, after the war ended.

Most German Americans stayed loyal to the United States. Some were torn two ways, such as this German American mother who said, "I love my Fatherland [Germany]. Why shouldn't I? . . . But— my three boys, they are Americans. . . . I would be a bad mother if I did not teach them to love and live and die for their country, America."

REVIEW **Why did the war cause the nation's iron and steel industry to grow?**

Growing weapon industry

The Great Migration

The war took millions of American men away from their jobs in the cities and on the farms. In addition, the number of immigrants dropped sharply because of the war. How could the United States produce enough goods when much of its workforce was gone?

One answer came from the nation's African Americans. Those who were not in the military moved by the tens of thousands from the South to the North to take jobs in the northern factories. So many African Americans moved north during the World War I years that the time is known as the Great Migration.

Together, these African Americans worked for the war effort and started new lives in the North. The artist Jacob Lawrence and his family were part of the Great Migration. He wrote about how life changed for those families that, like his, moved to the North:

> 66 Life in the North brought many challenges, but the migrants' lives had changed for the better. The children were able to go to school, and their parents gained the freedom to vote. 99

REVIEW **What was the Great Migration?**

The time when African American move from South to North to work in n factories

The painting (right) by Jacob Lawrence depicts the Great Migration. Many of those who moved to the North settled in Harlem in New York City. These Harlem children (below) are enjoying a community dance.

Some women helped the war effort by building weapons.

Women in the War

The nation's women also helped fill the jobs left empty by departing soldiers. Women became elevator operators and airplane builders and streetcar conductors. They plowed the nation's farm fields. They repaired automobiles and directed traffic. They took over many other jobs that were once done only by men. By 1918 the number of working women had reached 10 million.

The women in the workforce often earned good wages in their new jobs. However, many women worked for no pay. These women volunteered for the Red Cross, the Salvation Army, and other groups that helped make the lives of the nation's soldiers better.

Women also served in the military as office workers, translators, and nurses. Some nurses worked under battle conditions. Some were wounded, and some were captured by the Germans.

REVIEW By the end of World War I, about how many women were in the nation's workforce?

10 million

The War Ends

When the United States entered the war, people did not think United States troops would be trained and ready to sail for Europe until the spring of 1918. However, the war was going badly for the Allies and the morale of the fighting troops was very low. So the United States sent the first troops a whole year earlier than planned. These troops, who would finish their training in France, were the first of the American Expeditionary Forces. That is what United States troops in Europe were called during the war. By the end of 1917, fewer than 200,000 United States soldiers were in Europe. They did not see much fighting that year.

In 1918, however, the nation's soldiers poured across the Atlantic and into Europe. They were needed now more than ever because Russia had dropped out of the war. Its people had revolted against their leader, Czar Nicholas II. By the end of 1917, the communists were in charge of Russia's government. **Communism** is a political and economic system in which all industries, land, and businesses are owned by the government.

Many women joined the army as clerks or telegraph operators.

The communists faced many challenges as they set up their new government. They did not want to be at war, too. So they signed a peace agreement with Germany. Suddenly, the German soldiers who had been battling Russia in the east moved west. They joined the German troops fighting the remaining Allies.

World War I

Allied Powers
Central Powers
Neutral countries
🔥 Major battle

0   250   500 Miles
0   250   500 Kilometers
Azimuthal Equal-Area Projection

ICELAND (Denmark)
Arctic Circle
SWEDEN
NORWAY
RUSSIA
Moscow
North Sea
IRELAND (BRITAIN)
BRITAIN
DENMARK
Baltic Sea
Tannenberg
Aral Sea
London
NETHERLANDS
Berlin
ATLANTIC OCEAN
BELGIUM
GERMANY
Paris
Versailles
LUXEMBOURG
Argonne Forest
Vienna
Château-Thierry
SWITZERLAND
AUSTRIA-HUNGARY
Caspian Sea
FRANCE
ITALY
Caporetto
ROMANIA
Black Sea
Lisbon
PORTUGAL
Madrid
Sarajevo
MONTENEGRO
SERBIA
BULGARIA
Corsica
Rome
ALBANIA
Constantinople
Gallipoli
SPAIN
Sardinia
GREECE
OTTOMAN EMPIRE
ASIA
Sicily
Malta
Crete
Cyprus
MOROCCO (FRANCE)
ALGERIA (FRANCE)
TUNISIA (FRANCE)
Mediterranean
Sea
SPANISH SAHARA
AFRICA

GEOGRAPHY THEME

Regions This map shows the regions controlled by the Central Powers, the Allied Powers, and the neutral countries in Europe during World War I.

❓ What problems do you think Germany had because of having Allied Powers on both its eastern and western borders?

Germany was now sure it could win the war. Its troops attacked again and again. However, the Allies had hundreds of thousands of newly trained United States soldiers. Together, the United States soldiers and the Allies first held off the Germans. Then they pushed them farther and farther back until Germany had lost all the land it had won that year. The German army had begun to crumble.

Germany sent word that it wanted an armistice to end the fighting. The other major Central Powers had already asked for peace. On November 11, 1918, the representatives of the Allied and the Central Powers met in northern France. There they signed the document that ended the war. According to the agreement all fighting would cease at 11:00 A.M. on November 11.

As word of peace spread, celebrations broke out in many Allied cities. In Paris, people rushed into the streets to celebrate. "It is the 11th of November! The real Armistice Day!" wrote one member of the American Expeditionary Forces.

Word was slower to get to the United States, where it was still early morning.

After three major battles of World War I were fought there, the town of Ypres (EE•pruh), Belgium, lay in ruins.

Then President Wilson said these words: "The armistice was signed this morning. Everything for which Americans fought has been accomplished." The United States joined in the world's celebration.

The Allies had won the war. But the cost of winning was great. Almost 10 million soldiers belonging to both the Allied and the Central Powers had died. The United States, which had joined the war late, had lost more than 110,000 soldiers. In addition, millions more soldiers had been wounded in battle, and countless civilians had been injured or killed.

REVIEW When was the armistice that ended World War I signed?

Nov 11, 1918

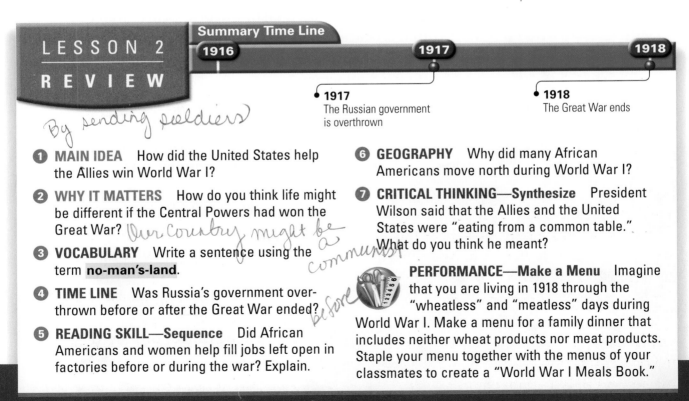

LESSON 2 REVIEW

Summary Time Line

1916 — 1917 — 1918

1917
The Russian government is overthrown

1918
The Great War ends

By sending soldiers

1 MAIN IDEA   How did the United States help the Allies win World War I?

2 WHY IT MATTERS   How do you think life might be different if the Central Powers had won the Great War? *Our country might be a communist*

3 VOCABULARY   Write a sentence using the term **no-man's-land**.

4 TIME LINE   Was Russia's government overthrown before or after the Great War ended? *before*

5 READING SKILL—Sequence   Did African Americans and women help fill jobs left open in factories before or during the war? Explain.

6 GEOGRAPHY   Why did many African Americans move north during World War I?

7 CRITICAL THINKING—Synthesize   President Wilson said that the Allies and the United States were "eating from a common table." What do you think he meant?

PERFORMANCE—Make a Menu   Imagine that you are living in 1918 through the "wheatless" and "meatless" days during World War I. Make a menu for a family dinner that includes neither wheat products nor meat products. Staple your menu together with the menus of your classmates to create a "World War I Meals Book."

MAIN IDEA
The outcome of World War I affected countries around the world.

WHY IT MATTERS
The outcome of World War I helped bring about many changes in the United States.

VOCABULARY
isolation
labor union
strike

After the War

| 1865 | 1885 | 1905 | 1925 |

1918–1924

World War I changed life for many people. In Europe even the political geography changed. Nine new nations were formed. These were Finland, Estonia, Latvia, Lithuania, and Poland—most of which had been part of Russia—and Austria, Hungary, Czechoslovakia, and Yugoslavia, which together had made up Austria-Hungary. In addition, Romania, Italy, and France gained more land.

The United States also saw changes after the war. Some of these changes were good for its people. Others were not.

Wilson's Fourteen Points

Long before the war was over, President Wilson began thinking about the peace to come. On January 8, 1918, he presented his peace ideas to Congress. He made a speech in which he described his Fourteen Points. These points, he hoped, would help bring about a lasting world peace. Indeed, he hoped that a peace based on the Fourteen Points would fulfill the promise he had made to the nation's people to "make the world safe for democracy."

In the Fourteen Points speech, Wilson spoke in favor of open diplomacy instead of the secret talks that had led to Europe's alliances before the war. He also favored ending trade barriers between countries and making sure the seas remained free for anyone to travel. Peace also would be lasting, he said, if all countries reduced their military power. The fourteenth point of Wilson's Fourteen Points called for a "general association of nations" to be formed. This League of Nations, as it would come to be called, promised "political

President Woodrow Wilson

World leaders met at the Palace of Versailles, near Paris, to sign the treaty that officially ended World War I.

independence . . . to great and small states [countries] alike."

As the fighting continued in 1918, many people in the United States and people from other Allied nations cheered Wilson's plan. After the war ended and it was time to write a peace treaty, people began to question parts of the Fourteen Points. Some countries went to the treaty talks not to build peace but to punish Germany.

In January 1919, representatives from more than 30 countries met near Paris to write a peace treaty. It took them five months. The treaty that came out of the negotiations was called the Treaty of Versailles (ver•SY) for the palace in which the treaty was signed.

The finished Treaty of Versailles contained few of Wilson's Fourteen Points. To many, it seemed that this was not a peace agreement but a list of punishments. It seemed that the purpose of the treaty was to hurt Germany.

The treaty said that Germany alone was responsible for the war and should pay for all the damages done to all the Allies. The Allies said the damages amounted to about $32 billion. Of course, even those writing the treaty knew that Germany could never repay this large amount of money.

Attempts to pay these billions of dollars also brought financial ruin to Germany. Some of the payments were made in German goods such as coal. Germany was told to send 25 million tons of coal to France, Belgium, and Italy every year. This left Germany with not enough coal to power its own industries.

REVIEW What promise did President Wilson hope to fulfill with his Fourteen Points?

World peace

POINTS OF VIEW
League of Nations

WOODROW WILSON, President of the United States

> "That is what the League of Nations is for—to end this war justly, and then to serve notice on other governments which might consider trying to do the same things Germany attempted. The League of Nations is the only thing that can prevent another dreadful catastrophe and fulfill our promises...."

HENRY CABOT LODGE, senator from Massachusetts

> "I object in the strongest possible way to having the United States agree, directly or indirectly, to be controlled by a League which may at any time ... be drawn in to deal with internal conflicts in other countries.... It must be made perfectly clear that no American soldiers ... can ever be engaged in war or ordered anywhere except by the constitutional authorities of the United States."

Analyze the Viewpoints

❶ What views about the League of Nations did each person hold?

❷ **Make It Relevant** Look at the Letters to the Editor section of your newspaper. Find two letters that express different viewpoints about the same issue. Then write a paragraph that summarizes the viewpoints of each letter.

The League of Nations

One of Wilson's Fourteen Points that did get into the Treaty of Versailles was the idea of a League of Nations. Countries that signed the treaty agreed to be part of the League.

Now it was time for the United States Senate to vote on the treaty. Many senators wanted to return to the isolation of earlier days. **Isolation** is the policy of remaining separate from other countries. The senators worried that joining the League would force the United States to get involved in European problems.

Many members of the Senate did not want the United States to join the League of Nations. Still, Wilson would not give up. He believed that "The League of Nations . . . was the only hope for mankind." He decided to take his case in favor of the treaty and the League directly to the nation's people.

Wilson started his League of Nations tour on September 3, 1919. In less than a month, he traveled more than 8,000 miles (about 13,000 km) and spoke to people in dozens of cities. Once his wife asked him to stop to rest for a few days. However, Wilson would not stop. He said, "I have caught the imagination of the people. They are eager to hear what the League stands for." He continued traveling across the country until he became very ill.

On October 2, Wilson suffered a paralyzing stroke. The next month, while the President was still sick in bed, the Senate voted against approving the Treaty of Versailles. The United States did not join the League of Nations.

REVIEW What was the League of Nations?

general association of countries political independence to countries

Changes at Home

When the war ended, millions of United States soldiers returned home. Suddenly there were more workers than jobs. As the demand for war supplies ended, many workers were laid off. Other workers' wages were cut.

Many workers protested these changes by joining labor unions. A **labor union** is a group of workers who join together to improve their working conditions.

There had been labor unions before World War I. The nation's first labor unions formed in the 1800s. Ironworkers formed an early labor union in 1859. Other unions helped blacksmiths, printers, and railroad-car makers.

A strike was an effective means used by labor unions to get companies to improve working conditions. A **strike** is the stopping of work to protest poor working conditions. One of the most violent strikes during this time took place at a steel mill in Pennsylvania. This strike was called the Homestead Strike.

Still more unions formed when many unions banded together into one large union. The

Samuel Gompers founded the American Federation of Labor.

American Federation of Labor (AFL) was an example of this kind of union. Carpenters, cigarmakers, bricklayers, and plumbers were among its many members.

Like other unions, the AFL wanted to improve working conditions by asking for higher wages and a shorter workday. AFL workers sang,

> **Eight hours for work, eight hours for rest, eight hours for what we will.**

After World War I, when there were many layoffs and wage cuts, strikes again took place. This time, rumors spread through the country that communists were starting the strikes. People became even more worried when, in 1919, Boston's police officers went on strike and gangs made the city unsafe.

One of the demands of these New York City workers was an eight-hour workday. Many of the workers in this photograph were immigrants and carried signs in their own languages, including Italian, Yiddish, and Russian.

The governor of Massachusetts at the time was Calvin Coolidge. He believed that "There is no right to strike against the public safety by anybody, anywhere, any time." He brought order back to Boston by calling out state troops. Coolidge became well known for the way he handled the police strike. The next year, he became Vice President of the United States. He became President when Warren G. Harding died in office in 1923.

With the strikes came the fear that communism would sweep the nation in the same way that it had swept Russia in the Revolution of 1917. In many states, teachers were made to take loyalty oaths to prove they were loyal to the United States. Thousands of people were wrongly arrested and imprisoned for being communists, or "Reds," as communists often were called.

In one single night—the night of January 2, 1920— Department of Justice raids in dozens of United States cities led to the arrests of more than 2,500 people. The country was in the middle of what many called the Red Scare.

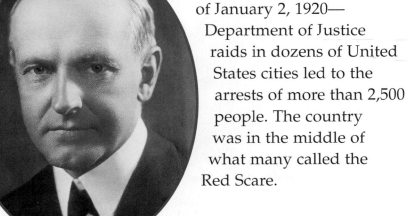

President Calvin Coolidge

The years after World War I were also a time when Congress limited immigration. Many people feared that too many immigrants would come to the United States. During the war, Congress already had passed a law that limited the number of immigrants that could move to the nation.

Once the war was over, more limitations were placed on immigrants. A new law in 1920 said that any immigrants thought to be "enemies" could be deported, or sent back to their home countries. A year later, another law said that no more than 375,000 immigrants could enter the United States each year. In 1924 Congress cut this number in half. As a result, the number of European immigrants greatly decreased.

REVIEW What was the Red Scare?

1920 the people worried that communist were trying to take over the world.

Police often collected and got rid of any literature they felt discussed communist ideas.

Women Demand Their Right to Vote

The fight for women's suffrage in the United States began many years before World War I. In 1878, an amendment to the Constitution was proposed to Congress. The amendment would have guaranteed suffrage to the nation's women. The amendment failed to pass, but many women continued their fight. The amendment was introduced in Congress every year for the next 40 years. Every year for 40 years, it failed to pass.

The amendment fight lasted longer than the lives of some of the movement's early leaders. Elizabeth Cady Stanton died in 1902. Susan B. Anthony died in 1906. Other women took their places in the fight for women's suffrage. One of those women was Carrie Lane Chapman Catt.

This program was for a march for women's suffrage held in Washington, D.C., in 1913.

Catt served as a leader of a number of suffrage groups, including the International Woman Suffrage Alliance.

Lucy Haessler's mother worked for the suffrage movement. Haessler was just ten years old when she first marched with her mother in 1914. Haessler remembers that first march:

"[My mother] told me, 'Oh, you're too young, you can't go.' But I said, 'I *am* going, because you're going to win the right to vote and I'm going to vote when I'm grown-up.' So she let me march. . . . In my heart, I knew that this movement was going to go somewhere, and it was going to help with the struggles of women."

Then came World War I. The nation's women helped keep the country running while many of the men were away at war. The work they did made many people think again about how they felt about women's suffrage.

Woodrow Wilson was one whose mind was changed by the war. He had at first been against the suffrage amendment. In 1919 he began to support women's suffrage. He explained that "the services of women during the supreme crisis [World War I] have been of the most signal usefulness and distinction. It is high time that part of our debt [to women] should be acknowledged and paid."

In 1918 the Amendment was approved by Congress. It was then sent to the states to be ratified.

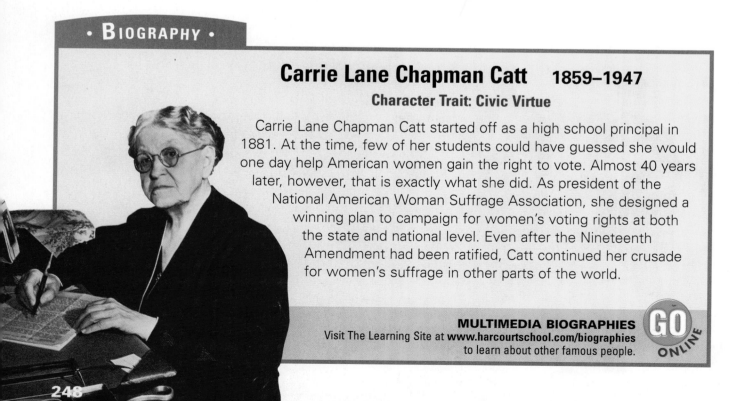

• BIOGRAPHY •

Carrie Lane Chapman Catt 1859–1947

Character Trait: Civic Virtue

Carrie Lane Chapman Catt started off as a high school principal in 1881. At the time, few of her students could have guessed she would one day help American women gain the right to vote. Almost 40 years later, however, that is exactly what she did. As president of the National American Woman Suffrage Association, she designed a winning plan to campaign for women's voting rights at both the state and national level. Even after the Nineteenth Amendment had been ratified, Catt continued her crusade for women's suffrage in other parts of the world.

MULTIMEDIA BIOGRAPHIES
Visit The Learning Site at **www.harcourtschool.com/biographies**
to learn about other famous people.

GO ONLINE

The last parade for women's suffrage was held in New York.

On August 26, 1920, enough states had voted for ratification, and the Nineteenth Amendment was added to the Constitution. The amendment states: "The right of citizens of the United States to vote shall not be denied or abridged [taken away] by the United States or by any state on account of sex [male or female]."

Afterward, the *Kansas City Star* newspaper reported that "the victory [passage of the amendment] is not a victory for women alone, it is a victory for democracy and the principle of equality upon which the nation was founded."

REVIEW In what year was the Nineteenth Amendment ratified?   1920

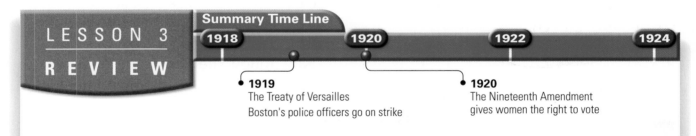

LESSON 3 REVIEW

Summary Time Line

1918 — 1920 — 1922 — 1924

1919
The Treaty of Versailles
Boston's police officers go on strike

1920
The Nineteenth Amendment
gives women the right to vote

1. **MAIN IDEA** What happened to Germany after World War I ended?

2. **WHY IT MATTERS** What important changes did the outcome of World War I help bring about in the United States?

3. **VOCABULARY** Write a sentence explaining how the belief in isolation led senators to vote against the Treaty of Versailles.

4. **TIME LINE** In what year did the Boston police strike take place?

5. **READING SKILL—Sequence** Was a suffrage amendment first proposed to Congress before or after World War I?

6. **ECONOMICS** Why did some groups decide to go on strike after World War I ended?

7. **CRITICAL THINKING—Synthesize** Carrie Lane Chapman Catt called the Nineteenth Amendment "the greatest thing that came out of the war." What do you think she meant by that?

 PERFORMANCE—Write a Speech Imagine that you are a speechwriter for President Woodrow Wilson. You will accompany him on his League of Nations train trip. Write a speech the President could give in favor of the United States' joining the League of Nations. Read your speech aloud to the class.

· SKILLS ·

CHART AND GRAPH

Read a Flow Chart

VOCABULARY

flow chart

➡ WHY IT MATTERS

Some information is easier to understand when it is explained in a drawing. The kind of drawing shown on page 251 is called a flow chart. A **flow chart** is a diagram that uses arrows to show the process that leads to an event or outcome.

➡ WHAT YOU NEED TO KNOW

The Constitution of the United States uses an Article—Article V—to explain how the document can be amended. This Article provides a good example of when a flow chart may be easier to read than the document. For example, the first part of Article V describes who can propose a new amendment. Here is what it says: "The Congress, whenever two-thirds of both houses shall deem it necessary, shall propose amendments to this Constitution, or, on the application of the legislatures of two-thirds of the several states, shall call a convention for proposing amendments. . . . "

Now examine the flow chart on page 251. The part of the flow chart that appears at the top gives the same information as the first part of Article V. By looking at the flow chart, you can tell that there are two ways an amendment can be proposed because two boxes are at the top of the chart. One way is by a two-thirds vote in both houses of Congress. The other is by a national convention called at the request of two-thirds of the states.

Now follow the arrows on the flow chart to find out how an amendment is added to the Constitution of the United States.

➡ PRACTICE THE SKILL

Use the flow chart on page 251 to answer these questions.

① How can the states propose an amendment to the Constitution?

② According to the arrows, how many ways can a proposed amendment to the Constitution be ratified?

The Nineteenth Amendment gave women the right to vote.

How an Amendment Is Added to the Constitution

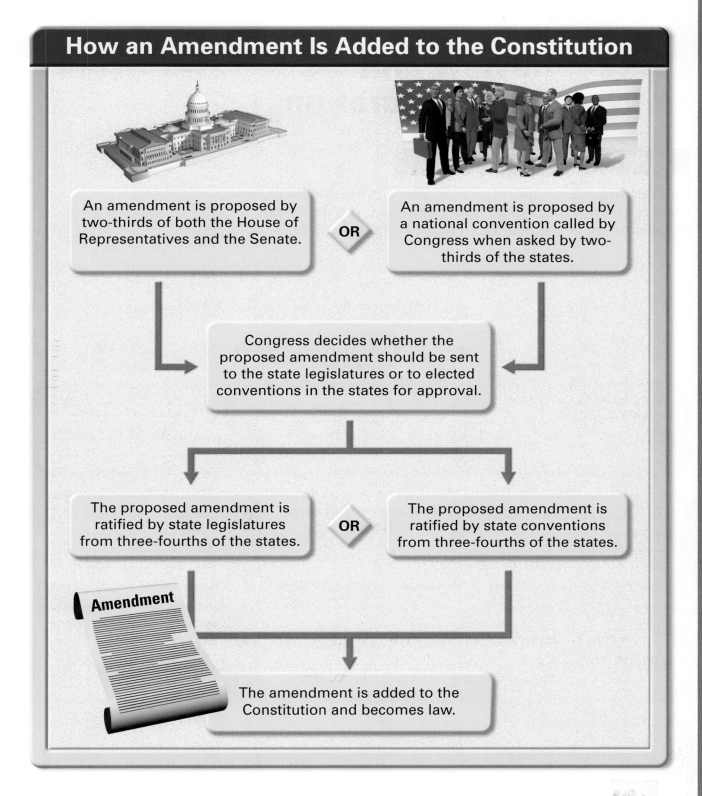

An amendment is proposed by two-thirds of both the House of Representatives and the Senate.

OR

An amendment is proposed by a national convention called by Congress when asked by two-thirds of the states.

Congress decides whether the proposed amendment should be sent to the state legislatures or to elected conventions in the states for approval.

The proposed amendment is ratified by state legislatures from three-fourths of the states.

OR

The proposed amendment is ratified by state conventions from three-fourths of the states.

Amendment

The amendment is added to the Constitution and becomes law.

❸ How many steps does it take to add an amendment to the Constitution?

➡ **APPLY WHAT YOU LEARNED**

Work with a partner to make a flow chart that explains your class schedule from the time you get to school until it is time for lunch. List all the classes and any activities you have each morning, connecting them with arrows to show the order in which they happen. Share your completed flow chart with the class.

6 Review and Test Preparation

Summary Time Line
1912

1913
Woodrow Wilson
becomes President

1914
World War I begins

USE YOUR READING SKILLS

Use this graphic organizer to help you put the events of World War I in the order in which they happened. A copy of this graphic organizer appears on page 64 of the Activity Book.

World War I

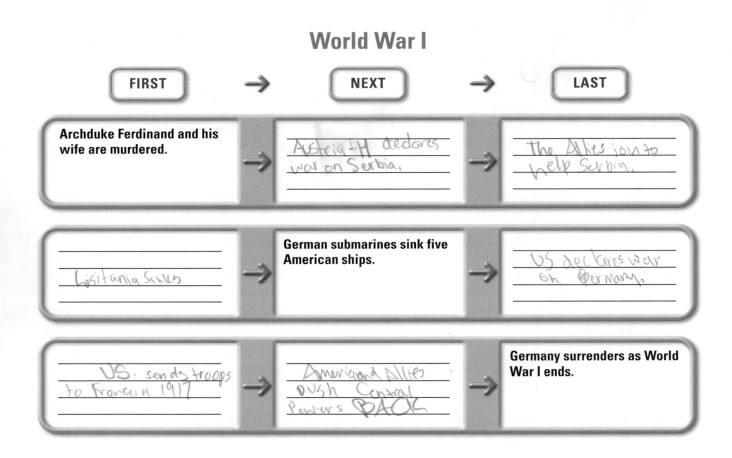

FIRST →	NEXT →	LAST
Archduke Ferdinand and his wife are murdered.	*Austria-H declares war on Serbia.*	*The Allies join to help Serbia.*
Lusitania Sinks	German submarines sink five American ships.	*US declares war on Germany.*
U.S. sends troops to France in 1917	*American and Allies push Central Powers BACK*	Germany surrenders as World War I ends.

THINK & WRITE

Write a Journal Entry Imagine you are an American student during World War I. Write a journal entry describing how the military draft, the food shortage, and the workforce shortage are affecting your life.

Write a Biography Write a biography about an important person mentioned in Chapter 6. Be sure to include where and when the person was born and why his or her life was important.

1917
The United States
enters World War I

1918
World War I ends

1920
The Nineteenth Amendment
is ratified

USE THE TIME LINE

Use the chapter summary time line to
answer these questions.

Woodrow Wilson

1 Who was President during World War I?

2 Was the Nineteenth Amendment ratified
before or after World War I? *After*

USE VOCABULARY

Write a definition
for each of these
terms.

alliance (p. 227)

no-man's-land
(p. 235)

labor union (p. 245)

strike (p. 245)

RECALL FACTS

Answer these questions.

France

3 In which European country did much of the
fighting during World War I take place?

4 What were German submarines called? *U-boat*

5 When did World War I end? *Nov 11, 1918*

6 What was the fourteenth point of President
Wilson's Fourteen Points? *League of Nations*

Write the letter of the best choice.

7 **TEST PREP** Which of the following were
not allies during World War I?
A Germany and Serbia
B the United States and France
C Britain and France
D Germany and Austria-Hungary

8 **TEST PREP** Which of the following
amendments gave women the right to vote?
F the Thirteenth Amendment
G the Fifteenth Amendment
H the Nineteenth Amendment
J the Twenty-second Amendment

THINK CRITICALLY

9 Why did soldiers in World War I fight from
trenches?

10 How did the Great Migration affect life in the
United States?

APPLY SKILLS

Predict a Likely Outcome
Review the information
on pages 232 and 233 to
answer these questions.

11 What is a prediction based on?

12 Why do people make predictions?

13 What four steps can you follow to make
a prediction?

Read a Flow Chart
Use the flow chart on
page 251 to answer
these questions.

14 What happens after an amendment is
proposed?

15 What two ways can the amendment be
ratified?

16 What is the final step before the amendment
becomes law?

VISIT

THE PANAMA CANAL

GET READY

Since its opening in 1914, the Panama Canal has helped move people and goods around the world. If you visit the Panama Canal, you can travel 50 miles (80 km) on the waterway. This 50 miles saves ships the journey of nearly 8,000 miles (12,874 km) that it would take to sail around South America.

Sets of locks, or water-filled chambers, move boats through the canal. When a boat enters a lock, water is slowly added so that the boat rises. When the water is at the same level as the water in the next chamber, gates open and the ship moves into the next lock. This process is repeated until the ship has moved through all of the locks. Tolls, or fees, are charged to boats using the canal according to the size of the ship. One of the highest fees ever charged was $141,344.91! A visit to the Panama Canal gives visitors an exciting look at this complex and historic waterway.

LOCATE IT

Panama Canal

PANAMA

WHAT TO SEE

A large ship moves through a lock.

This diagram shows the steps required for a boat to go through a system of locks.

The Panama Canal links the Atlantic Ocean with the Pacific Ocean.

Small trains called *mules* run on tracks along the sides of the locks. They help pull and guide boats.

TAKE A FIELD TRIP

GO ONLINE

A VIRTUAL TOUR
Visit The Learning Site at **www.harcourtschool.com/tours** to find virtual tours of other places of interest.

CNN Turner Le@rning®

A VIDEO TOUR
Check your media center or classroom library for a videotape tour of the Panama Canal.

3 Review and Test Preparation

VISUAL SUMMARY

Write Captions Look at the events on the Visual Summary below. Carefully read the captions that go with each event. Then use what you have learned in your reading to write new captions to go along with each event. As you write, be sure to answer the questions "When?", "Who?", and "Where?".

USE VOCABULARY

Identify the correct term that completes each sentence.

panhandle (p. 189)

armistice (p. 194)

skyscraper (p. 209)

communism (p. 239)

isolation (p. 244)

1 The world's first _____ was built in Chicago.

2 Under _____ the government owns all businesses, land, and industries.

3 When one country decides to stay separate from other countries it is called _____.

4 Alaska's _____ is a portion of land that sticks out like the handle on a pan.

5 The Spanish-American War ended when Spanish leaders signed an _____.

RECALL FACTS

Answer these questions.

6 What is yellow journalism?

7 Where is Hawaii located?

8 Why did Henry Ford search for ways to build automobiles faster?

9 What event led to the start of World War I?

10 Who was involved in the Great Migration?

Write the letter of the best choice.

11 **TEST PREP** Before the United States bought Alaska to which of the following countries did it belong?
A Russia
B Britain
C France
D China

Visual Summary

1865   1885

1867 **The United States purchases Alaska** p. 189

THE MAP OF ALASKA

256

1879 **Thomas Edison invents the light bulb** p. 201

1903 **The Wright brothers fly at Kitty Hawk** p. 204

12 TEST PREP The time following World War I in which some American citizens were wrongly arrested for being communists was called—

F the Communist Era.

G the Red Scare.

H suffrage.

J the Revolution of 1917.

THINK CRITICALLY

13 How did the Spanish-American War change the United States?

14 Why did more people live in the countryside than in the cities in the mid-1800s? *They were farmers*

15 What changes brought about by World War I still affect Americans today?

APPLY SKILLS

MAP AND GLOBE SKILLS

Compare Map Projections
Use the maps of Alaska on this page to answer the following questions.

16 On which map are the lines of longitude equal distances apart? *cylindrical*

17 On which map is the size of Alaska more accurate? A

18 On which map does Alaska appear to be larger? B

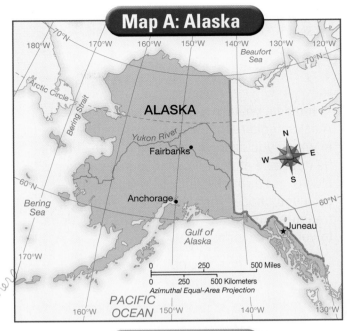

Map A: Alaska

PACIFIC OCEAN

Azimuthal Equal-Area Projection

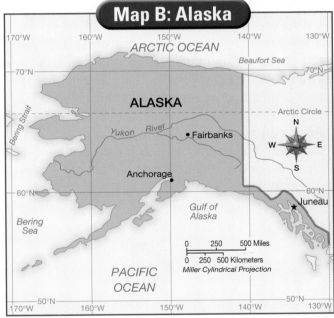

Map B: Alaska

ARCTIC OCEAN

ALASKA

PACIFIC OCEAN

Miller Cylindrical Projection

1905

1925

1908 Henry Ford introduces the Model T p. 202

1914 World War I begins p. 228

1920 The Nineteenth Amendment gives American women the right to vote p. 249

Unit Activities

Draw a Treasure Map

Imagine you are a gold miner during the Alaskan gold rush. Choose an area in Alaska in which you discover gold. That area should be near one of the following cities—Juneau, Nome, or Fairbanks. Look at a map of the area you chose. Then draw your own treasure map of the area, showing directions to your gold claim.

Give a Presidential Speech

Work as a group to write, edit, and deliver a Presidential State of the Union speech. Choose a President discussed in this unit. Then research that President and the important events that occurred during his time in office. Next, write and edit a speech to the American people, describing the state of the union and outlining goals for the upcoming year. Finally, select a member of your group to deliver your speech to the class.

GO ONLINE

Visit The Learning Site at www.harcourtschool.com/socialstudies/activities for additional activities.

VISIT YOUR LIBRARY

■ *Alexander Graham Bell* by Leonard Everett Fisher. Atheneum.

■ *Yukon Gold* by Charlotte Foltz Jones. Holiday House.

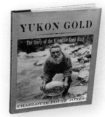

■ *Theodore Roosevelt Takes Charge* by Nancy Whitelaw. Albert Whitman & Company.

COMPLETE THE UNIT PROJECT

Make a Scrapbook   Work as a class to complete the unit project—make a scrapbook. Review the list you made during your reading. Then, make artwork that portrays the items on your list. You can make drawings and paintings, write poems and essays, and cut out pictures from magazines and newspapers. Combine your artwork with your classmates' artwork in a scrapbook.

Good Times and Bad

"Lucky Lindy"
gold coin

The *Spirit of St. Louis* in the National Air and Space Museum, Washington, D.C.

4

Good Times and Bad

> **❝ The greatest feat of a solitary man in the records of the human race. ❞**
>
> —description of Charles Lindbergh's flight across the Atlantic Ocean, May 21, 1927

Preview the Content

Read the title and the Main Idea for each lesson in the unit. Then use what you have read to make a web for each chapter. Write down words or phrases that will help you identify the main topics to be covered in the unit.

MAIN TOPICS

Preview the Vocabulary

Context Clues Context clues are words that can help you figure out the meanings of unfamiliar words or terms in sentences. Skim the unit, and find the terms **installment buying**, **unemployment**, and **depression**. For each term, write a sentence explaining how context clues help you understand the term's meaning.

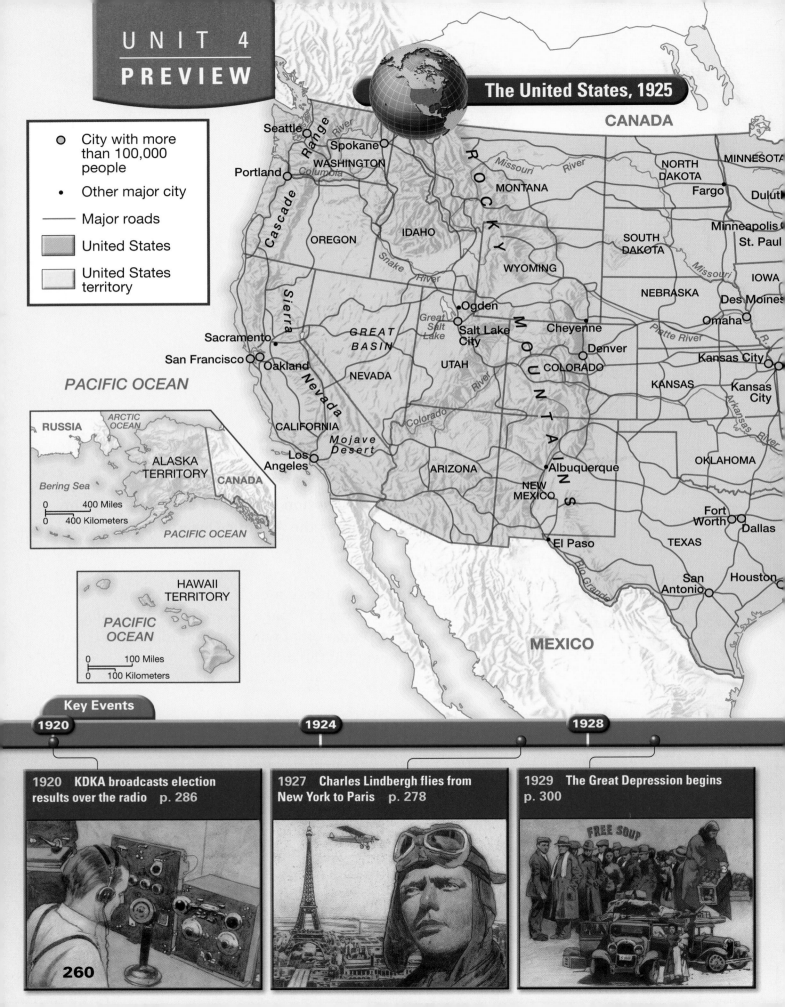

The United States, 1925

Legend
- City with more than 100,000 people
- Other major city
- Major roads
- United States
- United States territory

CANADA

Seattle
Spokane
WASHINGTON
Portland
Cascade Range
Columbia River
OREGON
IDAHO
Snake River
MONTANA
NORTH DAKOTA
Fargo
MINNESOTA
Duluth
Minneapolis
St. Paul
SOUTH DAKOTA
WYOMING
ROCKY MOUNTAINS
Missouri River
IOWA
Des Moines
NEBRASKA
Omaha
Sierra Nevada
Sacramento
San Francisco
Oakland
GREAT BASIN
NEVADA
Great Salt Lake
Ogden
Salt Lake City
UTAH
Cheyenne
Denver
COLORADO
Platte River
Kansas City
KANSAS
Kansas City
CALIFORNIA
Mojave Desert
Los Angeles
Colorado River
ARIZONA
NEW MEXICO
Albuquerque
OKLAHOMA
Arkansas River
PACIFIC OCEAN

Alaska inset
RUSSIA
ARCTIC OCEAN
Bering Sea
ALASKA TERRITORY
CANADA
PACIFIC OCEAN
0   400 Miles
0   400 Kilometers

Hawaii inset
HAWAII TERRITORY
PACIFIC OCEAN
0   100 Miles
0   100 Kilometers

El Paso
Rio Grande
TEXAS
Fort Worth
Dallas
San Antonio
Houston
MEXICO

Key Events

1920 — 1924 — 1928

1920 KDKA broadcasts election results over the radio   p. 286

1927 Charles Lindbergh flies from New York to Paris   p. 278

1929 The Great Depression begins p. 300

FREE SOUP

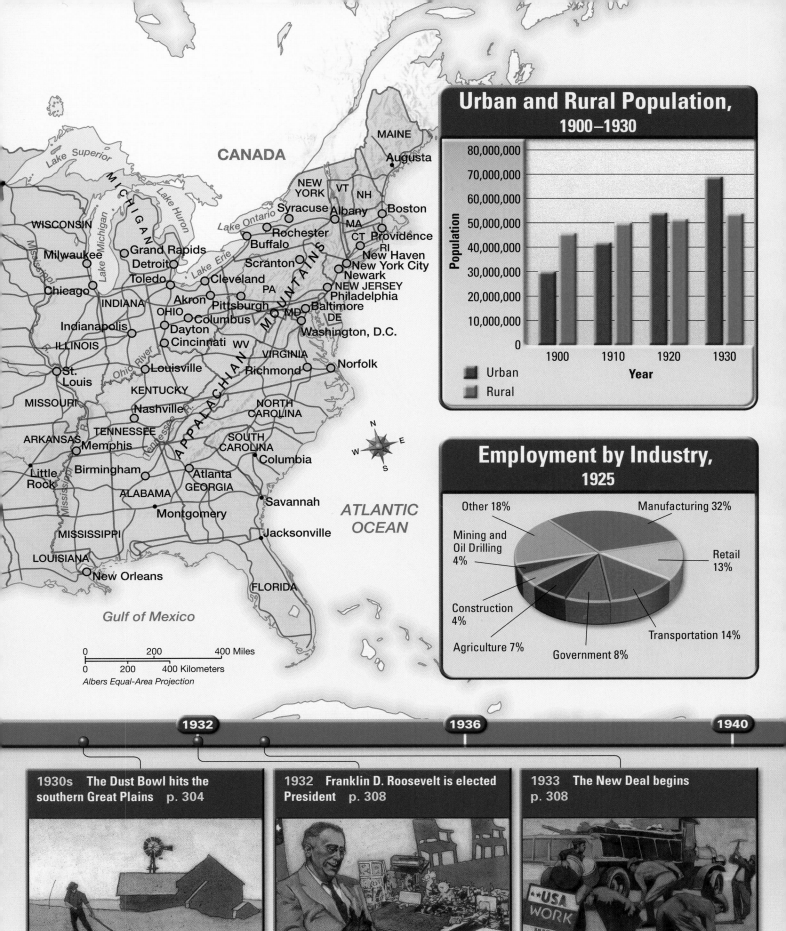

Urban and Rural Population, 1900–1930

Population (y-axis): 0 to 80,000,000

Year	Urban	Rural
1900	~30,000,000	~45,000,000
1910	~41,000,000	~49,000,000
1920	~54,000,000	~51,000,000
1930	~68,000,000	~53,000,000

■ Urban
▨ Rural

Employment by Industry, 1925

- Manufacturing 32%
- Retail 13%
- Transportation 14%
- Government 8%
- Agriculture 7%
- Construction 4%
- Mining and Oil Drilling 4%
- Other 18%

ATLANTIC OCEAN

Gulf of Mexico

0   200   400 Miles
0   200   400 Kilometers
Albers Equal-Area Projection

Timeline: **1932**   **1936**   **1940**

1930s The Dust Bowl hits the southern Great Plains   p. 304

1932 Franklin D. Roosevelt is elected President   p. 308

1933 The New Deal begins p. 308

★ USA WORK WPA

Rose's Journal

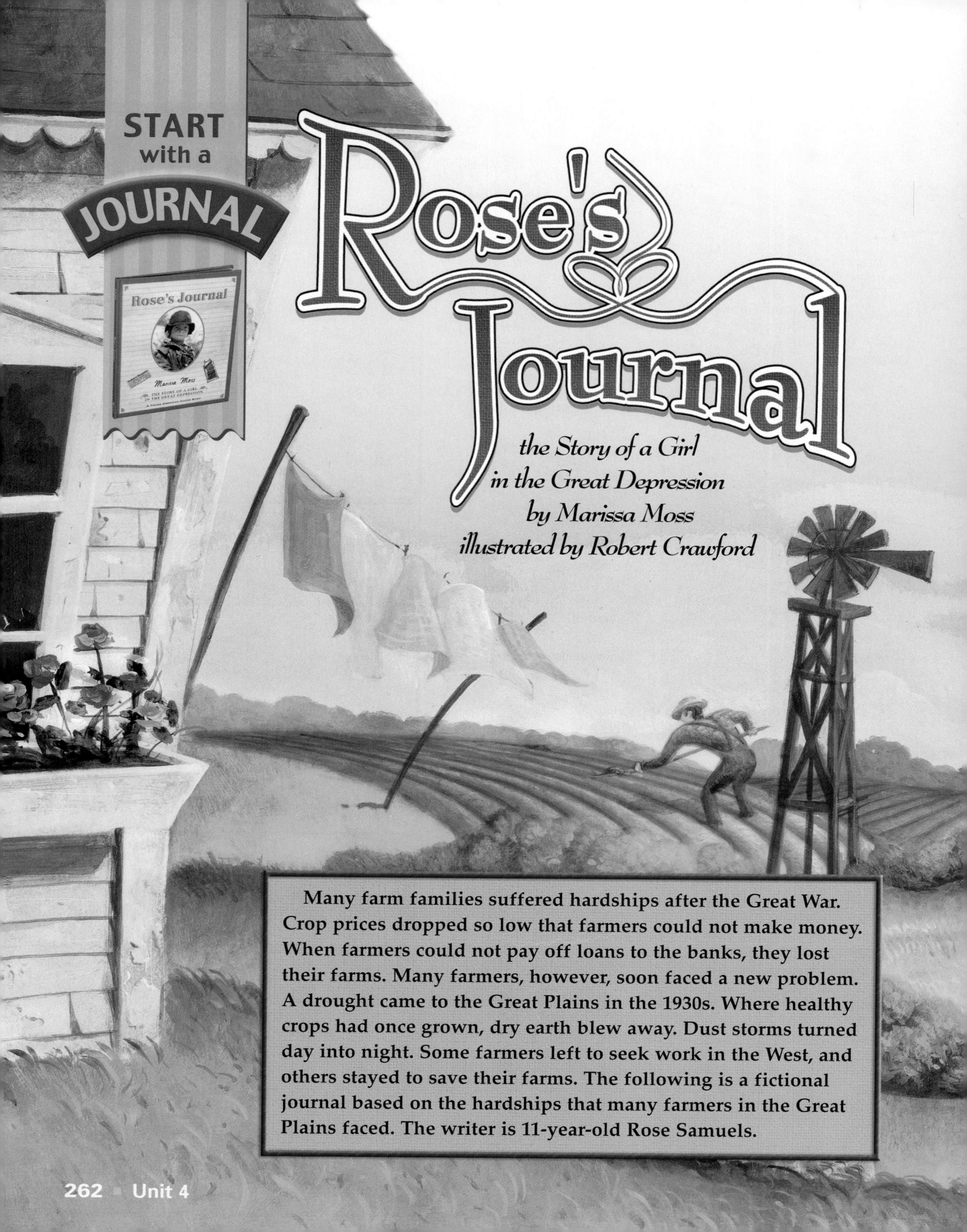

Rose's Journal

the Story of a Girl
in the Great Depression
by Marissa Moss
illustrated by Robert Crawford

Many farm families suffered hardships after the Great War. Crop prices dropped so low that farmers could not make money. When farmers could not pay off loans to the banks, they lost their farms. Many farmers, however, soon faced a new problem. A drought came to the Great Plains in the 1930s. Where healthy crops had once grown, dry earth blew away. Dust storms turned day into night. Some farmers left to seek work in the West, and others stayed to save their farms. The following is a fictional journal based on the hardships that many farmers in the Great Plains faced. The writer is 11-year-old Rose Samuels.

April 1, 1935

If it wasn't for the radio, I'd feel like the world was one big pepper shaker, and I was a little grain of pepper inside it. Father's wheat crop is long gone now. At least Mother has somehow kept her kitchen garden alive. Between dusters she waters the tomatoes, cucumbers, watermelons, potatoes, and beans. She wipes the dirt off the leaves and feeds the ground with eggshells and chicken manure. Father takes it as a sign not to give up, that we can still grow things here. Our farm isn't dead, and we won't let it die.

April 14, 1935

After so many gray days, today dawned clear and fresh, and I thought Father was right—there's hope for us here. It was such a beautiful day, everyone wanted to be outside. Mother and I did a wash, and it was a pleasure to hang the clothes in the bright sun.

Father thought it wasn't too late to try for a second crop of wheat, so he decided to sow the seed he'd saved. There still was no rain, but the sun was enough to give us all hope.

When we finished hanging out the wash, the day was so fine and Mother was so happy, we decided to take the horses and visit Gramma and Grampa. It looked like everyone was on the road, paying visits or having picnics, like we were all celebrating our good fortune in simply having the gift of a normal spring day.

As we got closer to Grampa's farm, the air got suddenly colder, much colder. The sky was thick with quiet, and then there was the sound of thousands of birds, more and more each moment, as if they were trying to outfly an invisible monster.

Mother yelled at me to hurry—we had to get to Grampa's. We kicked up the horses, but they were so skittish and fretful, I could barely get Flit's nose pointed in the right direction. Mother's horse, Lucky, was worse—she reared up and threw Mother off. I jumped off Flit to help Mother, and in a flash both horses were gone, racing off in a panic. Mother wasn't hurt, but we were both plenty scared. The wind was rising.

On the horizon we could see a great black smudge. Mother grabbed my hand and we ran. I've never been so scared, trying to outrace that giant black hand stretching out toward us. The wind pushed us forward, and just as we got to Grampa's gate, the first bits of dust whirled around us. We were so close, but it only took seconds for darkness to fill the air. I couldn't see, I couldn't breathe, I couldn't cry. All I could do was hold on to Mother's hand as she pulled me along. I choked on the thick, gritty air and squeezed my eyes tight shut to keep out the stinging dirt. The roar of the wind filled my ears and I thought, "I should have gone with Pearl, with Floyd, with anyone."

I don't know how she found her way, but over the howling wind, I heard a

pounding—it was Mother pounding on wood, pounding on the farmhouse, pounding as hard as she could, until Gramma opened the door and we blew in along with buckets and buckets of dirt. Gramma slammed the door shut, and only then did Mother let go of me. We were both coughing and gasping, tears streaming out of our eyes.

In time, better plowing methods, more rainfall, and the planting of windbreaks, or rows of large trees, ended the terrible dust storms. Families on the Great Plains were able to farm their land once again.

Analyze the Literature

1 Why was Rose happy to be able to listen to the radio?

2 Why did Rose's father decide to plant a second crop?

3 Work with a partner to write a list of reasons people might stay on their farms and reasons they might leave to find work elsewhere.

READ A BOOK

START THE UNIT PROJECT

Create a Mural Work with classmates to draw a mural that shows the good and bad times of the 1920s and 1930s. As you read the unit, take notes on the key people, places, and events. These notes will help you decide which items to include in your mural.

USE TECHNOLOGY

Visit The Learning Site at **www.harcourtschool.com/ socialstudies** for additional activities, primary sources, and other resources to use in this unit.

FOX THEATRE

The Fox Theatre in Atlanta, Georgia, was built in the 1920s to appear like a Middle Eastern courtyard. During the Roaring Twenties people flocked to the theatre to watch movies. Ever since, people have been fascinated by the rich sound of the music that is played in the theatre. People also continue to enjoy the lifelike sky, complete with twinkling stars and moving clouds, displayed on the ceiling.

LOCATE IT

Atlanta

GEORGIA

The Roaring Twenties

" The chief business of the American people is business. "

—Calvin Coolidge, speech to the American Society of Newspaper Editors, January 17, 1925

CHAPTER READING SKILL

Compare and Contrast

To **compare** people, places, events, or ideas, you find the ways in which they are alike. To **contrast** people, places, events, or ideas, you find ways in which they are different.

As you read this chapter, compare and contrast the people, places, events, and ideas that you find.

DIFFERENCES	SIMILARITIES	DIFFERENCES

MAIN IDEA
Read to find out why the United States economy was booming in the early 1920s.

WHY IT MATTERS
The lives of many Americans changed in the 1920s as factories produced more goods for home use.

VOCABULARY
consumer good
installment buying
interest
stock market
stock

The Boom Economy Brings Change

1920   1930   1940

1920–1930

The early 1920s were good times for many people in the United States. People wanted to forget about the hardships of World War I. They looked forward to new opportunities and wanted to enjoy themselves. For this reason, the 1920s are often called the Roaring Twenties. Many people thought these good times would go on forever.

New Prosperity

In the decade that followed World War I, the United States economy seemed to be getting stronger and stronger. The restrictions that had been placed on businesses during World War I were lifted when the war ended. Factories that had produced weapons and other war supplies went back to making

FAST FACT The first vacuum cleaner was invented in 1901. It sat on a horse-drawn cart and had a long hose connected to a gasoline engine.

Electric lamps on display in the store window (below) and vacuum cleaners (right) were some of the electric appliances people bought after the war.

During the 1920s many people bought items like radios (shown next to the lamp).

consumer goods. **Consumer goods** are products made for personal use. Factories made vacuum cleaners, washing machines, radios, and all kinds of new electric appliances for the home. Never before had consumers had so many ways to spend their money.

The government encouraged the nation's businesses to grow during this time. To help them, the government raised the taxes on consumer goods coming into the United States from other countries. These higher tariffs, or taxes on imports, made foreign goods more expensive to buy than goods that were made in the United States. The lower prices of American goods made them more affordable for people and kept the nation's factories busy.

Other industries grew very fast during this time as well. One of these industries was the business of producing electricity. This new source of power first became available in the late 1800s. By 1920 the United States was using almost ten times

as much electricity as it had used in 1900. By 1929 two out of every three homes in the United States had been wired to receive electricity.

> **REVIEW** How did high tariffs encourage businesses in the United States?
> Made foreign goods more expensive to buy.

New Patterns of Buying

After making sacrifices during the war, people wanted many of the consumer goods that were available, and they wanted them quickly. This was especially true of the automobile.

Installment buying made it possible for people to buy automobiles and other items without having to pay the whole price at one time. **Installment buying** allows a buyer to take home a product after paying only part of the price. The buyer then makes monthly payments, or installments, until the full price of the product has been paid.

"Pay as you ride!" urged automobile sellers across the country. People did.

During the Florida land boom, posters (right) encouraged people to move to or visit the state. In cities such as Coral Gables (above), busloads of people arrived to buy land.

More than three-fourths of all the automobiles bought in 1925 were paid for in installments.

Installment buying made many consumer goods affordable to most people in the nation. For example, in 1929 a person could buy a piano that cost $450 by paying only $15 at the time of the purchase and then $12 each month until the full price had been paid. A person could bring home a new couch by paying just $5 and then making the monthly payments. Part of each monthly payment went to pay for the item. The rest helped to pay the **interest**, or the money a borrower pays to a lender for the use of money.

People did not worry about promising their future earnings to get something today. However, some fell deeper and deeper into debt. People were spending more and more money that they did not have. This included money spent on real estate. People were especially eager to buy land in Florida, where prices had recently soared. Florida real estate companies promised everything from a perfect climate to a healthy old age to those who would buy land and live in Florida.

At the beginning of 1922, plots of land in Miami Beach, Florida, were selling for $16,000 each. Six months later the same plots of land were selling for as much as $150,000. Florida's boom reached its high point in the mid-1920s. On October 4, 1924, a real estate company in Tampa put 300 plots of land up for sale. In just three hours, all 300 plots had been sold. People bought land so quickly that they did not take the time to look at it before they bought it. Some people found that the land they had bought was under water!

Florida's land boom did not last long. It began to slow down in 1926 when a terrible hurricane hit Florida. Within two years an even more damaging hurricane

This stock certificate is for a mining company in Montana.

hit the state, and the land boom soon came to an end.

In the 1920s people also spent their money by putting it in the stock market. The **stock market** is a place where people buy and sell shares in the ownership of a company or business. These shares are called **stock**. The price of a company's stock is based on what people will pay for it. If more people want to buy the stock than want to sell it, the price will go up. In the same way, if more people want to sell the stock than want to buy it, the price will drop.

As the 1920s continued, businesses continued to boom and stock prices continued to go up. More and more people invested in the stock market. They hoped to make money from the growth of businesses. Some people even borrowed money to invest in stocks. They thought the stocks would make more money than it cost them to borrow the money.

REVIEW What effect did installment buying have on consumers? *Debt.*

Challenges for Some Americans

Everyone did not share in the good times of the 1920s. One example was the American farmer. During World War I, the United States and the rest of the Allies used all of the crops that the nation's farmers were able to grow.

Many farmers bought farm machinery, like this combine (KAHM•byn), during the war. Combines are both reapers that cut the crops and threshers that separate the grain from the straw.

This photograph shows an immigrant at Ellis Island being tested.

During those years, many farmers borrowed money to buy more farmland and more farm machinery. They hoped to produce more and make money from the high crop prices caused by the war.

After the war ended, the Allied countries no longer needed to buy crops raised in the United States. Suddenly, crop prices dropped. Many farmers found they could not make enough money to pay back the money they had borrowed.

Farmers began to organize political groups such as the American Farm Bureau Federation. The groups supported laws that would boost crop prices, which would lower farmers' debts. Still, farmers continued to struggle all during the 1920s.

Fewer farmworkers were needed, and many workers left farms and looked for jobs in cities. At the same time, immigrants from Europe were moving to cities in the United States.

During the war, Congress already had passed a law that said immigrants had to have basic skills in reading and writing in English or another language to move to the United States. Congress had also limited immigration each year to a certain number of people from each country. In 1924 another law limited immigration even more. Many people in the United States supported these limits. Some feared a flood of immigrants would take Americans' jobs. Others were suspicious of anyone whose way of life seemed "un-American," or different from their own.

This suspicion was one reason that during the 1920s, the Ku Klux Klan (KKK) again grew in the United States. KKK members wore white robes and hid their faces behind hooded masks. They used threats

Some people had to pass a literacy test before they could immigrate to the United States. This test showed whether a person could read and write.

Some people who immigrated to the United States during the 1920s started farms in the southwestern part of the country.

and violence to scare or drive away people they felt prejudice toward, such as African Americans and people of other religions, such as Jews and Catholics. During the 1920s, the number of KKK members reached into the millions. No one is sure exactly how many members there were because the KKK is a secret organization.

The KKK soon gained political power in several states. Some of these states were in the South, where the KKK had earlier been strong. However, the group also had members in midwestern and western states such as Ohio, Indiana, Colorado, and Oregon.

REVIEW Why did many people support limits on immigration?

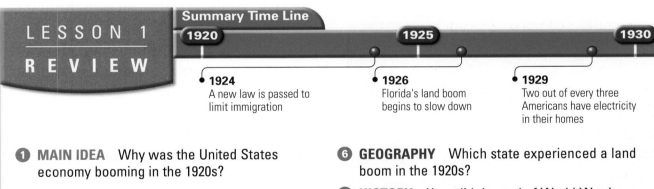

LESSON 1 REVIEW

Summary Time Line

1920 — 1925 — 1930

1924 A new law is passed to limit immigration

1926 Florida's land boom begins to slow down

1929 Two out of every three Americans have electricity in their homes

1. **MAIN IDEA** Why was the United States economy booming in the 1920s?

2. **WHY IT MATTERS** How did the production of more goods for home use change the lives of many people in the 1920s?

3. **VOCABULARY** Write a sentence explaining how **installment buying** boosted the nation's businesses.

4. **TIME LINE** In which year was a new immigration law passed?

5. **READING SKILL—Compare and Contrast** How might a farmer's view of the 1920s have differed from a factory worker's view?

6. **GEOGRAPHY** Which state experienced a land boom in the 1920s?

7. **HISTORY** How did the end of World War I affect farmers in the United States?

8. **CRITICAL THINKING—Evaluate** Do you think installment buying is a good idea? Explain.

 PERFORMANCE—Make a Collage Look through magazines and other sources, and cut out pictures of consumer goods that are important to you in your everyday life. Paste the pictures onto posterboard to create a collage. Name the collage "My Favorite Consumer Goods." Place your collage with those of your classmates in a wall display.

Use a Land Use and Resource Map

VOCABULARY
land use
generalization

▶ WHY IT MATTERS

Symbols provide people with helpful information every day. If you see the symbol of a telephone receiver on a sign, for example, you know that a telephone is nearby. Map symbols also provide helpful information. They tell you such things as the locations of a country's natural resources. This information can help you understand more about the economy of a place.

▶ WHAT YOU NEED TO KNOW

The map on page 275 is a land use and resource map. Both the colors and the symbols tell you things about a place. The map key shows which color indicates **land use**, or the way in which most of the land is used. For example, farming was an important land use in 1920 in the places colored light green. The map key also shows which symbol represents each natural resource. For example, if a place on the map has the symbol of an oil derrick, you know that oil or natural gas can be found there.

A land use and resource map shows only the most common land use and the most common resources in a place. This kind of map can help you make generalizations about a place's economy. A **generalization** is a statement that summarizes the facts. It is also used to summarize groups of facts and to show relationships between them. For example, the oil derrick symbols in Texas and Oklahoma show that oil was important to the economies of these states.

Among the many items manufactured in factories in the 1920s was this cloth tire.

274

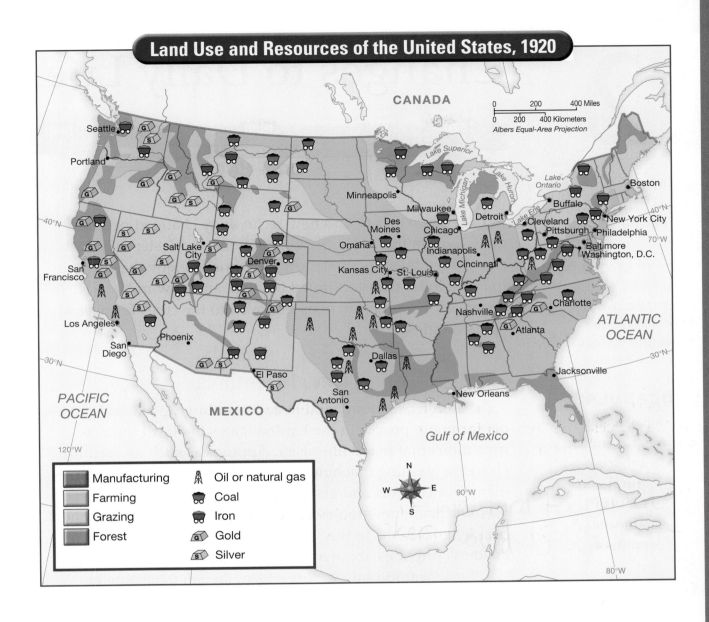

Land Use and Resources of the United States, 1920

Legend:
- Manufacturing
- Farming
- Grazing
- Forest
- Oil or natural gas
- Coal
- Iron
- G Gold
- S Silver

PRACTICE THE SKILL

Use the land use and resource map to answer these questions.

1. Were most of the nation's farms in the East or in the West?

2. In which states were gold and silver mined?

3. Suppose you were in the oil business in 1920. Near which cities might you have lived?

APPLY WHAT YOU LEARNED

Draw a land use and resource map of your state. Working with a partner, use encyclopedias and library books to find out how people use the land in your state. Also find out what resources are found there. Then use your completed map to write a generalization about the economy of your state.

Practice your map and globe skills with the **GeoSkills CD-ROM.**

Changes to Daily Life

1920   1930   1940

1920–1940

MAIN IDEA
Read to find how people's lives changed in the 1920s.

WHY IT MATTERS
The economic decisions people made during the 1920s would determine the shape of the nation's economy in the future.

VOCABULARY
advertising
commercial industry
urban
rural
suburb
commute
architect

New prosperity and new technology changed people's daily lives in the 1920s. New inventions and faster ways of travel gave many people more free time to enjoy their lives. Existing industries continued to grow, and new industries began. More and more people moved to the cities for new opportunities.

New Inventions

A booming economy and installment buying made it possible for many people in the United States to afford the new inventions that made life easier. Appliances such as vacuum cleaners, washing machines, and refrigerators brought convenience, or comfort and ease, to many households.

Advertising now took on a larger role in helping consumers decide what items to buy. **Advertising** is information that a business provides about a product or service to make people want to buy it. Advertising began to change in the 1920s. Earlier advertisements had usually just given facts about a product. An early ad for an automobile might have discussed the automobile's strong engine or its good brakes. In the 1920s an ad for an automobile often said little or nothing about how well the car was made. Instead, it described how a driver would feel driving such an automobile.

Inventions that saved time—along with the newly won right to vote—changed life for the nation's women. With the 1920s came a new

Her habit of measuring time in terms of dollars gives the woman in business keen insight into the true value of a Ford closed car for her personal use. This car enables her to conserve minutes, to expedite her affairs, to widen the scope of her activities. Its low first cost, long life and inexpensive operation and upkeep convince her that it is a sound investment value. And it is such a pleasant car to drive that it transforms the business call which might be an interruption into an enjoyable episode of her busy day.

TUDOR SEDAN, $590   FORDOR SEDAN, $685   COUPE, $575   (All prices f. o. b. Detroit)

Ford
CLOSED CARS

This ad explained some of the ways a Ford could make life easier for businesspeople.

Analyze Graphs   As automobile sales increased during the 1920s, so did traffic (above).

❖ About how many automobiles were sold in 1929?

Automobile Sales, 1920–1929

Year	
1920	🚗🚗🚗🚗
1921	🚗🚗🚗
1922	🚗🚗🚗🚗🚗
1923	🚗🚗🚗🚗🚗🚗🚗
1924	🚗🚗🚗🚗🚗🚗
1925	🚗🚗🚗🚗🚗🚗🚗
1926	🚗🚗🚗🚗🚗🚗🚗
1927	🚗🚗🚗🚗🚗🚗
1928	🚗🚗🚗🚗🚗🚗🚗
1929	🚗🚗🚗🚗🚗🚗🚗🚗🚗

🚗 = 500,000 automobiles

sense of independence for women. Many decided to work outside the home.

REVIEW How did advertising change during the 1920s?

A Land of Automobiles

In the 1920s automobile sales continued to grow. By 1930 there were more than 26 million automobiles on the roads in the United States. That meant that about one out of every five Americans owned an automobile.

As automobile sales boomed, so did the building of roads. In 1915 less than $300 million was spent to build roads. Just 10 years later more than $1 billion was spent to build roads. About a billion dollars was spent every year for the next five years.

The popularity of automobiles also helped automobile-related industries grow. Steel sales doubled in the 20 years after Henry Ford created the Model T. During the same 20-year period, the making of rubber became a huge industry because rubber is used to make tires.

In addition, automobiles caused new businesses to spring up. The first service stations were built around 1913. Car owners could buy gasoline and get their automobiles fixed at these stations.

By 1929 more than 121,000 service stations all across the country were open for business.

The industry of transporting goods by truck also developed at this time. More than 3 million trucks were on the roads by 1929, and taxis and buses soon became common on city streets.

REVIEW What businesses grew because of the automobile?

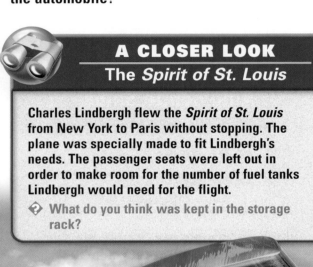

A CLOSER LOOK
The *Spirit of St. Louis*

Charles Lindbergh flew the *Spirit of St. Louis* from New York to Paris without stopping. The plane was specially made to fit Lindbergh's needs. The passenger seats were left out in order to make room for the number of fuel tanks Lindbergh would need for the flight.

◆ What do you think was kept in the storage rack?

Aviation Grows

The development of the airplane was important during World War I. Interest in planes continued to grow after the war ended. Charles Lindbergh had much to do with the growing popularity of planes. Lindbergh worked delivering mail by plane between the cities of St. Louis and Chicago. He predicted that "in a few years the United States will be covered with a network of passenger, mail and express lines."

In 1927 Lindbergh decided to try something that had never been done before. He would try to fly from New York to Paris, France, alone and without making any stops. If he succeeded, he would get a $25,000 prize at the end of the trip. The prize money had been offered eight years earlier by a New York hotel owner. For the trip, Lindbergh would fly a newly built airplane that he named the *Spirit of St. Louis*. Its name honored a group of

Periscope

Engine

Storage Rack

Compass

Fuel Tanks

NX-211

Spirit of St. Louis

Raft

NYP

Food

St. Louis businesspeople who had helped pay for the plane.

On May 20, 1927, early in the morning, Lindbergh and the *Spirit of St. Louis* took off from an airfield near New York City. After flying more than 3,600 miles (5,790 km) in more than 30 hours without stopping, Lindbergh landed safely at a Paris airfield. Thousands of people swarmed the runway when he landed. They had all come to witness this historic moment. He stepped out of his plane and said only these four words: "I am Charles Lindbergh." The crowd cheered loudly.

Millions of people cheered Lindbergh's achievement. Lindbergh became an instant hero to many. His flight also helped convince the world that airplane travel could become important. Soon, aviation became an important commercial industry. A **commercial industry** is an industry that is run to make a profit. Between 1926 and 1930 the number of people traveling by plane each year grew from about 6,000 to about 400,000. By 1935 there were four major airlines making regular flights in the United States.

Amelia Earhart also helped boost people's interest in aviation. In 1932 she became the first woman to fly alone across the Atlantic. Earhart successfully flew from Newfoundland, in Canada, to Ireland, where she landed in a pasture.

Charles Lindbergh (right and on button above) flew from New York to Paris. This map (below) shows the route he traveled.

Amelia Earhart was the first woman to fly alone across the Atlantic Ocean.

When a farmer approached her plane, Earhart said, "I've come from America." The farmer asked, "But who was with you? Who flew the plane?" He could not believe that a woman had piloted a plane across the Atlantic Ocean by herself. At that time very few women were pilots.

Earhart's fame grew even more when, in 1937, she decided to try to fly around the world. She and her navigator, Frederick Noonan, completed about 20,000 miles (32,200 km) of the trip. On July 1, they flew out of New Guinea (GIH•nee), near

This newspaper announces the disappearance of Amelia Earhart.

Australia, to continue their trip. The next day a United States ship picked up a weak radio signal from Earhart. She said she had run into trouble—her fuel tanks were empty. Then radio contact stopped. Earhart and Noonan were never heard from or seen again. A large search turned up no sign of Earhart, her navigator, or her plane. To this day, no one is certain what happened.

REVIEW Why did Charles Lindbergh call his plane the *Spirit of St. Louis*?

St Louis business people who help him pay for the plane.

Changing Cities

While big changes were happening in the way people traveled, life in the nation's cities was also changing. In 1920, for the first time, the United States census found that more people lived in **urban**, or city, areas than in **rural**, or country, areas.

As cities grew, their skylines changed. One reason for this change was the construction of more and more skyscrapers. Buildings that were called skyscrapers had been built before the war. Chicago, for example, had several 10-story buildings. After the war, skyscrapers started to live up to their name. Many more people and businesses were moving into the cities, and the price of urban land was rising. Builders began to build higher and higher to make the most of the

Place **Many people lived in cities in the 1920s.**

❖ **Which cities shown had the largest populations?**

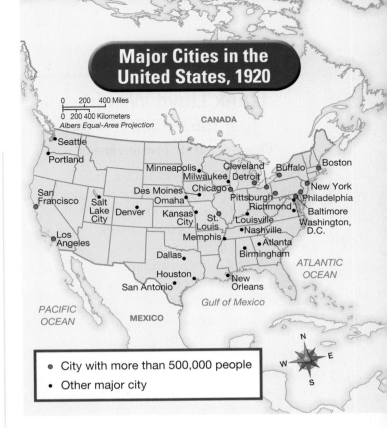

Major Cities in the United States, 1920

0   200   400 Miles
0 200 400 Kilometers
Albers Equal-Area Projection

CANADA

Seattle
Portland
Minneapolis
Milwaukee
Cleveland
Detroit
Buffalo
Boston
San Francisco
Salt Lake City
Denver
Des Moines
Omaha
Chicago
Pittsburgh
Richmond
New York
Philadelphia
Baltimore
Washington, D.C.
Los Angeles
Kansas City
St. Louis
Louisville
Nashville
Memphis
Atlanta
Dallas
Birmingham
ATLANTIC OCEAN
Houston
San Antonio
New Orleans
Gulf of Mexico
PACIFIC OCEAN
MEXICO

N E W S

● City with more than 500,000 people
● Other major city

land they had. In the 1920s three new skyscrapers that reached heights of 40 stories or more were built in Chicago!

Cities also grew outward. Automobiles allowed people to travel longer distances in shorter amounts of time. Therefore, people who worked in urban areas could move away from the cities and into the surrounding suburbs. A **suburb** is a community or neighborhood that lies outside a city. People who lived in the suburbs used their automobiles to **commute**, or travel back and forth, to work.

Architects, or people who design buildings, changed how cities and suburbs looked during the 1920s. For example, architect Frank Lloyd Wright designed everything from single-family houses to a mile-high skyscraper that was

never built. Wright designed many of his buildings to blend the outdoors with the indoors. The Wright style became known as the prairie style. Other architects developed a new style called art deco.

People who lived in the suburbs often commuted to cities to work.

Frank Lloyd Wright
1867–1959

Character Trait: Inventiveness

During the 1700s and 1800s, most architects in the nation designed buildings that followed European styles. Starting in the early 1900s, Frank Lloyd Wright helped create a new kind of American architecture. Wright's most famous early buildings were long, horizontal structures. This type of design came to be known as prairie style architecture, because it was inspired by the wide, open spaces of the Midwest. After the age of 70, Wright designed many of his best-known buildings, such as the Guggenheim Museum in New York City, shown here.

MULTIMEDIA BIOGRAPHIES
Visit The Learning Site at
www.harcourtschool.com/biographies
to learn about other famous people.

GO ONLINE

Art deco buildings often had bold outlines and used geometric shapes. Pottery, furniture, clothing, and other items of the 1920s also showed an art deco influence.

REVIEW How did automobiles encourage the growth of suburbs?

Prohibition

The 1920s are sometimes known as the Prohibition Era. In 1919, soon after the war ended, the Eighteenth Amendment was added to the Constitution of the United States. It made the production, sale, and transportation of alcoholic beverages against the law. Making these activities illegal was called Prohibition.

The purpose of the amendment was to stop people from drinking alcoholic beverages.

The ratification of the amendment seemed to make sense at the time. After all, many people had stopped drinking alcoholic beverages during the war so that the grain used to make them could be used to feed the troops. By the time the amendment was sent to the states for their approval, 19 states already had laws that banned the sale of alcoholic beverages.

After the war, however, the attitudes of many people began to change. They no longer wanted to sacrifice as they had during the war. Some citizens regularly broke the law by drinking alcoholic beverages in secret bars known as speakeasies. The people who supplied the speakeasies with alcoholic beverages were called bootleggers.

This illegal activity led to a rise in organized crime conducted by groups called gangs. These gangs grew as the demand for alcoholic beverages grew, because a lot of money could be made.

One of the most famous gangsters, or gang members, of the Prohibition Era was Al Capone. Capone and his gang worked, against the law, to supply people with alcoholic beverages.

Some people showed their support for Prohibition by wearing miniature hatchets (right). Hatchets were used to break open barrels of alcoholic beverages so that they could be emptied (far right).

Capone and other gangsters also broke other laws. Gangsters often threatened, harmed, and even killed people who got in their way.

The Eighteenth Amendment was different from earlier amendments. Most earlier amendments had to do with protecting the rights of the nation's people. The Eighteenth Amendment took away a right that people had held since the nation began. In addition, this amendment became the first amendment to be repealed. It was repealed by the Twenty-first Amendment, which was ratified in 1933. The drinking of alcoholic beverages was again legal.

REVIEW What amendment brought Prohibition to the United States? 18

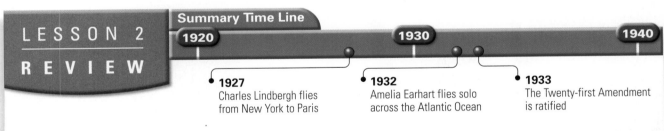

LESSON 2 REVIEW

Summary Time Line

1920 — 1930 — 1940

1927 Charles Lindbergh flies from New York to Paris

1932 Amelia Earhart flies solo across the Atlantic Ocean

1933 The Twenty-first Amendment is ratified

1. **MAIN IDEA** How did the automobile affect where some people chose to live in the 1920s?

2. **WHY IT MATTERS** How does advertising affect what people buy today?

3. **VOCABULARY** Use the term **commercial industry** in a sentence about Charles Lindbergh's contributions to aviation.

4. **TIME LINE** Who first flew across the Atlantic Ocean—Charles Lindbergh or Amelia Earhart?

5. **READING SKILL—Compare and Contrast** How were urban and suburban areas different?

6. **CIVICS AND GOVERNMENT** What amendment repealed the Prohibition amendment?

7. **ECONOMICS** How did the amount of money spent to build new roads change over time?

8. **CRITICAL THINKING—Analyze** Why do you think well-known pilots such as Amelia Earhart helped people become interested in aviation?

PERFORMANCE—Write an Advertisement Choose one of the goods that changed life at home during the 1920s. Then write an advertisement that would make consumers want to buy the product. Use both pictures and words. Show your finished advertisement to the class.

EXAMINE
PRIMARY SOURCES

Advertisements

During the 1920's Atwater Kent, like other makers of consumer products, spent millions of dollars on advertisements. Most advertisements were heard on the radio or seen in newspapers and the popular magazines of the day. Atwater Kent stopped making radios in 1936.

 FROM THE ATWATER KENT MUSEUM IN PHILADELPHIA, PENNSYLVANIA

Advertisements often showed products in glamorous settings.

The horn-shaped radio speaker and the receiver (bottom) were sold separately.

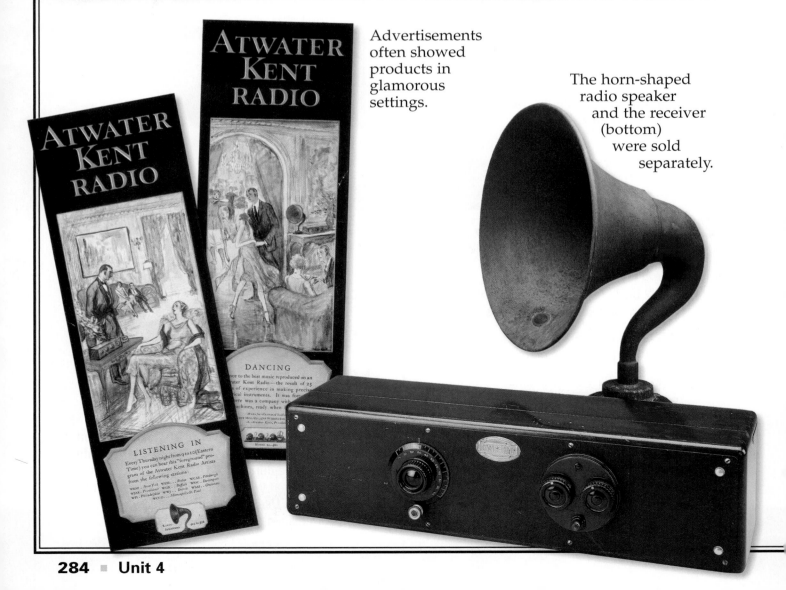

The Receiving Set illustrated is Atwater Kent Model 30, $85. (Including battery cable.) Radio Speaker is Model H, $21.

Prices slightly higher west of the Rockies and in Canada.

Read the headlines of the air - and choose whatever you like best

JUST AS YOU scan newspaper headlines and select what you want to read, so with this ONE DIAL receiver, you sample the radio programs and select what you want to hear.

In a few seconds you can cover all that's on the air within range—and then you can settle down to the program you prefer.

Think of it! No hunting—no juggling—no delay. Merely turn ONE DIAL with the finger tips of one hand, and listen. Whatever is on the air and within range the ONE DIAL summons instantly—you can't miss!

Quick, sure and reliable in operation, powerful in performance, charming in appearance, compact in size, sensible in price. That's Atwater Kent Radio with ONE DIAL.

Any Atwater Kent dealer will let you try it with an Atwater Kent Radio Speaker. And you'll be glad you asked him to.

Every Sunday Evening
—The Atwater Kent Radio Artists bring you their summer program at 9:15 Eastern Daylight Time, 8:15 Central Daylight Time, through:

WEAF . . . New York		WCCO . . .	{ Mpls. St. Paul
WEEI . . . . Boston			
WSAI . . . Cincinnati		WGN . . . . Chicago	
WCAP . . Washington		WGR . . . . Buffalo	
KSD . . . St. Louis		WWJ . . . . Detroit	

Write for illustrated booklet telling the complete story of Atwater Kent Radio.

ATWATER KENT MANUFACTURING COMPANY, A. Atwater Kent, President, 4701 WISSAHICKON AVENUE, PHILADELPHIA, PA.

This is the kind of advertisement that Atwater Kent published during the 1920s. This particular ad appeared in the September 1926 *The Ladies' Home Journal.*

Analyze the Primary Source

1. **What is the most important information the advertiser wanted readers to know about Atwater Kent radios?**

2. **Where could a reader get more information about Atwater Kent radios?**

3. **In which cities could listeners hear the Atwater Kent Radio Artists?**

ACTIVITY

Compare and Contrast Gather a variety of advertisements from current magazines. What do they have in common with the advertisements shown from the 1920s? How are they different?

RESEARCH

Visit The Learning Site at **www.harcourtschool.com/ primarysources** to research other primary sources.

MAIN IDEA
Read to learn how the spirit of the 1920s affected the arts in the United States.

WHY IT MATTERS
Many of the Roaring Twenties influences on arts and entertainment can still be seen.

VOCABULARY
jazz
renaissance

Entertainment and the Arts

1920 — 1930

During the Roaring Twenties nearly every part of life in the United States changed, including the arts. Radio and the movies made the arts available to more of the nation's people than ever before.

Popular Entertainment

Until the 1920s, radios were used as wireless telephones. They enabled people to speak to one another over long distances. People such as David Sarnoff, a radio operator, soon saw other uses for radio. His plan was to broadcast music to the radios in people's homes. Businesspeople in other parts of the country also saw the benefits of broadcasting news and entertainment into people's homes.

Many people say that the very first broadcast by a radio station was done on November 2, 1920. From the top of an office building in Pittsburgh, Pennsylvania, two announcers for the radio station KDKA broadcast the results of the presidential election. Warren G. Harding had won against James M. Cox. Radio soon became very popular. By the end of the 1920s, more than 600 stations had joined KDKA on the air, and more than

These actors are performing one of the many radio shows that were broadcast in the 1920s.

13 million people in the United States owned radios.

With radios, people could listen to music and news. Radios also brought sporting events from around the country into people's homes. Millions listened as boxing matches, baseball games, tennis matches, and golf tournaments were broadcast over the radio. They heard such history-making events as the moment Gene Tunney won a 10-round boxing match against Jack Dempsey. They listened while slugger George Herman "Babe" Ruth hit his sixtieth home run in 1927.

Listening to sports on the radio helped encourage people to go to sporting events. Attendance at football games, basketball games, and other competitions went up during the 1920s. Listening to sports also encouraged people to play sports themselves. Tennis and golf were just two of the sports that gained popularity in the 1920s.

Like radio, the movies began before the 1920s. But early movies were silent. It was during the 1920s that movies got sound. *The Jazz Singer,* shown in 1927, was

People flocked to baseball games to see players like "Babe" Ruth (left). They also enjoyed watching movies like *Wings* (above left) and *The Kid* (above).

the first movie with voices. Within three years, millions of people were going to "talkies," or movies with sound, each week.

Both radio and the movies brought a common culture to the people of the United States. For the first time, people from Maine to California could hear the same music and the same shows on the radio. Americans could also learn what life was like in other parts of the United States.

REVIEW What new kinds of entertainment were popular in the 1920s? Radio sport movies-talkies

Georgia O'Keeffe   1887–1986

Character Trait: Inventiveness

Georgia O'Keeffe was a painter who drew inspiration for her artwork from the different places where she lived. Born on a farm near Sun Prairie, Wisconsin, she lived there until 1902. She then moved with her family to Williamsburg, Virginia. She went to college in Chicago and later moved to New York City. During the 1920s she painted many city scenes of tall buildings and crowds. After spending some time in New Mexico, O'Keeffe began painting scenes that reflected the landscape of the south-western United States. Many of her paintings show images of animal bones, flowers, and deserts. Eventually, O'Keeffe moved to New Mexico, where she continued to paint.

MULTIMEDIA BIOGRAPHIES
Visit The Learning Site at
www.harcourtschool.com/biographies
to learn about other famous people.

GO ONLINE

Changes in the Arts

New styles of writing also developed in the 1920s. For example, Ernest Hemingway became famous for his plain but vivid writing style. Other writers, such as F. Scott Fitzgerald and Sinclair Lewis, wrote about society's problems.

Artists, too, were producing art that told about the 1920s. Georgia O'Keeffe, Edward Hopper, Charles Burchfield, and others often painted realistic pictures of everyday scenes and of exciting events of the time.

Jazz was the music of the 1920s. **Jazz** was deeply influenced by the traditional music of West Africa as well as by ragtime, spirituals, and blues music sung by African Americans such as Bessie Smith. Yet jazz was something more than just the combination of other forms of music. Some believe jazz started in clubs on the south side of Chicago. Others think it began in New Orleans with the music that African Americans played during funeral marches.

Louis Armstrong and Jelly Roll Morton were two of jazz's earliest performers.

A Georgia O'Keeffe painting of the desert in New Mexico

Jazz

Jazz was the first truly American form of music. It began in the South and the Midwest in the early 1900s and can now be heard around the world. What makes jazz unique is improvised playing—playing in which musicians create different melodies as they play. During the 1900s jazz developed many styles, including swing, bebop, and fusion. It also influenced rock and roll and other kinds of popular music. Today jazz continues to change and to surprise its listeners. As saxophone player John Coltrane said, "There are always new sounds to imagine; new feelings to get at."

Duke Ellington and his band

Their music and the music of other jazz artists were well liked by both black and white Americans. Jazz was so popular that the 1920s are sometimes referred to as the Jazz Age.

George Gershwin was one of the decade's most popular composers, or music writers. Gershwin, too, liked jazz. Although Gershwin did not write jazz music, his music was influenced by jazz. Gershwin became famous for songs like "Someone to Watch Over Me" and for long musical pieces like *Rhapsody in Blue*.

Other composers of the time were also influenced by the sounds and rhythms of jazz. Aaron Copland, a composer known for his modern style, used jazz in his *Music for the Theater* and *Piano Concerto*.

In addition to listening to new music, people tried new dances. In earlier times, many people had

A flapper

enjoyed ballroom dances. Now the "flappers," as stylish women of the time were called, danced the Charleston with their dates. The Charleston had fast movements and high kicks. People also flocked to theaters to see plays. Musical comedies, such as those written by George M. Cohan, were very popular. Cohan wrote the words and music for 20 musicals. He starred in them as well.

REVIEW Why are the 1920s also known as the Jazz Age?

Harlem Renaissance

During the Roaring Twenties, a neighborhood called Harlem, in northern Manhattan in New York City, became a center for African American writers, musicians, and artists. So many artists lived and worked in Harlem during the 1920s that this period has yet another nickname—the Harlem Renaissance (REH•nuh•sahns).

A **renaissance** is a time of great interest and activity in the arts. *Renaissance* is French for "rebirth."

Many people went to Harlem clubs to see performances by singers like Billie Holiday and Ethel Waters, dancers like Bill "Bojangles" Robinson, and band leaders like Duke Ellington. Many others read the works of writers such as Countee Cullen, Claude McKay, and Zora Neale Hurston.

Langston Hughes was another popular Harlem writer. Like other writers of the Harlem Renaissance, Hughes often wrote about what it was like to be African American in the United States.

REVIEW **What was the Harlem Renaissance?**

Zora Neale Hurston (left) and Langston Hughes (above) were popular writers of the Harlem Renaissance.

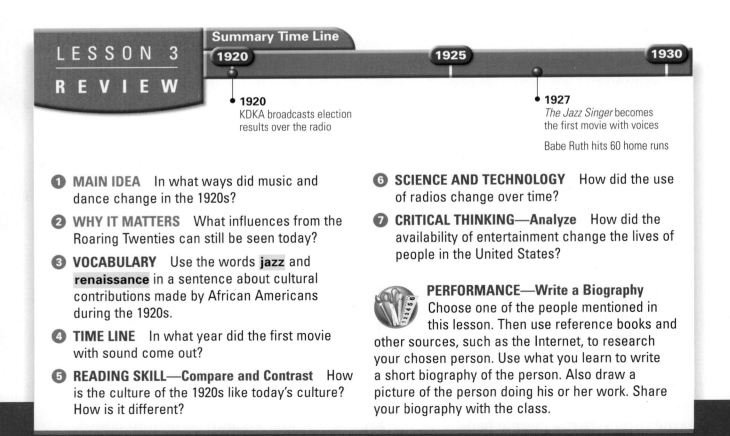

LESSON 3
REVIEW

Summary Time Line

1920 — 1925 — 1930

1920
KDKA broadcasts election results over the radio

1927
The Jazz Singer becomes the first movie with voices

Babe Ruth hits 60 home runs

1 **MAIN IDEA** In what ways did music and dance change in the 1920s?

2 **WHY IT MATTERS** What influences from the Roaring Twenties can still be seen today?

3 **VOCABULARY** Use the words **jazz** and **renaissance** in a sentence about cultural contributions made by African Americans during the 1920s.

4 **TIME LINE** In what year did the first movie with sound come out?

5 **READING SKILL—Compare and Contrast** How is the culture of the 1920s like today's culture? How is it different?

6 **SCIENCE AND TECHNOLOGY** How did the use of radios change over time?

7 **CRITICAL THINKING—Analyze** How did the availability of entertainment change the lives of people in the United States?

PERFORMANCE—Write a Biography
Choose one of the people mentioned in this lesson. Then use reference books and other sources, such as the Internet, to research your chosen person. Use what you learn to write a short biography of the person. Also draw a picture of the person doing his or her work. Share your biography with the class.

Tell Fact from Opinion

VOCABULARY

fact
opinion

▶ WHY IT MATTERS

Every day new information is presented to you. It is important to know whether to believe what you read. One way to decide is to find out whether the information contains facts or opinions. A **fact** is information that can be checked and proved true. An **opinion** is what a person thinks or believes. An opinion cannot be proved. Knowing how to tell a fact from an opinion can help you better understand what you hear or read.

▶ WHAT YOU NEED TO KNOW

Here is a statement from the lesson you just read: "*The Jazz Singer*, shown in 1927, was the first movie with voices." To tell whether this statement is a fact, ask yourself these questions: *Do I know from a reliable source that this idea is true? Can the idea be proved true by testing?*

Word clues can also help you decide whether a statement presents a fact or an opinion. For example, opinion statements often include phrases like *I think, I feel,* and *in my opinion.* In addition, watch

for words like *best, worst, wonderful,* or *terrible.* These words also signal that a statement is an opinion, not a fact.

Even though opinions cannot be proved, they can still be helpful. Historians, for example, use facts to help them form opinions about the past. Thoughtful opinions can help people understand the past or prepare for the future.

▶ PRACTICE THE SKILL

Read the following statements. Decide whether each statement is a fact or an opinion. Use the questions and clues listed on this page.

1 By the end of the 1920s, more than 13 million Americans owned radios.

2 Gene Tunney was the greatest boxer who ever lived.

3 The Charleston was a popular dance of the 1920s.

▶ APPLY WHAT YOU LEARNED

Many people rely on newspapers for information. Look at a recent newspaper. Underline three facts and circle three opinions that you read there. Explain to classmates how you were able to tell the facts from the opinions.

This couple is dancing the Charleston.

7 Review and Test Preparation

1920
First radio
station
broadcast

USE YOUR READING SKILLS

Complete this graphic organizer to compare and contrast radio and the movies in the 1920s. A copy of this graphic organizer appears on page 73 of the Activity Book.

Radio and the Movies in the 1920s

RADIO

MOVIES

DIFFERENCES

DIFFERENCES

SIMILARITIES

Both radio and movies brought a common culture to the people of the United States.

1._____

2._____

3._____

1._____

2._____

3._____

THINK & WRITE

Write a Short Story Imagine that you are living in the 1920s. Write a short story about your family getting its first automobile. In your story describe what it is like to ride in a car for the first time. Also tell how the car has changed your family's life.

Write a Poem Write a poem about what you think life was like in the United States during the 1920s. Your poem can be about some of the important people, places, and events you learned about in your reading.

1930 ——————————————————————————— 1940

1927
Charles Lindbergh flies across the Atlantic

1930
More than 26 million automobiles in the United States

1932
Amelia Earhart flies across the Atlantic

1933
The Twenty-First Amendment is ratified

USE THE TIME LINE

Use the chapter summary time line to answer these questions.

1 When was the first radio station broadcast? *1920*

2 How many years after Charles Lindbergh's flight did Amelia Earhart fly across the Atlantic?

USE VOCABULARY

Use each of the following terms in a sentence that will help explain its meaning.

interest (p. 270)

advertising (p. 276)

suburb (p. 281)

commute (p. 281)

jazz (p. 288)

RECALL FACTS

Answer these questions.

3 What helped keep American products affordable to Americans after World War I? *Tariff*

4 Which state had a land boom in the mid-1920s? *Florida*

5 How did advertising change in the 1920s?

Write the letter of the best choice.

6 **TEST PREP**   Which test did immigrants in the early 1900s have to take before they could enter the United States?
A math test
B literacy test
C history test
D lie-detector test

7 **TEST PREP**   During prohibition, it was against the law to—
F drive cars.
G listen to music.
H buy alcoholic beverages.
J sell products to foreign nations.

THINK CRITICALLY

8 How did the popularity of automobiles change American life in the 1920s?

9 Why do you think new styles in writing, art, and music developed during the 1920s?

APPLY SKILLS

Use a Land Use and Resource Map
Use the map on page 275 to answer these questions.

MAP AND GLOBE SKILLS

10 Which natural resources are represented on the map on page 275?

11 How was most of the land in the United States used in the 1920s?

Tell Fact from Opinion
Use the information on page 291 to decide whether each statement is fact or opinion.

READING SKILLS

12 The 1920s was the most exciting decade in American history. *O*

13 In the 1920s many people invested their money in the stock market. *F*

14 The Ku Klux Klan is a secret organization. *F*

15 By 1930 about one in every five Americans had a car. *F*

16 Amelia Earhart was not as good a pilot as Charles Lindbergh was. *O*

Chapter 7 ■ 293

EMPIRE STATE BUILDING

The construction of the Empire State Building began in 1930, during the Great Depression. Upon its completion 11 months later, the Empire State Building was the tallest building in the world. It remained so until 1972. Today millions of people each year journey up to the Observatory on the 86th floor to see a view of New York City.

LOCATE IT

NEW YORK

New York City

The Great Depression and the New Deal

" With the slow menace of a glacier, depression came on. No one had any measure of its progress; no one had any plan for stopping it. Everyone tried to get out of its way. "

—Frances Perkins, *People at Work*, 1934

CHAPTER READING SKILL

Generalize

When you **generalize**, you make a broad statement. Words such as *many, some,* and *most* usually signal a generalization.

As you read, use facts and details from each lesson to write generalizations.

 → → GENERALIZATION

FACT → FACT → GENERALIZATION

MAIN IDEA
Read to learn how the good times of the Roaring Twenties came to an end when the stock market crashed in 1929.

WHY IT MATTERS
Understanding the causes of economic problems can help the United States prevent them from happening again.

VOCABULARY
investor

President Hoover hoped the economy of the United States would stay strong.

The Good Times End

1920	1930	1940

1925–1930

Many people in the United States thought that the good times of the 1920s would never end. President Herbert Hoover, who was elected in 1928, shared that hope. He boasted about the nation's economic strength. "We are nearer today to the ideal of the abolition [ending] of poverty and fear from the lives of men and women than ever before in any land," he said. He did not know that the good times of the 1920s would soon come to an end.

The Economy Weakens

The economic problems that started in the late 1920s surprised many people. Yet there had been signs that the economy was weakening. The nation's wealth was growing, but most of that wealth was going to just a few people in the United States. This meant that a few Americans had a lot of control over the economy. If those few decided to stop spending money, it could mean financial trouble for the whole country. It also meant that some people were still poor.

By the end of the 1920s, many consumers already had washing machines, vacuum cleaners, and radios. Those who had bought these goods on installment plans continued to pay them off. However, they were not buying many new goods. As a result, consumer spending slowed. Suddenly, companies found that they had too many goods that they could not sell.

FAST FACT In 1929, over 1 1/2 million Americans had put part or all of their savings in the stock market.

As the nation's economy weakened, more and more companies laid off some of their workers. These unemployed workers hoped to get jobs with the city of New York.

Many companies soon cut workers' hours and wages. Some companies began to lay off workers. Other companies closed.

For farmers, too, the 1920s were very difficult years. At the beginning of the 1920s, prices for farm products dropped sharply, and they were still low at the end of the 1920s. Many farmers did not have enough money to make the payments for their land. They were forced to give up their farms. The country's economy was weakening.

REVIEW **Why did some companies begin to lay off workers?** They had too many goods that they could not sell

The Stock Market Crashes

While some people faced hardships, others expected to become rich by putting their money into the stock market. The stock market is a place where people can buy and sell stocks, or shares in businesses. People began to buy stocks at high prices, guessing that the stock would soon be worth more than they paid for it. They hoped others would be willing to buy it later at a higher price. If so, the seller would make money. The prices on most stocks kept going higher. Some people began to borrow money to buy stocks.

Beginning in the fall of 1929, stock prices began to drop. Some investors began to sell their stocks before the prices dropped any further. An **investor** is someone who uses money to buy or make something that will make more money. Other people then began to sell their stocks. Suddenly, there were many people selling stocks but very few buyers. That caused stock prices to drop sharply. Soon panicked stockholders hurried to sell their stocks.

Then, on Thursday, October 24, people began selling their stocks at a very fast rate. Stocks were selling so fast and prices were dropping so quickly that the ticker— the machine whose ticker tape tells the prices of stock—ran an hour behind, then two hours, and then three and four.

That same day, a group of wealthy bankers tried to stop stock prices from dropping any lower. They bought up large amounts of stocks in several important companies, such as United States Steel. Despite their efforts, almost 13 million shares of stock were sold on October 24 and stock prices continued to drop.

Stockholders continued to sell their stocks. For the next few days the prices did not drop as much as they had on Black Thursday, as October 24 came to be known. But on Monday, prices dropped again. Tuesday, October 29, was the worst of all. About 16 million shares were sold that day. Still prices continued to drop. Some stocks were worth just a small part of what they had cost. Other stocks were worth nothing at all. The stock market had "crashed."

The crash of the stock market hurt not only stockholders but also other people. For example, Solomon Hancox worked in the flooring business in New York City. He had an order to make all the floors in a skyscraper that was going to be built. He went to a bank and took out a loan. With the loan money, he bought the materials he would need to make the floors.

Then the stock market crashed. The people who had hired Hancox lost their money and could not build the skyscraper. Hancox found himself with a lot of unused building materials and a loan he could not pay back.

After the stock market crash, many people needed to spend their savings in order to live. As is true today, banks did not just keep the money locked away. Instead, they loaned people's money to

On the day of the stock market crash, people gathered on New York City's Wall Street (left) where stocks are traded. Nearly everyone who owned stocks lost money (below).

After the stock market crash, some people without jobs sold apples for money (above). Others sold their belongings (right).

businesses so the businesses could grow. They loaned the money to people so they could buy houses and other goods. Before the stock market crash, many people had borrowed money to buy stocks. When the market crashed, they could not pay back the money they owed. This also helped weaken the economy.

As the economy got worse, many people went to their banks to get their savings out. The banks, of course, did not have all the money on hand. When banks began to close, people with money in those banks lost all their savings.

REVIEW What happened to the stock market on October 29, 1929?

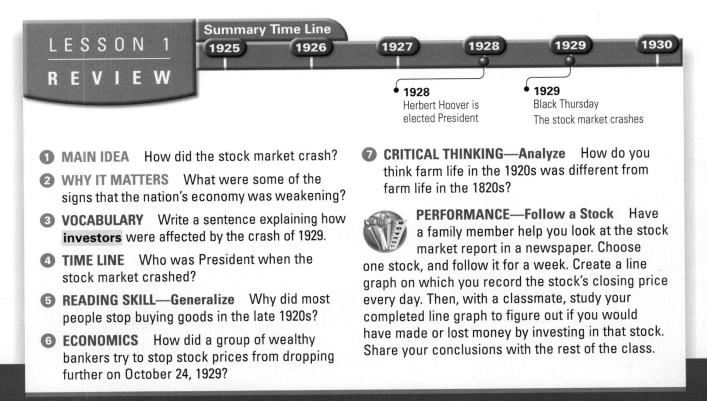

LESSON 1 REVIEW

Summary Time Line

1925   1926   1927   1928   1929   1930

1928
Herbert Hoover is elected President

1929
Black Thursday
The stock market crashes

1 **MAIN IDEA** How did the stock market crash?

2 **WHY IT MATTERS** What were some of the signs that the nation's economy was weakening?

3 **VOCABULARY** Write a sentence explaining how **investors** were affected by the crash of 1929.

4 **TIME LINE** Who was President when the stock market crashed?

5 **READING SKILL—Generalize** Why did most people stop buying goods in the late 1920s?

6 **ECONOMICS** How did a group of wealthy bankers try to stop stock prices from dropping further on October 24, 1929?

7 **CRITICAL THINKING—Analyze** How do you think farm life in the 1920s was different from farm life in the 1820s?

PERFORMANCE—Follow a Stock Have a family member help you look at the stock market report in a newspaper. Choose one stock, and follow it for a week. Create a line graph on which you record the stock's closing price every day. Then, with a classmate, study your completed line graph to figure out if you would have made or lost money by investing in that stock. Share your conclusions with the rest of the class.

2

MAIN IDEA
Read to learn about the hardships millions of people in the United States suffered during the Great Depression.

WHY IT MATTERS
Reading about the effects of the Great Depression helps us understand why the government takes steps to keep the nation's economy running smoothly.

VOCABULARY
depression
economist
unemployment
balanced budget

The Great Depression

1920   1930   1940

1925–1935

A **depression** is a time when industries do not grow and many people are out of work. Our nation has gone through several depressions. Many **economists**, or people who study the economy, believe that depressions are a natural part of an economic cycle of good times and hard times.

In 1929 another depression started. However, this depression was different from those in the past. By the time it ended, it had become deeper and lasted longer than any depression before it. It touched most of the world. That is why this time became known as the Great Depression.

Hard Times

In 1929, the year the stock market crashed, more than 22,000 businesses in the United States failed. Over the next ten years, thousands more businesses failed. Between 1929 and 1932, industrial production in the nation dropped by half.

Bank failures also continued in the country. In 1923 there were more than 30,000 banks across the nation. By 1933 only 14,700 banks were still in business.

During the Great Depression, **unemployment**—the number of workers without jobs—grew quickly. By 1932 so many businesses had closed that one in every four people in the United States was out of work. People who could not make their house payments lost their homes. In 1932 more than 248,000 people lost their homes. Another 250,000 lost their homes the following year. On top of that, many people were evicted, or put out of their apartments, for not paying their rent. This added thousands more to the number of people who now had no jobs, no money, and no homes.

Some homeless people stayed with family or friends. Others built their own homes using whatever they could find, such as tents, flattened tin cans, cardboard boxes, and even old automobiles. Whole towns of these homemade shelters grew in many of the nation's cities. These towns became known as shantytowns.

Food was also a big worry for many people. All over the country, hungry people lined up for free meals given by religious missions or local welfare groups. Sometimes lines stretched all the way around a block. One woman remembers a time her mother sent her to wait in line for free soup: "If you happened to be one of the first ones in line, you didn't get anything but the water on top. So we'd ask the guy that was putting the soup into the buckets . . . to please dip down to get some meat and potatoes from the bottom of the kettle. But he wouldn't do it."

Many people who had fallen on hard times were people who wanted to work.

This girl's family moved in search of work.

During the Great Depression many people lost their jobs and had little money. Many stood in long lines to receive free bread.

PIPE, VALVES, FITT
Offices 452 WATER
Phone ORCHARD 970

However, they could not find jobs. Many had worked hard all of their lives. The song "Brother, Can You Spare a Dime?" expressed what many of these people were going through:

> 66 Once I built a railroad, I made it run, made it race against time.

> Once I built a railroad, now it's done. Brother, can you spare a dime? 99

Farmers' troubles also continued to grow. Crop prices dropped so low that some farmers found it cheaper to burn grain than coal for heat.

REVIEW Why did so many people lose their homes during the Great Depression?

They could not make pymts

The President's Policies

President Hoover did not believe that giving government money directly to the nation's people was the answer to the depression. Hoover thought that it would hurt people's morale, or spirit. In addition, Hoover thought the government should keep a **balanced budget**. That is, he believed the government should not spend more money than it made. Hoover also thought that help should come first from the state and local levels of government and from individual Americans. Only after that should the national government give help. Because of these beliefs, he did not support giving out government aid to hungry citizens.

Even as the depression got worse, President Hoover kept telling people, "Prosperity is just around the corner." In 1930 he even said, "The depression is over." He may have spoken that way because he thought the economy was

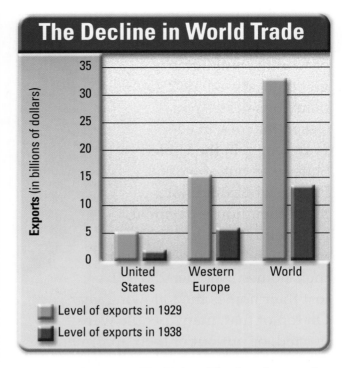

The Decline in World Trade

Exports (in billions of dollars)

Level of exports in 1929
Level of exports in 1938

Analyze Graphs The high tariffs placed on goods coming into the United States affected many of the nation's trading partners.

◆ About what was the worth of the goods exported from Western Europe in 1938?

getting stronger. He had once said, "ninety percent of our difficulty in depressions is caused by fear." However, his words did nothing to stop the hardships that so many people in the United States were facing.

In trying to protect the nation's businesses and help the economy, Hoover signed a new tariff act. It was called the Smoot-Hawley Tariff, after Utah Senator Reed Smoot and Oregon Congress Representative Willis Chatman Hawley. This law placed the highest tariff ever on goods coming into the country. Soon other countries also raised their tariffs and stopped buying goods made in the United States. In 1932, because of the tariffs on goods coming in and going out, United States imports and exports both dropped to below $1 billion for the first time in more than 20 years. The tariff hurt the economies of both the United States and Europe.

When Congress met in early 1932, its members knew that the economy was not improving. Something had to be done. President Hoover agreed that the economy needed help. However, he still thought that such help should go to businesses and not to individuals. Congress set up the Reconstruction Finance Corporation (RFC), which gave loans to banks, insurance companies, and railroads. The RFC helped some companies stay in business, but it did not help workers directly.

Congress also passed the Federal Home Loan Bank Act. This act started a number of new banks that offered loans to people trying to keep their homes. The act did help many people, but hundreds of thousands of others were still left with no place to live.

Despite his attempts at improving the economy, many people blamed President Hoover for the depression. Jackrabbits caught for dinner were called "Hoover hogs." Empty pockets turned inside out were called "Hoover flags." The newspapers with which people wrapped themselves to protect against the cold were called "Hoover blankets," and the shantytowns the homeless built became known as "Hoovervilles."

In 1932 a Hooverville appeared near Washington, D.C. It was made by as many as 15,000 to 20,000 World War I veterans. These veterans had been promised a bonus. This bonus was to be paid in 1945.

A large group of World War I veterans (below) gathered in Washington, D.C., to ask for their bonuses. Some (left) lived in shantytowns near the capital.

The veterans and their families had traveled to Washington, D.C., to ask for their bonuses early.

The government turned down the request of the Bonus Army, as this group of veterans came to be known. Most returned home. However, about 2,000 of the veterans with no homes stayed on in Washington, D.C.

President Hoover did not want the Bonus Army to stay in Washington. After veterans fought with the police, Hoover sent troops against the veterans and their families. General Douglas MacArthur, who had become a hero during World War I, now led soldiers against the veterans. Armed with tanks, tear gas, and machine guns, the soldiers drove out the Bonus Army and destroyed their shantytown. Both Hoover and MacArthur feared that these veterans were going to try to take over the government. But most people believed the veterans were just a group of homeless, hopeless people.

REVIEW In what ways did President Hoover and Congress try to improve the economy?

RFC
Loan Bank Act

Dust Bowl Region
Understanding Environment and Society

The Dust Bowl was the name given to a section of the southern Great Plains that suffered many bad droughts, or periods with little or no rain, through the 1930s. The Dust Bowl region was spread out over parts of Colorado, Kansas, Texas, Oklahoma, and New Mexico. The dust storms that developed in this area were known as "black blizzards" because the swirling dirt often blocked out the light of the sun. The storms forced thousands of farm families to leave their homes.

John Steinbeck, a writer from California, was concerned about the Dust Bowl families. In his novel *The Grapes of Wrath*, he told the story of the Joad family. His book describes the hardships the Joads faced as they traveled west from Oklahoma and after they reached California.

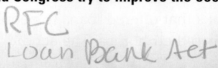

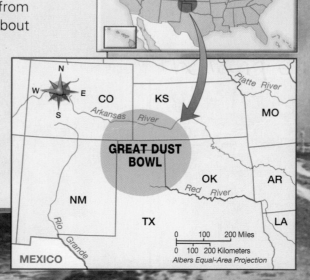

People on the Move

Farmers in the southern Great Plains were suffering, just as farmers all over the country were suffering. Then, just when these farmers thought their lives could not get any worse, the wind began to blow. It blew, on and off, year after year. As the wind howled across the land, it picked up the soil and blew it right off the farms. Because of these dry, dirt-filled winds, the southern Great Plains became known as the Dust Bowl.

One farmer listed the states that were part of this Dust Bowl when he described how the storms hit the Texas Panhandle, where he lived: "If the wind blew one way, here came the dark dust from Oklahoma. Another way and it was the gray dust from Kansas. Still another way, the brown dust from Colorado and New Mexico. Little farms were buried. And the towns were blackened." The states of Texas, Oklahoma, Kansas, Colorado, and New Mexico were parts of the Dust Bowl.

Dust covered everything. It smothered farm animals and clogged farm machinery. People slept with washcloths over their faces. Even then, when they woke, their mouths would be caked with dust.

Dust storms (below) turned day into night. To escape the Dust Bowl, many families (right) left their farms to start new lives in California.

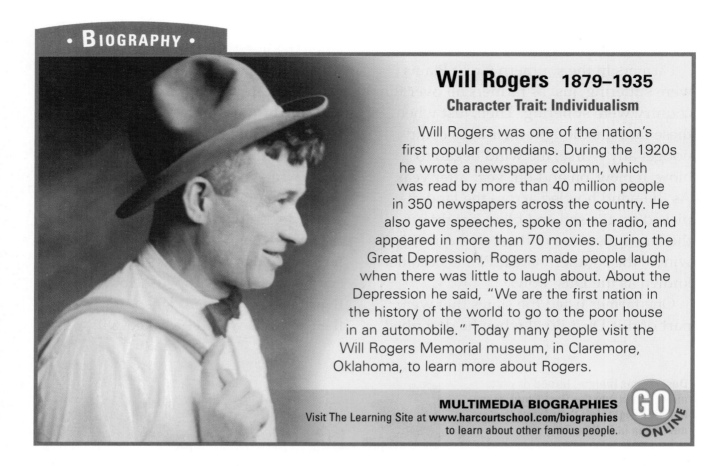

Will Rogers 1879–1935

Character Trait: Individualism

Will Rogers was one of the nation's first popular comedians. During the 1920s he wrote a newspaper column, which was read by more than 40 million people in 350 newspapers across the country. He also gave speeches, spoke on the radio, and appeared in more than 70 movies. During the Great Depression, Rogers made people laugh when there was little to laugh about. About the Depression he said, "We are the first nation in the history of the world to go to the poor house in an automobile." Today many people visit the Will Rogers Memorial museum, in Claremore, Oklahoma, to learn more about Rogers.

MULTIMEDIA BIOGRAPHIES
Visit The Learning Site at **www.harcourtschool.com/biographies**
to learn about other famous people.

GO ONLINE

Some people even died from breathing in the dust because the dust damaged their lungs.

No one could farm the land anymore, and thousands of farms went out of business. In Oklahoma, for example, almost half the farmers lost their farms during the 1930s. In some Dust Bowl states, almost one-third of the workers were out of work.

Thousands of people left the Dust Bowl states during the 1930s. Many of them headed to California, where they heard there were jobs. "All you could hear was 'Goin' to Californ-I-A! Goin' to Californ-I-A!'" remembered one Oklahoma man.

The families packed up everything that would fit into or onto their cars and headed west. Often they took odd jobs along the way to pay for gas, car repairs, or food. When travelers finally reached California, most did not find the work they hoped for. Instead, signs saying "No Jobs" greeted them at many California towns and farms. Instead of finding a better life, most Dust Bowl farmers found they had traded one place of hardships for another.

REVIEW Why did many people leave the Dust Bowl states during the 1930s? *no jobs the land could not be farm.*

Other Changes

Some people in the United States prospered during the Great Depression. Those who were able to keep their jobs found that as prices dropped, their money actually could buy more than it could before the Great Depression started. For just a few pennies, people could pay admission into one of the bright palaces built as movie theaters during the 1920s and 1930s. In 1933 five-year-old, curly-haired

Shirley Temple sang and tap-danced her way into many people's hearts in her first movie, *Stand Up and Cheer*. Walt Disney made the animated *Snow White and the Seven Dwarfs* in 1937. Just two years later both *The Wizard of Oz* and *Gone with the Wind* were released.

People also counted on their radios for entertainment. Across the nation people now looked forward to regularly scheduled shows. Radio shows offered everything from news to storytelling to big-band music.

Music played by big bands became more and more popular in the 1930s. Trumpets, saxophones, drums, and many other instruments were played together to make the sound that made the big bands famous. Many people enjoyed dancing to the music of the big bands.

REVIEW **Why did some people prosper during the 1930s?** *because as prices dropped, their money could buy more than b/f*

Thousands of people flocked to theaters to see movies starring Shirley Temple.

LESSON 2 REVIEW

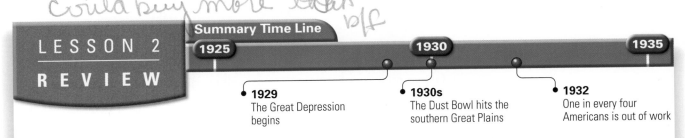

Summary Time Line

1925 — 1930 — 1935

1929
The Great Depression begins

1930s
The Dust Bowl hits the southern Great Plains

1932
One in every four Americans is out of work

1. **MAIN IDEA** What kinds of hardships did people suffer during the Great Depression?

2. **WHY IT MATTERS** In what ways did President Hoover and Congress try to improve the economy during the Great Depression?

3. **VOCABULARY** Write a sentence explaining how the **depression** caused **unemployment**.

4. **TIME LINE** How many years after the Great Depression began were one in every four Americans out of work?

5. **READING SKILL—Generalize** Why did many people face hardships in the 1930s?

6. **ECONOMICS** Why was the depression that started in 1929 known as the Great Depression?

7. **CRITICAL THINKING—Analyze** Did the Smoot-Hawley Tariff do what President Hoover hoped it would do? Why or why not?

PERFORMANCE—Draw a Picture Draw a picture illustrating one of the topics in this lesson. You might choose to illustrate an example of the hard times people experienced during the Great Depression, or you may wish to draw a picture of one of the kinds of entertainment people enjoyed during this time. Share your picture with the class.

MAIN IDEA

Read to learn how Franklin D. Roosevelt's New Deal helped put people in the United States back to work and eased the effects of the Great Depression.

WHY IT MATTERS

The government continues to provide programs to help the nation's people in times of need.

VOCABULARY

bureaucracy
pension
minimum wage
hydroelectric dam

Franklin D. Roosevelt and the New Deal

1930–1940

In 1932 United States citizens elected Franklin D. Roosevelt as President. Roosevelt believed that in order to end the Great Depression, the federal government needed to take bold, new action. On his inauguration day, he said, "This great nation will endure as it has endured, will revive, and will prosper. So, first of all, let me assert my firm belief that the only thing we have to fear is fear itself. . . ." Roosevelt's words gave people hope that the economy would improve.

The Promise of a New Deal

The term *New Deal* came from a statement that Franklin D. Roosevelt made when he was campaigning for the presidency. "I pledge you, I pledge myself, to a new deal for the American people," he promised. Roosevelt meant what he said about a

On his inauguration day, Franklin D. Roosevelt promised that the government would help end the Great Depression.

"new deal." In the first three months after Roosevelt's inauguration, Congress passed many of President Roosevelt's New Deal plans. During this time, which came to be known as the Hundred Days, more new laws were passed in the United States than at any other time since the founding of the nation.

One of President Roosevelt's first acts was designed to bring back people's faith in the nation's banks. He declared a four-day "bank holiday" during which all banks would close for four days. The government then used the Emergency Banking Act to check the records of all banks. Then it allowed only the strongest and most stable banks to open again.

In June Congress passed an act that created the Federal Deposit Insurance Corporation (FDIC). This organization put the strength of the federal government behind the nation's banks. It meant that an individual could place up to a certain amount of money in a bank, and the money would be insured by the federal government. If the bank lost the person's money, the federal government would pay him or her back.

President Roosevelt did not enact the New Deal by himself. He had the help of a group of advisers, and he also had help from members of Congress. These people helped Roosevelt create the programs. He also depended on a growing bureaucracy (byoo•RAH•kruh•see) to put his plan into action. A **bureaucracy** is the many workers and groups of people who are needed to run the government's programs.

REVIEW What was President Roosevelt's plan to end the Great Depression?

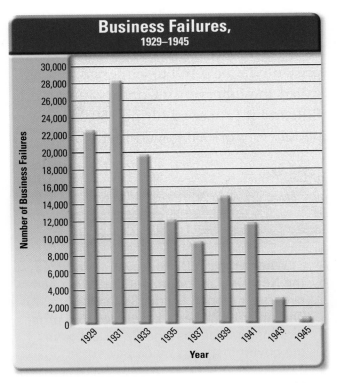

Analyze Graphs This graph shows the number of companies that went out of business from 1929 to 1945.

◆ About how many companies went out of business in 1931?

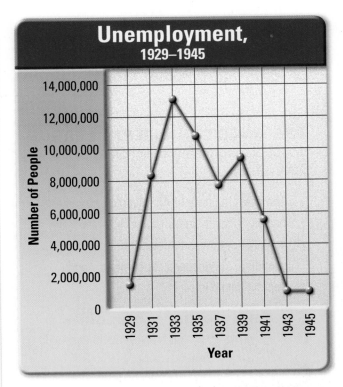

Analyze Graphs This graph shows the number of people who lost their jobs between 1929 and 1945.

◆ How did the number of unemployed people change over time?

Putting People Back to Work

On March 21, 1933, President Roosevelt presented a new bill to Congress. It was called the Emergency Conservation Work Bill, and it proposed hiring 250,000 people to work on government lands.

POINTS OF VIEW
The New Deal

When Franklin D. Roosevelt introduced the New Deal program, nothing like it had ever been tried in United States history. The American Liberty League was an organization that felt that the New Deal gave the government too much power.

FRANKLIN D. ROOSEVELT, speaking during the 1932 presidential campaign

66 The country needs . . . bold, persistent experimentation. It is common sense to take a method and try it: If it fails, admit it frankly and try another. But above all, try something. 99

THE AMERICAN LIBERTY LEAGUE, responding to the introduction of the New Deal

66 The great majority of American citizens believe in sanity in government . . . [and] are against . . . government waste, foolish spending, . . . unsound experiments, [and] impractical policies. 99

Analyze the Viewpoints

❶ What views about the New Deal did each side hold?

❷ **Make It Relevant** Look at the Letters to the Editor section of a newspaper. Find two letters that express different viewpoints about the same issue. Then write a paragraph summarizing the viewpoints of each letter.

One goal of this group, Roosevelt said, would be to work for "the prevention of forest fires, floods, and soil erosion" and for "plant, pest, and disease control." Congress voted to pass the bill, and on March 31, Roosevelt signed it into law. About two weeks later, the first Civilian Conservation Corps (CCC) camp opened in Virginia. Within three months, 250,000 new CCC employees were at work in more than 1,300 camps across the nation. In time, more than 3 million workers served in the CCC.

The workers who enrolled in the CCC had to meet certain requirements. As a rule, they had to be single, unemployed men between 17 and 23 years of age. Once chosen, each worker had to promise to send $22 or more of his $30-a-month salary to family members back home. This was not difficult for most workers, because the CCC paid for food, clothes,

A land surveyor works for the CCC to create one of Florida's state parks.

Analyze Primary Sources

Posters like these advertised some of the opportunities provided by Roosevelt's New Deal programs.

1. This poster is advertising an opportunity to see some of the paintings done by women who worked for the WPA.

2. This poster explains why people might enjoy working in the CCC.

? What other information is provided on these posters?

shoes, tools, and medical care for all its workers. In addition, most CCC camps offered free job training in subjects ranging from automobile mechanics and carpentry to welding.

The CCC opened camps all over the United States. The CCC workers built wildlife preserves, planted trees, maintained forest roads and trails, and built lookout towers to help spot forest fires.

In 1935 Congress passed a bill that set up a program called the Works Progress Administration (WPA). Like the CCC, the WPA put people back to work. More than 8 million men and women were part of the WPA's operation. Many of those workers helped build more than 650,000 miles (1,046,073 km) of roads and highways. They also built or repaired thousands of bridges, parks, landing strips at the nation's airports, and public buildings such as schools, libraries, and post offices.

The WPA also hired artists, including painters, sculptors, writers, and musicians, to record life during the Great Depression. These artists made thousands of murals and sculptures for public buildings. Their music and theater programs introduced many Americans to the arts.

The government helped get work for the nation's people in other ways, too. One example was the National Industrial Recovery Act (NIRA). Part of the NIRA set up the Public Works Administration (PWA). The PWA spent more than $3 billion for the construction of public roads and buildings. In all, the PWA sponsored about 34,000 public projects, each of which gave jobs to Americans.

Eleanor Roosevelt 1884–1962

Character Trait: Civic Virtue

Eleanor Roosevelt was one of the most active First Ladies in the nation's history. During the Great Depression, she wanted to let people know what the government was doing to help them. To do this, she held press conferences and wrote a regular newspaper column. After the United States entered World War II, she traveled around the world to visit United States troops. When the war ended, she was named a delegate to the United Nations. There she helped write and pass the Universal Declaration of Human Rights.

MULTIMEDIA BIOGRAPHIES
Visit the The Learning Site at www.harcourtschool.com/biographies to learn about other famous people.

Another part of the NIRA helped labor unions by promising workers the right "to organize and bargain collectively [together] through representatives of their own choosing." Labor unions also helped people protect their jobs once they were employed.

Another New Deal law was passed to help people who had retired from working. It was called the Social Security Act. Part of the act established a new tax, to be paid by both employers and employees. The money raised by this tax would be used to pay **pensions**, or retirement

The Triborough Bridge in New York City was completed in 1936.

incomes, to Americans who stopped working at the age of 65 or older.

Roosevelt's concern for working Americans did not end with his first term as President. In 1936 Roosevelt was elected for a second term. For the next four years, his concern for the working American continued. In 1938 Roosevelt worked with Congress to pass the Fair Labor Standards Act. This act is also called the Wages and Hours Law, because it set the lowest amount that a person could make per hour—a **minimum wage**—and the greatest number of hours a person could be asked to work in a week. The first minimum wage was 25 cents. The greatest number of hours was set at 44, with plans to lower the number to 40 by 1940. The Fair Labor Standards Act also made it against the law for children under the age of 16 to work.

REVIEW How did the Fair Labor Standards Act affect working children?

Tennessee Valley Authority worker

Help for Farmers

The government passed the Agricultural Adjustment Act (AAA) to help farmers get higher prices for their products. The government offered payments to farmers if they would not grow certain crops. Some of these crops were wheat, corn, rice, and cotton. Because of these payments, fewer of these crops were grown and the crops' prices were higher. The AAA also made money available to help farmers keep their farms.

In 1933 the Tennessee Valley Authority Act was passed to help the farmers in the Tennessee River valley. This large region includes parts of Tennessee, Kentucky, Virginia, North Carolina, Georgia, Alabama, and Mississippi. The act created an agency called the Tennessee Valley Authority (TVA). The TVA cleared the river where sandbars had kept boats from sailing. Now farmers could ship their products along the length of the Tennessee River.

This painting, titled *Electrification,* by David Stone Martin, shows workers installing poles for electrical wires to bring electricity to a rural area.

In addition, the TVA built dams along the river. These dams helped control the flooding that often damaged farms.

The dams built by the TVA were **hydroelectric dams**. These dams use the water they store to make electricity. Now farmers and others of the region could enjoy electric lights and appliances. Electricity also attracted businesses to the Tennessee River valley.

Making electricity available to more people, especially farmers, was the goal of another New Deal agency. This agency was called the Rural Electrification Administration (REA). This program worked to take electricity into rural areas that were hard for many electric companies to reach.

REVIEW What brought electricity to the Tennessee River valley?

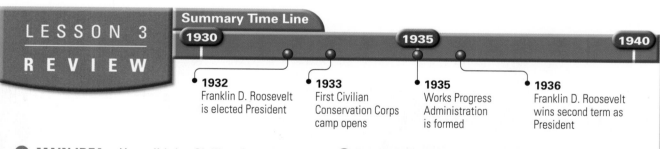

LESSON 3 REVIEW

Summary Time Line

1930 — 1935 — 1940

1932 Franklin D. Roosevelt is elected President

1933 First Civilian Conservation Corps camp opens

1935 Works Progress Administration is formed

1936 Franklin D. Roosevelt wins second term as President

1. **MAIN IDEA** How did the Civilian Conservation Corps help put Americans back to work?

2. **WHY IT MATTERS** How did the national government help people who were hurt by the Great Depression?

3. **VOCABULARY** Use the terms **pension** and **minimum wage** in a sentence about the New Deal programs.

4. **TIME LINE** Who was President when the Civilian Conservation Corps began?

5. **READING SKILL—Generalize** How did the New Deal programs change people's lives?

6. **GEOGRAPHY** How did hydroelectric dams change life in the Tennessee River valley?

PERFORMANCE—Make a Time Line Make a time line with the years 1933, 1934, and 1935 at equal distances. Add to the time line, in the appropriate places, all of the New Deal programs mentioned in the section titled Putting People Back to Work.

Compare Tables

VOCABULARY
classify

WHY IT MATTERS

Information can be easier to find if you **classify**, or group it. Knowing how to classify information can make facts easier to find.

WHAT YOU NEED TO KNOW

Using a table is one way to classify information. Look at the two tables below. Both classify information about some New Deal programs. In Table A, the programs are classified by the years in which they were founded. In Table B, the New Deal programs are classified in alphabetical order by their initials.

PRACTICE THE SKILL

Use the tables below to answer these questions.

1 Which table would you use to help you quickly identify the program founded in 1934?

2 Which table would you use to help you quickly find the name of the program that goes by the initials FCC?

APPLY WHAT YOU LEARNED

Write a paragraph that describes how each table classifies information about the New Deal programs.

Leading New Deal Programs

Table A

DATE FOUNDED	INITIALS	NAME	PURPOSE
1933	FDIC	Federal Deposit Insurance Corporation	insure bank deposits
1934	FCC	Federal Communications Commission	regulate radio and television systems
1937	FSA	Farm Security Administration	help farmers buy equipment

Table B

INITIALS	NAME	PURPOSE	DATE FOUNDED
FCC	Federal Communications Commission	regulate radio and television systems	1934
FDIC	Federal Deposit Insurance Corporation	insure bank deposits	1933
FSA	Farm Security Administration	help farmers buy equipment	1937

8 Review and Test Preparation

Summary Time Line
1925

● **1928**
Herbert Hoover is
elected President

● **1929**
The Great
Depression begins

USE YOUR READING SKILLS

Complete this graphic organizer by using facts you have
learned from the chapter to make generalizations about the
United States and the Great Depression. A copy of this graphic
organizer appears on page 82 of the Activity Book.

The United States and the Great Depression

1. The Economy Weakens

FACTS				GENERALIZATION
Only a few Americans had control over the economy.			→	

2. The Great Depression

FACTS				GENERALIZATION
On October 29, 1929, the stock market crashes.			→	

3. The New Deal

FACTS				GENERALIZATION
Franklin D. Roosevelt is elected President of the United States.			→	

THINK & WRITE

Write an Informative Essay   Write
an informative essay in which you explain
the difference between a depression and the
Great Depression. You can use examples
from the text in your essay. Share your essay
with a classmate.

Write a Speech   Imagine you are a government leader during the Great Depression.
Write a speech that will help inspire the
people around you. In your speech,
give people hope that the Great Depression
will soon come to an end.

1930s
The Dust Bowl hits the southern Great Plains

1932
Franklin D. Roosevelt is elected President

1935
The Works Progress Administration is formed

1936
Franklin D. Roosevelt is reelected President

USE THE TIME LINE

Use the chapter summary time line to answer these questions.

1 Was Herbert Hoover elected President before or after the Great Depression began?

2 When did the Dust Bowl hit the southern Great Plains? *1930*

USE VOCABULARY

Use the following terms to write a short story.

investor (p. 297)

depression (p. 300)

economist (p. 300)

unemployment (p. 301)

bureaucracy (p. 309)

minimum wage (p. 313)

RECALL FACTS

Answer these questions.

3 What was Black Thursday? *stock market crash*

4 Which states made up the Dust Bowl region? *Texas, Oklahoma, Kansas, Colorado, N. Mexico*

5 What was the Works Progress Administration? *Put people back to work on the nation's road system*

Write the letter of the best choice.

6 **TEST PREP** By the end of the 1920s, most of the nation's wealth—
A was spread evenly among the people.
B was invested in farms.
C was going to just a few Americans.
D was invested in government bonds.

7 **TEST PREP** When a government has a balanced budget,—
F it is not spending more money than it makes.
G it stops collecting taxes from its citizens.
H its citizens share all the money equally.
J it is spending more money than it saves.

THINK CRITICALLY

8 How did the Dust Bowl affect the state of California? *Because people was migrating to California*

9 How were President Roosevelt's plans to restore the economy different than President Hoover's? *did not believe in gov. aid while Roosevelt did*

APPLY SKILLS

Compare Tables to Classify Information

Use the tables on page 315 to answer these questions.

10 How are the tables on page 315 different?

11 How are the tables on page 315 the same?

12 When was the Federal Communications Commission founded? Which table did you use?

WALL STREET

GET READY

The early Dutch settlers of New York built a wall to protect their settlement from enemies. Today the wall is gone and New York City is the financial capital of the world. At the heart of the financial district is Wall Street, named for the Dutch-built wall of long ago.

Visitors to Wall Street can take a tour of the New York Stock Exchange, where millions of stock trades take place every day. At the Museum of American Financial History, exhibits trace the financial history of the United States. Those who visit Wall Street leave with a greater understanding of our country's financial history as well as its financial future.

LOCATE IT

NEW YORK

New York City

WHAT TO SEE

Wall Street still bustles with people, just as it did in 1915.

A stock trader in the 1920s calls out information.

Inside the New York Stock Exchange, 1893

The trading floor is the hub of the Stock Exchange. It is where the trades are made.

This statue is located in the financial district. A bull stands for rising stock prices.

TAKE A FIELD TRIP

GO ONLINE

A VIRTUAL TOUR
Visit The Learning Site at **www.harcourtschool.com/tours** to find virtual tours of other places of interest in the United States.

CNN Turner Le@rning

A VIDEO TOUR
Check your media center or classroom library for a videotape tour of Wall Street and its role in the Great Depression.

4 Review and Test Preparation

Write Captions Review the events on the Visual Summary below. Then choose another event from Unit 4 that is not represented on the Visual Summary. Write a sentence or two about that event. Finish by drawing a picture to illustrate the event.

USE VOCABULARY

Identify the correct term that matches each definition.

consumer good (p. 269)

commercial industry (p. 279)

renaissance (p. 290)

investor (p. 297)

bureaucracy (p. 309)

1 an industry that is run to make a profit

2 someone who uses money to buy or make something that will yield a profit

3 a product made for personal use

4 the many workers and groups needed to run government programs

5 a time of great interest and activity in the arts

RECALL FACTS

Answer these questions.

6 Why did crop prices drop after World War I? *Because European did not need A. Crops*

7 Who was the first woman to fly alone across the Atlantic Ocean? *Amelia Earhart*

8 Which amendment repealed the Eighteenth Amendment? *21*

9 How did people lose their savings during the Great Depression?

10 What was the Social Security Act?

11 **TEST PREP** When a buyer makes regular payments on a product it is called—
 A installment buying.
 B planned payment.
 C repayment.
 D partial payment.

12 **TEST PREP** Which of the following programs was started by President Franklin D. Roosevelt?
 F the New Freedom
 G the New Deal
 H the Square Deal
 J the League of Nations

Visual Summary

1920 — 1924 — 1928

1920 KDKA broadcasts election results over the radio p. 286

1927 Charles Lindbergh flies from New York to Paris p. 278

1929 The Great Depression begins p. 300

13 How did cities change in the 1920s?

14 How did the stock market crash affect people across the country?

15 How did President Roosevelt restore people's confidence in banks?

APPLY SKILLS

Use a Land Use and Resource Map

Use the map on this page to answer the following questions.

MAP AND GLOBE SKILLS

16 In what eastern states was coal produced in 1920?

17 What farm products were grown in Virginia in 1920?

18 In what eastern states were dairy cattle raised?

19 What eastern states produced cotton in 1920?

20 What eastern state produced both iron and coal in 1920?

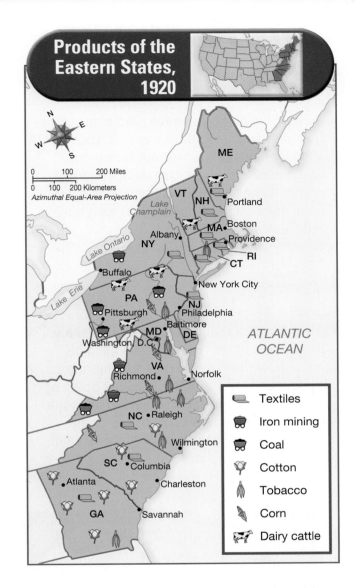

Products of the Eastern States, 1920

N E W S

0   100   200 Miles
0   100   200 Kilometers
Azimuthal Equal-Area Projection

Lake Champlain
Lake Ontario
Lake Erie

ME
VT
NH
Portland
Albany
MA
Boston
NY
Providence
CT
RI
Buffalo
New York City
PA
NJ
Pittsburgh
Philadelphia
Baltimore
MD
DE
Washington, D.C.
VA
Richmond
Norfolk
NC
Raleigh
Wilmington
SC
Columbia
Atlanta
Charleston
GA
Savannah

ATLANTIC OCEAN

Legend:
- Textiles
- Iron mining
- Coal
- Cotton
- Tobacco
- Corn
- Dairy cattle

1930s   The Dust Bowl hits the southern Great Plains   p. 304

1932   Franklin D. Roosevelt is elected President   p. 308

1933   The New Deal begins p. 308

1932   1936   1940

USA WORK WPA

Unit Activities

Paint a Scene

Choose a place you have read about in the unit that you would like to visit. Use encyclopedias or the Internet to find out more about that place. Use what you have learned to paint a picture. Include as much detail as possible to make it look as it does in real life.

Write a Radio Show

Work with a group to write a radio show. Choose one of the following events to be the topic of the radio show—the Roaring Twenties, Black Thursday, the Dust Bowl, or the New Deal. The radio show can be in the form of a story, a news broadcast, or an advertisement. Share a recorded version of the radio show in class.

Visit The Learning Site at www.harcourtschool.com/socialstudies/activities for additional activities.

VISIT YOUR LIBRARY

■ *Uncle Jed's Barbershop* by Margaree King Mitchell. Simon & Schuster.

■ *Georgia O'Keeffe* by Linda Lowery. Carolrhoda Books.

■ *Treasures in the Dust* by Tracey Porter. Joanna Cotler Books.

COMPLETE THE UNIT PROJECT

Create a Mural Work as a class to complete the unit project—create a mural. Review the notes you took during your reading. Then, choose one person, place, or event from your notes. Draw your chosen person, place, or event on the class mural.

World War II

D-Day Memorial, Bedford, Virginia

· U N I T ·

5

World War II

" The eyes of the world are upon you. The hopes and prayers of liberty-loving people everywhere march with you. **"**

—Dwight D. Eisenhower, order to troops preparing to invade Normandy, June 6, 1944

Preview the Content

Skim the unit. When you have finished, answer the following—*Who* and *What* is the unit about? *Where* are the places you will learn about? *When* did the events happen? *Why* are these events important? Make a graphic organizer, and fill in your responses.

| WHO → _____ |
| WHAT → _____ |
| WHERE → _____ |
| WHEN → _____ |
| WHY → _____ |

Preview the Vocabulary

Related Words   Use the Glossary to look up the vocabulary terms below. What do these terms have in common?

island hopping   front   D day   arms race

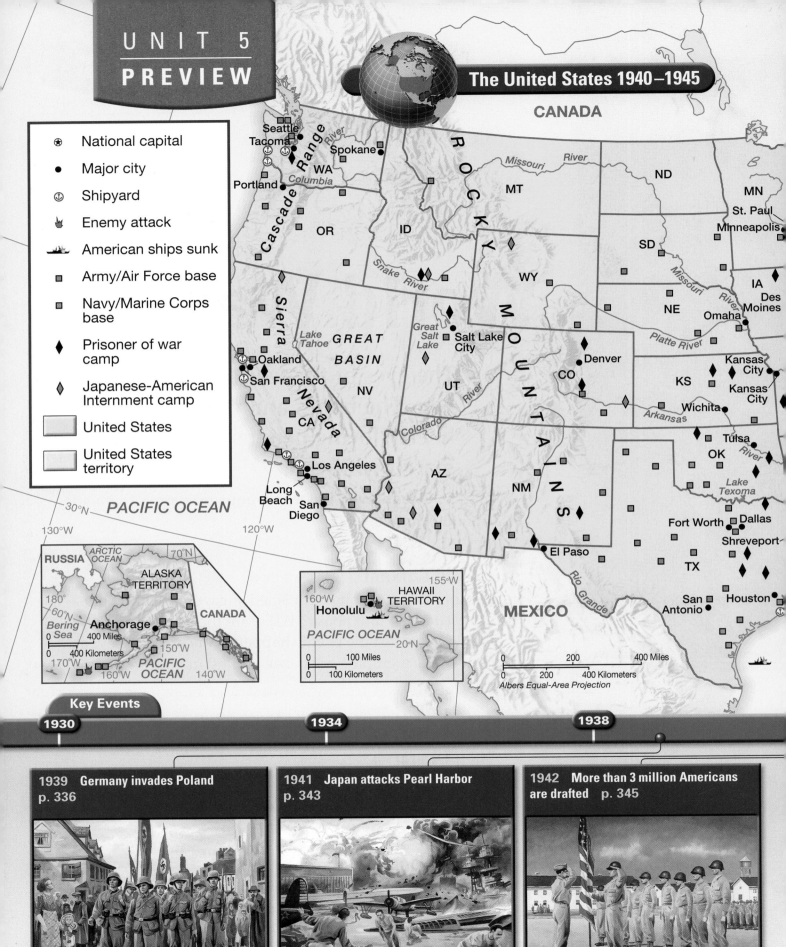

The United States 1940–1945

CANADA

Legend
- ⊛ National capital
- ● Major city
- ⚓ Shipyard
- ♨ Enemy attack
- ⚓ American ships sunk
- ▪ Army/Air Force base
- ▪ Navy/Marine Corps base
- ◆ Prisoner of war camp
- ◈ Japanese-American Internment camp
- ▭ United States
- ▭ United States territory

Main map labels:
Seattle, Tacoma, Spokane, Portland, Cascade Range, Columbia, WA, OR, ID, MT, ROCKY, Missouri River, ND, MN, St. Paul, Minneapolis, SD, WY, Snake River, NE, IA, Des Moines, Omaha, Platte River, Missouri River, Sierra Nevada, Lake Tahoe, GREAT BASIN, Great Salt Lake, Salt Lake City, Denver, CO, Kansas City, Kansas City, KS, Oakland, San Francisco, NV, UT, Colorado River, MOUNTAINS, Wichita, Arkansas, CA, AZ, NM, El Paso, Tulsa, OK, Lake Texoma, Los Angeles, Long Beach, San Diego, Fort Worth, Dallas, Shreveport, TX, Rio Grande, MEXICO, San Antonio, Houston

PACIFIC OCEAN
30°N
130°W
120°W

Alaska inset:
RUSSIA, ARCTIC OCEAN, 70°N, ALASKA TERRITORY, 180°, 60°N, Anchorage, CANADA, Bering Sea, 150°W, PACIFIC OCEAN, 170°W, 160°W, 140°W
0 400 Miles
0 400 Kilometers

Hawaii inset:
155°W, 160°W, HAWAII TERRITORY, Honolulu, PACIFIC OCEAN, 20°N
0 100 Miles
0 100 Kilometers

0 200 400 Miles
0 200 400 Kilometers
Albers Equal-Area Projection

Key Events

1930   1934   1938

1939 Germany invades Poland p. 336

1941 Japan attacks Pearl Harbor p. 343

1942 More than 3 million Americans are drafted p. 345

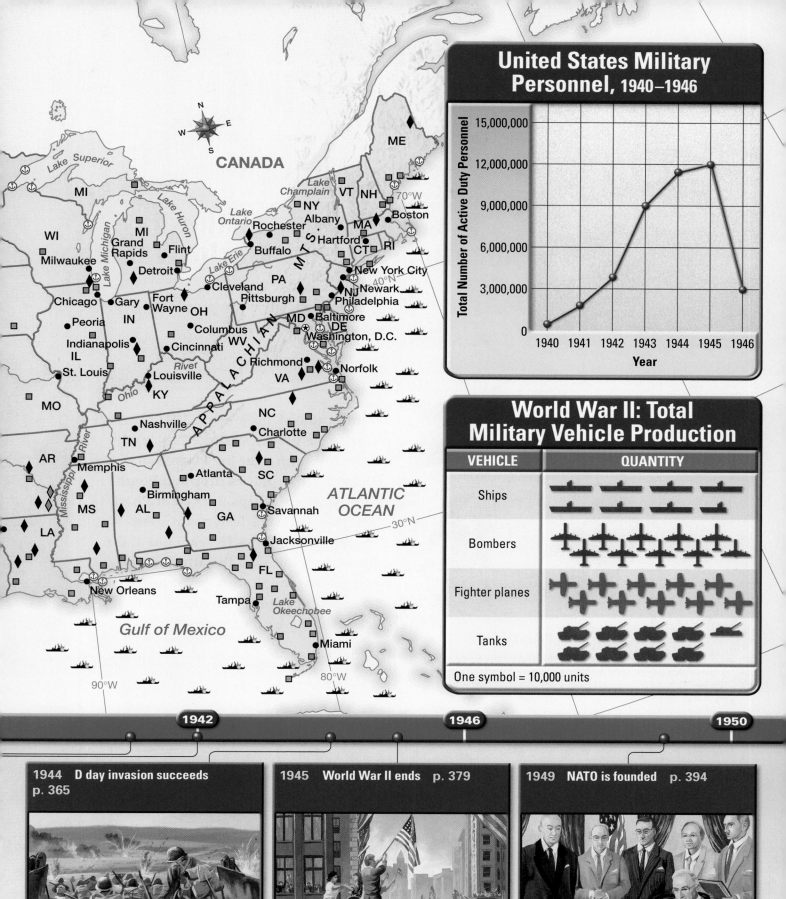

ATTACK ON PEARL HARBOR:

The True Story of the Day America Entered World War II

by Shelley Tanaka • paintings by David Craig

Peter Nottage

On Sunday, December 7, 1941, the roar of Japanese planes shattered the early-morning calm over the Hawaiian Islands. The planes dropped bombs on American ships docked at Pearl Harbor, an American naval base. Peter Nottage was 11 years old at the time. He witnessed the attack from nearby Kaneohe (kah·nay·OH·hay) Bay. Read now what Peter saw when World War II came to the United States.

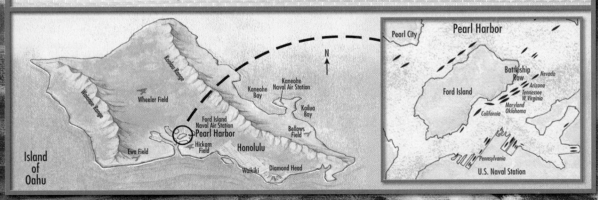

The Mitchell household was still asleep when Peter Nottage woke up. He slipped on a pair of shorts and an aloha shirt and went outside. Baby Girl shook herself awake and padded over to join him.

The house was built on a high bluff that overlooked Kaneohe (kah·nay·OH·hay) Bay. Across the water, the air station looked pretty quiet. Peter could see the two new hangars that housed the Navy's seaplanes. Most of the planes were neatly lined up on the ramp outside. Four planes were floating at anchor in the bay.

Peter heard a drone behind him. He looked up, and three silvery planes appeared above his head, coming in right over the house from the west. They were flying very close together and very low. He could see the goggled faces of the pilots.

Peter had never seen planes like these before. They weren't the usual P-26 fighters with the open cockpits, or even the sharp-nosed P-40s. Each plane had a big red circle painted on the underside of each wing. As he watched, the planes swerved over the bay and disappeared to the north.

Within minutes they swooped in again. This time they sprayed machine-gun fire. Peter could see the water jump as the bullets splashed into the bay.

Wow, he thought. This was great. The Navy was holding maneuvers right before his eyes. Must be the red team's planes against the blue team.

The door opened behind him and Mr. Mitchell came out, still wearing his pajamas. He squinted as a group of nine planes came in over the air station.

"Never seen one of those," he said. "What kind of plane do you suppose that is, Peter?"

"I don't know. I guess—"

One of the planes dropped a bomb right on the ramp of the seaplane hangar, setting it on fire. Metal, concrete, and glass exploded from the ground.

Peter started. Had one of the Navy pilots gone crazy? Somebody was really going to get it for that.

And then one of the seaplanes anchored in the bay was hit, and it blew up in a burst of fire.

Kaneohe was suddenly a sea of smoke and flames. All the seaplanes seemed to be burning.

Thick black smoke began to pour from one of the buildings. Alarms brayed.

A group of fighter planes swooped in again, but this time they faced fire from below. One of the attacking planes seemed to be hit. The pilot turned and waggled his wings at the rest of his squadron, which broke formation and peeled off. He came in alone, heading right for the station armory, as straight and deliberate as an arrow. Then, as Peter watched, the plane slammed into the ground and burst into flames.

Peter's mother flung open the door behind them. "It's on the radio. It's war!" she shouted. "Those are the Japanese! We're under attack!" And she grabbed Peter's arm and yanked him into the house.

brayed   called out loudly

Analyze the Literature

1 Why do you think Peter believed that the Navy was holding maneuvers?

2 Why did the pilot head toward the armory?

3 Write a paragraph explaining the clues that might have helped Peter realize that they were being attacked.

READ A BOOK

START THE UNIT PROJECT

Create an Illustrated Time Line
Work with your classmates to create an illustrated time line of World War II. As you read, make a list of the key events, people, and places you learn about. This list will help you decide which items to include on your time line.

USE TECHNOLOGY

Visit The Learning Site at **www.harcourtschool.com/ socialstudies** for additional activities, primary sources, and other resources to use in this unit.

USS *ARIZONA* MEMORIAL

The USS *Arizona* Memorial is anchored at Pearl Harbor. It was built to honor the 1,177 sailors who lost their lives on December 7, 1941. The memorial is positioned above the sunken battleship that still lies on the ocean floor. President Dwight D. Eisenhower approved the creation of the memorial, which was dedicated in 1962.

LOCATE IT

HAWAII

Pearl Harbor

The War Begins

❝ Yesterday, December 7, 1941—a date which will live in infamy. ❞

—Franklin D. Roosevelt, December 8, 1941, in a message to Congress

CHAPTER READING SKILL

Cause and Effect

An event or action that makes something else happen is a **cause**. What happens as a result of that event or action is the **effect**.

As you read this chapter, list the causes and effects of key events that led to World War II.

What Caused the Event	→	Event
CAUSE	→	EFFECT

MAIN IDEA
Read to learn how World
War II began.

WHY IT MATTERS
World War II was the
largest, costliest, and
deadliest war in history.

VOCABULARY
dictatorship
concentration camp
fascism

The Conflict Begins

1930 1940 1950

1930–1940

Franklin D. Roosevelt was reelected President in 1936. His New Deal programs had raised many people's spirits, but the worldwide depression continued. Europeans were still rebuilding their countries after World War I. Many of them had a hard time finding jobs to support their families. Also, food and other goods were scarce, making prices very high. In Asia some countries were running out of the resources needed to make their economies grow.

Powerful new leaders in some European and Asian countries promised to solve their countries' economic problems. They were willing to use force to do it.

The Rise of Dictators

The Treaty of Versailles marked the end of World War I. It made Germany pay other European countries for war damages. Germany could not afford to pay this debt. Like the economies of other countries, its economy had been badly damaged by the war. The Great Depression that soon followed left it unable to recover.

German leader Adolf Hitler addresses German soldiers at Nuremberg, Germany, in 1937.

FAST FACT In 1923 German money became so low in value that German children were allowed to use bundles of German paper money as building blocks.

Italian soldiers (at left) salute Benito Mussolini (center) with their knives.

Beginning in the 1920s an Austrian-born man who had fought in World War I started making angry speeches. His name was Adolf Hitler. He said that Germany had not been treated fairly after the war. He also said that Germans were better than all other peoples of the world. He was not speaking about all Germans, though. He blamed the Jewish people in Germany for many of the country's problems.

By 1932 the National Socialist party, or Nazis, who were led by Hitler, had become the most powerful political party in Germany. By 1933 Hitler was Germany's chancellor, or prime minister. Soon he had taken control of all of Germany and named himself its *führer* (FYOOR•er), which means "leader." Germany was now a dictatorship. A **dictatorship** is a government in which the dictator, or head of the government, has total authority.

Hitler soon took away the German people's right to vote and outlawed all political parties except the Nazi party. He also took control of the press and took away the rights of German Jews.

Hitler kept control by using a private army that he set up. Its soldiers, called storm troopers, arrested anyone who was even thought to disagree with Hitler. They put many of these people in terrible prisons called **concentration camps.**

Dictators rose to power in other European countries, too. This happened because of the rise of fascism. **Fascism** is a political idea in which power is given to a dictator and the freedoms of individuals are taken away. Since 1925 Italy had been under the rule of the fascist dictator Benito Mussolini (buh•NEE•toh moo•suh•LEE•nee). Mussolini wanted the nation to get back the power and glory it had had in ancient times, when it was the center of the Roman Empire.

In Spain, Francisco Franco set up a dictatorship with help from Hitler and Mussolini.

In 1924 in the Soviet Union, Joseph Stalin took control as a dictator. The Soviet Union had formed after the Russian Revolution in 1917. Stalin did not believe in fascism, but he did believe in communism. Communism is a political and economic system in which all industries, land, and businesses are owned by the government and in which people have few freedoms.

Dictators also ruled Japan, in Asia. The Japanese emperor, Hirohito (hir•oh•HEE•toh), lost much of his power. Instead, military leaders had seized the government, and General Hideki Tojo was named prime minister. To get the resources Japan's industries needed, military leaders decided to conquer other nations in Asia and the Pacific.

REVIEW **What countries were ruled by dictators before World War II?**

Hitler – Germany   Franco – Spain
Mussolini – Italy   Stalin – Soviet Union

Worldwide Troubles

In the 1920s and 1930s, China was torn by trouble. Communists were fighting to take over the nation. Japan made use of China's troubles to invade Chinese land. In 1931 Japan took Manchuria, a region in northeastern China. Manchuria was rich in resources such as coal and iron, which Japan needed. In 1937 Japan invaded the

Hirohito, the emperor of Japan, salutes as he inspects Japanese troops. The hat (right) was worn by a Japanese officer in World War II.

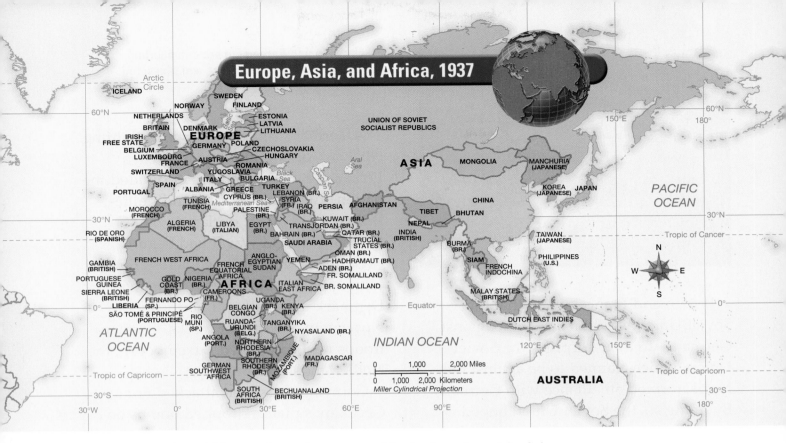

Europe, Asia, and Africa, 1937

Location This map shows the names and the borders of countries in Europe, Asia, and Africa as they were in 1937.

 Which places in Asia were taken over by Japan?

rest of China. By the end of 1938, much of eastern China had been taken over by the Japanese.

Italy had also begun to take over other countries. In 1935 Italy took over the African nation of Ethiopia. Then, in 1939, Mussolini sent his soldiers to invade the European country of Albania.

Germany began to move against other countries in 1938. In March of that year, Hitler's troops marched into neighboring Austria and quickly took over.

Because of painful memories of World War I, other countries, including the United States, did little to stop these warlike acts. Most people hoped there would be no war.

REVIEW Why did other countries do little to stop the warlike acts of some nations?

no one wanted war. painful memories.

War Breaks Out in Europe

After taking over Austria, Hitler next planned to invade the neighboring country of Czechoslovakia. Britain's prime minister, Neville Chamberlain, hoped to prevent the invasion. He met several times with both Hitler and Mussolini. At their last meeting in Munich, Germany, the three leaders and the leader of France signed the Munich Agreement. This treaty gave western Czechoslovakia to Germany. Britain and France hoped that in return, there would be no war. Hitler, however, did not stop at western Czechoslovakia. Within six months, he had broken the treaty. He sent German troops to take over the rest of Czechoslovakia.

Signing the Munich Agreement are Chamberlain, Edouard Daladier of France, Hitler, and Mussolini.

Britain and France hoped that the Soviet Union would take action against Germany. To their surprise, the Soviet Union, which claimed to be against the Nazis, formed an alliance with Germany. By doing so, the Soviet Union hoped to keep Hitler from attacking it.

On September 1, 1939, nearly 2 million German soldiers invaded Poland from the west. At the same time, Soviet soldiers invaded from the east. The Germans attacked with tanks on land and planes in the air, and Poland was quickly defeated.

The Germans called this style of fighting *blitzkrieg*, or "lightning war." When Poland fell, Stalin and Hitler divided the nation. Two days later Poland's allies, Britain and France, declared war on Germany. World War II had begun.

German forces stormed across Europe with unbelievable speed, taking over Denmark in a matter of hours and Norway in a matter of weeks. German troops next conquered Luxembourg, the Netherlands, and Belgium.

German forces then attacked France. Germany's planes dropped bombs on France's cities and countryside for hours at a time, and France soon surrendered. One French soldier described the effects of these bombings: "This bombing has tired even the toughest. What can one do with light machine-guns against 150 bombers? . . . Not to see the enemy face

German soldiers march to the Polish front during Germany's invasion of Poland in 1939. An American newspaper (right) announces the news.

Parts of London (left) burn during the Battle of Britain. Winston Churchill (above) spoke to the British people about never giving up.

to face, to have no means of defense, not to see the shadow of a French or Allied plane during the hours of bombing, this was one of the prime reasons for the loss of our faith in victory."

Although France had fallen, some French people kept up their fight. Many went to Africa or to Britain, where they set up a free French government. Within three months, much of western Europe had fallen to Hitler's forces. Events were happening so fast that one American warned that "before the snow flies again we may stand alone and isolated, the last great democracy on earth."

After the fall of France, Britain continued to fight, even though it was nearly alone. In August 1940 Germany took to the air to conquer Britain. For the next few months, wave after wave of German planes crossed the narrow

English Channel to bomb Britain. London alone saw German bombers in the air for 57 nights in a row! In fact, at times more than 1,000 German bombers filled the skies above Britain. This long air war became known as the Battle of Britain.

The British would not give up. Night after night, pilots from Britain's Royal Air Force (RAF) tried to stop the German bombers. By the end of the Battle of Britain, RAF pilots had shot down almost two German planes for every plane the RAF lost. Later, British Prime Minister Winston Churchill would honor those pilots when he said, "Never in the field of human conflict was so much owed by so many to so few."

Just as British pilots would not give up, neither would the British people. Edward R. Murrow was an American reporter in London during the Battle of Britain.

He explained how the British acted when faced with Germany's air war:

> 66 The politicians who called this a 'people's war' were right. . . . I've seen some horrible sights in this city during these days and nights, but not once have I heard man, woman, or child suggest that Britain should throw in her hand [give up]. 99

REVIEW What action by Germany started World War II? *taking over of Poland*

THIS SUBWAY IS NOT SAFE AS A SHELTER

Nearest air raid shelter

War Breaks Out in Asia

Across the Pacific Ocean from the United States, another war was raging. Japan had continued its conquests in Asia. After Germany conquered France, Japan got Germany to agree to let the Japanese take over French Indochina. This East Asian region is in the southeastern corner of the Asian continent, on the edge of the South China Sea. It includes the present-day countries of Vietnam, Cambodia, and Laos. With control of this region, Japan

People of London spend the night in the basement of a large store during a German air raid. The sign (above) guided the city's people to safety.

Japanese tanks cross the Xinjiang (SHIN•JYAHNG) River in China in 1941. These special tanks traveled through water as well as on land.

could stop trains from taking needed supplies to China. The war between Japan and China went on as Japanese forces kept taking more of China's land.

For many years France had been in control of Indochina. However, at the time of the Japanese invasion, French forces there numbered only about 13,000 soldiers. This was too few to fight off the larger Japanese army.

REVIEW How did the fall of France help Japan?

Japan got Germany to agree To let the Japanese take over French Indonesia.

LESSON 1 REVIEW

Summary Time Line

| 1930 | 1935 | 1940 |

1933
Nazi party takes control of Germany's government

1939
World War II begins

1940
The Battle of Britain begins

① **MAIN IDEA** What events led to World War II?

② **WHY IT MATTERS** Why do you think World War II was to be the largest war in history?

③ **VOCABULARY** Write a sentence explaining the relationship between the terms **fascism** and **dictatorship**.

④ **TIME LINE** In which year did the Battle of Britain begin?

⑤ **READING SKILL—Cause and Effect** What caused Britain and France to declare war on Germany?

⑥ **GEOGRAPHY** Do you think Britain's location helped the nation in the war with Germany? Explain.

⑦ **CRITICAL THINKING—Analyze** What do you think is the relationship between the rise of dictators and the coming of World War II?

PERFORMANCE—Write an Article
Imagine that you are an American newspaper reporter in Germany in the 1930s. Write an article describing the events in Europe. Then share your article with the class.

MAIN IDEA
In 1941 world events forced the United States into World War II.

WHY IT MATTERS
Until the United States entered World War II, Britain stood alone against the German forces.

VOCABULARY
civilian

The United States Enters the War

1930   1940   1950

1940–1942

The United States had planned to stay out of World War II. In fact, as late as October 1940, President Roosevelt told the American people, "I have said this before, but I shall say it again and again and again: Your boys are not going to be sent into any foreign wars." Soon, however, the actions of other countries would make it impossible for the United States to stay neutral, or take no sides, in the conflicts.

The United States Takes Action

Many Americans believed in a policy of isolation, or remaining separate from other countries. It soon became clear that even if the United States was neutral, its people were not. As the nation tried to stay out of the war, Americans began to take sides. Many of them sided with Britain.

President Roosevelt hoped for peace. Yet he knew the country should get ready for war, in case the United States was attacked. In his 1940 budget he asked for almost $2 billion for national defense. Five months later he asked for another $1 billion. Roosevelt also got the country ready for war by calling for the nation's first peacetime draft. He wanted to make sure there were enough American soldiers.

Through the Lend-Lease Act, Roosevelt helped Britain get war supplies without spending its limited amount of cash.

340

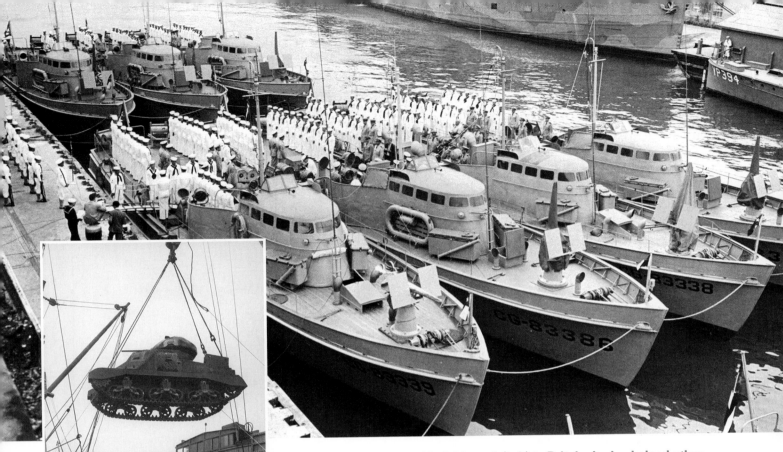

The Lend-Lease Act provided this tank (left) to Britain. It also helped other countries get supplies such as the American warships (above) given to the Cuban navy in 1943 to protect the Caribbean from German submarines.

President Roosevelt also looked for ways in which the United States could help Britain but stay out of the war. In September 1940 he announced the Destroyer-Bases Agreement. In this agreement the United States gave about 50 American warships to Britain in exchange for the right to use 8 British naval bases in Bermuda and the Caribbean. Then in March 1941 Roosevelt approved the Lend-Lease Act. This law allowed the United States to lend or rent supplies to warring countries whose defense was important to the United States. Soon the much-needed supplies of food and weapons were being sent to Britain.

REVIEW What was the purpose of the Lend-Lease Act?

Pearl Harbor

All during the 1930s, relations between Japan and the United States grew worse. The United States protested when Japan took over Manchuria. It protested again when Japan kept on fighting for more of China's land. Then, when Japan invaded Indochina, the United States decided to take action. Indochina is close to the Philippine Islands, which belonged to the United States at that time. Many American leaders feared that Japan would soon try to take over the Philippines and other places in the Pacific.

The United States government answered Japan's invasion of Indochina by placing a ban on resources, such as oil, that the United States exported to Japan.

Japan depended on the United States for more than half of its oil. The United States government hoped that cutting off part of Japan's oil supply would stop the Japanese from invading more countries. However, that did not stop them.

Pearl Harbor is a large natural harbor on the Hawaiian island of Oahu (oh•WAH•hoo). Its size and location made it a perfect home harbor for many of the ships in the United States Pacific Fleet. In December 1941 about 130 of those ships were at Pearl Harbor.

Many Americans believed the Pacific Fleet was so strong that no other country would attack it. However, the Japanese wanted to make sure the United States would not try to stop them from forming a huge empire.

In November 1941 a fleet of Japanese ships and aircraft carriers, or ships from which aircraft can take off and land,

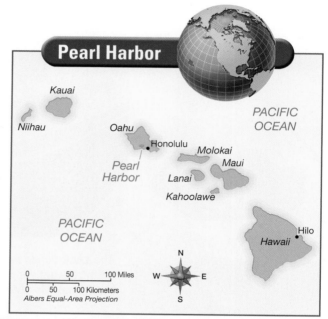

Pearl Harbor

Kauai
Niihau
Oahu
Honolulu
Molokai
Maui
Pearl Harbor
Lanai
Kahoolawe
PACIFIC OCEAN
PACIFIC OCEAN
Hilo
Hawaii

N W E S

0   50   100 Miles
0 50   100 Kilometers
Albers Equal-Area Projection

GEOGRAPHY THEME

Location Pearl Harbor is about 4,000 miles (6,400 km) from Japan. The planes that attacked the United States ships there (below) came most of the way on aircraft carriers.

❖ Why do you think the planes did not fly all the way from Japan to Pearl Harbor?

The battleships USS *West Virginia* and USS *Tennessee* burn after the attack on Pearl Harbor. Both were later repaired.

arrived about 230 miles (370 km) north of Oahu. They had kept strict radio silence so no one would know they were there. On December 2 they received the order to attack the United States Pacific Fleet in five days.

On the morning of December 7, 1941, the calm at Pearl Harbor was shattered when Japanese forces attacked the Pacific Fleet. Hundreds of planes armed with thousands of pounds of bombs took off from the Japanese aircraft carriers. Some Japanese also attacked from the sea in small, two-person submarines. Together they attacked the ships and planes of the Pacific Fleet.

A few minutes after the first Japanese planes had dropped their first bombs, one hit the USS *Arizona*. The *Arizona* seemed to buck into the air as the bomb exploded hundreds of tons of gunpowder stored in the front of the battleship. It took less than nine minutes for the *Arizona* to sink into the harbor. Almost all its crew—more than 1,100 sailors—went down with the ship. Another 400 sailors were lost when the USS *Oklahoma* was hit by Japanese torpedoes, causing it to turn over in the water. During the raid, the USS *California* and the USS *West Virginia* also sank. Other ships, like the *Maryland*, the *Pennsylvania*, and the *Tennessee*, were badly damaged.

Two Navy servicemen watch flames and smoke rise from Hickam Airfield during the attack on Pearl Harbor. Admiral Chester W. Nimitz pins the Navy Cross on Doris "Dorie" Miller (right) to honor him for his great courage during the attack.

Jack Kelley was a seaman aboard the USS *Tennessee*. He was below deck when the attack started. He said,

66 **When I came topside . . . the *West Virginia* was settling on the bottom beside us, and I looked behind, and the *Arizona* was just one big ball of fire, and up ahead to the left the *Oklahoma* had turned upside down with the screws sticking up in the air. It made me wonder where we ever got the idea that we were so secure. 99**

Some American sailors were able to fight back. Seaman Doris "Dorie" Miller was an African American cook on board the USS *West Virginia*. When the ship's commanding officer was wounded, Miller dragged him out of the line of fire.

Then Miller manned a machine gun and shot down four Japanese planes.

The Japanese attack lasted less than two hours. During the attack 19 warships were sunk or damaged in the harbor. About 150 planes were destroyed at nearby Hickam Airfield. More than 2,000 sailors and soldiers and 68 civilians were killed. A **civilian** is a person who is not in the military. As terrible as the losses were, they could have been even worse. The Japanese bomber planes did not hit the valuable oil supplies nearby. Also, the Pacific Fleet's three aircraft carriers were out of port on training exercises and escaped the attack.

The United States was shocked by the Japanese surprise attack on Pearl Harbor. President Roosevelt made a speech before Congress the next day to ask the members to declare war on Japan. He said,

> "Yesterday, December 7, 1941—a date which will live in infamy—the United States of America was suddenly and deliberately attacked by naval and air forces of the Empire of Japan. . . . I ask that the Congress declare that since the . . . attack by Japan . . . a state of war has existed between the United States and the Japanese Empire."

Three days later, Germany and Italy declared war on the United States, and Congress declared a state of war with them, too. Germany, Italy, and Japan were known as the Axis Powers. The United States joined with the Allies, which included Britain, France, and the Soviet Union. The Soviet Union had once sided with Germany. However, Adolf Hitler had ordered Joseph Stalin to stay out of affairs in Europe. When Stalin did not agree, Germany invaded the Soviet Union in the summer of 1941.

REVIEW What event led the United States to enter the war? *Pearl Harbor*

The United States Prepares for War

One of the biggest mistakes that the Japanese made while trying to take over lands and form an empire was to attack the United States. The surprise attack united most of the American people, even some who had been strongly against joining the war.

Thousands of men lined up to enlist, and thousands of others answered the draft's call. By 1942 more than 3 million American men had been drafted. Military camps and bases were soon built across the country to train pilots and soldiers.

DEMOCRATIC VALUES
The Common Good

CITIZENSHIP

The Japanese attack on Pearl Harbor brought together millions of Americans. They decided to put aside any differences they may have had and work together for the good of the country. This pulling together made it possible for the United States to supply the Allies with food, guns, bombs, tanks, medical equipment, and the other supplies that they needed in their fight against the Axis Powers.

Like Americans of the 1940s, Americans today often put aside their differences for the good of their community, their state, or their nation. Working together for the common good can help citizens overcome their differences.

Analyze the Value

1 Why was it important for Americans to work together during World War II?

2 **Make It Relevant** Ask your teacher or principal to name one change that would help your school be a better place. Then draw a poster that will encourage all the students to work for this common goal.

This United States flag was rescued from the sunken USS *California*.

After recruits were sworn in (left), their training began. In Miami, Florida, troops (above) exercise while wearing gas masks.

Some of the camps and bases did not have enough housing for all the troops, so hotels were used. In other camps, soldiers slept in tents.

During World War II, more than 15 million Americans—including about 338,000 women—served in the armed forces. Many women in the armed forces made maps, drove ambulances, and worked as mechanics, clerks, and nurses.

REVIEW Where were soldiers trained?

military camps & bases.

LESSON 2 REVIEW

Summary Time Line

1940 — President Roosevelt announces the Destroyer-Bases Agreement

1941 — Japan attacks Pearl Harbor and the United States enters World War II

1942 — More than 3 million American men are drafted into military service

1 **MAIN IDEA** How did poor relations with the Japanese lead the United States into the war?

2 **WHY IT MATTERS** What might have happened if the United States had not entered the war?

3 **VOCABULARY** What is a **civilian**?

4 **TIME LINE** When was Pearl Harbor attacked?

5 **READING SKILL—Cause and Effect** What caused many Americans to change their minds about becoming involved in the war?

6 **GEOGRAPHY** Why was Japan's attack on Indochina upsetting to the United States?

7 **CRITICAL THINKING—Evaluate** One sailor who was there during the Pearl Harbor attack said, "I finished growing up on that day and learned that life was more than just a good-time roller coaster." What do you think he meant by that?

PERFORMANCE—Write a Memorial
Write a memorial paragraph honoring the American men and women who defended Pearl Harbor during the attack. In your memorial, also discuss the importance of the event in United States history.

Life at Home

1930   1940   1950

1941–1945

MAIN IDEA
American soldiers relied on the people at home to produce the supplies and weapons they needed.

WHY IT MATTERS
During the war almost all Americans worked together toward one goal—to protect the United States and its Allies from enemies.

VOCABULARY
rationing
recycling
relocation camp

Supplying war materials to the Allies had already helped the United States get ready for war. After the bombing at Pearl Harbor, however, the United States suddenly had to come up with even more airplanes, tanks, and other war supplies. This work provided jobs for many more Americans. The Great Depression was over.

Wartime Industries

Now that the United States had joined in the war, it found it had to help supply the Allied forces with food, weapons, and everything else they needed. This meant supplying goods to millions of people. To make sure the country could supply all these things, the government took control of many businesses and stopped the production of many consumer goods. Instead, manufacturers were asked to make weapons and other war materials.

Workers built ships in many coastal cities. This shipyard was in Tampa, Florida.

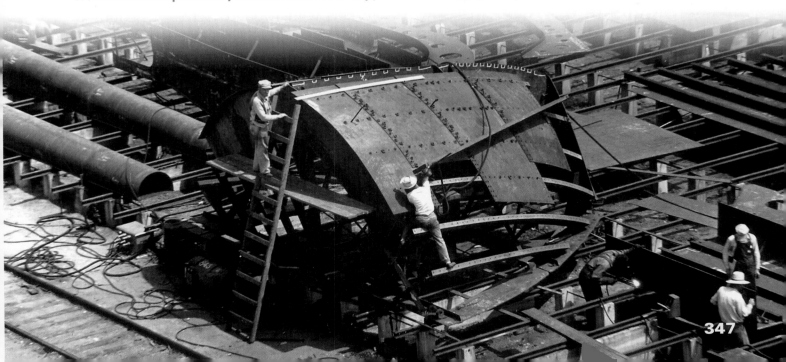

347

Blood Storage

Before World War II, scientists were unable to store supplies of blood for long periods of time. As a result, many injured people who had lost too much blood died. Charles Drew, an African American doctor, helped change this. Drew discovered that the plasma, or liquid portion of blood, could be separated from the red blood cells. The two could then be frozen and stored for a long time. When a person needed a transfusion, or transfer of blood, the two parts could be put together again to form human blood. During the war Drew helped begin the American Red Cross Blood Program. It saved the lives of thousands of wounded soldiers.

Charles Drew

Government actions also helped the growth of new industries. Before the war the United States had depended on Asian countries for the rubber used in making tires. After Japan took control of many of those countries, the supply of rubber nearly stopped. This might have caused a major problem for the United States military, which needed huge amounts of rubber for tires on trucks and airplanes. However, new industries were soon developed that made synthetic, or human-made, rubber.

To make the goods needed during wartime, hundreds of thousands of new workers were needed. Across the country people went to work in factories, steel mills, shipyards, and aircraft plants.

Working around the clock, American workers were able to produce huge amounts of war materials at record speed. At the beginning of the war, President Roosevelt asked American industries to produce as many as 60,000 aircraft a year. Many people believed this was impossible, but in 1943 alone, American workers built almost 86,000 aircraft.

REVIEW How did the government get businesses to produce enough war supplies?

Analyze Graphs The production of aircraft went up sharply during the first years of the war.

◆ About how many aircraft were produced in 1944?

United States Aircraft Production, 1941–1945

(y-axis: Aircraft Produced, 0 to 100,000; x-axis: Year, 1941 to 1945)

Women During the War

As they had in World War I, American women rushed to take the jobs left empty as men became soldiers. In fact, between 1941, when the United States joined the war, and 1945, when the war ended, the number of working women in the nation increased by nearly 3 million!

Many of the jobs taken by women had been held mostly by men before the war. For example, in 1941 women made up only about 1 percent of all workers in the aviation industry. Just two years later, in 1943, 65 percent of the workers in that industry were women. Women worked building planes, ships, and tanks for use by American and other Allied soldiers. At this time, more women also entered professional careers as lawyers, doctors, and chemists.

Rosina Bonavita was one of the millions of women assembling airplanes. She and a partner welded 3,345 rivets in place to put together one wing of a bomber— and they did it in just one workday!

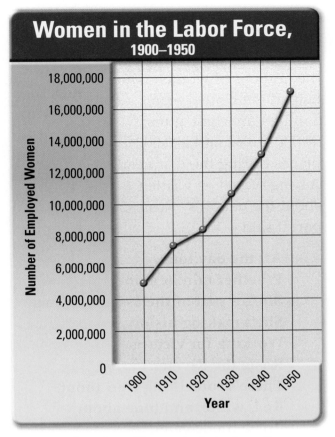

Women in the Labor Force, 1900–1950

Analyze Graphs The graph shows how the number of women working outside the home grew between 1900 and 1950. The photograph below shows women building aircraft. At left men and women work on B-17F bombers.

◈ By 1950, about how many women had become part of the labor force?

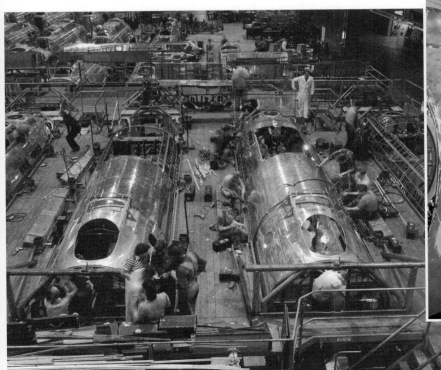

This feat helped earn Bonavita the nick-name "Rosie the Riveter." In time, "Rosie the Riveter" came to stand for the millions of women who helped the United States produce 3 million machine guns, 89,000 tanks, and 300,000 planes during the war years. A song was even written about the nation's "Rosies." In part it said,

> 66 **All the day long,**
> **Whether rain or shine,**
> **She's a part of the assembly line.**
> **She's making history,**
> **Working for victory,**
> **Rosie the Riveter. . . .**
> **There's something true about,**
> **Red, white, and blue about,**
> **Rosie the Riveter.** 99

Other women joined American men in military service during the war. These

women were not allowed to fight in battle. Instead, they carried out many important support tasks, which freed men for fighting. For example, pilot Jacqueline Cochran per-suaded the government to start the WASPs, or Women's Air Force Service Pilots. These pilots flew military missions around the United States, which left male pilots free for war duties. Women also served as nurses. Those who worked near the battlefields helped in camp hospitals where the men who had been wounded in battle were brought. In all, more than 60,000 American women served as nurses during the war.

REVIEW Whom did "Rosie the Riveter" come to stand for?

millions of women who help the U.S produce war supplies

American women held many different jobs during the war. Some (below) worked as nurses overseas. Others (right) trained as pilots to fly military missions in the United States.

Analyze Primary Sources

Ration books like the one shown here were used during World War II to enable people to buy rationed goods. Each family received books of coupons or stamps for certain goods. The buyer turned in the coupons as he or she paid for the goods.

1. ration book stamps
2. name of the ration book's owner
3. traits that identify the ration book's owner

◈ How do you think rationing helped the United States during World War II?

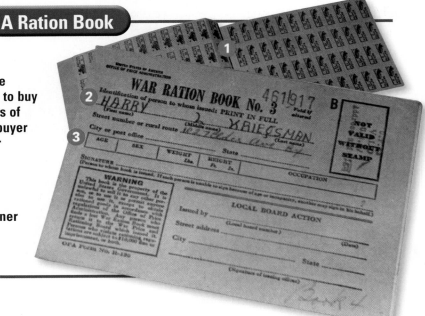

The Home Front

World War II, like World War I, caused shortages of goods. To make sure there were enough goods for soldiers, new government rules in 1942 called for **rationing**, or limiting, what people could buy. For certain goods, people needed not only the money to buy them, but also government coupons. People could buy only the amount of butter, sugar, coffee, and meat that the coupons allowed. That way the government could control the amounts of these goods that were sold on the home front.

Among the most difficult things for Americans to get used to was the rationing of sugar and gasoline. The government limited the amount of gasoline people could buy by giving stamps to drivers. Most drivers were allowed to buy 3 gallons of gas a week. People who traveled in their line of work could get more. Other rationed items included fruits, vegetables, shoes, and tires.

People at home also helped by **recycling** items, or using them again.

In fact, recycling became a way of life during World War II. Recycled bacon grease and other fats, for example, were used in making bullets and tanning leather. Scrap iron from old lawn mowers, radiators, and shovels was used to make guns and grenades. Recycled paper was used to make cartons that were used to ship goods to soldiers overseas.

To help feed the thousands of people serving in the military, farmers planted more crops and raised more livestock.

Both coupons and money were needed to buy rationed goods.

351

Children helped in the war effort by gathering paper to recycle.

This demand for food brought about good times for many farmers.

There were many other ways that Americans helped the war effort. For example, millions of volunteers helped protect the nation's borders by working for the Office of Civilian Defense. Most of the volunteers were adults, but some were children. For example, Neil Shine was 11 years old and living in Detroit, Michigan, when the United States entered the war. He remembers how he and other children he knew pitched in to help protect the United States: "We had to protect our shores from this 'enemy.' We learned the silhouettes [outlines] of all the airplanes, and we spent countless hours lying on our backs at the playground, looking skyward, watching for Messerschmitts and Stukas [German planes] and Mitsubishis and Zeros [Japanese planes]. But all we ever saw were the planes from the local air base. If

they [the Germans or Japanese] had ever tried to slip one airplane over Detroit airspace, . . . some kid in my neighborhood would have sounded the alarm."

Americans helped pay for the war by paying higher taxes and by buying war bonds. A war bond is a piece of paper showing that the buyer had loaned the government money to help pay the cost of the war. When people bought war bonds, they were letting the government use their money for a certain amount of time. After the time was up, people turned in their bonds and got their money back with interest. Interest is the money a bank or borrower pays to a lender for the use of money.

These $50 war bonds were bought in 1942.

Companies and state and local governments also bought war bonds. Even children bought them. For 25 cents, children could buy a war-bond stamp. Then they pasted it into a stamp book. When the stamp book was filled, the child could turn it in for a $25 bond. To help sell bonds, movie stars and other famous people appeared at rallies. The effort was a huge success, raising more than $180 billion.

All over the nation, World War II caused families to pull together. However, many families also suffered because of the war. After all, millions of American men were fighting in Europe and the Pacific. When the men went overseas, many women were left alone to take care of their families. Worse yet, some of those men never came home.

REVIEW How did Americans help pay for the war? *by paying higher taxes by buying war bonds*

Japanese Americans

The war caused changes in people's lives. It also led to terrible problems for Japanese Americans. At the time of the attack on Pearl Harbor, about 125,000 Japanese Americans lived in the United States. Most had been born here and were citizens. The attack on Pearl Harbor had shocked them too.

After Pearl Harbor, however, anger against Japanese Americans grew. Some United States military officials believed that Japanese Americans might even help Japan invade the United States.

In February 1942 President Roosevelt ordered the army to put about 110,000 Japanese Americans in relocation camps. **Relocation camps** were army-style settlements in which the Japanese Americans were forced to live. All Japanese Americans had to wear identification tags. They also had to sell their homes, businesses, and belongings.

A Japanese American business (right) closes before its owner goes to a relocation camp. Below, Japanese Americans wait to enter a camp near Los Angeles.

Many of the soldiers in the 442nd Regimental Combat Team were Japanese Americans. They fought in Italy and Germany and received many service awards like the medal shown here.

Some of the camps were in California, Arizona, Wyoming, and Arkansas. "Our home was one room in a large . . . barracks, measuring 20 by 25 feet," remembers one woman. "The only furnishings were an iron pot-belly stove and cots."

While their families and friends were in the relocation camps, more than 17,000

Japanese Americans served in the armed forces. Most became members of the 442nd Regimental Combat Team, which fought in Italy and Germany. This unit received more service awards than any other unit its size in World War II.

REVIEW Why were many Japanese Americans sent to relocation camps?

afraid Japan will help invade the U.S.

LESSON 3 REVIEW

Summary Time Line

1941 ———————— **1943** ———————— **1945**

1942
Japanese Americans are put into relocation camps

1943
American workers build almost 86,000 aircraft

1945
Fifteen million American women are employed in the labor force

1 **MAIN IDEA** What did the government do to make sure it had the food and supplies American soldiers needed? *ration*

2 **WHY IT MATTERS** How did American women help with the war effort?

3 **VOCABULARY** Use the term **rationing** in a sentence about life at home during World War II.

4 **TIME LINE** When were Japanese Americans placed in relocation camps? *1942*

5 **READING SKILL—Cause and Effect** What caused a shortage of goods for Americans?

6 **ECONOMICS** In what ways did the United States government control businesses?

7 **CRITICAL THINKING—Analyze** During World War II, the United States government called working women "soldiers without guns." What do you think the government meant by that?

PERFORMANCE—Draw a Poster
Imagine that it is 1942. Make a poster urging Americans to follow the rules for rationing any of the goods mentioned in this lesson. Display your poster in the classroom.

· SKILLS · Make Economic Choices

VOCABULARY

trade-off

opportunity cost

▶ WHY IT MATTERS

When you buy something at a store, you are making an economic choice. Choosing between items to buy can be difficult. In order to buy something you want now, you must spend money that you cannot use to buy something in the future. This giving up of one thing in return for another is called a **trade-off**. What you give up is the **opportunity cost** of what you get. Understanding trade-offs and opportunity costs can help you make thoughtful economic choices.

▶ WHAT YOU NEED TO KNOW

You have read that in World War II, Americans supported the war effort by buying war bonds. The money helped the armed forces fight the war. Later, bond owners got their money back with interest.

▶ PRACTICE THE SKILL

Imagine that you are an American factory worker in 1944. At the end of every week you receive your paycheck. After paying your bills, you have some money left over. You might use it to buy something you want now, such as a

new sweater, or you might use it to buy a war bond.

1. Think of the trade-offs. You could use the sweater, but you would not get any money back from this purchase. By buying war bonds, you are helping the war effort, but you would have to wait a while to earn interest on your bonds. What are the trade-offs of buying war bonds?

2. Think of the opportunity costs. You don't have enough money to buy both, so you have to give up one. If you buy the sweater, you give up the chance to get back more than what you spent. What are the opportunity costs of buying war bonds?

▶ APPLY WHAT YOU LEARNED

Imagine that you want to buy a book and rent a movie, but you do not have enough money for both. Explain to a partner the trade-off and the opportunity costs of your choices.

Americans everywhere lined up to buy war bonds.

CITIZENSHIP SKILLS

War Posters

During World War II United States government agencies, businesses, and private organizations printed posters to support the war effort. Wartime posters were described as a visual call to arms—a way for making American war aims the personal goals of every citizen. Study the war posters on these pages, and identify the purpose of each one.

FROM THE SMITHSONIAN INSTITUTION, NATIONAL MUSEUM OF AMERICAN HISTORY, ONLINE EXHIBIT "PRODUCE FOR VICTORY"

Many posters encouraged all workers to participate in the war effort.

Keep us flying!

BUY WAR BONDS

Analyze the Primary Source

1 What is the message of each of the four wartime posters on these pages?

2 Which poster or posters do you think may have worked the best?

3 Why do you think posters were an effective way to show the nation's wartime aims for its citizens?

War bond posters asked citizens to share in the cost of the war. This poster shows one of the corps of fighter pilots trained at Tuskegee Institute in Alabama.

Some posters encouraged citizens to grow food or conserve resources.

GROW IT YOURSELF

PLAN A FARM GARDEN NOW

Rural Electrification Administration, U. S. Department of Agriculture

ACTIVITY

Make a Poster   Imagine that you are working for the United States government during World War II. Design and make a poster of your choice. It should either encourage workers to help in the war effort or ask citizens to buy war bonds.

RESEARCH

Visit The Learning Site at **www.harcourtschool.com/ primarysources** to research other primary sources.

Review and Test Preparation

Summary Time Line
1930

• **1933**
Nazi party takes control
of Germany's government

USE YOUR READING SKILLS

Complete this graphic organizer to show that you understand
the causes and effects of some of the key events that started
World War II. A copy of this graphic organizer appears on
page 90 of the Activity Book.

World War II Begins

CAUSE	→	EFFECT
Adolf Hitler becomes chancellor of Germany.	→	_____
_____	→	Democracy in Europe and Asia comes under attack.
On September 1, 1939, German forces invade Poland.	→	_____
_____	→	French Indochina falls to the Japanese.
On December 7, 1941, Japanese forces attack Pearl Harbor.	→	_____

THINK & WRITE

Write a Diary Entry   Imagine that you
are living during World War II. Write a diary
entry about going shopping with your family.
Tell how the war has affected what you can
buy. Also describe other ways the war has
affected your family.

Write About a Career   Reread the
section in Lesson 3 called Women During
the War. Choose a job that women began
doing during World War II. Write a short
report about that job. Tell about what it is
like to do that job today.

1939
World War II begins

1941
The United States
enters World War II

1942
Japanese Americans are
ordered into relocation
camps

1945
Fifteen million American
women are employed in
the labor force

USE THE TIME LINE

Use the chapter summary time line to answer these questions.

1 Was the United States a nation at war in 1939? *No*

2 In which year were there fifteen million working women in the United States? *1945*

USE VOCABULARY

Identify the term that correctly completes each sentence.

dictatorship (p. 333)

concentration camps (p. 333)

civilians (p. 344)

recycling (p. 351)

3 In a war, soldiers and _civilians_ can be hurt or killed.

4 In a _dictatorship_, the head of the government has total authority.

5 Hitler put people who did not agree with him into _conc. camps_.

6 Many people helped by _recycling_ items rather than throwing them away.

RECALL FACTS

Answer these questions.

7 Who was the dictator in Italy in the 1920s and 1930s? *Benito Mussalini*

8 What event brought the United States into World War II? *Pearl Harbor*

9 Why did American industries begin making synthetic rubber during World War II?
Because Japan took over the countries that supply rubber

Write the letter of the best choice.

10 TEST PREP A political idea in which the power is given to a dictator is—
A democracy.
B capitalism.
C fascism.
D socialism.

11 TEST PREP The American government responded to Japan's invasion of Indochina by—
F invading Japan.
G placing a ban on resources that the United States exported to Japan.
H sending the United States Pacific Fleet to the South China Sea.
J issuing a written warning to Japan.

THINK CRITICALLY

12 Why do you think Japanese forces chose to attack the United States at Pearl Harbor rather than somewhere else?

13 Why did the Allies depend on the United States for supplies such as food and weapons?

APPLY SKILLS

Make Economic Choices
Read the following paragraph. Then use the information on page 355 to answer these questions.

Imagine you earn $6 for doing chores. You must choose between buying a new toy or putting the money into an interest-earning savings account.

14 What are the trade-offs of your choices?

15 What is the opportunity cost of each choice?

U.S. MARINE CORPS WAR MEMORIAL

The Marine Corps War Memorial at Arlington National Cemetery shows the American flag being raised during the terrible battle for the Japanese island of Iwo Jima. It was designed by Felix W. de Weldon and is based on a photograph by Joe Rosenthal that became one of the most famous images of World War II.

LOCATE IT

Washington, D.C.

UNCOMMON VALOR WAS A COMMON VIRTUE

10

The Allies Win the War

" Uncommon valor was a common virtue. "

—Admiral Chester Nimitz, referring to United States soldiers in World War II, 1945

MAIN IDEA
Read to learn how World War II affected countries in Africa and Europe.

WHY IT MATTERS
World War II greatly changed the world.

VOCABULARY
front
segregated
D day
Holocaust

War in Africa and in Europe

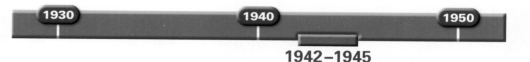

1930   1940   1950

1942–1945

World War II was a new kind of war. Instead of fighting from trenches, as in World War I, soldiers used tanks, ships, and airplanes to move quickly from battle to battle. Bombs that were dropped from larger, faster airplanes destroyed whole cities.

World War II was also fought over a much larger area than any other war was—almost half the world. It was fought on two major **fronts**, or battle lines, at the same time. The first was in Africa and in Europe. The second was in the Pacific. The war would need to be won on both fronts.

North Africa and Italy

To defeat the Axis Powers in Europe, the Allied Powers decided that they would need first to win control of the Mediterranean Sea. To do that, they would have to defeat the German and Italian forces in North Africa and then invade Italy.

In June 1942 President Roosevelt put Dwight D. Eisenhower (EYE•zin•how•er) in command of all the American troops in Europe. A respected leader and a skilled military planner, General Eisenhower led the Allied forces in their attack against the Axis forces in North Africa.

FAST FACT
During World War II, Dwight D. Eisenhower quickly advanced through the ranks of the United States Army. In 1942 he was a lieutenant colonel stationed in the Philippines. Less than two years later, he was a general commanding the most powerful military force in history.

In November 1942 American forces landed in Morocco and Algeria in northwestern Africa. The American troops slowly fought their way east. At the same time, the British pushed the Axis forces west, out of Egypt. On April 8, 1943, after five months of fighting, the American and the British troops met. Five weeks later, the Axis troops in North Africa surrendered. With that surrender, 240,000 German and Italian soldiers became prisoners of war.

The Allies then pushed north into Italy. They thought Italy might be close to surrendering, which would weaken the Axis Powers. They also thought that the Mediterranean Sea would be safer for Allied ships if the Allies pushed the Axis Powers out of Italy.

The Italian campaign began on July 10, 1943, on the island of Sicily. Fighting was fierce, but the Italian people were tired of the war. Cries of "Long live America!" and "Down with Mussolini!" greeted Allied soldiers as they took the Sicilian city of Palermo. On July 24 Mussolini was told, "The soldiers don't want to fight anymore. At this moment, you are the most hated man in Italy." That same day, Mussolini was arrested and put into prison. However, the fighting in Italy did not end with Mussolini's arrest. Hitler sent more German troops to defend Italy and free Mussolini. As a result, it took Allied forces almost another year to reach Rome, Italy's capital.

One of the military units from the United States that helped the Allies in their battle for Italy was the 92nd Division. This division was made up of African American soldiers. During the war African American soldiers had to serve in **segregated**, or separate, units.

REVIEW Why did the Allies need to invade North Africa?

African American soldiers of the 92nd Division load a gun behind sandbags during a battle in Italy.

The D Day Invasion

While the Allies were fighting in Italy, they were planning other invasions of Europe. General Eisenhower, now the commander of the Allied forces, would lead the largest of these invasions.

For months the Allies prepared for the attack. In fact, more than 170,000 soldiers and thousands of tanks, trucks, jeeps, and planes turned the southern part of Britain into one big army camp. The plan was for the Allied troops to cross the English Channel on June 4. They would come ashore on the beaches at Normandy, in France, and attack German forces there.

On Sunday, June 4, a terrible storm blew into the channel. However, weather forecasters told Eisenhower that there would be a break in the hurricane-like weather on Tuesday morning. General Eisenhower held off the attack. Now June 6, 1944, would be **D day**—the day the Allies would work together in the largest water-to-land invasion in history.

On June 6, in the early-morning darkness, the first of more than 4,000 ships began to leave Britain's coast to cross the English Channel. The slower ships went first, followed by the faster ships and airplanes, so that all the ships and planes would arrive at the same time in one giant striking force.

By 6:30 A.M., the first Allied soldiers had made it onto the beaches at Normandy. One soldier remembered:

"Everything was confusion. Shells were coming in all the time; boats burning, vehicles with nowhere to go bogging down, getting hit; supplies getting wet; boats trying to come in all the time, some hitting mines, exploding."

Many soldiers died on D day, but the invasion was successful. The Allies broke through the German lines and began moving inland from the west, pushing the Germans back. One sailor said, "I felt thankful, of course, that I seemed to have survived the worst part. I took a few deep breaths and felt suddenly elated [joyful], proud to be having even a tiny part in what was maybe the biggest battle of all history. At that moment, soaked to the skin, seasick, dead tired, cold, still scared, I would not have wanted to be anywhere else."

In December 1944 the Germans fought back at the Battle of the Bulge, in Belgium, but American General George Patton and his troops turned the Germans back. In March 1945 Patton's troops were the first to enter Germany.

REVIEW On what date did the Allies attack the Germans at Normandy?

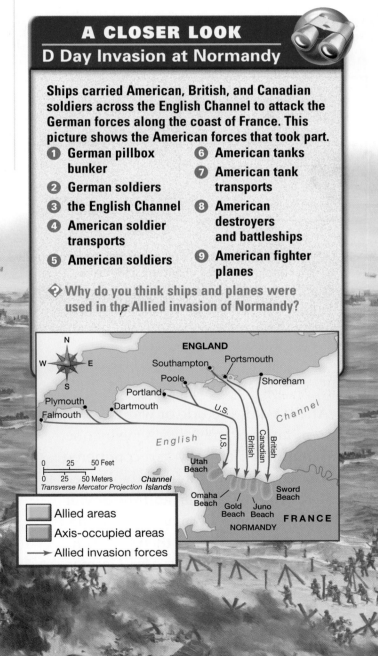

A CLOSER LOOK
D Day Invasion at Normandy

Ships carried American, British, and Canadian soldiers across the English Channel to attack the German forces along the coast of France. This picture shows the American forces that took part.

1 German pillbox bunker
2 German soldiers
3 the English Channel
4 American soldier transports
5 American soldiers
6 American tanks
7 American tank transports
8 American destroyers and battleships
9 American fighter planes

◈ Why do you think ships and planes were used in the Allied invasion of Normandy?

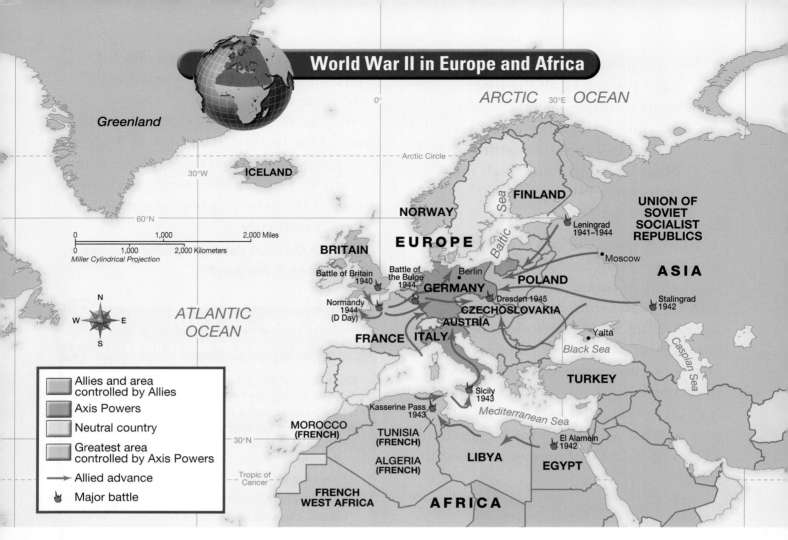

World War II in Europe and Africa

Greenland

ARCTIC 30°E OCEAN

Arctic Circle

30°W ICELAND

60°N

0   1,000   2,000 Miles

0   1,000   2,000 Kilometers
Miller Cylindrical Projection

FINLAND

NORWAY

EUROPE

BRITAIN

Battle of Britain 1940

Battle of the Bulge 1944

Normandy 1944 (D Day)

ATLANTIC OCEAN

FRANCE ITALY

AUSTRIA

GERMANY

Berlin

Dresden 1945

CZECHOSLOVAKIA

POLAND

Leningrad 1941–1944

UNION OF SOVIET SOCIALIST REPUBLICS

Moscow

ASIA

Stalingrad 1942

Yalta

Black Sea

Caspian Sea

TURKEY

Sicily 1943

Kasserine Pass 1943

Mediterranean Sea

El Alamein 1942

MOROCCO (FRENCH)

TUNISIA (FRENCH)

30°N

ALGERIA (FRENCH)

LIBYA

EGYPT

Tropic of Cancer

FRENCH WEST AFRICA

AFRICA

Baltic Sea

Legend:
- Allies and area controlled by Allies
- Axis Powers
- Neutral country
- Greatest area controlled by Axis Powers
- → Allied advance
- Major battle

GEOGRAPHY THEME

Location During the war, the areas controlled by the Axis Powers included much of Europe and Africa.

❖ Which European countries shown on the map were Axis Powers?

Victory in Europe

After D day, the tide of war began to turn in favor of the Allies. One by one, the countries Germany had conquered were freed as soldiers from the United States, Britain, Canada, and the Soviet Union forced the Germans out. In the fall of 1944, France and then Belgium were freed. Five months later, German troops in the Netherlands and Denmark surrendered to the Allies.

One Dutch woman, who was a little girl when the Netherlands was freed,

remembered what it was like when the Allies came. She said, "Big tanks rolled through the streets, and for the very first time I saw people who smiled and waved to us. They were soldiers! It was like a miracle."

The Allies were closing in on Berlin, the capital of Germany. Hitler knew the war was lost. Mussolini had been captured and killed. The Axis Powers' control over Europe was gone. In May 1945 the Allied troops from the east and the west met near Berlin. There they learned that Hitler had killed himself.

Berlin fell to the Soviets on May 2, 1945, and the German military leaders asked to surrender. On May 8, the Allies accepted their surrender. This day was called Victory in Europe Day, or V-E Day. It marked the end of the war in Europe.

President Roosevelt's health had grown worse. He did not live to see the end of the war. On April 12, 1945, Roosevelt died. Vice President Harry S. Truman became President.

REVIEW What happened to Axis leaders Hitler and Mussolini as World War II came to an end?

The Holocaust

Not until the war in Europe was over did people discover all that Hitler and the Nazis had done. As Allied troops marched across Central Europe toward Berlin, they freed people in the Nazis' concentration camps. The largest group of victims was the Jews, the people Hitler had blamed for Germany's problems.

The Nazis had made life difficult for Jews in every country they controlled. The Nazis began arresting Jews in 1938, sending between 20,000 and 30,000 of them to concentration camps. In 1939 after Germany invaded Poland, the Nazis gained control of that country's more than 3 million Jews. Millions more came under Nazi control in 1940 and 1941, as German armies invaded Belgium, Denmark, France, Norway, the Netherlands, and the Soviet Union.

Anne Frank was a young Jewish girl living in the Netherlands when World War II began. After the Nazis invaded the Netherlands in 1940, Anne and her family went into hiding. They lived in secret rooms in a building in the Dutch city of Amsterdam. Then, on August 4, 1944, their hiding place was discovered. Anne and her family were sent to concentration camps.

Prisoners in concentration camps suffered horribly. The Nazis forced Jewish people to wear a yellow Star of David to make them stand out.

Seven months later, Anne died at a camp named Bergen-Belsen.

In those small secret rooms, Anne kept a diary of her days in hiding. One diary entry described what was happening to Jews on the streets of Amsterdam after the Nazi invasion:

> **" It is terrible outside. Day and night more of those poor miserable people are being dragged off, with nothing but a rucksack [backpack] and a little money. . . . Families are torn apart, the men, women, and children all being separated. "**

In 1941 Hitler had begun what he called the "final solution to the Jewish question." It was the mass murder of all European Jews and other people he called "undesirable." The mass murder became known as the **Holocaust** (HOH•luh•kawst).

More than 6 million men, women, and children had been murdered in the camps. One of the largest camps was at Auschwitz (OWSH•vits), in Poland. About 1 1/2 million people were killed at this

Anne Frank (second from right) with family and friends in the Netherlands

camp. The Nazis killed people for many reasons. Many were killed for their religious or political beliefs. Others were killed because they were ill or disabled and could not work.

Beginning in late 1945, Nazi leaders accused of these crimes were brought to trial by the Allies. The most important trials were held in the German city of Nuremberg. Many Nazi leaders were found guilty and sentenced to death for their crimes.

REVIEW What was Hitler's "final solution"?

Changes in Technology

During World War II, new technology changed the way war was fought. Improvements to airplanes made them an even more important part of warfare than they had been in World War I. In World War II planes were used in battle and put to many other uses.

Bombers dropped bombs from the sky. Special planes called drones flew without pilots and dropped bombs on cities. Transport planes parachuted soldiers into battle. Aircraft carriers launched planes from the sea to attack places that soldiers could not reach easily by land.

Other military inventions were also used in World War II. To fight the attacks by airplanes, special cannons called anti-aircraft guns were developed. They could

Many Nazi leaders were tried for their crimes in Nuremberg, Germany.

Radar

Radar was developed in the 1930s by several countries. It was a way to use radio waves to locate faraway or hidden objects. Germany was one of the countries working to develop radar. However, Hitler ordered that the research be stopped. As a result, Allied radar systems were more advanced. By 1940, during the Battle of Britain, radar showed the Allies the number of German planes or ships that were approaching, as well as their speed and direction.

shoot large, exploding bullets to hit planes.

Another new invention helped find planes and ships in bad weather, at night, or over long distances. It was called radio detection and ranging, or radar. In addition, two-way radios let soldiers call for help or receive orders during battle.

Battlefield medicine also improved greatly during World War II. New drugs such as penicillin and sulfa helped keep soldiers' wounds from getting infected. In the Pacific a new chemical, DDT, was used to kill disease-carrying insects.

REVIEW **What new technologies were used for the first time in World War II?**

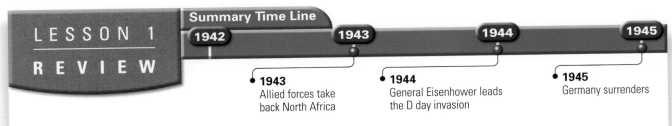

LESSON 1 REVIEW

Summary Time Line

1942 — 1943 — 1944 — 1945

1943 Allied forces take back North Africa

1944 General Eisenhower leads the D day invasion

1945 Germany surrenders

1 **MAIN IDEA** In what ways did World War II affect countries around the world?

2 **WHY IT MATTERS** What might have been different for the United States if the Axis Powers had won the war in Europe?

3 **VOCABULARY** Use the terms **D day** and **Holocaust** in a sentence about the war in Europe.

4 **TIME LINE** Did the Allies win in North Africa before or after the D day invasion?

5 **READING SKILL—Predict a Likely Outcome** How do you think the Allies would treat Germany after the war?

6 **SCIENCE AND TECHNOLOGY** How did weather forecasters affect D day?

7 **HISTORY** Who led the D day invasion?

8 **CRITICAL THINKING—Evaluate** What do you think would have been most difficult for Anne Frank and her family during their time of hiding from the Germans?

 PERFORMANCE—Write a Diary Entry Imagine that you are among the Allied troops freeing one of Germany's concentration camps. Write a diary entry in which you talk about what you saw when you entered the camp. Share your diary entry with a family member.

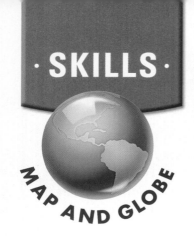

Compare Historical Maps

VOCABULARY
historical map

▶ WHY IT MATTERS

The end of World War II changed the map of Europe. The historical maps on pages 370 and 371 show those changes. A **historical map** provides information about a place at a certain time in history. Knowing how to use historical maps can help you learn how a region's borders have changed or how names given to an area changed at different times in history.

▶ WHAT YOU NEED TO KNOW

History books and many atlases contain historical maps. Often the title or key of a historical map tells what year or time period is shown on the map.

Map A: Europe in 1937

⊛ National capital

0   250   500 Miles
0   250   500 Kilometers
Azimuthal Equal-Area Projection

Map B: Europe in 1945

★ National capital

0   250   500 Miles
0   250   500 Kilometers
Azimuthal Equal-Area Projection

As you can tell from the titles, both these maps are of Europe. Each shows the continent in a different year. Map A shows Europe in 1937 before World War II began. Map B shows Europe after World War II ended.

Colors are important map symbols. Sometimes colors help you tell water from land on a map. Colors on a map can also show you the areas claimed by different countries.

▶ **PRACTICE THE SKILL**

Compare Map A with Map B. Use what you learn to answer these questions about how World War II changed Europe.

❶ Was Germany broken into East Germany and West Germany before or after World War II was fought?

❷ Did Finland gain or lose land because of World War II?

❸ Did Portugal's borders change or stay the same after World War II ended?

❹ What happened to the country of Estonia between 1937 and 1945?

▶ **APPLY WHAT YOU LEARNED**

Write a paragraph that describes what these historical maps show. In your paragraph, also explain why historical maps are useful. Then share your paragraph with a classmate.

Practice your map and globe skills with the **GeoSkills CD-ROM**.

MAP AND GLOBE SKILLS

MAIN IDEA

Read to learn why it took the Allies longer to win the war in the Pacific.

WHY IT MATTERS

The war in the Pacific brought about the end of World War II.

VOCABULARY

island hopping
V-J Day

War in the Pacific

1930   1940   1950

1942–1945

In the United States and in Europe, people cheered when they heard of Germany's surrender. However, they knew that although the Axis Powers had been defeated in Europe, the war was not yet over. Japan still had to be defeated.

Battles in the Pacific

Within days after the attack on Pearl Harbor, Japanese forces attacked and took over Hong Kong, Guam, Wake Island, and the Philippines. Other islands, too, fell to the Japanese. By the spring of 1942, it seemed that Japan might win the war in the Pacific.

After attacks from Japanese planes, the United States aircraft carrier *Lexington* burns during the Battle of the Coral Sea.

Then two battles turned the war in favor of the Allies. One was the Battle of the Coral Sea. This battle took place when Allied ships sailed to the Coral Sea to try to stop Japan from advancing toward Australia. It was the first naval battle in history in which enemy ships did not see each other. Instead, the whole battle was fought by planes that had been launched from aircraft carriers. The Battle of the Coral Sea ended with no real victory. However, the Allies had stopped Japan from invading Australia.

Soon Japanese leaders sent a coded message to their navy. The message ordered Japan's forces to attack Midway Island, about 1,000 miles (1,609 km) west of Hawaii. If Japan won Midway, it would have a base from which its ships, submarines, and planes could threaten not only Hawaii but also the western coast of the United States.

However, the Allies learned what the Japanese were planning. The Allies had broken the Japanese codes and were able now to read Japan's plans. Admiral Chester Nimitz was in charge of the Allied fleet that rushed to meet the Japanese fleet. From June 4 to June 8, 1942, the Battle of Midway raged. When it was over, four of Japan's aircraft carriers had been destroyed with more than 200 planes aboard. For the first time since Pearl Harbor, the Japanese were on the run.

Naval Admiral Chester Nimitz served as the commander in chief of the United States fleet in the Pacific.

Breaking Japan's codes was one reason the Allies won the Battle of Midway. Admiral Nimitz later said that ". . . the Battle of Midway would have ended differently" if the United States had not broken Japan's codes.

After Midway the Allies began to force the Japanese out of the islands they had conquered. However, the Allies would not take back every island. Instead, they followed a plan of island hopping. **Island hopping** meant that the Allies would fight for only certain key islands as they worked their way toward an invasion of Japan.

FAST FACT During World War II, battleships were named after states, submarines after fish and marine animals, cruisers after cities or territories, and destroyers after military heroes.

One group of islands they wanted to take back was the Philippine Islands because they had been a United States territory for many years. In early 1942, American and Philippine troops, led by General Douglas MacArthur, had fought the Japanese for four months but finally were forced to surrender. General MacArthur was ordered to leave the islands before the surrender. As he left, he made this promise to the people of the Philippines: "I shall return."

Two years later General MacArthur kept his promise. In October 1944 General MacArthur and his troops landed in the

United States soldiers raise the United States flag after the battle of Iwo Jima.

Philippines. By July 1945 the Allies had taken the Philippine Islands back from the Japanese.

Victory in the Philippines did more than push the Japanese out of the islands. It left the southernmost island of Japan unprotected. It also gave the Allies a land base from which they could attack Japan.

REVIEW **What was island hopping?**

Iwo Jima and Okinawa

Battles for the islands of Iwo Jima (EE•woh JEE•muh) and Okinawa (oh•kuh•NAH•wah) followed the victory in the Philippines. In both battles, the Allies won. However, the cost of these victories in human lives was very high. At Iwo Jima more than 25,000 United States Marines—almost one out of every three Marines fighting there—were killed. Almost all of the 21,000 Japanese defending the island died. At Okinawa more than 7,600 Allied soldiers

A CLOSER LOOK
An Aircraft Carrier

With the ability to carry large numbers of aircraft and troops, aircraft carriers played an important role in victories for the United States during World War II.

1. The bridge acts as the control center for navigation and communication.

2. The flight deck provides a runway for the carrier's aircraft.

3. Elevators lift aircraft from the hangar deck to the flight deck.

4. Besides acting as a storage area for aircraft, the area below the flight deck also includes living space for the crew and the ship's support systems and engines.

❓ Why is the deck of an aircraft carrier almost completely flat?

and Marines were killed or reported missing in action. Many thousands more were injured. More than 107,000 Japanese soldiers and civilians were killed.

The war in the Pacific was very different from the war in the Atlantic. The islands of the Pacific Ocean had a different geography from either Europe or North Africa. In the Pacific, soldiers faced tropical rain forests. One American soldier wrote of the difficulties of fighting in the heat, humidity, and heavy rains of the rain forests of the Pacific Islands: "[There was] always the rain and the mud, torrid heat and teeming [swarming] insect life. . . ." Because of the harsh conditions and the fierce battles, the numbers of those killed or wounded grew as the Allies moved closer to Japan.

REVIEW **Who won the Battle of Iwo Jima?**

The Atom Bomb

On August 2, 1939, a scientist named Albert Einstein wrote a letter to President Franklin D. Roosevelt. In the letter, he warned of Germany's plans to build a new kind of bomb. This bomb, Einstein wrote, was an "extremely powerful bomb of a new type . . . [that when] carried by boat and exploded in a port might well destroy the whole port together with some of the surrounding territory."

Because of this letter, President Roosevelt created a secret group of scientists. The group was so secret that Vice President Harry S. Truman did not know of it until he himself became President! The goal of this group was to get ahead of Germany in creating this new kind of bomb.

Dr. J. Robert Oppenheimer was named to lead the scientists. He went from university to university, asking the nation's top scientists to come to Los Alamos, New Mexico, to help him with the Manhattan Project. This was the name by which this secret work would be known.

By July 1945 the Manhattan Project's scientists had built a new bomb. They called it an atom bomb, because its explosive power came from splitting atoms. On July 16 they tested it in the New Mexico desert.

The explosion from this first atom bomb was very large. It had the force of more than 18,000 tons of dynamite, enough to shake the earth! Along with the explosion came a blinding flash and a cloud of smoke the shape of a giant mushroom. One scientist who watched

J. Robert Oppenheimer

the test bomb explode in New Mexico said, "I am sure that at the end of the world—in the last millisecond of the earth's existence—the last man will see something very similar to what we have seen."

REVIEW **Why did Albert Einstein write President Roosevelt a letter?**

Victory over Japan

By July 1945 Japan was in a difficult position. Its navy had been destroyed. Its air force was weakened. It had lost most of the territories it had invaded. With those losses came the loss of the raw materials Japan got from those territories. For example, in 1942 Japan got 40 percent of all the oil drilled in lands it had invaded. In 1943, as the Allies took back islands, they cut Japan off from those oil supplies.

In addition, Allied planes were fire-bombing Japanese cities, including Tokyo, in early March of 1945. High winds fanned the flames of the fires caused by the bombs until they had burned up 16 square miles (41 sq km) of Tokyo. The fires killed more than 80,000 people. They also left more than 1 million people homeless. One newspaper reporter wrote, "The city was as bright as at sunrise . . . . Clouds of smoke, soot, even sparks driven by the storm flew over it. That night we thought the whole of Tokyo was reduced

This photo shows United States and Filipino troops held in a Japanese prison camp.

to ashes." Similar damage was done during firebombing raids on other Japanese cities.

On July 26, 1945, the Allies sent Japan a message. It said that Japan had to surrender immediately. If it did not, the Allies would continue the bombing. Still, Japan would not surrender. President Harry S. Truman then made the difficult decision to drop an atom bomb on Japan. He said he wanted to end the war quickly and save American lives.

On August 6, 1945, the American bomber *Enola Gay* flew over the industrial city of Hiroshima (hir•uh•SHEE•muh),

Japan. It dropped a single bomb. The bomb destroyed almost all of Hiroshima and killed more than 70,000 people, mostly civilians who lived there.

The Allies were sure that the terrible destruction caused by the atom bomb would force Japan to surrender right away. Yet Japan still did not surrender. On August 9 the United States dropped a second atom bomb, this time on the city of Nagasaki (nah•guh•SAH•kee).

At that time Clarence Graham of the United States was a prisoner of war being held in Japan, just east of Nagasaki. He described the atomic explosion on the city.

Regions **Several major battles of World War II were fought in the Pacific, where the war ended.**

❯ In what general direction shown on the map did the Allied forces advance?

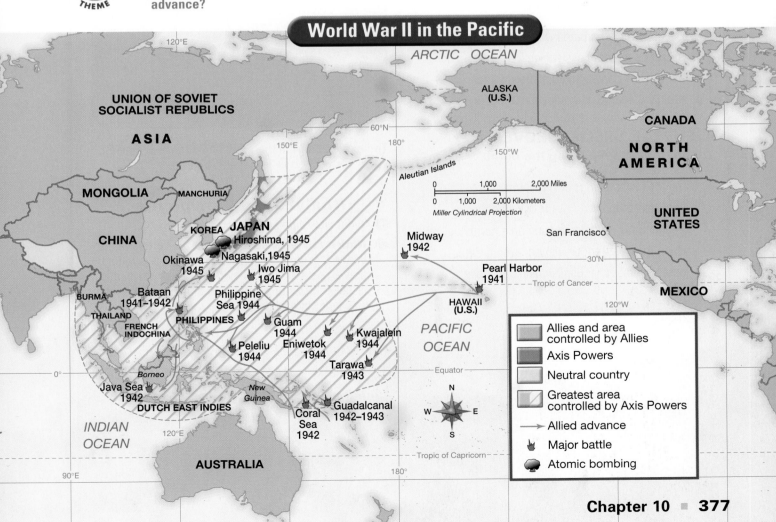

World War II in the Pacific

He said, "We saw a brilliant flash—there's no way to describe the brightness. You couldn't tell where the flash came from—just brilliant brightness. Then seconds later . . . you could feel the ground shaking."

Japan then agreed to surrender, and fighting stopped. That day, August 15, 1945, became known as **V-J Day**—Victory over Japan Day.

The Allies cheered and laughed and wept. One American soldier fighting in

POINTS OF VIEW
Dropping the Atom Bomb

The question of whether or not to use atom bombs was a difficult one to answer. President Truman asked a committee of scientists and officials whether the United States should use them. After reviewing the options, the committee said it should. Others opposed this advice.

ADMIRAL WILLIAM LEAHY, a top adviser to President Truman

❝The use of this barbarous [cruel] weapon . . . was of no material assistance [real help] in our war against Japan. The Japanese were already defeated and ready to surrender.❞

GENERAL LESLIE GROVES, the chief of the project developing the bomb

❝The atomic bombings of Hiroshima and Nagasaki ended World War II. While they brought death and destruction on a horrifying scale, they averted [prevented] even greater losses—American, English, and Japanese.❞

The explosion from the atom bomb (above) caused mass destruction in Nagasaki (below).

Analyze the Viewpoints
❶ What views did each person hold?
❷ **Make It Relevant** Look at the Letters to the Editor section of your newspaper. Find two letters that express different viewpoints about the same issue. Then write a paragraph that summarizes the viewpoint of each letter.

All across the United States, Americans celebrated V-J Day at the end of World War II.

the Pacific remembered what happened after the atom bombs were dropped: "We . . . cried with relief and joy."

On September 2, 1945, representatives from Japan's government came aboard the USS *Missouri*, which was anchored in Tokyo Bay. There they and representatives of the United States government signed the surrender papers. The end of World War II had finally come.

REVIEW Why did Japan finally surrender to the United States?

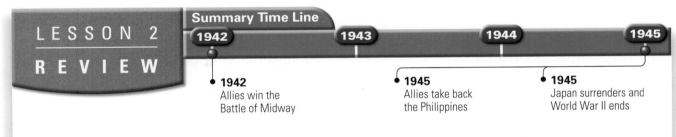

LESSON 2
REVIEW

Summary Time Line

1942   1943   1944   1945

1942
Allies win the Battle of Midway

1945
Allies take back the Philippines

1945
Japan surrenders and World War II ends

1 **MAIN IDEA** What two battles were the turning point in the war in the Pacific?

2 **WHY IT MATTERS** What was V-J Day?

3 **VOCABULARY** Write a sentence explaining the Allied plan of **island hopping**.

4 **TIME LINE** Which happened first, the Battle of Midway or the battles to take back the Philippines?

5 **READING SKILL—Predict a Likely Outcome** How do you think other countries reacted to the United States dropping the atom bomb?

6 **GEOGRAPHY** How was the geography of many of the Pacific islands different from the geographies of Europe and Africa?

7 **CRITICAL THINKING—Synthesize** What might have been different about World War II if the Japanese had surrendered after the battle for Okinawa?

PERFORMANCE—Give a Speech
Imagine that World War II has just ended. Your family has received word that your uncle, a United States soldier, is on his way home from serving in the Pacific. In fact, he is due home tomorrow! You have been chosen to give a speech, thanking him for his service during the war. Write the speech you would give. Practice giving the speech aloud. Then share your speech with the class.

·SKILLS· Read Parallel Time Lines

▶ WHY IT MATTERS

When there are many events happening at the same time in different places, it can be difficult to put the events in order on one time line. Parallel time lines can help. **Parallel time lines** are two or more time lines that show the same period of time. Parallel time lines can also show events that happened in different places.

▶ WHAT YOU NEED TO KNOW

The parallel time lines on these pages show events that took place during World War II, from 1941 to 1945. Time Line A shows the important events that affected the European front. Time Line B shows the important events that affected the Pacific front. You can use these parallel time lines to compare when different events in different places happened.

▶ PRACTICE THE SKILL

Use these parallel time lines to answer the following questions:

1 Which occurred first, D day or V-J Day?

2 Why do you think the label *Harry S. Truman becomes President of the United States* is shown on both time lines?

3 Did the Allies capture Guam before or after they won in North Africa?

4 In what year did V-E Day and V-J Day occur?

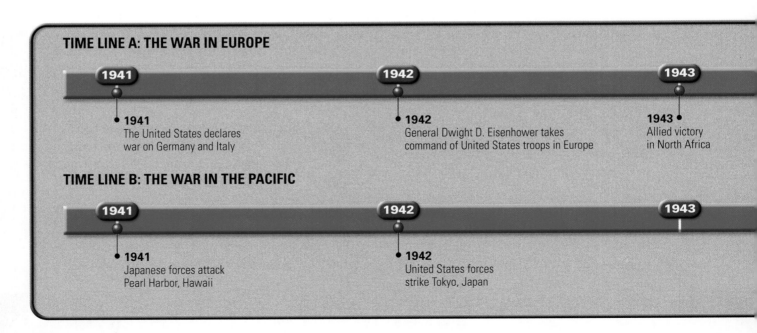

TIME LINE A: THE WAR IN EUROPE

1941

1941
The United States declares war on Germany and Italy

1942

1942
General Dwight D. Eisenhower takes command of United States troops in Europe

1943

1943
Allied victory in North Africa

TIME LINE B: THE WAR IN THE PACIFIC

1941

1941
Japanese forces attack Pearl Harbor, Hawaii

1942

1942
United States forces strike Tokyo, Japan

1943

On board the USS *Missouri*, a Japanese delegate signs the surrender papers that ended World War II.

▶ APPLY WHAT YOU LEARNED

Create parallel time lines of events that have happened in your lifetime. On one time line show the important events in your life, beginning with the year you were born and ending with the present year. On the other time line, show important events that have taken place in the United States during these same years. Share your time lines with a classmate.

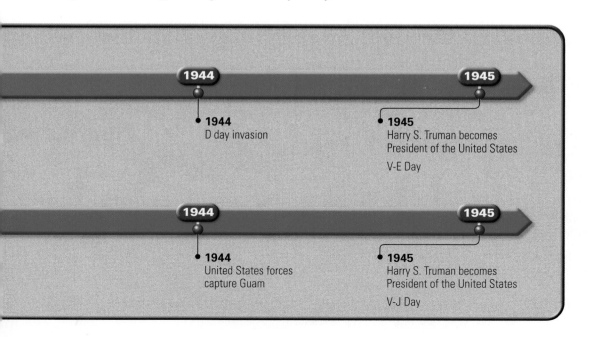

1944
1945

1944
D day invasion

1945
Harry S. Truman becomes
President of the United States

V-E Day

1944
1945

1944
United States forces
capture Guam

1945
Harry S. Truman becomes
President of the United States

V-J Day

MAIN IDEA
Read to learn how life in the United States changed after World War II.

WHY IT MATTERS
The American economy, made strong by the war, remained strong after the war ended.

VOCABULARY
refugees
veteran
baby boom

American soldiers from many wars, including World War II, are buried in Arlington National Cemetery in Arlington, Virginia.

Life After World War II

1930   1940   1950

1944–1950

Many Americans were afraid that the end of the war might also mean the end of the jobs and money the war had brought to the United States. They wondered if there would be enough work for everyone. Yet Americans were to find that the end of the war did not bring economic hardships with it.

The Cost of the War

The cost of World War II in terms of human lives was great for all the countries involved. About 400,000 American soldiers and close to 17 million soldiers from other countries had died in the fighting. Germany alone lost more than 3 million soldiers. Millions of civilians also died in the fighting. Some died in fires caused by the bombing raids. Others died from diseases.

When the war ended, cities and towns in Europe and Japan and in other places where fighting had taken place were in ruins. In some cities nine out of every ten buildings were too badly damaged to be used. Many of the people who survived had no homes, no jobs, and often nothing to eat. Some of these

Millions of American soldiers returning home after the war had a large effect on the country's economy.

people were prisoners of war, some had been freed from concentration camps, and some had fled cities that were being invaded. All these people became **refugees**—people who seek shelter and safety elsewhere. Some traveled from place to place in search of food and a safe place to live.

To help the refugees, the Allies set up camps and provided them with food, shelter, and medical care until they could find homes. The United States also worked with other nations to create agencies to help these millions of people. People in the United States gave much of the money spent by these agencies.

REVIEW How did the United States help those who were left homeless by the war?

Soldiers Return

The war was over. Millions of soldiers were returning home. To help them re-adjust to civilian life, or settle into it, the government passed the Servicemen's Readjustment Act. Americans were soon calling it the GI Bill—the Government Issue Bill of Rights. The GI Bill was passed in 1944. Just as the United States had planned for the war, the nation also had planned for peace.

The GI Bill helped many **veterans**, or those who had served in the armed forces. It stated that veterans could get government money to pay for a college education or for job training. In addition, veterans would receive a monthly allowance while they were in school.

Many veterans returned to school under the GI Bill. This photo shows veterans applying for educational courses.

Almost half of all the veterans took advantage of the GI Bill to get more education. In fact, General Dwight D. Eisenhower himself went back to school on the GI Bill.

With so many veterans going to school, many colleges and universities often ran out of room for housing and classes. The government helped by taking apart unused military buildings and sending them in pieces to be rebuilt and used by the nation's colleges.

The GI Bill also provided loans that had low interest rates. Because of the low interest rates, veterans would not have to pay back as much money as they would to repay a loan from a bank. Many veterans used these loans to buy houses and to start businesses. The government also provided one year of income to veterans who could not find work.

REVIEW **What was the GI Bill?**

The use of automobiles increased after gas rationing ended.

After the war, drive-in movie theaters became a popular place for entertainment. Some drive-in theaters, like this one in New York, held up to 1,200 cars!

Changes at Home

Most rationing ended with the end of the war. Many people were very happy that gasoline was no longer rationed. They could now get back in their automobiles and not worry about being able to get enough gas to go places.

A new place that people drove to was the drive-in movie theater. Between 1947 and 1950, about 2,000 drive-in theaters were built across the country. In these theaters people drove up to a parking spot in front of a huge movie screen, attached a speaker to their car, and then watched the movie.

Technology brought another new form of entertainment after the war. It was called the television. The first television sets were used in 1941, but it was not until after the war that television became popular. By 1949 Americans were buying almost 100,000 sets a week! In that same year, many TV stations started up. These stations broadcast everything from variety shows to sports games. Television also began to be used for education. For the first time, New York City high school students were able to watch a live meeting of national leaders on television.

People who had saved money during the war were ready to buy products. They wanted everything from houses to appliances to automobiles. Factories that had been making war supplies went back to producing consumer goods.

These factories could hardly keep up with consumers' demands. In fact, sometimes there were shortages of the goods that people wanted.

New industries did well after the war. The electronics industry grew rapidly, mainly because of the number of television sets people were buying. Other industries, such as the plastics and the frozen foods industries, also grew. Farm production stayed high after the war. For a while, the American farmer was also needed to provide the animals and the feed that would help start farms in war-torn countries.

The nation's economy remained strong. Some workers lost their jobs to returning soldiers, and many women left jobs at factories to care for their families. Still, the number of unemployed people stayed low. To make sure that unemployment stayed low, the government passed the Employment Act of 1946. This law created a council to advise the President on economic matters. This council also encouraged the government to take steps to keep Americans working.

REVIEW What product caused the electronics industry to grow after the war?

The Baby Boom

After the war, soldiers returned home to their families. Others started families with wives they had met and married while they were away from home. In the years right after the war many babies were born. In fact, about 50 million babies were born in the United States during the 15 years after the war ended! So many babies were born that this period became known as the **baby boom**.

Many of these new and growing families went to live in housing developments in the suburbs. Suburbs were growing as fast as they could be built. Many suburbs

This photo (left) shows the wedding of a United States Army sergeant and a Red Cross worker from Northern Ireland. After World War II, the couple started a new life and a new family in Arlington, Virginia (below).

The demand for housing became so strong in the postwar United States that new neighborhoods sprang up all over the country.

offered people new houses, playgrounds, swimming pools, and schools. Shopping centers were also built nearby. In the suburb of Levittown, on Long Island, New York, more than 17,000 new homes were built after the war. Sometimes as many as 36 houses were built in one day.

Life in the suburbs made Americans need their cars more than ever. Many people lived in the suburbs but worked in the cities. They needed their cars to get to and from work.

REVIEW What encouraged American families to move to the suburbs?

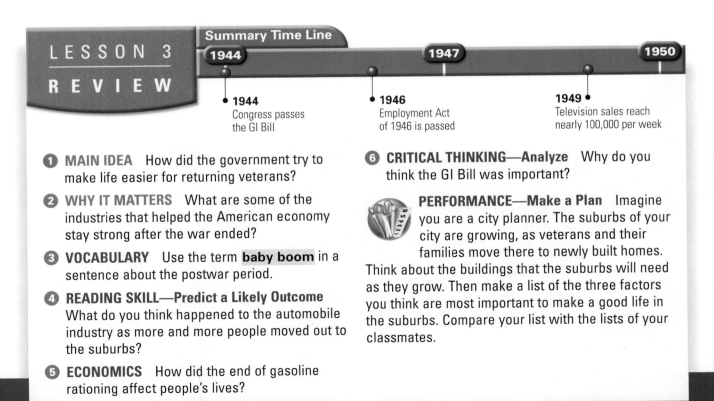

LESSON 3 REVIEW

Summary Time Line

| 1944 | 1947 | 1950 |

1944
Congress passes the GI Bill

1946
Employment Act of 1946 is passed

1949
Television sales reach nearly 100,000 per week

1 **MAIN IDEA** How did the government try to make life easier for returning veterans?

2 **WHY IT MATTERS** What are some of the industries that helped the American economy stay strong after the war ended?

3 **VOCABULARY** Use the term **baby boom** in a sentence about the postwar period.

4 **READING SKILL—Predict a Likely Outcome** What do you think happened to the automobile industry as more and more people moved out to the suburbs?

5 **ECONOMICS** How did the end of gasoline rationing affect people's lives?

6 **CRITICAL THINKING—Analyze** Why do you think the GI Bill was important?

PERFORMANCE—Make a Plan Imagine you are a city planner. The suburbs of your city are growing, as veterans and their families move there to newly built homes. Think about the buildings that the suburbs will need as they grow. Then make a list of the three factors you think are most important to make a good life in the suburbs. Compare your list with the lists of your classmates.

A Changed World

1930   1940   1950

1945–1950

MAIN IDEA
Read to learn how some nations of the world faced a new threat—the threat of communism.

WHY IT MATTERS
Without aid from the United States, many countries that are now democracies might have had communist governments after the war.

VOCABULARY
superpower
arms race
free world
cold war

At the end of World War II, General Douglas MacArthur was present when Japan surrendered. Afterward, MacArthur spoke of his hopes for the future. He said, "It is my earnest hope . . . that from this solemn occasion a better world shall emerge."

In the years after the war, the United States and the Soviet Union became the world's most powerful nations. They were called the **superpowers** because of the important role they played in world events. The two superpowers were very different from each other, so there were many conflicts between them. Although the two nations never went to war with each other, the threat of war was always present. For this reason, the years following World War II were a frightening time for many people.

The United Nations

Just as world leaders did after World War I, they turned to the idea of an organization of nations after World War II. This time the United States supported the idea. In April 1945,

Representatives of countries discuss the formation of the United Nations.

Divisions of the United Nations

GENERAL ASSEMBLY
- Each member nation has one vote.
- Makes decisions by two-thirds majority on important matters such as international peace and security, admitting new members, and the UN budget

SECURITY COUNCIL
- Fifteen council members, five of which are permanent members from the United States, Britain, France, Soviet Union, and China
- Is responsible for maintaining international peace and security
- Can order negotiations, economic bans, or military actions

ECONOMIC AND SOCIAL COUNCIL
- Fifty-four members elected by the General Assembly
- Works to improve economic and social conditions worldwide
- Individual groups work on issues such as human rights, crime prevention, and environmental protection.

INTERNATIONAL COURT OF JUSTICE
- Fifteen judges elected by the General Assembly and the Security Council
- Decides disputes among nations

SECRETARIAT
- Headed by the Secretary General, who is appointed by the General Assembly
- Is responsible for managing United Nations offices throughout the world

Analyze Charts The United Nations is organized into different areas of responsibility. Today almost 200 nations are members of the organization.

◈ Which division of the United Nations is responsible for deciding disputes between nations?

delegates from 50 countries met in San Francisco, California. They formed the United Nations, or UN. The purpose of the UN is to keep world peace and to promote cooperation among nations.

The United Nations soon found that keeping the peace was going to be a difficult task. The Nazis no longer threatened Europe or the rest of the world. Yet a new danger to the world's democracies had appeared—communism.

The United States and the Soviet Union had been allies during World War II.

British Prime Minister Winston Churchill works at his desk.

After the war this quickly changed. The Soviet Union was a communist country. It set up communist governments in the Eastern European countries it had invaded during the war. Joseph Stalin, the Soviet leader, felt that the Soviet Union had to control Eastern Europe to protect itself. He said that in this region, any "freely elected government would be anti-Soviet, and that we cannot allow." By 1948 Bulgaria, Czechoslovakia, Hungary, Poland, Romania, Albania, and Yugoslavia were communist countries. This happened so fast that Winston Churchill, the prime minister of Britain, said with alarm that the Soviets "are spreading across Europe like a tide."

Churchill was one of the first leaders to express concern about the spread of communism. In 1946 he spoke of his concerns at a university in the United States. He said that "an iron curtain has descended across the continent" between Eastern Europe and the West. He warned that the United States should remain ready for military conflict with the Soviet Union.

People across the world were also thinking about what the atom bombs had done to the Japanese cities of Hiroshima and Nagasaki. The Soviet Union feared the power of the United States, which had shown its ability to destroy a whole city with one bomb. Soon the Soviet Union was building its own atom bomb.

After the Soviet Union had the atom bomb, however, the United States made an even more powerful bomb—the hydrogen bomb. Scientists said that this bomb was 1,000 times more powerful than the atom bomb.

An arms race had begun. In an **arms race** one country builds up weapons to protect itself against another country. The other country then builds even more weapons to protect itself. Both the United States and the Soviet Union believed that having the most and the strongest weapons would keep their people safe.

REVIEW **Why did Stalin want to control Eastern Europe?**

Scientists Albert Einstein (left) and J. Robert Oppenheimer (right) had played roles in the development of the atom bomb.

President Harry S. Truman (left) meets with Secretary of State George C. Marshall (right).

A New Role for the United States

President Truman watched the spread of communism. He wrote, "Unless Russia [the Soviet Union] is faced with an iron fist and strong language, another war is in the making." He felt that the spread of communism was a threat to freedom. In 1947 the United States began to help countries fight communism by giving them military and economic aid. In the fight against communism, the United States and its allies were known as the **free world**.

The policy of helping countries fight communism became known as the Truman Doctrine. The economic aid offered by the Truman Doctrine helped the United States contain, or hold back, the Soviet threat. This policy was necessary, Truman said, because "the free peoples of the world look to us for support in maintaining their freedoms."

In 1948 Secretary of State George C. Marshall developed the Marshall Plan. This plan was to provide more aid to nations in war-torn Europe. According to the plan, the United States would help the nations of Europe rebuild their businesses, factories, roads, and airports over the next four years.

The Marshall Plan was a success. By the end of the four years, $12 billion had been sent to European countries in the form of money, machinery, livestock, and other materials that would help them rebuild. Many Europeans were pleased with the results of the plan.

REVIEW Why was the Marshall Plan considered a success?

New Threats to Peace

At the end of World War II, the Allies divided Germany into four parts. Each of the major Allies controlled one part. The United States, Britain, and France worked together to build a strong West Germany out of their parts. The Soviet Union took charge of East Germany and formed a communist government there.

Berlin, the capital of Germany, was in East Germany. It was divided into four parts, too. In June 1948 the Soviet Union challenged the other Allies by blocking all the highway, rail, and water routes into West Berlin. The Soviets hoped to drive the Western Allies out of Berlin by cutting off the routes by which food and other supplies were delivered.

Some Americans wanted to ignore what was happening in Berlin and pull out of the city. Others agreed with General Lucius Clay, who commanded American forces stationed in Germany after the war. He said, "If we mean . . . to hold [protect] Europe against communism, we must not budge. . . . I believe the future of democracy requires us to stay."

No one wanted to send supplies over land, because armed vehicles would be needed to break through the Soviet

United States Air Force pilots were trained to fly cargo transport planes (left) to deliver food and supplies to the people of West Berlin (below).

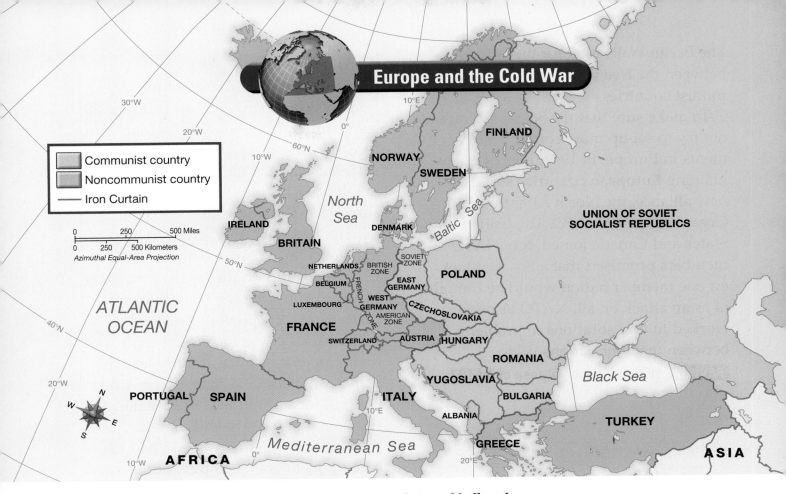

Europe and the Cold War

Communist country

Noncommunist country

Iron Curtain

0   250   500 Miles

0   250   500 Kilometers

Azimuthal Equal-Area Projection

NORWAY

FINLAND

SWEDEN

North Sea

DENMARK

Baltic Sea

UNION OF SOVIET SOCIALIST REPUBLICS

IRELAND

BRITAIN

NETHERLANDS

BRITISH ZONE

SOVIET ZONE

EAST GERMANY

POLAND

BELGIUM

FRENCH ZONE

WEST GERMANY

CZECHOSLOVAKIA

LUXEMBOURG

AMERICAN ZONE

ATLANTIC OCEAN

FRANCE

SWITZERLAND

AUSTRIA

HUNGARY

ROMANIA

YUGOSLAVIA

Black Sea

PORTUGAL

SPAIN

ITALY

BULGARIA

ALBANIA

TURKEY

GREECE

Mediterranean Sea

AFRICA

ASIA

Place   **World War II changed Europe in ways that would affect the world for years to come.**

❓ **What does this map show about changes that took place in Germany after World War II?**

GEOGRAPHY THEME

blockade. That could mean war. General Clay thought about this problem. Then he called General Curtis LeMay of the Air Force. "Curt, can you transport coal by air?" he asked. The answer was "yes." Soon the United States was delivering coal and other supplies by plane.

Using three airports, American and British pilots made more than 272,000 flights over East Germany to West Berlin. They carried more than 2 million tons of food and supplies to the people there. On some days, planes landed on an average of once every 3 minutes all day long. This way of bringing supplies by plane became known as the Berlin Airlift. Six months later, the Soviet Union backed down and

ended the blockade. Supplies could again be delivered over land to West Berlin.

After the blockade ended, many people tried to leave East Berlin to escape from communist rule. In time, the East German government, with Soviet help, built a fence to keep people from leaving. Then East Germany took down the fence and put up a concrete wall with barbed wire on the top. The Berlin Wall, as it came to be known, was guarded by soldiers who were ready to shoot anyone who tried to cross it. The Berlin Wall became one of the best-known symbols of the Cold War. A **cold war** is a war that is fought mostly with ideas and money instead of with soldiers and weapons.

The Berlin Wall stood for the division between the free world and the communist countries.

To make sure that the Soviet Union did not try to set up more communist governments in Europe, in 1949 most of the remaining European countries started a new alliance, the North Atlantic Treaty Organization, or NATO. The United States and Canada joined, too. NATO members promised that a Soviet attack on one member nation would be thought of as an attack on all. NATO also worked to find solutions to problems between member nations.

REVIEW What was the purpose of NATO?

Changes in Japan

After the war many Allied forces remained in Japan. They were under the command of General Douglas MacArthur. Most of these troops were American, since the United States had been the most involved in bringing about the Japanese surrender. The troops disarmed the Japanese military and stayed to help transform Japan into a democracy. In 1947 a constitution for Japan, written by MacArthur's advisers, went into effect. By its terms, the power to rule would be in the hands of the Japanese people, not their emperor or their military leaders.

In September 1951 most of the Allied nations, including the United States, signed a peace treaty with Japan. According to the treaty, Japan had to give up its overseas empire, but it was allowed to rebuild its military forces.

This treaty (left) created the North Atlantic Treaty Organization. Representatives of NATO (below) give a press conference on the treaty.

General MacArthur (center) inspects the Honor Guard (left) outside the American Embassy during Japan's transformation to democracy.

Most of the Allied forces were then sent home. However, another treaty permitted the United States to keep some troops in Japan to help the Japanese change to a democratic government.

The war left many of Japan's factories and cities destroyed. Many of Japan's trading ships were also destroyed, leaving Japan cut off from the rest of the world. People were left homeless and jobless. In time, people began to move from farming villages to cities to find work. In the cities, they worked in the new industries that were being developed. It took almost ten years for Japan to fully recover from the war.

Over time, relations between Japan and the United States improved. Japan became an important trading partner and ally of the United States.

REVIEW Why did Allied forces remain in Japan after the Japanese surrendered?

LESSON 4 REVIEW

Summary Time Line

1945 — 1946 — 1947 — 1948 — 1949 — 1950

1945 The United Nations is founded

1947 The Truman Doctrine is issued

1949 NATO is formed

1. **MAIN IDEA** What kind of government was a threat to freedom after World War II?

2. **WHY IT MATTERS** What was the purpose of the Marshall Plan?

3. **VOCABULARY** Use the terms arms race and free world in a sentence about the start of the Cold War.

4. **TIME LINE** When was the United Nations founded?

5. **READING SKILL—Predict a Likely Outcome** What do you think people in West Berlin thought would happen to the Soviet blockade?

6. **HISTORY** Why did the Soviet Union blockade West Berlin?

7. **CRITICAL THINKING—Analyze** How did the differences between the United States and the Soviet Union cause problems after World War II?

PERFORMANCE—Draw a Picture During the Berlin Airlift, pilots sometimes attached candy to little parachutes and dropped them to the waiting children of West Berlin. Draw a picture of children getting candy in this way during the Berlin Airlift. Share your drawing with the class.

10 Review and Test Preparation

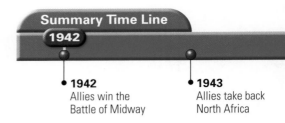

Summary Time Line
1942

● **1942**
Allies win the
Battle of Midway

● **1943**
Allies take back
North Africa

USE YOUR READING SKILLS

Complete this graphic organizer by predicting outcomes about Allied victories in World War II. A copy of this graphic organizer appears on page 100 of the Activity Book.

Allied Victories in World War II

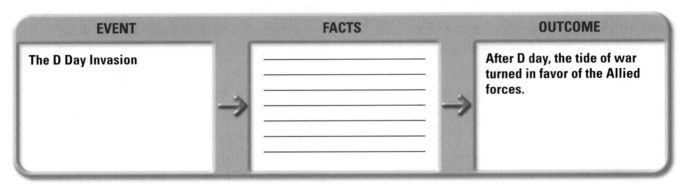

EVENT	FACTS	OUTCOME
The D Day Invasion		After D day, the tide of war turned in favor of the Allied forces.

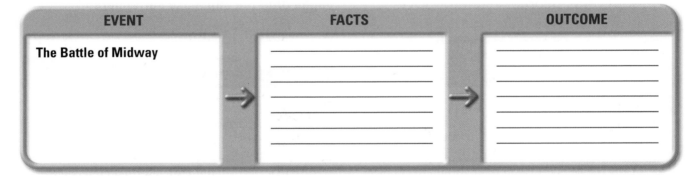

EVENT	FACTS	OUTCOME
The Battle of Midway		

THINK & WRITE

Write a Compare and Contrast Essay
Write an essay comparing and contrasting World War I with World War II. Include in your essay why the wars began, who fought in the wars, what weapons were used in the wars, and where the wars took place.

Write a Letter   Imagine you are an American soldier in World War II. You are stationed on an island in the Pacific. Write a letter home describing an average day. Your letter could include information about the weather, the food, and the sleeping conditions.

1946

1950

● **1945**
World War II ends

● **1947**
The Truman Doctrine
is issued

● **1949**
NATO is formed

USE THE TIME LINE

Use the chapter summary time line to answer these questions.

1 When did World War II end?

2 When was NATO formed?

USE VOCABULARY

Use each of the following terms in a sentence that will help explain its meaning.

front (p. 362)

V-J Day (p. 378)

refugee (p. 383)

veteran (p. 383)

cold war (p. 393)

RECALL FACTS

Answer these questions.

3 Where did the D day invasion take place?

4 Who was Anne Frank?

5 Why did Albert Einstein write a letter to President Franklin D. Roosevelt in 1939?

6 What was the GI Bill?

Write the letter of the best choice.

7 **TEST PREP** World War II was fought on two main fronts in—
  A the United States and Asia.
  B Europe and Africa, and in the Pacific.
  C Australia and South America.
  D Canada and Mexico.

8 **TEST PREP** The United States' policy of helping countries fight communism was called—
  F Americans Against Communism.
  G the Free World Plan.
  H the Truman Doctrine.
  J the Marshall Plan.

THINK CRITICALLY

9 How do you think the scientists on the Manhattan Project felt about building such a destructive weapon?

10 Why did President Truman feel that the spread of communism was a threat to freedom?

APPLY SKILLS

Compare Historical Maps
Use the information and maps on pages 370 and 371 to help answer these questions.

11 When would you use historical maps?

12 Where can you find historical maps?

13 How can you tell if a map is a historical map?

Read Parallel Time Lines
Use the information and time lines on pages 380 and 381 to answer these questions.

14 What is shown on Time Line A? Time Line B?

15 How does using two time lines help you in viewing the events?

VISIT

BERLIN,
GERMANY

GET READY

Berlin, Germany, is a large city that covers an area of 341 square miles (883 sq km). The city was divided in 1945 at the end of World War II, and it later became East Berlin and West Berlin. The United States occupied a part of West Berlin. The city officially became one again in 1990, when the governments of East and West Germany were united.

Today, visitors to Berlin can see many historic sites. Museums, memorials, and landmarks offer reminders of the United States' presence in Berlin during the war.

The Brandenburg Gate is a famous Berlin landmark.

LOCATE IT

GERMANY

Berlin

A memorial honors members of the United States Air Force who participated in the Berlin Airlift.

During the Berlin Airlift transport planes unloaded food and supplies at Tempelhof Airport.

The Berlin Wall was built in 1961.

Visitors can see Checkpoint Charlie, a famous guard station of the Berlin Wall.

Work to tear down the Berlin Wall began in 1989. Today visitors can see pieces of the wall that have been preserved as part of history.

TAKE A FIELD TRIP

GO ONLINE

A VIRTUAL TOUR
Visit The Learning Site at **www.harcourtschool.com/tours** to find virtual tours of parks and scenic areas.

A VIDEO TOUR
Check your media center or classroom library for a videotape tour of Berlin, Germany.

CNN Turner Le@rning®

5 Review and Test Preparation

VISUAL SUMMARY

Write Descriptions   Imagine that you are a radio announcer. Your job is to describe the events in the Visual Summary to your audience. Write a description for each event. Make sure you include enough detail that someone could match the description with its event.

USE VOCABULARY

Use each pair of terms in a sentence that explains the meanings of the terms.

concentration camp, Holocaust (pp. 333, 368)

civilian, veteran (pp. 344, 383)

rationing, recycling (p. 351)

superpowers, arms race (pp. 388, 390)

RECALL FACTS

Answer these questions.

1 What were the main messages in Hitler's speeches?

Germany was met treaty failed Germans were better than other people

2 What was one of the biggest mistakes the Japanese made while trying to build an empire? *to attack the U.S.*

3 What happened to Japanese Americans during World War II? *Relocation camps*

4 Who was the commander of the Allied forces in Europe after the Americans entered World War II?

5 In the years after World War II, which nations became superpowers?

Write the letter of the best choice.

6 **TEST PREP**   Which of the following events brought the United States into World War II?
  A Japan's attack on Pearl Harbor
  B D day
  C Germany's invasion of Austria
  D Japan's attack on Midway Island

7 **TEST PREP**   The period after World War II in which the United States' population grew by about 50 million became known as—
  F the population explosion.
  G the bountiful era.
  H the post-war expansion.
  J the baby boom.

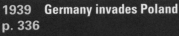
Visual Summary

1930   1934   1938

1939   Germany invades Poland   p. 336

400

1941   Japan attacks Pearl Harbor   p. 343

1942   More than 3 million Americans are drafted   p. 345

THINK CRITICALLY

8 What impact did the Treaty of Versailles have on the beginning of World War II?

9 What do you think would have happened if Germany had taken control of Britain before the United States entered World War II?

10 Why do you think World War II was fought over a larger area than World War I?

11 Do you think it was difficult for American soldiers returning from the war to readjust to everyday life? Explain.

APPLY SKILLS

Compare Historical Maps
Use the maps of Germany on this page to answer the following questions.

12 What city became the capital of West Germany?

13 Why do you think the land area of Germany in 1937 is larger than the combined land areas of West and East Germany?

Germany, 1937

Germany, 1949

1942

1946

1950

1944 D day invasion succeeds
p. 365

1945 World War II ends p. 379

1949 NATO is founded p. 394

401

Unit Activities

Visit The Learning Site at
www.harcourtschool.com/
socialstudies/activities
for additional activities.

Make a Newspaper

Work in a group to make a newspaper that could have been printed during World War II. Your newspaper should include news stories, editorials, letters to the editor, feature articles, cartoons, advertisements, and illustrations. Share your newspaper with the class.

Develop a Secret Code

Work in groups to develop a secret code. The secret code can either use whole words or letters. Be sure to include a translation for your secret code. Use your secret code to write about one of the major events of World War II. Give your finished secret code and writing to another group to translate.

VISIT YOUR LIBRARY

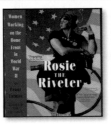

■ *Rosie the Riveter: Women Working on the Home Front in World War II* by Penny Colman. Crown Publishers.

■ *Foster's War* by Carolyn Reeder. Scholastic Press.

■ *My Wartime Summers* by Jane Cutler. Farrar, Straus, & Giroux.

COMPLETE THE UNIT PROJECT

Create an Illustrated Time Line
Work as a class to complete the unit project—create an illustrated time line. Review the events, people, and places that you listed during your reading. Make sure that each item on your list has a date. Next, create a variety of scenes and captions to go with your items. Complete the project by placing dates, scenes, and captions on a time line.

The Cold War and Beyond

A 1950s television

A suburban neighborhood in Riverside, California

The Cold War and Beyond

66 **We stand today at the edge of a new frontier.** 99

—John F. Kennedy, presidential nomination acceptance speech, Democratic National Convention, Los Angeles, July 15, 1960

Preview the Content

Skim the chapter and lesson titles. Use them to make an outline of the unit. Write down any questions that occur to you about the time in United States history known as the Cold War years.

Preview the Vocabulary

Multiple Meanings A word can often have several meanings. You may know one meaning but not another. Use the Glossary or a dictionary to look up each of the terms listed below. Then use each term in two sentences that show its different meanings.

HAWK ⇒ _____   DOVE ⇒ _____

SATELLITE ⇒ _____   RECESSION ⇒ _____

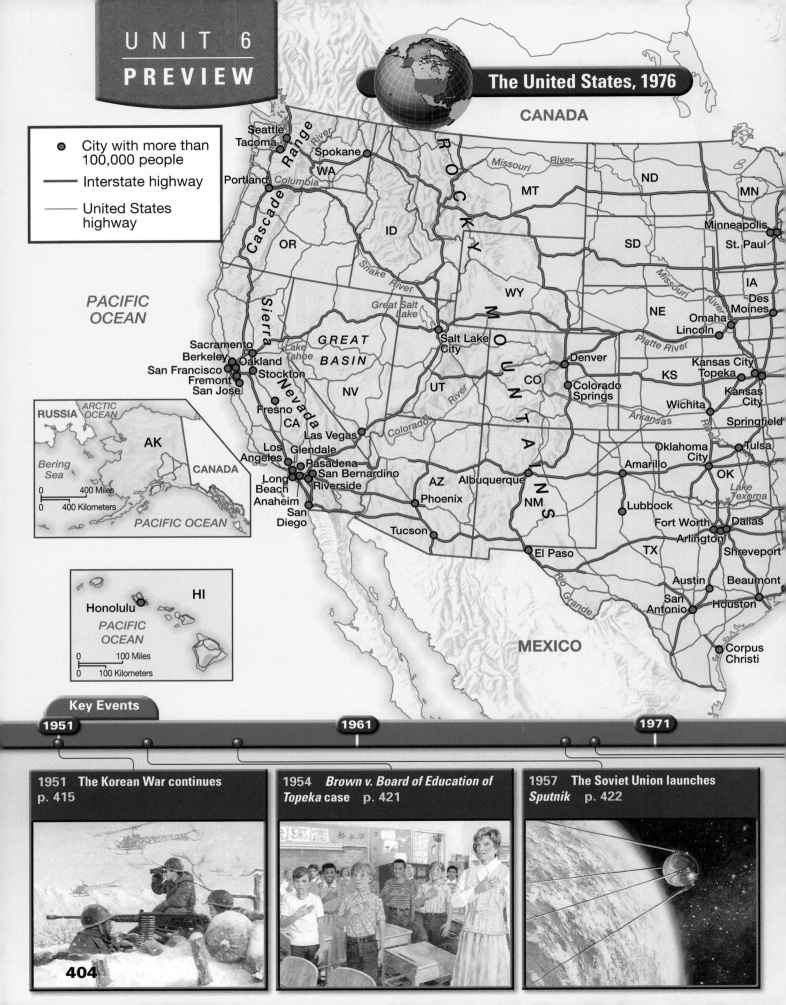

The United States, 1976

CANADA

City with more than 100,000 people

Interstate highway

United States highway

PACIFIC OCEAN

RUSSIA

ARCTIC OCEAN

AK

Bering Sea

CANADA

0   400 Miles

0   400 Kilometers

PACIFIC OCEAN

HI

Honolulu

PACIFIC OCEAN

0   100 Miles

0   100 Kilometers

CANADA

Seattle
Tacoma
Spokane
WA
Portland
Columbia
Cascade Range
OR
Snake River
ID
MT
ND
MN
Minneapolis
St. Paul
Missouri River
SD
IA
Des Moines
WY
Great Salt Lake
NE
Omaha
Lincoln
Platte River
Sacramento
Berkeley
Oakland
San Francisco
Fremont
San Jose
Stockton
Lake Tahoe
GREAT BASIN
Salt Lake City
Denver
CO
Colorado Springs
Kansas City
Topeka
KS
Kansas City
Sierra Nevada
Fresno
NV
UT
Colorado River
Wichita
Arkansas River
Springfield
CA
Las Vegas
Colorado
Los Angeles
Glendale
Pasadena
Long Beach
Anaheim
San Diego
San Bernardino
Riverside
AZ
Albuquerque
NM
Phoenix
Tucson
El Paso
Oklahoma City
Amarillo
OK
Tulsa
Lake Texoma
Lubbock
Fort Worth
Arlington
Dallas
Shreveport
TX
Austin
Beaumont
San Antonio
Houston
Rio Grande
Corpus Christi

MEXICO

Key Events

1951 — **1961** — **1971**

1951   The Korean War continues   p. 415

1954   *Brown v. Board of Education of Topeka* case   p. 421

1957   The Soviet Union launches *Sputnik*   p. 422

404

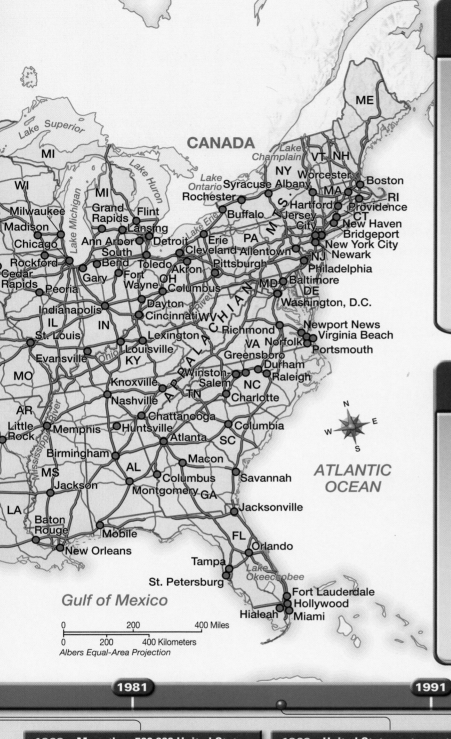

CANADA

MI
WI
Milwaukee
Madison
Chicago
Rockford
Cedar Rapids
Peoria
MI
Grand Rapids
Flint
Lansing
Ann Arbor
South Bend
Gary
Fort Wayne
Detroit
Toledo
Akron
OH
Columbus
Dayton
Cincinnati
Erie
PA
Cleveland
Pittsburgh
Allentown
Indianapolis
IL
IN
St. Louis
Evansville
MO
Lexington
Louisville
KY
Knoxville
Nashville
TN
Chattanooga
Huntsville
AR
Little Rock
Memphis
Birmingham
MS
AL
Jackson
Montgomery
LA
Baton Rouge
New Orleans
Mobile
Columbus
GA
Macon
Atlanta
SC
Columbia
Savannah
Jacksonville
FL
Orlando
Tampa
St. Petersburg
Lake Okeechobee
Fort Lauderdale
Hollywood
Hialeah
Miami

ME
Lake Champlain
VT NH
NY
Syracuse
Rochester
Buffalo
Albany
Worcester
MA
Hartford
CT
New Haven
Bridgeport
Jersey City
New York City
Newark
NJ
Philadelphia
Baltimore
MD
DE
Washington, D.C.
Richmond
VA
Newport News
Virginia Beach
Norfolk
Portsmouth
Greensboro
Durham
Raleigh
Winston-Salem
NC
Charlotte
Boston
RI
Providence
Rochester

Lake Superior
Lake Huron
Lake Michigan
Lake Ontario
Lake Erie
APPALACHIAN MTS.
Ohio River
Mississippi River

ATLANTIC OCEAN

Gulf of Mexico

N
W E
S

0   200   400 Miles
0   200   400 Kilometers
Albers Equal-Area Projection

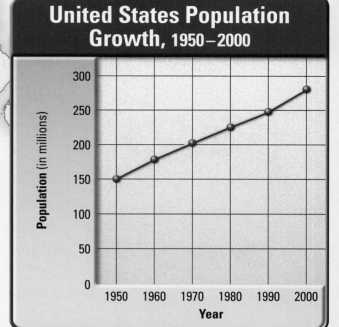

United States Population Growth, 1950–2000

Population (in millions) vs Year (1950, 1960, 1970, 1980, 1990, 2000)

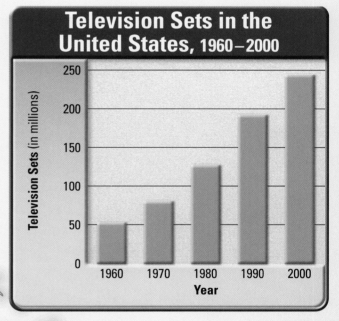

Television Sets in the United States, 1960–2000

Television Sets (in millions) vs Year (1960, 1970, 1980, 1990, 2000)

1981   1991   2001

1968   More than 500,000 United States troops in Vietnam   p. 449

1969   United States astronauts land on the moon   p. 432

1986   United States and Soviet leaders work to end the Cold War   p. 460

I HAVE A DREAM

by Dr. Martin Luther King, Jr.

illustrated by Leonard Jenkins

In the years after World War II, many people across the country worked for civil rights. Martin Luther King, Jr., became a leader of the Civil Rights movement in the United States. He worked hard for racial justice, and his peaceful protests caught the attention of people around the world. In 1963 about 250,000 people gathered for a march in Washington, D.C. The marchers were supporting a proposed civil rights bill that was in Congress. As the crowd stood in front of the Lincoln Memorial, King spoke to them about his dream for African Americans. Read now part of King's speech.

I say to you today, my friends, that in spite of the difficulties and frustrations of the moment I still have a dream. It is a dream deeply rooted in the American dream.

I have a dream that one day this nation will rise up and live out the true meaning of its creed: "We hold these truths to be self-evident; that all men are created equal. . . ."

This will be the day when all of God's children will be able to sing with new meaning, "My country 'tis of thee, sweet land of liberty, of thee I sing. Land where my father died, land of the Pilgrims' pride, from every mountainside, let freedom ring."

And if America is to be a great nation, this must become true. So let freedom ring from the prodigious [gigantic] hilltops of New Hampshire. Let freedom ring from the mighty mountains of New York. Let freedom ring from the heightening Alleghenies of Pennsylvania!

Let freedom ring from the snowcapped Rockies of Colorado! Let freedom ring from the curvaceous peaks of California! But not only that; let freedom ring from Stone Mountain of Georgia! Let freedom ring from Lookout Mountain of Tennessee!

Let freedom ring from every hill and molehill of Mississippi. From every mountainside, let freedom ring.

Analyze the Literature

1 What was King's dream?

2 Imagine that you are one of the marchers in Washington, D.C., and write an article describing people's reactions to King's words.

READ A BOOK

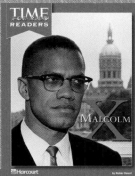

START THE UNIT PROJECT

Make a Class Magazine With your classmates, create a class magazine about the United States during the Cold War. As you read the unit, make a list of the key people, places, and events discussed. This list will help you decide what to include in your magazine.

USE TECHNOLOGY

GO ONLINE Visit The Learning Site at **www.harcourtschool.com/ socialstudies** for additional activities, primary sources, and other resources to use in this unit.

...UNTIL JUSTICE ROLLS DOWN
AND RIGHTEOUSNESS LIKE A
11·MAR·1965
REV. JAMES REEB
BEATEN TO DEATH
7·MAR·1965
STATE TROOPERS BEAT BACK MARCHERS
EDMUND PETTUS BRIDGE·SELMA, AL
26·FEB·1965
JIMMIE LEE JACKSON·CIVIL RIGHTS MARCHER
KILLED BY STATE TROOPER·MARION, AL
LT. COL. LEMUEL PENN·KILLED BY KLAN
CIVIL RIGHTS MARCH FROM SELMA TO
MONTGOMERY COMPLETED

CIVIL RIGHTS MEMORIAL

The Civil Rights Memorial was built to honor those who died in the fight for equal rights and justice. Inscribed in the memorial is a time line of events that took place during the Civil Rights movement in the United States. On November 5, 1989, over 6,000 people gathered for the dedication of the memorial.

LOCATE IT

ALABAMA

Montgomery

At Home and Abroad

" . . . until justice rolls down like water and righteousness like a mighty stream. "

—Martin Luther King, Jr., speech at the Lincoln Memorial in Washington, D.C., August 28, 1963

CHAPTER READING SKILL

Draw Conclusions

A conclusion is a decision or an idea reached by using evidence from what you read and what you already know about a subject. To draw a conclusion, you combine new facts with the facts you already know.

As you read this chapter, use evidence and what you already know to draw conclusions about the United States.

EVIDENCE

KNOWLEDGE

CONCLUSION

Chapter 11 ■ 409

MAIN IDEA
Read to learn about how the United States entered the Korean War to stop the spread of communism in the world.

WHY IT MATTERS
The United States' entry into the Korean War showed that the nation wanted to defend freedom.

VOCABULARY
desegregate

The Korean War Years

1951	1976	2001

1950–1953

The Berlin crisis was just the beginning of the conflict between the free world and communism. In 1950, the United States, along with other members of the United Nations, entered a war to stop communist forces from taking control of Korea. This conflict became known as the Korean War. The Korean War showed the world that the United States still wanted to defend freedom.

The 1948 Election

When Harry S. Truman became President after the death of Franklin D. Roosevelt, he understood the great challenge of his new office. During his first years as President, he worked hard to meet that challenge. Still, many people did not think he could win the 1948 presidential election.

FAST FACT
Late on election night in 1948, the editors of the *Chicago Daily Tribune* realized that they had incorrectly predicted the election's winner. However, thousands of morning newspapers had already been delivered.

Many people, including the editors of the *Chicago Daily Tribune*, did not think Truman (below) had enough support to win the presidential election.

Chicago Daily Tribune
HOME
DEWEY DEFEATS TRUMAN
G.O.P. Sweep Indicated in State; Boyle Leads in City

Prior to 1948, African American soldiers had to serve in separate units.

As Election Day drew near, most reporters predicted Truman's opponent, Republican Thomas E. Dewey, would win. After voting ended on Election Day, the *Chicago Daily Tribune* printed a headline for the next day's paper. It read, "Dewey Defeats Truman." The next morning, however, after all the votes had been counted, Truman had won the election by just over 2 million votes. Harry Truman had won one of the biggest surprise victories in the history of United States presidential elections.

REVIEW Why were many people surprised by Harry Truman's victory in the 1948 presidential election?

Changes Continue at Home

President Truman was a strong believer in the New Deal. He wanted to expand the programs that Franklin D. Roosevelt had begun. Soon after his election he said, "Every individual has a right to expect from his government a fair deal."

In 1949 Truman presented to Congress a plan that became known as the Fair Deal. It extended many of the economic programs the New Deal had created. Under the Fair Deal, for example, the minimum wage was increased. Social Security payments for the elderly continued. In addition, federal funds were used to help rebuild run-down areas in many of the nation's cities.

President Truman also believed in civil rights. In 1946 he formed the Presidential Committee on Civil Rights to advise him about civil rights in the country. Then, in 1948, he desegregated the nation's armed forces. To **desegregate** is to remove racial barriers. This meant that African Americans, for example, would no longer be put in separate units.

Truman's relations with other countries were influenced by the fact that he did not trust communism. He believed that communism was the opposite of democracy. He believed, too, that the United States should stop the spread of communism. He said, "I believe that it must be the policy of the United States to support free peoples who are resisting attempted subjugation [control] by armed minorities or by outside pressures."

A Divided Korea

SOVIET UNION

CHINA

0   50   100 Miles

0   50   100 Kilometers
Conic Projection

Chongjin

⊛ National capital

42°N

40°N

NORTH
KOREA

Hŭngnam

Sea of
Japan

Pyongyang ⊛

Cease-fire
line, 1953

Yalu River

38°N

Prewar boundary

38°N

Panmunjom

Inchon   Seoul

Yellow

Sea

SOUTH

KOREA

N

W   E

S

36°N   36°N

Pusan   132°E

Korea Strait

130°E

34°N

126°E   Cheju
Island

JAPAN

GEOGRAPHY THEME

Regions After World War II, Korea was divided into two parts—North Korea and South Korea.

❓ Where was the prewar boundary?

The division of Korea was supposed to last only a short time. So, in 1947, the United Nations called for elections that would choose a government for all of Korea. However, the Soviet Union was against the plan. Instead, each part of Korea chose a government. Each government said it was the lawful government for both North Korea and South Korea.

North Korea, which set up a communist government, was known as the People's Democratic Republic of Korea. South Korea, which set up a free government, became known as the Republic of Korea. Between 1948 and 1950, troops from both sides often battled near the border. These battles would soon lead to a much larger conflict.

REVIEW What two countries sent troops to occupy Korea after World War II?

The policy of stopping communism from spreading became known as the Truman Doctrine. In 1950 the United States went to war to uphold the Truman Doctrine and to defend the people of South Korea.

REVIEW How did President Truman change the armed forces?

Causes of the War

Like Germany, the Asian country of Korea was divided after World War II. The border that divided the country was known as the thirty-eighth parallel. Soviet troops occupied the northern part, and United States troops occupied the southern part.

The War Begins

On June 25, 1950, North Korean soldiers crossed the thirty-eighth parallel and invaded South Korea. Immediately, the United Nations called for a cease-fire. When North Korean troops would not stop fighting, the United Nations voted to send in troops to restore peace. For the first time in history, a world organization went to war to stop one country's attack on another country. Many of the member nations sent troops to South Korea. Most of the troops, however, were from the United States or were South Korean.

This Congressional Medal of Honor was awarded to a soldier who fought in the Korean War.

The United Nations named United States General Douglas MacArthur as commander of all UN forces in Korea. MacArthur had commanded troops in the Pacific during World War II and knew the region well.

North Korea's surprise attack had driven South Korean troops farther and farther south. By September 1950 the South Koreans held only the area around the city of Pusan, in the southeast corner of the nation. However, UN troops held the line around Pusan. This proved to be a turning point in the war.

REVIEW Why did the United Nations vote to send troops to South Korea?

UN Forces Move North

General MacArthur had a plan to cut off North Korean forces. According to this plan, some UN troops would attack North Korean forces at the line around Pusan. Others would approach secretly from the sea. They would surprise communist troops at a city called Inchon, 150 miles (241 km) deep into communist-held South Korea.

The attack at Inchon would be very dangerous, for each day the city had tides 30 feet (9 m) high. If the troops missed high tide, their ships would be stuck in mud. Then escape would be impossible. However, Inchon remained the target. A victory there would cut some of the North Korean forces' supply lines.

General MacArthur (left) commanded the UN troops in South Korea. The soldiers (right) are watching for North Korean troops.

The attack on the troops at Inchon started early in the morning on September 15. It so surprised the North Koreans that the battle was over in one day. At the same time, UN troops broke through enemy lines around Pusan and started heading north. By the end of September, UN soldiers had recaptured the city of Seoul, South Korea's capital. And by early October, UN forces had pushed the North Koreans back above the thirty-eighth parallel.

REVIEW Why was the attack on Inchon dangerous?

LOCATE IT

Heartbreak Ridge

NORTH KOREA

SOUTH KOREA

Advance and Retreat

For several weeks UN troops kept moving northward, pushing communist forces up toward the Yalu River. The Yalu River forms the border between North Korea and China. Most people did not believe China would become involved in the war. However, China's communist government supported North Korea. Soon Chinese troops and equipment were moving across the border. By the end of November more than 300,000 Chinese troops had entered North Korea.

On November 26, 1950, Chinese and North Korean forces attacked. UN troops were forced to fall back below the thirty-eighth parallel. Soon UN troops made another try and pushed the communist forces back into North Korea.

REVIEW How did China become involved in the Korean War?

This ridge (below) near the thirty-eighth parallel was called Heartbreak Ridge because of the great number of soldiers who were killed defending the position. These soldiers (left) were at the ridge and were only 45 yards (41 m) from North Korean troops.

The Korean War Ends

The Korean War became a war fought in feet, not in miles. The front lines moved very little in either direction for the next two years as UN troops battled the North Koreans and the Chinese. The weather, too, became a problem. Freezing cold winters made it hard to get supplies to the troops. Under these difficult conditions, soldiers had a hard time staying prepared for battle.

So many American soldiers lost their lives in Korea that the war became a major issue in the 1952 presidential election. General Dwight D. Eisenhower, who had commanded troops in World War II, promised that he would work to end the war if elected. Soon after his election he kept his promise. By 1953 communist troops had been pushed back into North Korea. That same year, an

General Dwight D. Eisenhower (above, with his wife, Mamie) was elected President in 1952. Supporters carried signs with his nickname, Ike.

armistice was signed, ending the fighting. The Korean War was over, and South Korea remained an independent country.

REVIEW Why did the Korean War become an issue in the 1952 presidential election?

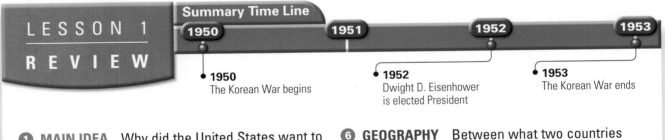

LESSON 1 REVIEW

Summary Time Line

1950 — 1951 — 1952 — 1953

1950 The Korean War begins

1952 Dwight D. Eisenhower is elected President

1953 The Korean War ends

① **MAIN IDEA** Why did the United States want to stop the spread of communism?

② **WHY IT MATTERS** What did the United States' decision to enter the war show to the world?

③ **VOCABULARY** Write a sentence using the term **desegregate**.

④ **TIME LINE** How long did the Korean War last?

⑤ **READING SKILL—Draw Conclusions** Why do you think President Truman removed racial barriers in the armed forces?

⑥ **GEOGRAPHY** Between what two countries does the Yalu River form a border?

⑦ **HISTORY** What was President Truman's view of communism?

⑧ **CRITICAL THINKING—Hypothesize** What do you think might have happened if China had not entered the Korean War?

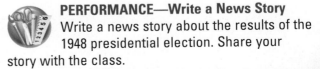

PERFORMANCE—Write a News Story Write a news story about the results of the 1948 presidential election. Share your story with the class.

Identify Changing Borders

➡ WHY IT MATTERS

Historical maps give important information about places as they were in the past. By studying a historical map, you can see how a place and its borders have changed over time. Seeing those changes on a historical map can help you better understand the changes and how they came about.

➡ WHAT YOU NEED TO KNOW

In Lesson 1 you read that when World War II ended, Korea was broken into two parts—North Korea and South Korea. You also read that the border was set on a line of latitude—the thirty-eighth parallel, or 38°N.

The two maps on page 417 show how the border between North Korea and South Korea changed over time. One map shows the national border before the Korean War. The second map shows the border after the war.

This soldier is standing guard at the border of South Korea.

➡ PRACTICE THE SKILL

Use the two maps to answer these questions:

❶ What color is used to show North Korea?

❷ What color is used to show South Korea?

❸ Which map shows North and South Korea's prewar border?

❹ Is North and South Korea's present-day border mostly north or mostly south of the prewar border?

Korea, 1945

⊛ National capital

0 50 100 Miles
0 50 100 Kilometers
Conic Projection

CHINA

Yalu River

NORTH KOREA

• Chongjin — 42°N

• Hŭngnam — 40°N

Pyongyang ⊛

Sea of Japan

— 38°N

• Panmunjom
⊛ Seoul
Inchon •

Yellow Sea

SOUTH KOREA

— 36°N

N
W   E
S

• Pusan

Korea Strait

— 34°N

124°E 126°E Cheju Island 128°E 130°E

JAPAN

Korea, 1953

⊛ National capital

0 50 100 Miles
0 50 100 Kilometers
Conic Projection

CHINA

Yalu River

NORTH KOREA

• Chongjin — 42°N

• Hŭngnam — 40°N

Pyongyang ⊛

Sea of Japan

— 38°N

• Panmunjom
⊛ Seoul
Inchon •

Yellow Sea

SOUTH KOREA

— 36°N

N
W   E
S

• Pusan

Korea Strait

— 34°N

124°E 126°E Cheju Island 128°E 130°E

JAPAN

5 According to the maps, did South Korea win or lose land at the end of the Korean War?

▶ APPLY WHAT YOU LEARNED

Many states today do not have the same borders they had when they joined the United States. Find a historical map of the United States, and choose one of the states it illustrates. Then use an encyclopedia or an atlas to find a map showing the state's present-day borders. On a sheet of paper, draw a map showing the original borders of the state. Then draw another map showing the present-day borders of the state. Share your maps with the class.

Practice your map and globe skills with the **GeoSkills CD-ROM**.

MAP AND GLOBE SKILLS

MAIN IDEA
Read to learn about the challenges the United States faced both outside and inside the nation during the 1950s.

WHY IT MATTERS
The challenges faced by the United States would help shape life at home and around the world.

VOCABULARY
integration
nonviolence
satellite

The 1950s

1950–1960

The 1950s were years when many Americans were doing well. Thanks to the GI Bill, the men and women who had served in World War II were given the chance to go to college. Many found good jobs and were able to buy homes in suburbs. Suburbs grew rapidly during the 1950s, and so did many Americans' sense of community. However, throughout the 1950s, Americans also were worried about communism, the arms race, and equal rights for all.

Life in the 1950s

Suburbs that began after World War II grew even more in the 1950s. In fact, of the 13 million houses built between 1948 and 1958, 11 million were in suburbs. Suburbs changed the look of the United States. As more people moved out to suburbs,

The popularity of television grew in the 1950s (left). Children (below) of families who moved to suburbs walked to neighborhood schools.

By 1960, millions of people in the United States had television sets.

the population of many older cities dropped. Cities near suburbs, however, grew and did well as new businesses, schools, and churches opened there.

Family life also changed in the 1950s. New appliances such as washers and dryers and dishwashers made life easier and gave people more free time. Watching television became a thing to do as a family. By the end of the decade, nine out of ten homes in the United States had televisions.

Television also brought a new kind of music into the nation's homes. It was called rock and roll. It combined country music and rhythm and blues. Teenagers of the 1950s danced to the rock and roll songs of musicians and singers such as Elvis Presley, Buddy Holly, and Chuck Berry.

During the 1950s the economy of the United States boomed. Homes, cars, and appliances were all being built and sold faster than ever before. Many of these items were bought on credit, which meant they were paid for over time. As the number of Americans buying goods on credit grew, the nation's economy grew. The first credit cards were introduced in the 1950s. Soon many people were using them.

One reason for the growth of the economy during this time was the growing number of building projects. In 1956 President Eisenhower signed the Federal Aid Highway Act. This led to the building of highways across the country. These new highways helped the number of automobile sales grow. They also led to the building of thousands of new hotels, restaurants, and gas stations across the country.

The growing number of automobiles and highways also led to the growth of shopping centers. In 1945 there were only 8 shopping centers in the United States. By 1960 there were almost 4,000. New shopping centers and malls became places where families from the suburbs gathered.

REVIEW How did the United States economy grow during the 1950s?

Chuck Berry was a popular rock and roll singer.

WBO55 DL PD

RENO NEV FEB 11 1139A

THE PRESIDENT

THE WHITE HOUSE

IN A LINCOLN DAY SPEECH AT WHEELING THURSDAY NIGHT
I STATED THAT THE STATE DEPARTMENT HARBORS A NEST OF
COMMUNISTS AND COMMUNIST SYMPATHIZERS WHO ARE HELPING TO
SHAPE OUR FOREIGN POLICY. I FURTHER STATED THAT I HAVE IN
MY POSSESSION THE NAMES OF 57 COMMUNISTS WHO ARE IN THE
STATE DEPARTMENT AT PRESENT. A STATE DEPARTMENT SPOKESMAN

The White House
Washington

1950 FEB 11 PM 7 31

Senator Joseph McCarthy (near left) sent a telegram (above) to the President to warn him of communists in the United States government.

Fears of Communism

During the 1950s Americans had more money than ever before. At the same time, people were worried about the future. Much of this concern had to do with the spread of communism around the world. However, the events in China and North Korea were not the only ones that troubled people in the United States. At home several citizens were tried for and found guilty of being communist spies.

In 1950 Senator Joseph McCarthy began holding hearings to look into possible communist threats in the United States. McCarthy made people's fears grow by saying that communist spies were working in every branch of the national government. He also ruined the lives of many innocent people by falsely accusing them of being communists.

However, for several years few people dared to say anything against McCarthy and his hearings. Those who did were often accused of being communists themselves. In time, people fought back against McCarthy. In 1954 he said that communist spies were working in the United States Army. Joseph Welch, the lawyer for the Army, challenged McCarthy during a hearing shown on television. Soon most Americans refused to believe McCarthy any longer.

REVIEW Who was Joseph McCarthy?

A Supreme Court Ruling

In the early 1950s Linda Brown of Topeka, Kansas, wanted to go to school with other children in her neighborhood. She did not understand why state laws in Kansas said that African American children had to attend separate schools.

In 1896 the United States Supreme Court had made a ruling in a case called *Plessy v. Ferguson*. The court said that separate public places for whites and African Americans were lawful as long as the places were equal. In most cases, however, they were not equal. This ruling applied to all public places, including schools. As a result, African American children often had to attend run-down schools. Their schools sometimes did not have books and other materials.

Linda Brown's family and 12 other African American families decided to fight laws that upheld segregated schools. The NAACP agreed to help in 1951. One of its lawyers, Thurgood Marshall, presented the case before the Supreme Court. The case, which became known as *Brown v. Board of Education of Topeka*, would help change history. Marshall argued that separate schools did not provide an equal education. He called for **integration**, or the bringing together of people of all races, in public schools.

In 1954 the Supreme Court Chief Justice Earl Warren said, "In the field of education the doctrine of 'separate but equal' has no place." The court ordered an end to segregation in public schools. However, many states were slow to carry out that order. Their schools and other public places remained segregated.

REVIEW What did the Supreme Court say about segregation in public schools?

Rosa Parks is fingerprinted after her arrest for refusing to move to the back of the bus.

The Montgomery Bus Boycott

On December 1, 1955, a young African American woman named Rosa Parks got on a bus in Montgomery, Alabama. She took a seat in the middle of the bus. Under Alabama law, African Americans had to sit in the back. They could sit in the middle section only if the seats were not needed for white passengers.

When the bus filled up, the bus driver told Rosa Parks to give up her seat to a white man. She refused. The bus driver called the police, and Parks was arrested.

After Parks's arrest, the African Americans of Montgomery decided to boycott, or refuse to ride, the city buses until they were integrated. A minister named Dr. Martin Luther King, Jr., led the boycott. He believed in **nonviolence**, or peaceful actions to bring about change.

Thurgood Marshall (far left) argued against school segregation so that students like Linda Brown (left) could get an equal education.

For more than a year, African Americans stayed off the buses. Finally, in November 1956 the Supreme Court ruled that all public transportation companies had to end segregation. The bus company had to change its rules. Rosa Parks had helped change the law.

REVIEW What was the purpose of the Montgomery bus boycott?

Cold War Tensions Grow

As people like Rosa Parks and Dr. Martin Luther King, Jr., worked to change laws in the nation, the Cold War tensions between the United States and the Soviet Union grew. Both nations continued to build up the number of weapons they had. People in the United States and around the world closely followed the actions of both nations.

Some people in the United States feared that a Soviet bombing raid could come at any moment. They built underground bunkers, or bomb shelters, and filled them with food and supplies. There they hoped they could survive any bombs that were dropped. Government officials also wanted people to be prepared. They made comic books to illustrate to schoolchildren what they should do in case of an attack.

The two superpowers also took the Cold War into space. In 1957 the Soviet Union surprised the United States by launching *Sputnik* (SPUT•nik). *Sputnik* was

People prepared for bombing raids by building bomb shelters (below). During drills (right), students were trained to take cover.

After the launching of *Sputnik* (model shown at right), the United States formed NASA (above).

the world's first space **satellite**. A satellite is an object that orbits a planet.

Because of *Sputnik*, the United States sped up its own efforts to explore space. In 1958 the National Aeronautics and Space Administration, or NASA, was formed to develop the nation's space program.

REVIEW Why was NASA formed?

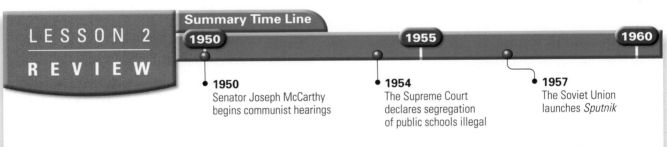

LESSON 2 REVIEW

Summary Time Line

1950 — **1955** — **1960**

1950
Senator Joseph McCarthy begins communist hearings

1954
The Supreme Court declares segregation of public schools illegal

1957
The Soviet Union launches *Sputnik*

1. **MAIN IDEA** What challenges did the United States face during the 1950s?

2. **WHY IT MATTERS** How did these challenges shape life in the United States?

3. **VOCABULARY** Write a sentence explaining how Dr. Martin Luther King, Jr., and others used **nonviolence** to achieve **integration**.

4. **TIME LINE** In what year was *Sputnik* launched?

5. **READING SKILL—Draw Conclusions** Why do you think the bus boycott in Montgomery, Alabama, helped change the bus company's rules?

6. **HISTORY** Why did some people build underground bunkers?

7. **CRITICAL THINKING—Analyze** How do you think Rosa Parks's actions helped the Civil Rights movement?

PERFORMANCE—Simulation Activity
Imagine that it is December 1, 1955, and you are on the bus with Rosa Parks. With a partner, role-play a conversation between you and a fellow passenger.

·SKILLS· Compare Graphs

CHART AND GRAPH

▶ WHY IT MATTERS

Suppose you want to prepare a report on the population of the United States after World War II. You want to show a lot of information in a brief, clear way. One way you might do this is by making graphs. Knowing how to read and make graphs can help you compare large amounts of information.

▶ WHAT YOU NEED TO KNOW

Different kinds of graphs show information in different ways. A line graph shows change over time. The line graph to the right shows how the number of people living in the United States changed between 1930 and 1960.

Bar graphs make it easy to compare a lot of information quickly. The bar graph to the right shows the number of immigrants in the United States between 1930 and 1960.

A circle graph, or pie chart, can also help you make comparisons. The circle graphs on page 425 show the percentage of Americans living in urban and rural areas in two different years.

▶ PRACTICE THE SKILL

Use the information in these four graphs to answer the following questions.

As you work, think about the advantages and disadvantages of each kind of graph.

1 In 1960, about how many people lived in this country?

2 Did the United States population get bigger or smaller between 1930 and 1960?

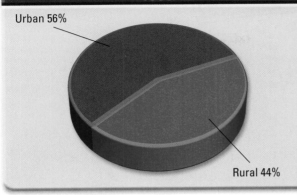

Urban and Rural Population, 1930

Urban 56%

Rural 44%

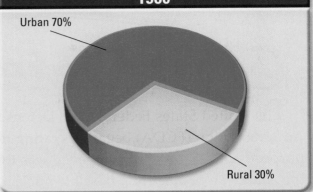

Urban and Rural Population, 1960

Urban 70%

Rural 30%

3 In which year was this statement true? *About two-thirds of all Americans live in cities.*

4 About how many people who were foreign born lived in the United States in 1960?

5 When the percentage of the urban population increases, why does the percentage of the rural population decrease?

➡ **APPLY WHAT YOU LEARNED**

Use the graphs on these pages to write a paragraph summarizing information about changes in the United States population between 1930 and 1960. Share your paragraph with a partner, and compare your summaries.

In 1960 most of the people in the United States lived in or near cities.

Civil Defense

The United States Federal Civil Defense Administration (FCDA) began operating in 1951. The purpose of this government agency was to prepare the American people for a possible nuclear war with the Soviet Union. It did so through programs during the 1950s and 1960s. The FCDA encouraged citizens to build fallout shelters as protection from the tiny radioactive particles that fall to Earth after a nuclear explosion. The agency also provided printed information.

 FROM THE NATIONAL ARCHIVES AND RECORDS ADMINISTRATION IN WASHINGTON, D.C.

A fallout shelter

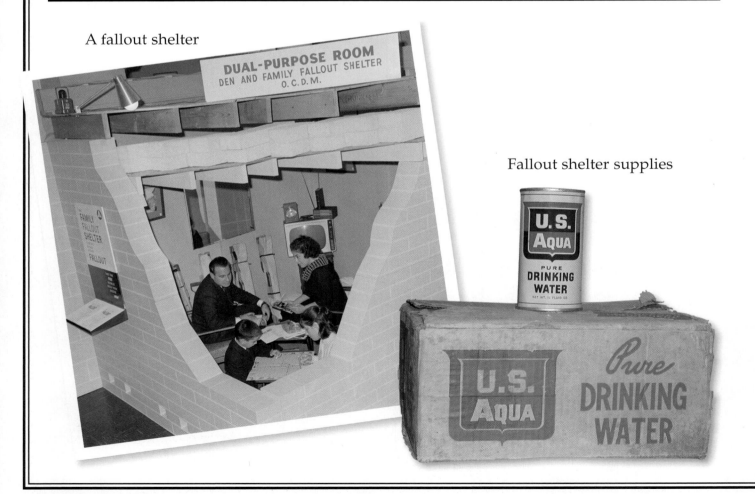

Fallout shelter supplies

Analyze the Primary Source

1. How would people know if the United States was being attacked by the Soviet Union?

2. What were people supposed to do to protect themselves in an attack?

Civil Defense officials and weather experts will estimate the probable path and speed of approaching fallout and keep you posted.

Tune your AM radio to 640 or 1240 kilocycles, your Conelrad stations, for official Civil Defense news and instructions.

HERE'S HOW YOU'LL KNOW IT

Civil Defense radiological monitoring teams will detect fallout if it is present in your area. They will tell you when it is safe and when you must take protective measures.

Brochures like this were distributed in schools and community centers.

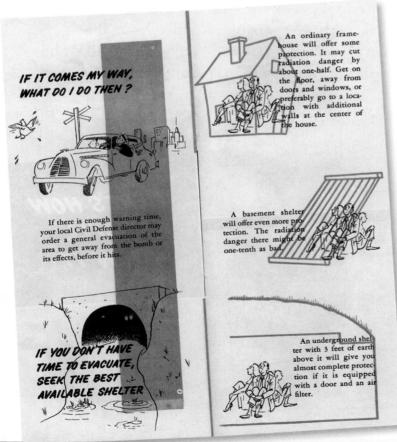

IF IT COMES MY WAY, WHAT DO I DO THEN?

An ordinary frame-house will offer some protection. It may cut radiation danger by about one-half. Get on the floor, away from doors and windows, or preferably go to a location with additional walls at the center of the house.

If there is enough warning time, your local Civil Defense director may order a general evacuation of the area to get away from the bomb or its effects, before it hits.

A basement shelter will offer even more protection. The radiation danger there might be one-tenth as bad.

IF YOU DON'T HAVE TIME TO EVACUATE, SEEK THE BEST AVAILABLE SHELTER

An underground shelter with 3 feet of earth above it will give you almost complete protection if it is equipped with a door and an air filter.

ACTIVITY

Compare and Contrast Identify ways in which the FCDA was similar to and different from the present-day Office of Homeland Security. Compare and contrast the purposes of these government agencies.

RESEARCH

Visit The Learning Site at **www.harcourtschool.com/ primarysources** to research other primary sources.

MAIN IDEA

Read to learn how the actions of the United States and the Soviet Union shaped world events in the 1960s.

WHY IT MATTERS

The competition between the United States and the Soviet Union led to great advances in space travel.

VOCABULARY

developing country
blockade

President Kennedy takes the oath of office at his inauguration.

New Opportunities and New Challenges

| 1951 | 1976 | 2001 |

1960–1969

All during the 1960s, the United States and the Soviet Union challenged each other both on Earth and in space. The election of a new President in 1960 raised the hopes of many Americans. Then a tragic event just three years later would forever change the nation. Even before then, however, people worried about what was going on in Cuba and the possibility of war. Yet, the accomplishments of the space program inspired people everywhere.

A "New Frontier"

In 1961 John F. Kennedy took the oath of office as President of the United States. Only 43 years old, Kennedy was the youngest person ever elected President. Young people liked his energy and enthusiasm. At his inauguration, the new President

urged Americans to work for the good of their country: "And so, my fellow Americans: Ask not what your country can do for you—ask what you can do for your country."

President Kennedy wanted to bring people with new ideas into the government. To fill his Cabinet he chose people who shared his views. Among them was his 35-year-old brother, Robert Kennedy. He became attorney general and the President's closest adviser.

President Kennedy's program to improve life in the United States and elsewhere became known as the New Frontier. Among the successes of the New Frontier was an increase in the minimum wage. Also, Congress voted to spend more money on rebuilding poor areas in the nation's older cities. Kennedy also signed a European trade deal that made trade between the United States and Europe easier.

One of the best-known and longest-lasting parts of the New Frontier remains the Peace Corps. Started in 1961, the Peace Corps is a program that sends volunteers from the United States to live and work with people in developing countries. A **developing country** is a country that does not have modern conveniences such as good housing, roads, schools, and hospitals. Many people in developing countries are very poor. Peace Corps volunteers teach classes in everything from farming to reading and writing English. Since 1961 more than 150,000 Peace Corps volunteers have worked in countries around the world.

REVIEW What was the New Frontier?

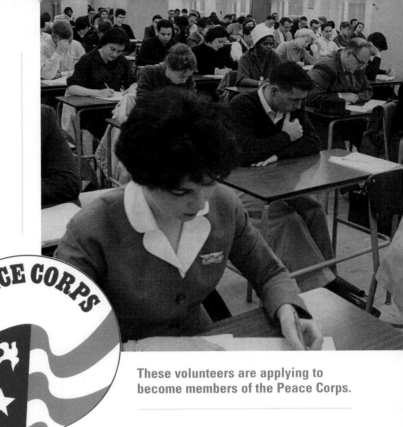

These volunteers are applying to become members of the Peace Corps.

The Cuban Missile Crisis

Soon after President Kennedy took office, the problems of the Cold War began to take up much of his time. In October 1962 he learned that the Soviet Union had built several launch sites for missiles on the island of Cuba, just 90 miles (145 km) off the tip of Florida. Fidel Castro had taken control of Cuba in 1959. With the help of the Soviet Union, he had formed a communist government. The missiles that Castro let the Soviets set up in Cuba had a range of more than 1,000 miles (1,609 km). This meant that these missiles could reach many of the United States' largest cities.

Kennedy demanded that the Soviets remove the missiles. When they did not, he ordered United States Navy ships to **blockade**, or prevent other ships from entering or leaving, the island nation. Their orders were to stop Soviet ships carrying missiles from reaching Cuba.

Cuban Missile Crisis, 1962

UNITED STATES

Gulf of Mexico

FLORIDA

• Miami

Key West ■

24°N

BAHAMAS

ATLANTIC OCEAN

• Havana

CUBA

MEXICO

Guantánamo Bay

HAITI

DOMINICAN REPUBLIC

BELIZE

Caribbean

JAMAICA

72°W

16°N

Sea

0   200   400 Miles

HONDURAS

0   200   400 Kilometers

Azimuthal Equal-Area Projection

N

NICARAGUA

W   E

S

■ U.S. military base

COSTA RICA

80°W

U.S. blockade zone

U.S. aircraft carrier

PANAMA

○ Soviet missile site

GEOGRAPHY THEME

Human-Environment Interactions
This map shows the naval blockade of Cuba during the Cuban Missile Crisis.

❖ Why do you think United States aircraft carriers were placed where they were?

already there. The United States agreed to end the blockade and to remove United States missiles from near the Soviet Union. The world had narrowly kept out of a nuclear war.

Once the crisis had passed, the United States took steps to try to ease tensions. One of these steps was to put in an emergency telephone line between Washington, D.C., and Moscow, the capital of the Soviet Union. Then, in 1963, the two nations signed a treaty. This treaty banned, or did not allow, nuclear tests above ground and underwater.

REVIEW What caused the Cuban Missile Crisis?

Americans worried as they listened to the news on the radio and television. What if the Soviet ships refused to stop? Would there be a war?

After 13 tense days, the Soviet Union agreed to stop sending missiles to Cuba and to remove all the missiles that were

This United States Navy ship (below, left) is blocking a Soviet Ship (below, right) from reaching Cuba. Soviet missiles (right) were being set up in Cuba.

878

A National Tragedy

President Kennedy became more and more well liked. He knew, however, that he would have to work hard to be reelected. On November 22, 1963, the President and Jacqueline, his wife, visited Dallas, Texas, to meet with supporters there. They were waving to the crowds as their car drove through the streets. Suddenly shots rang out. President Kennedy had been assassinated.

A couple of hours later, Vice President Lyndon Johnson took the oath of office and became the thirty-sixth President of the United States. Kennedy's sudden death shocked the world. Thousands of people lined the streets of Washington, D.C., as his coffin was taken for burial to Arlington National Cemetery.

REVIEW Who became President after John F. Kennedy's death?

The Space Race

Starting in 1958, the United States began to launch satellites into orbit. Many of these satellites contained devices that did scientific experiments in space. The United States was behind the Soviet Union in the space race, but NASA scientists were catching up fast.

In 1961 President Kennedy had set a goal for the United States. Kennedy wanted scientists to put a person on the moon by the end of the 1960s. Many people thought this would not be possible. However, the scientists in the space program immediately began working toward President Kennedy's goal.

In April 1961 the Soviet Union became the first nation to launch a spacecraft with a person on board. The spacecraft's

· GEOGRAPHY ·

GEOGRAPHY ESSENTIAL ELEMENTS

John F. Kennedy Space Center
Understanding Places and Regions

Most of our nation's spacecraft are sent into space from the launch pads located at the Kennedy Space Center. People come to watch as space shuttles and rockets are launched into orbit around Earth. A special part of the center, named Spaceport U.S.A., has exhibits and activities that teach people about the space program.

Gulf of Mexico

Canaveral National Seashore
Shuttle Landing Facility
ATLANTIC OCEAN
Titusville
JOHN F. KENNEDY SPACE CENTER
Shuttle Launch Complex
Indian River
50
Vehicle Assembly Building
Titan IV Complex
U.S. Astronaut Hall of Fame
405
Spaceport U.S.A.
CAPE CANAVERAL AIR STATION
407
3
Merritt Island
Banana R.
Cape Canaveral
95
1
401
Space and Missile Museum
528
Cape Canaveral
520
Cocoa
Merritt Island
0   4   8 Miles
0   4   8 Kilometers

The *Freedom 7* was launched into space with Alan Shepard, Jr., on board. The flight lasted 15 minutes.

name was the *Vostok,* and its pilot's name was Yury Gagarin. Gagarin orbited Earth one time before returning to Earth's surface. His flight became international news. Many Americans began to worry that the Soviet Union would control space. However, the United States was preparing a manned mission of its own.

In May 1961 United States astronaut Alan Shepard, Jr., climbed aboard the *Freedom 7* spacecraft. The *Freedom 7* was not designed to orbit Earth. Instead, it rocketed more than 115 miles (185 km) into the sky and then curved back down. A parachute helped the *Freedom 7* land safely in the ocean. This flight marked the first time the United States had managed to put a person into space.

One year later John Glenn, Jr., became the first United States astronaut to orbit Earth. Glenn orbited the Earth three times in the *Friendship 7* spacecraft.

In 1965 NASA launched the *Gemini 4* spacecraft. While the *Gemini 4* was orbiting Earth, Edward H. White became the first United States astronaut to venture outside of a spacecraft. A 26-foot (8-m) cord connected White to the spacecraft during his spacewalk. White moved in space by using a handheld device filled with gas. The United States had caught up to the Soviet Union in the space race.

President Kennedy had been one of the strongest supporters of the space program. After his death, NASA continued working to land a person on the moon.

A series of explorations called the Apollo program prepared for a moon landing. In 1968 astronauts in *Apollo 8* first circled the moon. By the next year, NASA was ready to attempt a landing.

On July 16, 1969, *Apollo 11* blasted off from Cape Canaveral, Florida. On board were astronauts Neil Armstrong, Edwin "Buzz" Aldrin, Jr., and Michael Collins. Four days later, on July 20, Armstrong and Aldrin became the first two people to walk on the moon.

The astronauts used television cameras to record their moonwalk. People all around the world watched with amazement as the historic event was broadcast on television. Eight years after Kennedy had challenged scientists to put a person on the moon, his goal had been met.

REVIEW **What was the Apollo program?**

When the *Apollo 11* astronauts began their mission to the moon on July 20, 1969, NASA scientists at Mission Control in Houston, Texas, followed events closely.

1 *Apollo 11* blasted off from Cape Canaveral.

2 The *Eagle* lander was launched from the orbiter.

3 The *Eagle* landed on the moon.

4 Armstrong and Aldrin walked on the moon.

5 Collins piloted the orbiter around the moon while the *Eagle* was on the moon's surface.

◆ What was Collins's job during the moon walk?

LESSON 3
REVIEW

Summary Time Line

| 1960 | 1963 | 1966 | 1969 |

1960
John F. Kennedy is elected President

1962
United States astronaut John Glenn, Jr., orbits the Earth

The Cuban Missile Crisis begins

1969
United States astronauts land on the moon

1 **MAIN IDEA** How did the actions of the United States and the Soviet Union shape life in the 1960s?

2 **WHY IT MATTERS** What was one outcome of the competition between the United States and the Soviet Union?

3 **VOCABULARY** Write a sentence explaining why President Kennedy ordered a **blockade** of Cuba.

4 **TIME LINE** In what year did John Glenn, Jr., orbit the Earth?

5 **READING SKILL—Draw Conclusions** Why did President Kennedy want to put a person on the moon?

6 **HISTORY** What did Edward H. White do?

7 **CRITICAL THINKING—Analyze** How do you think people in the United States felt about the Soviet Union during the Cold War?

PERFORMANCE—Write an Essay
Imagine that you are living during the Cold War. Write an essay telling how you feel about the space race.

Resolve Conflicts

WHY IT MATTERS

There are many ways to handle a disagreement. You can walk away and let the strong feelings fade over time. You can talk about the disagreement and explain your thoughts about it. You also can compromise. Knowing how to compromise gives you another way to resolve, or settle, conflicts.

WHAT YOU NEED TO KNOW

To resolve a conflict through compromise, you can follow these steps:

Step 1 Tell the other person clearly what you want.

Step 2 Decide which of the things you want are most important to you.

Step 3 Present a plan for a possible compromise and listen to the other person's plan.

Step 4 Talk about differences in the two plans.

Step 5 Present another plan, this time giving up one of the things that is important to you.

Step 6 Continue talking until the two of you agree on a plan. If either of you becomes angry, take a break and calm down.

Step 7 Plan a compromise that will work for a long time.

PRACTICE THE SKILL

Lesson 3 explained the events that took place during the Cuban Missile Crisis. The Soviet Union was threatening the United States by putting missiles in Cuba. The United States answered by blockading the island. How did the United States and the Soviet Union resolve this conflict?

APPLY WHAT YOU LEARNED

With your classmates, think of an issue on which not all the students agree. Form groups to talk about the issue, using the steps outlined on this page. Have each group share with the class how any conflicts were resolved.

Government officials met during the Cuban Missile Crisis to try to find a way to get the Soviets to take their missiles out of Cuba.

Working for Equal Rights

1951   1976   2001

1960–1980

MAIN IDEA
Read to learn how individuals and groups in the United States worked to gain equal rights.

WHY IT MATTERS
The movement for equal rights made it possible for more people to participate fully in government.

VOCABULARY
demonstration
migrant worker

The Civil Rights movement that began in the 1950s continued in the decades that followed. As the movement grew and got national attention, other groups joined African Americans in the fight for equal rights. Among these groups were Hispanic Americans, Native Americans, and women. During the 1960s and 1970s, Americans saw the nation change greatly.

Civil Rights Demonstrations

After the Montgomery bus boycott, the actions of Martin Luther King, Jr., and his followers got thousands of people in the United States to protest segregation laws. These civil rights demonstrations were reported in newspapers and on radio and television. A **demonstration** is a public show of group feelings about a cause. As more Americans learned about the demonstrations, they began to center their attention on the problems that caused them.

These people attended a march in Washington, D.C., to show their support for a bill that was in Congress.

435

In 1960 black and white college students formed the Student Nonviolent Coordinating Committee. These students challenged segregation laws at places such as restaurants, churches, and movie theaters. They also set an example by riding together on buses all over the South. The students and those who joined them were known as freedom riders. However, not everyone agreed with the students' actions. Sometimes the students were threatened by angry mobs.

Dr. Martin Luther King, Jr., Day

Dr. Martin Luther King, Jr., was born on January 15, 1929, in Atlanta, Georgia. With the Montgomery bus boycott, he became a leader in the Civil Rights movement. He worked tirelessly for racial justice, in spite of many arrests and many threats against his life. On April 4, 1968, King was assassinated. Just four days later, members of Congress began working to make his birthday a federal holiday. However, it was not until 1983 that such a law was signed. The third Monday in January became Dr. Martin Luther King, Jr., Day. The holiday was first celebrated on January 20, 1986. Today people celebrate the day with parades and other events. The special activities remind Americans of the continuing fight for equality, justice, and peace.

In April 1963 Martin Luther King, Jr., led a series of marches in Birmingham, Alabama. Much of the city was segregated, and the marchers wanted to put a stop to it. For eight days there were marches. Many of the marchers were arrested. King was one of those taken to jail. While he was in jail, he wrote, "We know through painful experience that freedom is never voluntarily given. . . . It must be demanded."

Later that year, close to 250,000 people gathered for a march in Washington, D.C. The marchers were there to show they were for a civil rights bill that Congress was debating. Standing in front of the Lincoln Memorial, Martin Luther King, Jr., gave one of the most unforgettable speeches in United States history. He spoke about his dream for the nation's future. He said,

> **❝I have a dream that one day on the red hills of Georgia the sons of former slaves and former slaveowners will be able to sit down together at the table of brotherhood. . . .❞**

King's words brought hope to millions of people. The year after the march in Washington, he was awarded the Nobel Peace Prize for his work.

REVIEW How did Martin Luther King, Jr., work for civil rights?

Working for Change

Shortly after he became President, Lyndon Johnson asked Congress to pass the civil rights bill that President Kennedy had introduced. Congress agreed. In 1964 both Democrats and Republicans voted to pass what became

People in Selma, Alabama, marched in support of voting rights for African Americans.

known as the Civil Rights Act of 1964. This law made segregation in public places against the law. It also said that people of all races should have equal job opportunities.

Even after the Civil Rights Act was passed, not all Americans were treated the same. In many places African Americans were kept from voting or were threatened if they tried to vote. Once again, Martin Luther King, Jr., led a march to try to bring about change. The march took place in Selma, Alabama. Those who were against it used violence to break up the march. The events in Selma were broadcast on television and troubled many Americans.

In response to the events in Selma, President Johnson appeared before Congress to ask for a vot-

ing rights law. He wanted to make sure that every United States citizen had the chance to vote. Afterward, in a speech broadcast on television, President Johnson said, "There is no issue of states' rights or national rights. There is only the struggle for human rights." Working together, Congress and President Johnson passed the Voting Rights Act of 1965. By 1968 more than half of all African Americans who were old enough to vote were registered voters.

REVIEW What did the Civil Rights Act of 1964 do?

Many civil rights workers helped African Americans register to vote.

After traveling to Mecca, Malcolm X encouraged groups to cooperate with one another.

Other Ideas, Other Leaders

Some African American leaders disagreed with Martin Luther King, Jr.'s, belief in nonviolent protest. Malcolm X was one of them. He was a member of the Nation of Islam, or Black Muslims. He wanted change to happen faster.

Malcolm X was born Malcolm Little, but he changed his last name to X to stand for the unknown African name his family had lost through slavery. In his early speeches, Malcolm X called for strict separation between white people and African Americans. Only in this way, he said, could African Americans truly be free. Later, after a trip to the Islamic holy city of Mecca in 1964, he talked less about separation and more about cooperation among groups. Malcolm X had little time to act on his new ideas. He was assassinated in 1965. Three years later, in April 1968, Martin Luther King, Jr., was also assassinated. Even though African Americans had lost two important leaders, other leaders continued to work for equal rights.

In 1966 Robert Weaver became the first African American to serve in the President's Cabinet when he became secretary of housing and urban development. In 1967 Thurgood Marshall became the first African American justice to sit on the Supreme Court of the United States. Two years later Shirley Chisholm became the first African American woman elected to Congress. These leaders worked for change from inside the government rather than from outside.

REVIEW How did Malcolm X's ideas change over time?

Robert Weaver was the first African American Cabinet member.

Civil Rights for Other Groups

Following the lead of the African American Civil Rights movement, other groups in the United States began to organize for change. They, too, wanted equal rights under the law.

To help improve the lives of farm workers, Cesar Chavez, Dolores Huerta (HWAIR•tah), and others organized a group that would become the United Farm Workers. Most of its members were Mexican American migrant workers. A **migrant worker** is someone who moves from place to place with the seasons, harvesting crops.

Like Martin Luther King, Jr., Cesar Chavez called for nonviolent action to solve problems. In 1965 he organized a strike by California grape pickers and started a nationwide boycott of grapes. Chavez's goal was to get better wages and improve working conditions for migrant workers. Many of the nation's people showed their support for the movement by not buying grapes. In 1970 Chavez reached an agreement with California's grape growers and helped the migrant workers get greater rights.

American Indians also formed groups to work for the rights that they had been promised in earlier treaties with the United States government. In many cases those treaties had not been honored. Then, in 1975, Congress passed the Self-Determination and Educational Assistance Act. For the first time, Indian tribes could run their own businesses and health and education programs.

REVIEW What did Cesar Chavez accomplish?

Cesar Chavez worked to improve conditions for migrant workers.

The Women's Rights Movement

Although the Civil Rights Act of 1964 said that all people should have equal job opportunities, many jobs were still not open to women. When men and women did have the same kinds of jobs, women were often paid less than men. To help women achieve equal rights, Betty Friedan and others started the National Organization for Women, or NOW, in 1966.

NOW and other women's rights groups helped elect many women to public office. These groups felt that having women in the government would make it easier to change unfair laws.

By the 1970s new laws had been passed saying that employers must treat men and women equally. No job could be open to men only or to women only.

Analyze Graphs In the 1970s women worked for equal rights (above) and equal pay. During this time the number of women in the labor force continued to increase.

◈ About how many women were employed in 2000?

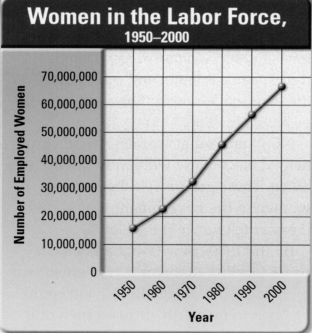

Women in the Labor Force,
1950–2000

Number of Employed Women

70,000,000
60,000,000
50,000,000
40,000,000
30,000,000
20,000,000
10,000,000
0

1950 1960 1970 1980 1990 2000

Year

As a result, many women began careers in fields such as law, medicine, and business. Some became astronauts, construction workers, and firefighters.

Many women also called for a new amendment to the Constitution. The amendment that was introduced in Congress became known as the Equal Rights Amendment. The purpose of this amendment was to make sure that women would always have equal rights under the law.

The Equal Rights Amendment was passed by Congress. However, it did not become part of the Constitution. For an amendment to be added to the Constitution, it must be ratified by three-fourths of the states. Since the Equal Rights Amendment was not ratified by the required number of states, it was never adopted.

Although the Equal Rights Amendment failed to pass, a number of education laws were passed in 1972. These laws helped guarantee women equal treatment in colleges. As a result, the number of women in law schools and medical schools went up.

In addition, women's sports programs also were helped by these new laws. For the first time, colleges and universities had to fund and support women's sports just as they did men's sports.

Today American women have the same rights and responsibilities as American men. In 1981 Sandra Day O'Connor became the first woman appointed to the United States Supreme Court. In the 1990s Madeleine Albright became the first woman secretary of state, and Janet Reno became the first woman attorney general. Women also serve their country in the armed forces.

REVIEW What did NOW do to help women gain equal rights?

Justice Sandra Day O'Connor

LESSON 4 REVIEW

Summary Time Line

1960 — 1970 — 1980

1964
The Civil Rights Act is signed into law

1965
Cesar Chavez organizes migrant workers

1972
Congress passes education reforms

1. **MAIN IDEA** How did individuals and groups try to get equal rights?

2. **WHY IT MATTERS** What did the movement for equal rights make possible?

3. **VOCABULARY** Write a sentence explaining how Cesar Chavez helped improve the lives of **migrant workers**.

4. **TIME LINE** When was the Civil Rights Act signed into law?

5. **READING SKILL—Draw Conclusions** Why do you think marches were a good way for groups to show support for civil rights?

6. **CULTURE** What group was helped by the Self-Determination and Educational Assistance Act?

7. **CRITICAL THINKING—Analyze** Why is it important for everyone to be treated equally?

 PERFORMANCE—Create a Time Line Create a year-by-year time line of the 1960s. On the time line, include all the dates in this lesson that marked important events in Americans' struggle for equal rights. Compare your completed time line with the time line of a classmate.

·SKILLS· Act as a Responsible Citizen

Dr. Martin Luther King, Jr., led people in the civil rights march in Washington, D.C.

➤ WHY IT MATTERS

Democratic nations depend on their citizens to act responsibly. For a democracy to work, its citizens must learn about important issues, choose wise leaders, and take part in government. In addition, when a nation faces a problem, its citizens must take responsible action to solve it.

➤ WHAT YOU NEED TO KNOW

You have read about the fight for civil rights in the United States during the 1950s and 1960s. Many citizens took part in the Civil Rights movement. The peaceful protests of Dr. Martin Luther King, Jr., and others caught the attention of people around the world.

Acting as a responsible citizen is not always as difficult as it was during the fight for civil rights. It can be as simple as voting or sitting on a jury. It does, however, require both thought and action.

Some of the steps that citizens working for civil rights followed to

442

Cesar Chavez (center) was still working for the rights of farm workers when he died in 1993.

act as a responsible citizen are listed below. They followed these steps to bring about change.

Step 1 **They learned about problems of injustice that affected people in the nation.**

Step 2 **They thought about what could be done to bring about change.**

Step 3 **They decided how to bring about change in a way that would be good for the whole country.**

Step 4 **Each person decided what contribution he or she could best make.**

Step 5 **People worked as individuals or with others to bring about change.**

▶ PRACTICE THE SKILL

Those citizens and the others who took part in the Civil Rights movement risked their lives to fight injustice. Some even died in the fight for civil rights.

In Lesson 4, you read about people who acted responsibly as they worked for civil rights. Choose two of them, and explain how they showed they were responsible citizens.

▶ APPLY WHAT YOU LEARNED

Some acts of citizenship, such as voting, can be done only by adults. Others can be done by citizens of almost any age. Use the five steps on this page as you decide on ways you and your classmates might act as responsible citizens of your community.

11 Review and Test Preparation

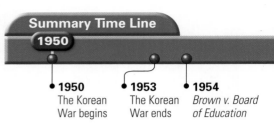
Summary Time Line
1950

• 1950
The Korean
War begins

• 1953
The Korean
War ends

• 1954
*Brown v. Board
of Education*

USE YOUR READING SKILLS

Use this graphic organizer to help you draw conclusions about the 1950s. A copy of this graphic organizer appears on page 112 of the Activity Book.

The 1950s

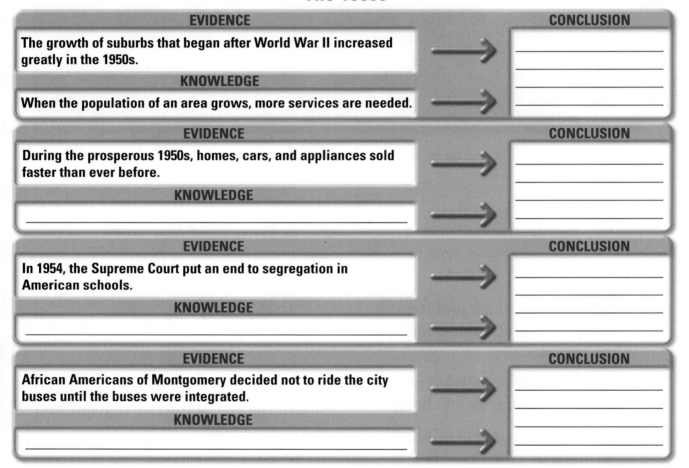

EVIDENCE		CONCLUSION
The growth of suburbs that began after World War II increased greatly in the 1950s.	→	
KNOWLEDGE		
When the population of an area grows, more services are needed.	→	

EVIDENCE		CONCLUSION
During the prosperous 1950s, homes, cars, and appliances sold faster than ever before.	→	
KNOWLEDGE		
	→	

EVIDENCE		CONCLUSION
In 1954, the Supreme Court put an end to segregation in American schools.	→	
KNOWLEDGE		
	→	

EVIDENCE		CONCLUSION
African Americans of Montgomery decided not to ride the city buses until the buses were integrated.	→	
KNOWLEDGE		
	→	

THINK & WRITE

Write a Story Imagine you are living in the early 1950s. Your family has just bought its first black-and-white television set. Write a story about how the television set has affected your family life. Share your story with a classmate.

Write a Descriptive Paragraph
Imagine you are either Neil Armstrong or Buzz Aldrin. Write a descriptive paragraph about your first step onto the moon's surface. Describe what you see, what you hear, and how you feel.

1962 The Cuban missile crisis

1964 The Civil Rights Act is passed

1965 Cesar Chavez begins a nationwide grape boycott

1966 The National Organization for Women is formed

1969 *Apollo 11* astronauts land on the moon

1972 Congress passes education reforms

USE THE TIME LINE

Use the chapter summary time line to answer these questions.

1 When was the Civil Rights Act passed?

2 When did the moon landing happen?

USE VOCABULARY

Use each term in a complete sentence that will help explain its meaning.

3 **desegregate** (p. 411)

4 **satellite** (p. 423)

5 **migrant worker** (p. 439)

RECALL FACTS

Answer these questions.

6 What kind of government ruled North Korea in 1950?

7 Who was the commander of all UN forces in Korea?

8 What was the Civil Rights Act of 1964?

Write the letter of the best choice.

9 **TEST PREP** Shortly after his election, President Harry S. Truman presented a plan to Congress that became known as—
A the New Deal.
B the Big Deal.
C the Fair Deal.
D the Truman Deal.

10 **TEST PREP** Which of the following was the name of the United States space program to land astronauts on the moon?
F Apollo
G Discovery
H Explorer
J Atlantis

THINK CRITICALLY

11 Why do you think most people felt that Harry S. Truman could not win the 1948 presidential election?

12 How did the Civil Rights movement inspire change in people around the United States?

APPLY SKILLS

Identify Changing Borders
Use the maps on page 417 to answer the question.

13 Where was the border between North Korea and South Korea set in 1945?

Compare Graphs
Use the information and graphs on pages 424 and 425 to answer these questions.

14 How are bar graphs different from circle graphs? How are they the same?

Resolve Conflicts
Use the information on page 434 to answer the question.

15 How can compromise solve conflicts?

Act as a Responsible Citizen

16 Identify a person who you think is a responsible citizen. Write a paragraph explaining why you think that person is acting responsibly.

LOCATE IT

CALIFORNIA

Simi Valley

RONALD REAGAN PRESIDENTIAL LIBRARY

The Ronald Reagan Presidential Library is one of ten presidential libraries. In this photograph taken from inside the library, a piece of the Berlin Wall is displayed. The original wall was 96 miles (154 km) long and divided Germany for almost 30 years. Helping bring down the wall was one of President Reagan's greatest accomplishments.

12

Into Modern Times

 Mr. Gorbachev, tear down this wall. "

—Ronald Reagan, in a speech at the Berlin Wall, June 12, 1987

CHAPTER READING SKILL

Make Inferences

When you read, sometimes you need to make inferences. An **inference** is an educated guess based on the facts you have read and your own knowledge and experience.

As you read each lesson in the chapter, use the details and your own knowledge and experience to make inferences.

WHAT YOU HAVE READ ←→ WHAT YOU KNOW

INFERENCE

MAIN IDEA
Read to learn how the
Vietnam War and the
events of the 1970s
changed the United States.

WHY IT MATTERS
The Vietnam War and the
events of the 1970s
divided Americans.

VOCABULARY

inflation
hawk
dove
arms control
détente
cease-fire
scandal

The Vietnam War Years

| 1951 | | 1976 | | 2001 |

1963–1975

While many groups were trying to win better treatment and equal rights, President Lyndon Johnson was working on government programs to make life better for all Americans. These programs were part of Johnson's dream—what he called the Great Society. However, Johnson also faced challenges outside the nation as the United States became involved in the Vietnam War. This war and the events of the 1970s divided the American people.

The Vietnam War

Like Korea, Vietnam was divided into two countries after World War II. North Vietnam became a communist country, and South Vietnam became a republic. In the late 1950s South Vietnamese communists, called the Vietcong, tried to take over

FAST FACT Lyndon Johnson's Great Society program was the largest expansion of government efforts since the New Deal. Altogether, the program resulted in the passage of 435 bills through Congress.

The Job Corps (below) was part of President Johnson's Great Society program.

GEOGRAPHY THEME

Movement The Ho Chi Minh Trail was a supply route from North Vietnam to South Vietnam. It was named for the communist leader of North Vietnam.

❖ Why do you think the trail went through other countries?

A Divided Vietnam

CHINA

Red River

Hanoi ⊛

BURMA

NORTH VIETNAM

Gulf of Tonkin

Hainan

LAOS

Vientiane ⊛

HO CHI MINH TRAIL

Demilitarized Zone

Mekong River

South China Sea

THAILAND

Bangkok ⊛

SOUTH VIETNAM

CAMBODIA

Gulf of Thailand

Phnom Penh ⊛

Saigon ⊛

0   100   200 Miles
0   100   200 Kilometers
Mercator Projection

Mekong Delta

⊛ National capital

the South Vietnamese government. North Vietnam helped the Vietcong. Between 1956 and 1962 the United States sent money, war supplies, and soldiers to help South Vietnam fight the Vietcong.

By the time Johnson became President in November 1963, the Vietcong were winning the war. Then in August 1964 it was reported that a North Vietnamese gunboat had attacked a United States Navy ship in the Gulf of Tonkin near Vietnam. Johnson sent more soldiers to South Vietnam, hoping they could help defeat the Vietcong.

When United States and South Vietnamese troops failed to defeat the Vietcong quickly, the United States sent planes to bomb North Vietnam. Johnson thought the bombing would stop the flow of supplies from North Vietnam to the Vietcong. He also sent more troops to South Vietnam. By 1968 more than

500,000 United States soldiers were serving there.

The Vietnam War now was costing the United States billions of dollars each year. At the same time, President Johnson was building many of his Great Society programs. Johnson said that the nation could afford both. It turned out that he was wrong.

To pay for both the Vietnam War and the programs of the Great Society, the government had to borrow a lot of money. This borrowing led to inflation. When there is **inflation**, people need more money to buy the same goods and services. This weakens a country's economy.

REVIEW **Why did the government have to borrow money in the 1960s?**

Citizens Are Divided

The Vietnam War divided American public opinion. Some people felt that the war was needed to stop the spread of communism. Others said that it was a civil war that should be settled by the Vietnamese without outside help.

The nation's leaders were also divided. Most government leaders were either hawks or doves. **Hawks**—named for the fierce bird of prey—were people who supported the war. They thought that if South Vietnam became a communist country, its neighbors—Laos and Cambodia—would soon also become communist. The idea that once one country fell to communism, neighboring countries would follow was called the domino theory. **Doves**, named for the traditional symbol of peace, were those who wanted the war to end. They believed that people were dying needlessly in a war that South Vietnam could not win. Each side believed that it was right and that the other side was wrong.

Some Americans (above, left) wanted the United States to leave Vietnam. Others (below) supported American involvement.

During the Vietnam War, United States soldiers joined with South Vietnamese troops to fight communist forces.

As the number of Americans killed in Vietnam climbed into the thousands, more and more people began to oppose the war. All over the United States, protests and marches against the war took place. Some young Americans resisted being drafted. They burned their draft cards in protest. Some even moved out of the United States to avoid military service. Many of them went to Canada.

By the end of Johnson's term as President, only 25 percent of Americans—just one in four—thought that he was doing a good job in Vietnam. For that reason and others, Johnson announced that he would not run for President again. In 1968 the American people elected a new President—Richard M. Nixon. Nixon promised Americans, "I'm going to end that war. Fast." The war, however, did not end, and the protests against it grew and spread across the country.

As the war continued, Nixon developed his plan to end the war as quickly as possible. He wanted to prevent more American soldiers from being injured or killed. He also wanted to keep South Vietnam from becoming a communist country.

Nixon's plan was to train the South Vietnamese troops better. Then they could fight the Vietcong and the North Vietnamese on their own. This would allow the United States to bring some American soldiers home. Other soldiers would stay and continue the bombing raids on North Vietnam. As the number of troops that were sent home grew, Nixon announced a new plan. After learning the Vietcong were launching some of their attacks from neighboring Cambodia, Nixon ordered an invasion of Cambodia. Soon troops were sent there to destroy the Vietcong bases.

REVIEW What was the domino theory?

DEMOCRATIC VALUES
Popular Sovereignty

During the 1960s many of the nation's high school and college students began a movement to give 18- to 20-year-olds the right to vote. Before this time the minimum voting age was 21. In 1971, West Virginia Senator Jennings Randolph proposed a constitutional amendment to lower the voting age to 18. The amendment was quickly approved by Congress and was ratified by the states in less than four months—faster than any earlier constitutional amendment. The Twenty-sixth Amendment states that the voting rights of citizens 18 years or older "shall not be denied or abridged by the United States or by any state on account of age."

Analyze the Value

1. What did the Twenty-sixth Amendment do?
2. **Make It Relevant** Write an essay explaining how you think elections have or have not changed since the passage of the Twenty-sixth Amendment.

After the Twenty-sixth Amendment was ratified, President Nixon signed the new law.

Improved Relations

In 1972, as the war raged on, President Nixon accepted an invitation from China's leader, Mao Zedong (MOW zeh•DUNG), to visit China. The United States had not traded or carried on foreign relations with China since 1949 when China became a communist country. As a result of Nixon's visit, the two nations agreed to trade with each other and to allow visits from each other's scientific and cultural groups.

Three months after visiting China, President Nixon flew to Moscow to meet with Soviet leader Leonid Brezhnev (BREZH•nef). This was the first time a United States President had visited both China and the Soviet Union. As a result of the meeting in Moscow, the United States and the Soviet Union agreed to increase trade and to work together on scientific and cultural projects.

During their 1972 visit to China, President Nixon and his wife, Patricia, visited the Great Wall of China.

During the meeting Nixon and Brezhnev also agreed to **arms control**, or limiting the number of weapons that each nation could have. This marked the beginning of a period of **détente** (day•TAHNT), or an easing of tensions, between the United States and the Soviet Union. However, that did not last long.

REVIEW What was détente?

Nixon Resigns and the War Ends

In 1972 Nixon was reelected President. The next year he agreed to a cease-fire in Vietnam. A **cease-fire** is a temporary end to a conflict. He also agreed to bring the remaining American soldiers home. The last ground troops left Vietnam in March 1973.

During the election campaign, some people working to help Nixon, a Republican, had done some things that were against the law. One thing they did was to break into an office of the Democratic party in the Watergate building in Washington, D.C. It was later shown that when Nixon learned about this unlawful act, he tried to cover it up.

Nixon announced his decision to resign in a national television speech.

The Watergate scandal ended Nixon's presidency. A **scandal** is an action that brings disgrace. On August 9, 1974, Nixon became the first United States President to resign, or give up, the presidency. On that same day, Vice President Gerald Ford became President.

Soon after the last American ground troops had left Vietnam, fighting broke out yet again. Without the support of American troops, South Vietnam could not win the war. On April 30, 1975, the government of South Vietnam surrendered.

When United States forces left the city of Saigon in South Vietnam, there was much confusion. Thousands of South Vietnamese people asked to leave on United States helicopters.

Veterans Day

To celebrate the signing of the armistice that ended World War I, Armistice Day was first observed on November 11, 1919. In 1954 President Dwight D. Eisenhower changed the name of Armistice Day to Veterans Day. This day honors all veterans of the United States armed forces.

Today Veterans Day is still observed on November 11. People celebrate with parades and speeches that honor the service that members of the military have given their country. Veterans Day is a time for families and friends of Vietnam veterans to visit the Vietnam Veterans Memorial. Volunteers help visitors find the names of friends and relatives on the memorial's wall.

A Vietnam veteran and his son search for people's names on the Vietnam Veterans Memorial.

The government of North Vietnam gained control of the whole country. The Vietnam War was over.

On Veterans Day in 1982, the Vietnam Veterans Memorial in Washington, D.C., was opened to visitors. The memorial's wall lists the names of more than 58,000 American men and women who lost their lives or were reported missing during the Vietnam War.

REVIEW Who became President after Nixon resigned?

LESSON 1 REVIEW

Summary Time Line

1963 — 1969 — 1975

1968 More than 500,000 United States troops in Vietnam

1974 President Nixon resigns

1975 The Vietnam War ends

1. **MAIN IDEA** How did the Vietnam War and the events of the 1970s change the nation?

2. **WHY IT MATTERS** Why did the Vietnam War and the events of the 1970s divide Americans?

3. **VOCABULARY** Write a sentence explaining the political difference between a **hawk** and a **dove**.

4. **TIME LINE** Did the Vietnam War end before or after President Nixon resigned?

5. **READING SKILL—Make Inferences** How do you think Americans reacted when President Nixon resigned?

6. **CRITICAL THINKING—Analyze** Why do you think President Nixon chose to go to China and the Soviet Union?

PERFORMANCE—Write a Report Use the Internet or library sources to write a report about the Vietnam Veterans Memorial. Share your report with the class.

The Cold War Ends

1951   1976   2001

1975–1991

· LESSON ·

2

MAIN IDEA
Read to learn about the events that brought about the end of the Cold War.

WHY IT MATTERS
The end of the Cold War marked the start of a new period in world history.

VOCABULARY
hostage
deficit

Although the Watergate scandal ended his time in office, President Nixon accomplished many things. His most important achievement may have been reducing tensions between the free world and communist nations. However, the Cold War did not end until 1991.

A New President

Just a few weeks after taking office, President Ford granted Richard Nixon "a full, free and absolute [total] pardon." This pardon included forgiveness "for all offenses against the United States which he . . . has committed or may have committed or taken part in." Ford said that putting Nixon on trial would have divided the American people even more than they were already.

President Ford also faced a troubled economy during his presidency. The nation was still paying for the Vietnam War. Businesses were making less money, and prices continued to rise.

As Gerald Ford took office as President, the nation's economy faced many problems. Unemployed workers seeking benefits and new jobs formed long lines at employment offices throughout the country.

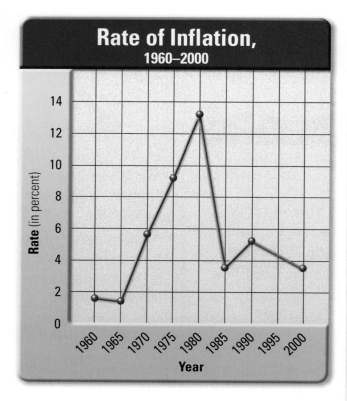

Rate of Inflation,
1960–2000

Rate (in percent)

14
12
10
8
6
4
2
0

1960 1965 1970 1975 1980 1985 1990 1995 2000

Year

Analyze Graphs This graph shows how the rate of inflation has changed over time.

◈ By how many points did the percent of inflation decrease from 1980 to 1985?

The number of people who were unemployed grew and inflation was high. Ford tried to lower inflation by slowing down the economy. He also started a program called Whip Inflation Now, or WIN, to help lower inflation. However, the nation still faced economic problems.

President Carter (center) is shown shaking hands with President Sadat of Egypt (left) and Prime Minister Begin of Israel at the signing of their peace agreement.

People soon stopped supporting President Ford. Many were angry that he had given Nixon a pardon. Others were unhappy with the poor economy.

In 1976 the American people elected Jimmy Carter President. Carter had been the governor of Georgia. He promised to restore trust in our nation's government. In his inauguration speech, he asked Americans to help him fulfill that promise. He said, "You have given me a great responsibility—to stay close to you, to be worthy of you, and to exemplify [stand for] what you are. Let us create together a new national spirit of unity and trust."

REVIEW Why did President Ford decide to not put Richard Nixon on trial?

Tensions Rise

Two years after Carter was elected President, he helped bring peace to the countries of the Middle East. Together, Southwest Asia and Northeast Africa are often called the Middle East. For centuries people in this region have been divided by religious, cultural, and political differences. In 1978 Carter brought the prime minister of Israel, Menachem Begin (BAY•guhn), and Egypt's president, Anwar Sadat (suh•DAT), to Camp David in Maryland.

Together they set up a peace agreement for these longtime enemies. The agreement became known as the Camp David Accords.

The following year President Carter faced another challenge in the Middle East. In February 1979 a revolution took place in the nation of Iran. The leaders of the revolution caused the shah, the country's ruler, to flee from Iran. These leaders became angry when the United States supported the shah.

To show their anger, the revolutionaries attacked the United States embassy in Teheran, the capital of Iran. They captured 53 Americans and made them hostages. A **hostage** is a prisoner held until the captors' demands are met. The captors demanded that the United States make the shah return to Iran for punishment. The United States, however, refused.

For more than a year, President Carter tried, but failed, to get the hostages freed. At the same time, the nation's economy slowed and unemployment rose. Inflation remained very high, and there were fuel shortages.

The United States did not produce as much oil as Americans needed. In fact, by 1972 almost one-third of the nation's oil needs were met by countries in the Middle East. In 1973 many Middle Eastern leaders were angered when the United States supported Israel in a war against Arab countries. This anger was one reason that Arab leaders decided to join together to control the amount of oil shipped to the United States.

Looking exhausted, the American hostages sit inside the United States embassy during a press conference.

Since gasoline is made from oil, Americans now had to wait in long lines to get gasoline for their cars. The price of traveling by car and of heating a home rose as oil prices soared.

To conserve energy, people made many sacrifices during this time. Americans heated their homes less. In some areas, schools met only every other day, and factories closed early. Americans also began buying smaller cars that used less gasoline.

The United States also had to deal with troubles outside the nation. In 1979 Soviet troops invaded the country of Afghanistan (af•GA•nuh•stan) in Southwest Asia. The invasion moved Soviet troops much closer to the region's rich oil fields. President Carter called the invasion a threat to world peace.

Carter demanded that the Soviets leave Afghanistan. When they refused, he cut back American trade with the Soviet Union and stopped supporting arms control. He also kept American athletes from taking part in the 1980 Olympic Games, because they would be held in the Soviet Union's capital city, Moscow.

The fighting in Afghanistan continued for years. The Afghan rebels fought so hard that it was difficult for the Soviets to win control of the country. Finally, in 1988, the Soviet Union began to remove its troops.

REVIEW **What were the Camp David Accords?**

Into the 1980s

Many people blamed President Carter for the nation's troubles. He ran for President again in 1980 but lost the election to the former governor of California Ronald Reagan. The day that Reagan

This photo shows a busy day of trading in the New York Stock Exchange. The United States economy began to grow stronger after Ronald Reagan took office.

Analyze Primary Sources

Newspapers across the country reported on the inauguration of President Ronald Reagan. On the day Reagan took office, the hostages that were being held in Iran were released.

1 the masthead, or title of the newspaper

2 the date the newspaper was published

3 the headline of the front page news story

4 photograph of the front page news story

❓ What other information can you find on the front page of this newspaper?

became President, the Iranians finally freed the hostages.

When Ronald Reagan ran for President, he had promised to help the economy. He quickly won approval from Congress for large tax cuts. He also cut some government programs. The economy slowly grew stronger, and high inflation ended. At the same time, however, the government's budget **deficit**, or shortage, increased. When there is a deficit, the government spends more money than it takes in each year in taxes and other income.

President Reagan soon increased defense spending. He believed that to win the Cold War the nation needed a stronger military. He said that the Cold War was a "struggle between right and wrong, good and evil." In that struggle, Reagan said, the Soviet Union was "the evil empire."

The Soviet Union continued to build more weapons, too, and it helped communist governments all over the world. Then, in 1985, a new leader named Mikhail Gorbachev (mee•KAH•eel gawr•buh•CHAWF) came to power in the Soviet Union. Nothing would be the same again.

REVIEW What causes a deficit in the government's budget?

Reduced Tensions

When Gorbachev took over, President Reagan said he would welcome the chance to meet the new Soviet leader in the "cause of world peace." In April 1985 Gorbachev agreed to a meeting. He said that better relations between the United States and the Soviet Union were "extremely necessary—and possible."

Soviet leader Gorbachev (left) and President Reagan (right) shake hands at their first meeting. They met each year from 1985 through 1988.

Reagan later spoke of the meeting with Gorbachev:

> 66 Here we were, I said, two men from humble beginnings. Now we were probably the only two men in the world who could bring about World War III. At the same time, I said, we were possibly the only two men who might be able to bring peace to the world. 99

The meeting between the two leaders marked a change in the Cold War. President Reagan called it a "fresh start" in United States–Soviet relations. Soon the United States and the Soviet Union agreed to more treaties limiting nuclear missiles.

In the Soviet Union, Gorbachev was already changing many of the old ways of doing things. He called for *perestroika* (pair•uh•STROY•kuh), or a restructuring of the Soviet government. Under perestroika,

Soviet people could start their own businesses. Gorbachev also called for *glasnost* (GLAZ•nohst), or openness. He wanted the Soviet people to have more freedoms. Soviet citizens could now speak out without fear of being punished.

Reforms in the Soviet Union led to changes in many other communist nations. In Poland, Czechoslovakia, and Hungary, people gained new freedoms. In time these nations became independent. In 1989 the government leaders of East Germany removed the armed guards from the Berlin Wall and opened its gates. As East Germans poured into West Berlin, people from both sides of the wall began to use hammers, bricks, and anything else they could find to start breaking down the wall. The following year Germany was reunited.

перестройку!

A political poster in Moscow, Russia, shows support for perestroika.

Tearing down the Berlin Wall became an important part of the celebration of West Germans and East Germans after their border opened.

In 1989 George Bush became the new President of the United States. That year he met with Mikhail Gorbachev.

The leaders talked about the many changes taking place in Europe and the Soviet Union. At the end Gorbachev looked Bush in the eye. "I have heard you say that you want *perestroika* to succeed," he said, "but frankly I didn't know this. Now I know." The Cold War was finally ending. On July 31, 1991, Bush and Gorbachev signed a new agreement called the Strategic Arms Reduction Treaty. This treaty was aimed at reducing each country's number of short-range nuclear weapons. As 1991 went on, Bush reduced the number of weapons in the United States even more, and he challenged Gorbachev to do the same in the Soviet Union.

REVIEW What new policies did Gorbachev bring to the Soviet Union?

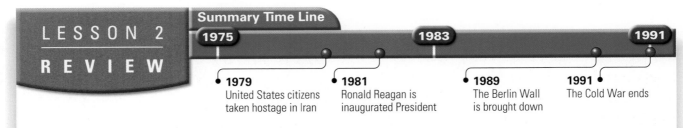

LESSON 2 REVIEW

Summary Time Line

1975 — 1983 — 1991

1979 United States citizens taken hostage in Iran

1981 Ronald Reagan is inaugurated President

1989 The Berlin Wall is brought down

1991 The Cold War ends

1 **MAIN IDEA** What events helped bring about the end of the Cold War?

2 **WHY IT MATTERS** How did the end of the Cold War change the world?

3 **VOCABULARY** Write a sentence explaining what a **deficit** is.

4 **TIME LINE** What year was the Berlin Wall brought down?

5 **READING SKILL—Make Inferences** How do you think relations between the United States and the Soviet Union changed after the Cold War ended?

6 **CRITICAL THINKING—Analyze** Why do you think reforms in the Soviet Union led to changes in other communist nations?

PERFORMANCE—Create a Time Line The Cold War between the United States and the Soviet Union lasted almost 50 years. Create a time line that shows the major events of the Cold War.

MAIN IDEA
Read to learn about some of the new challenges the United States faced after the Cold War ended.

WHY IT MATTERS
The United States continues to work to ensure stability at home and around the world.

VOCABULARY

recession
candidate

Vice President George Bush speaks at the Republican National Convention before being elected President.

New Challenges

1951   1976   2001

1989–1995

President George Bush faced many challenges during his presidency. One of the biggest was trying to improve the nation's economy. Also during this time, the United States emerged as the world's only superpower. As such, the United States played an important role in the conflicts that took place in other nations.

Challenges at Home

In his 1989 inauguration speech, President Bush urged Americans to volunteer their time to help one another. He described those that do so as "a thousand points of light . . . spread like stars throughout the nation." To encourage Americans to become more involved in their communities, President Bush helped begin the Points of Light Foundation to promote volunteer work.

President George Bush (seated in the chair on the right) meets with his advisers, including General Colin Powell (far left).

Bush wanted to improve life for all Americans, but he had difficulty improving the nation's economy. In 1990 the United States entered a **recession**, or a period of slow economic activity. This recession lasted for more than two years. During that time millions of Americans lost their jobs.

President Bush tried to boost the nation's economy by passing laws to help failing industries. However, the changing world economy meant that many jobs were moving. Factory jobs once done by workers in the United States were now being done by workers elsewhere. Bush had promised not to raise taxes, but he hoped that by raising some taxes, he would be able to lower the deficit.

Although President Bush was busy with problems at home, he also dealt with world events. Talking about the idea of a world without the Cold War, he said, "Now we can see . . . the very real prospect of a new world order." By "a new world order," Bush meant a world without the conflicts of the past. Despite his hopes, new conflicts soon developed.

REVIEW What is a recession?

The Gulf War

In August 1990 the nation of Iraq, led by its dictator, Saddam Hussein (hoo•SAYN), invaded and took control of the small country of Kuwait (koo•WAYT). Kuwait, a major producer of oil in the Middle East, borders Iraq and Saudi Arabia. Since Kuwait and Saudi Arabia were both allies of the United States, Bush quickly sent troops to Saudi Arabia to help defend it in case it, too, was attacked.

When Iraq refused to remove its troops from Kuwait, allied forces from 27 countries, including the United States, attacked Iraq. The United States led this attack, called Operation Desert Storm, or the Gulf War. Among President Bush's advisers during Operation Desert Storm was General Colin L. Powell. He was Chairman of the Joint Chiefs of Staff—the leaders of all the branches of the military. General Powell, who had commanded troops in the Vietnam War, had military experience and leadership qualities.

Allied planes bombed the country of Iraq, and Iraqi forces in Kuwait. Then ground troops swept into Kuwait and drove out the Iraqi forces. Within seven months the allied forces had defeated the Iraqis and returned Kuwait's leaders to power. Saddam Hussein, however, stayed in power in Iraq.

General Powell won fame during the Gulf War and became a national hero. In 2001 he became the United States secretary of state.

REVIEW What event caused the Gulf War to begin?

A New Eastern Europe

The early 1990s marked the end of communism in Eastern Europe. In 1991 Soviet president Gorbachev outlawed the Communist party. Once communism was gone, there was little to unite the many different peoples in the Soviet Union. Each of its 15 republics declared its

General Colin Powell (left) helped the United States win the Gulf War. During the war, burning oil fields (below) were a common sight.

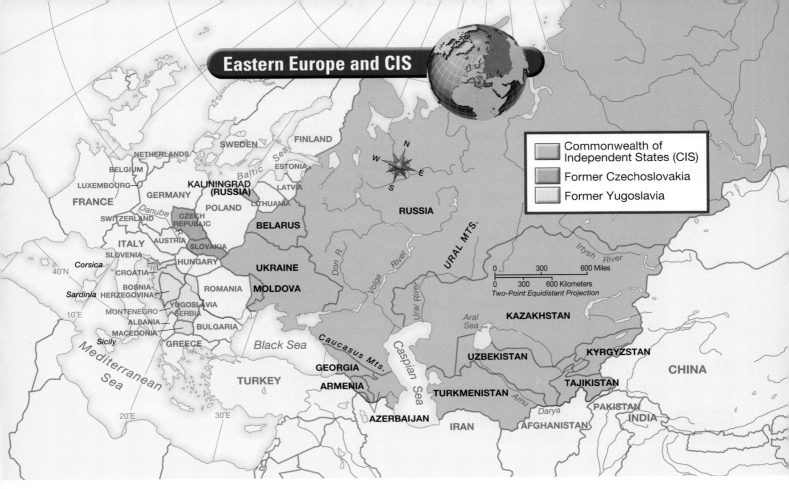

Eastern Europe and CIS

Commonwealth of Independent States (CIS)
Former Czechoslovakia
Former Yugoslavia

Regions After the Soviet Union collapsed, each of the former Soviet republics declared independence. New countries were also formed in what were once Czechoslovakia and Yugoslavia.

❖ How does the size of Russia compare with the size of the CIS?

independence. Most of the newly independent countries—including the largest, Russia—joined to form a loose confederation called the Commonwealth of Independent States (CIS).

The new countries in the former Soviet Union and Eastern Europe faced terrible problems. Communism had left their economies in ruins. Civil wars had also broken out in some places. Without communist control, old hatreds between people came to the surface.

REVIEW Why did many Eastern European countries face problems after the end of communism?

The 1992 Election

The 1992 presidential election was different from most because it featured three major candidates. A **candidate** is a person chosen by a political party to run for office. In 1992 George Bush was the Republican candidate. Bill Clinton was the Democratic candidate. And H. Ross Perot was the Reform party candidate.

Perot, a Texas businessperson, was popular with voters who wanted a change from the two major parties. Perot's decision to enter the race greatly changed the election. Early on, he appeared to be leading both Bush and Clinton.

As Election Day drew near, however, Clinton and Bush were the two leading candidates.

After all the votes had been counted, Bill Clinton was the winner. Clinton received only 43 percent of the popular vote, but he won 370 electoral votes. The rest of the popular vote was divided between Bush's 38 percent and Perot's 19 percent. Perot's percent was the highest ever for a third-party candidate.

Also, more voters voted in this election than ever before. More than 104 million Americans cast their votes in the election. Altogether 55 percent of all those who could vote did so.

REVIEW How was the 1992 presidential election different from most elections?

Conflicts in Eastern Europe

The United States tried to protect the freedom of people in many parts of the world. In 1993 President Bill Clinton faced serious challenges in Bosnia, a small country located near Yugoslavia. One group there, called the Serbs, wanted to clear the country of the other two groups, the Croats (KRO•atz) and the Muslims. The Serbs forced members of those groups into concentration camps.

President Clinton said Americans had a responsibility to help the Bosnians. In 1995 he sent 20,000 United States soldiers to join troops led by NATO. The NATO forces stopped the killing of Bosnian civilians and maintained a cease-fire. Clinton told Americans, "We stood for peace in Bosnia."

President George Bush (on stage at left) and Bill Clinton (on stage at right) look on as H. Ross Perot (on stage at center) speaks during the 1992 presidential debates.

Children of Kosovo watch United States peacekeepers set up a soccer goal at a school.

In 1998 another problem arose in Kosovo, a small region controlled by Yugoslavia. The people of Kosovo wanted independence, but the Yugoslav leader Slobodan Milosevic (mil•OH•seh•vitch) refused their request. Milosevic sent troops into Kosovo to destroy its people. In 1999 President Clinton again sent United States troops to join NATO forces. After NATO air strikes, Yugoslavia agreed to withdraw its forces from Kosovo. Once again, the United States had stepped in to protect the rights and freedoms of people in other nations.

REVIEW **Why did the United States send troops to Bosnia and Kosovo?**

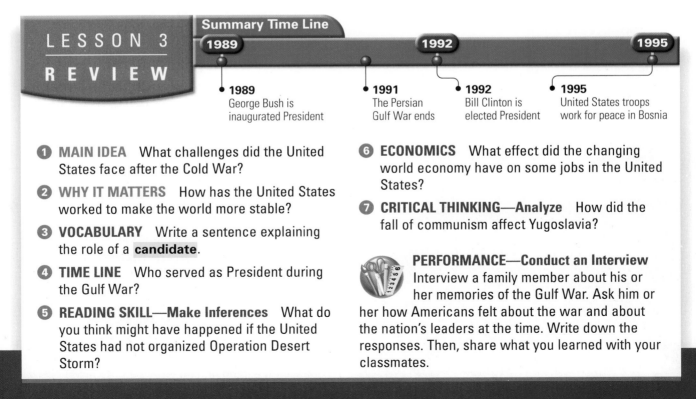

LESSON 3
REVIEW

Summary Time Line

1989 — 1992 — 1995

1989
George Bush is inaugurated President

1991
The Persian Gulf War ends

1992
Bill Clinton is elected President

1995
United States troops work for peace in Bosnia

1. **MAIN IDEA** What challenges did the United States face after the Cold War?

2. **WHY IT MATTERS** How has the United States worked to make the world more stable?

3. **VOCABULARY** Write a sentence explaining the role of a **candidate**.

4. **TIME LINE** Who served as President during the Gulf War?

5. **READING SKILL—Make Inferences** What do you think might have happened if the United States had not organized Operation Desert Storm?

6. **ECONOMICS** What effect did the changing world economy have on some jobs in the United States?

7. **CRITICAL THINKING—Analyze** How did the fall of communism affect Yugoslavia?

PERFORMANCE—Conduct an Interview
Interview a family member about his or her memories of the Gulf War. Ask him or her how Americans felt about the war and about the nation's leaders at the time. Write down the responses. Then, share what you learned with your classmates.

MAIN IDEA
Read to learn how
Americans worked to
make changes in the
United States and
the world at the end
of the twentieth century.

WHY IT MATTERS
Americans have faced
challenges as they worked
to build a better nation.

VOCABULARY

veto
impeach
terrorism
hijack

The End of the Twentieth Century

1951   1976   2001

1992–2001

The end of the twentieth century brought many changes to the United States. Americans watched as the nation's economy grew stronger and stronger. Americans also saw how important each person's civic responsibilities are. During this time the United States worked with other nations to help resolve conflicts. At home, Americans came together as they faced new dangers.

Changes at Home

President Clinton's programs helped change life in America. However, not all of his programs were successful. In his first year in office, Clinton promised to find a way to offer health care to the 30 million Americans who had no health insurance. Clinton's plan was presented before Congress, but it was not approved.

Other Clinton programs ran into problems after the 1994 congressional election. That election gave Republicans a majority of members in both the House and the Senate. Many times Congress passed bills that Clinton had **vetoed**, or rejected. Also, Clinton suggested bills that Congress did not pass.

One of the issues the President and Congress began to work on together was the national budget. A part of the budget dealt with money spent on the welfare program of

President Clinton worked with Congress to help balance the national budget.

Analyze Graphs   During the 1990s, the number of unemployed people steadily decreased.

❖ What does this graph tell you about the nation's economy in the 1990s?

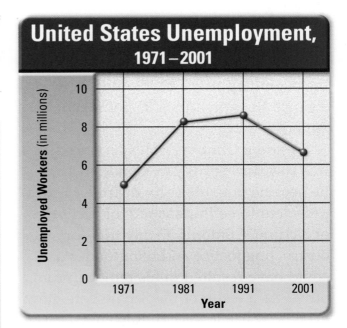

United States Unemployment, 1971–2001

the nation. Welfare is aid that needy people can receive from the government. Some people apply for welfare to help feed their families. Others rely on welfare for housing. The law was not exactly what either Congress or the President wanted. Yet both the Congress and the President were able to reach a compromise and change welfare spending. The new law put a time limit on welfare benefits. People could receive welfare for a period of only two years.

As President, Clinton oversaw one of the greatest periods of economic growth in the nation's history. Businesses created millions of new jobs, and unemployment dropped to its lowest level in many years.

When Clinton left office in 2001, the strong economy was one reason he had the support of many Americans.

Clinton also worked with Boris Yeltsin, the new president of Russia, to further reduce the number of nuclear weapons.

During the 1990s jobs were created in many new industries. These workers are helping put together computers.

In his 1995 State of the Union Address, Clinton said, "Tonight . . . is the first State of the Union Address ever delivered since the beginning of the Cold War when not a single Russian missile is pointed at . . . America."

President Clinton also experienced controversy during his presidency. In 1999 he became only the second United States president to be **impeached**, or accused of a crime. Clinton's 37-day trial for obstructing justice and lying under oath could have resulted in his removal from office. As a result of the Senate vote, however, he was allowed to finish his term.

REVIEW **Why did President Clinton work with Russian leader Boris Yeltsin?**

The 2000 Election

The presidential election of 2000 showed how important each person's vote is. Texas Governor George W. Bush was the Republican party's candidate. Vice President Al Gore was the Democratic party's candidate. When the more than 100 million votes had been counted, both candidates were very close to winning the presidency. In fact, it was the closest presidential election in 40 years.

The winner would be decided by votes in the state of Florida. But the numbers of votes were so close that for five weeks nobody could tell who had won. During that time, many counties in Florida began to recount their citizens' votes to make

The voting system (left) used in Palm Beach County, Florida, confused some voters. Palm Beach election officials (below) had to recount thousands of votes by hand.

On January 20, 2001, George W. Bush was sworn in as President. He became the first President of the twenty-first century.

sure the totals were correct. On December 12, 2000, the United States Supreme Court ruled that the counting must stop. The officials in Florida who recounted the votes found that George W. Bush had won by about 600 votes. He became President of the United States.

President George W. Bush began working on issues he had discussed during his campaign for the presidency. He proposed laws for tax cuts and worked to make changes in education. However, Bush soon faced challenges in foreign relations. Communist China is a powerful nation. The United States and China are not enemies, but they also are not allies. On April 1, 2001, a spy plane from the United States was flying off the coast of China. A Chinese fighter jet collided with the spy plane. The jet crashed, and its pilot was killed. The spy plane was also badly damaged. The crew had to make an emergency landing at a Chinese military base on the island of Hainan [HY•NAHN].

China's leaders were angry about the accident, and they kept the 24 members of the American crew as prisoners.

United States leaders asked the Chinese government to send the plane and its crew back home, but the Chinese refused. They demanded that the United States government apologize for the incident. Many Americans did not believe that the United States was at fault, but President Bush knew that he needed to avoid war with China. The two nations reached a compromise, and the plane and its crew were soon returned to the United States.

President Bush also dealt with problems in the Middle East when war broke out between Israel and the Palestinian people. The two groups had fought each other many times before, and other nations had volunteered to help bring about a peace agreement. President Bush agreed to attend talks between Israeli and Palestinian representatives. He hoped to play a role in bringing peace to the Middle East. Part of the President's job is to help other nations. It is a way to make the world better for citizens of every nation.

REVIEW How did the presidential election of 2000 show that each person's vote counts?

Facing New Dangers

At the end of the twentieth century, the United States faced new dangers from both outside and inside its borders. The nation's military forces continued to defend democratic values in missions around the world—from Haiti in the Caribbean to Bosnia in Europe. The nation also experienced acts of terrorism as bombs exploded at two United States embassies in Africa and next to a United States Navy ship in the Middle East. **Terrorism** is the deliberate use of violence to promote a cause.

Acts of terrorism occurred inside the United States, too. In the early 1990s, a bomb rocked the World Trade Center in New York City. Then, in 1995, an American citizen who was angry with the government set off a bomb outside the federal office building in Oklahoma City, Oklahoma. That blast killed 168 men, women, and children.

However, the worst act of terrorism in the nation's history occurred on September 11, 2001. That morning, terrorists **hijacked**, or illegally took control of, four American commercial airplanes. Again, terrorists targeted the World Trade Center. Two of the hijacked planes were flown directly into the center's twin towers, causing huge explosions. The third plane was flown into the side of the Pentagon, the nation's military headquarters, near Washington, D.C. The fourth

After the terrorist attacks on September 11, 2001, the twin towers of the World Trade Center caught fire and later collapsed. Firefighters (right) stand among the ruins and raise the American flag as a symbol of patriotism.

In the days after the terrorist attacks, Americans around the nation came together in public ceremonies to remember the victims.

plane crashed in an empty field near Pittsburgh, Pennsylvania.

Less than two hours after the attacks on the World Trade Center, both towers collapsed, killing thousands of people. At the Pentagon, nearly 200 people died.

President Bush, with the support of Congress, pledged that the United States would lead the world in a war against terrorism. As the United States works to make our nation and the world more secure, the Constitution will continue to make sure that our basic freedoms as Americans are protected.

REVIEW In what ways has terrorism affected the United States?

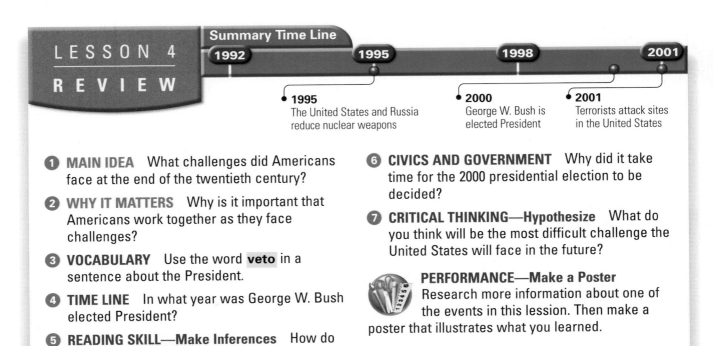

LESSON 4 REVIEW

Summary Time Line

1992 — 1995 — 1998 — 2001

1995
The United States and Russia reduce nuclear weapons

2000
George W. Bush is elected President

2001
Terrorists attack sites in the United States

1 **MAIN IDEA** What challenges did Americans face at the end of the twentieth century?

2 **WHY IT MATTERS** Why is it important that Americans work together as they face challenges?

3 **VOCABULARY** Use the word **veto** in a sentence about the President.

4 **TIME LINE** In what year was George W. Bush elected President?

5 **READING SKILL—Make Inferences** How do you think the 2000 election affected voters and non-voters in the United States?

6 **CIVICS AND GOVERNMENT** Why did it take time for the 2000 presidential election to be decided?

7 **CRITICAL THINKING—Hypothesize** What do you think will be the most difficult challenge the United States will face in the future?

PERFORMANCE—Make a Poster
Research more information about one of the events in this lession. Then make a poster that illustrates what you learned.

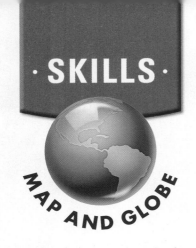

·SKILLS·
MAP AND GLOBE

Read a Population Map

VOCABULARY

population density

⮕ **WHY IT MATTERS**

Like most other geographic information, population can be shown on maps in many different ways. One way to show the population of a place is with color. Knowing how to read a population map can make it easier for you to find out the number of people who live in different areas of the United States and the world.

⮕ **WHAT YOU NEED TO KNOW**

The map below is a population map of the United States. A population map shows where people live. It also shows the population density of each place. **Population density** is the number of people who live in 1 square mile or 1 square kilometer of land. A square mile is a square piece of land. Each of its four

---

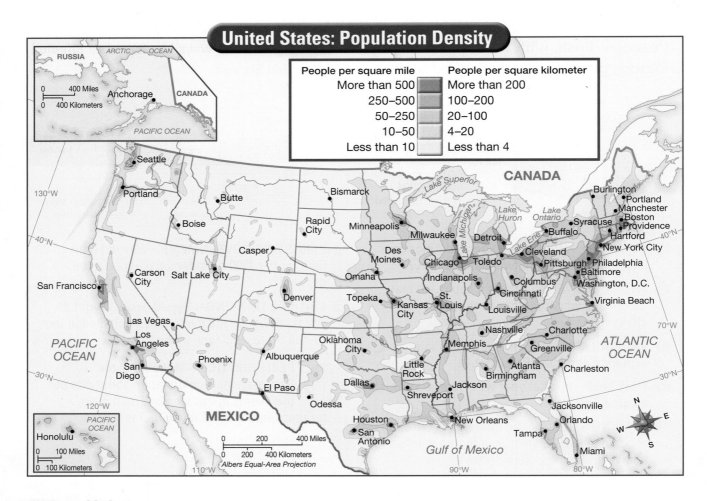

United States: Population Density

People per square mile	People per square kilometer
More than 500	More than 200
250–500	100–200
50–250	20–100
10–50	4–20
Less than 10	Less than 4

---

474 ▪ **Unit 6**

Many people today live in large cities like Seattle, Washington (left). Others live in small, rural communities like this New England town (right).

sides is 1 mile long. A square kilometer is a square piece of land with sides that are each 1 kilometer long.

Look at the key on the map. It shows colors that stand for different population densities.

On the map, the light-tan color stands for the least crowded areas. Red stands for the most crowded areas. Use the map key to find areas that have more than 500 people per square mile or fewer than 10 people per square mile.

▶ PRACTICE THE SKILL

Use the map on page 474 to answer the following questions:

❶ What is the lowest population density shown on the map?

BROADLY?

❷ What is the highest population density shown on the map? ← *BROADLY*

❸ Do most people live in the eastern half of the country or the western half?

❹ Which city has greater population density—Miami, Florida, or Los Angeles, California?

▶ APPLY WHAT YOU LEARNED

Study the population information given on the map on page 474. Then show some of the same information by using a chart, graph, or table.

Practice your map and globe skills with the **GeoSkills CD-ROM**.

MAP AND GLOBE SKILLS

Summary Time Line
1961

1968
More than 500,000
United States troops
in Vietnam

1974
President Nixon
resigns

USE YOUR READING SKILLS

Complete this graphic organizer by using information you have learned from the chapter to make inferences about the end of the Soviet Union and communist rule in Europe. A copy of this graphic organizer appears on page 122 of the Activity Book.

The End of the Soviet Union and Communist Rule in Europe

WHAT YOU HAVE READ

As leader of the Soviet Union, Mikhail Gorbachev introduces reforms that give the Soviet people more freedom.

WHAT YOU KNOW

_____
_____
_____
_____

INFERENCE

_____
_____
_____

WHAT YOU HAVE READ

In 1991, Soviet President Gorbachev outlaws the communist party.

WHAT YOU KNOW

_____
_____
_____
_____

INFERENCE

_____
_____
_____

THINK & WRITE

Write an Interview   Interview a grandparent, parent, or other family member who was alive during one of the following presidencies: Nixon, Ford, Carter, Reagan, or Bush. Ask questions about what life was like during that time period. Write out the interview questions and answers.

Write a Report   Research one of the countries you read about in Chapter 12. Write a report about that country. Include in your report information about the country's geography, people, cultures, religions, and economy. Share your report with a classmate.

1981　　　　　　　　　　　　　　　　　　　　　　　　　　　2001

1975
The Vietnam War ends

1981
Ronald Reagan becomes President

1989
The Berlin Wall is brought down

1991
The Persian Gulf War ends

1995
NATO forces end fighting in Bosnia

2000
George W. Bush is elected President

2001
Terrorists attack sites in the United States

USE THE TIME LINE

Use the chapter summary time line to answer these questions.

1 In what year did the Vietnam War end?

2 When was George W. Bush elected president?

USE VOCABULARY

Identify the correct term that completes each sentence.

> **arms control** (p. 453)
>
> **cease-fire** (p. 452)
>
> **deficit** (p. 459)
>
> **candidate** (p. 465)
>
> **impeached** (p. 470)

3 A _____ temporarily stops a conflict but does not end a war.

4 In 1992 Bill Clinton was chosen to be the presidential _____ for the Democrats.

5 Nations that agree to _____ must limit the number of weapons that they have.

6 The government caused a _____ when it spent more money than it had.

7 The representatives wanted the President to be _____ after he was caught lying.

RECALL FACTS

Answer these questions.

8 Why did the United States support South Vietnam during the Vietnam War?

9 How did the Vietnam War divide people in America?

10 What meeting marked the beginning of the end of the Cold War?

11 What was Operation Desert Storm?

12 Who was the second American President to be impeached?

Write the letter of the best choice.

13 **TEST PREP** The first American President to resign was—
A George Bush.
B Bill Clinton.
C Richard Nixon.
D Jimmy Carter.

14 **TEST PREP** In 2001 President George W. Bush, supported by Congress, declared a war on—
F drugs.
G crime.
H terrorism.
J fraud.

THINK CRITICALLY

15 How do you think citizens of the Soviet Union felt about *perestroika* and *glasnost*?

16 Why do you think the 2000 presidential election was so close?

APPLY SKILLS

Read a Population Map
Use the information on pages 474 and 475 and the map on page 474 to help answer these questions.

17 What do population maps show?

18 When would you use a population map?

19 According to the map, which region of the United States has the lowest population density, the Northeast or the West?

VISIT

Civil Rights Institute

GET READY

The Birmingham Civil Rights Institute celebrates the many people who worked to gain full rights for African Americans. On a visit there, you seem to travel back in time. You will see, feel, and hear what it was like in this important time in American history. After you explore the life-size scenes and watch the video presentations in the institute's different galleries, you will feel as if you lived through the events of the Civil Rights movement.

LOCATE IT

Birmingham

ALABAMA

Life-size figures and a time line walk you through important events of the Civil Rights movement.

The lunch counter exhibit at the Birmingham Civil Rights Institute illustrates a time of segregation.

TAKE A FIELD TRIP

A VIRTUAL TOUR
Visit The Learning Site at **www.harcourtschool.com/tours** to take virtual tours of other historic sites in the United States.

CNN
Turner Le@rning®

A VIDEO TOUR
Check your media center or classroom library for a videotape tour of the Birmingham Civil Rights Institute.

6 Review and Test Preparation

VISUAL SUMMARY

Write a Poem Look at the Visual Summary below and choose one of the events to write a poem about. Use the captions, your imagination, and what you have learned in your reading to interpret what is taking place in the picture. In your poem, describe what is happening in the picture and how the picture makes you feel.

USE VOCABULARY

Identify the term that correctly matches each definition.

| integration (p. 421) |
| blockade (p. 429) |
| détente (p. 453) |
| recession (p. 463) |

1 a period of slow economic activity

2 the bringing together of people of all races

3 an easing of tensions

4 to isolate a place

RECALL FACTS

Answer these questions.

5 Which United States President created the Presidential Committee on Civil Rights?

6 How did Martin Luther King, Jr., protest segregation?

7 Who was the first United States astronaut to orbit Earth?

8 Why did President Nixon resign from the presidency?

9 Why did the Soviet Union break up in 1991?

10 **TEST PREP** Which President helped bring peace to the Middle East in 1978?
 A Jimmy Carter
 B Gerald Ford
 C Richard Nixon
 D Bill Clinton

11 **TEST PREP** Which group of people demanded independence from the Yugoslavian government in 1998?
 F the Serbs
 G the Croats
 H the people of Bosnia
 J the people of Kosovo

Visual Summary

1951   1961   1971

1951 The Korean War continues p. 415

1954 *Brown v. Board of Education of Topeka* case p. 421

1957 The Soviet Union launches *Sputnik* p. 422

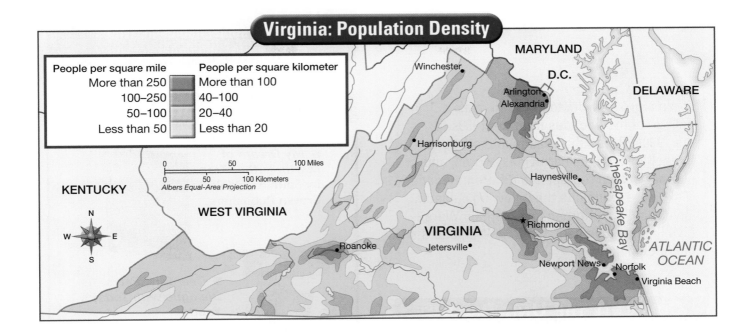

Virginia: Population Density

People per square mile
More than 250
100–250
50–100
Less than 50

People per square kilometer
More than 100
40–100
20–40
Less than 20

0   50   100 Miles
0   50   100 Kilometers
Albers Equal-Area Projection

N W E S

MARYLAND
Winchester
D.C.
Arlington
Alexandria
DELAWARE
Harrisonburg
Haynesville
Chesapeake Bay
KENTUCKY
WEST VIRGINIA
VIRGINIA
Roanoke
Jetersville
Richmond
ATLANTIC OCEAN
Newport News
Norfolk
Virginia Beach

THINK CRITICALLY

⓬ How were the Korean War years similar to the Vietnam War years? How were they different?

⓭ Why do you think it was important to President Kennedy to put an astronaut on the moon by the end of the 1960s?

⓮ How do you think the American people felt when they learned President Nixon was resigning?

APPLY SKILLS

Read a Population Map
Use the map on this page to answer the following questions.

MAP AND GLOBE SKILLS

⓯ Which city has a higher population density—Winchester or Virginia Beach?

⓰ Which city has a lower population density—Norfolk or Harrisonburg?

1981   1991   2001

1968 More than 500,000 United States troops in Vietnam p. 449

1969 United States astronauts land on the moon p. 432

1986 United States and Soviet leaders work to end the Cold War p. 460

481

Unit Activities

Make a Collage

In a group, work together to make a collage of the decades from the 1950s to the 1990s. Divide the collage into sections. In each section, use drawings, words, and photographs to represent a different decade. Make sure to include the following subjects in your collage: Korean and Vietnam Wars, Civil Rights movement, the Cold War, and the fall of Communism.

COMPLETE THE UNIT PROJECT

Make a Class Magazine   Work as a class to complete the unit project—make a class magazine. Review the list you took during your reading. Then, choose one key person, place, or event to write a magazine article about. You can also draw pictures and design advertisements to go along with your article.

GO ONLINE

Visit The Learning Site at
www.harcourtschool.com/
socialstudies/activities
for additional activities.

VISIT YOUR LIBRARY

- **My Dream of Martin Luther King** by Faith Ringgold. Crown Publishers.

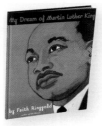

- **Dear Mrs. Parks: A Dialogue with Today's Youth** by Rosa Parks and Gregory J. Reed. Lee and Low Books.

- **President George W. Bush: Our Forty-third President** by Beatrice Gormley. Aladdin Paperbacks.

The United States and the World

Patriotic folk art

Statue of Liberty, Liberty
Island, New York

7

The United States and the World

66 **History and destiny have made America the leader of the world that would be free.** 99

—Colin Powell, Chairman of the United States Joint Chiefs of Staff, in a speech, September 28, 1993

Preview the Content

Read the title and the Main Idea for each lesson. Then write a short paragraph for each lesson, telling what you think it is about.

Preview the Vocabulary

Suffixes   A suffix is a word part that is added to the end of a root word. Use the root words and suffixes in the chart below to learn the meaning of each vocabulary word.

SUFFIX	ROOT WORD	VOCABULARY WORD	POSSIBLE MEANING
-ity	responsible	**responsibility**	
-ism	patriot	**patriotism**	

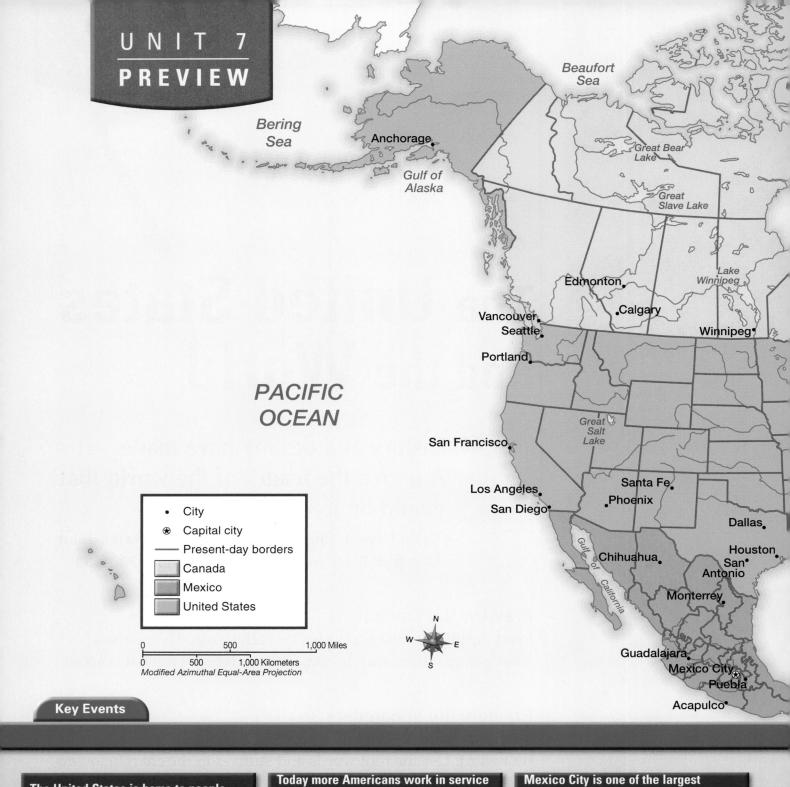

Beaufort
Sea

Bering
Sea

Anchorage

Gulf of
Alaska

Great Bear
Lake

Great
Slave Lake

Lake
Winnipeg

Edmonton

Calgary

Vancouver
Seattle

Winnipeg

Portland

PACIFIC
OCEAN

Great
Salt
Lake

San Francisco

Santa Fe

Los Angeles

Phoenix

San Diego

Dallas

Houston
San
Antonio

Chihuahua

Monterrey

Guadalajara

Mexico City

Puebla

Acapulco

- • City
- ⊛ Capital city
- — Present-day borders
- Canada
- Mexico
- United States

0		500		1,000 Miles

0	500	1,000 Kilometers

Modified Azimuthal Equal-Area Projection

N
W—E
S

Key Events

The United States is home to people from all over the world. p. 492

Today more Americans work in service jobs than in any other kinds of jobs. p. 505

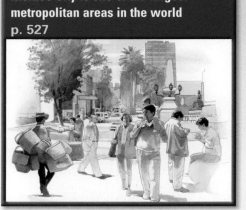

Mexico City is one of the largest metropolitan areas in the world p. 527

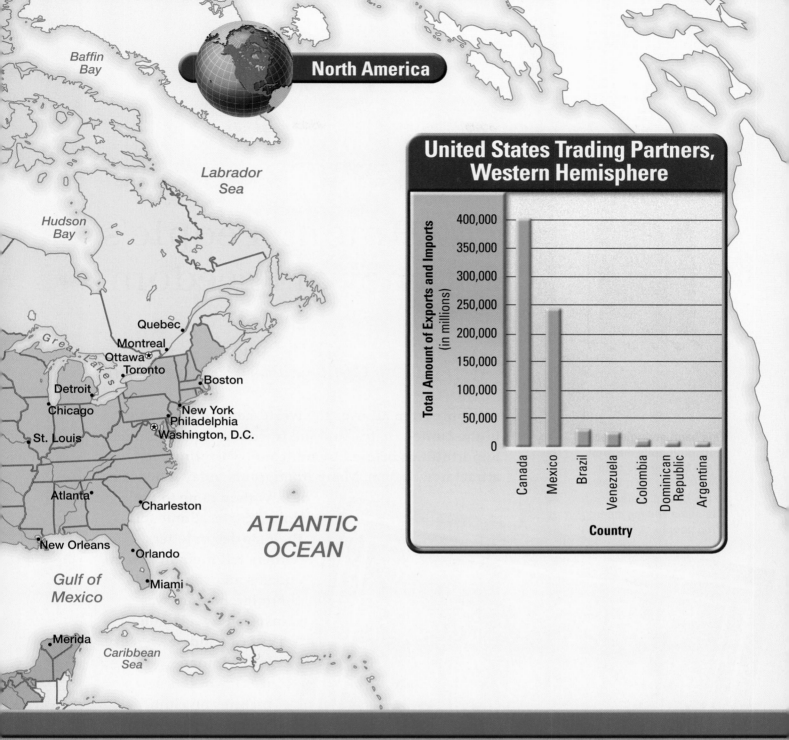

North America

Baffin Bay

Labrador Sea

Hudson Bay

Great Lakes

Quebec
Montreal
Ottawa ✪
Toronto
Boston
Detroit
Chicago
New York
Philadelphia
✪ Washington, D.C.
St. Louis
Atlanta
Charleston

ATLANTIC OCEAN

New Orleans
Orlando
Miami

Gulf of Mexico

Merida

Caribbean Sea

United States Trading Partners, Western Hemisphere

Total Amount of Exports and Imports (in millions)

400,000
350,000
300,000
250,000
200,000
150,000
100,000
50,000
0

Canada
Mexico
Brazil
Venezuela
Colombia
Dominican Republic
Argentina

Country

Jean-Bertrand Aristide becomes Haiti's president. p. 533

Simón Bolívar helps win independence for many present-day Latin American countries. p. 538

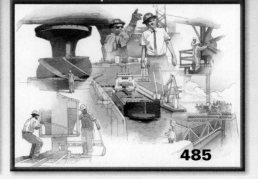

The St. Lawrence Seaway allows ships to travel from the Atlantic Ocean to the Great Lakes. p. 545

485

Dia's Story Cloth

The Hmong People's Journey of Freedom

by Dia Cha
stitched by Chue and Nhia Thao Cha

This hand-embroidered story cloth tells the story of the Hmong and their long journey from Laos to the United States. The name *Hmong* means "free people."

People from all over the world have come to live in the United States, and the freedoms and economic opportunities offered by our country continue to attract newcomers. Many immigrants today tell stories of how they came to the United States. Some tell their stories in letters. Others tell their stories in poems and songs. This immigrant story was inspired by a Hmong [MONG] hand-sewn story cloth. Hmong needleworkers sew pictures on cloth, using no patterns or measurements, to remember their past. The story cloth on these pages tells the story of how Dia Cha [DEE·ah CHAY] and her family left Asia, to come to the United States in 1979.

Only 15 years old when she arrived in the United States, Dia Cha found life in America very different from life in Laos.

When my people first arrived in America, most didn't speak or write English. Many families had sponsors, who picked us up at the airport.

Everything about life in America was different for the Hmong.

I was 15 years old when I came to this country. I'd never been to school, so I had to start everything from scratch. They wanted to put me in high school, but I didn't know anything. Then they wanted to put me in adult school, but the teachers said I was too young.

Shoulder baskets (left) are made in adult and child sizes for carrying crops and other items. The stool, gourd water jar, and bamboo table (right) are like those found in many Hmong households.

The Hmong are known for their beautiful needlework, which is called *pa'ndau* (pan•DOW), or "flower cloth." Each design follows a theme. Those shown above, from left to right, are called "lightning", "snail house," and "frog legs."

Finally, I started high school. Thirteen years later, I received my master's degree from Northern Arizona University. I went back to Laos as an anthropologist in 1992 to work with Hmong and Lao women in the refugee camps in Thailand.

This story cloth reminds me of the history of my family and of my people. Some of the memories it brings are good, and some are bad. But it is important for me to remember everything the Hmong have been through.

Dia Cha believes that each memory sewn into the story cloth is important. This part of the story cloth shows Cha's home in Laos.

The Hmong's heavily embroidered clothes set them apart from neighboring peoples in Asia. Hmong clothes sometimes combine green, pink, black, dark blue, and white, as seen in the child's jacket and sash above.

Hmong women in America continue to stitch new story cloths. We all have vivid memories about our lives and culture and history. The story cloth is a bridge to all the generations before us. When I show the story cloth to my niece and nephew, who were both born here in the United States, I point to different pictures and tell them that this is what it was like.

Analyze the Literature

① What is the purpose of a Hmong story cloth?

② Why do you think many people feel it is important to remember their past?

READ A BOOK

START THE UNIT PROJECT

A Cultural Fair   With your classmates, hold a cultural fair. As you read the unit, take notes about the different cultures discussed. Your notes will help you decide what to include in your cultural fair.

USE TECHNOLOGY

Visit The Learning Site at **www.harcourtschool.com/ socialstudies** for additional activities, primary sources, and other resources to use in this unit.

THE WHITE HOUSE

For over two hundred years, the White House has symbolized the executive branch. In 1800, President John Adams and his wife Abigail became the White House's first residents. Since then, the building has been home to 41 United States Presidents. On average, the White House receives hundreds of visitors a day.

LOCATE IT

MARYLAND

Washington, D.C.

VIRGINIA

White House

13

The United States Today

"I pray Heaven to bestow the best of blessings on this house and all that shall hereafter inhabit it."

—John Adams, letter to Abigail Adams, November 2, 1800

CHAPTER READING SKILL

Tell Fact from Opinion

A **fact** is a statement that can be proven to be true. An **opinion** is an individual's view of something that is shaped by that person's feelings.

As you read this chapter, separate facts from opinions about the modern United States.

MAIN TOPIC

| FACT | | OPINION |

MAIN IDEA
Read to learn how technology and diversity have affected the way people in the United States live and work.

WHY IT MATTERS
Advances in technology and increased cultural diversity often change people's ways of life.

VOCABULARY
Sun Belt
ethnic group
Internet
teleconference

FAST FACT Today about one of every ten people in the United States was born in another country.

The American People Today

People have been coming to the Americas since before history was recorded. Over time, the United States has become a nation of many cultures. The nation has changed in other ways, too.

A Growing Nation

More than 281 million people live in the United States today, and that number is rising fast. During the 1990s alone, the population of the United States grew by almost 33 million people—the largest ten-year increase in the country's history.

The population of the United States is growing for two reasons. More people are being born in the United States, and more people are moving to this country. People who are born in the United States or who have at least one parent who is a United States citizen are automatically citizens of our country.

Many immigrants have become naturalized citizens. To become a naturalized citizen, a person must have lived in the United States for at least five years (or three if married to a citizen). Then that person must apply for citizenship and pass a test to show that he or she understands United States history and government. Finally, the person must take part in a ceremony in which he or she promises to be loyal to the United States.

Many immigrants become citizens of the United States each year.

The Sun Belt of the United States

GEOGRAPHY THEME

Regions Many Americans are attracted to the warm and sunny weather of the Sun Belt.

❓ What cities in Texas are growing fast?

In the past, most immigrants came to the United States from Europe. Today, most immigrants come from countries in Asia and Latin America. Like immigrants in the past, they come seeking freedom and new opportunities for a better life. Many seek refuge from war, weak economies, and poor living conditions in their homelands.

Most new immigrants, like most other Americans, live in metropolitan areas. In fact, about four of every five people in the United States live in metropolitan areas. About one-third of all Americans live in metropolitan areas of more than 5 million people.

More than half of the American people live in the ten states with the greatest populations—California, Texas, New York, Florida, Illinois, Pennsylvania, Ohio, Michigan, New Jersey, and Georgia. However, the population of every state is growing.

Although the population of every region of the United States is growing, different regions are growing at different rates. Much of the nation's growth has taken place in the **Sun Belt**, a wide area of the southern United States that has a mild climate all year. The Sun Belt stretches from the Atlantic coast to the Pacific coast. Places in the Sun Belt region began growing during World War II. One reason for this growth was the development of air conditioning.

Air conditioning was introduced in the early twentieth century. It was first used in movie theaters and railroad cars.

Immigrants who share a culture sometimes choose to settle in the same neighborhood. One example of this is Chinatown in San Francisco, California.

In the 1920s, the first fully air-conditioned office building, the Milam Building in San Antonio, Texas, was constructed. As air conditioning spread across the Sun Belt in the 1950s, it helped make living there more comfortable. Millions of people moved to the region, built homes and started businesses, and forever changed the environment.

The Sun Belt stretches across parts of both the South and the West. In recent years, both of these regions have grown faster than other regions of the United States. The West is the fastest-growing region of the United States, but the South has the largest population of any region. Almost 100 million people live in states in the South.

REVIEW How did the use of air-conditioning change the Sun Belt?

A Diverse Nation

The population of the United States is growing quickly. At the same time, the United States is becoming a more diverse nation. In fact, the United States has one of the world's most diverse populations in terms of ancestry. Today about 210 million Americans are of European background. Almost 35 million are African Americans, and more than 10 million are of Asian background. About two and a half million people in the United States are Native Americans.

Hispanic Americans make up the fastest-growing ethnic group in the nation. An **ethnic group** is a group of people from the same country, of the same race, or with a shared culture. A little more than 1 in 10 Americans, or about 35 million people, are of Hispanic descent. More than three-fourths of them live in the South or West. California and Texas have the largest Hispanic populations, but the state with the highest percentage of Hispanic residents is New Mexico. In New Mexico more than 4 of every 10 people are of Hispanic background.

Many Americans of Greek heritage attend Greek Orthodox churches.

Most people in the United States are either immigrants or descendants of immigrants. Some people's families have been living in the United States for hundreds of years. Others have come to live in this country only recently. Instead of arriving on ships, as immigrants often did in the past, most immigrants today arrive by plane at one of the nation's international airports.

Some people who have immigrated to this country still speak the language of the country in which they were born. So do some of their descendants. In fact, about one-fifth of all schoolchildren in the United States today speak a language other than English at home. Most of them speak Spanish.

Some Americans continue to dress in the styles of their homelands or take part in customs, celebrations, or traditions that are unique to their culture. Cultural differences among Americans can also be seen in the kinds of music people listen to, the foods they eat, and the religious groups they belong to.

Having so many different cultures has made the United States a more diverse place. At the same time, it has given Americans a richer life. Over the years, people from each culture have contributed to American life. Cultural differences help explain why people in the United States often seem so different from one another in so many ways.

Although Americans are different from one another, they also have much in common. Americans share a deep belief in individual rights. Most Americans support the government, which is based on representation and the consent of the people. Americans also value our economic system, which supports free enterprise and the ideas of competition, open opportunity, and private property. These common beliefs help unite Americans.

REVIEW **In what ways can one see cultural differences among Americans?**

• HERITAGE •

Epiphany

For many Hispanic families in the United States, the Christmas season does not end on December 25. It continues with Epiphany, or Three Kings Day, which is celebrated on January 6. According to tradition, 12 days after the birth of Jesus, the Three Kings, or Wise Men, arrived to present the newborn child with gifts. The night before Epiphany, many Hispanic children leave snacks out for the Kings. The children hope to find candy and presents waiting for them the next day. Other Epiphany traditions include eating special ring-shaped cakes called roscones and attending Three Kings Day parades.

Changing Ways of Life

As the United States is becoming more diverse, it is changing in other ways, too. Advances in technology, such as computers, cellular telephones, and facsimile, or fax, machines, have affected how people in the United States live, work, communicate, and travel. These machines have made it possible for people to communicate and conduct business faster and more easily.

Computers first came into widespread use after World War II. At that time computers were so big that just one would fill an entire room. Then, in 1958, scientists working independently in Texas and California each invented the silicon chip. This tiny device can now store millions of bits of computer information. Silicon chips have allowed businesses to make smaller, faster, and cheaper computers.

Today millions of computers are used in businesses and in homes and schools throughout the world. Many people even run their own businesses from their homes with the use of the Internet. The **Internet** is a network that links computers around the world for the exchange of information.

The United States Department of Defense set up a computer network in the late 1960s for military communications. The network changed and grew over the years. In 1992, the World Wide Web came into use. It allows millions of people to send and receive electronic mail, or e-mail, as well as electronic documents, pictures, and sounds.

· **S**CIENCE AND **T**ECHNOLOGY ·

The Microchip

The integrated circuit, or microchip, was one of the twentieth century's greatest inventions. Introduced in 1959, the microchip helped reduce the size of all types of electronic machines. It did so by letting hundreds of electronic parts be put on a single silicon chip half the size of a paper clip. Starting in the early 1970s, microchips were used to run handheld calculators. Over the years, microchips grew more and more powerful. Today they are used in everything from personal computers to space satellites.

Today many computers like the one above are very compact. Early computers, however, were bulky machines (below). They often filled an entire room.

Using the Internet, people can shop for clothing, cars, or any other item online. They can check on bank accounts, transfer money, pay bills, make reservations, and do many other tasks. They can also reach government agencies, libraries, and other online sites to research almost any subject.

Another change in people's lives is the ability to travel much faster from one place to another. Each year more than 700 million people travel on jet airplanes. In just a few hours they can travel from city to city or halfway around the world to visit family members. People also travel to attend business meetings. However, people do not have to travel at all to communicate directly with others. They can hold a **teleconference**—a conference, or meeting, that uses electronic machines to connect people. Having a teleconference allows people from all over the world to

Satellites such as this one make it possible for people around the world to communicate with one another instantly.

communicate directly with one another by turning on a computer or dialing a telephone.

Advances in technology have changed people's lives in other ways, too. Doctors can use tiny video cameras attached to plastic tubes to see inside a person. Eye doctors now use laser beams to help correct eye problems. The way some automobile drivers find out how to get where they want to go has changed, too. Today, automobiles can be equipped with a Global Positioning System (GPS) receiver. These receivers use satellites to help find a driver's location anywhere on Earth. Drivers can also receive directions through the GPS.

REVIEW What is the Internet?

LESSON 1
REVIEW

1 **MAIN IDEA** How have technology and diversity affected the way Americans live and work?

2 **WHY IT MATTERS** What parts of people's lives have changed the most as a result of technology and diversity?

3 **VOCABULARY** Write a description of the **Sun Belt**.

4 **READING SKILL—Tell Fact from Opinion** The United States has one of the world's most diverse populations in terms of ancestry. Is this statement a fact or an opinion? How do you know?

5 **SCIENCE AND TECHNOLOGY** How have advances in technology helped people?

6 **CRITICAL THINKING—Analyze** Compare and contrast today's immigrant groups and immigrant groups from 100 years ago.

PERFORMANCE—Write a Report Use library or Internet sources to research information about different cultures in the United States. Then write a report about the similarities and differences among the cultures you researched.

Use a Cartogram

VOCABULARY

cartogram

▶ WHY IT MATTERS

One way to show the population of different places is to use a cartogram. A **cartogram** is a diagram that gives information about places by the size shown for each place. Knowing how to read a cartogram can help you quickly compare information about different places.

▶ WHAT YOU NEED TO KNOW

Some maps of the United States base the size of each state on its land area. With a cartogram, a state's size is based on a geographical statistic. On the cartogram on page 499, size is based on population.

A population cartogram shows the states as their sizes would be if each

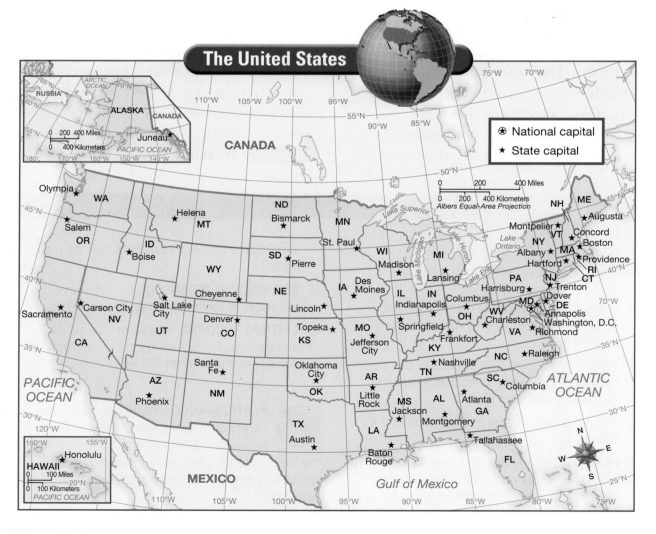

The United States

National capital
★ State capital

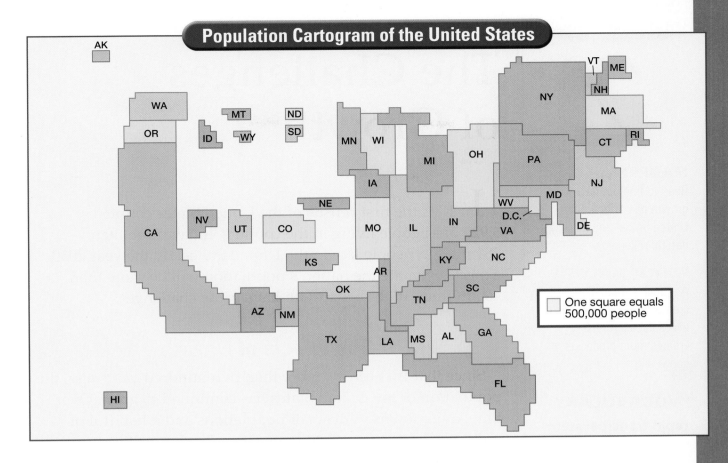

Population Cartogram of the United States

One square equals 500,000 people

---

person had the same amount of land. A state with many people would be much bigger than a state with few people. When states are shown this way, you can quickly compare populations around the country.

➡ PRACTICE THE SKILL

The map on page 498 is a political map of the United States. The size of each state is based on its land area. Compare the size of New Jersey with the size of South Dakota. South Dakota is larger in land area. The cartogram on this page is a population cartogram. The size of each state is based on population. Compare the sizes of New Jersey and South Dakota again. Although New Jersey has a smaller land area than South Dakota, it is shown larger than South Dakota on the cartogram because it has more people.

Continue to compare land area and population to answer these questions.

1 Which state has more land area, Pennsylvania or Montana?

2 Which of those states is shown larger on the cartogram? Why is it shown larger?

3 What does the cartogram tell about Alaska when you compare its size on the political map?

➡ APPLY WHAT YOU LEARNED

With a partner, brainstorm other ideas for cartograms. What other statistics could be shown in this way to help people compare and contrast states? Make a cartogram of the United States that is based on other statistics besides population statistics. Then prepare a list of questions that could be answered by looking at your cartogram.

MAIN IDEA
Read to find out how growth has affected the United States and its natural resources.

WHY IT MATTERS
A growing population creates more consumers of resources. It also creates more producers of goods and services.

VOCABULARY
rapid-transit system

The Challenges of Growth

In 1790 the first census of the United States counted 3,929,214 people living in the country. Today more than 281 million people live in the United States. By the year 2050, experts estimate the nation's population will be more than 400 million. With this growth have come challenges.

The Effects of Growth

Since that first census more than two hundred years ago, the population of the United States has continued to grow. Over time, quiet towns with small populations and a handful of buildings have grown into large cities. As those cities and the suburbs around them continue to grow, they often spread out over larger and larger areas. Land that was once used for farming is now used for houses, stores, office buildings, and highways.

Across the country many communities are choosing to manage urban growth by passing laws to control it. These laws not only limit where buildings may go, but what kinds of buildings may be built in an area. The laws set aside areas of land to be used only for homes, offices, or businesses, such as shopping centers. In some cases, the laws say the land cannot be used for buildings.

About eight out of every ten people live in or near large cities. Areas that were once undeveloped, such as this Florida neighborhood, are now home to large communities.

As the population grows and the spread of urban areas continues, the need for more services, such as fire protection, also increases.

Some people disagree with placing limits on how land can be used. They believe that it is unfair to restrict use of land that has valuable resources. Some believe that private ownership of land also can help to conserve it. This is because the land's owner usually wants to protect his or her land and use its resources wisely so it will remain valuable in the future.

Rapid population growth has presented many other challenges for the American people. As the nation's population has grown, so has the number of vehicles on its highways and city streets. In many places roads are often jammed with cars, trucks, and buses. This is especially true during rush hour, the time when people are going to work or going home. To help keep traffic moving, some cities now use computers to control traffic lights. Others use electronic highway signs to warn drivers of problems and to suggest other routes they can take.

To help reduce the number of vehicles on their streets, many cities have worked to improve their public transportation systems. These cities have added more bus lines and built rapid-transit systems. A **rapid-transit system** is a passenger transportation system that uses elevated or underground trains or both.

A growing population means growth in the amount of services that are needed. For example, more electricity is needed for people to run their homes and businesses. More people also means that increases are needed in other services.

Directing traffic helps keep city streets from jamming up.

Water, garbage collection, education, health care, and police and fire protection must meet the demands of a growing population.

Changes in population mean changes in government. An increase in population can affect a state's representation in Congress. When a state's population changes, the number of seats it has in the House of Representatives can change also.

Population growth also has its benefits. Having more people helps increase the number of new ideas that can lead to new inventions and new and better ways of doing things. Population growth can also help businesses grow by increasing the market for many goods and services. Having more people also encourages improvements in transportation and communication systems.

REVIEW **How have many cities reduced the number of vehicles on their streets?**

Challenges for the Environment

As the population continues to grow, so does a greater need for natural resources. As a nation it is our responsibility to use our natural resources wisely. Over the years some people's actions have damaged the country's natural resources. Water, land, and even wildlife have been affected.

However, through conservation efforts, some of the damage has been repaired. For example, at one time the American bald eagle was on the endangered species list. There were only about 417 pairs of the eagles left in the United States.

This slide is made of recycled materials. Many everyday products can be made from recycled materials.

To help save the endangered birds, laws were passed banning a chemical that was getting into the water supply. This chemical poisoned the fish eaten by the eagles. By 1998 there were more than 5,000 pairs of American bald eagles in the United States.

Another way to help preserve natural resources is to recycle. Countries with large populations, such as the United States, produce large amounts of trash. To solve this problem, many communities across the nation recycle.

Trash containing materials such as metal, glass, plastic, and paper is used to make new products. Many factories use recycled materials instead of new natural resources to make their products. Everyday items such as videocassettes, playground equipment, and clothing, can be made from recycled materials.

As in the past, Americans continue to rely on natural resources to meet their wants and needs. Today, however, most

National preserves, such as this one in Alabama, help to protect natural resources.

people understand the need to help protect the nation's natural resources for future Americans and to make sensible plans about how those natural resources are used.

REVIEW How do many communities try to solve their trash problems?

LESSON 2 REVIEW

1 MAIN IDEA How has the growth of the United States population affected the land and its natural resources?

2 WHY IT MATTERS How does a growing population create more producers of goods and services?

3 VOCABULARY What are the benefits of using a rapid-transit system ?

4 READING SKILL—Tell Fact from Opinion In the lesson, find examples of one statement that is fact and one that is opinion.

5 HISTORY What helped save the American bald eagle?

6 GEOGRAPHY Why do some people disagree with placing limits on how land can be used?

7 CRITICAL THINKING—Hypothesize By the year 2050 over 400 million people may be living in the United States. What new problems do you think Americans will have in that time? How might the increase in population benefit Americans?

PERFORMANCE—Interview a Person Interview a parent, a grandparent, or someone else older than you to find out what your city or town was like when he or she was your age. Have your questions ready before the interview. Write down the answers and present them to your class.

3

MAIN IDEA

Read to learn how the economy of the United States has changed in recent years.

WHY IT MATTERS

Our nation's diverse economy has changed the way many Americans earn a living.

VOCABULARY

diverse economy
high-tech
Information Age
e-commerce
interdependent
international trade
free-trade agreement
global economy

The American Economy

Just as the people of the United States have become more and more diverse over time, so has the nation's economy. A **diverse economy** is one that is based on many kinds of industries. Our nation's diverse economy has created many new kinds of jobs for American workers. It has also changed the kinds of jobs that most of them do to earn a living.

A Changing Economy

Many American workers continue to do the traditional jobs that they have always done. Some people farm the land, fish the waters, cut down trees, and mine the earth for mineral resources. Others construct highways and buildings. Many others—more than 18 million—work in factories, where together they produce more manufactured goods than any other nation in the world.

While all of those jobs remain important parts of the American economy today, more Americans now work in

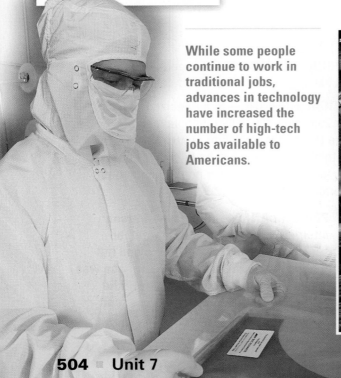

While some people continue to work in traditional jobs, advances in technology have increased the number of high-tech jobs available to Americans.

◈ About how many more Americans work in the service industry than in the trade and transportation industry?

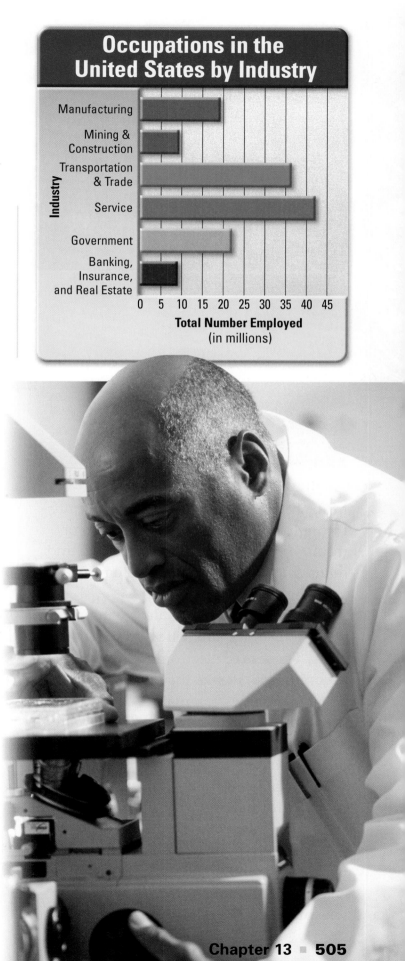

Occupations in the United States by Industry

Manufacturing

Mining & Construction

Transportation & Trade

Service

Government

Banking, Insurance, and Real Estate

Industry

0 5 10 15 20 25 30 35 40 45

Total Number Employed (in millions)

service jobs than in any other kinds of jobs. In fact, about one-third of all workers have service jobs, such as working in restaurants, repairing cars and appliances, or providing health care. If other groups of workers who provide services are included, such as government and transportation workers and people who work in stores, banks, and insurance companies, then about four of every five workers in the United States hold service jobs.

Many of the changes in the kinds of jobs that people do have come about because of advances in technology. In recent years, high-technology, or high-tech, industries have been of growing importance to the American economy. **High-tech** industries are those that invent, build, or use computers and other kinds of electronic equipment. These new devices have made it easier for businesspeople to communicate, travel, trade goods and services, and organize information.

The early 1970s marked the beginning of the **Information Age**. This period in history has been defined by the growing amount of information available to people. In fact, most of what is known about the human body has been learned in the past 40 years.

Today, organizing and storing information and getting the information to people when they need it is a major industry.

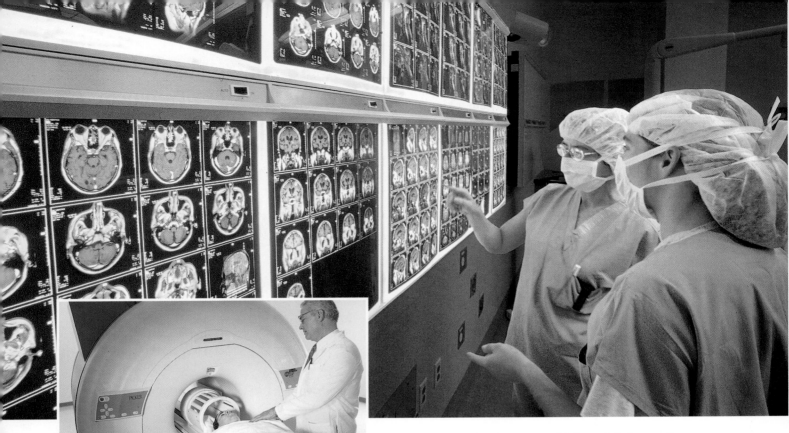

Health care has become a high-tech industry. Doctors can use advanced technology to scan a patient's brain to find out what may be wrong with the patient.

Much of this work is done electronically, through private computer networks or through public Web sites. Setting up and managing these computer systems is a growing field for workers.

New technologies are also changing the way people buy and sell goods and services. The rise of electronic commerce, or **e-commerce**, means that both large and small companies can market their products worldwide. E-commerce has greatly increased the number of goods and services available to American consumers. It has also enabled thousands of Americans to run full-time or part-time businesses from their homes. In 1999, American businesses and individual consumers spent a total of $659 billion on e-commerce purchases. More than 90 percent of this total was made up of business-to-business

sales, or businesses selling things to one another.

New technologies are also changing the part of the American economy that relates to medicine and science. High-tech advances in the field of medicine have already changed the way doctors treat disease. For example, the use of lasers in surgery has helped millions of people.

As technology and knowledge advance, the possibility of additional scientific discoveries increases. Scientific discoveries will likely change the American economy even more in time. Technology used in the area of space exploration has already given the United States many new pictures of different parts of space.

REVIEW How have new technologies changed people's lives?

A Global Economy

Each day, people in different states and in different regions of the United States exchange natural resources, finished products, and services. That is because no one state or region has all the natural resources that people and businesses there may need or want. And no one state or region can produce all the goods and services that people may need or want.

North Carolina, for example, grows too little cotton to supply all of its textile mills, so mill owners there buy cotton grown in other states, such as California and Texas. In turn, farmers in those states may buy products such as cotton blankets, towels, and clothing made by workers in mills and factories in North Carolina. In this way people in different states and regions are **interdependent**—they depend on one another for natural resources, finished products, and services.

The United States and other countries are also interdependent. Modern transportation and communication systems have made it easier for people in one country to trade with people in other countries. Goods from the United States are exported to places all over the world. At the same time, the United States imports many goods from other countries. This **international trade**, or trade among nations, allows people in the United States and in other countries to buy goods that their own countries do not make or grow. The United States' most important international trading partners are Canada, China, Britain, Germany, Japan, and Mexico.

This man is working on an American brand of automobile in a factory in Beijing, China. Below, cars in Japan await shipment overseas.

To increase international trade, many countries, including the United States, have signed free-trade agreements. A **free-trade agreement** is a treaty in which countries agree not to charge tariffs, or taxes, on goods they buy from and sell to each other. Such an agreement gives industries in each of the trading nations the chance to compete better. In 1994, Mexico, Canada, and the United States put the North American Free Trade Agreement, or NAFTA, into effect. One of NAFTA's goals has been to assist the movement of goods and services across national borders. As a result, the number of goods and services available to people in all three nations has increased.

International trade adds much to the economy of the United States. The United States also interacts with other countries in other ways. Many companies in the United States have offices and factories in other countries. Many companies from other countries also have businesses in the United States. Almost 5 million people in the United States work in businesses owned by people in other countries. This means that the nations of the world are now part of a **global economy**, the world market in which companies from different countries buy and sell goods and services.

REVIEW What is a free-trade agreement?

A Free Enterprise Economy

In a free enterprise economy, such as that of the United States, producers offer goods or services that consumers want to buy. Companies produce a greater supply when demand rises. Price affects demand, and demand affects price. For example, if a computer game cost $1,000, very few people would be willing to buy it. Demand for the product will be low, and the company will produce only a small number of games. If the price of the game is $10, many more people will be interested in buying it. Demand for the product will be high, and the company will produce many of the games.

In a free enterprise economy, people own and run their own businesses. In other kinds of economies, the government owns businesses. It tells factory

Many people in the United States, such as this Virginia couple, run their businesses from their homes.

Under the free enterprise system, Americans can open a wide variety of businesses, such as this store in Waitsfield, Vermont.

managers what goods to produce, how to produce them, and how much to charge for them. In the United States, these decisions are made by business owners.

The freedom that American businesses have has led to the creation of many new products. For example, some of today's largest computer companies were started in people's homes. The people who began these businesses were free to design their products any way they wished. As a result, consumers have been able to choose from a wide variety of products.

Another benefit of a free enterprise economy is that anyone, even a young person, can start a business. Some of the many businesses young people have started include everything from dog-walking services to Web site design companies.

REVIEW In what kind of economy are people allowed to own and run their own businesses?

LESSON 3 REVIEW

1 MAIN IDEA How has the economy of the United States changed in recent years?

2 WHY IT MATTERS What kinds of new jobs has our nation's diverse economy created for American workers?

3 VOCABULARY Explain how **e-commerce** is a part of the nation's **diverse economy**.

4 READING SKILL—Tell Fact from Opinion Price affects demand, and demand affects price. Is this statement a fact or an opinion? Explain.

5 HISTORY When did the Information Age begin?

6 ECONOMICS In what ways is the United States part of a global economy?

7 CRITICAL THINKING—Analyze How has e-commerce changed the American economy?

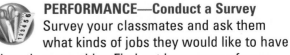 **PERFORMANCE—Conduct a Survey** Survey your classmates and ask them what kinds of jobs they would like to have when they are older. Find out how many of your classmates want to have traditional jobs and compare that to how many of your classmates want to have either high-tech or service jobs.

Government and the People

MAIN IDEA
Read to learn about the role of government and the main rights and responsibilities of American citizens.

WHY IT MATTERS
For the United States to remain strong, government and citizens must each meet their responsibilities.

VOCABULARY

responsibility
register
informed citizen
jury
volunteer
patriotism

The Constitution of the United States of America, which became law in 1788, set up the government for the nation. More than 200 years later, government leaders still look to the Constitution to help guide their actions. The American people also look to the Constitution to protect their rights and freedoms.

The Federal System

The federal system created by the Constitution divides political power between the national, or federal, government and the state governments. The federal government is the country's largest government system.

From the United States capital in Washington, D.C., the federal government conducts thousands of activities that affect the lives of Americans. It runs programs to help people who are poor, aged, or disabled. It tests foods and drugs for safety, conducts research on diseases, and sets

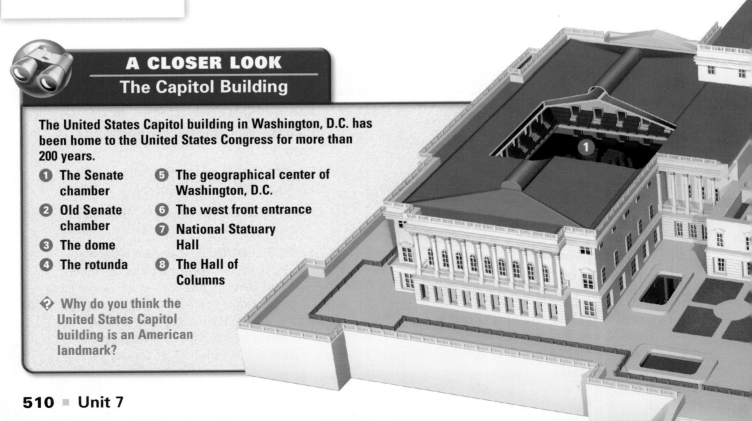

A CLOSER LOOK
The Capitol Building

The United States Capitol building in Washington, D.C. has been home to the United States Congress for more than 200 years.

❶ The Senate chamber
❷ Old Senate chamber
❸ The dome
❹ The rotunda
❺ The geographical center of Washington, D.C.
❻ The west front entrance
❼ National Statuary Hall
❽ The Hall of Columns

❖ Why do you think the United States Capitol building is an American landmark?

standards to control pollution. It deals with the governments of other nations, and it sets trade rules with them. The federal government is also in charge of space exploration, air travel safety, and national parks, forests, historic sites, and museums.

Many famous landmarks across the country are associated with the federal government. These include the Statue of Liberty in New York Bay, the White House in Washington, D.C., and Mount Rushmore in South Dakota. They are not just places to visit. They are patriotic symbols that remind Americans of the things that unite them as a people.

Many Americans of different backgrounds are also united by the political party to which they belong. The two main political parties are the Republican and Democratic parties. In Congress, the party with the most members in each house is known as the majority party. The party with fewer members is called the minority party.

The most powerful officer of the House of Representatives is the Speaker of the House. No member of the House may speak until called upon by the Speaker. The Speaker is always a member of the majority party and has usually served in Congress for many years.

The most powerful officers of the Senate are the majority leader and the minority leader. These people help direct the actions of their party in the Senate.

Uncle Sam

American history is filled with heroes, but only a few of them have been preserved as cartoons. During the War of 1812, Samuel Wilson, owner of a New York meat-packing business, helped supply the United States Army with beef. Wilson's supply wagons were marked with the initials *U.S.* It was reported that U.S. stood for "Uncle Sam" Wilson. In fact, the letters stood for *United States*. The name caught on and in 1868 the great political cartoonist Thomas Nast created the first Uncle Sam cartoon. In 1961 Congress passed a resolution honoring Samuel Wilson as the person who inspired America's national symbol.

federal treaties. Through the years, the role of the federal government has increased in traditional state government activities, such as regulating businesses and providing for public schools.

On every level of government federal, state, and local leaders attempt to fulfill their roles as government officials. Some of these leaders, such as state representatives to Congress, are elected by the voters. Others, such as federal judges, are appointed, or named, by a specific governing body. For example, in 2000 Hillary Rodham Clinton was elected to the United States Senate by the voters of New York. Supreme Court Justice Sandra Day O'Connor, on the other hand, was nominated to her position by the President of the United States.

REVIEW What are some powers that the federal and state governments share?

Civic Affairs

The Constitution says that citizens who meet the age requirements have the right to vote and the right to hold public office. All residents in the United States—citizens and noncitizens alike—have freedom of speech, freedom of the press, freedom of religion, and freedom to gather in groups. Laws passed by the United States Congress and by state governments can give people other rights, too.

With these rights come responsibilities. A **responsibility** is a duty—something that a person is expected to do. With the right to vote, for example, comes the responsibility of voting. Most state

Since most state congresses are modeled after the federal Congress, these offices also exist at the state level.

The federal and state governments both have some of the same powers. These include the rights to tax and to spend and borrow money.

Each state has its own constitution, its own laws, and its own legislative, executive, and judicial branches. However, state laws and activities must not conflict with the United States Constitution or governments say that a citizen who wants to take part in an election must **register** to vote, or show that he or she lives where the voting takes place. This is an important responsibility because every vote matters in an election. This was very clear in the 2000 Presidential election when only a few hundred votes made the difference in George W. Bush's win over Al Gore.

With freedom of speech and freedom of the press comes the responsibility of being an informed and active citizen. An **informed citizen** is one who knows what is happening in the community, the state, the nation, and the world. An informed citizen is more likely to understand why things happen and to see other people's points of view.

Citizens who feel strongly about an issue can always contact their representatives by writing letters or making phone calls. Today e-mail makes staying in touch with government leaders simpler than ever.

The responsibilities of citizens are not written in the Constitution, but they follow naturally from what is written there. For example, the Constitution says that every person charged with a crime will be judged by a jury. A **jury** is a group of citizens who decide a case in court. Citizens must be willing to be members of a jury if called upon to serve. The Constitution gives Congress the authority to raise money to run the nation. Citizens must be willing to pay taxes if the nation is to run smoothly.

Besides voting, obeying the laws, defending the nation, serving on a jury, and paying taxes, some citizens take a more active part in the government. One way citizens take action is by taking part in political campaigns.

Volunteers (right) help to register voters before the 2000 Presidential election. Other volunteers (below) work in the campaign office of California Representative Loretta Sanchez.

Some citizens go from door to door, handing out information on their candidates or on issues. Other citizens telephone voters to remind them to go to the polls on election day. Most campaign workers are **volunteers**, or people who work without pay.

The most common way citizens take part in politics is by joining a political party. Most registered voters are members of either the Republican or Democratic party. However, a growing number of voters are choosing to register as independents. These voters are not connected to any organized party.

Members of organized parties can be chosen to serve as delegates to their party's national convention. These conventions, which take place every four years, are where presidential candidates are selected. Every state sends a certain number of delegates to each convention. The greater the state's population, the more delegates it can send. These delegates then vote on who their party will nominate as its Presidential candidate.

Citizens can also be candidates themselves. One person who decided to take an active part in government is Patty Murray. As a parent volunteer, she lobbied for more money for education. In 1992 she ran for office and won, becoming the first woman to represent the state of Washington in the United States Senate.

REVIEW How can people today contact government leaders?

Working Together

The writers of the United States Constitution were not sure their government would last. No other nation had ever had a government quite like the one described by the Constitution. No other people had ever had all of the rights that

Elected officials and local citizens hold a city council meeting in Gloucester, Massachusetts.

American citizens enjoyed. But would the people be able to keep their government going and protect their freedoms over time? The country would need good citizens—citizens who would work for the common good.

Past republics, like that of ancient Rome, broke up partly because the people grew greedy and selfish. To keep the nation strong, Americans would have to keep the spirit that had given the nation its independence and its Constitution. They would need to show **patriotism**, or love of country. Patriotism is more than simply waving the American flag at special times. The writers of the Constitution knew that Americans would have to be good citizens all the time.

 **What are good citizens?**

LESSON 4 REVIEW

1. **MAIN IDEA** What are the roles of government and citizens in the United States?

2. **WHY IT MATTERS** Why must government and citizens both meet their responsibilities?

3. **VOCABULARY** Use the word **register** in a sentence about voting.

4. **READING SKILL—Tell Fact from Opinion** The most powerful officer of the House of Representatives is the Speaker of the House. Is this statement a fact or an opinion? Explain.

5. **CIVICS AND GOVERNMENT** What are some of the responsibilities that come with the rights of United States residents?

6. **CRITICAL THINKING—Analyze** What is the meaning of the Pledge of Allegiance?

 PERFORMANCE—Write a Letter The role of government leaders is to work for the good of the people they represent. Write a letter to one of your local, state, or national leaders telling this person how he or she could improve life in your community.

·SKILLS· Identify Political Symbols

➡ WHY IT MATTERS

People often recognize sports teams, clubs, and other organizations by their symbols. The same is true for political parties, the President, Congress, the Supreme Court, and even voters. Being able to identify political symbols and what they stand for can help you better understand news reports, political cartoons, and other sources of information.

➡ WHAT YOU NEED TO KNOW

Two of the country's most famous political symbols are animals. The donkey represents the Democratic party. The elephant represents the Republican party. The donkey was probably first used to represent President Andrew Jackson, a Democrat, in the 1830s. Later the donkey became a symbol for the entire party. Cartoonist Thomas Nast introduced the elephant as a symbol of the Republican party in 1874. Both of these symbols are still used today.

One of the symbols for the national government is Uncle Sam. The bald eagle and the Statue of Liberty are other symbols for our government. Buildings are often used as political symbols. The White House is a symbol for the President, and the United States Capitol is a symbol for Congress.

PRACTICE THE SKILL

When you see a political symbol, answer the following questions to help you understand its meaning.

1 Do you recognize the symbol? Does it stand for the whole national government or only part of the national government? Does it stand for a person or group that is involved in government, such as a political party or organization?

2 Where did you see the symbol? If it appeared in a magazine, did the writer give you any clues about its meaning?

3 Does it include any captions or other words that help explain what the symbol means? A symbol labeled "To Protect and Serve," for example, might tell you that it stands for the police.

4 Why do you think the symbol is a good representation of the person or group it stands for?

5 When do you think you are most likely to see the symbol?

APPLY WHAT YOU LEARNED

Look through current news-magazines, in the editorial pages of newspapers, or on the Internet. Cut or print out an example of a political symbol and paste it on a sheet of paper. Below the symbol, write a brief description of what it stands for.

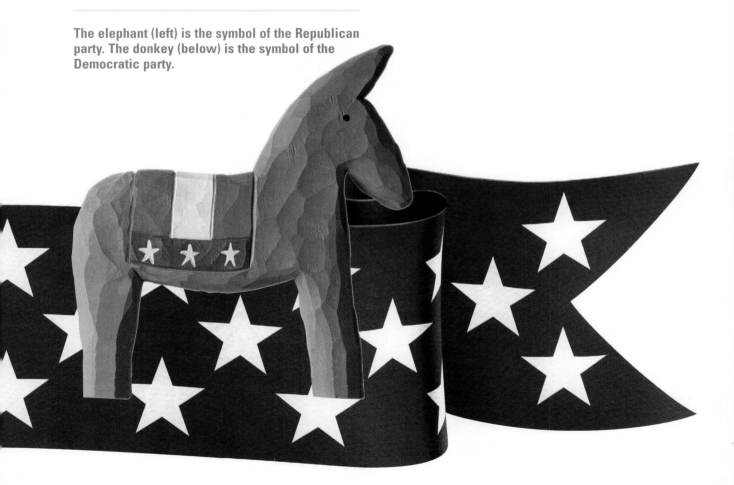

The elephant (left) is the symbol of the Republican party. The donkey (below) is the symbol of the Democratic party.

Political Buttons

Political candidates often think of clever ways to make themselves known to voters. They distribute buttons and other materials to rally enthusiasm and support of voters. Political buttons can list or show ideas that are important to a candidate's campaign. Many people wear political buttons to show their support for a candidate. Some people choose to wear political buttons to show they support an elected leader.

This title identifies the button's purpose.

The photographs on this button show who was elected.

The eagle is a patriotic symbol of the United States.

The elephant is a political symbol of the Republican party.

Red, white, and blue are the colors of the American Flag.

INAUGURATION DAY
JAN. 20th 1981
PRESIDENT · VICE-PRESIDENT
RONALD REAGAN · GEORGE BUSH

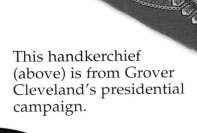

Analyze the Primary Source

1. How do you think a voter wearing a political button can help a candidate become better known? Why would a candidate or elected official want to picture their face on a political button?

2. Can you think of other campaign items a candidate might use?

3. List the patriotic symbols you see on the political buttons and campaign items.

This handkerchief (above) is from Grover Cleveland's presidential campaign.

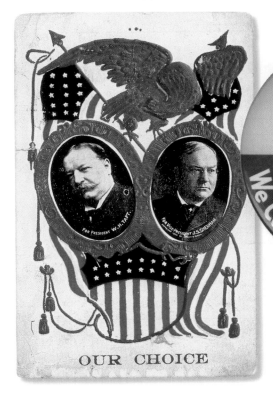

Political buttons show a variety of information. The postcard (left) is from William Taft's presidential campaign.

ACTIVITY

Write to Explain Imagine you are running for an elected office. Design a political button for your supporters to wear. Write a paragraph that explains the information on your button.

RESEARCH

Visit The Learning Site at **www.harcourtschool.com/primarysources** to research other primary sources.

13 Review and Test Preparation

USE YOUR READING SKILLS

Complete this graphic organizer by identifying facts and opinions about the United States. A copy of this graphic organizer appears on page 132 of the Activity Book.

Facts and Opinions About the United States

THE POPULATION OF THE UNITED STATES

FACT:

More than 281 million people live in the United States

➡️

OPINION:

_____

_____

FACT:

_____

➡️

OPINION:

_____

THE UNITED STATES GOVERNMENT AND THE PEOPLE

FACT:

_____

➡️

OPINION:

_____

FACT:

_____

➡️

OPINION:

_____

THINK & WRITE

Write a List of Questions   Imagine that the President of the United States has scheduled a trip to visit your school and to spend time with your class. Write a list of questions you would like to ask the President.

Write a Poem   Many patriotic poems have been written about the United States over the course of its history. Think of the things that make the United States a great nation, and then write a poem that honors the country.

USE VOCABULARY

For each pair of terms, write a sentence that explains how the terms are related.

1 **Internet** (p. 496), **teleconference** (p. 497)

2 **interdependent** (p. 507), **global economy** (p. 508)

3 **register** (p. 513), **informed citizen** (p. 513)

RECALL FACTS

Answer these questions.

4 In what ways can people contact their representatives?

5 Why was the Pledge of Allegiance written?

Write the letter of the best choice.

6 **TEST PREP**   Today most new immigrants to the United States come from countries in—
  A Europe and South America.
  B Asia and Europe.
  C Asia and Latin America.
  D Africa and South America.

7 **TEST PREP**   Under a free enterprise system—
  F people can own and run their own businesses.
  G the government owns most businesses.
  H most people work in agriculture.
  J the government tells businesses what to charge for goods and services.

8 **TEST PREP**   The two main political parties in the United States today are the—
  A Republican and Federalist parties.
  B Federalist and Democratic parties.
  C Republican and Democratic parties.
  D Democratic and Whig parties.

9 **TEST PREP**   The most common way American citizens take part in politics is by—
  F running for office.
  G volunteering as campaign workers.
  H joining a political party.
  J serving on a jury.

THINK CRITICALLY

10 How does immigration continue to shape the United States today?

11 What do you think might happen if cities did not try to manage urban growth?

12 How have American jobs changed over the last 100 years?

13 Why do you think the United States has remained a strong nation for so long?

APPLY SKILLS

Use a Cartogram
Review the map and the cartogram in the skill on pages 498–499. Then answer the following questions.

14 Why is New Jersey shown larger than Maine on the cartogram?

15 Which West Coast state has the smallest population?

Identify Political Symbols

16 Write down the names of the last five United States Presidents. Then use the Almanac in the back of your textbook to find out their political parties. Decide which party symbol would be used to represent each President.

ORGANIZATION OF AMERICAN STATES FLAG GARDEN

The Organization of American States, or OAS, was formed in 1890. It is the world's oldest regional organization. Today, the OAS is made up of 35 Western Hemisphere nations. It has four official languages—English, Spanish, French, and Portuguese.

LOCATE IT

MARYLAND

Washington, D.C.

VIRGINIA

Organization of American States Flag Garden

14

Partners in the Hemisphere

❝ Our future cannot be separated from the future of our neighbors. ❞
—George W. Bush, State Department speech, February 15, 2001

CHAPTER READING SKILL

Compare and Contrast

To **compare** two things is to find out how they are alike. To **contrast** them is to find out how they are different.

As you read this chapter, compare and contrast the issues and events involving the United States and its neighbors.

KEY ISSUES OR EVENTS

SIMILARITIES   DIFFERENCES

MAIN IDEA
Read to find out about the land, people, history, and economy of Mexico.

WHY IT MATTERS
As our nearest neighbor to the south, Mexico has played an important role in the history and economy of the United States.

VOCABULARY
middle class
interest rate

Mexico

1800	1900	PRESENT

In 1521 the Spanish conquistador Hernando Cortés conquered the Aztec Empire and claimed Mexico for Spain. For the next 300 years, Mexico remained under Spanish rule. Then, in 1821, a revolution ended Spain's rule, and Mexico became an independent country.

Independence, however, did not immediately bring peace. For many years afterward, the people of Mexico struggled to build an orderly society. The Mexican Constitution of 1917 reorganized the country's government and led to closer ties with the United States. Today, the two countries are major trading partners.

The Land and People of Mexico

Mexico is a land with many mountains. Two mountain ranges, the Sierra Madre Occidental on the west and the Sierra Madre Oriental on the east, stretch along Mexico's coast. Between these mountains lies the Mexican Plateau, a region of rich farmland

FAST FACT — Two states in Mexico share part of their names with a state in the United States—California.

Mexico

	State	Capital City
1.	AGUASCALIENTES	Aguascalientes
2.	QUERÉTARO	Querétaro
3.	TLAXCALA	Tlaxcala
4.	MÉXICO	Toluca
5.	DISTRITO FEDERAL	Mexico City
6.	MORELOS	Cuernavaca

⊛ National capital
★ State capital
— National border
— State border

Place Mexico is divided into 31 states.

❖ Which Mexican states border the United States?

and major cities. North of the Mexican Plateau, the land is mostly desert. To the south on the Yucatán Peninsula, there are both rain forests and grassy plains.

Most people in Mexico today trace their cultural heritage to two main groups—Native American and Spanish. In fact, more than 60 percent of the people are mestizos, people of mixed Indian and Spanish ancestry. Mexicans continue to honor the contributions of both groups with public history displays and celebrations.

REVIEW What two groups have mainly influenced Mexico's culture and people?

These hikers (left) are in the rugged desert of Mexico's Baja Peninsula.

Mexico, a Republic

Most of the wealth and power in colonial Mexico belonged to people of pure Spanish ancestry. Other Mexicans had few opportunities. In September 1810, Father Miguel Hidalgo (mee•GAYL ee•DAHL•goh) gave a speech in his church calling for a revolution against Spain. Hidalgo's rebel army was later defeated, but his actions were not forgotten. The revolution continued, and in 1821 Mexico gained its independence.

In time, Mexico became a republic. The Mexican people, however, had little experience with self-government. Presidents were no sooner elected than they were forced out of office by their enemies. During those same years, Mexico lost most of its northern lands to the United States. Texas, which won its independence from Mexico in 1836, became part of the United States in 1845.

Fiestas Patrias

Each year the Mexican people celebrate two national holidays known as the *Fiestas Patrias*, or festivals of the country. The first of these holidays, *Cinco de Mayo*, or May 5, honors Mexico's victory over the French at Puebla on May 5, 1862. The second holiday, *Diez y Seis de Septiembre*, or September 16, is Mexico's national independence day. Both celebrations often feature speeches, patriotic songs, dances, and parades.

Three years later, following a war with the United States, Mexico agreed to give up most of its remaining northern lands to the United States. These lands included present-day California, Utah, and Nevada and parts of New Mexico, Arizona, Colorado, and Wyoming. In return, the United States paid Mexico $15 million. Mexico later sold the southern parts of present-day Arizona and New Mexico to the United States.

In 1861 Benito Juárez (HWAHR•ays), a Zapotec Indian, became president. As president, Juárez helped bring about many reforms, including the private ownership of land.

From the start, Juárez had enemies who wanted him out of office. Those enemies looked to France for help. On May 5, 1862, French soldiers invaded Mexico and attacked the city of Puebla. Though greatly outnumbered, the Mexicans at Puebla defeated the French.

Despite their loss at Puebla, the French eventually took control of Mexico and removed Juárez from office. Within a few years, however, the Mexican people rebelled. Juárez became president again.

After Juárez died, the dictator Porfirio Díaz (pour•FEER•yoh DEE•ahs) ruled for more than 30 years. Díaz ordered railroads built and factories enlarged. Díaz brought economic growth to Mexico, but problems remained. Many poor farmers lost their land. When Díaz took control, 20 percent of the people owned land. Thirty years later, only 2 percent of the people owned land.

In 1910 many Mexican farmers and other groups fought against the dictatorship. Díaz resigned, but the fighting continued in Mexico. When the fighting ended, the leaders of the revolution took control of Mexico. They wrote a new constitution that limited the time a president could serve to a six-year term.

Benito Juárez

Mexico City, like all large cities, has crowded streets. Air pollution from automobile exhaust is often a problem in the city.

LOCATE IT

Mexico City

MEXICO

Many government-owned farms were divided among farm families.

While more people owned land, they still had few political choices. For more than 70 years, a single party controlled the presidency. Candidates from other political parties were elected to the Mexican Congress, but only those from the Partido Revolucionario Institucional (PRI) became president.

The election of July 2000 changed everything. Mexicans chose Vicente Fox, from the Partido Acción Nacional (PAN), as their new president. When asked how difficult his job as president would be, Fox replied, "The challenge is gigantic, but so are our resources. In Mexico we have a saying, 'Every newborn child comes with a gift.' Democracy will bring us lots of benefits and hope."

REVIEW How does the Mexican constitution limit a president's power?

A Growing Middle Class

Mexico is divided into 31 states and one federal district. The federal district contains Mexico City, Mexico's capital. About 9 million people live in Mexico City. About 9 million more people live in its metropolitan area, making Mexico City one of the world's most populated metropolitan areas.

Mexico City is just one of the large cities that lie on the Mexican Plateau. In fact, more than half of Mexico's population lives in this region. Other large cities on the Mexican Plateau include Monterrey, Guadalajara, and Puebla. Each of these cities has more than a million people.

Many cities in Mexico have grown as people have moved from rural areas to cities to find new jobs and better wages. In recent years, many new factories have been built in northern Mexico.

George W. Bush's first international trip as President of the United States was to visit with Mexican president Vicente Fox. The trip emphasized the strong ties between the two nations.

As a result, Ciudad Juárez, Matamoros, Tijuana, and other cities near the United States border have all grown quickly.

The growth of manufacturing and other industries in Mexico also led to the growth of a large **middle class**, an economic level between the poor and the wealthy. Today, Mexico's middle class is one of the largest in the Americas.

In 1994, however, even middle-class families found buying most products difficult. The value of the peso, Mexico's basic unit of money, suddenly dropped because of inflation and the government's need to pay its debts. That caused prices in Mexico to rise sharply. Some doubled. Others tripled. **Interest rates**, the amounts that banks charge to loan money, rose as high as 80 percent. To help stabilize the Mexican economy, the United States arranged $52 billion in loans to Mexico. Had the Mexican economy collapsed, it would have had a terrible effect on the world economy.

Another major economic change occurred in 1994 when Canada, Mexico, and the United States put the North American Free Trade Agreement into effect. The year before NAFTA began, trade between the United States and Mexico totaled $80 billion a year. By 2000 that figure was $230 billion.

REVIEW Why did Mexico's middle class grow larger?

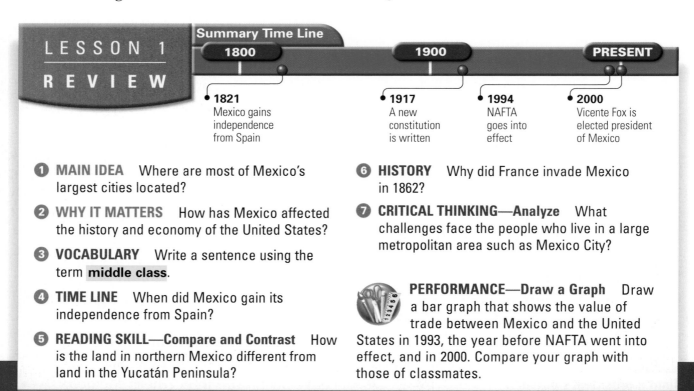

LESSON 1 REVIEW

Summary Time Line

1800	1900	PRESENT

1821 Mexico gains independence from Spain

1917 A new constitution is written

1994 NAFTA goes into effect

2000 Vicente Fox is elected president of Mexico

1. **MAIN IDEA** Where are most of Mexico's largest cities located?

2. **WHY IT MATTERS** How has Mexico affected the history and economy of the United States?

3. **VOCABULARY** Write a sentence using the term **middle class**.

4. **TIME LINE** When did Mexico gain its independence from Spain?

5. **READING SKILL—Compare and Contrast** How is the land in northern Mexico different from land in the Yucatán Peninsula?

6. **HISTORY** Why did France invade Mexico in 1862?

7. **CRITICAL THINKING—Analyze** What challenges face the people who live in a large metropolitan area such as Mexico City?

PERFORMANCE—Draw a Graph Draw a bar graph that shows the value of trade between Mexico and the United States in 1993, the year before NAFTA went into effect, and in 2000. Compare your graph with those of classmates.

Central America and the Caribbean

| 1880 | 1940 | PRESENT |

Like the United States, many nations in Central America and the Caribbean have a history of democracy. Costa Rica has a long democratic tradition. So does Puerto Rico, with its ties to the United States. In some places in the region, however, people continue to struggle for democracy and economic security.

The Land and People

The geography of the nations of Central America and the Caribbean is as varied as the backgrounds of the people who live there. Towering mountains, sandy beaches, dense forests, and remote islands are just some of the features that mark these two regions.

MAIN IDEA
Read to find out about the various regions, common heritages, and similar challenges facing Central American and Caribbean countries.

WHY IT MATTERS
Events in Central America and the Caribbean often affect not only the countries in those regions but also the United States.

VOCABULARY
commonwealth
embargo
free election

On the outskirts of Guatemala City, a large volcano looms.

LOCATE IT

MEXICO

GUATEMALA

Guatemala City

Central America and the Caribbean

Location Seven countries make up the region known as Central America, while hundreds of islands are found in the Caribbean.

◆ Which Caribbean country lies farthest north?

Traveling south from Mexico, a visitor would pass through Belize (buh•LEEZ), Guatemala (gwah•tuh•MAH•luh), Honduras, El Salvador, Nicaragua (nih•kuh•RAH•gwah), Costa Rica, and Panama. These seven countries form the 202,000 square miles (523,180 sq km) called Central America. Almost all the Central American countries have mountains. Volcanoes, some still active, formed the mountains. Ash from the volcanoes made the surrounding land fertile.

The Pacific Ocean forms the western borders of all the Central American countries except Belize. The Caribbean Sea, which is part of the Atlantic Ocean, forms the eastern borders of all the Central American countries except El Salvador.

Rain forests brighten the landscapes of Guatemala and Costa Rica. Costa Rica especially wants to preserve its rain forests' rich variety of plant and animal life. About 25 percent of Costa Rica's land has been set aside as nature preserves.

The fertile land of Central America is farmed to produce crops such as bananas, sugarcane, coffee, corn, cotton, and beans. Fishing is an important industry in Belize. Some countries, such as Guatemala and Panama, also have mineral resources.

People who live on islands in the Caribbean grow many of the same kinds of crops as people in Central America, and they earn their livings in similar ways. Among the hundreds of islands in the Caribbean are Cuba, Puerto Rico, the Bahamas, Jamaica, and Hispaniola.

European explorers first visited these islands in the late 1400s and early 1500s. The beauty of the tropical islands and the rich land impressed the explorers. Today, visitors come for the islands' lovely beaches and warm climates.

Despite the beauty and the rich land, places in the Caribbean and Central America face special challenges. Earthquakes are common in Central America, and tropical storms often bring heavy rains to both regions. Hurricane Georges, for example, hit the eastern Caribbean, Haiti, and the Dominican Republic in September 1998. The storm caused more then $1.5 billion in damages. One month later, Hurricane Mitch roared into the western Caribbean, with winds that reached 180 miles (290 km) per hour. The storm then came ashore in Honduras, where its heavy rains caused mudslides in Central America. The storm killed more than 10,000 people and injured about 13,000.

Many of the people who live in Central America and the Caribbean are of Spanish and Native American descent. Many people of African descent also live in the regions. Their ancestors were brought from Africa as slaves. The main language in most of the countries is Spanish, but in some countries most people speak either English, French, or Dutch.

REVIEW **What are two major challenges to living in Central America and the Caribbean?**

In 1998 Hurricane Mitch (below) hit the Caribbean island of Guanaja (right), destroying most buildings and boat docks.

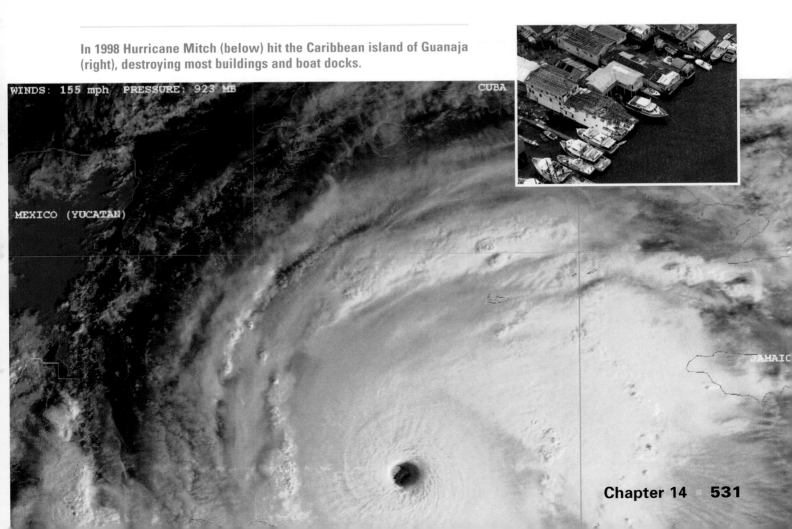

WINDS: 155 mph   PRESSURE: 923 MB

CUBA

MEXICO (YUCATAN)

JAMAIC

Fidel Castro has ruled Cuba since 1959.

Government in the Regions

For the first time in recent history, almost all the nations in Central America and the Caribbean have some form of democratic government. Cuba, which is a communist dictatorship, is the exception.

Both Puerto Rico and Cuba came under United States control in 1898, after the Spanish-American War. Puerto Rico was made a United States territory, but Cuba became an independent country in 1902. In 1952 Puerto Rico became a **commonwealth**, a kind of territory that governs itself. As citizens of a territory, Puerto Ricans hold United States citizenship. The United States Virgin Islands is another United States territory in the Caribbean.

Since 1959 Fidel Castro has ruled Cuba as a communist dictator. In an effort to end communism in Cuba, the United States government set up an economic embargo against the nation in 1960. An **embargo** is one nation's refusal to trade goods with another. Cuba's economy has been weakened by the embargo, but Cuba still remains a communist nation. Meanwhile, many Cuban Americans in the United States continue to hope that Cuba will become a democracy.

At Castro's request, Pope John Paul II visited Cuba in January 1998. Although

• SCIENCE AND TECHNOLOGY •

The Arecibo Observatory

In the late 1950s, American scientist William E. Gordon was searching for a site to build a space observatory. Because of what Gordon wished to study, the observatory had to be able to see a certain part of the sky, near the equator. The site finally chosen was Arecibo (ah•rah•SEE•boh) in northwest Puerto Rico. Today, the Arecibo Observatory has the world's largest single-dish radio telescope. The dish has a 1000-foot (305 m) diameter and covers 20 acres. The telescope has helped locate planets outside our solar system.

the Roman Catholic Church is not outlawed, its members cannot join the Communist party, which controls housing and jobs. In honor of the Pope's visit, Castro allowed Christmas to be celebrated in public for the first time in many years.

Many democratic governments in Central America and the Caribbean have struggled to survive. Costa Rica has been the most stable democracy. Like the United States, Costa Rica has three branches of government.

Despite being the second-oldest republic in the Western Hemisphere, after the United States, Haiti has had a history of military takeovers of its government. For much of its history, Haiti was ruled by dictators.

Former president of Haiti, Jean-Bertrand Aristide

At other times, however, the people of Haiti have freely elected their leaders. In 1990 Haiti held a **free election**—one that offers a choice of candidates, instead of a single candidate. Jean-Bertrand Aristide (air•ih•STEED) was elected, but military leaders soon took over. Aristide escaped to the United States. To help end military rule and return Aristide to office, the United States sent troops to Haiti in 1994. Soon Aristide returned to office.

Since that time, Haiti has held other free elections. Most people in Haiti are hopeful that their government will remain a democracy.

REVIEW **What nation in the Caribbean continues to be a communist country?**

LESSON 2 REVIEW

Summary Time Line

1880 — 1940 — PRESENT

1898
Cuba, the Philippines, and Puerto Rico are under United States control

1952
Puerto Rico becomes a United States commonwealth

1990
Haiti holds free elections

1998
Pope John Paul II visits Cuba

1. **MAIN IDEA** What do all the countries in Central America and the Caribbean, except Cuba, have in common?

2. **WHY IT MATTERS** How has the United States been affected by events in Central America and the Caribbean?

3. **VOCABULARY** What is a **commonwealth**?

4. **TIME LINE** When did Puerto Rico become a commonwealth?

5. **READING SKILL—Compare and Contrast** How are the governments of Costa Rica and Cuba different?

6. **HISTORY** Why did the United States send troops to Haiti in 1994?

7. **CRITICAL THINKING—Analyze** How might an embargo affect a country?

 PERFORMANCE—Make a Mobile Make a mobile about the land and the people of Central America and the Caribbean. Include pictures that represent the regions' physical features and products. Use your mobile to describe the regions to other students.

Read Population Pyramids

▶ WHY IT MATTERS

A graph that shows the division of a country's population by age is called a **population pyramid**. Each side of the graph is divided by age. One side of the graph shows the female population. The other side of the graph shows the male population.

Two factors affect the shape of the population pyramid—a country's birth rate and its death rate. The birth rate is the number of children born each year for every 1,000 people in the country. The death rate is the number of people who die each year for every 1,000 people in the country.

A population pyramid also gives a picture of a country's **life expectancy**, the number of years people can expect to live. This number varies from country to country. It tells in general how long people in a country live, but it does not say how long any one person will live.

A population pyramid also shows the country's median age. The word *median* means "middle." Half the people in the country are older than the **median age**, and half are younger.

Four generations of the same family can be seen in this photograph.

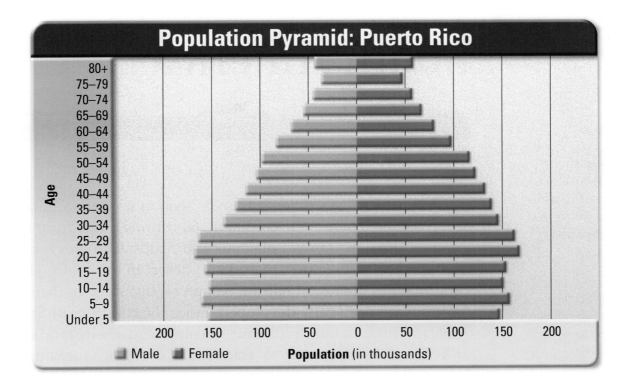

Population Pyramid: Puerto Rico

Age / Population (in thousands)
■ Male ■ Female

WHAT YOU NEED TO KNOW

The population pyramid shown above gives the population of Puerto Rico. Notice how it is divided into age groups, with the youngest at the bottom and the oldest at the top. The left side of the population pyramid shows the number of males in each age group. The right side shows the number of females. If you want to know the number that a whole age group represents, add together the number of males and the number of females in that age group. For example, in the 10–14 age group, there are about 152,000 males and about 150,000 females. So there are about 302,000 persons age 10–14 in Puerto Rico.

The pyramid's shape indicates how rapidly Puerto Rico's population is growing. The very wide parts of the pyramid show that the greatest number of people are under 29 years of age. The top of the pyramid indicates that fewer people are over 70 years of age.

PRACTICE THE SKILL

Use the population pyramid to answer the following questions.

1. Find your age group on the population pyramid. About how many boys in Puerto Rico are in that age group? About how many girls?

2. In which age groups are there more females than males?

3. Which age group is the largest?

4. About how many people in Puerto Rico have lived 80 years or longer?

5. What general statement can you make about Puerto Rico's population from this pyramid?

APPLY WHAT YOU LEARNED

Think about the ages of people in your own family or in your class at school. Draw a population pyramid that shows the number of people of different ages in your family or class.

CHART AND GRAPH SKILLS

MAIN IDEA
Read to find out about the land and people of South America and how countries there gained independence.

WHY IT MATTERS
Countries in South America have an important effect on the world's health and economy.

VOCABULARY
standard of living
liberate
deforestation

South America

1800   1900   PRESENT

South America's diversity can be seen in its lands, climates, and resources. Across the continent, landforms range from towering mountains to broad plateaus and plains. Climates range from tropical in the north to arid and desert in the south. The continent has abundant natural resources, but some of them have not yet been fully developed. Since the countries of South America differ in their economic development, their standards of living also vary widely. A **standard of living** is a measure of how well people in a country live.

South America and Its People

South America, the fourth largest continent, covers more than twice the area of the continental United States. Only Africa has a less indented coastline than South America. Because of this, there are few good harbors along most of South America's coasts.

The Andes Mountains extend 4,500 miles (7,250 km) along the western side of South

LOCATE IT

VENEZUELA
Caracas
Angel Falls

America, from the Caribbean in the north to the continent's southern tip. East of the Andes are areas of plateaus and plains, including the Guiana Highlands in the north and the Pampus and Patagonia to the south. Three major river systems—the Río de la Plata, the Orinoco (ohr•ee•NOH•koh), and the Amazon—run like veins through the continent's lowlands. Many of these lowlands lie in the tropics. Rain forests, with unique animals and plants, cover much of the land along the Amazon and along many of the other rivers in the region.

While much of South America is hot and humid, some areas are dry and cold. West of the snowcapped Andes, along the coast of northern Chile, is the Atacama Desert. It is the world's driest desert. So little rain falls there that people have found ways to capture moisture from the early morning fogs. The southern part of the continent is cold for much of the year.

Native peoples lived in South America for thousands of years. Then, in the 1500s, Spain, Portugal, and other European countries began to build colonies there.

South America

GEOGRAPHY THEME

Location There are 13 countries on the continent of South America. Of those 13, Brazil is the largest.

❓ How are Bolivia and Paraguay different from the other countries of South America?

FAST FACT

South America has the world's highest waterfall, longest mountain range, and largest river by volume of water. Angel Falls, the Andes Mountains, and the Amazon River are three A's to remember!

The Valley of the Moon is an arid region in Chile. Angel Falls (left), in Venezuela, is the world's highest waterfall.

Simón Bolívar   1783–1830

Character Trait: Leadership

Simón Bolívar fought for nine years for his homeland's independence. In 1821, he and his troops defeated the Spanish in Venezuela. Two years earlier Bolívar had helped Colombia win its freedom. He and his troops later defeated the Spanish in Bolivia and Peru. Because of his contributions to the independence of many nations, he is known as *El Libertador*, or The Liberator.

MULTIMEDIA BIOGRAPHIES
Visit The Learning Site at
www.harcourtschool.com/biographies
to learn about other famous people.

GO ONLINE

Europeans soon ruled most of the continent.

During the late 1700s and early 1800s, political independence became a goal for many people in South America. They had observed the success of the 13 British colonies in North America in breaking free of British rule and forming the United States. In the early 1800s, colony after colony in South America declared its independence—usually through revolution.

Simón Bolívar (see•MOHN boh•LEE•var) in Venezuela and José de San Martín (sahn mar•TEEN) in Argentina were key figures in the struggle to **liberate**, or set free, these colonies. By 1828 all of Spain's and Portugal's colonies in South America had become independent. By the mid-1800s most parts of South America had been liberated.

Bolívar hoped for a single nation in South America but knew how unlikely that would be. "[South] America is separated by climatic differences, geographical diversity, conflicting interests, and dissimilar characteristics," he said. Each country developed on its own, often fighting over borders with its neighbors.

REVIEW What was the goal of many people in South America in the early 1800s?

Old Problems in New Countries

Even after independence, most of the people in South America had little say in government. Wealth was concentrated in the hands of a few landowners, and political matters were in the hands of dictators or armies. The people lacked the education necessary to make changes. They were also unschooled in the ways of self-government.

Various reformers throughout South America began working to solve these problems.

This statue of José de San Martín is in Cordoba, Argentina.

One solution was to redistribute the land so that individuals could own small farms. During the colonial period large haciendas, which were similar to plantations in the southern United States, were common. Since the 1960s, land reform supporters have enjoyed some victories, but many farmers still do not own the land on which they work.

REVIEW What were some problems the newly independent countries faced?

New Problems for All Countries

Many South American countries continue to face the problems of poverty, unemployment, and keeping their democracies. Land use has once again become a major issue. In some places, Indian tribes have protested land development, which they believe disturbs

Many scientists are working to solve problems related to the destruction of the rain forests.

centuries-old patterns of life. These tribes are beginning to take legal measures to regain their ancestral lands.

In addition, many scientists are concerned over the destruction of the rain forests in some areas of South America.

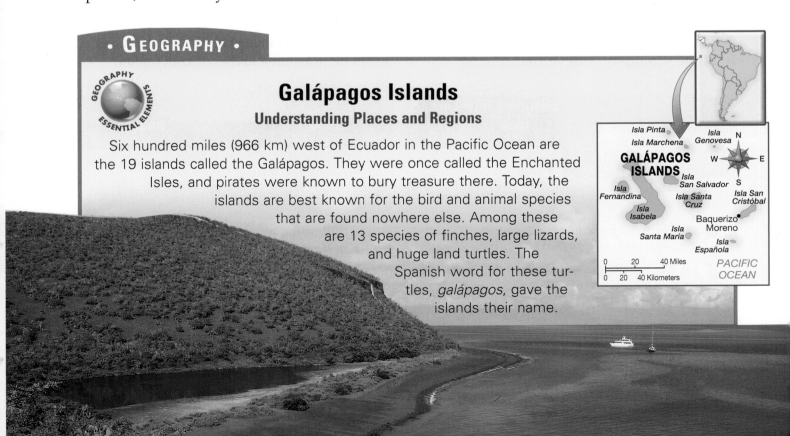

· **GEOGRAPHY** ·

GEOGRAPHY ESSENTIAL ELEMENTS

Galápagos Islands
Understanding Places and Regions

Six hundred miles (966 km) west of Ecuador in the Pacific Ocean are the 19 islands called the Galápagos. They were once called the Enchanted Isles, and pirates were known to bury treasure there. Today, the islands are best known for the bird and animal species that are found nowhere else. Among these are 13 species of finches, large lizards, and huge land turtles. The Spanish word for these turtles, *galápagos*, gave the islands their name.

GALÁPAGOS ISLANDS

Isla Pinta
Isla Marchena
Isla Genovesa
Isla Fernandina
Isla San Salvador
Isla Santa Cruz
Isla San Cristóbal
Isla Isabela
Baquerizo Moreno
Isla Santa María
Isla Española

N W E S

0   20   40 Miles
0   20   40 Kilometers

PACIFIC OCEAN

more carbon dioxide in the atmosphere leads to warmer temperatures, which scientists term the *greenhouse effect*.

Scientists have begun to explore the use of rain forest plants for medicine. Although less than 1 percent of the plants in the rain forest have been tested for medical benefits, about 25 percent of western medicines come from rain forest plants. Destroying these plants may prevent new medicines from being discovered.

Brazil has worked to slow this **deforestation**, or the widespread cutting down of forests. Not only has the rate of cutting slowed, but lands have been set aside for protection. The Amazon region now has several plant and animal reserves, national parks, and national forests.

REVIEW **What kinds of lands have been set aside for protection in the Amazon region?**

Across South America, rain forests are cleared for their valuable wood or to build new farms, towns, and roads. As the forests are cut down, and burned, carbon dioxide is released into the atmosphere and there are fewer trees to absorb it. Some scientists believe that having

LESSON 3 REVIEW

Summary Time Line

| 1800 | 1900 | PRESENT |

1828
All of Spain and Portugal's South American colonies are independent

1 **MAIN IDEA** How did most countries in South America gain independence?

2 **WHY IT MATTERS** How does South America influence the world's health?

3 **VOCABULARY** Use the word **liberate** in a sentence that explains its meaning.

4 **TIME LINE** When did the last of Spain's and Portugal's South American colonies gain independence?

5 **READING SKILL—Compare and Contrast** How is the climate of southern South America different from the climate along the Amazon?

6 **HISTORY** Who were Simón Bolívar and José de San Martín?

7 **CRITICAL THINKING—Analyze** Why might production increase if farmers own small plots of land, rather than having the government own all the land?

 PERFORMANCE—Write a Packing List The climate and geography of parts of South America are very different. Imagine that you will be taking a trip across the continent. Tell where you will visit, and write a packing list of the clothes and supplies you might need there.

Canada

| 1600 | 1800 | PRESENT |

Canada's red and white maple leaf flag is a familiar symbol to many Americans. Canada and the United States share one of the longest borders in the world, and about two-thirds of all Canadians live within 100 miles of the United States border. Geography, however, is just one reason why the two nations have such strong ties to each other.

A Varied Landscape

In land area, Canada is the second-largest country in the world. It covers more than 40 percent of North America. Canada, like the United States, stretches from the Atlantic Ocean to the Pacific Ocean, and from a 3,987-mile (6,416-km) southern border shared with the continental United States to islands in the Arctic Ocean. Canada's people may live near mountains, lakes, forests, prairies, or tundra.

MAIN IDEA
Canada is a land of great variety and has strong ties to the United States.

WHY IT MATTERS
Canada and the United States share a long border and similar landforms. The two neighbors are also major trading partners.

VOCABULARY

province
separatist

A wide variety of climates and landforms can be found in Canada. Cattle graze on fertile prairie land. This glacier (inset) is in northern Alberta.

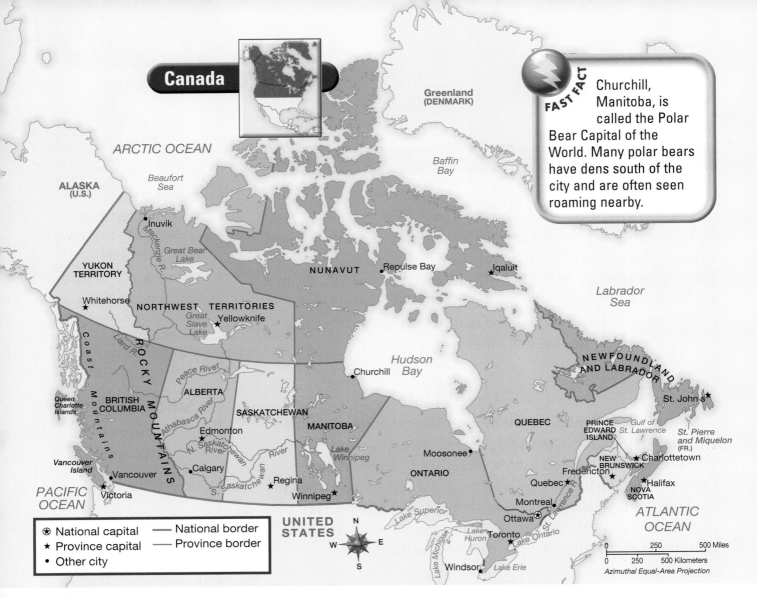

Canada

ARCTIC OCEAN

ALASKA (U.S.)

Greenland (DENMARK)

Churchill, Manitoba, is called the Polar Bear Capital of the World. Many polar bears have dens south of the city and are often seen roaming nearby.

Beaufort Sea

Baffin Bay

Inuvik

Mackenzie R.

Great Bear Lake

YUKON TERRITORY

Whitehorse

NORTHWEST TERRITORIES

Great Slave Lake

Yellowknife

NUNAVUT

Repulse Bay

Iqaluit

Labrador Sea

Coast Mountains

Liard River

R O C K Y   M O U N T A I N S

Peace River

Hudson Bay

Churchill

NEWFOUNDLAND AND LABRADOR

Queen Charlotte Islands

BRITISH COLUMBIA

ALBERTA

Athabasca River

Edmonton

SASKATCHEWAN

N. Saskatchewan River

MANITOBA

Lake Winnipeg

Moosonee

QUEBEC

St. John's

PRINCE EDWARD ISLAND

Gulf of St. Lawrence

St. Pierre and Miquelon (FR.)

Vancouver Island

Vancouver

Calgary

Saskatchewan River

S. Saskatchewan

Regina

Winnipeg

ONTARIO

Fredericton

Quebec

NEW BRUNSWICK

Charlottetown

Halifax

NOVA SCOTIA

PACIFIC OCEAN

Victoria

Montreal

St. Lawrence

ATLANTIC OCEAN

⊛ National capital
★ Province capital
• Other city

── National border
── Province border

UNITED STATES

Lake Superior

Ottawa

Toronto

Lake Ontario

N
W   E
S

Lake Michigan

Lake Huron

Lake Erie

Windsor

0   250   500 Miles
0   250   500 Kilometers
Azimuthal Equal-Area Projection

GEOGRAPHY THEME

Regions   **This map shows the 10 provinces and 3 territories of Canada.**

↪ **Which Canadian province is the largest? Which territory is the largest?**

Canada is a land of variety. The low Coast Mountains extend along the Pacific coast, while farther inland are the towering Rockies. The Interior Plains cover the central part of Canada. To the northeast is the Canadian Shield, a huge region of poor, rocky soil. Southeast of the Canadian Shield is the St. Lawrence Lowlands. This region has most of Canada's people and industries. The Appalachian Mountains extend into southeastern Canada.

Canada has many rivers and lakes that provide beauty and natural resources for the country. Four of the five Great Lakes help define its southern border.

Canada has 10 provinces and 3 territories. A **province** is a political region similar to a state in the United States. Each province has its own government, and it can take many actions without the approval of the national government.

REVIEW How is western Canada different from central Canada?

Journey to Self-Government

Thousands of years ago, Canada's first settlers entered the region, probably over a land bridge from Asia. Many of the descendants of these early settlers still live in Canada today. They are known as the First Nation peoples.

The Vikings first explored what is now eastern Canada around A.D. 1000, but other European explorers did not reach Canada until about 500 years later. Both Britain and France wanted to control Canada's vast lands, and each nation sent explorers to claim land. After wars in Europe and North America, France lost its Canadian holdings to Britain. In the Quebec Act of 1774, Britain agreed that French settlers in Canada could keep their own laws, language, and religion.

In 1867 the British Parliament passed the British North American Act. This act, which united all of Canada into one nation, also served as Canada's first constitution. It gave Canada a representative government, but Britain held the final word in Canadian affairs.

In 1931 the British Parliament passed the Statute of Westminister. It allowed Canada to conduct its own foreign affairs, but Canada still remained partly under British rule. Canada also became a partner in the British Commonwealth of Nations, the name given to territories that give allegiance to the British crown.

Canadians wanted more control over their own government and decisions. A new constitution in 1982 permitted constitutional amendments without approval from the British Parliament.

Canada's flag

LOCATE IT

Ottawa

ONTARIO

Great Lakes

Members of the Canadian Senate (inset) meet inside the Parliament Building, in Ottawa.

POINTS OF VIEW
Should Quebec Secede?

Almost since Britain won control of New France in 1763, Quebec has struggled to hold on to its French heritage. Some French Canadians of Quebec have tried to win Quebec's independence from Canada.

MARC-ANDRE BEDARD, a leader of the separatist movement

❝Are we a people or are we not? If we are, we should be sovereign. We should be at the table with the international community.❞

PIERRE TRUDEAU, former Canadian prime minister

❝It would be disastrous. . . . It would mean a major setback in the course of history. And the burden would lie with those who would like to break up one of history's greatest achievements—the Canadian federation.❞

Analyze the Viewpoints

❶ What views does each person hold?

❷ **Make it Relevant** Choose an issue about which the people in your class or community have different views. Find out what people think about the issue.

In Montreal (below), signs such as this one are in both French and English.

The constitution also included a Charter of Rights and Freedoms, similar to the United States Bill of Rights. Canada's independence was complete.

Canada's executive branch is still headed by Britain's monarch, who appoints a representative, the governor-general. Daily governmental affairs, however, are handled by the prime minister. He or she is a member of the ruling majority party of the House of Commons. Along with the Senate, the House of Commons makes up the Canadian Parliament.

REVIEW What did the Constitution of 1982 do?

New Solutions to Old Problems

For a long time, many Quebec citizens, called **separatists**, have wanted to form a separate country in order to preserve their French culture. In 1998, a vote to secede from Canada failed. The Canadian Supreme Court then ruled that Quebec could not secede unless the rest of Canada agreed.

Like the people of Quebec, the native peoples of Canada want to preserve their culture. In 1999 Nunavut, part of the Northwest Territories, became Canada's third territory. Most of the people who live in Nunavut are Inuit. They plan to govern the territory of Nunavut according to the traditional means of consensus, or the agreement of the community.

REVIEW Why do separatists want to secede from Canada?

A World Partner

Canada has economic partnerships with many countries, but it has the greatest cooperation with the United States. The United States and Canada are major trading partners. In 1987 the two countries signed a free trade agreement that was a forerunner to NAFTA. Today, more than 80 percent of Canada's exports go to the United States, and Canada gets about 70 percent of its imports from the United States.

One of the greatest examples of cooperation between the two neighbors was the construction of the St. Lawrence Seaway. The St. Lawrence River flows nearly 800 miles (1,287 km) from Lake Ontario to the Atlantic Ocean, but parts of the river are not deep enough for large ships to navigate. The St. Lawrence Seaway also includes the Welland Ship Canal, built between Lake Ontario and Lake Erie to bypass Niagara Falls. Construction of the

This photograph shows the first ship to enter the locks of the St. Lawrence Seaway in April of 1959.

St. Lawrence Seaway was completed in 1959. This allowed large ships to reach the Great Lakes from the Atlantic Ocean.

REVIEW What is one example of cooperation between Canada and the United States?

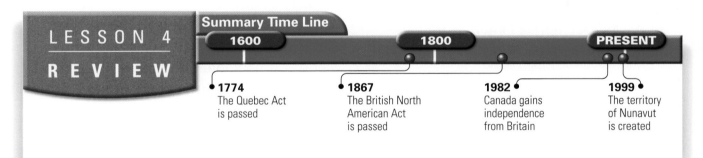

LESSON 4 REVIEW

Summary Time Line

1600	1800	PRESENT

1774
The Quebec Act is passed

1867
The British North American Act is passed

1982
Canada gains independence from Britain

1999
The territory of Nunavut is created

1. **MAIN IDEA** Why does Canada have strong ties to the United States?

2. **WHY IT MATTERS** How do Canada and the United States affect each other's economy?

3. **VOCABULARY** What is a **province**?

4. **TIME LINE** Which occurred first, the Quebec Act or the British North American Act?

5. **READING SKILL—Compare and Contrast** Compare and contrast the residents of Quebec and the residents of Nunavut.

6. **GEOGRAPHY** What are the three main mountain ranges in Canada?

7. **CRITICAL THINKING—Analyze** Why do you think Canada and the United States cooperated to build the St. Lawrence Seaway?

PERFORMANCE—Draw a Map Use your textbook, library books, and the Internet to draw a map of Canada. Find the location of each of Canada's major landforms, and label them on your map. Also show each of Canada's provinces and territories.

Use a Time Zone Map

WHY IT MATTERS

"What time is it?" The answer depends on where you are. That is because people who live in different parts of the world set their clocks at different times.

For centuries people used the sun to determine time. When the sun was at its highest point in the sky, it was noon. However, the sun cannot be at its highest point all around the Earth at the same time. As the Earth rotates, the sun is directly overhead in different places at different times. The sun is past its highest point at places east of where you are, and it has not yet reached its highest point at places west of you.

In the 1800s Charles Dowd of the United States and Sandford Fleming of

Canada developed the idea of dividing the Earth into time zones. A **time zone** is a region in which a single time is used. To figure out the time in a place, you can use a time zone map like the one on page 547.

WHAT YOU NEED TO KNOW

Dowd and Fleming divided the Earth into 24 time zones. A new time zone begins every fifteenth meridian, starting at the prime meridian. In each new time zone to the west, the time is one hour earlier than in the time zone before it.

The map on page 547 shows the time zones in the Western Hemisphere. Find Dallas, in the central time zone. Now find New York City. It is in the eastern time zone, which is just east of the central time zone. The time in the central time zone is one hour earlier than the time in the eastern time zone. If it is 5:00 P.M. in the central time zone, it is 6:00 P.M. in the eastern time zone.

PRACTICE THE SKILL

Use the time zone map of the Western Hemisphere to answer these questions.

1. In which time zone is Los Angeles?
2. If it is 10:00 A.M. in Los Angeles, what time is it in San Antonio?
3. In which time zone is Puerto Rico?

While the sun sets in Honolua Bay, Hawaii, it is already dark in other places in the United States.

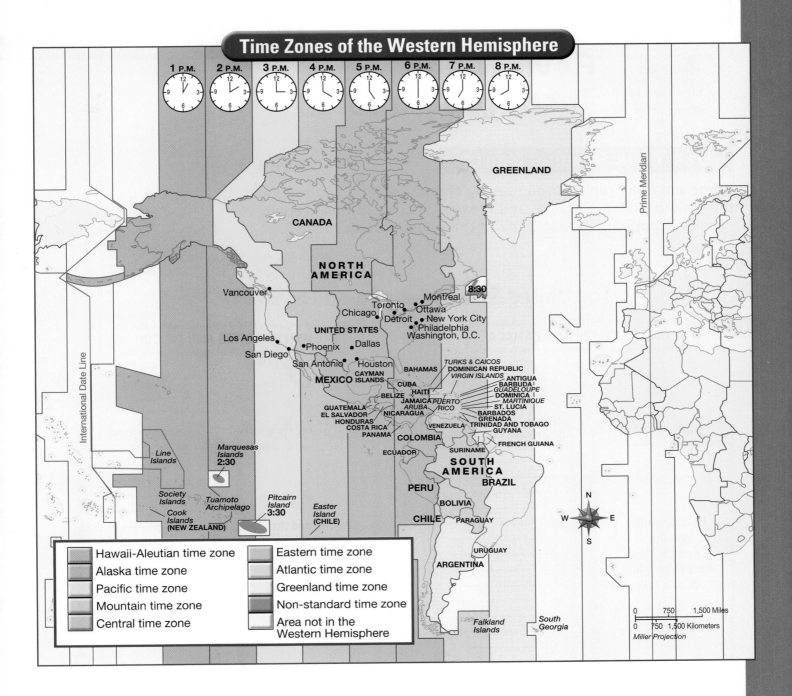

Time Zones of the Western Hemisphere

1 P.M. 2 P.M. 3 P.M. 4 P.M. 5 P.M. 6 P.M. 7 P.M. 8 P.M.

GREENLAND

Prime Meridian

CANADA

NORTH AMERICA

Vancouver

Montreal 8:30
Toronto Ottawa
Chicago Detroit New York City
Philadelphia
Washington, D.C.

UNITED STATES

Los Angeles Phoenix Dallas
San Diego
San Antonio Houston

International Date Line

TURKS & CAICOS
BAHAMAS DOMINICAN REPUBLIC
VIRGIN ISLANDS ANTIGUA
CUBA BARBUDA
HAITI GUADELOUPE
BELIZE DOMINICA
JAMAICA PUERTO MARTINIQUE
GUATEMALA ARUBA RICO ST. LUCIA
EL SALVADOR NICARAGUA BARBADOS
HONDURAS GRENADA
COSTA RICA VENEZUELA TRINIDAD AND TOBAGO
PANAMA GUYANA
COLOMBIA FRENCH GUIANA
ECUADOR SURINAME

MEXICO
CAYMAN ISLANDS

Line Islands

Marquesas Islands
2:30

SOUTH AMERICA

PERU BRAZIL

Society Islands
Cook Islands
(NEW ZEALAND)
Tuamoto Archipelago

Pitcairn Island
3:30

Easter Island
(CHILE)

BOLIVIA

CHILE PARAGUAY

N
W   E
S

URUGUAY

ARGENTINA

Falkland Islands
South Georgia

0   750   1,500 Miles
0 750 1,500 Kilometers
Miller Projection

Legend	
Hawaii-Aleutian time zone	Eastern time zone
Alaska time zone	Atlantic time zone
Pacific time zone	Greenland time zone
Mountain time zone	Non-standard time zone
Central time zone	Area not in the Western Hemisphere

4 If it is 3:00 P.M. in Puerto Rico, what time is it in Philadelphia? in Houston?

5 If it is 6:00 A.M. in San Diego, what time is it in Toronto?

6 Imagine that you are in Honduras. Is the time earlier than, later than, or the same as in Chicago?

▶ APPLY WHAT YOU LEARNED

Record the current time where you live. Now figure out the time in Montreal, Canada; Vancouver, Canada; Venezuela; and Argentina. Explain why it might be useful to know the time in different places.

Practice your map and globe skills with the **GeoSkills CD-ROM.**

MAP AND GLOBE SKILLS

14 Review and Test Preparation

USE YOUR READING SKILLS

Complete this graphic organizer by comparing and contrasting the United States, Canada, and Mexico. A copy of this graphic organizer appears on page 142 of the Activity Book.

The United States, Canada, and Mexico

THE UNITED STATES AND CANADA

SIMILARITIES

Both Canada and the United States were once under British rule.

DIFFERENCES

THE UNITED STATES AND MEXICO

SIMILARITIES

Mexico and the United States each have democratic governments.

DIFFERENCES

THINK & WRITE

Write a Postcard Imagine you are traveling through South America on a family vacation. Write a postcard to a friend describing the natural wonders you have seen. Be sure to mention where these places are located.

Write a Wise Saying Having a good relationship with one's neighbors is important for both people and nations. Write a wise saying about the importance of the United States maintaining good relations with its neighbors.

1774 The Quebec Act is passed

1821 Mexico gains independence from Spain

1867 The British North American Act is passed

1917 Mexico writes a new constitution

1952 Puerto Rico becomes a United States commonwealth

1982 Canada gains independence from Britain

1990 Haiti holds free elections

1994 The NAFTA agreement is made

USE VOCABULARY

Identify the term that correctly matches each definition.

middle class (p. 528)	
interest rate (p. 528)	
free election (p. 533)	
province (p. 542)	

1 the amount that banks charge to loan money

2 a political region

3 people who are economically between the rich and the poor

4 a political race that offers a choice of candidates

RECALL FACTS

Answer these questions.

5 Why are *Fiestas Patrias* important for many Mexican Americans?

6 How is the territory of Nunavut different from other Canadian territories?

Write the letter of the best choice.

7 **TEST PREP** The purpose of NAFTA is to—
  A protect French Canadian culture.
  B continue an embargo on exports from Cuba.
  C increase trade among the United States, Canada, and Mexico.
  D bring democracy to all the nations of Central America and the Caribbean.

8 **TEST PREP** Benito Juárez was the first Native American president of—
  F Mexico.
  G Bolivia.
  H El Salvador.
  J Costa Rica.

9 **TEST PREP** Which of the following Canadian provinces has stated a wish to secede?
  A Alberta
  B New Brunswick
  C Quebec
  D British Columbia

THINK CRITICALLY

10 Why is immigration such an important issue for the United States and Mexico?

11 Why do you think some Latin American countries have had difficulty forming stable governments?

12 What might happen if Quebec decides to secede from Canada?

APPLY SKILLS

Read Population Pyramids
Review the population pyramid on page 535. Then answer the following questions.

13 What age group makes up the smallest part of the population?

14 In which age groups are there more males than females?

Use a Time Zone Map
Find the Bahamas on the time zone map on page 547. Then answer the following questions.

15 If it is 9:00 A.M. in the Bahamas, what time is it in Dallas?

16 If it is 12:00 P.M. in the Bahamas, what time is it in Vancouver?

VISIT Washington, D.C.

GET READY

Every year millions of people visit Washington, D.C. Visitors enjoy the city because, in addition to being the home of the national government, it is a beautiful city that is rich in history. If you visit Washington, D.C., you can tour important government buildings, such as the White House, where the President lives and works, and the Capitol, where Congress meets. You can visit museums, such as the National Museum of American History, or monuments, such as the Washington Monument. The many buildings, museums, and monuments of Washington, D.C. tell the story of America's past.

LOCATE IT

MARYLAND

VIRGINIA

Washington, D.C.

WHAT TO SEE

The White House

Visitors look at the *Gemini 4* space capsule at the Smithsonian National Air and Space Museum.

The Capitol

The Washington Monument

The Declaration of Independence is displayed at the National Archives.

The United States Botanic Garden has more than 10,000 varieties of plants.

TAKE A FIELD TRIP

GO ONLINE

A VIRTUAL TOUR
Visit The Learning Site at **www.harcourtschool.com/ tours** to take virtual tours of places of interest in the United States.

CNN Turner Le(@)rning®

A VIDEO TOUR
Check your media center or classroom library for a videotape tour of Washington, D.C.

7 Review and Test Preparation

USE VOCABULARY

Use a term from this list to complete each of the sentences that follow.

> Sun Belt (p. 493)
>
> rapid-transit system (p. 501)
>
> register (p. 513)
>
> embargo (p. 532)

1 A _____ moves passengers on an underground train.

2 Before a citizen can vote, that person must _____.

3 Much of the recent growth in the United States has taken place in the _____.

4 An _____ occurs when one nation refuses to trade goods with another.

RECALL FACTS

Answer these questions.

5 How has the Information Age affected science?

6 How has NAFTA affected trade between the United States, Canada, and Mexico?

Write the letter of the best choice.

7 **TEST PREP**   The fastest-growing ethnic group in the United States today is—
A Hispanic Americans.
B African Americans.
C Asian Americans.
D Irish Americans.

8 **TEST PREP**   About one-third of all American workers have jobs in the—
F federal government.
G banking, insurance, and real estate industry.
H service industry.
J medical profession.

Visual Summary

The United States is home to people from all over the world. p. 492

552

Today more Americans work in service jobs than in any other kinds of jobs. p. 505

Mexico City is one of the largest metropolitan areas in the world. p. 527

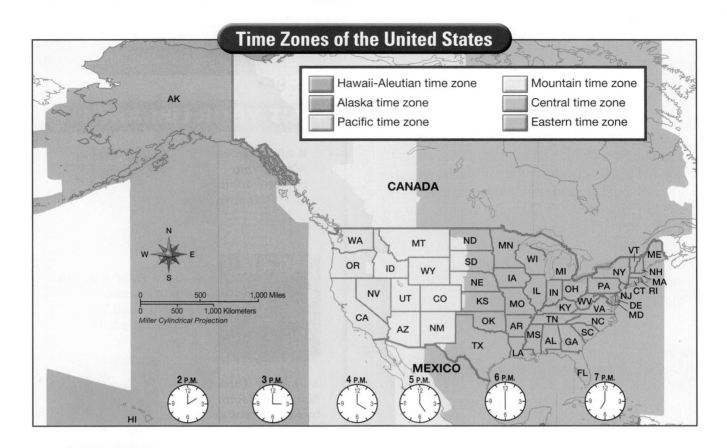

Time Zones of the United States

Hawaii-Aleutian time zone
Alaska time zone
Pacific time zone
Mountain time zone
Central time zone
Eastern time zone

AK

CANADA

N
W E
S

0   500   1,000 Miles
0   500   1,000 Kilometers
Miller Cylindrical Projection

WA MT ND MN VT ME
OR ID WY SD WI NY NH
NV UT CO NE IA MI PA MA
CA AZ NM KS MO IL IN OH WV VA NJ CT RI
OK AR KY NC DE MD
TX MS AL GA TN SC
LA

MEXICO

2 P.M.   3 P.M.   4 P.M.   5 P.M.   6 P.M.   FL 7 P.M.

HI

THINK CRITICALLY

9 Why is voting an important part of a citizen's responsibility?

10 Why do you think the Mexican people chose to elect Vicente Fox as president in 2000?

11 What might happen if Quebec decides to secede from Canada?

APPLY SKILLS

Use a Time Zone Map
Use the map to answer the following questions.

MAP AND GLOBE SKILLS

12 What is the time difference between New Jersey and New Mexico?

13 What is the time difference between Oklahoma and Montana?

Jean-Bertrand Aristide becomes Haiti's president. p. 533

Simón Bolívar helps win independence for many present-day Latin American countries. p. 538

The St. Lawrence Seaway allows ships to travel from the Atlantic Ocean to the Great Lakes. p. 545

Unit Activities

GO ONLINE Visit The Learning Site at www.harcourtschool.com/socialstudies/activities for additional activities.

Make a Mural

Work with a group of your classmates to create a mural of famous United States monuments. First, decide which monuments you want to show on your mural. Some examples include the Washington Monument, the Lincoln Memorial, the Statue of Liberty, and Mount Rushmore. After choosing the monuments you wish to show, draw or paint them on a posterboard. Remember to label each monument. Finally, display your mural with those of your classmates.

Prepare a Newscast

Work in a group to prepare a newscast on a meeting between the President of the United States and a leader of a Western Hemisphere nation. Each member of your group should have a job, such as researcher, writer, reporter, or anchorperson. When planning your newscast, include information about the other nation and its relationship with the United States. When you are finished, present your newscast to your class.

VISIT YOUR LIBRARY

■ *My Mexico—México mío* by Tony Johnston. G. P. Putnam's Sons.

My Mexico~México mío

ANGEL FALLS
A SOUTH AMERICAN JOURNEY
Martin and Tanis Jordan

■ *Angel Falls: A South American Journey* by Martin and Tanis Jordan. Kingfisher.

■ *Journey Through the Northern Rainforest* by Karen Pandell. Penguin Putnam Books for Young Readers.

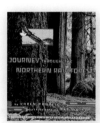

JOURNEY THROUGH THE NORTHERN RAINFOREST

COMPLETE THE UNIT PROJECT

A Cultural Fair   Work with a group of your classmates to finish the unit project—presenting a cultural fair. Look over your notes describing the different cultures discussed in this unit. Use these notes to decide what to include in your cultural fair. Your fair may feature posters representing different art forms or styles of dress. You may also wish to feature different kinds of foods or music. Finally, hold your cultural fair.

For Your Reference

Almanac

Facts About the States

State Flag	State	Year of Statehood	Population*	Area (sq. mi.)	Capital	Origin of State Name
	Alabama	1819	4,447,100	50,750	Montgomery	Choctaw, *alba ayamule*, "one who clears land and gathers food from it"
	Alaska	1959	626,932	570,374	Juneau	Aleut, *alayeska*, "great land"
	Arizona	1912	5,130,632	113,642	Phoenix	Papago, *arizonac*, "place of the small spring"
	Arkansas	1836	2,673,400	52,075	Little Rock	Quapaw, "the downstream people"
	California	1850	33,871,648	155,973	Sacramento	Spanish, a fictional island
	Colorado	1876	4,301,261	103,730	Denver	Spanish, "red land" or "red earth"
	Connecticut	1788	3,405,565	4,845	Hartford	Mohican, *quinnitukqut*, "at the long tidal river"
	Delaware	1787	783,600	1,955	Dover	Named for Lord de la Warr
	Florida	1845	15,982,378	54,153	Tallahassee	Spanish, "filled with flowers"
	Georgia	1788	8,186,453	57,919	Atlanta	Named for King George II of England
	Hawaii	1959	1,211,537	6,450	Honolulu	Polynesian, *hawaiki* or *owykee*, "homeland"
	Idaho	1890	1,293,593	82,751	Boise	Invented name with unknown meaning

State Flag	State	Year of Statehood	Population*	Area (sq. mi.)	Capital	Origin of State Name
	Illinois	1818	12,419,293	55,593	Springfield	Algonquin, *iliniwek*, "men" or "warriors"
	Indiana	1816	6,080,485	35,870	Indianapolis	*Indian + a*, "land of the Indians"
	Iowa	1846	2,926,324	55,875	Des Moines	Dakota, *ayuba*, "beautiful land"
	Kansas	1861	2,688,418	81,823	Topeka	Sioux, "land of the south wind people"
	Kentucky	1792	4,041,769	39,732	Frankfort	Iroquoian, *ken-tah-ten*, "land of tomorrow"
	Louisiana	1812	4,468,976	43,566	Baton Rouge	Named for King Louis XIV of France
	Maine	1820	1,274,923	30,865	Augusta	Named after a French province
	Maryland	1788	5,296,486	9,775	Annapolis	Named for Henrietta Maria, Queen Consort of Charles I of England
	Massachusetts	1788	6,349,097	7,838	Boston	Massachusett tribe of Native Americans, "at the big hill" or "place of the big hill"
	Michigan	1837	9,938,444	56,809	Lansing	Ojibwa, "large lake"
	Minnesota	1858	4,919,479	79,617	St. Paul	Dakota Sioux, "sky-blue water"
	Mississippi	1817	2,844,658	46,914	Jackson	Indian word meaning "great waters" or "father of waters"
	Missouri	1821	5,595,211	68,898	Jefferson City	Named after the Missouri Indian tribe. *Missouri* means "town of the large canoes."

* Census 2000 figures

State Flag	State	Year of Statehood	Population*	Area (sq. mi.)	Capital	Origin of State Name
	Montana	1889	902,195	145,566	Helena	Spanish, "mountainous"
	Nebraska	1867	1,711,263	76,878	Lincoln	From an Oto Indian word meaning "flat water"
	Nevada	1864	1,998,257	109,806	Carson City	Spanish, "snowy" or "snowed upon"
	New Hampshire	1788	1,235,786	8,969	Concord	Named for Hampshire County, England
	New Jersey	1787	8,414,350	7,419	Trenton	Named for the Isle of Jersey
	New Mexico	1912	1,819,046	121,365	Santa Fe	Named by Spanish explorers from Mexico
	New York	1788	18,976,457	47,224	Albany	Named after the Duke of York
	North Carolina	1789	8,049,313	48,718	Raleigh	Named after King Charles II of England
	North Dakota	1889	642,200	70,704	Bismarck	Sioux, *dakota*, "friend" or "ally"
	Ohio	1803	11,353,140	40,953	Columbus	Iroquois, *oheo*, "great water"
	Oklahoma	1907	3,450,654	68,679	Oklahoma City	Choctaw, "red people"
	Oregon	1859	3,421,399	96,003	Salem	Unknown; generally accepted that it was taken from the writings of Maj. Robert Rogers, an English army officer
	Pennsylvania	1787	12,281,054	44,820	Harrisburg	*Penn + sylvania*, meaning "Penn's woods"

State Flag	State	Year of Statehood	Population*	Area (sq. mi.)	Capital	Origin of State Name
	Rhode Island	1790	1,048,319	1,045	Providence	From the Greek island of Rhodes
	South Carolina	1788	4,012,012	30,111	Columbia	Named after King Charles II of England
	South Dakota	1889	754,844	75,898	Pierre	Sioux, *dakota*, "friend" or "ally"
	Tennessee	1796	5,689,283	41,220	Nashville	Name of a Cherokee village
	Texas	1845	20,851,820	261,914	Austin	Native American, *tejas*, "friend" or "ally"
	Utah	1896	2,233,169	82,168	Salt Lake City	From the Ute tribe, meaning "people of the mountains"
	Vermont	1791	608,827	9,249	Montpelier	French, *vert*, "green," and *mont*, "mountain"
	Virginia	1788	7,078,515	39,598	Richmond	Named after Queen Elizabeth I of England
	Washington	1889	5,894,121	66,582	Olympia	Named for George Washington
	West Virginia	1863	1,808,344	24,087	Charleston	From the English-named state of Virginia
	Wisconsin	1848	5,363,675	54,314	Madison	Possibly Algonquian, "the place where we live"
	Wyoming	1890	493,782	97,105	Cheyenne	From Delaware Indian word meaning "land of vast plains"
	District of Columbia		572,059	67		Named after Christopher Columbus

* Census 2000 figures

Almanac

Facts About the Western Hemisphere

Country	Population*	Area (sq. mi.)	Capital	Origin of Country Name
North America				
Antigua and Barbuda	66,970	171	St. Johns	Named for the Church of Santa María la Antigua in Seville, Spain
Bahamas	297,852	5,386	Nassau	Spanish, *bajamar*, "shallow water"
Barbados	275,330	166	Bridgetown	Means "bearded"—probably referring to the beard like vines early explorers found on its trees
Belize	256,062	8,867	Belmopan	Mayan, "muddy water"
Canada	31,592,805	3,851,809	Ottawa	Huron-Iroquois, *kanata*, "village" or "community"
Costa Rica	3,773,057	19,730	San José	Spanish, "rich coast"
Cuba	11,184,023	42,803	Havana	Origin unknown
Dominica	70,786	289	Roseau	Latin, *dies dominica*, "Day of the Lord"
Dominican Republic	8,581,477	18,815	Santo Domingo	Named after the capital city
El Salvador	6,237,662	8,124	San Salvador	Spanish, "the Savior"
Grenada	89,227	131	St. George's	Origin unknown
Guatemala	12,974,361	42,042	Guatemala City	Indian, "land of trees"
Haiti	6,964,549	10,714	Port-au-Prince	Indian, "land of mountains"
Honduras	6,406,052	43,277	Tegucigalpa	Spanish, "profundities" —probably referring to the depth of offshore waters
Jamaica	2,665,636	4,243	Kingston	Arawak, *xamayca*, "land of wood and water"
Mexico	101,879,171	761,602	Mexico City	Aztec, *mexliapan*, "lake of the moon"
Nicaragua	4,918,393	49,998	Managua	from *Nicarao*, the name of an Indian chief

Country	Population*	Area (sq. mi.)	Capital	Origin of Country Name
Panama	2,845,647	30,193	Panama City	From an Indian village's name
St. Kitts-Nevis	38,756	96	Basseterre	Named by Christopher Columbus—Kitts for St. Christopher, a Catholic saint; Nevis, for a cloud-topped peak that looked like *las nieves*, "the snows"
St. Lucia	158,178	238	Castries	Named by Christopher Columbus for a Catholic saint
St. Vincent and Grenadines	115,942	150	Kingstown	May have been named by Christopher Columbus for a Catholic saint
Trinidad and Tobago	1,169,682	1,980	Port of Spain	Trinidad, from the Spanish word for "trinity"; Tobago, named for tobacco because the island has the shape of a person smoking a pipe
United States of America	281,421,906	3,537,441	Washington, D.C.	Named after the explorer Amerigo Vespucci

South America

Country	Population*	Area (sq. mi.)	Capital	Origin of Country Name
Argentina	37,384,816	1,068,296	Buenos Aires	Latin, *argentum*, "silver"
Bolivia	8,300,463	424,162	La Paz/Sucre	Named after Simón Bolívar, the famed liberator
Brazil	174,468,575	3,286,470	Brasília	Named after a native tree that the Portuguese called "bresel wood"
Chile	15,328,467	292,257	Santiago	Indian, *chilli*, "where the land ends"
Colombia	40,349,388	439,735	Bogotá	Named after Christopher Columbus
Ecuador	13,183,978	109,483	Quito	From the Spanish word for *equator*, referring to the country's location
Guyana	697,181	83,000	Georgetown	Indian, "land of waters"
Paraguay	5,734,139	157,043	Asunción	Named after the Paraguay River, which flows through it
Peru	27,483,864	496,222	Lima	Quechua, "land of abundance"
Suriname	433,998	63,039	Paramaribo	From an Indian word, *surinen*
Uruguay	3,360,105	68,039	Montevideo	Named after the Uruguay River, which flows through it
Venezuela	23,916,810	352,143	Caracas	Spanish, "Little Venice"

*Census 2000 figures

Almanac

Facts About the Presidents

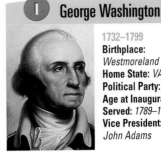

George Washington ①

1732–1799
Birthplace:
Westmoreland County, VA
Home State: *VA*
Political Party: *None*
Age at Inauguration: *57*
Served: *1789–1797*
Vice President:
John Adams

John Adams ②

1735–1826
Birthplace: *Braintree, MA*
Home State: *MA*
Political Party: *Federalist*
Age at Inauguration: *61*
Served: *1797–1801*
Vice President:
Thomas Jefferson

Thomas Jefferson ③

1743–1826
Birthplace:
Albemarle County, VA
Home State: *VA*
Political Party:
Democratic-Republican
Age at Inauguration: *57*
Served: *1801–1809*
Vice Presidents:
Aaron Burr,
George Clinton

James Madison ④

1751–1836
Birthplace:
Port Conway, VA
Home State: *VA*
Political Party:
Democratic-Republican
Age at Inauguration: *57*
Served: *1809–1817*
Vice Presidents:
George Clinton,
Elbridge Gerry

James Monroe ⑤

1758–1831
Birthplace:
Westmoreland County, VA
Home State: *VA*
Political Party:
Democratic-Republican
Age at Inauguration: *58*
Served: *1817–1825*
Vice President:
Daniel D. Tompkins

John Quincy Adams ⑥

1767–1848
Birthplace: *Braintree, MA*
Home State: *MA*
Political Party:
Democratic-Republican
Age at Inauguration: *57*
Served: *1825–1829*
Vice President:
John C. Calhoun

Andrew Jackson ⑦

1767–1845
Birthplace:
Waxhaw settlement, SC
Home State: *TN*
Political Party:
Democratic
Age at Inauguration: *61*
Served: *1829–1837*
Vice Presidents:
John C. Calhoun,
Martin Van Buren

Martin Van Buren ⑧

1782–1862
Birthplace: *Kinderhook, NY*
Home State: *NY*
Political Party:
Democratic
Age at Inauguration: *54*
Served: *1837–1841*
Vice President:
Richard M. Johnson

William H. Harrison ⑨

1773–1841
Birthplace: *Berkeley, VA*
Home State: *OH*
Political Party: *Whig*
Age at Inauguration: *68*
Served: *1841*
Vice President:
John Tyler

John Tyler ⑩

1790–1862
Birthplace: *Greenway, VA*
Home State: *VA*
Political Party: *Whig*
Age at Inauguration: *51*
Served: *1841–1845*
Vice President: *none*

James K. Polk ⑪

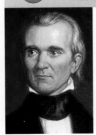

1795–1849
Birthplace:
near Pineville, NC
Home State: *TN*
Political Party:
Democratic
Age at Inauguration: *49*
Served: *1845–1849*
Vice President:
George M. Dallas

Zachary Taylor ⑫

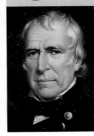

1784–1850
Birthplace:
Orange County, VA
Home State: *LA*
Political Party: *Whig*
Age at Inauguration: *64*
Served: *1849–1850*
Vice President:
Millard Fillmore

Millard Fillmore ⑬

1800–1874
Birthplace: *Locke, NY*
Home State: *NY*
Political Party: *Whig*
Age at Inauguration: *50*
Served: *1850–1853*
Vice President: *none*

Home State refers to the state of residence when elected.

14 Franklin Pierce

1804–1869
Birthplace: *Hillsboro, NH*
Home State: *NH*
Political Party:
Democratic
Age at Inauguration: *48*
Served: *1853–1857*
Vice President:
William R. King

15 James Buchanan

1791–1868
Birthplace:
near Mercersburg, PA
Home State: *PA*
Political Party:
Democratic
Age at Inauguration: *65*
Served: *1857–1861*
Vice President:
John C. Breckinridge

16 Abraham Lincoln

1809–1865
Birthplace:
near Hodgenville, KY
Home State: *IL*
Political Party:
Republican
Age at Inauguration: *52*
Served: *1861–1865*
Vice Presidents:
*Hannibal Hamlin,
Andrew Johnson*

17 Andrew Johnson

1808–1875
Birthplace: *Raleigh, NC*
Home State: *TN*
Political Party:
National Union
Age at Inauguration: *56*
Served: *1865–1869*
Vice President: *none*

18 Ulysses S. Grant

1822–1885
Birthplace:
Point Pleasant, OH
Home State: *IL*
Political Party:
Republican
Age at Inauguration: *46*
Served: *1869–1877*
Vice Presidents:
*Schuyler Colfax,
Henry Wilson*

19 Rutherford B. Hayes

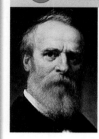

1822–1893
Birthplace:
near Delaware, OH
Home State: *OH*
Political Party:
Republican
Age at Inauguration: *54*
Served: *1877–1881*
Vice President:
William A. Wheeler

20 James A. Garfield

1831–1881
Birthplace: *Orange, OH*
Home State: *OH*
Political Party:
Republican
Age at Inauguration: *49*
Served: *1881*
Vice President:
Chester A. Arthur

21 Chester A. Arthur

1829–1886
Birthplace: *Fairfield, VT*
Home State: *NY*
Political Party:
Republican
Age at Inauguration: *51*
Served: *1881–1885*
Vice President: *none*

22 Grover Cleveland

1837–1908
Birthplace: *Caldwell, NJ*
Home State: *NY*
Political Party:
Democratic
Age at Inauguration: *47*
Served: *1885–1889*
Vice President:
Thomas A. Hendricks

23 Benjamin Harrison

1833–1901
Birthplace: *North Bend,
OH*
Home State: *IN*
Political Party:
Republican
Age at Inauguration: *55*
Served: *1889–1893*
Vice President:
Levi P. Morton

24 Grover Cleveland

1837–1908
Birthplace: *Caldwell, NJ*
Home State: *NY*
Political Party:
Democratic
Age at Inauguration: *55*
Served: *1893–1897*
Vice President:
Adlai E. Stevenson

25 William McKinley

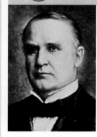

1843–1901
Birthplace: *Niles, OH*
Home State: *OH*
Political Party:
Republican
Age at Inauguration: *54*
Served: *1897–1901*
Vice Presidents:
*Garret A. Hobart,
Theodore Roosevelt*

26 Theodore Roosevelt

1858–1919
Birthplace: *New York, NY*
Home State: *NY*
Political Party:
Republican
Age at Inauguration: *42*
Served: *1901–1909*
Vice President:
Charles W. Fairbanks

27 William H. Taft

1857–1930
Birthplace: *Cincinnati, OH*
Home State: *OH*
Political Party:
Republican
Age at Inauguration: *51*
Served: *1909–1913*
Vice President:
James S. Sherman

28 Woodrow Wilson

1856–1924
Birthplace: *Staunton, VA*
Home State: *NJ*
Political Party:
Democratic
Age at Inauguration: *56*
Served: *1913–1921*
Vice President:
Thomas R. Marshall

29 Warren G. Harding

1865–1923
Birthplace:
Blooming Grove, OH
Home State: *OH*
Political Party:
Republican
Age at Inauguration: *55*
Served: *1921–1923*
Vice President:
Calvin Coolidge

30 Calvin Coolidge

1872–1933
Birthplace:
Plymouth Notch, VT
Home State: *MA*
Political Party:
Republican
Age at Inauguration: *51*
Served: *1923–1929*
Vice President:
Charles G. Dawes

31 Herbert Hoover

1874–1964
Birthplace: *West Branch, IA*
Home State: *CA*
Political Party:
Republican
Age at Inauguration: *54*
Served: *1929–1933*
Vice President:
Charles Curtis

32 Franklin D. Roosevelt

1882–1945
Birthplace: *Hyde Park, NY*
Home State: *NY*
Political Party:
Democratic
Age at Inauguration: *51*
Served: *1933–1945*
Vice Presidents:
John N. Garner,
Henry A. Wallace,
Harry S. Truman

33 Harry S. Truman

1884–1972
Birthplace: *Lamar, MO*
Home State: *MO*
Political Party:
Democratic
Age at Inauguration: *60*
Served: *1945–1953*
Vice President:
Alben W. Barkley

34 Dwight D. Eisenhower

1890-1969
Birthplace: *Denison, TX*
Home State: *NY*
Political Party:
Republican
Age at Inauguration: *62*
Served: *1953–1961*
Vice President:
Richard M. Nixon

35 John F. Kennedy

1917–1963
Birthplace: *Brookline, MA*
Home State: *MA*
Political Party:
Democratic
Age at Inauguration: *43*
Served: *1961–1963*
Vice President:
Lyndon B. Johnson

36 Lyndon B. Johnson

1908–1973
Birthplace:
near Stonewall, TX
Home State: *TX*
Political Party:
Democratic
Age at Inauguration: *55*
Served: *1963–1969*
Vice President:
Hubert H. Humphrey

37 Richard M. Nixon

1913–1994
Birthplace: *Yorba Linda, CA*
Home State: *NY*
Political Party:
Republican
Age at Inauguration: *56*
Served: *1969–1974*
Vice Presidents:
Spiro T. Agnew,
Gerald R. Ford

38 Gerald R. Ford

1913–
Birthplace: *Omaha, NE*
Home State: *MI*
Political Party:
Republican
Age at Inauguration: *61*
Served: *1974–1977*
Vice President:
Nelson A. Rockefeller

39 Jimmy Carter

1924–
Birthplace: *Plains, GA*
Home State: *GA*
Political Party:
Democratic
Age at Inauguration: *52*
Served: *1977–1981*
Vice President:
Walter F. Mondale

40 Ronald W. Reagan

1911–
Birthplace: *Tampico, IL*
Home State: *CA*
Political Party:
Republican
Age at Inauguration: *69*
Served: *1981–1989*
Vice President:
George Bush

41 George Bush

1924–
Birthplace: *Milton, MA*
Home State: *TX*
Political Party:
Republican
Age at Inauguration: *64*
Served: *1989–1993*
Vice President:
Dan Quayle

42 William Clinton

1946–
Birthplace: *Hope, AR*
Home State: *AR*
Political Party:
Democratic
Age at Inauguration: *46*
Served: *1993–2001*
Vice President:
Albert Gore

43 George W. Bush

1946–
Birthplace: *New Haven, CT*
Home State: *TX*
Political Party:
Republican
Age at Inauguration: *54*
Served: *2001–*
Vice President:
Richard Cheney

American Documents

THE DECLARATION OF INDEPENDENCE

In Congress, July 4, 1776.
The unanimous Declaration of the
thirteen United States of America,

When in the Course of human events it becomes necessary for one people to dissolve the political bands which have connected them with another, and to assume among the powers of the earth, the separate and equal station to which the Laws of Nature and of Nature's God entitle them, a decent respect to the opinions of mankind requires that they should declare the causes which impel them to the separation.

We hold these truths to be self-evident, that all men are created equal, that they are endowed by their Creator with certain unalienable Rights, that among these are Life, Liberty and the pursuit of Happiness.
That to secure these rights, Governments are instituted among Men, deriving their just powers from the consent of the governed,
That whenever any Form of Government becomes destructive of these ends, it is the Right of the People to alter or to abolish it, and to institute new Government, laying its foundation on such principles and organizing its powers in such form, as to them shall seem most likely to effect their Safety and Happiness. Prudence, indeed, will dictate that Governments long established should not be changed for light and transient causes; and accordingly all experience hath shown, that mankind are more disposed to suffer, while evils are sufferable, than to right themselves by abolishing the forms to which they are accustomed. But when a long train of abuses and usurpations, pursuing invariably the same Object evinces a design to reduce them under absolute Despotism, it is their right, it is their duty, to throw off such Government, and to provide new Guards for their future security.

Such has been the patient sufferance of these Colonies; and such is now the necessity which constrains them to alter their former Systems of Government. The history of the present King of Great Britain is a history of repeated injuries and usurpations, all having in direct object the establishment of an absolute Tyranny over these States. To prove this, let Facts be submitted to a candid world.

He has refused his Assent to Laws, the most wholesome and necessary for the public good.
He has forbidden his Governors to pass Laws of immediate and pressing importance, unless suspended in their operation till his Assent should be obtained; and when so suspended, he has utterly neglected to attend to them.

Preamble
The Preamble tells why the Declaration was written. It states that the members of the Continental Congress believed the colonies had the right to break away from Britain and become a free nation.

A Statement of Rights
The opening part of the Declaration tells what rights the members of the Continental Congress believed that all people have. All people are equal in having the rights to life, liberty, and the pursuit of happiness. The main purpose of a government is to protect the rights of the people who consent to be governed by it. These rights cannot be taken away. When a government tries to take these rights away from the people, the people have the right to change the government or do away with it. The people can then form a new government that respects these rights.

Charges Against the King
The Declaration lists more than 25 charges against the king. He was mistreating the colonists, the Declaration says, in order to gain total control over the colonies.

The king rejected many laws passed by colonial legislatures.

He has refused to pass other Laws for the accommodation of large districts of people, unless those people would relinquish the right of Representation in the Legislature, a right inestimable to them and formidable to tyrants only.

The king made the colonial legislatures meet at unusual times and places.

He has called together legislative bodies at places unusual, uncomfortable, and distant from the depository of their public Records, for the sole purpose of fatiguing them into compliance with his measures.

The king and the king's governors often dissolved colonial legislatures for disobeying their orders.

He has dissolved Representative Houses repeatedly, for opposing with manly firmness his invasions on the rights of the people.

He has refused for a long time, after such dissolutions, to cause others to be elected; whereby the Legislative powers, incapable of Annihilation, have returned to the People at large for their exercise; the State remaining in the mean time exposed to all the dangers of invasion from without, and convulsions within.

The king stopped people from moving to the colonies and into the western lands.

He has endeavored to prevent the population of these States; for that purpose obstructing the Laws for Naturalization of Foreigners; refusing to pass others to encourage their migrations hither, and raising the conditions of new Appropriations of Lands.

The king prevented the colonists from choosing their own judges. The king chose the judges, and they served only as long as the king was satisfied with them.

He has obstructed the Administration of Justice, by refusing his Assent to Laws for establishing Judiciary powers.

He has made Judges dependent on his Will alone, for the tenure of their offices, and the amount and payment of their salaries.

The king hired people to help collect taxes in the colonies.

He has erected a multitude of New Offices, and sent hither swarms of Officers to harass our people, and eat out their substance.

The king appointed General Thomas Gage, commander of Britain's military forces in the Americas, as governor of Massachusetts.

He has kept among us, in times of peace, Standing Armies without the Consent of our legislatures.

He has affected to render the Military independent of and superior to the Civil power.

He has combined with others to subject us to a jurisdiction foreign to our constitution, and unacknowledged by our laws; giving his Assent to their Acts of pretended Legislation:

For quartering large bodies of armed troops among us:

The king expected the colonists to provide housing and supplies for the British soldiers in the colonies.

For protecting them, by a mock Trial, from punishment for any Murders which they should commit on the Inhabitants of these States:

For cutting off our Trade with all parts of the world:

The king and Parliament demanded that colonists pay many taxes, even though the colonists did not agree to pay them.

For imposing Taxes on us without our Consent:

Colonists were tried by British naval courts, which had no juries.

For depriving us in many cases, of the benefits of Trial by Jury:

Colonists accused of treason were sent to Britain to be tried.

For transporting us beyond Seas to be tried for pretended offenses:

For abolishing the free System of English Laws in a neighboring Province, establishing therein an Arbitrary government, and enlarging its Boundaries so as to render it at once an example and fit instrument for introducing the same absolute rule into these Colonies:

For taking away our Charters, abolishing our most valuable Laws, and altering fundamentally the Forms of our Governments:

For suspending our own Legislatures, and declaring themselves invested with power to legislate for us in all cases whatsoever.

He has abdicated Government here, by declaring us out of his Protection and waging War against us.

He has plundered our seas, ravaged our Coasts, burnt our towns, and destroyed the lives of our people.

He is at this time transporting large Armies of foreign Mercenaries to complete the works of death, desolation and tyranny, already begun with circumstances of Cruelty & perfidy scarcely paralleled in the most barbarous ages, and totally unworthy the Head of a civilized nation.

He has constrained our fellow Citizens taken Captive on the high Seas to bear Arms against their Country, to become the executioners of their friends and Brethren, or to fall themselves by their Hands.

He has excited domestic insurrections amongst us, and has endeavored to bring on the inhabitants of our frontiers, the merciless Indian Savages, whose known rule of warfare, is an undistinguished destruction of all ages, sexes and conditions.

In every stage of these Oppressions We have Petitioned for Redress in the most humble terms: Our repeated Petitions have been answered only by repeated injury. A Prince, whose character is thus marked by every act which may define a Tyrant, is unfit to be the ruler of a free people.

Nor have We been wanting in attentions to our British brethren. We have warned them from time to time of attempts by their legislature to extend an unwarrantable jurisdiction over us. We have reminded them of the circumstances of our emigration and settlement here. We have appealed to their native justice and magnanimity, and we have conjured them by the ties of our common kindred to disavow these usurpations, which, would inevitably interrupt our connections and correspondence. They too have been deaf to the voice of justice and of consanguinity. We must, therefore, acquiesce in the necessity, which denounces our Separation, and hold them, as we hold the rest of mankind, Enemies in War, in Peace Friends.

We, therefore, the Representatives of the united States of America, in General Congress, Assembled, appealing to the Supreme Judge of the world for the rectitude of our intentions, do, in the Name, and by Authority of the good People of these Colonies, solemnly publish and declare, That these United Colonies are, and of Right ought to be Free and Independent States; that they are Absolved from all Allegiance to the British Crown, and that all political connection between them and the State of Great Britain, is and ought to be totally dissolved; and that as Free and Independent States, they have full Power to levy War, conclude Peace, contract Alliances, establish Commerce, and to do all other Acts and Things which Independent States may of right do.

The king allowed General Gage to take military action to enforce British laws in the colonies.

The king hired Hessian mercenaries and sent them to fight the colonists.

The king's governor in Virginia promised freedom to all enslaved people who joined the British forces. The British also planned to use Indians to fight the colonists.

The Declaration explained the efforts of the colonists to avoid separation from Britain. But the colonists said that the king had ignored their protests. Because of the many charges against the king, the writers of the Declaration concluded that he was not fit to rule free people.

A Statement of Independence The writers declared that the colonies were now free and independent states. All ties with Britain were broken. As free and independent states, they had the right to make war and peace, to trade, and to do all the things free countries could do.

To support the Declaration, the signers promised one another their lives, their fortunes, and their honor.

And for the support of this Declaration, with a firm reliance on the protection of divine Providence, we mutually pledge to each other our Lives, our Fortunes and our sacred Honor.

John Hancock

NEW HAMPSHIRE
Josiah Bartlett
William Whipple
Matthew Thornton

MASSACHUSETTS
John Adams
Samuel Adams
Robert Treat Paine
Elbridge Gerry

NEW YORK
William Floyd
Philip Livingston
Francis Lewis
Lewis Morris

RHODE ISLAND
Stephen Hopkins
William Ellery

NEW JERSEY
Richard Stockton
John Witherspoon
Francis Hopkinson
John Hart
Abraham Clark

PENNSYLVANIA
Robert Morris
Benjamin Rush
Benjamin Franklin
John Morton
George Clymer
James Smith
George Taylor
James Wilson
George Ross

DELAWARE
Caesar Rodney
George Read
Thomas McKean

MARYLAND
Samuel Chase
William Paca
Thomas Stone
Charles Carroll of Carrollton

NORTH CAROLINA
William Hopper
Joseph Hewes
John Penn

VIRGINIA
George Wythe
Richard Henry Lee
Thomas Jefferson
Benjamin Harrison
Thomas Nelson, Jr.
Francis Lightfoot Lee
Carter Braxton

SOUTH CAROLINA
Edward Rutledge
Thomas Heyward, Jr.
Thomas Lynch, Jr.
Arthur Middleton

CONNECTICUT
Roger Sherman
Samuel Huntington
William Williams
Oliver Wolcott

GEORGIA
Button Gwinnett
Lyman Hall
George Walton

Members of the Continental Congress stated that copies of the Declaration should be sent to all Committees of Correspondence and to commanders of the troops and that it should be read in every state.

Resolved, That copies of the Declaration be sent to the several assemblies, conventions, and committees, or councils of safety, and to the several commanding officers of the continental troops; that it be proclaimed in each of the United States, at the head of the army.

THE CONSTITUTION OF
THE UNITED STATES OF AMERICA

Preamble*

We the people of the United States, in order to form a more perfect Union, establish justice, insure domestic tranquillity, provide for the common defense, promote the general welfare, and secure the blessings of liberty to ourselves and our posterity, do ordain and establish this Constitution for the United States of America.

ARTICLE I
THE LEGISLATIVE BRANCH

SECTION 1. CONGRESS

All legislative powers herein granted shall be vested in a Congress of the United States, which shall consist of a Senate and House of Representatives.

SECTION 2. THE HOUSE OF REPRESENTATIVES

(1) The House of Representatives shall be composed of members chosen every second year by the people of the several states, and the electors in each state shall have the qualifications requisite for electors of the most numerous branch of the state legislature.

(2) No person shall be a Representative who shall not have attained to the age of twenty-five years, and been seven years a citizen of the United States, and who shall not, when elected, be an inhabitant of that state in which he shall be chosen.

(3) Representatives [*and direct taxes*]** shall be apportioned among the several states which may be included within this Union, according to their respective numbers [*which shall be determined by adding to the whole number of free persons, including those bound to service for a term of years, and excluding Indians not taxed, three-fifths of all other persons*]. The actual enumeration shall be made within three years after the first meeting of the Congress of the United States, and within every subsequent term of ten years, in such manner as they shall by law direct. The number of Representatives shall not exceed one for every 30,000, but each state shall have at least one Representative [; *and until such enumeration shall be made, the State of New Hampshire shall be entitled to choose three; Massachusetts eight; Rhode Island and Providence Plantations one; Connecticut five; New York six; New Jersey four; Pennsylvania eight; Delaware one; Maryland six; Virginia ten; North Carolina five; South Carolina five; and Georgia three*].

*Titles have been added to make the Constitution easier to read. They did not appear in the original document.

**The parts of the Constitution that no longer apply are printed in italics within brackets [ ]. These portions have been changed or set aside by later amendments.

Preamble
The introduction to the Constitution states the purposes and principles for writing it. The writers wanted to set up a fairer form of government and to secure peace and freedom for themselves and for future generations.

Congress
Congress has the authority to make laws. Congress is made up of two groups of lawmakers: the Senate and the House of Representatives.

(1) Election and Term of Members
Qualified voters are to elect members of the House of Representatives every two years. Each member of the House of Representatives must meet certain requirements.

(2) Qualifications
Members of the House of Representatives must be at least 25 years old. They must have been citizens of the United States for at least seven years. They must live in the state that they will represent.

(3) Determining Apportionment
The number of representatives a state may have depends on the number of people living in each state. Every ten years the federal government must take a census, or count, of the population in every state. Every state will have at least one representative.

(4) Filling Vacancies
If there is a vacancy in representation in Congress, the governor of the state involved must call a special election to fill it.

(5) Special Authority
The House of Representatives chooses a Speaker as its presiding officer. It also chooses other officers as appropriate. The House is the only government branch that may impeach, or charge, an official in the executive branch or a judge of the federal courts for failing to carry out his or her duties. These cases are tried in the Senate.

(1) Number, Term, and Selection of Members
Each state is represented by two senators. Until Amendment 17 was passed, state legislatures chose the senators for their states. Each senator serves a six-year term and has one vote in Congress.

(2) Overlapping Terms and Filling Vacancies
One-third of the senators are elected every two years for a six-year term. This grouping allows at least two-thirds of the experienced senators to remain in the Senate after each election. Amendment 17 permits state governors to appoint a replacement to fill a vacancy until the next election is held.

(3) Qualifications
Senators must be at least 30 years old. They must have been citizens of the United States for at least nine years. They must live in the state that they will represent.

(4) President of the Senate
The Vice President acts as chief officer of the Senate but does not vote unless there is a tie.

(5) Other Officers
The Senate chooses its other officers and a president pro tempore, who serves if the Vice President is not present or if the Vice President becomes President. *Pro tempore* is a Latin term meaning "for the time being."

---

(4) When vacancies happen in the representation from any state, the executive authority thereof shall issue writs of election to fill such vacancies.

(5) The House of Representatives shall choose their Speaker and other officers; and shall have the sole power of impeachment.

SECTION 3. THE SENATE

(1) The Senate of the United States shall be composed of two Senators from each state [*chosen by the legislature thereof*], for six years, and each Senator shall have one vote.

(2) [*Immediately after they shall be assembled in consequence of the first election, they shall be divided as equally as may be into three classes. The seats of the Senators of the first class shall be vacated at the expiration of the second year, of the second class at the expiration of the fourth year, and of the third class at the expiration of the sixth year, so that one-third may be chosen every second year; and if vacancies happen by resignation, or otherwise, during the recess of the legislature of any state, the executive thereof may make temporary appointments until the next meeting of the legislature, which shall then fill such vacancies.*]

(3) No person shall be a Senator who shall not have attained to the age of thirty years, and been nine years a citizen of the United States, and who shall not, when elected, be an inhabitant of that state for which he shall be chosen.

(4) The Vice President of the United States shall be President of the Senate, but shall have no vote, unless they be equally divided.

(5) The Senate shall choose their other officers, and also a President *pro tempore*, in the absence of the Vice President, or when he shall exercise the office of the President of the United States.

(6) The Senate shall have the sole power to try all impeachments. When sitting for that purpose, they shall be on oath or affirmation. When the President of the United States is tried, the Chief Justice shall preside; and no person shall be convicted without the concurrence of two-thirds of the members present.

(7) Judgment in cases of impeachment shall not extend further than to removal from office, and disqualification to hold and enjoy any office of honor, trust, or profit under the United States; but the party convicted shall nevertheless be liable and subject to indictment, trial, judgment and punishment, according to law.

SECTION 4. ELECTIONS AND MEETINGS

(1) The times, places, and manner of holding elections for Senators and Representatives shall be prescribed in each state by the legislature thereof; but the Congress may at any time by law make or alter such regulations, [*except as to the places of choosing Senators*].

(2) The Congress shall assemble at least once in every year, [*and such meeting shall be on the first Monday in December, unless they shall by law appoint a different day*].

SECTION 5. RULES OF PROCEDURE

(1) Each house shall be the judge of the elections, returns and qualifications of its own members, and a majority of each shall constitute a quorum to do business; but a smaller number may adjourn from day to day, and may be authorized to compel the attendance of absent members, in such manner and under such penalties as each house may provide.

(2) Each house may determine the rules of its proceedings, punish its members for disorderly behavior, and, with the concurrence of two-thirds, expel a member.

(3) Each house shall keep a journal of its proceedings, and from time to time publish the same, excepting such parts as may in their judgment require secrecy; and the yeas and nays of the members of either house on any question shall, at the desire of one-fifth of those present, be entered on the journal.

(6) Impeachment Trials
If the House of Representatives votes articles of impeachment, the Senate holds a trial. A two-thirds vote is required to convict a person who has been impeached.

(7) Penalty for Conviction
If convicted in an impeachment case, an official is removed from office and may never hold office in the United States government again. The convicted person may also be tried in a regular court of law for any crimes.

(1) Holding Elections
Each state makes its own rules about electing senators and representatives. However, Congress may change these rules at any time. Today congressional elections are held on the Tuesday after the first Monday in November, in even-numbered years.

(2) Meetings
The Constitution requires Congress to meet at least once a year. That day is the first Monday in December, unless Congress sets a different day. Amendment 20 changed this date to January 3.

(1) Organization
Each house of Congress may decide if its members have been elected fairly and are able to hold office. Each house may do business only when a quorum—a majority of its members—is present. By less than a majority vote, each house may compel absent members to attend.

(2) Rules
Each house may decide its own rules for doing business, punish its members, and expel a member from office if two-thirds of the members agree.

(3) Journal
The Constitution requires each house to keep records of its activities and to publish these records from time to time. The House Journal and the Senate Journal are published at the end of each session. How each member voted must be recorded if one-fifth of the members ask for this to be done.

(4) Adjournment
When Congress is in session, neither house may take a recess for more than three days without the consent of the other.

(1) Pay and Privileges
Members of Congress set their own salaries, which are to be paid by the federal government. Members cannot be arrested or sued for anything they say while Congress is in session. This privilege is called congressional immunity. Members of Congress may be arrested while Congress is in session only if they commit a crime.

(2) Restrictions
Members of Congress may not hold any other federal office while serving in Congress. A member may not resign from office and then take a government position created during that member's term of office or for which the pay has been increased during that member's term of office.

(1) Money-Raising Bills
All money-raising bills must be introduced first in the House of Representatives, but the Senate may suggest changes.

(2) How a Bill Becomes a Law
After a bill has been passed by both the House of Representatives and the Senate, it must be sent to the President. If the President approves and signs the bill, it becomes law. The President can also veto, or refuse to sign, the bill. Congress can override a veto by passing the bill again by a two-thirds majority. If the President does not act within ten days, two things may happen. If Congress is still in session, the bill becomes a law. If Congress ends its session within that same ten-day period, the bill does not become a law.

(3) Orders and Resolutions
Congress can pass orders and resolutions, some of which have the same effect as a law. Congress may decide on its own when to end the session. Other such acts must be signed or vetoed by the President.

(4) Neither house, during the session of Congress, shall, without the consent of the other, adjourn for more than three days, nor to any other place than that in which the two houses shall be sitting.

SECTION 6. PRIVILEGES AND RESTRICTIONS

(1) The Senators and Representatives shall receive a compensation for their services, to be ascertained by law and paid out of the Treasury of the United States. They shall in all cases, except treason, felony, and breach of the peace, be privileged from arrest during their attendance at the session of their respective houses, and in going to and returning from the same; and for any speech or debate in either house, they shall not be questioned in any other place.

(2) No Senator or Representative shall, during the time for which he was elected, be appointed to any civil office under the authority of the United States, which shall have been created, or the emoluments whereof shall have been increased, during such time; and no person holding any office under the United States shall be a member of either house during his continuance in office.

SECTION 7. MAKING LAWS

(1) All bills for raising revenue shall originate in the House of Representatives; but the Senate may propose or concur with amendments as on other bills.

(2) Every bill which shall have passed the House of Representatives and the Senate shall, before it become a law, be presented to the President of the United States; if he approve, he shall sign it, but if not, he shall return it, with his objections, to that house in which it shall have originated, who shall enter the objections at large on their journal, and proceed to reconsider it. If after such reconsideration two-thirds of that house shall agree to pass the bill, it shall be sent, together with the objections, to the other house, by which it shall likewise be reconsidered, and, if approved by two-thirds of that house, it shall become a law. But in all such cases the votes of both houses shall be determined by yeas and nays, and the names of the persons voting for and against the bill shall be entered on the journal of each house respectively. If any bill shall not be returned by the President within ten days (Sundays excepted) after it shall have been presented to him, the same bill shall be a law, in like manner as if he had signed it, unless the Congress by their adjournment prevent its return, in which case it shall not be a law.

(3) Every order, resolution, or vote to which the concurrence of the Senate and House of Representatives may be necessary (except on a question of adjournment) shall be presented to the President of the United States; and before the same shall take effect, shall be approved by him, or being disapproved by him, shall be repassed by two-thirds of the Senate and House of Representatives, according to the rules and limitations prescribed in the case of a bill.

SECTION 8. POWERS DELEGATED TO CONGRESS

The Congress shall have power

(1) To lay and collect taxes, duties, imposts and excises, to pay the debts and provide for the common defense and general welfare of the United States; but all duties, imposts and excises shall be uniform throughout the United States;

(2) To borrow money on the credit of the United States;

(3) To regulate commerce with foreign nations, and among the several states and with the Indian tribes;

(4) To establish an uniform rule of naturalization, and uniform laws on the subject of bankruptcies throughout the United States;

(5) To coin money, regulate the value thereof, and of foreign coin, and fix the standard of weights and measures;

(6) To provide for the punishment of counterfeiting the securities and current coin of the United States;

(7) To establish post offices and post roads;

(8) To promote the progress of science and useful arts by securing for limited times to authors and inventors the exclusive right to their respective writings and discoveries;

(9) To constitute tribunals inferior to the Supreme Court;

(10) To define and punish piracies and felonies committed on the high seas and offenses against the law of nations;

---

(1) Taxation
Only Congress has the authority to raise money to pay debts, defend the United States, and provide services for its people by collecting taxes or tariffs on foreign goods. All taxes must be applied equally in all states.

(2) Borrowing Money
Congress may borrow money for national use. This is usually done by selling government bonds.

(3) Commerce
Congress can control trade with other countries and between states.

(4) Naturalization and Bankruptcy
Congress decides what requirements people from other countries must meet to become United States citizens. Congress can also pass laws to protect people who are bankrupt, or cannot pay their debts.

(5) Coins, Weights, and Measures
Congress can coin money and decide its value. Congress also decides on the system of weights and measures to be used throughout the nation.

(6) Counterfeiting
Congress may pass laws to punish people who make fake money, bonds, or stamps.

(7) Postal Service
Congress can build post offices and make rules about the postal system and the roads used for mail delivery.

(8) Copyrights and Patents
Congress can issue patents and copyrights to inventors and authors to protect the ownership of their works.

(9) Federal Courts
Congress can establish a system of federal courts under the Supreme Court.

(10) Crimes at Sea
Congress can pass laws to punish people for crimes committed at sea. Congress may also punish United States citizens for breaking international law.

(11) Declaring War
Only Congress can declare war.

(12) The Army
Congress can establish an army, but it cannot vote enough money to support it for more than two years. This part of the Constitution was written to keep the army under civilian control.

(13) The Navy
Congress can establish a navy and vote enough money to support it for as long as necessary. No time limit was set because people thought the navy was less of a threat to people's liberty than the army was.

(14) Military Regulations
Congress makes the rules that guide and govern all the armed forces.

(15) The Militia
Each state has its own militia, now known as the National Guard. The National Guard can be called into federal service by the President, as authorized by Congress, to enforce laws, to stop uprisings against the government, or to protect the people in case of floods, earthquakes, and other disasters.

(16) Control of the Militia
Congress helps each state support the National Guard. Each state may appoint its own officers and train its own guard according to rules set by Congress.

(17) National Capital and Other Property
Congress may pass laws to govern the nation's capital (Washington, D.C.) and any land owned by the government.

(18) Other Necessary Laws
The Constitution allows Congress to make laws that are necessary to enforce the powers listed in Article I. This clause has two conflicting interpretations. One is that Congress can only do what is absolutely necessary to carry out the powers listed in Article I. The other is that Congress may stretch its authority in order to carry out these powers, but not beyond limits established by the Constitution.

(11) To declare war, grant letters of marque and reprisal, and make rules concerning captures on land and water;

(12) To raise and support armies, but no appropriation of money to that use shall be for a longer term than two years;

(13) To provide and maintain a navy;

(14) To make rules for the government and regulation of the land and naval forces;

(15) To provide for calling forth the militia to execute the laws of the Union, suppress insurrections and repel invasions;

(16) To provide for organizing, arming, and disciplining the militia, and for governing such part of them as may be employed in the service of the United States, reserving to the states, respectively, the appointment of the officers, and the authority of training the militia according to the discipline prescribed by Congress;

(17) To exercise exclusive legislation in all cases whatsoever, over such district (not exceeding ten miles square) as may, by cession of particular states, and the acceptance of Congress, become the seat of government of the United States, and to exercise like authority over all places purchased by the consent of the legislature of the state in which the same shall be, for the erection of forts, magazines, arsenals, dock-yards, and other needful buildings; —and

(18) To make all laws which shall be necessary and proper for carrying into execution the foregoing powers, and all other powers vested by this Constitution in the government of the United States, or in any department or officer thereof.

SECTION 9. POWERS DENIED TO CONGRESS

(1) [*The migration or importation of such persons as any of the states now existing shall think proper to admit shall not be prohibited by the Congress prior to the year 1808; but a tax or duty may be imposed on such importation, not exceeding 10 dollars for each person.*]

(2) The privilege of the writ of habeas corpus shall not be suspended, unless when in cases of rebellion or invasion the public safety may require it.

(3) No bill of attainder or ex post facto law shall be passed.

(4) [*No capitation or other direct tax shall be laid, unless in proportion to the census or enumeration herein before directed to be taken.*]

(5) No tax or duty shall be laid on articles exported from any state.

(6) No preference shall be given by any regulation of commerce or revenue to the ports of one state over those of another; nor shall vessels bound to, or from, one state, be obliged to enter, clear, or pay duties in another.

(7) No money shall be drawn from the Treasury, but in consequence of appropriations made by law; and a regular statement and account of the receipts and expenditures of all public money shall be published from time to time.

(1) Slave Trade
Some authority is not given to Congress. Congress could not prevent the slave trade until 1808, but it could put a tax of ten dollars on each slave brought into the United States. After 1808, when a law was passed to stop slaves from being brought into the United States, this section no longer applied.

(2) Habeas Corpus
A writ of habeas corpus is a privilege that entitles a person to a hearing before a judge. The judge must then decide if there is good reason for that person to have been arrested. If not, that person must be released. The government is not allowed to take this privilege away except during a national emergency, such as an invasion or a rebellion.

(3) Special Laws
Congress cannot pass laws that impose punishment on a named individual or group, except in cases of treason. Article III sets limits to punishments for treason. Congress also cannot pass laws that punish a person for an action that was legal when it was done.

(4) Direct Taxes
Congress cannot set a direct tax on people, unless it is in proportion to the total population. Amendment 16, which provides for the income tax, is an exception.

(5) Export Taxes
Congress cannot tax goods sent from one state to another or from a state to another country.

(6) Ports
When making trade laws, Congress cannot favor one state over another. Congress cannot require ships from one state to pay a duty to enter another state.

(7) Public Money
The government cannot spend money from the treasury unless Congress passes a law allowing it to do so. A written record must be kept of all money spent by the government.

(8) Titles of Nobility and Gifts
The United States government cannot grant titles of nobility. Government officials cannot accept gifts from other countries without the permission of Congress. This clause was intended to prevent government officials from being bribed by other nations.

(1) Complete Restrictions
The Constitution does not allow states to act as if they were individual countries. No state government may make a treaty with other countries. No state can print its own money.

(2) Partial Restrictions
No state government can tax imported goods or exported goods without the consent of Congress. States may charge a fee to inspect these goods, but profits must be given to the United States Treasury.

(3) Other Restrictions
No state government may tax ships entering its ports unless Congress approves. No state may keep an army or navy during times of peace other than the National Guard. No state can enter into agreements called compacts with other states without the consent of Congress.

(1) Term of Office
The President has the authority to carry out our nation's laws. The term of office for both the President and the Vice President is four years.

(2) The Electoral College
This group of people is to be chosen by the voters of each state to elect the President and Vice President. The number of electors in each state is equal to the number of senators and representatives that state has in Congress.

(3) Election Process
This clause describes in detail how the electors were to choose the President and Vice President. In 1804 Amendment 12 changed the process for electing the President and the Vice President.

(8) No title of nobility shall be granted by the United States; and no person holding any office of profit or trust under them, shall, without the consent of the Congress, accept of any present, emolument, office, or title, of any kind whatever, from any king, prince, or foreign state.

SECTION 10. POWERS DENIED TO THE STATES

(1) No state shall enter into any treaty, alliance, or confederation; grant letters of marque and reprisal; coin money; emit bills of credit; make anything but gold and silver coin a tender in payment of debts; pass any bill of attainder, ex post facto law, or law impairing the obligation of contracts, or grant any title of nobility.

(2) No state shall, without the consent of the Congress, lay any imposts or duties on imports or exports, except what may be absolutely necessary for executing its inspection laws; and the net produce of all duties and imposts, laid by any state on imports or exports, shall be for the use of the Treasury of the United States; and all such laws shall be subject to the revision and control of the Congress.

(3) No state shall, without the consent of Congress, lay any duty of tonnage, keep troops, or ships of war in time of peace, enter into any agreement or compact with another state, or with a foreign power, or engage in war, unless actually invaded, or in such imminent danger as will not admit of delay.

ARTICLE II
THE EXECUTIVE BRANCH
SECTION 1. PRESIDENT AND VICE PRESIDENT

(1) The executive power shall be vested in a President of the United States of America. He shall hold his office during the term of four years, and together with the Vice President, chosen for the same term, be elected as follows:

(2) Each state shall appoint, in such manner as the legislature thereof may direct, a number of electors, equal to the whole number of Senators and Representatives to which the state may be entitled in the Congress; but no Senator or Representative, or person holding an office of trust or profit under the United States, shall be appointed an elector.

(3) [*The electors shall meet in their respective states, and vote by ballot for two persons, of whom one at least shall not be an inhabitant of the same state with themselves. And they shall make a list of all the persons voted for, and of the number of votes for each; which list they shall sign and certify, and transmit sealed to the seat of the government of the United States, directed to the president of the Senate. The president of the Senate shall, in the presence of the Senate and House of Representatives, open all the certificates, and the votes shall then be counted. The person having the greatest number of votes shall be the President, if such number be a majority of the whole number of electors appointed; and if there be more than one who have such majority, and have an equal number of votes, then the House of Representatives shall immediately choose by ballot one of them for President; and if no person have*

a majority, then from the five highest on the list the said House shall in like manner choose the President. But in choosing the President the votes shall be taken by states, the representation from each state having one vote: A quorum for this purpose shall consist of a member or members from two-thirds of the states, and a majority of all the states shall be necessary to a choice. In every case, after the choice of the President, the person having the greatest number of votes of the electors shall be the Vice President. But if there should remain two or more who have equal votes, the Senate shall choose from them by ballot the Vice President.]

(4) The Congress may determine the time of choosing the electors, and the day on which they shall give their votes; which day shall be the same throughout the United States.

(5) No person except a natural-born citizen [*or a citizen of the United States, at the time of the adoption of this Constitution,*] shall be eligible to the office of the President; neither shall any person be eligible to that office who shall not have attained to the age of thirty-five years, and been fourteen years a resident within the United States.

(6) [*In case of the removal of the President from office, or of his death, resignation, or inability to discharge the powers and duties of the said office, the same shall devolve on the Vice President, and the Congress may by law provide for the case of removal, death, resignation or inability, both of the President and Vice President, declaring what officer shall then act as President, and such officer shall act accordingly, until the disability be removed, or a President shall be elected.*]

(7) The President shall, at stated times, receive for his services, a compensation, which shall neither be increased nor diminished during the period for which he shall have been elected, and he shall not receive within that period any other emolument from the United States, or any of them.

(8) Before he enter on the execution of his office, he shall take the following oath or affirmation:—"I do solemnly swear (or affirm) that I will faithfully execute the office of President of the United States, and will to the best of my ability, preserve, protect, and defend the Constitution of the United States."

SECTION 2. POWERS OF THE PRESIDENT
(1) The President shall be Commander in Chief of the Army and Navy of the United States, and of the militia of the several states, when called into the actual service of the United States; he may require the opinion, in writing, of the principal officer in each of the executive departments, upon any subject relating to the duties of their respective offices, and he shall have power to grant reprieves and pardons for offenses against the United States, except in cases of impeachment.

(4) Time of Elections
Congress decides the day the electors are to be elected and the day they are to vote.

(5) Qualifications
The President must be at least 35 years old, be a citizen of the United States by birth, and have been living in the United States for 14 years or more.

(6) Vacancies
If the President dies, resigns, or is removed from office, the Vice President becomes President.

(7) Salary
The President receives a salary that cannot be raised or lowered during a term of office. The President may not be paid any additional salary by the federal government or any state or local government. Today the President's salary is $400,000 a year, plus expenses for things such as housing, travel, and entertainment.

(8) Oath of Office
Before taking office, the President must promise to perform the duties faithfully and to protect the country's form of government. Usually the Chief Justice of the Supreme Court administers the oath of office.

(1) The President's Leadership
The President is the commander of the nation's armed forces and of the National Guard when it is in service of the nation. All government officials of the executive branch must report their actions to the President when asked. The President can excuse people from punishment for crimes committed.

(2) Treaties and Appointments
The President has the authority to make treaties, but they must be approved by a two-thirds vote of the Senate. The President nominates justices to the Supreme Court, ambassadors to other countries, and other federal officials with the Senate's approval.

(3) Filling Vacancies
If a government official's position becomes vacant when Congress is not in session, the President can make a temporary appointment.

Duties
The President must report to Congress on the condition of the country. This report is now presented in the annual State of the Union message.

Impeachment
The President, the Vice President, or any government official will be removed from office if impeached, or accused, and then found guilty of treason, bribery, or other serious crimes. The Constitution protects government officials from being impeached for unimportant reasons.

Federal Courts
The authority to decide legal cases is granted to a Supreme Court and to a system of lower courts established by Congress. The Supreme Court is the highest court in the land. Justices and judges are in their offices for life, subject to good behavior.

(1) General Authority
Federal courts have the authority to decide cases that arise under the Constitution, laws, and treaties of the United States. They also have the authority to settle disagreements among states and among citizens of different states.

(2) He shall have power, by and with the advice and consent of the Senate, to make treaties, provided two-thirds of the senators present concur; and he shall nominate, and by and with the advice and consent of the Senate, shall appoint ambassadors, other public ministers and consuls, judges of the Supreme Court, and all other officers of the United States, whose appointments are not herein otherwise provided for, and which shall be established by law; but the Congress may by law vest the appointment of such inferior officers, as they think proper, in the President alone, in the courts of law, or in the heads of departments.

(3) The President shall have power to fill up all vacancies that may happen during the recess of the Senate, by granting commissions which shall expire at the end of their next session.

SECTION 3. DUTIES OF THE PRESIDENT

He shall from time to time give to the Congress information of the state of the Union, and recommend to their consideration such measures as he shall judge necessary and expedient; he may, on extraordinary occasions, convene both houses, or either of them, and in case of disagreement between them, with respect to the time of adjournment, he may adjourn them to such time as he shall think proper; he shall receive ambassadors and other public ministers; he shall take care that the laws be faithfully executed, and shall commission all the officers of the United States.

SECTION 4. IMPEACHMENT

The President, Vice President and all civil officers of the United States, shall be removed from office on impeachment for, and conviction of, treason, bribery, or other high crimes and misdemeanors.

ARTICLE III
THE JUDICIAL BRANCH
SECTION 1. FEDERAL COURTS

The judicial power of the United States shall be vested in one Supreme Court, and in such inferior courts as the Congress may from time to time ordain and establish. The judges, both of the supreme and inferior courts, shall hold their offices during good behavior, and shall, at stated times, receive for their services a compensation, which shall not be diminished during their continuance in office.

SECTION 2. AUTHORITY OF THE FEDERAL COURTS

(1) The judicial power shall extend to all cases, in law and equity, arising under this Constitution, the laws of the United States, and treaties made or which shall be made, under their authority; to all cases affecting ambassadors, other public ministers and consuls; to all cases of admiralty and maritime jurisdiction; to controversies to which the United States shall be a party; to controversies between two or more states; [*between a state and citizens of another state;*] between citizens of different states; —between citizens of the same state claiming lands under grants of different states, [*and between a state or the citizens thereof, and foreign states, citizens, or subjects.*]

(2) In all cases affecting ambassadors, other public ministers and consuls, and those in which a state shall be party, the Supreme Court shall have original jurisdiction. In all the other cases before mentioned, the Supreme Court shall have appellate jurisdiction, both as to law and fact, with such exceptions, and under such regulations as the Congress shall make.

(3) The trial of all crimes, except in cases of impeachment, shall be by jury; and such trial shall be held in the state where the said crimes shall have been committed; but when not committed within any state, the trial shall be at such place or places as the Congress may by law have directed.

SECTION 3. TREASON
(1) Treason against the United States shall consist only in levying war against them, or in adhering to their enemies, giving them aid and comfort. No person shall be convicted of treason unless on the testimony of two witnesses to the same overt act, or on confession in open court.

(2) The Congress shall have power to declare the punishment of treason, but no attainder of treason shall work corruption of blood, or forfeiture except during the life of the person attainted.

ARTICLE IV
RELATIONS AMONG STATES
SECTION 1. OFFICIAL RECORDS
Full faith and credit shall be given in each state to the public acts, records, and judicial proceedings of every other state. And the Congress may by general laws prescribe the manner in which such acts, records, and proceedings shall be proved, and the effect thereof.

SECTION 2. PRIVILEGES OF THE CITIZENS
(1) The citizens of each state shall be entitled to all privileges and immunities of citizens in the several states.

(2) A person charged in any state with treason, felony, or other crime, who shall flee from justice, and be found in another state, shall on demand of the executive authority of the state from which he fled, be delivered up, to be removed to the state having jurisdiction of the crime.

(3) [*No person held to service or labor in one state, under the laws thereof, escaping into another, shall in consequence of any law or regulation therein, be discharged from such service or labor, but shall be delivered up on claim of the party to whom such service or labor may be due.*]

(2) Supreme Court
The Supreme Court can decide certain cases being tried for the first time. It can review cases that have already been tried in a lower court if the decision has been appealed, or questioned, by one side.

(3) Trial by Jury
The Constitution guarantees a trial by jury for every person charged with a federal crime. Amendments 5, 6, and 7 extend and clarify a person's right to a trial by jury.

(1) Definition of Treason
Acts that may be considered treason are making war against the United States or helping its enemies. A person cannot be convicted of attempting to overthrow the government unless there are two witnesses to the act or the person confesses in court to treason.

(2) Punishment for Treason
Congress can decide the punishment for treason, within certain limits.

Official Records
Each state must honor the official records and judicial decisions of other states.

(1) Privileges
A citizen moving from one state to another has the same rights as other citizens living in that person's new state of residence. In some cases, such as voting, people may be required to live in their new state for a certain length of time before obtaining the same privileges as citizens there.

(2) Extradition
At the governor's request, a person who is charged with a crime and who tries to escape justice by crossing into another state may be returned to the state in which the crime was committed.

(3) Fugitive Slaves
The original Constitution required that runaway slaves be returned to their owners. Amendment 13 abolished slavery, eliminating the need for this clause.

(1) Admission of New States
Congress has the authority to admit new states to the Union. All new states have the same rights as existing states.

(2) Federal Property
The Constitution allows Congress to make or change laws governing federal property. This applies to territories and federally owned land within states, such as national parks.

Guarantees to the States
The federal government guarantees that every state have a republican form of government. The United States must also protect the states against invasion and help the states deal with rebellion or local violence.

Amending the Constitution
Changes to the Constitution may be proposed by a two-thirds vote of both the House of Representatives and the Senate or by a national convention called by Congress when asked by two-thirds of the states. For an amendment to become law, the legislatures or conventions in three-fourths of the states must approve it.

(1) Public Debt
Any debt owed by the United States before the Constitution went into effect was to be honored.

(2) Federal Supremacy
This clause declares that the Constitution and federal laws are the highest in the nation. Whenever a state law and a federal law are found to disagree, the federal law must be obeyed so long as it is constitutional.

(3) Oaths of Office
All federal and state officials must promise to follow and enforce the Constitution. These officials, however, cannot be required to follow a particular religion or satisfy any religious test.

SECTION 3. NEW STATES AND TERRITORIES
(1) New states may be admitted by the Congress into this Union; but no new state shall be formed or erected within the jurisdiction of any other state; nor any state be formed by the junction of two or more states, or parts of states, without the consent of the legislatures of the states concerned as well as of the Congress.

(2) The Congress shall have power to dispose of and make all needful rules and regulations respecting the territory or other property belonging to the United States; and nothing in this Constitution shall be so construed as to prejudice any claims of the United States, or of any particular state.

SECTION 4. GUARANTEES TO THE STATES
The United States shall guarantee to every state in this Union a republican form of government, and shall protect each of them against invasion; and on application of the legislature, or of the executive (when the legislature cannot be convened) against domestic violence.

ARTICLE V
AMENDING THE CONSTITUTION
The Congress, whenever two-thirds of both houses shall deem it necessary, shall propose amendments to this Constitution, or, on the application of the legislatures of two-thirds of the several states, shall call a convention for proposing amendments, which, in either case, shall be valid to all intents and purposes, as part of this Constitution, when ratified by the legislatures of three-fourths of the several states, or by conventions in three-fourths thereof, as the one or the other mode of ratification may be proposed by the Congress; provided that [*no amendment which may be made prior to the year 1808 shall in any manner affect the first and fourth clauses in the Ninth Section of the First Article; and that*] no state, without its consent, shall be deprived of its equal suffrage in the Senate.

ARTICLE VI
GENERAL PROVISIONS
(1) All debts contracted and engagements entered into, before the adoption of this Constitution, shall be as valid against the United States under this Constitution, as under the Confederation.

(2) This Constitution, and the laws of the United States which shall be made in pursuance thereof, and all treaties made, or which shall be made, under the authority of the United States, shall be the supreme law of the land; and the judges in every state shall be bound thereby, anything in the Constitution or laws of any state to the contrary notwithstanding.

(3) The Senators and Representatives before mentioned, and the members of the several state legislatures, and all executive and judicial officers, both of the United States and of the several states, shall be bound by oath or affirmation, to support this Constitution; but no religious test shall ever be required as a qualification to any office or public trust under the United States.

ARTICLE VII
RATIFICATION

The ratification of the conventions of nine states, shall be sufficient for the establishment of this Constitution between the states so ratifying the same.

Done in convention by the unanimous consent of the states present the seventeenth day of September in the year of our Lord one thousand seven hundred and eighty seven and of the independence of the United States of America the Twelfth. In witness whereof we have hereunto subscribed our names.

George Washington—President and deputy from Virginia

DELAWARE
George Read
Gunning Bedford, Jr.
John Dickinson
Richard Bassett
Jacob Broom

MARYLAND
James McHenry
Daniel of St. Thomas Jenifer
Daniel Carroll

VIRGINIA
John Blair
James Madison, Jr.

NORTH CAROLINA
William Blount
Richard Dobbs Spaight
Hugh Williamson

SOUTH CAROLINA
John Rutledge
Charles Cotesworth Pinckney
Charles Pinckney
Pierce Butler

GEORGIA
William Few
Abraham Baldwin

NEW HAMPSHIRE
John Langdon
Nicholas Gilman

MASSACHUSETTS
Nathaniel Gorham
Rufus King

CONNECTICUT
William Samuel Johnson
Roger Sherman

NEW YORK
Alexander Hamilton

NEW JERSEY
William Livingston
David Brearley
William Paterson
Jonathan Dayton

PENNSYLVANIA
Benjamin Franklin
Thomas Mifflin
Robert Morris
George Clymer
Thomas FitzSimons
Jared Ingersoll
James Wilson
Gouverneur Morris

ATTEST: William Jackson, secretary

Ratification
In order for the Constitution to become law, 9 of the 13 states had to approve it. Special conventions were held for this purpose. The process took 9 months to complete.

Basic Freedoms
The Constitution guarantees our five basic freedoms of expression. It provides for the freedoms of religion, speech, the press, peaceable assembly, and petition for redress of grievances.

Weapons and the Militia
This amendment protects the right of the state governments and the people to maintain militias to guard against threats to their public order, safety, and liberty. In connection with that state right, the federal government may not take away the right of the people to have and use weapons.

Housing Soldiers
The federal government cannot force people to house soldiers in their homes during peacetime. However, Congress may pass laws allowing this during wartime.

Searches and Seizures
This amendment protects people's privacy and safety. Subject to certain exceptions, a law officer cannot search a person or a person's home and belongings unless a judge has issued a valid search warrant. There must be good reason for the search. The warrant must describe the place to be searched and the people or things to be seized, or taken.

Rights of Accused Persons
If a person is accused of a crime that is punishable by death or of any other crime that is very serious, a grand jury must decide if there is enough evidence to hold a trial. People cannot be tried twice for the same crime, nor can they be forced to testify against themselves. No person shall be fined, jailed, or executed by the government unless the person has been given a fair trial. The government cannot take a person's property for public use unless fair payment is made.

AMENDMENT 1 (1791)***
BASIC FREEDOMS

Congress shall make no law respecting an establishment of religion, or prohibiting the free exercise thereof; or abridging the freedom of speech, or of the press; or the right of the people peaceably to assemble, and to petition the government for a redress of grievances.

AMENDMENT 2 (1791)
WEAPONS AND THE MILITIA

A well-regulated militia, being necessary to the security of a free state, the right of the people to keep and bear arms shall not be infringed.

AMENDMENT 3 (1791)
HOUSING SOLDIERS

No soldier shall, in time of peace, be quartered in any house, without the consent of the owner; nor in time of war, but in a manner to be prescribed by law.

AMENDMENT 4 (1791)
SEARCHES AND SEIZURES

The right of the people to be secure in their persons, houses, papers, and effects, against unreasonable searches and seizures, shall not be violated; and no warrants shall issue but upon probable cause, supported by oath or affirmation, and particularly describing the place to be searched, and the persons or things to be seized.

AMENDMENT 5 (1791)
RIGHTS OF ACCUSED PERSONS

No person shall be held to answer for a capital, or otherwise infamous crime, unless on a presentment or indictment of a grand jury, except in cases arising in the land or naval forces, or in the militia, when in actual service in time of war or public danger; nor shall any person be subject for the same offense to be twice put in jeopardy of life or limb; nor shall be compelled in any criminal case to be a witness against himself; nor be deprived of life, liberty, or property, without due process of law; nor shall private property be taken for public use without just compensation.

*** The date beside each amendment is the year that the amendment was ratified and became part of the Constitution.

AMENDMENT 6 (1791)
RIGHT TO A FAIR TRIAL

In all criminal prosecutions, the accused shall enjoy the right to a speedy and public trial, by an impartial jury of the state and district wherein the crime shall have been committed, which district shall have been previously ascertained by law, and to be informed of the nature and cause of the accusation; to be confronted with the witnesses against him; to have compulsory process for obtaining witnesses in his favor, and to have the assistance of counsel for his defense.

AMENDMENT 7 (1791)
JURY TRIAL IN CIVIL CASES

In suits at common law, where the value in controversy shall exceed 20 dollars, the right of trial by jury shall be preserved, and no fact tried by a jury shall be otherwise re-examined in any court of the United States, than according to the rules of the common law.

AMENDMENT 8 (1791)
BAIL AND PUNISHMENT

Excessive bail shall not be required, nor excessive fines imposed, nor cruel and unusual punishments inflicted.

AMENDMENT 9 (1791)
RIGHTS OF THE PEOPLE

The enumeration in the Constitution, of certain rights, shall not be construed to deny or disparage others retained by the people.

AMENDMENT 10 (1791)
POWERS OF THE STATES AND THE PEOPLE

The powers not delegated to the United States by the Constitution, nor prohibited by it to the states, are reserved to the states respectively, or to the people.

AMENDMENT 11 (1798)
SUITS AGAINST STATES

The judicial power of the United States shall not be construed to extend to any suit in law or equity, commenced or prosecuted against one of the United States or citizens of another state, or by citizens or subjects of any foreign state.

Right to a Fair Trial
A person accused of a crime has the right to a public trial by an impartial jury, locally chosen. The trial must be held within a reasonable amount of time. The accused person must be told of all charges and has the right to see, hear, and question any witnesses. The federal government must provide a lawyer free of charge to a person who is accused of a serious crime and who is unable to pay for legal services.

Jury Trial in Civil Cases
In most federal civil cases involving more than 20 dollars, a jury trial is guaranteed. Civil cases are those disputes between two or more people over money, property, personal injury, or legal rights. Usually civil cases are not tried in federal courts unless much larger sums of money are involved or unless federal courts are given the authority to decide a certain type of case.

Bail and Punishment
Courts cannot treat harshly people accused of crimes or punish them in unusual or cruel ways. Bail is money put up as a guarantee that an accused person will appear for trial. In certain cases bail can be denied altogether.

Rights of the People
The federal government must respect all natural rights, whether or not they are listed in the Constitution.

Powers of the States and the People
Any powers not clearly given to the federal government or denied to the states belong to the states or to the people.

Suits Against States
A citizen of one state cannot sue another state in federal court.

Election of President and Vice President
This amendment replaces the part of Article II, Section 1, that originally explained the process of electing the President and Vice President. Amendment 12 was an important step in the development of the two-party system. It allows a party to nominate its own candidates for both President and Vice President.

AMENDMENT 12 (1804)
ELECTION OF PRESIDENT AND VICE PRESIDENT

The electors shall meet in their respective states, and vote by ballot for President and Vice President, one of whom, at least, shall not be an inhabitant of the same state with themselves; they shall name in their ballots the person voted for as President, and in distinct ballots the person voted for as Vice President, and they shall make distinct lists of all persons voted for as President, and of all persons voted for as Vice President, and of the number of votes for each, which lists they shall sign and certify, and transmit, sealed, to the seat of government of the United States, directed to the President of the Senate; the President of the Senate shall, in the presence of the Senate and House of Representatives, open all the certificates, and the votes shall then be counted; the person having the greatest number of votes for President shall be the President, if such a number be a majority of the whole number of electors appointed; and if no person have such majority; then from the persons having the highest numbers not exceeding three on the list of those voted for as President, the House of Representatives shall choose immediately, by ballot, the President. But in choosing the President, the votes shall be taken by states, the representation from each state having one vote; a quorum for this purpose shall consist of a member or members from two thirds of the states, and a majority of all the states shall be necessary to a choice. [And *if the House of Representatives shall not choose a President whenever the right of choice shall devolve upon them, before the fourth day of March next following, then the Vice President shall act as President, as in the case of the death or other constitutional disability of the President.*] The person having the greatest number of votes as Vice President, shall be the Vice President, if such number be a majority of the whole number of electors appointed, and if no person have a majority, then, from the two highest numbers on the list the Senate shall choose the Vice President; a quorum for the purpose shall consist of two thirds of the whole number of Senators, and a majority of the whole number shall be necessary to a choice. But no person constitutionally ineligible to the office of President shall be eligible to that of Vice President of the United States.

End of Slavery
People cannot be forced to work against their will unless they have been tried for and convicted of a crime for which this means of punishment is ordered. Congress may enforce this by law.

AMENDMENT 13 (1865)
END OF SLAVERY

SECTION 1. ABOLITION

Neither slavery nor involuntary servitude, except as a punishment for crime whereof the party shall have been duly convicted, shall exist within the United States, or any place subject to their jurisdiction.

SECTION 2. ENFORCEMENT

Congress shall have power to enforce this article by appropriate legislation.

Citizenship
All persons born or naturalized in the United States are citizens of the United States and of the state in which they live. State governments may not deny any citizen the full rights of citizenship. This amendment also guarantees due process of law. According to due process of law, no state may take away the rights of a citizen. All citizens must be protected equally under law.

AMENDMENT 14 (1868)
RIGHTS OF CITIZENS

SECTION 1. CITIZENSHIP

All persons born or naturalized in the United States and subject to the jurisdiction thereof, are citizens of the United States and of the state wherein they reside. No state shall make or enforce any law which shall abridge the privileges or immunities of citizens of the United States, nor shall any state deprive any person of life, liberty, or property, without due process of law; nor deny to any person within its jurisdiction the equal protection of the laws.

SECTION 2. NUMBER OF REPRESENTATIVES

Representatives shall be apportioned among the several states according to their respective numbers, counting the whole number of persons in each state, [*excluding Indians not taxed*]. But when the right to vote at any election for the choice of electors for President and Vice President of the United States, representatives in Congress, the executive and judicial officers of a state, or the members of the legislature thereof, is denied to any of the [*male*] inhabitants of such state, being [*twenty-one years of age and*] citizens of the United States, or in any way abridged, except for participation in rebellion or other crime, the basis of representation therein shall be reduced in the proportion which the number of such [*male*] citizens shall bear to the whole number of [*male*] citizens [*twenty-one years of age*] in such state.

SECTION 3. PENALTY FOR REBELLION

No person shall be a Senator or Representative in Congress, or elector of President and Vice President, or hold any office, civil or military, under the United States, or under any state, who, having previously taken an oath, as a member of Congress, or as an officer of the United States, or as a member of any state legislature, or as an executive or judicial officer of any state, to support the Constitution of the United States, shall have engaged in insurrection or rebellion against the same, or given aid or comfort to the enemies thereof. But Congress may, by a vote of two thirds of each house, remove such disability.

SECTION 4. GOVERNMENT DEBT

The validity of the public debt of the United States, authorized by law, including debts incurred for payment of pensions and bounties for services in suppressing insurrection or rebellion, shall not be questioned. But neither the United States nor any state shall assume or pay any debt or obligation incurred in aid of insurrection or rebellion against the United States, [*or any claim for the loss or emancipation of any slave;*] but all such debts, obligations, and claims shall be held illegal and void.

SECTION 5. ENFORCEMENT

The Congress shall have power to enforce, by appropriate legislation, the provisions of this article.

AMENDMENT 15 (1870)
VOTING RIGHTS

SECTION 1. RIGHT TO VOTE

The right of citizens of the United States to vote shall not be denied or abridged by the United States or by any state on account of race, color, or previous condition of servitude.

SECTION 2. ENFORCEMENT

The Congress shall have power to enforce this article by appropriate legislation.

AMENDMENT 16 (1913)
INCOME TAX

The Congress shall have power to lay and collect taxes on incomes, from whatever source derived, without apportionment among the several states, and without regard to any census or enumeration.

Number of Representatives
Each state's representation in Congress is based on its total population. Any state denying eligible citizens the right to vote will have its representation in Congress decreased. This clause abolished the Three-fifths Compromise in Article I, Section 2. Later amendments granted women the right to vote and lowered the voting age to 18.

Penalty for Rebellion
No person who has rebelled against the United States may hold federal office. This clause was originally added to punish the leaders of the Confederacy for failing to support the Constitution of the United States.

Government Debt
The federal government is responsible for all public debts. It is not responsible, however, for Confederate debts or for debts that result from any rebellion against the United States.

Enforcement
Congress may enforce these provisions by law.

Right to Vote
No state may prevent a citizen from voting simply because of race or color or condition of previous servitude. This amendment was designed to extend voting rights to enforce this by law.

Income Tax
Congress has the power to collect taxes on its citizens, based on their personal incomes rather than on the number of people living in a state.

Direct Election of Senators
Originally, state legislatures elected senators. This amendment allows the people of each state to elect their own senators directly. The idea is to make senators more responsible to the people they represent.

Prohibition
This amendment made it illegal to make, sell, or transport liquor within the United States or to transport it out of the United States or its territories. Amendment 18 was the first to include a time limit for approval. If not ratified within seven years, it would be repealed, or canceled. Many later amendments have included similar time limits.

Women's Voting Rights
This amendment protected the right of women throughout the United States to vote.

Terms of Office
The terms of the President and the Vice President begin on January 20, in the year following their election. Members of Congress take office on January 3. Before this amendment newly elected members of Congress did not begin their terms until March 4. This meant that those who had run for reelection and been defeated remained in office for four months.

AMENDMENT 17 (1913)
DIRECT ELECTION OF SENATORS

SECTION 1. METHOD OF ELECTION

The Senate of the United States shall be composed of two Senators from each state, elected by the people thereof, for six years; and each Senator shall have one vote. The electors in each state shall have the qualifications requisite for electors of the most numerous branch of the state legislatures.

SECTION 2. VACANCIES

When vacancies happen in the representation of any state in the Senate, the executive authority of such state shall issue writs of election to fill such vacancies: *Provided*, that the legislature of any state may empower the executive thereof to make temporary appointments until the people fill the vacancies by election as the legislature may direct.

SECTION 3. EXCEPTION

[*This amendment shall not be so construed as to affect the election or term of any Senator chosen before it becomes valid as part of the Constitution.*]

AMENDMENT 18 (1919)
BAN ON ALCOHOLIC DRINKS

SECTION 1. PROHIBITION

[*After one year from the ratification of this article the manufacture, sale, or transportation of intoxicating liquors within, the importation thereof into, or the exportation thereof from the United States and all territory subject to the jurisdiction thereof for beverage purposes is hereby prohibited.*]

SECTION 2. ENFORCEMENT

[*The Congress and the several states shall have concurrent power to enforce this article by appropriate legislation.*]

SECTION 3. RATIFICATION

[*This article shall be inoperative unless it shall have been ratified as an amendment to the Constitution by the legislatures of the several states as provided in the Constitution, within seven years from the date of the submission hereof to the states by the Congress.*]

AMENDMENT 19 (1920)
WOMEN'S VOTING RIGHTS

SECTION 1. RIGHT TO VOTE

The right of citizens of the United States to vote shall not be denied or abridged by the United States or by any state on account of sex.

SECTION 2. ENFORCEMENT

Congress shall have power to enforce this article by appropriate legislation.

AMENDMENT 20 (1933)
TERMS OF OFFICE

SECTION 1. BEGINNING OF TERMS

The terms of the President and Vice President shall end at noon on the 20th day of January, and the terms of Senators and Representatives at noon on the 3rd day of January, of the years in which such terms would have ended if this article had not been ratified; and the terms of their successors shall then begin.

SECTION 2. SESSIONS OF CONGRESS

The Congress shall assemble at least once in every year, and such meeting shall begin at noon on the 3rd day of January, unless they shall by law appoint a different day.

SECTION 3. PRESIDENTIAL SUCCESSION

If, at the time fixed for the beginning of the term of the President, the President-elect shall have died, the Vice President-elect shall become President. If a President shall not have been chosen before the time fixed for the beginning of his term, or if the President-elect shall have failed to qualify, then the Vice President-elect shall act as President until a President shall have qualified; and the Congress may by law provide for the case wherein neither a President-elect nor a Vice President-elect shall have qualified, declaring who shall then act as President, or the manner in which one who is to act shall be selected and such person shall act accordingly until a President or Vice President shall be qualified.

SECTION 4. ELECTIONS DECIDED BY CONGRESS

The Congress may by law provide for the case of the death of any of the persons from whom the House of Representatives may choose a President whenever the right of choice shall have devolved upon them, and for the case of the death of any of the persons from whom the Senate may choose a Vice President whenever the right of choice shall have devolved upon them.

SECTION 5. EFFECTIVE DATE

[*Sections 1 and 2 shall take effect on the 15th day of October following the ratification of this article.*]

SECTION 6. RATIFICATION

[*This article shall be inoperative unless it shall have been ratified as an amendment to the Constitution by the legislatures of three fourths of the several states within seven years from the date of its submission.*]

AMENDMENT 21 (1933)
END OF PROHIBITION

SECTION 1. REPEAL OF AMENDMENT 18

The eighteenth article of amendment to the Constitution of the United States is hereby repealed.

SECTION 2. STATE LAWS

The transportation or importation into any state, territory, or possession of the United States for delivery or use therein of intoxicating liquors, in violation of the laws thereof, is hereby prohibited.

SECTION 3. RATIFICATION

[*This article shall be inoperative unless it shall have been ratified as an amendment to the Constitution by conventions in the several states, as provided in the Constitution within seven years from the date of the submission hereof to the states by Congress.*]

Sessions of Congress
Congress meets at least once a year, beginning at noon on January 3. Congress had previously met at least once a year beginning on the first Monday of December.

Presidential Succession
If the newly elected President dies before January 20, the newly elected Vice President becomes President on that date. If a President has not been chosen by January 20 or does not meet the requirements for being President, the newly elected Vice President becomes President. If neither the newly elected President nor the newly elected Vice President meets the requirements for office, Congress decides who will serve as President until a qualified President or Vice President is chosen.

End of Prohibition
This amendment repealed Amendment 18. This is the only amendment to be ratified by state conventions instead of by state legislatures. Congress felt that this would give people's opinions about prohibition a better chance to be heard.

Two-Term limit for Presidents
A President may not serve more than two full terms in office. Any President who serves less than two years of a previous President's term may be elected for two more terms.

AMENDMENT 22 (1951)
TWO-TERM LIMIT FOR PRESIDENTS
SECTION 1. TWO-TERM LIMIT

No person shall be elected to the office of the President more than twice, and no person who has held the office of President, or acted as President, for more than two years of a term to which some other person was elected President shall be elected to the office of the President more than once. [*But this article shall not apply to any person holding the office of President when this article was proposed by the Congress, and shall not prevent any person who may be holding the office of President, or acting as President, during the term within which this article becomes operative from holding the office of President, or acting as President, during the remainder of such term.*]

SECTION 2. RATIFICATION

[*This article shall be inoperative unless it shall have been ratified as an amendment to the Constitution by the legislatures of three-fourths of the several states within seven years from the date of its submission to the states by the Congress.*]

Presidential Electors for District of Columbia
This amendment grants three electoral votes to the national capital.

AMENDMENT 23 (1961)
PRESIDENTIAL ELECTORS FOR DISTRICT OF COLUMBIA
SECTION 1. NUMBER OF ELECTORS

The District constituting the seat of Government of the United States shall appoint in such manner as Congress may direct:

A number of electors of President and Vice President equal to the whole number of Senators and Representatives in Congress to which the District would be entitled if it were a state, but in no event more than the least populous state; they shall be in addition to those appointed by the states, but they shall be considered, for the purposes of the election of President and Vice President, to be electors appointed by a state, and they shall meet in the District and perform such duties as provided by the twelfth article of amendment.

SECTION 2. ENFORCEMENT

The Congress shall have power to enforce this article by appropriate legislation.

Ban on Poll Taxes
No United States citizen may be prevented from voting in a federal election because of failing to pay a tax to vote. Poll taxes had been used in some states to prevent African Americans from voting.

AMENDMENT 24 (1964)
BAN ON POLL TAXES
SECTION 1. POLL TAX ILLEGAL

The right of citizens of the United States to vote in any primary or other election for President or Vice President, for electors for President or Vice President, or for Senator or Representative in Congress, shall not be denied or abridged by the United States or any state by reason of failure to pay any poll tax or other tax.

SECTION 2. ENFORCEMENT

The Congress shall have power to enforce this article by appropriate legislation.

Presidential Vacancy
If the President is removed from office or resigns from or dies while in office, the Vice President becomes President.

AMENDMENT 25 (1967)
PRESIDENTIAL SUCCESSION
SECTION 1. PRESIDENTIAL VACANCY

In case of the removal of the President from office or of his death or resignation, the Vice President shall become President.

SECTION 2. VICE PRESIDENTIAL VACANCY

Whenever there is a vacancy in the office of the Vice President, the President shall nominate a Vice President who shall take the office upon confirmation by a majority vote of both houses of Congress.

SECTION 3. PRESIDENTIAL DISABILITY

Whenever the President transmits to the President pro tempore of the Senate and the Speaker of the House of Representatives his written declaration that he is unable to discharge the powers and duties of his office, and until he transmits to them a written declaration to the contrary, such powers and duties shall be discharged by the Vice President as Acting President.

SECTION 4. DETERMINING PRESIDENTIAL DISABILITY

Whenever the Vice President and a majority of either the principal officers of the executive departments or of such other body as Congress may by law provide, transmit to the President pro tempore of the Senate and the Speaker of the House of Representatives their written declaration that the President is unable to discharge the powers and duties of his office, the Vice President shall immediately assume the powers and duties of the office as Acting President.

Thereafter, when the President transmits to the President pro tempore of the Senate and the Speaker of the House of Representatives his written declaration that no inability exists, he shall resume the powers and duties of his office unless the Vice President and a majority of either the principal officers of the executive department or of such other body as Congress may by law provide, transmit within four days to the President pro tempore of the Senate and the Speaker of the House of Representatives their written declaration that the President is unable to discharge the powers and duties of his office. Thereupon Congress shall decide the issue, assembling within 48 hours for that purpose if not in session. If the Congress, within 21 days after receipt of the latter written declaration, or, if Congress is not in session, within 21 days after Congress is required to assemble, determines by two-thirds vote of both houses that the President is unable to discharge the powers and duties of his office, the Vice President shall continue to discharge the same as Acting President; otherwise the President shall resume the powers and duties of his office.

AMENDMENT 26 (1971)
VOTING AGE

SECTION 1. RIGHT TO VOTE

The right of citizens of the United States, who are 18 years of age or older, to vote shall not be denied or abridged by the United States or any state on account of age.

SECTION 2. ENFORCEMENT

The Congress shall have the power to enforce this article by appropriate legislation.

AMENDMENT 27 (1992)
CONGRESSIONAL PAY

No law, varying the compensation for the services of the Senators and Representatives, shall take effect, until an election of Representatives shall have intervened.

Vice Presidential Vacancy
If the office of the Vice President becomes open, the President names someone to assume that office and that person becomes Vice President if both houses of Congress approve by a majority vote.

Presidential Disability
This section explains in detail what happens if the President cannot continue in office because of sickness or any other reason. The Vice President takes over as acting President until the President is able to resume office.

Determining Presidential Disability
If the Vice President and a majority of the Cabinet inform the Speaker of the House and the president pro tempore of the Senate that the President cannot carry out his or her duties, the Vice President then serves as acting President. To regain the office, the President has to inform the Speaker and the president pro tempore in writing that he or she is again able to serve. But, if the Vice President and a majority of the Cabinet disagree with the President and inform the Speaker and the president pro tempore that the President is still unable to serve, then Congress decides who will hold the office of President.

Voting Age
All citizens 18 years or older have the right to vote. Formerly, the voting age was 21 in most states.

Congressional Pay
A law raising or lowering the salaries for members of Congress cannot be passed for that session of Congress.

THE NATIONAL ANTHEM

The Star-Spangled Banner

"The Star-Spangled Banner" was written by Francis Scott Key in September 1814 and adopted as the national anthem in March 1931. The army and navy had recognized it as such long before Congress approved it.

During the War of 1812, Francis Scott Key spent a night aboard a British warship in the Chesapeake Bay while trying to arrange for the release of an American prisoner. The battle raged throughout the night, while the Americans were held on the ship. The next morning, when the smoke from the cannons finally cleared, Francis Scott Key was thrilled to see the American flag still waving proudly above Fort McHenry. It symbolized the victory of the Americans.

There are four verses to the national anthem. In these four verses, Key wrote about how he felt when he saw the flag still waving over Fort McHenry. He wrote that the flag was a symbol of the freedom for which the people had fought so hard. Key also told about the pride he had in his country and the great hopes he had for the future of the United States.

(1)

Oh, say can you see by the dawn's early light
What so proudly we hail'd at the twilight's last gleaming,
Whose broad stripes and bright stars through the perilous fight
O'er the ramparts we watch'd were so gallantly streaming?
And the rockets' red glare, the bombs bursting in air,
Gave proof through the night that our flag was still there.
Oh, say does that star-spangled banner yet wave
O'er the land of the free and the home of the brave?

(2)

On the shore dimly seen through the mists of the deep,
Where the foe's haughty host in dread silence reposes,
What is that which the breeze, o'er the towering steep,
As it fitfully blows, half conceals, half discloses?
Now it catches the gleam of the morning's first beam,
In full glory reflected now shines in the stream.
'Tis the star-spangled banner, oh, long may it wave
O'er the land of the free and the home of the brave!

(3)

And where is that band who so vauntingly swore
That the havoc of war and the battle's confusion
A home and a country should leave us no more?
Their blood has wash'd out their foul footstep's pollution.
No refuge could save the hireling and slave
From the terror of flight or the gloom of the grave,
And the star-spangled banner in triumph doth wave
O'er the land of the free and the home of the brave.

(4)

Oh, thus be it ever when freemen shall stand
Between their lov'd home and the war's desolation!
Blest with vict'ry and peace may the heav'n-rescued land
Praise the power that hath made and preserv'd us a nation!
Then conquer we must, when our cause it is just,
And this be our motto, "In God is our Trust,"
And the star-spangled banner in triumph shall wave
O'er the land of the free and the home of the brave.

THE PLEDGE OF ALLEGIANCE

I pledge allegiance to the Flag

of the United States of America,

and to the Republic

for which it stands,

one Nation under God, indivisible,

with liberty and justice for all.

The flag is a symbol of the United States of America. The Pledge of Allegiance says that the people of the United States promise to stand up for the flag, their country, and the basic beliefs of freedom and fairness upon which the country was established.

AMERICAN DOCUMENTS

Biographical Dictionary

The Biographical Dictionary lists many of the important people introduced in this book. The page number tells where the main discussion of each person starts. See the Index for other page references.

A

Adams, John *1735–1826* Second U.S. President and one of the writers of the Declaration of Independence. p. 62

Adams, Samuel *1722–1803* American Revolutionary leader who set up a Committee of Correspondence in Boston and helped form the Sons of Liberty. p. 50

Addams, Jane *1860–1935* American reformer who brought the idea of settlement houses from Britain to the United States. With Ellen Gates Starr, she founded Hull House in Chicago. pp. 207–208

Albright, Madeleine *1937–* First woman to be appointed U.S. secretary of state. p. 441

Aldrin, Edwin, Jr. *1930–* American astronaut who was one of the first people to set foot on the moon. p. 432

Anderson, Robert *1805–1871* Union commander of Fort Sumter; he was forced to surrender to the Confederacy. p. 118

Anthony, Susan B. *1820–1906* Women's suffrage leader who worked to enable women to have the same rights as men. p. 247

Aristide, Jean-Bertrand (air•ih•STEED, ZHAHN bair•TRAHN) *1953–* Freely elected president of Haiti; he was overthrown in 1991 but was returned to office in 1994. p. 533

Armstrong, Louis *1901–1971* Noted jazz trumpeter who helped make jazz popular in the 1920s. pp. 288–289

Armstrong, Neil *1930–* American astronaut who was the first person to set foot on the moon. p. 432

Austin, Stephen F. *1793–1836* Moses Austin's son. He carried out his father's dream of starting a United States colony in Texas. p. 71

B

Balboa, Vasco Núñez de (bahl•BOH•uh, NOON•yays day) *1475–1519* Spanish explorer who, in 1513, became the first European to reach the western coast of the Americas—proving to Europeans that the Americas were separate from Asia. p. 31

Banneker, Benjamin *1731–1806* African American mathematician and astronomer who helped survey the land for the new capital of the United States. p. 64

Barrett, Janie Porter *1865–1948* African American teacher who founded a settlement house in Hampton, Virginia. p. 208

Barton, Clara *1821–1912* Civil War nurse and founder of the American Red Cross. p. 127

Begin, Menachem (BAY•guhn) *1913–1992* Israeli prime minister; signed peace treaty with President Anwar Sadat of Egypt. p. 456

Bell, Alexander Graham *1847–1922* American inventor and educator; he invented the telephone in 1876. p. 201

Bellamy, Francis *1800s* Writer of patriotic oath that came to be called the Pledge of Allegiance. p. 515

Berlin, Irving *1888–1989* American songwriter who moved to New York City from Russia in 1893. p. 167

Berry, Chuck *1926–* American rock and roll performer. p. 419

Bessemer, Henry *1813–1898* British inventor of a way to produce steel more easily and cheaply than before. p. 159

Bolívar, Simón (boh•LEE•var, see•MOHN) *1783–1830* Leader of independence movements in Bolivia, Colombia, Ecuador, Peru, and Venezuela. p. 538

Bonaparte, Napoleon (BOH•nuh•part, nuh•POH•lee•uhn) *1769–1821* French leader who sold all of the Louisiana region to the United States. pp. 66–67

Bonavita, Rosina *1900s* American factory worker during World War II who became the model for "Rosie the Riveter," representing women working to produce goods needed for the war. pp. 349–350

Boone, Daniel *1734–1820* American who was one of the first pioneers to cross the Appalachians. p. 65

Booth, John Wilkes *1838–1865* Actor who assassinated President Abraham Lincoln. p. 141

Breckinridge, John *1821–1875* Democrat from Kentucky who ran against Abraham Lincoln in the 1860 presidential election. p. 117

Brezhnev, Leonid (BREZH•nef) *1906–1982* Leader of the Communist party of the Soviet Union from 1964 until his death in 1982. President Nixon's 1972 visit with him in the Soviet Union led to arms control and began a period of détente. pp. 452–453

Brown, John *1800–1859* American abolitionist who seized a weapons storehouse to help slaves rebel. He was caught and hanged. p. 113

Brown, Linda *1943–* African American student whose family was among a group that challenged public-school segregation. pp. 420–421

Bruce, Blanche K. *1841–1898* Former slave who became U.S. senator from Mississippi. p. 143

Burchfield, Charles *1893–1967* American painter. p. 288

Bush, George *1924–* Forty-first U.S. President. He was President at the end of the Cold War and during Operation Desert Storm. pp. 461, 462–464, 465–466, 523

Bush, George W. *1946–* Forty-third U.S. President; son of George Bush, he won the closest presidential election in history. pp. 470–471, 473, 513

C

Caboto, Giovanni (kah•BOH•toh, joh•VAH•nee) *1450?–1499?* Italian explorer who, in 1497, sailed from England and landed in what is now Newfoundland, though he thought he had landed in Asia. The English gave him the name John Cabot. p. 30

Calhoun, John C. *1782–1850* Vice President under John Quincy Adams and Andrew Jackson. He was a strong believer in states' rights. pp. 100, 117

Calvert, Cecilius *1605–1675* First proprietor of the Maryland Colony. p. 43

Capone, Alphonse *1899–1947* American gangster during Prohibition Era. pp. 282–283

Cardozo, Francis L. *1837–1903* African American who became secretary of state and state treasurer in South Carolina. p. 143

Carnegie, Andrew *1835–1919* Entrepreneur who helped the steel industry grow in the United States. pp. 159, 160

Carter, Jimmy *1924–* Thirty-ninth U.S. President. He brought about a peace agreement between Israel and Egypt. pp. 456–457, 458

Cartier, Jacques (kar•TYAY, ZHAHK) *1491–1557* French explorer who sailed up the St. Lawrence River and began a fur-trading business with the Hurons. p. 33

Castro, Fidel *1926–* Leader who took over Cuba in 1959 and made it a communist nation. pp. 429, 532

Catt, Carrie Chapman *1859–1947* President of the International Woman Suffrage Alliance. pp. 247–248

Cavelier, René-Robert (ka•vuhl•YAY) *See* La Salle.

Chamberlain, Neville *1869–1940* British prime minister; met with Hitler and Mussolini in hopes of preventing invasions and war. p. 335

Champlain, Samuel de (sham•PLAYN) *1567?–1635* French explorer who founded the first settlement at Quebec. p. 33

Charles I *1600–1649* English king who chartered the colonies of Massachusetts and Maryland. p. 43

Charles II *1630–1685* English king who granted charters for the New Hampshire Colony and the Carolina Colony. Son of Charles I and Henrietta Maria. pp. 41, 44

Chavez, Cesar *1927–1993* Labor leader and organizer of the United Farm Workers. p. 439

Chisholm, Shirley *1924–* First African American woman elected to Congress. p. 438

Churchill, Sir Winston Leonard Spencer *1874–1965* British prime minister during World War II. pp. 337, 390

Clark, William *1770–1838* American explorer who aided Meriwether Lewis in an expedition through the Louisiana Purchase. p. 67

Clay, Henry *1777–1852* Representative from Kentucky who worked for compromises on the slavery issue. p. 102

Clay, Lucius *1897–1978* U.S. Army officer; he oversaw Berlin Airlift. p. 392

Clinton, Hillary Rodham *1947–* Wife of William Clinton; senator of New York. p. 512

Clinton, William *1946–* Forty-second U.S. President. Economic recovery occurred during his presidency; second President to be impeached. pp. 465–467, 468–470

Cochran, Jacqueline *1910?–1980* American aviator; director of Women's Air Force Service Pilots, or WASPs. p. 350

Collins, Michael *1930–* American astronaut who remained in the lunar orbiter during the *Apollo 11* moon landing. p. 432

Columbus, Christopher *1451–1506* Italian-born Spanish explorer who, in 1492, sailed west from Spain and thought he had reached Asia but had actually reached islands near the Americas, lands that were unknown to Europeans. pp. 29–30

Coolidge, Calvin *1872–1933* Thirtieth U.S. President; as governor of Massachusetts, he restored order during a police strike. p. 246

Cooper, Peter *1791–1883* American manufacturer who built *Tom Thumb*, one of the first locomotives made in the United States. p. 80

Copland, Aaron *1900–1990* American composer. p. 289

Cornish, Samuel *1795–1858* African American who, in 1827, helped John Russwurm found an abolitionist newspaper called *Freedom's Journal*. p. 112

Coronado, Francisco Vásquez de (kawr•oh•NAH•doh) *1510?–1554* Spanish explorer who led an expedition from Mexico City into what is now the southwestern United States in search of the Seven Cities of Gold. p. 32

Cortés, Hernando (kawr•TEZ) *1485–1547* Spanish conquistador who conquered the Aztec Empire. pp. 32, 524

Crazy Horse *1842?–1877* Sioux leader who fought against General George Custer. p. 155

Cullen, Countee *1903–1946* African American writer and poet during the Harlem Renaissance. p. 290

D

da Gama, Vasco (dah GA•muh) *1460?–1524* Portuguese navigator who sailed from Europe, around the southern tip of Africa, and on to Asia between 1497 and 1499. p. 29

Davis, Jefferson *1808–1889* United States senator from Mississippi who became president of the Confederacy. p. 117

Dawes, William *1745–1799* American who, along with Paul Revere, warned the Patriots that the British were marching toward Concord. p. 50

de Soto, Hernando (day SOH•toh) *1496?–1542* Spanish explorer who led an expedition into what is today the southeastern United States. p. 31

Dempsey, William (Jack) *1895–1983* American boxer. p. 287

Dewey, George *1837–1917* American naval commander who destroyed the Spanish fleet and captured Manila Bay in the Spanish-American War. p. 194

Dewey, Thomas Edmund *1902–1971* Republican candidate who challenged Harry S. Truman for the presidency in 1948 election. p. 411

Dias, Bartolomeu (DEE•ahsh) *1450?–1500* Portuguese navigator who, in 1488, became the first European to sail around the southern tip of Africa. p. 29

Díaz, Porfirio *1830–1915* Mexican dictator. p. 526

Disney, Walter Elias *1901–1966* American film producer, cartoon creator, and builder of theme parks. p. 307

Douglas, Stephen A. *1813–1861* American legislator who wrote the Kansas-Nebraska Act and debated Abraham Lincoln in a race for a senate seat from Illinois. p. 115

Douglass, Frederick *1817–1895* Abolitionist speaker and writer who had escaped from slavery. p. 113

Drake, Edwin *1819–1880* American pioneer in oil industry; became first to drill for petroleum. p. 161

Drew, Charles *1904–1950* American physician who developed an efficient way to store blood plasma in blood banks. p. 348

Du Bois, W. E. B. (doo•BOYS) *1868–1963* African American teacher, writer, and leader who helped form the National Association for the Advancement of Colored People (NAACP). p. 218

E

Earhart, Amelia *1897–1937* American aviator; first woman to cross the Atlantic in an airplane. pp. 279–280

Edison, Thomas *1847–1931* American who invented the phonograph and the electric lightbulb; he also built the first power station to supply electricity to New York City. pp. 162–163, 164–165, 201

Eisenhower, Dwight D. *1890–1969* Thirty-fourth U.S. President and, earlier, American general who led the D day invasion. pp. 362, 364, 384, 415, 419, 454

Ellicott, Andrew *1754–1820* American clockmaker who helped survey the land for the new capital of the United States. p. 64

Ellington, Edward Kennedy (Duke) *1899–1974* Band leader who became well-known playing jazz during the 1920s. p. 290

F

Ferdinand, Francis *1863–1914* Archduke of Austria-Hungary; his assassination sparked the outbreak of World War I. pp. 227–228

Ferdinand II *1452–1516* King of Spain who—with Queen Isabella, his wife—sent Christopher Columbus on his voyage to find a western route to Asia. p. 30

Fitzgerald, F. Scott *1896–1940* American writer. p. 288

Fong, Hiram L. *1906–* Chinese immigrant who settled in Hawaii; became first Chinese American senator. p. 169

Ford, Gerald *1913–* Thirty-eighth U.S. President. He became President when Richard Nixon resigned. The Vietnam War ended during his term. pp. 453, 455-456

Ford, Henry *1863–1947* American automobile manufacturer who mass-produced cars at low cost by using assembly lines. pp. 202–204, 277

Fox, Vicente *1942–* Elected president of Mexico in 2000. p. 527

Franco, Francisco *1892–1975* Spanish dictator. p. 334

Frank, Anne *1929–1945* Jewish girl who kept a diary describing her family's hiding during Nazi occupation of the Netherlands; they were later found and sent to concentration camps. pp. 367–368

Franklin, Benjamin *1706–1790* American leader who was sent to Britain to ask Parliament for representation. He was a writer of the Declaration of Independence, a delegate to the Constitutional Convention, and a respected scientist and business leader. p. 59

Friedan, Betty *1921–* Writer who helped set up the National Organization for Women to work for women's rights. p. 439

Fulton, Robert *1765–1815* American engineer and inventor who created the first commercial steamboat. p. 79

G

Gagarin, Yury Alekseyevich *1934–1968* Soviet cosmonaut; first human to orbit Earth. p. 431

Gage, Thomas *1721–1787* Head of the British army in North America and colonial governor. p. 50

Garrison, William Lloyd *1805–1879* American abolitionist who started a newspaper called *The Liberator*. p. 112

George III *1738–1820* King of Britain during the Revolutionary War. p. 47

Gershwin, George *1898–1937* American composer. p. 289

Gibbs, Jonathan C. *1800s* African American who became secretary of state in Florida; helped set up public school system. p. 143

Glenn, John H., Jr. *1921–* American astronaut who was the first person from the United States to orbit Earth. Former U.S. senator. p. 432

Gorbachev, Mikhail (gawr•buh•CHAWF, mee•KAH•eel) *1931–* Leader of the Soviet Union from 1985 to 1991. He improved relations with the United States and expanded freedom in the Soviet Union. pp. 459–460, 461, 464

Gordon, William E. *1918–* American scientist who established the Arecibo Observatory in Puerto Rico. p. 532

Gore, Albert *1948–* Vice President under President William Clinton. Defeated by George W. Bush in the 2000 election—the closest presidential election in history. pp. 470, 513

Granger, Gordon *1822–1876* Union general who read the order declaring all slaves in Texas to be free. p. 146

Grant, Ulysses S. *1822–1885* Eighteenth U.S. President and, earlier, commander of the Union army in the Civil War. pp. 129, 132, 133, 135, 139

Greeley, Horace *1811–1872* American journalist and political leader; publisher of a newspaper called the *New York Tribune*. p. 125

Groves, Leslie *1896–1970* American general and head of the project to develop the atomic bomb. p. 378

H

Hallidie, Andrew S. *1836–1900* American inventor of the cable car. p. 209

Hamilton, Alexander *1755–1804* American leader in calling for the Constitutional Convention and winning support for it. He favored a strong national government. pp. 62, 63

Hammond, James Henry *1807–1864* Senator from South Carolina. p. 106

Hancock, John *1737–1793* Leader of the Sons of Liberty in the Massachusetts Colony. p. 50

Harding, Warren G. *1865–1923* Twenty-ninth U.S. President. p. 246

Haynes, Elwood *1857–1925* Indiana inventor who developed the first gasoline-powered automobile, in 1894. p. 202

Hearst, William Randolph *1863–1951* American newspaper publisher; owner of *New York Journal*; known for yellow journalism. p. 193

Hemingway, Ernest *1899–1961* American writer. p. 288

Henry *1394–1460* Henry the Navigator, prince of Portugal, who set up the first European school for training sailors in navigation. p. 29

Hidalgo, Miguel *1753–1811* Mexican priest who called for a revolution against Spain in 1810. p. 525

Hirohito *1901–1989* Emperor of Japan from 1926 until his death. p. 334

Hitler, Adolf *1889–1945* Nazi dictator of Germany. His actions led to World War II and the killing of millions of people. pp. 333, 335, 336, 363, 366, 368

Holiday, Eleanora (Billie) *1915–1959* American jazz singer. p. 290

Holly, Charles Hardin (Buddy) *1936–1959* American rock and roll performer. p. 419

Hooker, Thomas *1586?–1647* Minister who helped form the Connecticut Colony. His democratic ideas were adopted in the Fundamental Orders. pp. 40–41

Hoover, Herbert *1874–1964* Thirty-first U.S. President. When the Great Depression began, he thought that the economy was healthy and conditions would improve. pp. 296, 302–304

Hopper, Edward *1882–1967* American painter. p. 288

Houston, Sam *1793–1863* President of the Republic of Texas and, later, governor of the state of Texas. p. 117

Hudson, Henry *?–1611* Explorer who sailed up the Hudson River, giving the Dutch a claim to the area. p. 34

Huerta, Dolores *1930–* Labor leader and organizer, along with Cesar Chavez, of the United Farm Workers. p. 439

Hurston, Zora Neale *1903–1960* African American novelist and one of the best-known Harlem writers. p. 290

Hussein, Saddam *1937–* Leader of Iraq. p. 463

Hutchinson, Anne Marbury *1591–1643* English-born woman who left Massachusetts because of her religious beliefs. She settled near Providence, which joined with other settlements to form the Rhode Island Colony. p. 40

Isabella I *1451–1504* Queen of Spain who—with King Ferdinand, her husband—sent Columbus on his voyage to find a western route to Asia. p. 30

Jackson, Andrew *1767–1845* Seventh U.S. President and, earlier, commander who won the final battle in the War of 1812. As President he favored a strong Union and ordered the removal of Native Americans from their lands. pp. 69–70, 101

Jackson, Thomas (Stonewall) *1824–1863* Confederate general. pp. 122, 130

Jay, John *1745–1829* American leader who wrote letters to newspapers, defending the Constitution. He became the first chief justice of the Supreme Court. p. 62

Jefferson, Thomas *1743–1826* Third U.S. President and the main writer of the Declaration of Independence. pp. 51, 62, 63, 67

Jenney, William *1832–1907* American engineer who developed the use of steel frames to build tall buildings. pp. 160, 208–209

John I *1357–1433* King of Portugal during a time of great exploration. Father of Prince Henry, who set up a school of navigation. p. 29

Johnson, Andrew *1808–1875* Seventeenth U.S. President. Differences with Congress about Reconstruction led to his being impeached, though he was found not guilty. pp. 141, 143

Johnson, Lyndon B. *1908–1973* Thirty-sixth U.S. President. He started Great Society programs and expanded U.S. involvement in the Vietnam War. pp. 431, 436, 437, 448, 449, 451

Joliet, Louis (zhohl•YAY, loo•EE) *1645–1700* French fur trader who with Jacques Marquette and five others explored North American lakes and rivers for France. p. 33

Joplin, Scott *1868–1917* American composer; known as the King of Ragtime. p. 209

Joseph *1840?–1904* Nez Perce chief who tried to lead his people to Canada after they were told to move onto a reservation. p. 155

Juárez, Benito *1806–1872* Served twice as president of Mexico; made many reforms. p. 526

Kalakaua (kah•lah•KAH•ooh•ah) *1836–1891* Hawaiian king who tried but failed to keep Americans from taking over the Hawaiian Islands. p. 191

Kennedy, John F. *1917–1963* Thirty-fifth U.S. President. He made the Soviet Union remove its missiles from Cuba; later introduced the bill that became known as the Civil Rights Act of 1964. pp. 428–431, 432

Kennedy, Robert *1925–1968* American politician and attorney general. p. 429

King, Dr. Martin Luther, Jr. *1929–1968* African American civil rights leader who worked for integration in nonviolent ways. King won the Nobel Peace Prize in 1964. p. 421, 435–438

L

La Follette, Robert *1855–1925* Wisconsin governor who began many reforms in his state, including a merit system for government jobs. pp. 214–215

La Salle, René-Robert Cavelier, Sieur de (luh•SAL) *1643–1687* French explorer who found the mouth of the Mississippi River and claimed the whole Mississippi Valley for France. p. 34

Lawrence, Jacob *1917–2000* African American artist; his parents took part in the Great Migration. pp. 171, 238

Leahy, William *1875–1959* American navy admiral; opposed the use of the atom bomb. p. 378

Lee, Robert E. *1807–1870* United States army colonel who gave up his post to become commander of the Confederate army in the Civil War. pp. 125, 130, 135

LeMay, Curtis *1906–1990* American air force officer; directed Berlin Airlift. p. 393

L'Enfant, Pierre Charles *1754–1825* French-born American engineer who planned the buildings and streets of the new capital of the United States. p. 64

Lewis, Meriwether *1774–1809* American explorer chosen by Thomas Jefferson to be a pathfinder in the territory of the Louisiana Purchase. p. 67

Lewis, Sinclair *1885–1951* American novelist. p. 288

Liliuokalani, Lydia (lih•lee•uh•woh•kuh•LAH•nee) *1838–1917* Hawaiian queen who tried but failed to bring back the Hawaiian monarchy's authority. p. 191

Lincoln, Abraham *1809–1865* Sixteenth U.S. President, leader of the Union in the Civil War, and signer of the Emancipation Proclamation. pp. 114–119, 125, 126, 132, 140–141

Lincoln, Mary Todd *1818–1882* Wife of Abraham Lincoln. p. 141

Lindbergh, Charles *1902–1974* Airplane pilot who was the first to fly solo between the United States and Europe. pp. 278–279

Longstreet, James *1821–1904* Former Confederate general who wanted the South to build more factories; considered a scalawag. p. 148

M

MacArthur, Douglas *1880–1964* Commander of Allied forces in the Pacific during World War II. pp. 304, 388, 394, 413

Madison, James *1751–1836* Fourth U.S. President. He was a leader in calling for the Constitutional Convention, writing the Constitution, and winning support for it. p. 62

Magellan, Ferdinand (muh•JEH•luhn) *1480?–1521* Portuguese explorer who, in 1519, led a fleet of ships from Spain westward to Asia. He died on the voyage, but one of the ships made it back to Spain, completing the first trip around the world. p. 31

Malcolm X *1925–1965* African American leader who disagreed with the views of Dr. Martin Luther King, Jr., on nonviolence and integration. p. 438

Marconi, Guglielmo (mahr•KOH•nee, gool•YEL•moh) *1874–1937* Italian who invented the radio. p. 201

Marquette, Jacques (mar•KET, ZHAHK) *1637–1675* Catholic missionary who knew several American Indian languages. With Louis Joliet, he explored lakes and rivers for France. p. 33

Marshall, George C. *1880–1959* U.S. secretary of state who developed the European Recovery Program, also known as the Marshall Plan, after World War II. p. 391

Marshall, Thurgood *1908–1993* NAACP lawyer who argued the school segregation case that the Supreme Court ruled on in 1954 and, later, was the first African American to serve on the Supreme Court. pp. 421, 438

Martí, José (mar•TEE) *1853–1895* Cuban writer and patriot who worked for Cuban independence from Spain. p. 192

McCarthy, Joseph Raymond *1908–1957* American politician; accused many individuals of being communists. p. 420

McKay, Claude *1890–1948* African American writer during the Harlem Renaissance. p. 290

McKinley, William *1843–1901* Twenty-fifth U.S. President. The Spanish-American War was fought during his term. p. 195

Miller, Doris (Dorie) *1919–1944* African American seaman who was awarded the Navy Cross for his bravery during the Japanese attack on Pearl Harbor, December 7, 1941. p. 344

Monroe, James *1758–1831* Fifth U.S. President. He established the Monroe Doctrine, which said that the United States would stop any European nation from expanding its American empire. p. 69

Morton, Ferdinand Joseph La Menthe (Jelly Roll) *1885–1941* American jazz musician. p. 288

Motecuhzoma (maw•tay•kwah•SOH•mah) *1466–1520* Emperor of the Aztecs when they were conquered by the Spanish. He is also known as Montezuma. p. 32

Murrow, Edward Roscoe *1908–1965* American journalist who reported from London during Battle of Britain. p. 337

Mussolini, Benito (moo•suh•LEE•nee, buh•NEE•toh) *1883–1945* Ruler of Italy from 1922 until 1943, most of that time as dictator. pp. 333, 335, 363, 366

N

Nast, Thomas *1840–1902* American cartoonist who created the "Uncle Sam" character. p. 512

Nimitz, Chester W. *1885–1966* Commander of U.S. Pacific fleet during World War II. p. 373

Nixon, Richard M. *1913–1994* Thirty-seventh U.S. President. He tried to end the Vietnam War, he reduced tensions with communist nations, and he resigned the presidency because of the Watergate scandal. pp. 451–453, 455

O

O'Connor, Sandra Day *1930–* First woman to be appointed to the United States Supreme Court. p. 512

Oglethorpe, James *1696–1785* English settler who was given a charter to settle Georgia. He wanted to use debtors from England to help settle it. p. 44

O'Keeffe, Georgia *1887–1986* American painter who developed her own style of showing abstract studies of color and light. p. 288

Oppenheimer, Julius Robert *1904–1967* Director of the Manhattan Project, which developed the atom bomb. p. 376

Otis, James *1725–1783* Massachusetts colonist who spoke out against British taxes and called for "no taxation without representation." p. 48

P

Paine, Thomas *1737–1809* Author of a widely read pamphlet called *Common Sense,* in which he attacked King George III and called for a revolution to make the colonies independent. p. 50

Parks, Rosa *1913–* African American woman whose refusal to give up her seat on a Montgomery, Alabama, bus started a year-long bus boycott. p. 421

Paterson, William *1745–1806* Constitutional delegate from New Jersey who submitted the New Jersey Plan, under which each state would have one vote, regardless of population. p. 61

Penn, William *1644–1718* Proprietor of Pennsylvania under a charter from King Charles II of Britain. Penn was a Quaker who made Pennsylvania a refuge for settlers who wanted religious freedom. p. 42

Perot, H. Ross *1930–* Texas business person who ran for President in the 1992 election against George Bush and William Clinton. pp. 465–466

Pickett, George *1825–1875* Confederate general who led the charge at Gettysburg; he was forced to retreat. p. 130

Polo, Marco *1254–1324* Explorer from Venice who spent many years in Asia in the late 1200s. He wrote a book about his travels that gave Europeans information about Asia. p. 28

Ponce de León, Juan (POHN•say day lay•OHN) *1460–1521* Spanish explorer who landed on the North American mainland in 1513, near what is now St. Augustine, Florida. p. 31

Powell, Colin L. *1937–* Chairman of the Joint Chiefs of Staff during the Gulf War; became U.S. secretary of state in 2001. p. 464

Presley, Elvis *1935–1977* American rock and roll performer. p. 419

Pulitzer, Joseph *1847–1911* American journalist and newspaper publisher; owner of *New York World.* p. 193

R

Randolph, Edmund *1753–1813* Virginia delegate to the Constitutional Convention who wrote the Virginia Plan, which stated that the number of representatives a state would have in Congress should be based on the free population of the state. p. 61

Reagan, Ronald *1911–* Fortieth U.S. President. His meetings with Soviet leader Mikhail Gorbachev led to a thaw in the Cold War, including advances in arms control. pp. 459–460

Revels, Hiram R. *1822–1901* First African American elected to the U.S. Senate. p. 143

Revere, Paul *1735–1818* American who warned the Patriots that the British were marching toward Concord, where Patriot weapons were stored. p. 50

Riis, Jacob (REES) *1849–1914* Reformer and writer who described the living conditions of the poor in New York City. pp. 206–207

Robinson, Bill (Bojangles) *1878–1949* African American tap dancer. p. 290

Rockefeller, John D. *1839–1937* American oil entrepreneur who joined many refineries into one business, called the Standard Oil Company. pp. 161–162

Roebling, John *1806–1869* Engineer and industrialist who designed suspension bridges. p. 160

Rogers, Will *1879–1935* American comedian during the Great Depression. p. 306

Roosevelt, Eleanor *1884–1962* Wife of Franklin Delano Roosevelt; one of the most active First Ladies. p. 312

Roosevelt, Franklin Delano *1882–1945* Thirty-second U.S. President. He began New Deal programs to help the nation out of the Great Depression, and he was the nation's leader during most of World War II. pp. 308–310, 313, 332, 340–341, 344–345, 348, 362, 367, 375

Roosevelt, Theodore *1858–1919* Twenty-sixth U.S. President. Hero of the Spanish-American War. He showed the world America's strength, made it possible to build the Panama Canal, and worked for progressive reforms and conservation. pp. 194–195, 196, 215–217

Root, George Frederick *1820–1895* American composer and teacher. p. 99

Ross, Edmund G. *1826–1907* Senator from Kansas who voted to acquit President Andrew Johnson. p. 143

Ross, John *1790–1866* Chief of the Cherokee nation. He fought in U.S. courts to prevent the loss of the Cherokees' lands in Georgia. Though he won the legal battle, he still had to lead his people along the Trail of Tears to what is now Oklahoma. p. 70

Russwurm, John *1799–1851* Helped Samuel Cornish found an abolitionist newspaper called *Freedom's Journal* in 1827. p. 112

Ruth, George (Babe) *1895–1948* American baseball player. p. 287

BIOGRAPHICAL DICTIONARY

S

Sacagawea (sa•kuh•juh•WEE•uh) *1786?–1812?* Shoshone woman who acted as an interpreter for the Lewis and Clark expedition. p. 68

Sadat, Anwar (suh•DAT) *1918–1981* Egyptian president; signed peace treaty with Prime Minister Menachem Begin of Israel. p. 456

San Martín, José de (sahn mar•TEEN) *1778–1850* Leader of an independence movement in Argentina. p. 538

Santa Anna, Antonio López de *1794–1876* Dictator of Mexico; defeated Texans at the Alamo. p. 71

Sarnoff, David *1891–1971* American communications executive; he planned to broadcast music to radios in people's homes. p. 286

Scott, Dred *1795?–1858* Enslaved African who took his case for freedom to the Supreme Court and lost. p. 104

Seward, William H. *1801–1872* Secretary of state in the cabinet of Abraham Lincoln. pp. 107, 189

Shays, Daniel *1747?–1825* Leader of Shays's Rebellion, which showed the weakness of the government under the Articles of Confederation. p. 59

Shepard, Alan, Jr. *1923–1998* American astronaut; first American to fly in space. p. 432

Sherman, William Tecumseh *1820–1891* Union general who, after defeating Confederate forces in Atlanta, led the March to the Sea, on which his troops caused great destruction. pp. 132, 133

Sitting Bull *1831–1890* Sioux leader who fought against General George Custer. p. 155

Slater, Samuel *1768–1835* Textile pioneer who helped bring the Industrial Revolution to the United States by providing plans for a new spinning machine. p. 77

Smalls, Robert *1839–1915* African American who delivered a Confederate steamer to the Union forces. p. 127

Smith, Bessie *1894 or 1898–1937* African American blues singer. p. 288

Smith, John *1580–1631* English explorer who, as leader of the Jamestown settlement, saved its people from starvation. p. 34

Sprague, Frank *1857–1934* American inventor who built the trolley car, an electric streetcar. p. 211

Squanto *See* Tisquantum.

Stalin, Joseph *1879–1953* Dictator of the Soviet Union from 1924 until his death. pp. 334, 336, 390

Stanton, Elizabeth Cady *1815–1902* American reformer who organized the first convention for women's rights. pp. 111, 247

Starr, Ellen Gates *1860–1940* Reformer who, with Jane Addams, founded Hull House in Chicago. p. 208

Stowe, Harriet Beecher *1811–1896* American abolitionist who, in 1852, wrote the book *Uncle Tom's Cabin*. p. 112

T

Taft, William Howard *1857–1930* Twenty-seventh U.S. President; initiated dollar diplomacy with other nations. p. 228

Taney, Roger B. (TAW•nee) *1777–1864* Supreme Court chief justice who wrote the ruling against Dred Scott. p. 105

Tarbell, Ida *1857–1944* Reporter during the Progressive Era; investigated John D. Rockefeller's Standard Oil Company. p. 214

Tisquantum *1585?–1622* Native American who spoke English and who helped the Plymouth Colony. p. 35

Tojo, Hideki *1884–1948* Japanese general who was named prime minister when military seized Japan's government. p. 334

Tompkins, Sally *1833–1916* Civil War nurse who eventually ran her own private hospital in Richmond, Virginia. She was a captain in the Confederate army, the only woman to achieve such an honor. p. 127

Trudeau, Pierre *1919–2000* Twice-elected prime minister of Canada who helped defeat the separatist movement of Quebec. p. 544

Truman, Harry S. *1884–1972* Thirty-third U.S. President. He ordered the atom bomb to be dropped on Japan to end World War II; he later sent American soldiers to support South Korea in 1950. pp. 367, 375, 377, 390, 410–411

Truth, Sojourner *1797?–1883* Abolitionist and former slave who became a leading preacher against slavery. p. 113

Tubman, Harriet *1820–1913* Abolitionist and former slave who became a conductor on the Underground Railroad. She led about 300 slaves to freedom. p. 111

Tunney, Gene *1898–1978* American boxer. p. 287

Turner, Nat *1800–1831* Enslaved African who led a rebellion against slavery. p. 109

Tweed, William (Boss) *1823–1878* New York City political boss who robbed the city of millions of dollars. p. 214

V

Vespucci, Amerigo (veh•SPOO•chee, uh•MAIR•ih•goh) *1454–1512* Italian explorer who made several voyages from Europe to what many people thought was Asia. He determined that he had landed on another continent, which was later called America in his honor. pp. 30–31

W

Wald, Lillian *1867–1940* Reformer who started the Henry Street Settlement in New York City. p. 208

Warren, Earl *1891–1974* Chief justice of the Supreme Court; he wrote the 1954 decision against school segregation. p. 421

Washington, George *1732–1799* First U.S. President, leader of the Continental Army during the Revolutionary War, and president of the Constitutional Convention. pp. 50, 52, 53, 58, 62, 64

Waters, Ethel *1896–1977* African American singer and actress. p. 290

Weaver, Robert *1907–1997* Secretary of Housing and Urban Development; first African American to serve in a President's Cabinet. p. 438

Welch, Joseph *1890–1960* American lawyer; represented the U.S. Army in a televised hearing before Joseph McCarthy. p. 420

Westinghouse, George *1846–1914* American inventor who designed an air brake for stopping trains. p. 159

White, Edward Higgins, II *1930–1967* American astronaut; first U.S. astronaut to walk in space. p. 432

Whitney, Eli *1765–1825* American inventor who was most famous for his invention of the cotton gin and his idea of interchangeable parts, which made mass production possible. p. 77

Williams, Roger *1603?–1683* Founder of Providence, in what is now Rhode Island. He had been forced to leave Massachusetts because of his views. pp. 39–40

Wilson, Samuel *1766–1854* American meat packer who inspired the "Uncle Sam" national symbol. p. 512

Wilson, Woodrow *1856–1924* Twenty-eighth U.S. President. He brought the country into World War I after trying to stay neutral. He favored the League of Nations, but the Senate rejected U.S. membership in the league. pp. 228, 229, 230, 237, 241, 242–243, 244, 248

Winthrop, John *1588–1649* Puritan leader who served several times as governor of the Massachusetts Bay Colony. He helped form confederation among people of New England and served as its first president. p. 39

Woods, Granville T. *1856–1910* African American who improved the air brake and developed a telegraph system for trains. p. 159

Wright, Frank Lloyd *1867–1959* American architect known for producing unusual buildings. pp. 281, 282

Wright, Orville *1871–1948* Pioneer in American aviation who—with his brother, Wilbur—made and flew the first successful airplane, at Kitty Hawk, North Carolina. pp. 204–205

Wright, Wilbur *1867–1912* Pioneer in American aviation who—with his brother, Orville—made and flew the first successful airplane, at Kitty Hawk, North Carolina. pp. 204–205

Y

Yeltsin, Boris *1931–* President of Russia who worked with President Clinton to reduce the number of nuclear weapons. p. 469

Z

Zedong, Mao (MOW zeh•DUNG) *1893–1976* Communist leader of China who invited President Richard Nixon to visit his country in 1972. p. 452

Zimmermann, Arthur *1864–1940* Germany's foreign secretary; he sent a telegram during World War I to a German ambassador to Mexico offering Mexico an alliance with Germany and support in reconquering lost territory. p. 229

BIOGRAPHICAL DICTIONARY

Gazetteer

The Gazetteer is a geographical dictionary that will help you locate places discussed in this book. The page number tells where each place appears on a map.

A

Abilene A city in central Kansas on the Smoky Hill River; a major railroad town. (39°N, 97°W) p. 152

Alberta One of Canada's ten provinces; located in western Canada. p. 542

Amazon River The longest river in South America, flowing from the Andes Mountains across Brazil and into the Atlantic Ocean. p. 537

Andes Mountains (AN•deez) The longest chain of mountains in the world; located along the entire western coast of South America. p. 537

Antietam (an•TEE•tuhm) A creek near Sharpsburg in north central Maryland; site of a Civil War battle in 1862. (39°N, 78°W) p. 134

Antigua An island in the eastern part of the Leeward Islands, in the eastern West Indies. p. 530

Appomattox (a•puh•MA•tuhks) A village in central Virginia; site of the battle that ended the Civil War in 1865; once known as Appomattox Court House. (37°N, 79°W) p. 134

Atlanta Georgia's capital and largest city; located in the northwest central part of the state; site of a Civil War battle in 1864. (33°N, 84°W) pp. 134, 493

Austin The capital of Texas; located in south central Texas. (30°N, 97°W) p. 493

B

Bahamas An island group in the North Atlantic Ocean; located southeast of Florida and north of Cuba. p. 530

Baja California A peninsula in northwestern Mexico extending south-southeast between the Pacific Ocean and the Gulf of California. p. 525

Barbados An island in the Lesser Antilles, West Indies; located east of the central Windward Islands. p. 530

Barbuda A flat coral island in the eastern West Indies. p. 530

Baxter Springs A city in the southeastern corner of Kansas. (37°N, 94°W) p. 152

Belgrade The capital of Serbia. (44°N, 20°E) p. 227

Belmopan (bel•moh•PAN) A town in Central America; capital of Belize. (17°N, 88°W) p. 530

Bennington A town in the southwestern corner of Vermont; site of a major Revolutionary War battle in 1777. (43°N, 73°W) p. 52

Bogotá A city in South America, located on the plateau of the Andes; capital of Colombia. (4°N, 74°W) p. 537

Boise (BOY•zee) Idaho's capital and largest city; located in the southwestern part of the state. (44°N, 116°W) p. 493

Brandywine A battlefield on Brandywine Creek in southeastern Pennsylvania; site of a major Revolutionary War battle in 1777. (40°N, 76°W) p. 52

Brasília A city in South America on the Tocantins River; capital of Brazil. (15°S, 48°W) p. 537

British Columbia One of Canada's ten provinces; located on the west coast of Canada and bordered by the Yukon Territory, the Northwest Territories, Alberta, the United States, and the Pacific Ocean. p. 542

Buenos Aires A city in South America; the capital of Argentina. (34°S, 58°W) p. 537

Bull Run A stream in northeastern Virginia; flows toward the Potomac River; site of Civil War battles in 1861 and in 1862. p. 134

C

Calgary A city in southern Alberta, Canada; located on the Bow River. (51°N, 114°W) p. 542

Camden A city in north central South Carolina, near the Wateree River; site of a major Revolutionary War battle in 1780. (34°N, 81°W) p. 52

Canal Zone A strip of territory in Panama, through which the Panama Canal runs. p. 196

Canary Islands An island group in the Atlantic Ocean off the northwest coast of Africa. (28°N, 16°W) p. 37

Caracas (kuh•RAH•kuhs) A city in northern Venezuela; capital of Venezuela. (10°N, 67°W) p. 537

Caribbean Sea A part of the Atlantic Ocean between the West Indies and Central and South America. p. 530

Cayenne A city on the northwestern coast of Cayenne Island, in northern South America; capital of French Guiana. (5°N, 52°W) p. 537

Chancellorsville (CHAN•suh•lerz•vil) A location in northeastern Virginia, just west of Fredericksburg; site of a Civil War battle in 1863. (38°N, 78°W) p. 134

Charleston A city in southeastern South Carolina; a major port on the Atlantic Ocean; once known as Charles Town. (33°N, 80°W) pp. 52, 134

Charlotte The largest city in North Carolina; located in the south central part of the state. (35°N, 81°W) p. 493

Charlottetown The capital of Prince Edward Island, Canada; located in the central part of the island. (46°N, 63°W) p. 542

Chattanooga (cha•tuh•NOO•guh) A city in southeastern Tennessee; located on the Tennessee River; site of a Civil War battle in 1863. (35°N, 85°W) p. 134

Cheyenne (shy•AN) The capital of Wyoming; located in the southeastern part of the state. (41°N, 105°W) p. 152

Chicago A city in Illinois; located on Lake Michigan; the third-largest city in the United States. (42°N, 88°W) p. 152

Chickamauga (chik•uh•MAW•guh) A city in northwestern Georgia; site of a Civil War battle in 1863. (35°N, 85°W) p. 134

Chihuahua A city and state in northern Mexico. (28°N, 85°W) p. 525

Cold Harbor A location in east central Virginia, north of the Chickahominy River; site of Civil War battles in 1862 and in 1864. (38°N, 77°W) p. 134

Concord A town in northeastern Massachusetts, near Boston; site of a major Revolutionary War battle in 1775. (42°N, 71°W) p. 52

Cowpens A town in northwestern South Carolina; located near the site of a major Revolutionary War battle in 1781. (35°N, 82°W) p. 52

Cuba An island country in the Caribbean; the largest island of the West Indies. (22°N, 79°W) pp. 430, 530

D

Dallas A city in northeastern Texas; located on the Trinity River. (33°N, 97°W) p. 493

Denver Colorado's capital and largest city. (40°N, 105°W) pp. 152, 493

Dodge City A city in southern Kansas; located on the Arkansas River; once a major railroad center on the Santa Fe Trail. (38°N, 100°W) p. 152

Dominica (dah•muh•NEE•kuh) An island and a republic in the West Indies; located in the center of the Lesser Antilles between Guadeloupe and Martinique. p. 530

Dominican Republic A country in the West Indies, occupying the eastern part of Hispaniola. p. 530

Durango A city and state in northwestern central Mexico. (24°N, 104°W) p. 525

E

Edmonton The capital of Alberta, Canada; located in the south central part of the province on both banks of the North Saskatchewan River. (53°N, 113°W) p. 542

El Paso A city at the western tip of Texas; located on the Rio Grande. (32°N, 106°W) p. 493

Ellsworth A city in central Kansas. p. 152

F

Falkland Islands A British colony in the Atlantic Ocean; located east of the Strait of Magellan. p. 537

Fort Donelson A fort located in northwestern Tennessee; site of a major Civil War battle in 1862. p. 134

Fort Lauderdale A city in southeastern Florida along the Atlantic coast. p. 493

Fort Sumter A fort on a human-made island, off the coast of South Carolina, in Charleston Harbor; site of the first Civil War battle, in 1861. (33°N, 80°W) p. 134

Fort Wagner A fort near Charleston, South Carolina; site of a Civil War battle in 1863. p. 134

Fort Worth A city in northern Texas; located on the Trinity River. (33°N, 97°W) p. 493

Franklin A city in central Tennessee; site of a major Civil War battle in 1864. (36°N, 87°W) p. 134

Fredericksburg A city in northeastern Virginia; located on the Rappahannock River; site of a Civil War battle in 1862. (38°N, 77°W) p. 134

Fredericton The capital of New Brunswick, Canada; located in the southwestern part of the province. (46°N, 66°W) p. 542

G

Galápagos Islands Nineteen islands off the coast of Ecuador; home to many unique animal species. p. 539

Gatun Lake (gah•TOON) A lake in Panama; part of the Panama Canal system. p. 196

Georgetown A city in South America; located at the mouth of the Demerara River; capital of Guyana. (6°N, 58°W) p. 537

Germantown A residential section of present-day Philadelphia, on Wissahickon Creek, in southeastern Pennsylvania; site of a major Revolutionary War battle in 1777. (40°N, 75°W) p. 52

Gettysburg A town in southern Pennsylvania; site of a Civil War battle in 1863. (40°N, 77°W) p. 134

Grenada (grah•NAY•duh) An island in the West Indies; the southernmost of the Windward Islands. p. 530

Guadalajara A city in western central Mexico; capital of Jalisco state. (20°N, 103°W) p. 525

Guánica (GWAHN•ih•kah) A town in southwestern Puerto Rico; located on Guánica Harbor. (18°N, 67°W) p. 194

Guantánamo Bay (gwahn•TAH•nah•moh) A bay on the southeastern coast of Cuba. p. 430

Guatemala City Capital of Guatemala; largest city in Central America. (14°N, 90°W) p. 530

Guiana Highlands (gee•AH•nuh) Highland area in northern South America. p. 537

Guilford Courthouse (GIL•ferd) A location in north central North Carolina, near Greensboro; site of a major Revolutionary War battle in 1781. (36°N, 80°W) p. 52

Gulf of Panama A large inlet of the Pacific Ocean; located on the southern coast of Panama. p. 196

H

Haiti A country in the West Indies; occupies the western part of the island of Hispaniola. p. 530

Halifax The capital of the province of Nova Scotia, Canada; a major port on the Atlantic Ocean; remains free of ice all year. (44°N, 63°W) p. 542

Hampton Roads A channel in southeastern Virginia that flows into Chesapeake Bay; site of a Civil War naval battle in 1862 between two ironclad ships, the *Monitor* and the *Merrimack*. p. 134

Havana The capital of Cuba; located on the northwestern coast of the country. (23°N, 82°W) pp. 194, 430

Hiroshima The Japanese city upon which the first atom bomb was dropped in World War II. p. 377

Hispaniola (ees•pah•NYOH•lah) An island in the West Indies made up of Haiti and the Dominican Republic; located in the Caribbean Sea between Cuba and Puerto Rico. pp. 30, 530

Honolulu (hah•nuhl•OO•loo) Hawaii's capital and largest city; located on Oahu. (21°N, 158°W) pp. 190, 342

Houston A city in southeastern Texas; third-largest port in the United States; leading industrial center in Texas. (30°N, 95°W) p. 493

Iceland An island country in the North Atlantic Ocean; between Greenland and Norway. p. 366

Inchon (ihn•CHON) A city in northwestern South Korea. (36°N, 127°E) p. 412

Iqaluit (ee•KAH•loo•iht) The capital of Nunavut, Canada; located on the eastern coast. p. 542

Iron Curtain An imaginary barrier separating communist Eastern European countries from the West during the Cold War years. p. 393

Isthmus of Panama (IS•muhs) A narrow strip of land that connects North America and South America. p. 30

Iwo Jima A Japanese island; the site of major battles during World War II. p. 377

J

Jacksonville A city in northeastern Florida; located near the mouth of the St. Johns River. (30°N, 82°W) p. 493

Jamaica (juh•MAY•kuh) An island country in the West Indies; south of Cuba. p. 530

K

Kahoolawe (kah•hoh•uh•LAY•vay) One of the eight main islands of Hawaii; located west of Maui. pp. 190, 342

Kaskaskia (ka•SKAS•kee•uh) A village in southwestern Illinois; site of a major Revolutionary War battle in 1778. (38°N, 90°W) p. 52

Kauai (kah•WAH•ee) The fourth-largest of the eight main islands of Hawaii. pp. 190, 342

Kennesaw Mountain (KEN•uh•saw) An isolated peak in northwestern Georgia, near Atlanta; site of a Civil War battle in 1864. p. 134

Kings Mountain A ridge in northern South Carolina and southern North Carolina; site of a Revolutionary War battle in 1780. p. 52

Kingston A commercial seaport in the West Indies; capital of Jamaica. (18°N, 76°W) p. 530

L

La Paz A city in South America; capital of Bolivia. (16°S, 68°W) p. 537

Lanai (luh•NY) One of the eight main islands of Hawaii. pp. 190, 342

Las Vegas (lahs VAY•guhs) A city in southeastern Nevada. (36°N, 115°W) p. 493

Lexington A town in northeastern Massachusetts; site of the first battle of the Revolutionary War, in 1775. (42°N, 71°W) p. 52

Lima (LEE•mah) The capital of Peru; located on the Rímac River. (12°S, 77°W) p. 537

Little Bighorn A location near the Little Bighorn River in southern Montana; site of a fierce battle in 1876 between Sioux and Cheyenne Indians and United States Army soldiers led by General George Armstrong Custer. p. 154

Long Island An island located east of New York City and south of Connecticut; lies between Long Island Sound and the Atlantic Ocean. p. 52

Los Angeles The largest city in California; second-largest city in the United States; located in the southern part of the state. (34°N, 118°W) p. 493

M

Madeira (mah•DAIR•uh) An island group in the eastern Atlantic Ocean, off the coast of Morocco. p. 37

Managua A city in Central America; capital of Nicaragua; located on the south shore of Lake Managua. (12°N, 86°W) p. 530

Manitoba (ma•nuh•TOH•buh) A province in central Canada; bordered by Nunavut, Hudson Bay, Ontario, the United States, and Saskatchewan; located on the Interior Plains of Canada. p. 542

Maui (MOW•ee) The second-largest island in Hawaii. pp. 190, 342

Mérida A city in southeastern Mexico; capital of Yucatán state. (21°N, 89°W) p. 525

Mexico City A city on the southern edge of the Central Plateau of Mexico; the present-day capital of Mexico. (19°N, 99°W) p. 525

Minneapolis The largest city in Minnesota; located in the southeast central part of the state, on the Mississippi River; twin city with St. Paul. (45°N, 93°W) p. 162

Mobile Bay An inlet of the Gulf of Mexico; located off the coast of southern Alabama; the site of a Civil War naval battle in 1864. p. 134

Molokai (mah•luh•KY) One of the eight main islands of Hawaii. pp. 190, 342

Montenegro An independent state in southeastern Europe on the Balkan Peninsula. p. 227

Monterrey A city in northeastern Mexico; capital of Nuevo León state. (25°N, 100°W) p. 525

Montevideo (mon•tuh•vih•DAY•oh) A seaport city located in the southern part of the north shore of La Plata estuary; capital of Uruguay. (35°S, 56°W) p. 537

N

Nagasaki Japanese city upon which the second atom bomb was dropped, resulting in the end of World War II. p. 377

Nashville The capital of Tennessee; site of a Civil War battle in 1864. (36°N, 87°W) pp. 134, 493

Nassau A city on the northeastern coast of New Providence Island; capital of the Bahamas. (25°N, 77°W) p. 530

New Brunswick One of Canada's ten provinces; bordered by Quebec, the Gulf of St. Lawrence, Northumberland Strait, the Bay of Fundy, the United States, and Nova Scotia. p. 542

New Guinea (GIH•nee) An island of the eastern Malay Archipelago; located in the western Pacific Ocean, north of Australia. p. 377

New Orleans The largest city in Louisiana; a major port located between the Mississippi River and Lake Pontchartrain. (30°N, 90°W) p. 134

Newfoundland and Labrador (NOO•fuhn•luhnd) One of Canada's ten provinces; bordered by Quebec and the Atlantic Ocean. p. 542

Newton A city in south central Kansas. (38°N, 97°W) p. 152

Niihau (NEE•how) One of the eight main islands of Hawaii. pp. 190, 342

Normandy A region of northwest France; site of the Allied D day invasion on June 6, 1944. p. 366

Northwest Territories One of Canada's three territories; located in northern Canada. p. 542

Nova Scotia (NOH•vuh SKOH•shuh) A province of Canada; located in eastern Canada on a peninsula. p. 542

Nunavut (NOO•nuh•voot) One of Canada's three territories; formed in 1999 and inhabited mostly by Inuit peoples. p. 542

O

Oahu (oh•AH•hoo) The third-largest of the eight main islands of Hawaii; Honolulu is located there. pp. 190, 342

Oaxaca (wuh•HAH•kuh) A city and state in southern Mexico. (17°N, 96°W) p. 525

Ogallala (oh•guh•LAHL•uh) A city in western Nebraska on the South Platte River. (41°N, 102°W) p. 152

Ontario (ahn•TAIR•ee•oh) One of Canada's ten provinces; located between Quebec and Manitoba. p. 542

Orinoco River A river in Venezuela in northern South America. p. 537

Orlando A city in central Florida. (28°N, 81°W) p. 493

Ottawa (AH•tuh•wuh) The capital of Canada; located in Ontario on the St. Lawrence Lowlands. (45°N, 75°W) p. 542

P

Pampas (PAHM•puhs) The plains of South America; located in the southern part of the continent, extending for nearly 1,000 miles. p. 537

Panama Canal A canal across the Isthmus of Panama; extends from the Caribbean Sea to the Gulf of Panama. p. 196

Panama City The capital of Panama; located in Central America. (9°N, 80°W) p. 530

Paramaribo (par•ah•MAR•uh•boh) A seaport city located on the Suriname River; capital of Suriname. (5°N, 55°W) p. 537

Paraná River (par•uh•NAH) A river in southeast central South America; formed by the joining of the Rio Grande and the Paranaíba River in south central Brazil. p. 537

Patagonia A barren tableland in South America between the Andes and the Atlantic Ocean. p. 537

Pearl Harbor An inlet on the southern coast of Oahu, Hawaii; the Japanese attacked an American naval base there on December 7, 1941. p. 342

Pecos River (PAY•kohs) A river in eastern New Mexico and western Texas; empties into the Rio Grande. p. 152

Perryville A city in east central Kentucky; site of a major Civil War battle in 1862. (38°N, 90°W) p. 134

Petersburg A port city in southeastern Virginia; located on the Appomattox River; site of a series of Civil War battles from 1864 to 1865. (37°N, 77°W) p. 134

Philippine Islands A group of more than 7,000 islands off the coast of southeastern Asia, making up the country of the Philippines. p. 30

Phoenix Capital and largest city of Arizona; located in south central Arizona. (34°N, 112°W) p. 493

Port of Spain A seaport in the northwestern part of the island of Trinidad; capital of Trinidad and Tobago. (10°N, 61°W) p. 530

Port-au-Prince A seaport located on Hispaniola Island, in the West Indies, on the southeastern shore of the Gulf of Gonâve; capital of Haiti. (18°N, 72°W) p. 530

Portland (OR) Oregon's largest city and principal port; located in the northwestern part of the state on the Willamette River. (46°N, 123°W) p. 493

Prince Edward Island One of Canada's ten provinces; located in the Gulf of St. Lawrence. p. 542

Princeton A borough in west central New Jersey; site of a major Revolutionary War battle. (40°N, 75°W) p. 52

Puebla A city and state in southeastern central Mexico. (19°N, 98°W) p. 525

Pueblo (PWEH•bloh) A city in Colorado. p. 152

Pueblo Bonito (PWEH•bloh boh•NEE•toh) Largest of the prehistoric pueblo ruins; located in Chaco Culture National Historical Park, New Mexico. p. 23

Pusan (poo•SAHN) A city in the southeast corner of South Korea. (35°N, 129°E) p. 412

Q

Quebec (kwih•BEK) The capital of the province of Quebec, Canada; located on the northern side of the St. Lawrence River; the first successful French settlement in the Americas; established in 1608. (47°N, 71°W) p. 542

R

Raleigh (RAW•lee) The capital of North Carolina; located in the east central part of the state. (36°N, 79°W) p. 493

Regina (rih•JY•nuh) The capital of Saskatchewan, Canada; located in the southern part of the province. (50°N, 104°W) p. 542

Richmond The capital of Virginia; a port city located in the east central part of the state, on the James River; capital of the Confederacy. (38°N, 77°W) p. 134

Rio de Janeiro A city and commercial seaport in southeastern Brazil, on the southwestern shore of Guanabara Bay. (23°S, 43°W) p. 537

Río de la Plata A river on the southeastern coast of South America. p. 537

S

Sacramento The capital of California; located in the north central part of the state, on the Sacramento River. (39°N, 121°W) p. 493

Salt Lake City Utah's capital and largest city; located in the northern part of the state, on the Jordan River. (41°N, 112°W) p. 493

San Antonio A city in south central Texas; located on the San Antonio River; site of the Alamo. (29°N, 98°W) p. 493

San Diego A large port city in southern California; located on San Diego Bay. (33°N, 117°W) p. 493

San Francisco The second-largest city in California; located in the northern part of the state, on San Francisco Bay. (38°N, 123°W) pp. 196, 493

San José A city in Central America; capital of Costa Rica. (10°N, 84°W) p. 530

San Juan (SAN WAHN) Puerto Rico's capital and largest city. (18°N, 66°W) pp. 194, 530

San Juan Hill A hill in eastern Cuba; captured by Cuban and American troops during the Spanish-American War in 1898. p. 194

San Salvador One of the islands in the southern Bahamas; Christopher Columbus landed there in 1492. p. 37

Santa Fe (SAN•tah FAY) The capital of New Mexico; located in the north central part of the state. (36°N, 106°W) p. 493

Santiago (san•tee•AH•goh) A seaport on the southern coast of Cuba; second-largest city in Cuba. (20°N, 75°W) p. 194

Santo Domingo The capital of the Dominican Republic. (18°N, 70°W) p. 530

São Francisco River A river in eastern Brazil; flows north, northeast, and east into the Atlantic Ocean. p. 537

São Paulo (SOW POW•loh) A city in southeastern Brazil; capital of São Paulo state. p. 537

Saratoga A village on the western bank of the Hudson River in eastern New York; site of a major Revolutionary War battle in 1777; present-day Schuylerville. (43°N, 74°W) p. 52

Saskatchewan (suh•SKA•chuh•wahn) One of Canada's ten provinces; located between Alberta and Manitoba. p. 542

Savannah The oldest city and a principal seaport in southeastern Georgia; located in the southeastern part of the state, at the mouth of the Savannah River. (32°N, 81°W) pp. 52, 134

Seattle The largest city in Washington; a port city located in the west central part of the state, on Puget Sound. (48°N, 122°W) p. 493

Sedalia (suh•DAYL•yuh) A city in west central Missouri. (39°N, 93°W) p. 152

Seoul The capital of South Korea; located in the northwestern portion of nation. (37°N, 127°E) p. 412

Serbia An independent state in southeastern Europe on the Balkan Peninsula. p. 227

Shiloh (SHY•loh) A location in southwestern Tennessee; site of a major Civil War battle in 1862; also known as Pittsburg Landing. (35°N, 88°W) p. 134

Sierra Madre Occidental (see•AIR•ah MAH•dray ahk•sih•den•TAHL) A mountain range in western Mexico, running parallel to the Pacific coast. p. 525

St. John's A city on the southeastern coast of Canada, on the Atlantic Ocean; the capital of Newfoundland and Labrador. (47°N, 52°W) p. 542

St. Joseph A city in northwestern Missouri on the Missouri River. (40°N, 95°W) p. 152

St. Lucia An island and an independent state of the Windward Islands; located in the eastern West Indies, south of Martinique and north of St. Vincent. p. 530

St. Paul The capital of Minnesota; located in the eastern part of the state, on the Mississippi River. (45°N, 93°W) p. 162

Strait of Magellan (muh•JEH•luhn) The narrow waterway between the southern tip of South America and Tierra del Fuego; links the Atlantic Ocean with the Pacific Ocean. p. 30

Sucre (SOO•kray) A city in Bolivia, South America. (19°S, 65°W) p. 537

Suriname A country in north central South America. p. 537

T

Tallahassee The capital of Florida; located in the state's panhandle. (34°N, 84°W) p. 493

Tegucigalpa (teh•goo•see•GAHL•puh) A city in Central America; capital of Honduras. (14°N, 87°W) p. 530

Toledo (tuh•LEE•doh) A port city in northwestern Ohio located at the southwestern corner of Lake Erie. (42°N, 84°W) p. 162

Toronto The capital of the province of Ontario, Canada; located near the northwestern end of Lake Ontario; largest city in Canada. (43°N, 79°W) p. 542

Trenton The capital of New Jersey; located in the west central part of the state; site of a major Revolutionary War battle in 1776. (40°N, 75°W) p. 52

Trinidad and Tobago An independent republic made up of the islands of Trinidad and Tobago; located in the Atlantic Ocean off the northeastern coast of Venezuela. p. 530

Tucson (TOO•sahn) A city in southern Arizona; located on the Santa Cruz River. (32°N, 111°W) p. 493

V

Valley Forge A location in southeastern Pennsylvania, on the Schuylkill River; site of General George Washington's winter headquarters during the Revolutionary War. (40°N, 75°W) p. 52

GAZETTEER

Vancouver Canada's eighth-largest city; located where the northern arm of the Fraser River empties into the Pacific Ocean. (49°N, 123°W) p. 542

Veracruz (veh•rah•KROOZ) A state in Mexico; located in the eastern part of the country, on the Gulf of Mexico. (19°N, 96°W) p. 525

Vicksburg A city in western Mississippi; located on the Mississippi River; site of a major Civil War battle in 1863. (32°N, 91°W) p. 134

Victoria The capital of British Columbia, Canada; located on Vancouver Island. (48°N, 123°W) p. 542

Vincennes (vihn•SENZ) A town in southwestern Indiana; site of a Revolutionary War battle in 1779. (39°N, 88°W) p. 52

W

Wabash River (WAW•bash) A river in western Ohio and Indiana; flows west and south to the Ohio River, to form part of the Indiana-Illinois border. p. 52

West Indies The islands enclosing the Caribbean Sea, stretching from Florida, in North America, to Venezuela, in South America. p. 37

West Point A United States military post since the Revolutionary War; located in southeastern New York on the western bank of the Hudson River. p. 52

Whitehorse The capital of the Yukon Territory, Canada; located on the southern bank of the Yukon River. (60°N, 135°W) p. 542

Winnipeg The capital of the province of Manitoba, Canada; located on the Red River. (50°N, 97°W) p. 542

Y

Yellowknife The capital of the Northwest Territories in Canada; located on the northwestern shore of Great Slave Lake at the mouth of the Yellowknife River. (62°N, 114°W) p. 542

Yorktown A small town in southeastern Virginia; located on Chesapeake Bay; site of the last major Revolutionary War battle, in 1781. (37°N, 76°W) p. 52

Yucatán Peninsula (yoo•kah•TAN) A peninsula in southeastern Mexico and northeastern Central America. p. 525

Yukon Territory One of Canada's three territories; bordered by the Arctic Ocean, the Northwest Territories, British Columbia, and Alaska. p. 542

Glossary

The Glossary contains important social studies words and their definitions. Each word is respelled as it would be in a dictionary. When you see this mark ´ after a syllable, pronounce that syllable with more force than the other syllables. The page number at the end of the definition tells where to find the word in your book.

add, āce, câre, pälm; end, ēqual; it, īce; odd, ōpen, ôrder; tŏŏk, pōōl; up, bûrn; yōō as *u* in *fuse*; oil; pout; ə as *a* in *above*, *e* in *sicken*, *i* in *possible*, *o* in *melon*, *u* in *circus*; check; ring; thin; ~~th~~is; zh as in *vision*

A

abolitionist (a•bə•li´shən•ist) A person who wanted to end slavery. p. 112

absolute location (ab´sə•lōōt lō•kā´shən) The exact location of any place on Earth. p. 36

acquittal (ə•kwi´təl) A verdict of not guilty. p. 143

adapt (ə•dapt´) To adjust ways of living to land and resources. p. 6

address (ə•dres´) A formal speech. p. 131

advertisement (ad•vər•tīz´mənt) A public announcement that tells people about a product or an opportunity. p. 167

advertising (ad´vər•tīz•ing) Information that a business provides about a product or service to make people want to buy it. p. 276

agriculture (a´grə•kul•chər) Farming. p. 22

alliance (ə•lī´əns) A formal agreement. p. 227

ally (a´lī) A partner in an alliance. p. 227

amendment (ə•mend´mənt) A change. p. 62

analyze (a´nəl•īz) To look closely at how parts of an event connect with one another and how the event is connected to other events. p. 3

anarchist (a´nər•kist) A person who is against any kind of government. p. 195

architect (är´kə•tekt) A person who designs buildings. p. 282

armistice (är´mə•stəs) An agreement to stop fighting a war. p. 194

arms control (ärmz kən•trōl´) Limiting the number of weapons that each nation may have. p. 453

arms race (ärmz rās) A time during which one country builds up weapons to protect itself against another country. p. 390

assassinate (ə•sa´sən•āt) To murder a leader by sudden or secret attack. p. 141

assembly line (ə•sem´blē līn) System of building things in which a moving belt carries parts from worker to worker. p. 202

aviation (ā•vē•ā´shən) Air travel. p. 204

B

baby boom (bā´bē bōōm) The 15 years following World War II during which 50 million babies were born in the United States. p. 386

balanced budget (ba´lənst bu´jət) A government plan for spending in which it does not spend more money than it makes. p. 302

bias (bī´əs) A personal feeling for or against someone or something. p. 73

black codes (blak kōdz) Laws limiting the rights of former slaves in the South. p. 142

blockade (blä•kād´) To use ships to isolate a port or island. p. 429

boom (bōōm) A time of fast economic growth. p. 150

border state (bôr´dər stāt) During the Civil War, a state—Delaware, Kentucky, Maryland, or Missouri—between the North and the South that was unsure which side to support. p. 123

boycott (boi´kät) The refusal to buy certain goods. p. 48

bureaucracy (byōō•rä´krə•sē) The many workers and groups that are needed to run government programs. p. 309

bust (bust) A time of quick economic decline. p. 151

C

candidate (kan´də•dāt) A person chosen by a political party to run for office. p. 465

capital (ka´pə•təl) The money needed to set up or improve a business. p. 161

cardinal direction (kärd´nal də•rek´shən) One of the main directions: north, south, east, or west. p. A3

carpetbagger (kär´pət•ba•gər) A Northerner who moved to the South to take part in Reconstruction governments. p. 147

cartogram (kär´tə•gram) A diagram that gives information about places by the size shown for each place. p. 498

cash crop (kash krop) A crop that is grown to be sold. p. 43

casualty (ka´zhəl•tē) A person who has been wounded or killed in a war. p. 125

cause (kôz) An event or an action that makes something else happen. p. 27

cease-fire (sēs•fīr´) A temporary end to a conflict. p. 453

charter (chär´tər) An official paper in which certain rights are given by a government to a person or business. p. 39

chronology (krə•nä´lə•jē) Time order. p. 2

civics (si´viks) The study of citizenship. p. 9

civic participation (si´vik pär•ti´sə•pā´•shən) Being concerned with and involved in issues related to the community, state, country, or world. p. 9

civil rights (si´vəl rīts) The rights guaranteed to all citizens by the Constitution. p. 218

civilian (sə•vil´yən) A person who is not in the military. p. 344

civilization (si•və•lə•zā´shən) A culture that usually has cities and well-developed forms of government, religion, and learning. p. 23

classify (kla´sə•fī) To group. p. 315

climograph (klī´mə•graf) A chart that shows the average monthly temperature and the average monthly precipitation for a place. p. 156

code (kōd) A set of laws. p. 109

cold war (kōld wôr) A war fought mostly with propaganda and money rather than with soldiers and weapons. p. 393

colony (kä´lə•nē) A settlement ruled by another country. p. 32

commercial industry (kə•mûr´shəl in´dəs•trē) An industry that is run to make a profit. p. 279

commission (kə•mi´shən) A special committee. p. 214

commonwealth (kä´mən•welth) A kind of territory that governs itself. p. 532

communism (kä´myə•ni•zəm) A political and economic system in which all industries, land, and businesses are owned by the government. p. 239

commute (kə•myōot´) To travel back and forth to work. p. 281

compass rose (kum´pəs rōz) A circular direction marker on a map. p. A3

competition (käm•pə•ti´shən) The contest among companies to get the most customers or sell the most goods. p. 49

compromise (käm´prə•mīz) To reach an agreement by having each party give up some of what it wants. p. 60

concentration camp (kon•sən•trā´shən kamp) A prison camp. p. 333

Confederacy (kən•fe´də•rə•sē) The group of eleven states that left the Union, also called the Confederate States of America. p. 117

confederation (kən•fə•də•rā´shən) A loose group of governments working together. p. 26

conquistador (kän•kēs´tə•dôr) An explorer or soldier sent by Spain to conquer and claim large areas of North and South America. p. 31

conservation (kän•sər•vā´shən) The protection of the environment by keeping natural resources from being wasted or destroyed. p. 216

constitution (kän•stə•tōo´shən) A plan of government. p. 41

consumer good (kən•sōo´mər good) A product made for personal use. p. 269

D

D day (dē dā) June 6, 1944, the day the Allies worked together in Europe in the largest water-to-land invasion in history. p. 364

declaration (de•klə•rā´shən) An official statement. p. 48

deficit (de´fə•sət) A shortage. p. 459

deforestation (dē•fôr•ə•stā´shən) The widespread cutting down of forests. p. 540

democracy (di•mä´krə•sē) A government in which the people rule. p. 69

demonstration (de•mən•strā´shən) A public show of a group's feelings about a cause. p. 435

depression (di•pre´shən) A time when industries do not grow and many people are out of work. p. 300

desegregate (dē•se´gri•gāt) To remove racial barriers. p. 411

détente (dā•tänt´) An easing of tensions, especially between the United States and the Soviet Union. p. 453

developing country (di•ve´lə•ping kun´trē) A country that does not have modern conveniences such as good housing, roads, schools, and hospitals. p. 429

dictator (dik´tā•tər) A leader who has total authority to rule. p. 71

dictatorship (dik´tā•tər•ship) A government in which the dictator, or head of the government, has total authority. p. 333

distortions (di•stôr´shənz) The purposeful errors that enable cartographers to make flat maps. p. 198

diverse economy (də•vûrs´ i•kä´nə•mē) An economy based on many kinds of industries. p. 504

diversity (də•vûr´sə•tē) Great differences among the people. p. 24

doctrine (däk´trən) A government plan of action. p. 69

dollar diplomacy (dä´lər di•plō´mə•sē) A policy in which the United States government gave money to other nations in return for some U.S. control over the actions of those nations. p. 228

dove (duv) A person who was against the Vietnam War. p. 450

E

e-commerce (ē•kä´mərs) The buying and selling of goods and services through computers. p. 506

economics (e•kə•nä´miks) The study of how people use resources to meet their needs. p. 8

economist (i•kä´nə•məst) A person who studies the economy. p. 300

economy (i•kä´nə•mē) The way people of a state, region or country use resources to meet their needs. p. 8

effect (i•fekt´) Something that happens as a result of an event or action. p. 27

electoral college (i•lek´tə•rəl kä´lij) A group of electors who vote for the President and Vice President. p. 62

emancipation (i•man•sə•pā´shən) The freeing of enslaved peoples. p. 109

embargo (im•bär´gō) One nation's refusal to trade goods with another. p. 532

empire (em´pīr) A conquered land of many people and places governed by one ruler. p. 32

entrepreneur (än•trə•prə•nûr´) A person who sets up and runs a business. p. 159

equality (i•kwä´lə•tē) Equal rights. p. 112

ethnic group (eth´nik grōop) A group of people from the same country, of the same race, or with a shared culture. p. 494

executive branch (ig•ze′kyə•tiv branch) The part of government that carries out the laws. p. 60

expedition (ek•spə•di′shən) A journey. p. 30

F

fact (fakt) A statement that can be checked and proved true. p. 291

fascism (fa′shi•zem) A political idea in which power is given to a dictator and the freedoms of individuals are taken away. p. 333

federal system (fe′də•rəl sis′təm) A system of government in which national and state authorities share the responsibility of governing. p. 60

flow chart (flō chärt) A diagram that uses arrows to show the order in which events happen. p. 250

frame of reference (frām uv ref′•rəns) A set of ideas that determine how a person understands something. pp. 3, 106

free election (frē i•lek′shən) Election that offers a choice of candidates instead of a single candidate. p. 533

free enterprise (frē en′tər•prīz) An economic system in which people are able to start and run their own businesses with little control by the government. p. 158

free state (frē stāt) A state that did not allow slavery before the Civil War. p. 101

free world (frē wûrld) The United States and its allies. p. 391

freedmen (frēd′mən) The men, women, and children who had once been slaves. p. 145

free-trade agreement (frē•trād′ ə•grē′mənt) A treaty in which countries agree not to charge tariffs, or taxes, on goods they buy from and sell to each other. p. 508

front (frənt) A battle line. p. 362

fugitive (fyōō′jə•tiv) A person who is running away from something. p. 109

G

generalization (jen•ə•rə•lə•za′shən) A statement that summarizes the facts. p. 274

geography (jē•ä′grə•fē) The study of Earth's surface and the way people use it. p. 6

global economy (glō′bəl i•kä′nə•mē) The world market in which companies from different countries buy and sell goods and services. p. 508

government (gu′vərn•mənt) A system by which people of a community, state, or nation use leaders and laws to help people live together. p. 9

grid system (grid sis′təm) An arrangement of lines that divide something, such as a map, into squares. p. A3

H

hawk (hôk) Person who supported the Vietnam War. p. 450

high-tech (hī•tek′) Based on computers and other kinds of electronic equipment. p. 505

hijack (hī′jak) To illegally take control of an aircraft or other vehicle. p. 472

historical empathy (hi•stôr′i•kəl em′pə•thē) An understanding of the thoughts and feelings people of the past had about events in their time. p. 3

historical map (hi•stôr′i•kəl map) A map that provides information about a place at a certain time in history. p. 370

history (hi•stə•rē) Events of the past. p. 2

Holocaust (hō′lə•kôst) The mass murder during World War II of European Jews and other people whom Adolf Hitler called "undesirable." p. 368

homesteader (hōm′sted•ər) Person living on land granted by the government. p. 152

hostage (hos′tij) A prisoner held until the captors' demands are met. p. 457

human feature (hyōō′mən fē′chər) Something created by humans, such as a building or road, that alters the land. p. 6

human resource (hyōō′mən rē′sôrs) A worker who brings his or her own ideas and skills to a job. p. 163

hydroelectric dam (hī•drō•i•lek′trik dam) Dam that uses the water it stores to produce electricity. p. 314

I

immigrant (i′mi•grənt) A person from one country who comes to live in another country. p. 42

impeach (im•pēch′) To accuse a government official, especially the President, of a crime. p. 470

imperialism (im•pir′ē•ə•liz•əm) The building of an empire. p. 192

import (im′pôrt) A product brought in from another country. p. 42

indentured servant (in•den′chərd sûr′vənt) A person who agreed to work for another person for a certain length of time in exchange for passage to North America. p. 43

independence (in•də•pen′dəns) The freedom to govern on one's own. p. 51

Industrial Revolution (in•dus′trē•əl re•və•lōō′shən) A time of complete change in how things were made, in which people began using machines instead of hand tools. p. 76

inflation (in•flā′shən) An economic condition in which more money is needed to buy goods and services than was needed earlier. p. 450

Information Age (in•fər•mā′shən āj) A period of history defined by the growing amount of information available to people. p. 505

informed citizen (in•fôrmd′si′tə•zən) Someone who knows what is happening in the community. p. 513

inset map (in′set map) A smaller map within a larger one. p. A3

installment buying (in•stâl′mənt bī′ing) Taking home a product after paying only part of a price and then making monthly payments until the product is paid for. p. 269

GLOSSARY

integration (in•tə•grā´shən) The bringing together of people of all races. p. 421

interchangeable parts (in•tər•chān´jə•bəl pärts) Identical machine-made parts, any of which may be used to make or repair an item. p. 77

interdependent (in•tər•di•pen´dənt) Depending on other states and regions for natural resources, finished products, and services. p. 507

interest (in´trəst) The fee a borrower pays to a lender for the use of money. p. 270

interest rate (in´trəst rāt) An amount that a bank charges to lend money. p. 528

intermediate direction (in•tər•mē´dē•it də•rek´shən) One of the in-between directions: northeast, northwest, southeast, southwest. p. A3

international trade (in•tər•na´shə•nəl trād) Trade among nations. p. 507

Internet (in´tər•net) A network that links computers around the world for the exchange of information. p. 496

investor (in•ves´tər) Someone who uses money to buy or make something that will yield a profit. p. 297

island hopping (ī´lənd hä´ping) The fighting by the Allied forces to win only certain key islands as they worked their way toward an invasion of Japan. p. 373

isolation (ī•sə•lā´shən) The policy of remaining separate from other countries. p. 244

isthmus (is´məs) A narrow strip of land that connects two larger landmasses. p. 196

jazz (jaz) A music style influenced by the music of West Africa as well as by spirituals and blues. p. 288

judicial branch (jōō•di´shəl branch) The part of government that settles differences about the meaning of laws. p. 60

jury (jûr´ē) A group of citizens who decide a case in court. p. 513

labor union (lā´bər yōōn´yən) A group of workers who join together to improve their working conditions. p. 245

land use (land yōōs) The way in which most of the land in a place is used. p. 274

legislative branch (le´jəs•lā•tiv branch) The part of government that makes the laws. p. 60

legislature (le´jəs•lā•chər) The lawmaking branch of a government. p. 34

liberate (li´bə•rāt) To set free. p. 538

life expectancy (līf ik•spek´tən•sē) The number of years a person can expect to live. p. 534

lines of latitude (līnz uv la´tə•tōōd) Lines that run east and west on a map or globe. p. 36

lines of longitude (līnz uv lon´jə•tōōd) Lines that run north and south on a map or globe. p. 36

location (lō•kā´shən) The place where something can be found. p. 6

locator (lō´kā•tər) A small map or picture of a globe that shows where an area on the main map is found in a state, on a continent, or in the world. p. A3

long drive (lông drīv) A trip made by ranchers to lead cattle to market or to the railroads. p. 151

manifest destiny (ma´nə•fest des´tə•nē) The belief that the United States should someday stretch from the Atlantic Ocean to the Pacific Ocean. p. 71

map key (map kē) A part of a map that explains what the symbols on a map stand for. p. A2

map scale (map skāl) A part of a map that compares a distance on the map to a distance in the real world. p. A3

map title (map tī´təl) Words on a map that tell the subject of the map. p. A2

mass production (mas prə•duk´shən) The system of producing large amounts of goods at one time. p. 78

median age (mē´dē•ən āj) An age in years that half of the people in a country are older than and half are younger than. p. 534

meridians (mə•ri´dē•ənz) Lines of longitude. p. 36

merit system (mer´ət sis´təm) A system through which a person is tested to make sure he or she can do the job before the job is offered. p. 215

middle class (mi´dəl klas) An economic level between the poor and the wealthy. p. 528

migrant worker (mī´grənt wûr´kər) Someone who moves from place to place with the seasons, harvesting crops. p. 439

migration (mī•grā´shən) The movement of people. p. 21

militarism (mil´ə•tə•ri•zem) The idea that using military force is a good way to solve problems. p. 226

military draft (mil´ə•ter•ē draft) A way of making the people of a nation join the armed forces. p. 230

minimum wage (mi´nə•məm wāj) The lowest amount of money by law that a person can be paid per hour. p. 313

mission (mi´shən) A small religious settlement. p. 33

missionary (mi´shə•ner•ē) A person sent out by a church to spread its religion. p. 32

modify (mä´də•fī) To change. p. 6

monopoly (mə•no´pə•lē) A company that has little or no competition. p. 215

nationalism (na´shə•nel•i•zem) Pride in one's country. p. 69

navigation (na•və•gā´shən) The study or act of planning and controlling the course of a ship. p. 29

neutral (nōō´trəl) Not taking a side in a conflict. p. 229

GLOSSARY

new immigration (no͞o i•mə•grā′shən) People who came from southern and central Europe and other parts of the world after 1890 to settle in North America. p. 167

no-man's-land (nō′manz•land) In a war, land not controlled by either side and filled with barbed wire, land mines, or bombs buried in the ground. p. 235

nonviolence (nän•vī′ə•ləns) The use of peaceful ways to bring about change. p. 421

O

old immigration (ōld i•mə•grā′shən) People who came from northern and western Europe before 1890 to settle in North America. p. 166

open range (ō′pən rānj) Land on which animals can graze freely. p. 153

opinion (ə•pin′yən) A statement that tells what a person thinks or believes. p. 291

opportunity cost (ä•pər•to͞o′nə•tē kôst) The value of what a person gives up in order to get something else. p. 355

oral history (ôr′əl his′tə•rē) Stories, events, or experiences told aloud by a person who did not have a written language or who did not write down what happened. p. 2

P

panhandle (pan′han•dəl) A portion of land that sticks out like the handle of a pan. p. 189

parallel time lines (par′ə•lel tīm līnz) Two or more time lines that show the same period of time. p. 380

parallels (par′ə•lelz) Lines of latitude. p. 36

patriotism (pā′trē•ə•ti•zəm) Love of one's country. p. 515

pension (pen′shən) Retirement income paid to people who stop working at a certain age. p. 312

petroleum (pə•trō′lē•əm) Oil. p. 161

physical feature (fi′zi•kəl fē′chər) A land feature that has been made by nature. p. 6

pioneer (pī•ə•nir′) A person who first settles a place. p. 65

point of view (point uv vyo͞o) How a person sees things. p. 3

political boss (pə•li′ti•kəl bôs) An elected official—often a mayor—who has many dishonest employees and who is able to control the government with the help of those employees. p. 213

population density (po•pyə•lā′shən den′sə•tē) The number of people living in 1 square mile or 1 square kilometer of land. p. 474

population pyramid (po•pyə•lā′shən pir′ə•mid) A graph that shows the division of a country's population by age. p. 534

prediction (pri•dik′shən) A decision about what might happen next, based on the way things are. p. 232

prejudice (pre′jə•dəs) An unfair feeling of hate or dislike for members of a certain group because of their background, race, or religion. p. 168

primary source (prī′mer•ē sôrs) A record of an event made by a person who saw or took part in it. p. 4

prime meridian (prīm mə•ri′dē•ən) The meridian marked 0 degrees and that runs north and south through Greenwich, England. p. 37

progressive (prə•gre′siv) A person who worked to improve life for those who were not wealthy. p. 213

prohibition (prō•hə•bi′shən) The plan to stop people in the United States from drinking alcoholic beverages. p. 219

projections (prə•jek′shənz) The different kinds of maps cartographers use to show the Earth. p. 198

propaganda (prä•pə•gan′də) Information designed to help or hurt a cause. p. 232

proprietary colony (prə•prī′ə•tər•e kä′lə•nē) A colony owned and ruled by one person. p. 42

prospector (präs′pek•tər) A person who searches for gold, silver, or other mineral resources. p. 151

province (prä′vəns) A political region similar to a state in the United States. p. 542

R

rapid-transit system (ra′pəd tran′sət sis′təm) A passenger transportation system that uses elevated or underground trains or both. p. 501

ratify (ra′tə•fī) To approve. p. 61

rationing (rash′ən•ing) The limiting of the supply of what people can buy. p. 351

recession (ri•se′shən) A period of slow economic activity. p. 463

Reconstruction (rē•kən•struk′shən) The time during which the South was rebuilt after the Civil War. p. 140

recycling (rē•sī′kəl•ing) Using items again. p. 351

refinery (ri•fī′nə•rē) A factory in which materials, especially fuels, are cleaned and made into usable products. p. 151

refugee (ref′yo͞o•jē) A person who seeks shelter and safety in a country other than his or her own. p. 383

region (rē′jən) An area of Earth in which many features are similar. p. 7

register (re′jə•stər) To sign up to vote by showing proof that the voter lives where the voting takes place. p. 513

regulation (re•gyə•lā′shən) A rule or an order. p. 169

relocation camp (rē•lō•kā′shən kamp) During World War II, an army-style settlement in which Japanese Americans were forced to live. p. 353

renaissance (re′nə•säns) A time of great interest and activity in the arts. p. 290

representation (re•pri•zen•tā′shən) The action of having someone speaking for another. p. 48

republic (ri•pub′lik) A form of government in which people elect representatives to govern the country. p. 60

reservation (re•zər•va´shən) An area of land set aside by the government for use only by Native Americans. p. 154

resist (ri•zist´) To act against. p. 109

responsibility (ri•spän•sə•bi´lə•tē) A duty; something a person is expected to do. p. 512

retreat (ri•trēt´) To fall back. p. 122

revolution (re•və•loo´shən) A sudden, complete change, such as the overthrow of a government. p. 47

royal colony (roi´əl kä´lə•nē) A colony ruled directly by a monarch. p. 43

rural (rûr´əl) Of or like the country; away from the city. p. 280

S

satellite (sa´tə•līt) An object that orbits a planet. p. 423

scalawag (ska´li•wag) A rascal; someone who supports something for his or her own gain. p. 148

scandal (skan´dəl) An action that brings disgrace. p. 453

secede (si•sēd´) To leave. p. 117

secondary source (se´kən•der•ē sôrs) A record of an event written by someone who was not there at the time. p. 5

secret ballot (sē´kret ba´lət) A voting method in which no one knows how anyone else voted. p. 148

sectionalism (sek´shən•ə•li•zəm) Regional loyalty. p. 100

segregated (se´gri•gā•təd) Set apart or separated because of race or culture. p. 363

segregation (se•gri•gā´shən) The practice of keeping people in separate groups based on race or culture. p. 148

separatist (se´pə•rə•tist) A person in a province who wants his or her country to become a separate nation to preserve a culture. p. 544

settlement house (se´təl•mənt hous) A community center where people can learn new skills. p. 208

sharecropping (sher´kräp•ing) A system of working the land in which the worker was paid with a "share" of the crop. p. 147

siege (sēj) A long-lasting attack. p. 194

skyscraper (skī´skrā•pər) A tall steel-frame building. p. 209

slave state (slāv stāt) A state that allowed slavery before the Civil War. p. 101

slavery (slā´və•rē) The practice of holding people against their will and making them carry out orders. p. 33

standard of living (stan´dərd uv li´ving) A measure of how well people in a country live. p. 536

states' rights (stāts rīts) The idea that the states, rather than the federal government, should have final authority over their own affairs. p. 100

stock (stäk) A share of a business or company. p. 271

stock market (stäk mär´kət) A place where people buy and sell shares of a company or business. p. 271

strategy (stra´tə•jē) A long-range plan. p. 123

strike (strīk) The stopping of work in protest of poor working conditions. p. 245

suburb (su´•bərb) A community or neighborhood that lies outside a city. p. 281

Sun Belt (sun belt) A wide area of the southern United States that has a mild climate all year. p. 493

superpower (soo´pər•pou•ər) A nation that is one of the most powerful in the world. p. 388

T

tariff (tar´əf) A tax on goods brought into a country. p. 100

technology (tek•nä´lə•jē) The use of scientific knowledge or tools to make or do something. p. 22

teleconference (te´li•kän•frəns) A conference, or meeting, that uses electronic machines to connect people. p. 497

tenement (te´nə•mənt) A poorly built apartment building. p. 167

territory (ter´ə•tôr•ē) Land that belongs to a national government but is not a state and is not represented in Congress. p. 66

terrorism (ter´ər•i•zəm) The use of violence to promote a cause. p. 472

textile (tek´stīl) Cloth. p. 76

theory (thē´ə•rē) A possible explanation. p. 20

time zone (tīm zōn) A region in which a single clock time is used. p. 546

trade-off (trād´ôf) A giving up of one thing in return for another. p. 355

transcontinental railroad (trans•kän•tə•nen´təl rāl´rōd) The railway line that crossed North America. p. 158

treaty (trē´tē) An agreement between countries. p. 53

trial by jury (trī´əl bī jûr´ē) The judging of a person accused of a crime by a jury of fellow citizens. p. 42

U

underground (un´dər•ground) Done in secret. p. 110

unemployment (un•im•ploi´mənt) The number of workers without jobs. p. 301

urban (ûr´bən) Of or like a city. p. 280

V

veteran (ve´tə•rən) A person who has served in the armed forces. p. 383

veto (vē´tō) To reject. p. 468

V-J Day (vē•jā´ dā) Victory over Japan Day; August 15, 1945, the day in World War II on which Japan agreed to surrender and fighting stopped. p. 378

volunteer (vä•lən•tir´) A person who works without pay. p. 514

Y

yellow journalism (ye´lō jər´nəl•i•zəm) Style of newspaper writing in which reporters exaggerate the facts of a story in order to sell newspapers. p. 193

GLOSSARY

Index

Page references for illustrations are set in italic type. An italic *m* indicates a map. Page references set in boldface type indicate the pages on which vocabulary terms are defined.

D

INDEX

For permission to reprint copyrighted material, grateful acknowledgment is made to the following sources:

Atheneum Books for Young Readers, an imprint of Simon & Schuster Children's Publishing Division: Cover illustration from *Alexander Graham Bell* by Leonard Everett Fisher. Copyright © 1999 by Leonard Everett Fisher.

Candlewick Press, Inc., Cambridge, MA, on behalf of Walker Books Ltd., London: Cover illustration by P. J. Lynch from *When Jessie Came Across the Sea* by Amy Hest. Illustration copyright © 1997 by P. J. Lynch. Cover illustration by Gino D'Achille from *The Stone Age News* by Fiona Macdonald. Illustration copyright © 1998 by Walker Books Ltd.

Carolrhoda Books, Inc., a division of Lerner Publishing Group: Cover illustration by Rochelle Draper from *Georgia O'Keeffe* by Linda Lowery. Illustration copyright © 1996 by Linda Lowery.

Crown Publishers, a division of Random House, Inc.: Cover illustration from *My Dream of Martin Luther King* by Faith Ringgold. Copyright © 1995 by Faith Ringgold.

Dutton Children's Books, an imprint of Penguin Putnam Books for Young Readers, a division of Penguin Putnam Inc.: Cover photograph by Art Wolfe from *Journey Through the Northern Rainforest* by Karen Pandell. Photograph copyright © 1999 by Art Wolfe.

Farrar, Straus and Giroux, LLC: Cover illustration by David Wilgus from *My Wartime Summers* by Jane Cutler. Illustration copyright © 1994 by David Wilgus.

Harcourt, Inc.: From *Rose's Journal* by Marissa Moss. Copyright © 2001 by Marissa Moss. Cover photograph courtesy of the Library of Congress.

HarperCollins Publishers: From *Jason's Gold* by Will Hobbs. Text copyright © 1999 by Will Hobbs. Cover illustration by Mark Elliott from *Treasures in the Dust* by Tracey Porter. Illustration copyright © 1997 by Mark Elliott.

David Higham Associates Limited: Cover illustration by Martin Jordan from *Angel Falls: A South American Journey* by Martin and Tanis Jordan. Illustration copyright © 1995 by Martin Jordan. Published by Larousse Kingfisher Chambers Inc.

Henry Holt and Company, LLC: From *Betsy Ross: Patriot of Philadelphia* by Judith St. George, cover illustration by Sasha Meret. Text copyright © 1997 by Judith St. George; illustration copyright © 1997 by Sasha Meret.

Derek James: Cover illustration by Derek James from *Jason's Gold* by Will Hobbs. Illustration copyright © 1999 by Derek James.

Lee & Low Books, Inc., 95 Madison Avenue, New York, NY 10016: From *Dia's Story Cloth: The Hmong People's Journey to Freedom* by Dia Cha, illustrated by Chue and Nhia Thao Cha. Copyright © 1996 by Denver Museum of Natural History. Cover photograph by Mark T. Kerrin from *Dear Mrs. Parks: A Dialogue with Today's Youth* by Rosa Parks with Gregory J. Reed. Photograph copyright © 1996 by Mark T. Kerrin.

Madison Press Books: From *Attack on Pearl Harbor*, a Hyperion/Madison Press book by Shelley Tanaka, illustrated by David Craig. Copyright © 2001 by The Madison Press Limited.

Jack McMaster: Maps by Jack McMaster from *Attack on Pearl Harbor* by Shelley Tanaka, illustrated by David Craig.

Robin Moore and BookStop Literary Agency: Cover illustration by Robin Moore from *Across the Lines* by Carolyn Reeder. Illustration copyright © 1997 by Robin Moore.

Orion Books, a division of Random House, Inc.: From *All for the Union* by Robert Hunt Rhodes. Text and photograph copyright © 1985 by Robert Hunt Rhodes.

G. P. Putnam's Sons, an imprint of Penguin Putnam Books for Young Readers, a division of Penguin Putnam Inc.: Cover illustration by F. John Sierra from *My Mexico – México mío* by Tony Johnston. Illustration copyright © 1996 by F. John Sierra.

Scholastic Inc.: Cover illustration by Tim O'Brien from *Foster's War* by Carolyn Reeder. Illustration copyright © 1998 by Tim O'Brien.

Simon & Schuster Books for Young Readers, an imprint of Simon & Schuster Children's Publishing Division: Cover illustration by James Ransome from *Uncle Jed's Barbershop* by Margaree King Mitchell. Illustration copyright © 1993 by James Ransome.

Steck-Vaughn Company: Cover illustration by Debbe Heller from *Tales from the Underground Railroad* by Kate Connell. Illustration copyright © 1993 by Dialogue Systems, Inc.

Albert Whitman & Company: Cover illustration from *Theodore Roosevelt Takes Charge* by Nancy Whitelaw. Copyright © 1992 by Nancy Whitelaw.

Winslow Press: Cover illustration by Mark Summers from *Thomas Jefferson: Letters from a Philadelphia Bookworm* by Jennifer Armstrong. Illustration copyright © 2000 by Mark Summers.

Writers House LLC, on behalf of The Heirs to the Estate of Martin Luther King, Jr.: From "I Have a Dream" speech by Martin Luther King, Jr. Text copyright 1963 by Martin Luther King, Jr.; text copyright renewed 1991 by Coretta Scott King.

ILLUSTRATION CREDITS

Pages A18-A19, Studio Liddell; 12-13, Wayne Hovis; 20-21, Gregory Manchess; 24-25, Cliff Spohn; 44-45, Luigi Galante; 80-81, Don Foley; 88-89, Wayne Hovis; 92-93, Cliff Spohn; 94-97, George Gaadt; 118-119, Luigi Galante; 132, Bill Smith Studio; 158-159, Dennis Lyall; 176-177, Cliff Spohn; 180-181, Yuan Lee; 210-211, Nick Rotondo; 234-235, Jim Griffin; 251(t), Studio Liddell; 251(b), Patrick Gnan; 256-257, Yuan Lee; 260-261, Bill Maughan; 278-279, Don Foley; 279, Geoffrey McCormack; 320-321, Bill Maughan; 324-325, Andrew Wheatcroft; 364-365, Dennis Lyall; 374-375, Don Foley; 400-401, Andrew Wheatcroft; 404-405, Cliff Spohn; 432-433, Sebastian Quigley; 480-481, Cliff Spohn; 484-485, Rick Johnson; 510-511, Studio Liddell; 515, Bill Smith Studio; 516-517, Vincent Wakerley; 552-553, Rick Johnson.

All maps by MapQuest.com

PHOTO CREDITS

Cover: P. Frilet/Panoramic Images (astronaut); NASA (rocket); NASA (moon landing); H. Armstrong Roberts (pedestrians); Don Mason/Corbis Stock Market (computer chip).

PLACEMENT KEY: (t) top; (b) bottom; (l) left; (r) right; (c) center; (bg) background; (fg) foreground; (I) inset.

POSTER INSERT

Flag: Don Mason/Corbis Stock Market, Eagle: Minden Pictures

TITLE PAGE AND TABLE OF CONTENTS

Title page (fg) Ruth Dixon/Stock, Boston, (bg) Doug Armand/Stone; v Concord Museum; vi Smithsonian Institute; vii Stahlhelms Military Collectibles; viii Larry DeVito; ix Stahlhelms Military Collectibles; x The Image Bank.GRADE

INTRODUCTION

1(t) Ruth Dixon/Stock, Boston; (l) Doug Armand/Stone; 2 (t) Bettmann/Corbis; 2 (c) Brown Brothers; 2 (b) AP/Wide World Photos; 3 (t) Underwood & Underwood/Corbis; 3 (c) Bettmann/Corbis; 4 (b) W. L. Cenac; 5 (t) Bettmann/Corbis; 5 (tr) Owen Franken/Corbis; 7 (tl) Matthew Borkoski/Stock, Boston/PictureQuest; 7 (tr) Michael S. Yamashita/Corbis; 7 (bl) Kevin Alexander/Index Stock Imagery/PictureQuest; 7 (br) James Frank/Stock Connection/PictureQuest; 7 (cl) Peter Pearson/Stone; 7 (cr) Jeffrey Muir Hamilton/Stock, Boston/PictureQuest; 8 (c) Telegraph Colour Library/Getty Images; 8 (b) Gary Conner/PhotoEdit; 9 (b) Stone/Getty Images; 10 (t) Michael P. Gadomski/Photo Researchers; 10 (b) Bob Krist/Corbis.

UNIT 1

Unit Opener, (fg) Concord Museum; (bg) Eliot Cohen/Janelco Photographers; 14-15 The Granger Collection, New York; 15 (c) "Anonymous Loan", National Portrait Gallery, Smithsonian Institution/Art Resource, NY; 16 (b) The Granger Collection, New York; 16 (tr) Lee Snider/Corbis; 18-19 David Muench Photography; 20 (bl) Mark Newman/Alaska Stock Images; 22 (tl) Vera Lentz; 22 (tr) Place Stock Photo; 22 (b) Maxwell Museum of Anthropology Albuquerque, NM/Art Resource; 23 Dewitt Jones/Corbis; 24 (i) National Park Service, Sitka National Historical Park; 26 David Heald/National Museum of the American Indian; 28 (b) Werner Forman/Art Resource, NY; 28 (i) Made by Ivor Lawton, Courtesy of Regia/www.regia.org; 29 (t) Bibliotheque Nationale, Paris; 29 (b) Giraudon/Art Resource; 31 (b) Superstock; 31 (i) Courtesy of the Oakland Museum of California; 32 (b) George H. H. Huey Photography; 33 (tl) Library of Congress; 33 (tr) Canadian Museum of Civilization; 34 (t) Bettmann/Corbis; 34 (b) The Reformed Church of the Tarrytowns; 35 (t) Courtesy of the Pilgrim Society, Plymouth, Massachusetts; 38 Salem: Joseph Orme, c. 1765; Peabody Essex Museum; 39 (t) Blackwell History of Education Museum; 40 (t) Bettman/Corbis; 40 (b) Vince Streano/Corbis; 42 (b) Andre Jenny/Focus Group/PictureQuest; 43 (t) Hulton/Archive Photos; 43 (b) Hulton/Archive/Corbis; 46 (b) Bettmann Archive/Corbis; 47 (t) Courtesy of the National Portrait Gallery, London; 48 (tr) Contract Place Holder/Corbis; 48 (bl) Kevin Fleming/Corbis; 49 Hulton/Archive/Getty Images; 50 (b) Lee Snider Photo Images; 50 (tl) Bettman Archive/Corbis; 50 (tr) Hulton/Archive/Getty Images; 51 (tl) Barney Burstein/Corbis; 51 (bl) Corbis; 51 (br) Corbis; 53 (t) A detail, John Trumbull "The Surrender of Lord Cornwallis at Yorktown, 19 October 1781" Yale University Art Gallery, Trumbull Collection; 56-57 Tom Till Photography; 58 (bl) Hulton/Archive; 58 (br) Hulton/Archive Photos; 59 Bettmann/Corbis; 61 (b) North Wind Pictures Archives; 61 (bkgd) Harcourt; 62 Independence National Historical Park; 63 (t) Independence National Historical Park; 63 (b) Reprinted with permission of the Supreme Council, 33°, Scottish

Rite of Freemasonry, S.J., USA; 64 Lee Snider Photo Images; 65 (b) David Muench/Corbis; 65 (i) A detail of George Calieb Bingham, Daniel Boone Escorting Settlers Through The Cumberland Gap, 1851-52, detail. Oil on Canvas, 35 1/2 x 50 1/4'. Washington University Gallery of Art, St. Louis; 66 (b) David Muench/Corbis; 67 (t) National Park Service; 67 (bl) Independece National Historical Park; 67 (br) Independence National Historical Park; 68 (b) Bettmann/Corbis; 70 (t) Robert Holmes/Corbis; 70 (br) National Portrait Gallery, Smithsonian Institution/Art Resource, NY; 72 (t) Bettmann/Corbis; 73 (b) "Westward the course of Empire Takes its Way" ca. 1861, Oil on Canvas, 0126.1615, from the collection of Gilcrease Museum, Tulsa; 74-75 (b) Map Collection/Library of Congress; 74 (bl) Smithsonian Institution; 75 (t) Thomas Jefferson Papers/Library of Congress; 75 (c) National Numismatic Collection/Smithsonian Institution; 75 (cr) National Numismatic Collection/Smithsonian Institution; 76-77 (b) Bob Rowan, Progressive Image/Corbis; 77 (t) Bettmann/Corbis; 78 (t) Russ Poole Photography; 78-79 (b) Maryland Historical Society; 82 (b) Museum of the City of New York; 83 (b) Collection of the Oakland Museum of California, gift of Mr. and Mrs. Rollen Gaskill; 86 Joseph Sohm/ChromoSohm/Corbis; 87 (tl) Bettmann/Corbis; 87 (tr) Joseph Sohm/ChromSohm/Corbis; 87 (cr) Joseph Sohm/Chromosohm/Corbis; 87 (cl) Joseph Sohm/ChromoSohm/Corbis.

UNIT 2

Unit Opener (fg) Smithsonian Institution; (bg) Peter Gridley/FPG International; 91 (t) Smithsonian Institution; (l) Peter Gridley/FPG International; 94 All for the Union; 98-99 David Muench Photography; 100 The American Clock and Watch Museum; 101 Stock Montage/Hulton Archive/Getty Images; 102 Bettmann/Corbis; 105 Missouri Historical Society; 106 (bl) Courtesy of the South Carolina Library; 106 (br) Courtesy of the South Carolina Library; 107 (br) Hulton-Deutsch Collection/Corbis; 107 (br) Bettmann/Corbis; 108 (br) Scala/Art Resource, NY; 108 (cl) The Charleston Museum; 110 Library of Congress; 111 (t) Hulton/Archive Photos; 111 (b) National Museum of American Art, Washington DC/Art Resource, NY; 112 (bl) National Portrait Gallery, Smithsonian Institution/Art Resource, NY; 112 (i) Book cover slide of "Uncle Tom's Cabin" by Harriet Beecher Stowe. Courtesy of the Charles L. Blockson Afro-American Collection, Temple University; 113 (t) National Portrait Gallery, Smithsonian Institution/Art Resource, NY; 114 (b) Morton Beebe, S.F./Corbis; 115 Courtesy of the Illinois State Historical Library; 116 (bl) National Portrait Gallery, Smithsonian Institution/Art Resource, NY; 116 (bc) Corbis; 117 (t) National Portrait Gallery, Smithsonian Institution/Art Resource, NY; 117 (b) The Granger Collection; 122 (b) Brown Military Collection, Brown University; 122 (bl) National Portrait Gallery, Smithsonian Institution/Art Resource, NY; 124 James P. Rowan Photography; 125 Library of Congress; 126 (t) National Portrait Gallery; 126 (b) Library of Congress; 127 (b) Bettmann/Corbis; 128 Chicago Historical Society; 129 (bc) Salamander Books; 129 (br) National Portrait Gallery, Smithsonian Institution, Washington, D.C.; 130 (t) Courtesy of General Dynamics Corp., Electric Boat Div.; 131 (cl) Richmond, Virginia/Katherine Wetzel; 131 (b) New Hampshire Historical

Society; 133 (b) Tom Lovell©National Geographic; 135 Tom Prettyman/PhotoEdit/PictureQuest; 140 (bl) Corbis; 140 (bc) Library of Congress; 141 (t) Hulton Archive/Getty Images; 141 (i) Library of Congress; 142 Corbis; 143 (c) Library of Congress; 143 (tl) The Granger Collection, New York; 144 (tl) American Treasures of the Library of Congress; 144 (tr) Library of Congress; 145 (bl) Corbis; 145 (br) Southern Historical Collection; 146 (br) Bob Daemmrich Photography; 146 (cl) Bob Daemmrich Photography; 147 (t) The Metropolitan Museum of Art, Morris K. Jessup Fund; 147 (i) Smithsonian Institution, Division of Agriculture; 148 (t) Hulton/Archive/Getty Images; 148 (b) Smithsonian Institute; 149 The Granger Collection; 150 (i) The Bancroft Library; 150-151 Joseph Sohm/Visions of America/PictureQuest; 152 (b) Jeff Greenberg/PhotoEdit; 152 (tc) William Manns Photo/Zon International Publishing; 153 Solomon D. Butcher Collection, Nebraska State Historical Society; 154 Corbis; 155 Corbis; 156 Michael Forsberg; 160 Corbis; 161 Corbis; 163 From the Collections of Henry Ford Museum & Greenfield Village; 164 (t) Transfer from the National Museum of American Art; Gift of Dr. Eleanor A. Campbell to the Smithsonian Institution, 1942.; 164 (bl) Henry Ford Museum & Greenfield Village; 164 (br) Henry Ford Museum & Greenfield Village; 165 (t) Henry Ford Museum & Greenfield Village; 165 (c) Science Museum, London, UK/The Bridgeman Art Library International; 165 (br) Alfred Harrell/Smithsonian Institution; 166 (i) "By Courtesy of the Statue of Liberty National Monument"; 167 (tl) Corbis; 168-169 (b) Corbis; 169 (i) Corbis; 170 The Phillips Collection, Washington, DC; 171 (t) Corbis; 174 (c) Andre Jenny/Focus Group/PictureQuest; 174 (b) Thomas R. Fletcher/Stock, Boston; 174-175 (bg) Thomas R. Fletcher/Stock, Boston; 175 (tl) Mark E. Gibson; 175 (tl) Michael DiBella/Words & Pictures/PictureQuest; 175 (br) Andre Jenny/Focus Group/PictureQuest.

UNIT 3

Unit Opener; (fg) Stahlhelms Military Collectibles; (bg) Victoria A. Satterthwaite/Mira;186-187 Barbara Brundege/Accent Alaska; 188 (b) Corbis; 189 (t) Skagway Museum; 190 (b) Michele Burgess/Index Stock Imagery/PictureQuest; 191 (c) Bettmann/Corbis; 191 (i) Superstock; 192 (b) Bettmann/Corbis; 193 (t) The Granger Collection; 193 (tr) Bettmann/Corbis; 193 (i) Culver Pictures; 194 Culver Pictures; 195 (t) Bettmann/Corbis; 195 (b) Michael Freeman/Corbis; 197 Corbis; 200 (bl) Brown Brothers; 200 (i) Hulton/Archive; 201 (tl) Superstock; 201 (tc) Brown Brothers; 201 (tr) Hulton/Archive; 202 (t) Culver Pictures; 202 (bl) Hulton/Archive; 202 (br) AP Photo/Wide World Photos; 203 (tl) Brown Brothers; 203 (i) Hulton/Archive; 204 (c) Bettmann/Corbis; 204 (tr) Stacy Pick/Stock, Boston; 204 (cl) The Granger Collection; 205 (t) Franklin Institute; 206 (bl) Bettmann/Corbis; 206 (br) The Jacob A. Riis Collection, Museum of the City of New York; 207 (tl) Hulton/Archive; 207 (tr) Bettmann/Corbis; 208 Hulton/Archive; 209 (c) Hulton/Archive; 209 (b) Hulton/Archive; 209 (tr) Hulton/Archive; 211 Angelo Hornak/Corbis; 212 (b) Underwood & Underwood/Corbis; 213 (br) Bettmann/Corbis; 213 (i); 214 (t) Underwood & Underwood/Corbis; 214 (b) Underwood & Underwood/Corbis; 215 (b) Corbis; 216 (i) FPG International; 217 (t) Hulton/Archive; 217 (b)

Victoria Bowen/Harcourt; 218 (b) Hulton/Archive; 218 (i) The Library of Congress; 219 (t) Bettmann/Corbis; 220 (t) Museum of the City of New York; 220 (br) SuperStock; 220 (bl) The Jacob A. Riis Collection, The Museum of the City of New York/Museum of the City of New York; 221 The Jacob A. Riis Collection, The Museum of the City of New York/Museum of the City of New York; 224-225 Medford Taylor/National Geographic Society; 226 Bettmann/Corbis; 227 Liaison Agency, Inc.; 229 (t) The White House; 229 (b) Bettmann/Corbis; 229 (i) Bettmann/Corbis; 230 (bl) National Arcives; 230 (bc) National Archives; 230 (br) National Archives; 231 (t) Florida State Archives; 231 (i) Hulton/Archive; 233 (tl) Corbis; 233 (tr) Hulton/Archive; 235 Culver Pictures/PictureQuest; 236 Bettmann/Corbis; 237 (t) Georgetown University Library; 237 (br) PEMCO - Webster & Stevens Collection; Museum of History & Industry, Seattle/Corbis; 238 (i) Museum of Modern Art; 238 Brown Brothers; 239 (b) Hulton/Archive; 239 (tl) Corbis; 241 (t) Hulton Archive Photos; 242 (bl) Bettmann/Corbis; 243 (t) National Portrait Gallery, Smithsonian Institution/Art Resource, NY; 244 (cl) Brown Brothers; 244 (cr) Hulton/Archive; 245 (b) Bettmann/Corbis; 245 (i) George Meany Memorial Archives; 246 (t) Brown Brothers; 246 (b) Bettmann/Corbis; 247 (b) Hulton/Archive; 248 (t) LBJ Library Collection; 248 (b) Corbis; 249 (t) Brown Brothers; 250 Brown Brothers; 254-255 (t) Robert Frerck/Odyssey/Chicago; 254 (i),(cr) Joe Viesti; 255 (tr) Olivier Rebbot/Stock, Boston.

UNIT 4

Unit Opener; (fg) Larry DeVito; (bg) Richard Nowitz; 266-267 Stephen G. St. John/National Geographic Society; 268 Schenectady Museum; Hall of Electrical History Foundation/Corbis; 268 (i) Stock Montage; 269 (t) Brown Brothers; 271 (t) Bettmann/Corbis; 271 (b) Brown Brothers; 272 (t) Brown Brothers; 272 (b) Corbis; 273 (t) Brown Brothers; 274 (b) Corbis; 276 Hulton/Archive; 277 (t) Brown Brothers; 279 (t) David J. & Janice L. Frent Collection/Corbis; 279 (b) Hulton/Archive; 280 (t) Bettmann/Corbis; 280 (b) The New York Times; 281 (b) AP/Wide World Photos; 282 (bl) Angelo Hornak/Corbis; 282 (i) Corbis; 283 (tr) Underwood & Underwood/Corbis; 283 (i) Bettmann/Corbis; 284 (t) Brown Brothers; 284 (bl) Atwater Kent Museum; 284 (br) Atwater Kent Museum; 285 Atwater Kent Museum; 286 (bl) Brown Brothers; 287 (b) Bettmann/Corbis; 287 (t) Liaison Agency; 287 (i) Liaison Agency; 288 (c) Hulton/Archive; 288 (b) Art Resource, NY; 289 (t) Bettmann/Corbis; 289 (b) Hulton/Archive; 290 (tr) Hulton/Archive; 290 (i) Brown Brothers; 291 (b) Hulton-Deutsch Collection/Corbis; 294-295 Bill Ross/Corbis; 296 (bl) Corbis; 297 (t) Bettmann/Corbis; 298 (bl) Bettmann/Corbis; 298 (br) H. Armstrong Roberts, Inc.; 299 (tl) United Press International; 299 (tr) Bettmann/Corbis; 300-301 (b) Corbis; 301 (tc) Corbis; 303 (b) Bettmann/Corbis; 303 (i),(cl) Corbis; 304-305 (b) Corbis; 305 (i),(cr) Bettmann/Corbis; 306 (t) Bettmann/Corbis; 307 (tr) The Kobal Collection; 308 (b) Library of Congress; 310 (br) Florida State Archives; 311 (tl) Corbis; 311 (tr) Corbis; 312-313 (b) Franklin D. Roosevelt Library; 312 (tl) Bettmann/Corbis; 313 (tc) Corbis; 314 (t) Fine Arts Collection, General Services Administration/National Archives; 318 (c) Hulton/Archive; 318-319 Elizabeth Holmes/Omni-Photo Communications; 319 (c)

Ray Juno/Corbis Stock Market; 319 (tc) Hulton/Archive; 319 (tr) Hulton/Archive; 319 (cr) Tony Perrottet/Omni-Photo Communications.

UNIT 5

Unit Opener; (fg) Stahlhelms Military Collectibles; (bg) Dennis Brock/Black Star; 330-331 James Blank/Stock, Boston; 332 (b) Hulton/Archive; 333 (t) Bettmann/Corbis; 334 (b) Bettmann/Corbis; 334 (i),(cr) Stahlhelms Military Collectibles; 336 (b) Hulton-Deutsch Collection/Corbis; 336 (tl) Corbis; 336 (i),(cr) Culver Pictures; 337 (tl) William Vandivert/TimePix; 337 (tr) National Portrait Gallery, Smithsonian Institution/Art Resource, NY; 338 (b) William Vandivert/TimePix; 338 (tc) David E. Scherman/TimePix; 339 (t) Corbis; 340 (bl) Myron Davis/TimePix; 341 (t) Bettmann/Corbis; 341 (i),(cl) Bettmann/Corbis; 342 (b) TimePix; 343 (t) Bettmann/Corbis; 344 (tl) TimePix; 344 (tr) Corbis; 345 (br) Henry Groskinsky/TimePix; 346 (tl) Herbert Gehr/TimePix; 346 (i),(tr) Florida State Archives; 347 (b) George Strock/TimePix; 348 (tr) Scurlock Photo/Moorland-Spingarn Research Center/Howard University; 349 (bl) Library of Congress; 349 (br) Hulton/Archive; 350 (tc) Harcourt; 350 (bl) Peter Stackpole/TimePix; 350 (i),(br) Peter Stackpole/TimePix; 351 (tr) Hulton/Archive; 351 (br) Hulton/Archive; 352 (t) John Phillips/TimePix; 352 (br) Myron Davis/TimePix; 353 (b) Corbis; 353 (tr) Dean Wong/Corbis; 353 (i),(cr) Hulton-Deutsch Collection/Corbis; 354 (t) The Library of Virginia; 355 (br) Myron Davis/TimePix; 356 (b),(c) Corbis; 356 (tr) Hulton Archive/Getty Images; 357 (tl) Smithsonian Institution; 357 (cr) Smithsonian Institution; 358-359 Johnny Stockshooter/International Stock; 362 (bl) Corbis; 363 (b) Margaret Bourke-White/TimePix; 367 (b) Margaret Bourke-White/TimePix; 367 (cr) Yellow Star, Germany, 1930's. Printed cotton. Gift of Moriah Artcraft Judaica. Photograph by Greg Staley, Courtesy of B'nai B'rith Klutznick National Jewish Museum; 368 (tc) TimePix; 368 (bl) Hulton/Archive; 368-269 Stephen G. St. John/National Geographic Society; 369 (tl) Bettmann/Corbis; 372 (b) TimePix; 373 (tr) Bob Leavitt/TimePix; 374 (tc) Corbis; 376 (tc) Bettmann/Corbis; 376 (bl) Hulton/Archive; 378 (b) Bernard Hoffman/TimePix; 378 (cr) Office of War Information/National Archives/TimePix; 379 (tl) Hulton/Archive; 379 (tr) Hulton/Archive; 381 (t) Carl Mydans/TimePix; 382 (b) Yale Joel/TimePix; 383 (t) Hulton/Archive; 384 (b) Bettmann/Corbis; 384 (tl) Bettmann/Corbis; 385 (t) Bettmann/Corbis; 386 (bl) Catherine Redmond; 386 (br) Catherine Redmond; 387 (t) Margaret Bourke-White/TimePix; 388 (b) Gjon Mili/TimePix; 389 (br) Nat Farbman/TimePix; 390 (br) Alfred Eisenstaedt/TimePix; 391 (t) Bettmann/Corbis; 392 (b) Walter Sanders/TimePix; 392 (i),(cl) J. R. Eyerman/TimePix; 394 (b) Thomas D. McAvoy/TimePix; 394 (cl) Corbis; 395 (t) Bettman/Corbis; 398-399 Bill Bachmann/Mira; 399 (c) Carl Purcell/Mira; 399 (tc) Hulton-Deutsch Collection/Corbis; 399 (i),(tc) AP/Wide World Photos; 399 (i),(cr) AP/Wide World Photos; 399 (cr) AP/World Wide Photos.

UNIT 6

Unit Opener; (fg) The Image Bank; (bg) Lloyd Sutton/Masterfile; 408-409 Raymond Gehman/Corbis.; 411 (t) Corbis; 413 (b) Corbis; 413 (tc) William A. Bake/Corbis; 413 (i),(bl Carl Mydans/TimePix; 414 (b) John Dominis/TimePix; 414 (cl) Corbis; 415 (c) Bettmann/Corbis; 415 (tr) Bettmann/Corbis; 416 (b) Greg Mathieson/TimePix; 418 (b) Jack Moebes/Corbis; 418 (i),(cl Jack Moebes/Corbis; 419 (bc) Hulton/Archive; 419 (tl) Bettmann/Corbis; 420 (tl) Hank Walker/TimePix; 421 (bc) Carl Iwasaki/TimePix; 421 (tr) AP/Wide World Photos; 421 (br) Hank Walker/TimePix; 422 (b) Loomis Dean/TimePix; 422 (i) Bettmann/Corbis; 423 (i) Allan Grant/TimePix; 423 (tr) Howard Sochurek/TimePix; 425 (b) Bettmann/Corbis; 426 (tr) National Archives; 426 (bl) Bettmann/Corbis; 426 (br) Cold War Museum; 427 National Archives; 427 National Archives; 428 (b) John F. Kennedy Library; 429 (c) Peace Corps; 429 (tr) Al Fenn/TimePix; 430 (b) Carl Mydans/TimePix; 430 (i) UPI/Corbis; 431 (r) NASA; 432 (tl) Ralph Morse/TimePix; 434 (br) Corbis; 435 (b) Flip Schulke/Corbis; 436 (bl) UPI/Corbis; 437 (t) Flip Schulke/Corbis; 437 (br) Matt Herron/Black Star; 438 (tl) Ted Russell/TimePix; 438 (bl) Bettmann/Corbis; 439 (tr) Arthur Schatz/TimePix; 440 (t) Bettmann/Corbis; 441 (c) Theo Westenberger/Gamma Liasion International; 442 (b) Hulton Archive/TimePix; 448 (b) Corbis; 448 (i) Oscar White/Corbis; 449 (t) Bettmann/Corbis; 450 (b) Leif Skoogfors/Corbis; 450 (cl) Joe Munroe/TimePix; 451 (t) Larry Burrows/TimePix; 452 (tr) Bettmann/Corbis; 452 (bl) UPI/Bettmann/Corbis; 453 (b) Bettmann/Corbis; 455 (b) Bettmann/Corbis; 456 (bl) David Rubinger/TimePix; 457 (b) Bettmann/Corbis; 457 (tc) Owen Franklin/Corbis; 458 (b) Bettmann/Corbis; 460 (bc) Janet Wishnetsky/Corbis; 460 (tl) Dirck Halstead/Gamma Liaison International; 461 (tl) Chris Niedenthal/TimePix; 461 (i) David & Peter Turnley/Corbis; 462 (b) Dennis Brack/TimePix; 463 (t) David Valdez/TimePix; 464 (b) David Longstreath/AP/Wide World Photos; 464 (i) Terry Ashe/TimePix; 466 (b) Reuters NewMedia/Corbis; 467 (tl) Visar Kryeziu/AP/Wide World Photos; 468 (bl) AFP/Corbis; 469 (b) Mark Gibson/Index Stock Imagery/PictureQuest; 470 (b) Colin Braley/TimePix; 470 (i) Gary I. Rothstein/AP/Wide World Photos; 471 (tr) Reuters NewMedia/Corbis; 472 (b) AFP/Corbis; 472 (i) Thomas E. Franklin/The Record (Bergen County New Jersey)/Corbis SABA; 473 (t) Steve Liss/TimePix; 475 (tl) Alamy; 475 (tr) Alamy; 478 Mark Gibson; 479 (t) Raymond Gehman/Corbis; 479 (b) Birmingham Civil Rights Institute.

UNIT 7

Unit Opener, (bg) Werner J. Bertsch/Bruce Coleman, Inc.; 490-491 Miles Ertman/Masterfile; 492 Chuck Pefley/Stock, Boston; 494-495 (t) ML Sinibaldi/Corbis Stock Market; 494 (b) Steve Solum/Bruce Coleman Collection; 496 (b) Bettmann/Corbis; 497 (t) Denis Scott/Corbis Stock Market; 500 (b) Norman Owen Tomlin/Bruce Coleman Collection; 501 (t) Normwn Owen Tomlin/Bruce Coleman Collection; 501 (b) Debra P. Hershkowitz/Bruce Coleman Collection; 502 Tony Freeman/PhotoEdit/PictureQuest; 503 Robb Helfrick/Index Stock Imagery/PictureQuest; 504 (bl) Bob Daemmrich/Stock, Boston; 504 (br) Keith Bardin/Mira; 505 FPG International; 506 (t) Lester Lefkowitz/Corbis Stock Market; 506 (i) Pete Saloutos/Corbis Stock Market; 507 (b) Rei O'Hara/Black Star Publishing/PictureQuest; 507 (i) Erica Lanser/Black Star Publishing/PictureQuest; 508 Sonda Dawes/The Image Works; 509 Dave Bartruff/ Stock, Boston; 512 (c) Catherine Karnow/Corbis; 512 (tc) Corbis Stock Market; 513 (b) Jonathan Nourok/PhotoEdit; 513 (i) Dorothy Littel Greco/Stock, Boston; 514(b) Nubar Alexanian/Stock, Boston/PictureQuest; 515 (t) Raphael Macia/Photo Researchers, Inc.; 518(t) AP/Wide World Photos; 519(c) Bowling Green State University Library; 519(tr) Terry Heffernan/Kit Hinrichs and Delphine Hirasuna; 519(cr) Bowling Green State University Library; 519(cl) Terry Heffernan/Kit Hinrichs and Delphine Hirasuna; 522-523 Larry Luxner; 524 Greg Von Doersten/Outside Images/PictureQuest; 526 (b) Bettmann/Corbis; 654 526 (cl) Carlos S. Pereyra/DDB Stock Photo; 527 (t) Carlos S. Pereyra/DDB Stock Photo; 528 (t) Reuters NewMedia Inc./Corbis; 529 Bob Daemmrich/Stock, Boston/PictureQuest; 531 (b) NOAA/APWideWorld; 531 (i) Yann Arthus-Bertrand/Corbis; 532 (t) Tom Haley/Sipa; 532 (b) David Parker/Science Photo Library/Photo Researchers; 533 AP Photo/Lynne Sladky); 534(b) Suzanne Murphy-Larronde/DDB Stock Photo; 536-537(b) H. Mark Heidman; 536(i) Jacques Jangoux/Photo Researchers; 538 (t) D. Donne Bryant/DDB Stock Photo; 538(b) Larry Luxner; 539(t) Peter Menzel/Stock, Boston; 539(b) Francis E. Caldwell/DDB Stock Photo; 540 Walter Bibikow/Stock, Boston; 541(b) Pascal Quittemelle/Stock, Boston; 541(i) Martin Grosnick/Bruce Coleman, Inc.; 543(t) Owen Franken/Stock, Boston; 543(b) Walter Bibikow/Stock, Boston; 543 (i) The Parliament of Canada Photo Gallery; 544 (bl) J.A. Kraulis/Masterfile; 544 (bc) Mike Mazzaschi/Stock, Boston; 545 Public Archives, Canada/The St. Lawrence Seaway Management Corporation; 546 N. Devore/Bruce Coleman, Inc.; 550 (t) Miles Ertman/Masterfile; 550 (b) Russ Finley; 550-551 (bg) David R. Frazier; 551(tl) David R. Frazier; 551 (tr) Laurence Parent Photography; 551 (br) Lee Snider Photo Images; 551 (cl) National Geographic Society.

REFERENCE

R8-R10, All Presidential Portraits courtesy of National Portrait Gallery except page R10, (br) The Image Works

All other photos from Harcourt School Photo Library and/or Photographers: Weronica Ankarorn, Ken Kinzie, U. S. Color.

Home
304 268-7039-Terry